Western Philosophies of Religion

Western Philosophies of Religion

Great Religious Epistemologies from Augustine to Hick

Wayne P. Pomerleau
Gonzaga University

Ardsley House Publishers, Inc., New York

Address orders and editorial
correspondence to:
Ardsley House, Publishers, Inc.
320 Central Park West
New York, NY 10025

ISBN: 1-880157-62-4

Printed in the United States of America

10 9 8 7 6 5 4 3 2 1

to Martha,
my helpmeet

Contents

Preface

What is the purpose of this book? The book is designed to study the writings of important philosophers of Western civilization on matters concerning God and religion. As far as we know, religious beliefs have always played a significant role in human life. Many of us grew up believing in some God. But philosophy challenges us to ask what rational grounds, if any, there might be for such faith. We shall focus on answers to this question provided by some of the greatest, most influential thinkers of the Christian world over a period of some 1600 years—more specifically, on responses from the writings of Augustine at the end of the fourth century to the Gifford Lectures of John Hick, published in 1989. All the chapters of this book include biographical material designed to put philosophers' ideas in the context of their cultures, lives, activities, and interests. Such issues as the relationship between reason and religious faith, arguments for the existence of God, and the problem of evil, discussed from the perspectives of these philosophers' epistemologies (or theories of knowledge), will be emphasized. We shall consider the development of ideas, the historical connections among theories, the arguments used in support of conclusions, and suggestions for discriminating critically between strengths and weaknesses of various positions.

Why should we study great thinkers of the past? The quotation I like best about the importance of learning our intellectual heritage is from my favorite American philosopher, William James: "To know the chief rival attitudes towards life, as the history of human thinking has developed them, and to have heard some of the reasons they can give for themselves, ought to be considered an essential part of liberal education." We are fortunate to be able to read, consider, and benefit from the ideas of our predecessors. By studying their ideas in a critical manner, we can learn from their conflicts as well as their continuities, from their errors as well as their accurate insights. From the conflicts emerges a more refined truth; by coming to recognize the errors, we guard ourselves against repeating them. This is especially so in philosophy, which emphasizes the reasoning underlying conclusions every bit as strongly as the conclusions themselves.

What is "philosophy"? This is itself a controversial issue debated by philosophers, and it is not particularly helpful to point out that the etymology is from the Greek, meaning the "love of wisdom." I use the word to refer to a systematic, critical reflection on fundamental concepts, principles, and assumptions. These ideas can be in any area of human experience, so that we have philosophy of art, moral philosophy, philosophy of human nature, political philosophy, and so forth. Since this is a book on the philosophy of religion, we shall focus on concepts, principles, and assumptions from that area of human experience.

How should we conceive of "religion"? Those of us who grew up in cultures dominated by monotheistic traditions (e.g., Judaism, Christianity, and Islam) tend to think of "religion" in terms of belief in God. (The Latin roots of the word mean "to bind back," so that "religio" was conceived of as a bond or connecting link between man and the gods.) Yet I share John Hick's reluctance to subscribe to such a prejudicial analysis, which rules out by definition all nontheistic faiths (such as Theravada Buddhism) as genuinely religious. I accept his broader "working definition of religion as an understanding of the universe, together with an appropriate way of living in it, which involves reference beyond the natural world to God or gods or to the Absolute or to a transcendent order or process." This analysis leaves open the question of whether the object of a religious attitude is to be regarded monotheistically, polytheistically, or nontheistically. Yet it includes the theoretical dimension of interpreting reality in terms of that which transcends the natural world and the practical dimension of how such an interpretation affects our way of living.

Why study philosophies of religion this way? There is no better way to learn what great thinkers have taught than to work through all of their writings. But for most of us this is a highly impractical task. I have spent the last quarter of a century studying the history of philosophy. As a professional philosopher, I have far more time and resources for doing this than most people have. My hope is that the studies embodied in these ten chapters will facilitate the reader's understanding of the important and influential theories they cover.

For whom is this book intended? It is aimed at all students of the philosophy of religion who have not already mastered its history, whether they are formally enrolled in school courses or studying on their own. Because we shall focus on arguments offered in support of various theories, it is not likely to seem easy reading. Yet I believe that anyone who has already been exposed to some introduction to philosophy and/or logical reasoning should be able to handle it well enough.

How can one best use this book? The ideal would be to study these chapters in conjunction with the writings discussed. This book is designed to be a supplement to, rather than a substitute for, the reading of the great thinkers themselves. This is one reason for the heavy emphasis on textual references throughout—the Endnotes of each chapter (as well as the Bibliography) are designed to facilitate consultation of primary-source works. At the same time, I have tried to be careful in my expositions and analyses, so that these studies might accurately convey what these philosophers thought rather than present some distorted set of caricatures. This has been my other motive for so emphasizing documentation—to establish tight connections with primary-source writings. My frequent quotations are meant both to give the reader direct access to what these thinkers have written and to facilitate the relating of these studies to their works. Beyond consulting their writings in conjunction with this book, the reader might want to consider other published secondary sources on all of them. I have deliberately focused my attention on the primary-source writings of the influential thinkers and not on other contemporary secondary sources, since it is not my intention to become embroiled in wrangling over alternative scholarly interpretations or to comment on the commentators. Yet one secondary source I feel obliged to mention (and recommend) with affection and respect is the monumental, nine-volume *History of Philosophy*, by Frederick Copleston, S.J. Although I have made a concerted effort to avoid referring to it in the writing of these studies, I have nevertheless found it an extremely valuable resource since my undergraduate days and have no doubt that my understanding of the great theories has been significantly influenced by its interpretations.

Why these philosophers rather than others? I have tried to concentrate on the great philosophers of medieval and modern Christian cultures (as well as some provocative contemporary perspectives) because they are the ones who, for better or worse, have shaped our thinking. They constitute a significant part of our intellectual heritage; and, as the previous quotation from James indicates, a familiarity with their ideas has come to represent "an essential part of liberal education." But if superficiality is to be avoided, some theories must be selected over others. Such choices are always questionable, in the sense that there are important thinkers whose works get left out. My selections have been in favor of those views I consider most influential, comprehensive, and best argued, though I admit that this is, to a considerable extent, a subjective judgment. Beyond this, my Table of Contents reveals a bias in favor of great modern philosophers. I devote eight chapters to individual thinkers who span a three-century period from René Descartes (1637) through William James (1910). By contrast, only one chapter concerns philosophers of the Middle Ages, and only a single chapter discusses the work of contemporary philosophers. The reason for the bias is that I do not believe that any philosophy of religion before Descartes has a sufficiently well-developed epistemological foundation to stand comparison with the modern theories or that any of the thinkers after James has the philosophical stature of the great modern philosophers. (The Appendix considers two classic texts from Eastern thought and some relationships between them and Western theories.)

How are these theories approached here? I have tried to present all of the theories sympathetically, even those with which I largely disagree. Yet I have also offered lines of critical reflection on even those theories toward which I am quite favorably inclined. It is not my wish to prejudice the reader in favor of certain views on God and religion at the expense of others. I think that all of the philosophies of religion examined here have much of value to offer us today and that none of them should be above criticism. My hope is that readers will arrive at their own conclusions concerning the relative merits of different theories. (At the same time, the fact that these studies culminate in the thought of John Hick, with whose ideas they do not take issue, indicates something of my allegiances.) Readers might want to use my "*co*" test to assess various theories: in order for a philosophical theory to be *co*nvincing, it must be:

1. *co*herent (intelligible and making sense)
2. logically *co*nsistent (and not tainted by self-contradiction)
3. *co*mpatible with past and present experience (that is, corresponding to the facts, congenial to our needs and interests, and conducive to effective action)
4. able to *co*ntribute to the understanding of future experience
5. as *co*mprehensive as reasonably possible

Which of these philosophers' writings are recommended? Given the impracticality of consulting all the works in the Endnotes and Bibliography, I particularly recommend the following primary-source writings as relatively brief, clear, and dovetailing nicely with the discussions of theories in this book:

Augustine, *On Free Choice of the Will*
Anselm, *Proslogium*
Aquinas, Question II of *Summa Theologica*
Descartes, *Meditations*, II-V
Locke, *Essay concerning Human Understanding*, Book IV, Chapters X, XVIII, and XIX
Leibniz, "Monadology" and "The Theodicy: Abridgement of the Argument Reduced to Syllogistic Form"
Hume, *Dialogues concerning Natural Religion* and *Enquiry concerning Human Understanding*, Sections X-XI
Kant, "The Ideal of Pure Reason" from *Critique of Pure Reason* and *Critique of Practical Reason*, Book II, Chapter II
Hegel, *Phenomenology of Spirit*, sections on "Religion" and "Absolute Knowledge," or final section of *Philosophy of Mind*
Kierkegaard, *Concluding Unscientific Postscript*, Book II, Part II, Chapter II
James, "The Will to Believe" and Lectures XVIII, XX, and Postscript of *Varieties of Religious Experience*
Copleston, debates with B. Russell and A. J. Ayer
Ayer, *Language, Truth and Logic*, Chapter VI
Flew and others, "Theology and Falsification" discussion
Hick, *Philosophy of Religion*

It would be convenient if all these were combined in a single anthology, but no such collection presently exists. Two excellent anthologies do come close to this ideal, and I strongly encourage the use of either or both: *Historical*

Selections in the Philosophy of Religion, edited by Ninian Smart, offers superb coverage of thinkers from Augustine through James but includes none of the contemporary perspectives I discuss in my last chapter; and *Classical and Contemporary Readings in the Philosophy of Religion*, edited by John Hick, is splendid, except for the absence of Locke, Leibniz, and Hegel. At any rate, each of these anthologies contains a great amount of the magnificent material which we are about to examine as philosophical perspectives on God and religion.

* * *

The Glossary is provided to help the reader with technical terms—specifically, those terms concerned with philosophy and religion. The first appearance in the text of each glossary term is printed in boldface.

Acknowledgments

The spirit of this book is drawn from the tradition of Jesuit education, which has thoughtfully related faith and reason for more than four and a half centuries, and whose ideals of liberal learning have inspired me for three and a half decades.

I am grateful for the corrections and helpful suggestions proffered by Frank Fair of Sam Houston University and David Fox of Montgomery College, both of whom read all ten chapters of the text, and by Michael Myers of Washington State University, who read the entire text and the Appendix. I thank Gonzaga University for granting me a sabbatical leave, during which I was able to do the research and writing for much of this book. Quanhua Liu of Gonzaga and Gregory Fields of Southern Illinois University helped me with the Appendix. David Calhoun, William Ryan, S.J., and John Wagner of Gonzaga and Catherine Ann Pomerleau of the University of Arizona gave me constructive criticisms for the Glossary. More than twenty years after working with him, I still remain grateful to Errol E. Harris, who directed my doctoral dissertation at Northwestern University. Martha Pomerleau, my wife, helped me with word processing and proofreading. Finally, I thank Ardsley House for the smooth, painless, and salutary process leading to this finished product.

Western Philosophies of Religion

1

Medieval Perspectives

Augustine: Life and Writings

$\mathcal{A}$ugustine's life and writings were characterized by the intensity and commitment of the man himself. Aurelius Augustinus was born at Tagaste in the Roman colony of Numidia in North Africa (in present-day Algeria) on November 13, 354, the son of Patricius, a **pagan** (until converting to **Christianity** shortly before his death), and Monica, a Christian. This mixed marriage reflected the mixed state of the Roman world in the first half of the fourth century. In 303, the Roman Emperor Diocletian ordered Christian churches and texts to be burned. Ten years later, Emperor Constantine issued an edict of toleration mandating freedom of **religion**. During Augustine's life (in 394) Emperor Theodosius established Christianity as the official religion of the empire. Augustine himself was raised a Christian, although his **baptism** was deferred. He studied Latin, arithmetic, and some Greek (which he hated) under a schoolmaster in Tagaste before going to the pagan town of Madaura (about twenty miles away), around 365, to further his studies.

In his autobiographical *Confessions* Augustine writes of his early life in terms of "my past foulness and the carnal corruptions of my **soul**." He describes his sixteenth year as one of "idleness," and broods over the memory of his joining "a group of very bad youngsters" in the theft of some fruit from a neighbor (the infamous pear-tree incident), maintaining that they enjoyed doing it "for the reason that it was forbidden." In 370, the year of his father's death, he was sent to the great port city of Carthage (in present-day Tunisia) to study rhetoric. In Carthage, as he later wrote, "a caldron of shameful loves seethed and sounded about me on every side." It was an environment of licentiousness and sensuality, and the young Augustine wallowed in its fleshpots. He soon took a mistress, with whom he lived for more than a decade and by whom he had an illegitimate son, Adeodatus (which literally means "given by God").[1]

Meanwhile, however, he was successful in his studies of rhetoric, which "were directed to the practice of law." In 373, he read Cicero's *Hortensius*, which was an "exhortation to **philosophy**" and which, he says, "set me on fire for it"; thereafter his life was devoted to a search for **truth**. By contrast, he was very unimpressed with the worldview to be found in the **Scriptures**, which, he says, "seemed to me unworthy of comparison with the nobility of Cicero's writings."[2] He was dissatisfied with the orthodox Christian explanations of evil, the literalism of conventional Scriptural exegesis, and the foolish **anthropomorphism** of Christians he knew.

The temporarily preferable alternative he found was **Manicheanism**, of which he later spoke harshly: "And so I fell in with certain men, doting in their pride, too carnal-minded and glib of speech, in whose mouth were the snares of the devil and a very bird-lime" in which young men like himself could easily be trapped. Between 373 and 382, he was an auditor in this radically **dualistic sect**, which taught that there are two ultimate and irreducible absolute principles, Ormuzd, the God of light and goodness, and Ahriman, the source of darkness and evil; that these two eternal principles were engaged in endless strife; and that man is their battleground, his soul being the good product of Ormuzd and his body being the evil work of Ahriman. The young Augustine was temperamentally attracted to the carnal tendencies of the sect and intellectually taken with its solution to the **problem of evil**.[3] Meanwhile, he founded a school of rhetoric in Carthage in 376.

But in time, questions and doubts surfaced and grew in his **mind**. A famous Manichean **bishop** named Faustus visited Carthage, and Augustine was determined to ask his questions. The meeting was a serious disappointment to Augustine. Although he found Faustus "gracious and pleasant in his conversation," he also thought him shallow and his responses facile and unsatisfying. As Augustine writes,

> After it had become quite clear to me that Faustus was not well equipped in those arts in which I had supposed him to be outstanding, I began to despair that he could ever explain and solve the things that perplexed me.... So this

Faustus, who had been a fatal snare to so many men, now began, neither willing it nor knowing it, to loosen the snare in which I was caught.[4]

Meanwhile, he was becoming annoyed by the rowdy behavior of his Carthaginian students and had heard that students were more cooperative and sophisticated in Rome.

So, with his **enthusiasm** for Manicheanism "dulled" by the meeting with Faustus, he, his mistress, and his son journeyed to Rome in 383, where he opened a new school of rhetoric. That same year, he adopted the **skepticism** of the New Academy, becoming convinced "that those philosophers whom they call the Academics were wiser than the rest" in their views "that all things are doubtful" and "that no truth can be apprehended by man."[5] His students in Rome were adept at evading their tuition payments, so that an opportunity to move to Milan as municipal master of rhetoric in 384 seemed attractive enough to impel his moving again.

There he went to hear the preaching of Ambrose, the great Christian Bishop of Milan, who was renowned as a model of effective oratory. He found himself drawn to the content as well as to the style of Ambrose's sermons, from which he came to see that parts of the Scriptures could be interpreted "by way of **allegory**, by which same passages I was killed when I had taken them literally" (that is, a literal interpretation proved spiritually destructive).[6] That same year, he began reading the Latin translations of **Neoplatonists** (including the *Enneads* of Plotinus) by the Christian Victorinus, himself a Neoplatonist. These writings helped him overcome his **materialistic** tendencies and his **epistemological** skepticism, to achieve a less anthropomorphic conception of God, and to perceive a new way of solving the problem of evil. He became increasingly sympathetic to a Neoplatonic brand of Christianity. In the meantime, his mother, Monica, was pressing him not only to return to Christianity but to get married as a means of escaping his life of **sin**. She succeeded in separating Augustine from his long-time mistress, who returned to North Africa, leaving him with their twelve-year-old son (who died in 388 at the age of seventeen). But Augustine's developing intellectual conversion was yet unmatched by a moral conversion, and he quickly took another mistress.

He had yet to find the peace of which he writes in the first paragraph of his *Confessions*, while addressing God: "you have made us for yourself, and our heart is restless until it rests in you." But his conversion became complete in his garden in 386 when he heard a child's voice chanting "from a nearby house, . . . repeating over and over, 'Take up and read. Take up and read.'" As he says, "I interpreted this solely as a command given to me by God to open the book and read the first chapter I should come upon." The book was the Bible, and the passage, which he took most personally, was from Paul's Epistle, *Romans* (13:13–14): "I snatched it up, opened it, and read in silence the chapter on which my eyes first fell: 'Not in rioting and drunkenness, not in chambering and impurities, not in strife and envying; but put you on the Lord Jesus Christ, and make not provision for the flesh in its concupiscences. . . .' Instantly, . . . as if before a peaceful light streaming into my heart, all the dark shadows of doubt fled away."[7] In 387, after a year's retreat, he and Adeodatus were baptized by Ambrose the day before Easter. His mother, Monica, who had come to Italy for the occasion, died while they were awaiting a boat back to Africa. Augustine then delayed his return and, while in Rome, wrote several works, including *On Free Choice of the Will*.

In 388, he returned to Tagaste, sold his property, and founded a small **monastic** community. He reluctantly was ordained a priest in 391 in Hippo, a seaport (in modern-day Algeria). He established a **monastery** there and, in 395, was consecrated auxiliary Bishop of Hippo. The following year, Valerius, the Bishop of Hippo, died, and Augustine succeeded him, remaining in that position until his own death more than a third of a century later.

Most of his great writings were completed after his **ordination**. In 395, his *On Free Choice of the Will*, the book on which we shall mainly focus, was cast into its final form. *On the Advantage of Believing* (about 391), *On Christian Doctrine* (397), *On **Faith** in Things Unseen* (400), *Confessions* (about 400), *On the Trinity* (400–415), *The City of God* (413–426), *The Enchiridion on Faith, Hope and Love* (421), and his *Retractations* (426–427) all come from this period (after his ordination). Other works we shall briefly consider—*Against the Academicians* (386), *De Ordine* (386), his *Soliloquies* (387), and *Of True Religion* (390)—were written between his conversion and his ordination. Through much of the years between his ordination and his death, Augustine was engaged in polemical controversies with the Manicheans, the **Donatists**, and the **Pelagians**. In a sense his greatest work was inspired by another controversy. When Alaric and his Visigoths sacked Rome in 410, pagans blamed the Christians for the tribulations of Rome, which, they said, was being punished for deserting its ancient gods. *The City of God* includes a defense of Christianity against this accusation. In 430, the Vandals, under the command of Gaiseric, expanding their conquest of the crumbling Empire, swept through Spain, invaded North Africa, and laid siege to Hippo; during this siege Augustine died, while reciting the *Psalms*, on August 28, 430. About a year later, the Vandals burned much of Hippo, though not the cathedral or Augustine's library. His reputation as the most important Christian philosophical **theologian** would remain unchallenged for over eight centuries thereafter.

Augustine: Religious Philosophy

Faith and Reason. Augustine's position on faith and reason is developed, in the context of his break with the Manicheans, in his work *The Advantage of Believing*. Manicheanism was a **Gnostic** sect (founded in the third century by the Persian Mani and combining elements of **Zoroastrianism** and Christianity) that taught that redemptive **knowledge** is rationally attainable without reliance on **revelation**. Augustine criticizes the Manicheans for alluring him, as a youth "desirous of truth," with the false promise "that by pure and simple **reason**, apart from all formidable authority, they would lead their willing listeners on to God and free them from all error." Against them he insists that the authority of the Scriptures must be accepted as a foundation for religious understanding, although the Scriptures are handed down to us in a four-fold variety of ways: "according to history, according to **aetiology**, according to **analogy**, and according to allegory" (aetiology is the study of **causal** origins). Thus, he has come to recognize that the Scriptures are not always to be interpreted in a historically literal manner in order to remain authoritative; he now approvingly quotes Paul's Epistle, *II Corinthians* (3:6): "The letter killeth, but the spirit quickeneth."[8]

But if submission to the authority of the Scriptures requires their interpretation on our part, we must be sensitive to the possible ways in which we might interpret or misinterpret them.

> There are three kinds of mistakes according to which men err when they read anything. . . . The first kind is that in which what is false is thought to be true, though the writer has thought otherwise. The second kind, not so widespread but no less harmful, occurs when what is false is considered true and is so thought because the writer also thought so. The third is the perception of some kind of truth from the writing of another, though the writer himself did not understand it. In this kind there is no little profit.

Thus, if Scriptural revelation is to provide a basis for religious knowledge, it must be carefully interpreted. The purpose of such a pursuit is not purely theoretical or speculative but involves the practical consideration of the welfare of our souls. As Augustine says, "It is for the sake of the soul that all religion exists."[9] This echoes the earlier, more famous summary, in his *Soliloquies*, of the only two objects of knowledge that he seeks: "I desire to know God and the soul" (*Deum et animam scire cupio*); he proceeds to add that "up to now I love nothing except God and the soul, neither of which I know" (*nunc autem nihil aliud amo quam Deum et animam, quorum neutrum scio*).[10] Reason can help develop a philosophical understanding of these pivotal natural objects of our love.

In *Believing*, Augustine tries to define his theory of faith and reason. He begins by reminding us that there is a difference between legitimate belief and a foolish credulity, the problem being where to draw the line between the two: "you will perhaps say: I grant that at times we have to believe something; now, explain how in religion it is not base to believe before one knows. I shall do so, if I can."[11]

He attempts to reduce the Gnosticism of the Manicheans to absurdity by asking whether the majority of men, who are not intellectually capable of rational understanding, "should be denied religion" altogether; he suggests that it is intolerable to suppose that they "should in any way be deserted or rejected" because of a lack of intellectual ability for which they are not responsible. But, beyond this rhetorical appeal, he maintains that even the intellectual who is philosophically able must begin by submitting in faith: "unless he first believes that he will arrive at the goal which he has set for himself, and shows the mind of a suppliant, obeying certain important and necessary precepts, and completely purging himself by a certain way of life, he will not in any other way attain to that which is pure truth."[12]

There may seem to be some tension between what he is saying here and his endorsement of **Platonic** wisdom elsewhere. In *The City of God*, he says, "To Plato is given the praise of having perfected philosophy" and "It is evident that none come nearer to us than the Platonists," admitting, "Certain partakers with us in the **grace** of Christ wonder when they hear and read that Plato had conceptions concerning God, in which they recognize considerable agreement with the truth of our religion." Pagan philosophers such as Plato, Aristotle, and Plotinus were able to believe in God and rationally argue for God without having the benefit of the authority of the Judeo-Christian Scriptures. In *The City of God* Augustine maintains that we see that the world exists but believe that God exists. "That God made the world, we can believe from no one more safely than from God Himself. But where have we heard Him? Nowhere more distinctly than in the Holy Scriptures, where His prophet said, 'In the beginning God created the heavens and the earth.'" Aristotle, of course, did argue (in his *Metaphysics*) for the **necessary** existence of his Unmoved

Mover on the basis of reason alone. Indeed, Augustine himself admits that "though the voices of the prophets were silent, the world itself, by its well-ordered changes and movements, and by the fair appearance of all visible things, bears a testimony of its own, both that it has been created, and also that it could not have been created save by God."[13] Augustine is not necessarily guilty of **logical** self-**contradiction** here. His **ambiguity** seems to be due to the fact that he has failed clearly to distinguish (as Aquinas later did) between religious truths (such as those concerning God's existence and nature) that are philosophically arguable apart from traditional revelation and those (like those concerning the **Trinity** and the **Incarnation**) that must be believed on that latter basis alone.

In On Faith in Things Unseen, Augustine makes an important and valuable point (anticipating William James by about 1500 years), to the effect that we do commonly and reasonably believe in matters that can neither be literally seen nor intellectually known, "that even those things which are not seen ought to be believed." He rhetorically asks, against the Gnostics, "with what eyes do you see your friend's will toward you? For no will can be seen with bodily eyes. Or, indeed, do you also see in your mind that which is taking place in the mind of another?" He argues that the upshot of the Gnostic view is a pernicious collapse of interpersonal trust and confidence: "If this faith in human affairs is removed, who will not mark how great will be their disorder and what dreadful confusion will follow? For, who will be cherished by anyone in mutual charity, since love itself is invisible, if what I do not see I ought not to believe?" He proceeds to indict the Gnostics for themselves believing in historical events that they could not have witnessed, in geographical "places where they themselves have never been," and even in reports concerning their own parentage.[14]

Augustine shrewdly anticipates the objection that this is a lame analogy: "But, you will say, although I am not able to see the kindness of a friendly person toward me, I am able, nevertheless, to trace it by many indications; whereas you, on the **contrary**, can show no evidence of those things not seen which you wish us to believe." Against this objection Augustine responds, "They are very much in error who think that we believe in Christ without any **proofs** of Christ. For what evidences are more clear than those which have been foretold and fulfilled?" He goes on to discuss Scriptural **prophecies** that historically came to pass and allegedly provide evidence for the beliefs of Christianity—"things which you do not see have been long ago prophesied and are now so manifestly fulfilled." He also deftly parries the objection that these prophecies were concocted by Christians as *ad hoc* evidences, saying that, in fact, they derive from the Old Testament "books of our opponents, the Jews." How strong this leaves the analogy between believing on the basis of what we personally experience and faith based on traditional revelation remains, of course, a matter for critical consideration. For those of us who are skeptical about this analogy, Augustine has another consideration, appealing to the fact that Christianity has so remarkably eclipsed the old pagan religions: "Even if no testimonies concerning Christ and the Church had appeared in advance, ought not the unexpected illumination of the human race by divine brightness move every one to believe, when we behold false gods abandoned . . . ?"[15] But, if anything, this sort of appeal to popularity is even less convincing than the analogy that appeals to the fulfillment of Scriptural prophecies.

In *Believing*, Augustine distinguishes the two types of persons "who are praiseworthy" regarding religion—those who have already learned its truths and those who are conscientiously striving to do so—from the three types who are "worthy of censure"—"those who think that they know what they do not know," those who, realizing they do not know, nevertheless fail to seek the truth in such a way as to discover it, and "those who neither think they know nor wish to seek" the truth in any manner whatsoever. He also establishes a trichotomy among "understanding, belief, and opinion," saying that "the first is always without fault; the second is at times faulty; and the third is never without fault." Understanding and knowledge, by definition, can only be of truth, so that they are always good. Belief becomes "blameworthy" when it is either in that which is "unworthy" of belief or "too readily held." Mere "opinion is very base for two reasons: both in that he who has convinced himself that he already knows cannot learn (even if it were possible for the thing to be learned), and the very rashness is of itself a sign of a mind ill disposed."[16] This trichotomy (anticipating Kant's), although important, is critically valuable only to the extent that we have independent criteria concerning what is true, what is unworthy of our belief, and what is too rashly accepted. Unfortunately, Augustine does not develop a systematic epistemology to provide such criteria.

He proceeds to speak of the interrelationships among the three elements of his trichotomy:

> What we understand, accordingly, we owe to reason; what we believe, to authority; and what we have an opinion on, to error. But everyone who understands also believes, and everyone who has an opinion believes, too; but not everyone who believes understands, and no one who merely has an opinion understands.

In his *Retractations* he says that this passage should not be interpreted as suggesting that we cannot "*know* what we believe on the authority of suitable witnesses";[17] although knowledge based on reason and personal experience is different from knowledge based on authority, Augustine would hold that we can know matters of revealed faith through the acceptance of authority. But, then, we might ask, what is knowledge and what are its criteria? If it is justified, true belief, is traditional revelation an adequate criterion of its truth, and is the authority of such revelation adequate justification for believing? For Augustine the answer is affirmative, but a critical thinker should be cautious about agreeing with him too readily here.

Gnostics (including Manicheans) "who say that we are to believe nothing, except what we know" are properly "on their guard" against rash, irresponsible opinion. Yet, according to Augustine, they fail to acknowledge the value of an honest, searching faith: "if they consider carefully that there is a very great difference between, on the one hand, thinking one knows and, on the other, believing, under the influence of some authority, what one realizes he does not know, they would surely avoid errors and the charge of inhumanity and pride." Against the Gnostics, he claims that "for a man that cannot see the truth, authority is at hand to make him fit for this. . . . partly through **miracles**, partly through the crowds that accept it." Augustine uses these further appeals to authority and popular belief to support his major point, that "souls have no sure way to wisdom and health unless faith first prepares them for reason."[18] Even though Augustine does not convincingly establish that our belief in submission to the authority of revelation is a necessary propaedeutic to religious understanding or that such belief merits the title of knowledge, his analysis of the **Biblical** view of faith as "the evidence of things not seen" (*Hebrews* 11:1) is provocative and has proved to be historically influential.

In *Of True Religion* Augustine writes "that philosophy, i.e., the pursuit of wisdom, cannot be quite divorced from religion." Nevertheless, he distinguishes between their respective methods of reason and authority: "Authority demands belief and prepares man for reason. Reason leads to understanding and knowledge."[19] But perhaps the most famous statement of Augustine's position on faith and reason is that which says that "understanding is the reward of faith. Therefore do not seek to understand in order to believe, but believe that thou mayest understand."[20] This view of faith seeking understanding was to dominate Christian philosophy throughout the **medieval** period.

God's Existence. Augustine's **argument** for God, in his philosophical dialogue *On Free Choice of the Will*, deliberately **presupposes** this position on faith and reason. He quotes the Old Testament "prophet who says, 'Unless you believe, you shall not understand.' "[21] His argument for God's existence (like Descartes's twelve centuries later) builds on the **certainty** of the existence of the self. This is achieved through the recognition that even mistaken ideas and beliefs require that someone exists to conceive of them. We might conceivably be in error about everything else. "But if you did not exist, it would be impossible for you to be deceived."[22] It is important that some such certain truth be established as a basis for argumentation. In the famous *si fallor, sum* passage in *The City of God*, he develops the reasoning involved here against philosophical skeptics:

> I am not at all afraid of the arguments of the Academicians, who say, What if you are deceived? For if I am deceived, I am. For he who is not, cannot be deceived; and if I am deceived, by this same token I am. . . . Since, therefore, I, the person deceived, should be, even if I were deceived, certainly I am not deceived in this knowledge that I am.[23]

In *Free Choice* Augustine proceeds to argue that in order thus to know that I exist, I must also be alive and have understanding. But among these three—existence, life, and understanding—we can establish a hierarchy. Being alive is superior to merely existing, since the former presupposes the latter. Likewise, "it is very certain that he who understands both *is* and *lives*," so that understanding is superior to mere life. On the other hand, what is alive does not necessarily understand, and "what *is* does not necessarily live or understand."[24]

In understanding, we typically use the five external senses of "sight, hearing, smell, taste, and touch" as well as "a certain inner sense to which all things are referred by the five familiar senses." The inner sense is superior to the external senses in that it perceives not only the objects of the external senses (colors, sounds, odors, flavors, and textures) but also perceive the external senses perceiving those objects. Thus, the inner sense makes judgments concerning the external senses (e.g., that what I see, smell, and hear refer to the same common object—wood burning). Augustine introduces a principle at this point: "No one can doubt that what judges is better than what is judged." According to this principle, the inner sense is held to be "more excellent" than the external senses. Reason, in turn, makes judgments concerning the inner sense (e.g., that the sights, sounds, and smells associated by it are correctly referred to the common object of wood burning, that it constitutes an avoidable danger, etc.), so that it must be superior to the inner sense. Indeed, Augustine maintains that it is our most excellent **faculty**, denying that we "can find anything in man's nature which is more noble than reason."[25]

Yet even an understanding of our own nature is not adequate. For, as we have seen, Augustine says to God in his *Confessions*, "our heart is restless until it rests in you."[26] But the principle that that which judges is superior to that which is judged, combined with the realization that reason is the highest faculty in man, provides a basis for Augustine's proof of God's existence. In *Free Choice* he goes on to ask, "What if we should be able to find something which you would not doubt not only exists, but even is more excellent than our reason? Will you hesitate to say that, whatever it is, this is our God?" Evodius, his interlocutor, shrewdly responds, "I would not immediately say that this is God. I am not inclined to call God that to which my reason is inferior, but rather that to whom no one is superior. . . . I shall admit that this is God to which nothing is granted to be superior."[27] This formula for God, as that Being to Whom nothing is superior, is also indicated in other works of Augustine,[28] and it seems to have influenced Anselm in the construction of his **ontological argument**.

At any rate, in *Free Choice* Augustine proceeds to argue that if anything can be shown to be superior to human reason, God must exist. He considers mathematical certainties as examples of eternal, **immutable**, **universal**, and necessary truths: "But seven and three are ten, not only now, but forever. There has never been a time when they are not ten. Therefore, I have said that the truth of number is incorruptible and common to all who think." But since such truth is eternal, immutable, and common to all who know, Augustine argues, it must be "more excellent than our minds" that know it. He maintains that we do not judge such truth or make judgments about it but only judge *"according* to it," so that our minds are not superior to it. Second, if such "truth were equal to our minds, it would be subject to change," rather than being immutable. Yet since there are only three alternative possibilities—that truth is "more excellent than our minds, or equally so, or less"—by a logical **process of elimination**, "if truth is neither inferior nor equal to our minds, it follows that it is superior to them, and more excellent." Augustine maintains that this eternal, immutable, universal truth either is inferior to some other reality which is God or is itself God. "For if there is something more excellent than truth, this is God. If there is not, then truth itself is God. Whether or not truth is God, you cannot deny that God exists." He concludes his demonstration thus: "God exists, truly and in the highest degree. This indubitable fact we maintain, I think, not only by faith, but also by a sure though somewhat tenuous form of reasoning."[29]

This fascinating proof of God's existence does not fit neatly into the usual typology of ontological, **cosmological, teleological,** and **moral arguments.** However, it has also not been particularly influential in the history of philosophical theology. Why not? The structure of the argument can be expressed thus: If anything is superior to the rational mind, God must exist; eternal, immutable, universal truth is superior to the rational mind (since the latter judges according to it and not about it); therefore, God must exist. Although this is a **valid argument,** there are three problems with it. First, the principle that "what judges is better than what is judged" is stated **axiomatically** and not critically considered. If I were to encounter a finite being that is superior to me in every respect, I would make judgments about it and not according to it without altering its superiority to me. Second, Augustine's Neoplatonic conception of truth presupposes that it is independent of all human minds. This may be correct, but it is not **self-evident.** Mathematical truths, for example, may be merely a function of the way our minds interrelate their abstract ideas— either arbitrarily, in the sense that it is the way our minds happen to think, or necessarily, in the sense that our minds are constituted in such a way that they must thus conceive of such relationships. And, third, there is an important difference between saying that eternal truth exists and that the Judeo-Christian God exists. If the highest reality is impersonal truth, such as that of mathematics, it is a dubious candidate for religious worship and far from having the list of divine attributes to be found in the fourth chapter of Augustine's *Confessions:* "Most high, most good, most mighty, most almighty; most merciful and most just; . . . ever active, and ever at rest; . . . supporting, fulfilling, and protecting things; creating, nourishing, and perfecting them."[30] It is surely significant, from a religious perspective, whether there is a Being having such characteristics. Abstract, impersonal truth is no acceptable substitute. Of course, this is not to deny the Biblical notion of "a God of truth" (*Deuteronomy* 32:4; cf. *John* 14:6), to which Augustine beautifully refers in his *Soliloquies,* where he calls "God the Truth, in whom and by whom and through whom all those things are true which are true" (*Deus Veritas, in quo et a quo et per quem vera sunt, quae vera sunt omnia*).[31] However, to speak thus of God as the ground of truth is not to reduce God to an abstract principle.

The Problem of Evil. Augustine's solution of the problem of evil occupies much of the philosophical discussion of his *Free Choice.* Indeed, the first sentence of that book is the challenge presented to Augustine by Evodius: "Tell me, please, whether God is not the cause of evil." The problem of evil, in the context of Christian faith, might be formulated thus: if the perfect (e.g., **omnipotent**, **omniscient**, and absolutely good) God of the **monotheistic** religions exists and is the causal source of everything else that exists, including our free will, and our free will can choose evil, how can God escape ultimate causal responsibility for the evil done? Augustine, beginning to seek a solution to this problem, says: "Let us take up our search in the following order, if you will. First, how is it proved that God exists? Second, are all things whatsoever, insofar as they are good, from God? Finally, is free will to be counted as a good?"[32] We have already analyzed Augustine's answer to the first of these three questions.

Augustine argues that everything which has come to be must be "formable." "Nothing can give itself **form**, since nothing can give to itself what it does not have." He goes on to argue Platonically that whatever acquires form in coming to be must ultimately derive that form from "an immutable and eternal Form," which is God. This, he insists, holds true for all three of the sorts of beings we experience:

> If you can find any other kind of creature except that which exists and does not live, or that which lives and does not understand, or that which exists, lives, and understands—only then can you tell me that there exists some good which does not come from God.

Thus, the only three forms of being we can experience, all of which are **intrinsically** good but changeable creatures, "exist as a result of that Form which is always of the same nature. Therefore, all good things, whether great or small, can come only from God."[33] This argument presumes that no good being is coeternal with God but that each one other than God is a creature dependent on the divine Form for its form of being. It also requires that the three categories of creatures be **exhaustive** and that every member of each class be intrinsically good.

"Now let us turn to a third question: whether we can establish that free will is to be numbered among the goods." Can it be good when man uses it as a means for committing evil? Augustine reminds us that it is also a **necessary condition** for our being morally good and doing what is morally right, "that no righteous act could be performed except by free choice of the will, and . . . that God gave it for this reason." Even physical gifts, such as our eyes, hands, and feet, can be misused or abused.

> If, therefore, we find among the goods of the body some that a man can use wrongly, but that we cannot say ought not to have been given to man, since we have agreed that they are goods, why should we wonder if there are in the spirit certain goods, of which we can make wrong use, but which, because they are goods, could not have been given by anyone but Him from whom all good things proceed?

This analogy limps a bit because what misuses the goods of the body is the will, whereas it is the will itself which chooses wrongly. Still it does seem plausible that free will can be a good if it is the necessary condition for our choosing rightly, despite the fact that it can also choose wrongly. Augustine asks rhetorically, "will you think that free will is not a good when no one can live rightly without it?"[34] The question is whether the necessary condition of our being morally good is itself necessarily good. It may not seem obvious that this is the case, but Augustine's argument here rests on this assumption.

Of course, it follows logically that free will must come from God, if all good things come from God and free will is a good. But, then, what of evil? Augustine explains, "evil is a turning away from immutable goods and a turning toward changeable goods." This "turning" introduces the defect of evil into the will, though no amount of such defect abolishes the fact that the will is **essentially** good.

> Thus, if all good is completely removed, no vestige of reality persists; indeed, nothing remains. Every good is from God. There is nothing of any kind that is not from God. Therefore . . . the movement of turning away from good, which we admit to be sin, is a defective movement and . . . every defect comes from nothing.[35]

This is the Neoplatonic theory of evil as nothing. If God created all other things that exist, evil must be conceived as not a thing in order to avoid God's being responsible for it.

In his *Enchiridion* Augustine pursues this theory of evil as **privation** further. Although all things that exist are good, not all things are equally good; nevertheless, the "*ensemble*" of various types and levels of goods "constitutes the universe in all its wonderful order and beauty." Furthermore, he argues, "even that which is called evil, when it is regulated and put in its own place, only enhances our admiration of the good; for we enjoy and value the good more when we compare it with the evil." The apparent callousness of this **aesthetic** treatment of evil might seem somewhat mollified by Augustine's assurance that God "would never permit the existence of anything evil among His works, if He were not so omnipotent and good that He can bring good even out of evil. For what is that which we call evil but the absence of good?"[36]

Although they are intrinsically good, no creatures are absolutely and unchangeably good, so that "their good may be diminished and increased. But for good to be diminished is an evil." Yet, since all being is good, the corruption of evil can only occur in what is fundamentally good. Nothing which is thoroughly evil, or "wholly consumed by corruption," could exist. Augustine draws his **paradoxical conclusion**: "Nothing, then, can be evil except something which is good." Augustine, perhaps somewhat uncomfortably, admits that this violates the logical **law of excluded middle**:

> Accordingly, in the case of these contraries which we call good and evil, the rule of the logicians, that two contraries cannot be predicated at the same time of the same thing, does not hold. . . . But although no one can doubt that good and evil are contraries, not only can they exist at the same time, but evil cannot exist without good, or in anything that is not good.[37]

In his *Confessions* Augustine develops a subtle **reductio ad absurdum** argument against the view that anything can exist that is totally evil rather than at least somewhat good:

> beings that suffer corruption are nevertheless good. . . . unless they were good, they could not be corrupted. . . . if they were not good at all, there would be nothing in them to be corrupted. . . . whatever suffers corruption is deprived of some good. . . . If things are deprived of all good whatsoever, they will not exist at all. If they continue to be, and still continue incapable of suffering corruption, they will be better than before, because they will remain forever incorruptible. What is more monstrous than to claim that things become better by losing all their good? Therefore, if they are deprived of all good, they will be absolutely nothing. Hence, as long as they exist, they are good.[38]

We can cast this into **deductive** form thus: (1) If beings could be "deprived of all good" and "continue to be," then "they could not be corrupted" further. (2) If "they could not be corrupted" further, then they would "be better than before" they were "deprived of all good" (i.e., when they could still be corrupted). (3) If they would "be better than before" they were "deprived of all good," then they "become better by losing all their good." So if beings could be "deprived of all good" and "continue to be," they would "become better by losing all their good." But we must deny (as "monstrous") the **absurd** "claim that things become better by losing all their good." And thus we must also deny that beings could be "deprived of all good" and "continue to be." The logical problem with this formally valid **sorites** is that the apparent truth of the second **premise** hinges on an ambiguity regarding two different ways in which something might be incorruptible. Anything that (like God) is incorruptible because it is thoroughly good and in no way inclined to evil is indeed better than any corruptible thing. But a thing that is incorruptible because it is devoid of any good is, by definition, less good than something which is somewhat good and therefore corruptible.

More broadly, what is to be said of Augustine's famous theory of evil as nothing? We might begin by considering his own former reservations about it, which he summarizes and repudiates in his *Confessions*:

> I sought an answer to the question, "Whence is evil?" but I sought it in an evil way, and I did not see the evil in my very search. . . . Thus . . . I said: . . . has it no being whatsoever? Why then do we fear and shun what does not exist? If we fear it without cause, that very fear is evil . . . and that evil is all the more serious in so far as what we fear does not exist, and still we are fearful of it.[39]

What Augustine may have been recognizing in this "evil" critique of the privation theory of evil is that it dismisses evil in too facile a manner to call it nothing. But what he failed to see is that fear of nothing might be rationally appropriate to the extent that it involves the denial of reality that is good. Beyond this, though, his theory seems merely an *ad hoc* solution to the problem of evil, which becomes so thorny in a **monistic** system, such as Neoplatonism, or a Christian system based on an **omnicompetent** Creator. There is no independent experiential evidence to support this all-too-convenient theory that all being is good and that evil is mere privation.

At any rate, this theory allows Augustine to argue that free will, which is a good creation of God, is the ultimate cause of evil and therefore the responsibility of the creature who thus misuses this good. *The City of God* expresses the point thus: "And indeed evil had never been, had not the mutable nature—mutable, though good, and created by the most high God and immutable Good, who created all things good—brought evil upon itself by sin."[40] Augustine believes that God, though omnisciently aware that we would misuse the good faculty of free will to choose evil, cannot be held responsible for that abuse. As he says in *Free Choice*, "I cannot find, and assert there cannot be found, any way in which to attribute our sins to God the Creator." The fault, then, of our wrongdoing lies in our own will: "After all, what cause of the will could there be, except the will itself? . . . Either the will is the first cause of sin, or else there is no first cause. Sin cannot rightly be imputed to anyone but the sinner, nor can it rightly be imputed to him unless he wills it."[41] Thus, in the writings of Augustine, "faith seeking understanding" strives to achieve knowledge regarding God and evil.

Anselm: Life and Writings

$\mathscr{A}$nselm's life and writings extend significantly beyond the two pages or so of "ontological" argumentation for which he is deservedly famous. He was born in 1033 at Aosta in Piedmont (now in Italy, near its junction with France and Switzerland). Very little is known about his father, Gundulf, or Ermenburga, his mother, both of whom died when he was in his twenties.

Anselm (like Augustine before him and Aquinas after him) can be considered a medieval thinker. For our purposes, the medieval period (or "**middle ages**" between **antiquity** and **modern** times) can be viewed as lasting almost exactly a thousand years, from 410 A.D. (when Alaric I captured Rome) to 1453 (when Constantinople fell to the Turks, under Sultan Mohammed II). What some people refer to as the philosophical "Dark Ages" lasted for about half of this time, from the death of Boethius in 524 to the birth of Anselm; during these five centuries little philosophy of lasting importance seems to have emerged.

European history before and shortly after the turn of the millennium was hectic. Learning had progressed under the "Carolingian Renaissance" of Charlemagne, who encouraged Alcuin, an English churchman and educator, to help make France a new Athens. Alcuin had written a rhetoric text; through his influence the seven liberal arts, the "trivium" (logic, grammar, and rhetoric) and "quadrivium" (arithmetic, music, geometry, and astronomy), became the curriculum for medieval Western Europe. But after the death of Charlemagne in 814, his son Louis I, called "the Pious," uneasily ruled his empire, being formally deposed by his own sons and later restored as emperor; Louis died in 840. The Treaty of Verdun (843) split up the empire among his three sons, which perpetuated the instability and dissension. The ninth- and tenth-century invasions of the Vikings seriously disrupted intellectual life in Europe; and the **papacy** was so controlled by secular powers that it could do little to help. Conditions improved after the German king Otto I (called "the Great") became emperor in 962, when Pope John XII appealed to him for help against the aggressions of Berengar II. Otto thus united his German middle kingdom (carved out by the partition of the Treaty of Verdun) with Italy. The pope found Otto becoming alarmingly powerful and plotted against him. So in 963, Otto had John deposed and replaced with someone under his influence.

The year 1000 was anticipated with fear and trembling by those who imagined that it would mark the end of the world. Meanwhile, monastic life was undergoing a rebirth at monasteries, such as the one at Cluny, which preserved and handed down European learning, although the transcription of manuscripts was laborious and transportation and communication were extremely slow. The feudal system was being challenged, and the monasteries strove to effect moral reforms against **simony** and clerical marriages. The **Benedictine** monk Hildebrand, who became Pope Gregory VII, played a prominent role in such moral and political reform in the eleventh century, particularly condemning lay investiture, by means of which **abbacies** and **bishoprics** became subject to secular powers who could use them to their own advantage. As pope, for example, in 1076, he **excommunicated** Henry IV for opposing this reform; Henry became so unpopular as a result that the following year he saw fit to humble himself before Gregory at Canossa.

This is the historical background to Anselm's life. He left home in his early twenties, wandered through France, and reached Normandy in 1059. The Benedictine **abbey** of Bec, located southwest of Rouen, had been founded there seven years before Anselm's birth. He was drawn there by the reputation of the Italian logician and theologian Lanfranc, who was **prior** of the abbey and followed Alcuin in emphasizing the study of the trivium and quadrivium. When he decided to become a novice at the monastery at Bec the next year, he claims to have entered monastic life there rather than at Cluny in hopes that Lanfranc's intellectual achievements would leave him free of scholarly responsibilities so that he might devote his time and efforts to prayer and meditation. But three years later, Lanfranc left Bec to take a position at a new monastery established by William the Conqueror. Anselm, new as he was to monastic life, succeeded him as prior of the abbey. He remained in this position for fifteen years, becoming abbot in 1078. He enhanced the reputation of the school at Bec and won the admiration of William the Conqueror, who asked that Anselm hear his confession as he was dying at Rouen in 1087.

Most of Anselm's scholarly works were written during the three decades between his becoming prior and his leaving Bec. His *Monologium* was written about 1076 and was followed by *Proslogium* in 1077 or 1078. His three dialogues, *Concerning Truth, On Freedom of Choice*, and *The Fall of Satan*, seem to have been written in the eighties. His *Cur Deus Homo* was written in the mid- to late nineties (after he had gone to Canterbury). These writings, incorporating **dialectical** argumentation into theology, combined with his educational leadership at Bec, helped establish him as "the Father of **Scholasticism**."

In 1078, Anselm visited his friend and former master Lanfranc, who had become **Archbishop** of Canterbury after William's conquest of England. In 1093, about four years after Lanfranc's death, Anselm reluctantly left Bec and crossed the Channel to succeed his friend as Archbishop of Canterbury, being consecrated on September 25th. Then began his official struggle with the monarchy for control over the Church in England. William Rufus, the son of William the Conqueror, wished to maintain political control over the Norman church. Unlike Lanfranc, who had accommodated himself to such secular authority, Anselm had supported Pope Gregory VII's stand on behalf of the freedom of the church from nonecclesiastical control. Like Gregory and Pope Urban II, Anselm opposed lay investiture. When Anselm went to Rome (without William's permission) to get Urban's support in 1097, the king banished him and confiscated the diocesan properties. While in exile, Anselm was given places of honor at the councils of Bari in 1098 (where he ably defended the *Filioque* of the Creed in the East-West theological controversy over the Procession of the Holy Spirit in the Trinity) and in Rome in 1099.

Anselm remained in exile until 1100, when William Rufus was succeeded by Henry I, who recalled Anselm to his **see**. Anselm helped arrange Henry's marriage to Matilda of Scotland and worked to win the support of the barons for Henry. But soon, the conflict over lay investiture resurfaced, and Anselm refused to consecrate bishops and abbots nominated by Henry. In 1103, Anselm was in Rome getting the support of the new pope, Paschal II, and again was banished. Finally in 1107, after Rome threatened to excommunicate the king, Anselm secured Henry's agreement to surrender the claim to investiture in return for certain church revenues.

There is a story of Anselm's lying on his deathbed on Palm Sunday in 1109 and being told that he would probably spend Easter Sunday with God. Anselm's touching reply was that he would accept God's will in the matter, but that he would gratefully welcome a bit more time to solve the problem of the origin of the soul on which he had been working and on which he doubted anyone else would labor sufficiently to solve. But, in fact, he died four days before Easter, on April 21st.

Anselm: Religious Philosophy

Faith and Reason. Anselm's position on faith and reason is indicated in the Preface to *Proslogium*, where he explains that he has written it, like his earlier work *Monologium*, as one who "seeks to understand what he believes" and that "the first might be known as, An Example of Meditation on the Grounds of Faith, and its sequel as, Faith Seeking Understanding."[42] This theme of *Fides Quaerens Intellectum* is clearly Augustinian, and fidelity to that tradition is obviously important to Anselm. As he proudly writes in the Preface to *Monologium*, "after frequent consideration, I have not been able to find that I have made . . . any statement which is **inconsistent** with the writings of the Catholic Fathers, or especially with those of St. Augustine."[43] Perhaps Anselm's most famous statement on faith and reason appears at the end of the first chapter of *Proslogium*:

> For I do not seek to understand that I may believe, but I believe in order to under-stand. For this also I believe,—that unless I believed, I should not understand.[44]

This theme of employing reason to gain an understanding of doctrines of faith is elaborated in the first book of *Cur Deus Homo* (Why God Became Man), a dialogue between Anselm and Boso, a real (rather than fictitious) Christian monk. In the first chapter Anselm says that Christians seek rational grounds for religious beliefs, "not for the sake of attaining to faith by means of reason, but that they may be gladdened by understanding and meditating on those things which they believe; and that, as far as possible, they may be always ready to convince any one who demands of them a reason of that hope which is in us."[45] As we proceed to consider Anselm's arguments for God, it will be good to keep this in mind—the purpose of his argumentation is not to generate faith by means of understanding (hence not to convert "infidels"), but to confer on us the joy that comes from understanding what we believe, as well as to show that some rational grounds can be achieved for matters of faith already held.

Anselm has Boso take the issue even further, when he maintains that it would be negligent of us, who are confirmed in the faith, not to "seek to understand what we believe." Second, he avers, although both infidels and Christians seek an understanding of ultimate reality, "they appeal to reason because they do not believe, but we, on the other hand, because we do believe," so that the methodologies are different, the one starting from ignorance and/or doubt, the other from the convictions of faith. Third, Boso denies that those convictions depend on rational understanding, which is sought "not to strengthen me in the faith, but to gratify one already confirmed by the knowledge of the truth itself." This indicates that faith itself, like rational understanding, imparts a knowledge of the truth. And, fourth, Boso acknowledges that religious faith transcends the limits of rational understanding and asks Anselm "only to explain it according to your ability."[46] Thus, there is no arrogant presumption that human reason can comprehend the doctrines of faith, but only the appeal that it be employed to achieve what it can in the way of understanding.

In addition to being an epistemological **rationalist** (i.e., one who holds that we can have **a priori** knowledge of some matters of fact), Anselm is also a theological rationalist, maintaining that religious doctrines (including those of the Incarnation and the Trinity) can be defended by rational argumentation. Yet he is not so extreme a rationalist as to subordinate Scriptural revelation or ecclesiastical authority to the findings of reason. As he says in *Cur Deus Homo*,

> I wish all that I say to be received with this understanding, that, if I shall have said anything which higher authority does not corroborate, though I appear to demonstrate it by argument, yet it is not to be received with any further confidence, than as so appearing to me for the time, until God in some way make a clearer revelation to me.[47]

There is also a second sense in which Anselm is not extreme in his theological rationalism. Like Boso, he does not imagine that we can always rationally explain what reason shows to be true. As he writes in *Monologium*,

> nor ought assured belief to be the less readily given to these truths which are declared to be such by cogent proofs, and without the contradiction of any other reason, if, because of the incomprehensibility of their own natural sublimity, they do not admit of explanation.[48]

Reason adequately does its job by showing us the truth, even if it cannot explain why it is as it is. As Anselm says in *Cur Deus Homo*,

> For what is clearly made out by absolute reasoning ought by no means to be questioned, even though the method of it be not understood.[49]

A third respect in which Anselm is not an extreme rationalist is that he does not think that faith should be limited to what can be rationally established. As Boso says in *Cur Deus Homo*, "even were I unable in any way to understand what I believe, still nothing could shake my constancy." Far from admonishing Boso, as an extreme rationalist might do, Anselm affirms that "we must understand that for all that a man can say or know still deeper grounds of so great a truth lie concealed."[50]

The object of both faith and reason is truth. Through faith we adopt beliefs regarding truth, and through reason we try to understand the truth. Anselm (like Augustine) is committed to a Christian Neoplatonism which regards truth as having **ontological** status outside of and **transcendent** to our minds. As he says in his *Monologium*, "anything that is true cannot exist without truth," and the divine nature, the ground of all truth, "is itself the supreme Truth."[51]

In his dialogue *Concerning Truth*, Anselm adopts a traditional **correspondence theory** that a **proposition** (i.e., a statement) is "true" whenever "what it affirms to exist does exist, and when what it denies to exist does not exist," immediately adding the Platonic claim that "nothing is true except by its participation in truth," so that of every true proposition it can be said that "there is truth in it." Later, he defines the truth in which all true propositions participate in terms of intellectual correctness: "Therefore, unless I am mistaken we can define truth as the rightness perceptible only to the mind." Many propositions can be true; yet ultimately, for Anselm, "truth is one in all these things"; and, like Augustine, he identifies this unity of all truth with God, the "Supreme Truth."[52]

Anselm holds that we have access to even the truth about God not only through faith but also through reason. But how can we think or express such truth, since propositions concerning God must be interpreted differently than similar propositions concerning creatures? For example, Anselm believes that "God is free" and "man is free" are both true propositions. In his dialogue *On Freedom of Choice*, he provides a definition: "freedom of choice is the ability to keep uprightness of will for itself alone"; later, he adds, "nevertheless, the freedom of God is quite different from the freedom possessed by rational creatures."[53] Likewise, in *The Fall of Satan*, Anselm attributes goodness to "every being" as well as to God, adopting Augustine's views that nothing, or nonbeing, cannot come from God, "because from God come only being and good," "that evil is nothing," and that, although God is the cause of all being, "evil is only corruption, or defect, which has no being except as it is in some being," which is good to the extent that it is real.[54] But, again, Anselm would deny that God's goodness is the same as ours. Although "God is good" and "man is good" are both true propositions, what access can we have to the meaning of the former?

Anselm discusses this in *Monologium*. He begins with the recognition that our language regarding God and creatures cannot be **univocal**, when he says that "the supreme Being is so above and beyond every other nature that, whenever any statement is made concerning it in words which are also applicable to other natures, the sense of these words in this case is by no means that in which they are applied to other natures." On the other hand, theological language cannot be regarded as utterly **equivocal** without becoming meaningless. "For what sense have I conceived of, in all these words that I have thought of, except the common and familiar sense? If, then, the familiar sense of words is alien to that Being, whatever I have **inferred** to be attributable to it is not its property." How, then, can we truly think or say anything at all about God at the level of faith or at that of reason? Anselm's answer anticipates Aquinas's famous doctrine of analogy:

> For often we speak of things which we do not express with precision as they are. . . . And often we see a thing, not precisely as it is in itself, but through a likeness or image.

Thus, though the divine nature is "**ineffable**, because it is incapable of description in words" that are literally and precisely true, still "an inference regarding it . . . is not therefore necessarily false."[55] This would be an indirect and incomplete apprehension of the truth about the divine nature, yet it remains a positive achievement of the mind.

Anselm maintains that the mind is "the mirror and image" of God and draws an analogy between the mind, "remembering, conceiving of, and loving that Being," and the divine nature, "which through its memory and intelligence and love, is united in an ineffable Trinity." This leads to a final dimension of Anselm's conception of faith, that it should be "living" or dynamic, rather than "dead" or merely passive. We are not only to believe (and understand) the truth regarding God's existence and (to some extent) essence; we are to recognize that God "is to be hoped for," we are to " 'strive for' the supreme Being," and we are to "believe *in*" God. Such an active faith, informed by love, constitutes the essential difference between believing the truth and believing *in* the Truth.

> As that faith, then, which operates through love is recognized as living, . . . living faith believes *in* that *in* which we ought to believe; while dead faith merely believes that which ought to be believed.[56]

Thus, starting with faith, we can and should seek a rational understanding of the truth we believe and experience joy to the extent that we succeed. Both faith and reason provide us with a knowledge of the truth, though the former transcends the limits of the latter, which must submit to the "higher authority" of faith, which cannot always explain what is known, and which must employ what later came to be called an analogical use of language. Yet the ultimate Truth, which is the object of both faith and reason, is not merely to be known by our minds but loved. Although Anselm's treatment of faith and reason is not as systematically developed as this discussion would suggest, and though it is too indebted to Augustine to be called an original position, it remains an impressively rich one. Perhaps the most controversial and least convincing aspect of this view, however, is that Neoplatonic idea that any true proposition we can believe in and/or understand must participate in some truth independently existing outside our minds. It is not enough epistemologically to inherit this idea from Augustine; it requires argued justification, which is not achieved and which would considerably strengthen Anselm's arguments for God.

***A Posteriori* Arguments for God's Existence.** Anselm's arguments for God in *Monologium* are *a posteriori*, since they start with our **empirical** observations of varying degrees of perfection in the world about us. They presuppose the Platonic view that the relatively perfect participates in and is derived from the absolutely perfect. Anselm argues for God by way of degrees of perfection regarding goodness, greatness, and existence. He introduces these arguments with the claim that even a person who "has no knowledge of" a Being "which is best, and greatest, and highest of all existing beings" (that is, which is absolutely perfect regarding goodness, greatness, and existence) "can at least convince himself of these truths in great part, even if his mental powers are very ordinary, by the force of reason alone."[57] This last phrase is significant, for in these arguments Anselm does not explicitly appeal to the authority of Scriptural revelation or of other thinkers or of ecclesiastical **dogma**, so that these are presented as truly philosophical arguments.

Anselm's first argument reasons from our observation of the existence of manifold goods to a "supremely good" Being, which is the source, foundation, and measure of all good. We might formulate the argument thus: If "there are goods so innumerable, whose great diversity we experience by the bodily senses and discern by our mental faculties," then there must be "some one thing, through which all goods whatever are good" and which is "good through itself." There are such innumerable goods which we experience and discern. Therefore, there must be "some one thing, through which all goods whatever are good" and which is "good through itself." This is a perfectly valid **conditional argument** (of a *modus ponens* form), whose second premise seems to be true to our ordinary experience (although a skeptic might wish to protest that all value judgments, including those concerned with what is good, are merely derived from and relative to the persons making them). But why would anyone hold the first premise? For Anselm it follows from the Platonic axiom "that whatsoever things are said to possess any attribute in such a way that in mutual comparison they may be said to possess it in greater, or less, or equal degree, are said to possess it by virtue of some fact, which is not understood to be one thing in one case and another in another, but to be the same in different cases, whether it is regarded as existing in these cases in equal or unequal degree."[58] As applied here, this axiom requires that different things can only share the same quality, being more or less or equally good, if they all participate in the same reality, such as goodness, from which they derive that quality. Whether or not this is a plausible principle, it is not self-evident. Indeed, it presupposes the dubious Platonic view of metaphysical **realism**, which holds that qualities, such as goodness, themselves are realities outside the mind. Even if the principle is plausible, however, it should be noticed that Anselm says nothing to justify it, thus treating it as self-evident. Here is the point of greatest vulnerability for this first argument.

Anselm's second argument briefly applies the same reasoning to the relative greatness observed in things around us and the need for them to participate in and be derived from absolute greatness. As lesser degrees of goodness point to the supremely good, so from our experience of various degrees of greatness, says Anselm, "it is necessarily inferred that there is something supremely great, which is great through itself. But I do not mean physically great, as a material object is great, but that which, the greater it is, is the better or the more worthy—wisdom, for instance."[59] The concept of "greatness," then, is to be interpreted in terms of (qualitative) superiority or excellence rather than of (quantitative) size or magnitude. The argument might be **syllogistically** formulated thus: If there are diverse degrees of greatness observed by us, then there must be "something supremely great, which is great through itself." There are diverse degrees of greatness observed by us. So there must be "something supremely great, which is great through itself." This is merely a variant of our formulation of Anselm's first argument; the logical form is identical, so it too is valid. And the same evaluation of the premises would be appropriate.

Anselm's very complex third argument applies the degrees of perfection idea to our experience of being and our idea of the causal source of existence. "For everything that is exists either through something, or through nothing. But nothing exists through nothing. For it is altogether inconceivable that anything should not exist by virtue of something." This leads Anselm to the intermediate conclusion, which completes this valid alternative syllogism, "Whatever is, then, does not exist except through something." The second phase of his argument attempts to show that "there is one being" by virtue of which all other "things that are exist." The premises leading to this (intermediate) conclusion generate a valid **alternative argument**: "either there is one being, or there are more than one, through which all things that are exist"; but there cannot be more than one; hence there is one such being. The subsidiary argument offered to show that there cannot be more than one being through which all things that are exist is a valid complex conditional: "But if there are more than one, either these are themselves to be referred to some one being, through which they exist, or they exist separately, each through itself, or they exist mutually through one another." There cannot be many causes "which are themselves to be referred to some one being, through which they exist" without it being false that there is more than one ultimate cause. Nor, allegedly, can "they exist separately, each through itself" except by dint of some common "power or property of existing through self," which then would be the one ultimate cause, without it likewise being false that there is more than one ultimate cause. And it is impossible that beings should mutually cause one another's existence, "since it is an irrational conception that anything should exist through a being on which it confers existence." Thus, by a logical process of elimination, Anselm supposedly shows that there cannot be more than one ultimate cause of all being. From a critical perspective, the most dubious element of this ingenious subsidiary argument is Anselm's Platonic notion that several separate beings, each existing through itself, would have to participate in "some power or property of existing through self," which would itself be real and the causal source of their being. As we have observed, Anselm has not rationally justified his adoption of the Platonic metaphysics employed here. At any rate, by this point he thinks he has established that "that being, through which all exist, must be one." But since this one being is the ultimate cause of all other beings (and since we have already ruled out the possibility of two or more beings mutually causing each other's existence), "doubtless this one being exists through itself" as the only self-existent being. The final phase of this intricate argument goes like this: Only "this one being exists through itself," and all other beings ultimately "exist through this one being. . . . But whatever exists through another is less than that, through which all things are, and which alone exists through itself. Therefore, that which exists through itself exists in the greatest degree of all things."[60] Anselm treats that final premise as self-evident and thus offers no justification in its behalf. But, far from being self-evident, it seems false that every efficient cause is greater or more excellent than (or qualitatively superior to) all of its effects.

These three arguments from *Monologium* build on each other neatly, each conclusion absorbing the preceding one. If there is only one self-existent being which is the ultimate cause of all other beings, then Anselm maintains that it must be "greatest of all"; and the greatest being must be greatest in all respects, including being best or most good. So the ultimate being, supposedly proved in his third argument, must be identified with the greatest being, supposedly proved in his second, which, in turn, must be identified with the "supremely good" being, supposedly proved in his first.

It is difficult to say whether the next argument should be regarded as a new one or a reformulation or a **synthesis** of the previous three. But, for our purposes, it does not really matter. It proceeds from the experiential fact that "if one observes the nature of things he perceives, whether he will or no, that not all are embraced in a single degree of dignity." We do recognize that some beings are superior to others in degrees of perfection. Now since it is absurd to suppose that "the distinction of degrees is **infinite**" (which would render the number of existing natures unlimited), there must be some degree of perfection "than which no higher can be found." This is an absolutely superior being in the sense that "there is none in comparison with which it is ranked inferior." Is Anselm correct in his claim that an infinite number of degrees of perfection entails an infinite number of existing natures? Only on his Platonic conception of perfections as metaphysically real is he correct. Is he correct in his claim that an infinite number of existing natures is an "absurdly foolish" idea? It is surely unimaginable by us. But Anselm does not suppose that reality is limited by the powers of our human imagination. At any rate he continues the argument by maintaining that either there is only one such preeminent nature or there are more than one of equal degree of perfection. But, if the latter were true, then they would be equal "only through some cause which is one and the same," which cause is either identical with their nature (in which case they are essentially one after all) or extrinsic to their nature (in which case they are subordinate in dignity to that cause, since "whatever is great through something else is less than that through which it is great" and therefore not really absolutely superior after all). "We conclude, then, that there is some nature which is one and single, and which is so superior to others that it is inferior to none."[61] Again, we see Anselm invoking the dubious Platonic view that beings that participate in the same perfection are inferior to that perfection, which is itself a reality outside the mind. (This last argument of Anselm's, we should note, is the one which closely resembles the fourth of Aquinas's "five ways" of proving God's existence.)

Anselm's command of logic is superb, and his reasoning is powerful in each of these arguments. But each of the arguments presupposes controversial axioms of Platonic metaphysics, which Anselm does not rationally substantiate. He does connect the absolutely perfect nature with that which is preeminent in goodness, greatness, and being:

> There is, therefore, a certain Nature, or Substance, or Essence, which is through itself good and great, and through itself is what it is; and through which exists whatever is truly good, or great, or has any existence at all; and which is the supreme good being, the supreme great being, being or subsisting as supreme, that is, the highest of all existing beings.

In the Preface to *Monologium* Anselm describes this work as a "meditation on the Being of God."[62] We have seen that the arguments of its first four chapters rationally attempt to establish that Being in terms of both God's existence and God's essence and, indeed, that the two are intertwined.

Ontological Argument for God's Existence. Anselm's "ontological" argument for God in *Proslogium* is what he is most famous for in the history of philosophy. Anselm declares that he is seeking

> a single argument which would require no other for its proof than itself alone; and alone would suffice to demonstrate that God truly exists, and that there is a supreme good requiring nothing else, which all other things require for their existence and well-being.

This "single argument" thus contrasts with "the linking of many arguments" in *Monologium*.[63] Unlike all those arguments, this single argument is *a priori*, proceeding from the very meaning of the concept of God to establish the necessary existence of a being corresponding to that concept.

Anselm tells God that he seeks "to understand that thou art as we believe; and that thou art that which we believe." Thus, he signals that the argument is designed to prove both God's existence and something about the divine nature. Anselm introduces the argument with a conceptual definition and a factual claim based on experience. God, the object of religious belief, is defined as "a being than which nothing greater can be conceived" (*aliquid quo maius nihil cogitari potest*)—a conception of God derived from Augustine. Next, it is asserted that even the nonbeliever (i.e., "the fool" who says "there is no God"—*Psalms* 14:1) understands the idea of God; so "what he understands is in his understanding."[64] With this accomplished, Anselm is ready to develop his argument.

Anselm's argument can be cast into the form of a conditional syllogism: If God existed "in the understanding alone," then a God existing also "in reality" would be greater than that God existing "in the understanding alone." But, since the God existing in the understanding is "that, than which nothing greater can be conceived," it "is impossible" that anything exists which is greater than the God existing in the understanding. Therefore, God cannot exist "in the understanding alone" but must exist "both in the understanding and in reality."[65] This is a *modus tollens* conditional (or hypothetical) argument; as such, it is necessarily, by the rules of deductive logic, formally valid. Consequently, possible objections must focus on its premises.

Let us consider the first premise of Anselm's argument, then, which claims that a God existing outside the mind ("in reality") as well as mentally ("in the understanding") would be "greater" than a God existing only mentally ("in the understanding alone"). In what sense is such a God "greater"? We would say that it cannot have "more" existence, since something either does or does not exist, existence not being a matter of degree but an absolute fact. Perhaps one would speak of "higher levels" of existence, as when we say that a tortoise is "higher" than a dandelion but "lower" than a person; but we must recognize that we are here comparing types of things, in terms of what they are (their essence), and not in terms of the fact that they are (their existence). Indeed, we would do well to wonder whether any cogent and **coherent** meaning can be assigned to the claim that a mental existent is "greater" than a reality outside the mind; for such a claim involves a comparison of two disproportionate realms of "existence." What basis could we have for comparing two such radically incompatible orders of being as the purely mental and that which is outside the mind? The key word of the first premise, then, "greater," is undefined; and its application presumes the correctness of Platonic metaphysics, which views ideas as real, but for which Anselm does not argue. Thus, we are not given adequate reason to accept the truth of this premise.

But what about the second premise? We should notice its dependence on Anselm's definition and empirical claim, both of which are dubious. The definition of God assumes an understanding of God's nature—an understanding presumably culled from Anselm's prior belief. Yet we might well question the possibility of finite man's understanding the nature of Anselm's infinite God at all. There may, indeed, be an instance of **circular reasoning** here, since Anselm's argument is itself intended to provide an understanding of God. Next, we should question the definition that Anselm uses as a linchpin of his argument. Although this would have sounded **blasphemous** to the medieval Christian, we can conceive of (and could believe in) a finite God as (to paraphrase Anselm) something than which nothing greater actually exists, even though a greater might be theoretically conceivable. Anselm rashly assumes that there is no alternative to his conception of God. His empirical claim is equally suspicious, since we who have not already accepted Platonic metaphysics would say that it is not God that "is understood," but the meaning of the concept of God, that it is not God that "exists in the understanding," but merely the idea of God. Therefore, Anselm's minor premise is unsubstantiated on two counts: we have not been shown that God (as opposed to the idea of God) does, in fact, exist in the understanding; nor has the crucial definition of God been justified.

Thus, because the **truth-value** of each of Anselm's premises is questionable and unjustified, the argument as a whole—despite its logical **validity**—remains unconvincing and may be **unsound**. But he proceeds to argue, even more radically, that God's nonexistence is inconceivable:

> For, it is possible to conceive of a being which cannot be conceived not to exist; and this is greater than one which can be conceived not to exist. Hence, if that, than which nothing greater can be conceived, can be conceived not to exist, it is not that, than which nothing greater can be conceived. But this is an irreconcilable contradiction. There is, then, so truly a being than which nothing greater can be conceived to exist, that it cannot even be conceived not to exist.[66]

This is a brilliant argument, which can again be construed in a (valid) *modus tollens* conditional form; even though Anselm derives this conception of God from Augustine, the argument itself is highly original. This statement of the argument can be viewed as a negative formulation of the earlier one and is subject to comparable criticisms. All versions of (what Kant later labeled) the "ontological" argument can be seen as defining God into existence, here by conceiving of God as necessarily existing. (For historical purposes, it should be observed that Anselm's formulations of the argument, unlike the modern Cartesian formulations, nowhere maintain the controversial claim that existence is a perfection.)

Anselm raises a curious question as to how "the fool" can deny the existence of a God whose nonexistence is inconceivable. His immediate answer is the **ad hominem** response that it is because "he is dull and a fool." Anselm explains that, though "no one who understands what God is can conceive that God does not exist," people who conceive only the word "God," rather than understanding the being signified by that word, can deny God's existence. Anselm unpacks the **implications** his conception of God has for the divine nature, maintaining that it requires that God be "just, truthful, blessed, and whatever it is better to be than not to be."[67] This approach to the divine nature assures Anselm that his argumentation will not merely lead us to an abstract metaphysical principle (this is a shortcoming of most arguments for God) but rationally points to the perfect personal God of monotheistic religion.

Anselm's argumentation in *Proslogium* was criticized during his own lifetime by Gaunilon, another perspicacious Benedictine monk from Marmoutier (Tours), who wrote a pamphlet "In Behalf of the Fool," to which Anselm then replied at some length. Gaunilon's pamphlet comprises eight sections, averaging about a page in length apiece. We shall focus on the criticisms contained in four of these sections, as well as Anselm's responses to them.

Gaunilon cuts to the core of Anselm's argumentation in maintaining,

> I, so far as actual knowledge of the object, either from its specific or general character, is concerned, am as little able to conceive of this being when I hear of it, or to have it in my understanding, as I am to conceive of or understand God himself: whom, indeed, for this very reason I can conceive not to exist. For I do not know that reality itself which God is, nor can I form a conjecture of that reality from some other like reality. For you yourself assert that that reality is such that there can be nothing else like it.

By contrast, he avers, I can conceive of "a man absolutely unknown to me, of whose very existence I was unaware," by reference to my knowledge of other men and my understanding of what it is to be a man. The only way in which the idea of God is in our understanding is that we do have a conceptual grasp of the meaning of the words "a being greater than all other conceivable beings." But we have no experience of any object corresponding to such an idea and can form no adequate mental image of it.[68] In reply, Anselm claims that, by reflecting on lesser degrees of greatness in the things about us and rationally "ascending from the lesser good to the greater, we can form a considerable notion of a being than which a greater is inconceivable."[69] It seems that Gaunilon is correct against Anselm here, that the "considerable notion" of God we can achieve is inadequate to support Anselm's *a priori* argument.

Gaunilon objects that, even if we were to grant that a conceptual understanding of God "is in the understanding," it does not follow that it must "attain to real existence also," as long as that existence is in question. This concession, even if granted, gives us only a conceptual reality in the mind.

> For I do not say, no, I even deny or doubt that this being is greater than any real object. Nor do I concede to it any other existence than this (if it should be called existence) which it has when the mind, according to a word merely heard, tries to form the image of an object absolutely unknown to it.[70]

Anselm's response is little more than an insistence that if the idea of God is possibly one to which no reality outside the mind corresponds, it is the idea of a being than whom a greater (namely one that also exists in reality) can be conceived and, hence, not an accurate idea of God at all.[71] Anselm seems simply to have missed the point of Gaunilon's acute critique, that more argumentation is needed to show that "existence" in the mind can ever necessitate existence outside the mind. Again Gaunilon seems correct against Anselm.

Gaunilon raises his most famous objection, that the argument, if accepted, can be used to prove the existence of the greatest conceivable anything. For example, we can conceive that "somewhere in the ocean is . . . the lost island," which "is more excellent than all other countries" and, indeed, is the greatest conceivable land. But, then, Anselm's argument allegedly might be used to show that, since this idea exists in the mind, the lost island must also exist in reality. Otherwise, "any land which really exists will be more excellent than it; and so the island already understood by you to be more excellent will not be more excellent." But, as Gaunilon says, if someone tried to convince us, by means of such an argument, of the existence of that "lost island," we would either "believe that he was jesting" or that he was trying to make fools of us or that he is himself a fool.[72] Anselm's brief response is that his argument only works for the greatest conceivable being.[73] Even the ideal island is limited because it is physical; not being a person, for example, it necessarily lacks intelligence and moral goodness and, therefore, cannot possibly be the greatest conceivable being. Here, Anselm is probably correct against Gaunilon; the ontological argument is conceptually set up in such a way that it can legitimately apply only to God.

Gaunilon objects that it is premature to claim that God's nonexistence is inconceivable until God's existence has been conclusively proved and that, rather than calling God's nonexistence "inconceivable," it "might better be said" that it "is unintelligible."[74] In response, Anselm holds that God's existence could not be **contingent**, that either it is absolutely necessary (so that it "cannot be conceived not to be") or God "would not exist at all." Presumably he thinks this dichotomy to be necessitated by the very conception of God. A contingent being, whose existence is not necessary, would not be Anselm's God—i.e., would not be the greatest conceivable. It appears that Gaunilon is correct, that Anselm gives us a false dichotomy, ruling out, by dubious definition, a third alternative of God contingently existing—for example, as the greatest actual (though not the greatest conceivable) being. In response to Gaunilon's claim that God's nonexistence is "unintelligible" rather than "inconceivable," Anselm points out that this would not be uniquely true of God's nonexistence.[75] For example, it would be unintelligible (logically irrational) for me to say that I do not exist or that the chair on which I am sitting doesn't exist; but it is conceivable (theoretically possible) that neither I nor the chair might have come to be. Anselm has a point here against Gaunilon—he is trying to make a claim that uniquely applies to God—even if he has failed logically to justify that claim.

The debate between Anselm and Gaunilon regarding the argumentation of *Proslogium* seems quite cordial. In the final paragraph of his pamphlet, Gaunilon praises Anselm's book as arguing "with such truth, such brilliancy, such grandeur" and as being "so replete with usefulness" in other parts than those he has criticized.[76] Anselm begins his reply by observing that Gaunilon "is by no means a fool" and ends it by thanking him "for your kindness both in your blame and in your praise for my book."[77]

Although, as we have seen, the famous ontological argument is far from Anselm's only significant contribution to philosophical theology, it is his most original example of "faith seeking understanding" and more gripping than the "many arguments" of his earlier work. Yet this argument had relatively little impact until the thirteenth century, when it was adopted by Bonaventure and criticized by Thomas Aquinas.

Aquinas: Life and Writings

*T*homas Aquinas's life and writings were those of a successfully productive thirteenth-century scholar and friar. He was born in the family castle of Roccasecca, near Aquino (hence his name) in southern Italy, in early 1225, the seventh (and youngest) son of Landulfo, the Count of Aquino, and his wife, Countess Theodora. That area, located between Rome and Naples, was then part of the Kingdom of Sicily, which was ruled by the Emperor Frederick II, to whom Thomas's father was related and in whose armies Landulfo and his older sons served. Theodora was descended from the Norman conquerors of Sicily. So he was of good stock on both sides of this feudal noble family.

In 1230, when he was five years old, he was presented by his parents to the Benedictine Abbey of Monte Cassino as an oblate (one offered for religious life, if he later so chose). Thomas's uncle was abbot at the monastery, which was located near Roccasecca. He remained a student at Monte Cassino until 1239, when political turmoil made the place unsafe. The difficulty was a dispute between Emperor Frederick II and the pope. Frederick's Sicilian troops occupied Monte Cassino and ultimately expelled the monks; and, in 1239, Frederick was excommunicated. So, the teenaged Thomas returned to Roccasecca for a few months.

Next, Thomas was sent to the University of Naples, founded in 1224 by Frederick II, where he studied the seven liberal arts and philosophy, between 1239 and 1244. It was probably here that Thomas was first exposed to the ideas of Aristotle, which were to become such an essential element of his own philosophical position. It was also during this period that he met members of the new **Dominican** order (the Order of Preachers), which had been granted papal approval in 1216. During this time, the Dominicans' master general visited Naples, where a house of Dominican friars was located. In 1244, a short time after his father's death, contrary to his mother's wishes, Thomas entered the Dominican order. While he was traveling with the master general to Paris, the young novice was kidnapped by two of his brothers, who belonged to the Emperor's army, and was held prisoner at Aquino for about a year. His family hoped he would give up his commitment to the Dominicans and perhaps return to the Benedictines, with whom he might rise to a position of greater influence. There is a story that his brothers, in their determination to convince Thomas, sent an attractive woman to his room one night to seduce him but that Thomas scared her away. At any rate, in 1245 he was released from captivity and resumed his trip to Paris, where he stayed as a novice in the house of the Dominican order until 1248.

In Paris Thomas studied theology with Albert the Great, who influenced his intellectual development more than anyone else whom he was ever to know personally. Albert believed in the value of the works of Aristotle and, no doubt, communicated this commitment to the young novice. In the summer of 1248, Thomas went with Albert to Cologne to help him organize a Dominican house of studies. Thomas worked as Albert's assistant until 1252, being ordained a priest in 1250 or 1251. He was a very large man, one of the few philosophers to be both fat and famous (the other who immediately comes to mind is David Hume), mild-mannered and shy, tending to be so quiet that, in his student days, his schoolmates, mistakenly assuming him a dunce, called him "the Dumb Ox." (Albert is said to have exclaimed that one day the bellowing of this "dumb ox" would be heard throughout the whole world.)

At the age of twenty-seven, Thomas, referred to as Aquinas from now on, returned to Paris, where he continued his studies at the University of Paris (which had been chartered in 1200 and had a Faculty of Arts comparable to the one at the University of Naples), where the theology program was particularly good. It used a combination of lecture and disputation in its pedagogy, which Aquinas was to master. In 1256, he received his Licentiate, a license to teach theology; a bit later, he received a master's degree in theology. He then taught in Paris at the Dominican convent of St. James until 1259. He was a very capable and popular teacher. During this period in Paris from 1252 to 1259, Aquinas produced some important writings, including *De Ente et Essentia* (*On Being and Essence*) and *De Veritate* (*On Truth*).

In 1259, the thirty-four-year-old Aquinas returned to Italy, where he was preacher general for almost a decade, teaching theology in several houses of Dominican studies. Among these was the monastery in Orvieto, where Urban IV had his papal court in which Albert the Great was in residence. A Flemish Dominican named William of Moerbeke was also there. William was adept in Greek, as Aquinas was not; and, at the latter's suggestion, William translated Aristotelian works and revised some earlier translations of Aristotle into Latin. These careful, accurate translations were most helpful to Aquinas, who was synthesizing Aristotle's thought into his own Christian philosophy and writing extended commentaries on Aristotle's works during this period. (When Aquinas writes of "the Philosopher," it is Aristotle to whom he refers.) Pope Urban IV encouraged the blending of Aristotle's philosophy with Christian faith. It was also during this time (1259–64) that Aquinas completed his great *Summa contra Gentiles*, which he had begun in Paris and had intended for Dominican missionaries to use in Spain to help convert "infidels" of the Islamic faith. During this Italian period of almost a decade, Aquinas produced a prodigious amount of scholarly and original work, keeping quite a few fellow Dominicans busy as his secretaries, sometimes dictating to several at once.

In late 1268, Aquinas was reassigned to one of the Dominican chairs of theology at the University of Paris, which was in turmoil at the time. There were disputes between the secular clergy and the mendicant orders, and classes were suspended during the Lenten season of 1272. Much of the writing of Aquinas's greatest work, *Summa Theologica*, was completed during this period of some three years in Paris. In 1272, Aquinas was assigned to establish a new Dominican house of studies in Naples. In Italy he continued work on the *Summa Theologica*; but it seems that, by 1273, his health was deteriorating. A few months before his death, Aquinas stopped writing and teaching; he seems to have had a religious experience which led him to consider all his professorial and scholarly efforts insignificant. In 1274, Pope Gregory X summoned Aquinas to participate in the Council of Lyons in France. He only got to the Cistercian monastery at Fossanuova, where he died on March 7, 1274.

In January of 1277, Pope John XXI asked Etienne Tempier, the Bishop of Paris, to investigate the orthodoxy of recent theological teachings. The Bishop's commission of sixteen theologians collected 219 propositions, which the Bishop condemned on March 7, 1277 (three years to the day after Aquinas's death). Some of these condemned propositions were theses included in the philosophy of Aquinas, although he was not mentioned by name. A few days later, Robert Kilwardby, the Dominican Archbishop of Canterbury, condemned a shorter list of thirty propositions, including the Thomistic thesis that man has a single substantial form. Nevertheless, from 1278 on, Thomism became increasingly recommended in the Dominican order. Aquinas was canonized a saint on July 18, 1323 by Pope John XXII and was proclaimed "the Angelic Doctor" by Pope Pius V in 1567. After the canonization of Aquinas, attacks against his thought decreased; in 1325, the man who was then Bishop of Paris revoked the condemnation. In his papal **encyclical** of 1879, *Aeterni Patris*, Leo XIII recommended the philosophy of Aquinas, calling him the master and prince of Scholastic Doctors and praising him for carefully distinguishing, while also synthesizing, faith and reason.

Aquinas's Latin writings fill up some twenty-five volumes. Unlike those of Augustine earlier and of Descartes later, his writing assumes an impersonal style. The form of his *Summa Theologica*, the book on which we shall focus most of our attention (which will sometimes be referred to here simply as "the *Summa*"), comprises articles formally divided into five sections: (1) a statement of the question at issue; (2) a list of objections against the position Aquinas himself is maintaining; (3) a section "On the contrary" in which he quotes Scriptural, theological, and philosophical authorities with whom he agrees on the issue at hand; (4) an "I answer that" section presenting his own position and arguments for it; and (5) his replies to the objections given in the second section. A rare example of a personal statement contained in his writings is in his *Summa contra Gentiles*, where he humbly says, "I have set myself the task of making known, as far as my limited powers will allow, the truth that the Catholic faith professes, and of setting aside the errors that are opposed to it."[78] So his work as philosophical theologian is that of Christian **apologetics**. Our critical consideration of this work will start with an examination of his views on the relation between philosophical reason and theological faith.

Aquinas: Religious Philosophy

Faith and Reason. Aquinas's position on faith and reason is suggested in the very first article of the *Summa Theologica*, where he argues that divine revelation, independent of philosophical reasoning, was needed because our eternal **salvation** requires that we have theological truths "which exceed human reason"; furthermore, even those truths about God within the capacities of reason "would only be known by a few, and that after a long time, and with the admixture of many errors," apart from divine revelation. He distinguishes revealed (or **dogmatic**) theology from rational (or **philosophical**) theology, indicating that they do overlap.[79] Because God is the end (or goal) of man's being, as well as his beginning (or source), because human salvation requires that man know God, and because of the natural limitations of the human intellect, divine revelation, to be appropriated in faith, was needed to supplement what man can learn through natural experience and reason.

Despite their difference, Aquinas maintains that dogmatic theology, based on divine revelation, is as genuine a science, or organized body of knowledge, as is philosophical theology, which is based on natural experience and reason; it is a single speculative science concerned with the knowledge of God. Because of both "its greater certitude" and "the higher dignity of its subject-matter," Aquinas considers revealed theology to be "nobler" than any other science, including philosophical theology:

> in point of greater certitude, because other sciences derive their certitude from the natural light of reason, which can err, whereas this derives its certitude from the light of the divine knowledge, which cannot err; in point of the higher dignity of its subject-matter, because this science treats chiefly of those things which by their sublimity transcend human reason, while other sciences consider only those things which are within reason's grasp.

But if it is the highest and most certain science, any apparent conflict between its truths and those of any other science must be decisively resolved in favor of revealed theology; as Aquinas firmly puts it, "whatsoever is found in the other sciences contrary to the truth of this science must be condemned as false."[80]

We have seen that God is "the subject-matter of this science." But a science must have basic principles as well as subject-matter; and these, according to Aquinas, are "the articles of faith." Revealed theology is an "argumentative" science in two ways: first, if given certain articles of faith as basic principles, it can supposedly proceed to prove other truths; and, second, even if no articles of faith are granted as starting points, it can allegedly **refute** objections raised against the faith. Aquinas emphasizes the first of these argumentative tasks more in his *Summa Theologica* and the second more in his *Summa contra Gentiles*. Whereas the methodology of philosophical theology is purely rational and shuns appeals to authority, that of revealed theology is committed "to argue from authority, inasmuch as its principles are obtained by revelation"; yet this does not detract from the "dignity" of this science because, whereas appeals to human authority are "the weakest" sorts of reasons, that to "authority based on divine revelation is the strongest." Second, revealed theology's use of authority is not at the expense of reason, which is employed to articulate the meaning and implications of articles of faith.[81]

So revealed theology is a science concerned with the knowledge of God, based on articles of faith; it differs from philosophical theology in its methodology, although they deal with the same subject matter. Let us now consider Aquinas's discussion, in his *Summa contra Gentiles*, of the two sorts of truths about God of which we can allegedly be aware. "Some truths about God exceed all the ability of the human reason. Such is the truth that God is triune." In what sense do some theological doctrines "exceed all the ability of the human reason"? Man's intellect "depends on" sense experience "for the origin of knowledge" that is natural to it, "and so those things that do not fall under the senses cannot be grasped by the human intellect except in so far as the knowledge of them is gathered from sensible things." But sense experience, by the limitations of its nature, could never lead us to the truth of such theological doctrines as those of the Trinity, God's creation of the world from nothing, and the Incarnation. Nor is the nature of human reason such that we can ever understand these doctrines even if we maintain them as certain matters of faith; in this sense also they "absolutely surpass its power." On the other hand, "there are some truths" about God "which the natural reason also is able to reach. Such are that God exists, that He is one, and the like."[82] In addition to being revealed to us by God, these truths can be rationally proved from the findings of experience and can be understood by the human mind. In contrast to the articles of faith we have been discussing, Aquinas calls these "preambles" of faith in the *Summa Theologica*: "The existence of God and other like truths about God, which can be known by natural reason, are not articles of faith, but are preambles to the articles."[83]

Not only is the truth about God the subject matter of theology, but, more generally, the object of both faith and reason, for Aquinas, is truth, an extremely long discussion of which he develops in his *De Veritate*. Our brief consideration of this issue here will be necessarily restricted to those elements that seem most obviously germane to his treatment of faith and reason—specifically, the analyses of truth, knowledge, and the relationship between both of these and faith. Aquinas defines truth as "the conformity of thing and intellect" (*adaequatio rei et intellectus*), explaining that it involves judgments "corresponding to" reality.[84] This later came to be called the "correspondence theory" and has been the dominant theory of truth in Western philosophy from the time of the ancient Greeks to that of the German **idealists** (i.e., for well over two millennia); for example, even though John Locke, more than four centuries after Aquinas, recognized the problem with the theory (that we have no certain way of verifying that the correspondence or conformity has been established), he continued to hold it.

Aquinas's theory of human knowledge is clearly empirical, seeing it (differently from Augustine and Anselm) as always originating in sense experience of real things: "Our knowledge, taking its start from things, proceeds in this order. First, it begins in sense; second, it is completed in the intellect. As a consequence, sense is found to be in some way an intermediary between the intellect and things." Yet knowledge, beginning with sense experience, is an intellectual act. The senses perceive surface appearances of things, whereas in knowledge the intellect must grasp "the most profound elements of a thing; for to understand (*intelligere*) means to read what is inside a thing (*intus legere*). Sense and imagination know only external accidents, but the intellect alone penetrates to the interior and to the essence of a thing."[85] Later, Aquinas discusses how the intellect, potentially capable of acquiring knowledge, does so in two ways, by discovering previously unknown things and by instruction from someone else who already knows.[86]

Having examined Aquinas's analyses of truth and knowledge in *De Veritate*, let us briefly consider how he then relates them to faith. He says, "The act of faith consists essentially in knowledge"; but this is the sort of knowledge that consists of the mind's assenting to what is not "seen" or understood as true. "But, in so far as there is certainty of assent, faith is knowledge." As knowledge is oriented towards truth, so, says Aquinas, "The essential object of faith is first truth." When we assent to truth in faith, we do so on the "witness" or accepted testimony of another, rather than on the authority of our own understanding. By contrast, scientific knowledge requires understanding. "Hence, it is impossible to have faith and scientific knowledge about the same thing" in the same person at the same time, even though faith is a kind of knowledge.

Aquinas distinguishes two types of objects of faith—the absolute sort, which "exceeds the intellectual capacity of all men who exist in this life, for instance, that there is trinity and unity in God," and the relative sort, which "does not exceed the capacity of all men, but only of some men"—for example, the existence and perfection of God, which some people can demonstrate and others merely accept on faith. "There is nothing to prevent those who have scientific proofs of these things from knowing them scientifically, and others who do not understand these proofs from believing them. But it is impossible for the same person to know and believe them" at the same time.[87]

Aquinas discusses the relationship between faith and reason, regarding the truth about God, further in *Summa contra Gentiles*. He argues that it is appropriate that even truths about God that are within the scope of human reason should be given for belief because otherwise "few men would possess the knowledge of God" needed for salvation, even those few, who are philosophically gifted, would come to do so only "after a great deal of time" and effort, and even then the fruits of their labor would be limited and subject to error because of the fallibility of our human intellect.[88] Aquinas argues that "even those truths that are above the human reason" are fittingly revealed as objects of religious belief for several reasons: we should be called to something higher than the human reason here and now can reach," since our ultimate good and goal is supernatural; we need a greater knowledge of God, the beginning and end of all reality, than natural experience and reason could provide; and the acceptance of revealed truths that exceed the powers of reason helps us to curb our tendencies to arrogant "presumption, which is the mother of error."[89] Aquinas claims that, even though articles of faith are above human reason and "exceed natural knowledge," God also "gives visible manifestation to works that surpass the ability of all nature";[90] there are, for example, miracles, which we shall consider near the end of this section on Aquinas. He argues that there can be no ultimate opposition between truths of faith and truths of reason, since "only the false is opposed to the true" and since God, the ultimate Truth, is the source of both kinds of truth.[91] Aquinas maintains that "human reason is related to" the truth of theological faith "in such a way that it can gather certain likenesses of it, which are yet not sufficient so that the truth of faith may be comprehended as being understood demonstratively";[92] later we shall discuss his theory of analogy as a means of gaining and expressing some understanding of God.

In his treatise on faith in the *Summa*, Aquinas characterizes the object of faith as "nothing else than the First Truth" and analyzes faith itself as "a mean between science and opinion." It is a "mean," or middle ground, between natural science and mere opinion, in that, like the former, its object is always truth and, like the latter, it has not been verified by natural experience. He appeals to the Scriptures on behalf of this view that faith, by its very nature, does not admit of empirical verification: "*On the contrary*, The Apostle says (*Heb.* 11:1) that *faith is the evidence of things that appear not.*" Indeed, Aquinas goes beyond this to maintain that it is "impossible for one and the same thing to be an object of science and of belief for the same person."[93] Yet he has already claimed that revealed theology, based on articles of faith, is the most certain science. It seems that he is either using "science" now in the restricted sense of natural science or is inconsistent in his treatment of its relationship to faith.

Later, Aquinas endorses Augustine's definition, which holds that "to believe" is "to think with assent" (*credere est assensione cogitare*). It is to be distinguished from every sort of demonstrative "inquiry of natural reason" and is "an act of the intellect" determined "not by the reason, but by the will." And he accepts the Augustinian view that such an act of religious faith involves a commitment "*to believe in a God*," "*to believe God*," and "*to believe in God.*" Because faith is not naturally compelled by empirical evidence, it is to the credit of the believer: "Now the act of believing is an act of the intellect assenting to divine truth at the command of the will moved by the grace of God, so that it is subject to free choice in relation to God; and consequently the act of faith can be meritorious." He argues that it must be an intellectual act because its object is truth. Finally, since it is a habit leading to good actions, "faith is a virtue"; for "any habit that is always the principle of a good act may be called a human virtue."[94] Indeed, earlier, Aquinas had defined **virtue** as "a good habit, productive of good works," had approvingly analyzed Augustine's definition of virtue, and had argued that there are "theological virtues," in addition to the natural (intellectual and moral) ones, "so called, first, because their object is God . . .; secondly, because these virtues are not made known to us, save by divine revelation." Appealing to the Scriptures (I *Cor.* 13:13), he holds that the three theological virtues are faith, hope, and charity, faith being first among the three in "the order of generation" (although charity has priority "in the order of perfection").[95] This summarizes Aquinas's analysis of faith.

He discusses man's knowledge of God in the *Summa*. Although we will not be able to follow all the details of this discussion here, we will focus on a few key points that are most relevant to Aquinas's philosophical theology. He agrees with Augustine (and with *Jeremiah* 32) that "It is impossible for any created intellect to comprehend God" in the sense of achieving a perfect understanding. But he argues that, since "the more perfectly a cause is seen, the more of its effects can be seen in it" and, since God is the ultimate cause of all other reality, the more perfectly any intellect understands God, the greater will be its knowledge of "the things that God does or can do." He agrees with the Old Testament (*Exodus* 33:20) that no person in this life naturally experiences the divine essence, since the human mind "knows naturally only what has a form in matter, or what can be known by such a form" and since "it is evident that the divine essence cannot be known through the nature of material things."[96] Now what would *seem* to follow from this is that man can have no natural knowledge of God, since without any knowledge of God's essence (what God is) any purported knowledge of God's existence (that God is) would be vacuous—in which case philosophical theology would be a fraud.

But, as we might guess, this is not at all the conclusion Aquinas draws: "*On the contrary*, It is written (*Rom.* 1:19), *That which is known of God*, namely, what can be known of God by natural reason, *is manifest in them*" (i.e., in the things of God's creation). He again maintains his empirical position that all our natural knowledge begins in sense experience and extends only as far as our intellect "can be led by sensible things"—and, thus, not to the divine essence. Nevertheless, he holds, because the things of this world are the effects of God's creative causality, "we can be led from them so far as to know of God *whether He exists*, and to know of Him what must necessarily belong to Him, as the first cause of all things, exceeding all things caused by Him." Finally, he describes faith itself as "a kind of knowledge, inasmuch as the intellect is determined by faith to some knowable object"; yet he says it is not scientific knowledge because it is not based on "the vision and understanding of first principles."[97]

From a critical perspective, what are we to make of this position on faith and reason? Each of us must judge for himself, but it may very well be the best such position ever worked out by any medieval Christian philosopher. Aquinas does a cleaner, clearer job of distinguishing religious faith from philosophical reason than do, for example, Augustine and Anselm, and he avoids having to make their dubious Platonic assumptions, giving us, instead, a more easily digestible empiricism which nevertheless allows for a philosophical theology, rather than **positivistically** ruling it out. Yet this also seems to be the major problem with Aquinas's position, that it would try to justify knowledge of that which transcends natural experience, while remaining faithful to the principles of empiricism. We might object that science is indeed a body of knowledge, that human knowledge, by its nature, is limited within the parameters of concrete experience, which does not naturally extend to God—so that theology, the study of God, cannot yield knowledge and thus cannot be a science. (Of course, it is far easier to state this view than to justify it; good reasons for holding it are those carefully developed more than half a millennium after Aquinas by Immanuel Kant.) Our admiration for Aquinas's theory on faith and reason is compatible with the view that it is flawed, as is medieval philosophy in general, by not being built on an adequately developed theory of knowledge. This is the enormous advantage of modern philosophical theologies, starting with that of Descartes, that they are based on explicitly and painstakingly developed epistemologies. One might reasonably become skeptical whenever Aquinas (and all the more so with Augustine and Anselm, given their unjustified Platonic assumptions) makes knowledge claims in connection with God and religious faith or tries to present theology (revealed and philosophical alike) as a "science." For example, why should we, from a critical perspective, accept his assurance that we can be led from an experience of God's effects to a knowledge of God's existence and some knowledge of the divine essence? Can this claim be cogently justified? This is the topic of our next subsection.

God's Existence. Aquinas's argumentation for God is ample material for book-length treatment by itself. Nevertheless, in this subsection, we can critically analyze some of it, beginning with the extremely important and highly influential short question on the existence of God.

The first of the three articles comprising this question asks "whether the existence of God is self-evident." The second objection within the article is particularly interesting in that it presents an Anselmian argument for answering the question affirmatively: since the name God means "that thing than which nothing greater can be conceived," and since "that which exists actually and mentally is greater than that which exists only mentally," it must follow that "the proposition *God exists* is self-evident." Against this view Aquinas observes, "*On the contrary*," that it is impossible that we "mentally admit the opposite of what is self-evident, as the Philosopher states"; and, since some people, such as "the fool" of the Old Testament (*Psalms* 52:1), hold that there is no God, the divine existence cannot be self-evident. Aquinas's own "answer" involves a distinction regarding two ways in which something can be self-evident: something can be either "self-evident in itself, though not to us" or both "self-evident in itself and to us." The proposition "God exists" is "self-evident in itself" insofar as the concept of "the predicate is included in the essence of the subject," since, according to Aquinas, God's essence and existence are identical. However, "because we do not know the essence of God, the proposition is not self-evident to us, but needs to be demonstrated." Against the Anselmian objection, Aquinas presents a three-pronged "Reply": first, not everyone understands the name "God" to mean "something than which nothing greater can be thought," so the argument cannot be self-evident to all; secondly, even if everyone did understand the name in this way, it would not be self-evident to everyone "that what the name signifies exists actually, but only that it exists mentally"; and, thirdly, to argue that God's existence is self-evident is to presume that God "actually exists," which is precisely the point at issue.[98] Aquinas seems generally right against Anselm here and correct that God's existence is not self-evident to us. But one point which seems uncertain is whether God's existence is "self-evident in itself." For can we really even understand what it means to say that God's existence and essence are identical, let alone claim to know that it is true?

The second article asks "whether it can be demonstrated that God exists." Two of the various objections are particularly interesting: the first holds that God's existence cannot be demonstrated because "it is an article of faith" rather than the matter of "scientific knowledge" it would become if demonstrated; and the third maintains that, since the Anselmian *a priori* argument has been ruled out, any demonstration of God's existence would be from God's effects, which "are not proportioned to Him, since He is infinite and His effects are finite, and between the finite and infinite there is no proportion" and since no cause can be demonstrated by utterly incommensurable effects. "*On the contrary*," Aquinas interprets Paul's claim, "*The invisible things of Him are clearly seen, being understood by the things that are made*" (*Rom.* 1:20) to mean that God's existence is demonstrable from the effects of divine creation. (By the way, in the nineteenth century the first Vatican Council declared in favor of this position, that God is certainly knowable by natural human reason by means of created things. This does not mean, however, that the position has ever been—or could ever be—philosophically justified or that any such cogent demonstration has actually been worked out.) Aquinas's "answer" here again involves a distinction, this time between two kinds of demonstration: "One is through the cause, and is called *propter quid*, and this is to argue from what is prior absolutely. The other is through the effect, and is called a demonstration *quia*; this is to argue from what is prior relatively only to us." The first sort of argument, from the cause ("because of which") to the effect, is unavailable to us since we do not naturally experience God. The second sort of argument reasons that "since" the experienced effects are as they are, the cause needed to account for those effects must be such and so; this is the sort of demonstration that Aquinas holds is available to us. "When an effect is better known to us than its cause, from the effect we proceed to the knowledge of its cause." In "Reply" to the first objection, Aquinas says that God's existence is not among the articles of faith distinguished from scientific demonstration; it is rather among the "preambles to the articles." In "Reply" to the third objection, Aquinas admits that the effects of divine creation are disproportionate to God as cause but insists that all that follows from this fact is that "no perfect knowledge of that cause can be obtained."[99] Aquinas's distinction between arguments that reason from cause to effect and those that reason from effect back to cause seems a valuable one, and he seems correct that, *if* it were possible for us to demonstrate God's existence, it would have to be by means of the second sort. But neither Aquinas nor anyone else has produced a generally convincing philosophical argument that even this sort of demonstration can be logically cogent. And it seems there is a great deal more force and merit to the third objection than Aquinas's rather facile "Reply" would indicate. (The devastating objections to causal arguments raised in the eighteenth century by Hume and Kant impel many people to take this objection a good deal more seriously than Aquinas does.)

The third article, asking the question "whether God exists," comprises three of the most famous pages in Aquinas's writings and is worthy of considerable attention. Both objections are important. The first is in terms of the problem of evil—to the effect that, since "there is evil in the world" and "if one of two contraries be infinite, the other would be altogether destroyed," God could not exist because God is "infinite goodness." The second objection is the position of **naturalism**, that we can adequately account for everything in the world of our experience by means of naturalistic principles without needing to have recourse to a supernatural one, so that "there is no need to suppose God's existence." Against these objections, Aquinas quotes the Old Testament, "*On the contrary*, It is said in the person of God: *I am Who am*" (*Exodus* 3:14); and his own "answer" is, "The existence of God can be proved in five ways."[100] We shall critically analyze these "five ways" individually before discussing them collectively.

"The first and more manifest way is the argument from motion" or change. Through our senses we experience things in the world as "in motion" or changing. Something can be "moved" or changed from what it was capable of becoming to what it will actually be only by something which already actually is. For example, "wood, which is potentially hot," can only be "moved" or changed to become "actually hot" by something, such as fire, which is already actually hot. But nothing can be simultaneously "in actuality and **potentiality** in the same respect"—for example, something is either actually hot or potentially hot at any given time, but cannot be both at once. Therefore, nothing can move or change itself from potentiality to actuality—for instance, make itself hot by itself. "Therefore, whatever is moved must be moved by another." But if that which moves or changes it is itself moved or changed, then it too requires an external "mover" or source of change, and so forth. "But this cannot go on to infinity," since a never-ending chain of that which moves and that which is moved would have no beginning from which everything else could be derived; the chain must be suspended from some ultimate hook or "first mover," which is not itself "moved" from potentiality to actuality; "and this everyone understands to be God."[101] Now consider whether this "argument from motion" seems cogent. If you do not find it convincing, why not? If you do, from the perspective of critical thinking, should you? Don't we all experience things in our environment, including you and Ling-Ling, the giant panda, which are self-moved, changing themselves from what they are potentially (a student of the philosophy of religion or the consumer of this pile of bamboo shoots rather than that one) to what they will actually be? Second, why can there not be the sort of infinite regress that Aquinas rules out? Why, for example, could change not have occurred from all eternity in the matter-energy continuum that we call the universe, without any (temporal or ontological) starting point? (This second critical question will apply to Aquinas's second and third arguments also.) Third, why, as on the analogy of the chain, must we view change as derived from a single source, or "first mover," rather than admitting the possibility of a more or less extensive constellation of ultimate sources of change? And, fourth, if there is, indeed, a "first mover," is it necessarily what "everyone understands to be God"? There being a "first mover" is a necessary, but not **sufficient, condition** for the existence of Aquinas's sort of God. But, as he challenged the universality of the Anselmian conception of God, so we might (even while remembering that he is addressing fellow medieval Christians) question that of his. (Such a critique as this one can be addressed to all of Aquinas's "five ways.")

"The second way is from the nature of efficient cause" and is rather similar to the first. "In the world of sensible things" we experience beings (and events) as related to each other as cause to effect. You were caused to be by your parents, they by your grandparents, and so forth. "There is no case known (neither is it, indeed, possible) in which a thing is found to be the efficient cause of itself; for so it would be prior to itself, which is impossible." So nothing can be self-caused, and, again, as in the "first way," an infinite regress of efficient causes is allegedly impossible, because "if there be no first cause," which is itself uncaused, there could never come to be the caused causes which produce the effects we experience. "Therefore it is necessary to admit a first efficient cause, to which everyone gives the name of God."[102] At the risk of oversimplifying it, we might cast this argument into the form of a (valid, *modus tollens*) syllogism: If there were no "first efficient cause," no effects could exist. But we experience effects as existing in "the world of sensible things." Therefore, there must be a "first efficient cause." Critically speaking, the problem is with the first (hypothetical) premise, which assumes too much—that we have a clearer cognitive understanding of cause-effect relationships than Aquinas appears prepared to demonstrate, that what we know about causality extends beyond the natural realm of things in the world to the world as a whole (for example, could *it* be the uncaused first efficient cause?) and its relationship to that which supernaturally transcends it, and (again) that there is only one ultimate first cause on which everything else depends.

"The third way is taken from possibility and necessity" and again bears a resemblance to the first two (these first three demonstrations are collectively considered "cosmological arguments" because they all are derived from general features that we experience in the cosmos, or world as an organized whole). All the things that we encounter in our world, even though they exist, do so in a contingent manner; that is to say, they could conceivably *not* have existed, or it was not absolutely necessary that they should come to exist.

> But it is impossible for these always to exist, for that which can not-be at some time is not. Therefore if everything can not-be, then at one time there was nothing in existence.

But if there had ever been "nothing in existence," that would have to be the case "even now," since nothing can come to be from nothing. But this "is absurd," for we know from experience that things do, in fact, exist.

> Therefore, not all beings are merely possible, but there must exist something the existence of which is necessary.

But if it derived its necessity from another, that other must also be a necessary being, which may or may not derive its necessity from another, and so forth. But again there cannot be an infinite regress of necessary beings or else nothing would be explained. Thus, we must "admit the existence of some being having of itself its own necessity, and not receiving it from another, but rather causing in others their necessity." This absolutely necessary being, Aquinas concludes, "all men speak of as God."[103] Because of the similarities of these first three arguments, it is difficult to come up with new criticisms. But let us focus on the two complete consecutive sentences quoted (the third and fourth sentences of this paragraph). Suppose that everything that ever existed were contingent (i.e., could conceivably never have been; even though it happened to exist, its existence was not absolutely necessary). Why could some of these contingent beings not merely happen "always to exist"? Why, for example, could there not be some piece of matter (perhaps of a chemical composition foreign to our planetary system) in some remote, distant galaxy, which always has been and always will be there. Suppose that if we ever discovered it and wanted to destroy it, we could cause it not to be but that, in fact, neither we nor anything else of any significance will ever interact with it. Why should we accept Aquinas's dogmatic claim that "that which can not-be at some time is not"? Furthermore, even if we grant (for the sake of argument) that all contingent beings at some time do not exist, why should it logically follow (as Aquinas would have us believe with his use of the word "Therefore") that if everything were contingent, "then at one time there was nothing in existence"? Again, this is a *non sequitur* on his part. A contingent being may have existed *from* all eternity, generated other causes (which will continue to generate others *for* all eternity), and subsequently itself have ceased to be. Thus, everything would exist contingently and nothing eternally, but with times in existence overlapping in such a way that there never is a time when nothing exists.

"The fourth way is taken from the gradation to be found in things"— that is, qualitative degrees of perfection experienced in things. "Among beings there are some more and some less good, true, noble, and the like." (This is reminiscent of Anselm's argumentation in *Monologium*.) But the meaningfulness of degrees of perfection allegedly presupposes "something which is the maximum." Therefore there must be a maximum degree of each sort of perfection (a best, truest, noblest, etc.). "Now the maximum in any genus is the cause of all in that genus," as Aristotle says fire, "the maximum of heat, is the cause of all hot things." Thus, it is necessary that there be "something which is to all beings the cause of their being, goodness, and every other perfection; and this we call God."[104] First, although it is a painfully skeptical question to consider, we must ask whether the perfections we perceive in the world are there objectively or are attributed to (imposed on) things by us. Second, it might seem that there must be some actually best being, some actually truest being, some noblest being, etc. (however difficult it would be to measure and determine them), though not necessarily a best possible being, truest possible being, noblest possible being, etc., which is what the traditional monotheistic believer would want to predicate of God. Third, why should we follow Aquinas's example in accepting the authority of Aristotle to the effect that "the maximum in any genus is the cause of all in that genus"? It is hard to imagine how that can be shown to be true. The example of fire and heat inspires no confidence at all, given that fire is neither "the maximum of heat" nor "the cause of all hot things"; but even if the example worked, the sweeping **generalization** derived from it is staggering. Fourth, we should notice that Aquinas does not here justify the consolidation, in his final sentence, of all the maxima into a single most perfect being.

"The fifth way is taken from the governance of the world" and is a version of the teleological argument or what, in modern times, has come to be called the "**argument from design**." We experience things in the world about us as acting for purposes, in regular fashions designed to bring about their good. For example, on our planet, plants routinely sink their roots into the ground (to derive nourishment from the soil) and raise their leaves towards the sun (to benefit from the light); it does not naturally happen the other way around, which would kill the plant rather than helping it to thrive. It is incredible to imagine that the immense order of so many things in the universe has happened merely by chance. "Hence it is plain that they achieve their end, not fortuitously, but designedly." Yet most things (for example, dandelion plants) are not intelligent and cannot envision the reasons for which they act. "Now whatever lacks knowledge cannot move towards an end, unless it be directed by some being endowed with knowledge and intelligence, as the arrow is directed by the archer." Only intelligent thought can adequately account for the overwhelming design of reality. "Therefore some intelligent being exists by whom all natural things are directed to their end; and this being we call God."[105] The argument from design seems the most psychologically persuasive of the arguments for God (particularly when what is to be accounted for is the intelligent activity of personal life). But is this the logically cogent demonstration Aquinas intends? Unfortunately, it is not. For over one hundred twenty-five years now, Darwin's theory of **natural selection** has stood as a credible logical alternative to the hypothesis of an intelligent Designer. This, then, vitiates the force of Aquinas's final premise ("Now whatever . . .") and erodes the logical credibility of the argument.

Having analyzed each of the "five ways" systematically and critically, let us now consider them collectively and comparatively. First, they are all empirical (*a posteriori*) attempts to demonstrate God's existence on the basis of experienced facts about the world—that it is one of change, involving cause-effect relationships, of contingently existing things, exhibiting manifold degrees of perfection, and being regularly ordered toward specifiable ends. Second, they all (Hume might say, presumptuously) involve a connection of things experienced in the natural world to a supernatural reality transcending the world by means of cause-effect reasoning of some sort. Third, in each case, the causal reasoning terminates in a metaphysical principle—(a) first mover, (b) ultimate efficient cause, (c) absolutely necessary being, (d) maximum source of perfection, and (e) intelligent governor of the world—which is allegedly unique, radically different from everything it is designed causally to explain, and not itself requiring any explanation (self-sufficient). Fourth, each argument ends with a phrase which tries to identify that metaphysical principle with the personal God of monotheistic religions, as if each metaphysical principle represents one aspect of God.

What of Aquinas's responses to each of the two important objections in Article Three? Both appear to be disappointing. In "Reply" to the problem of evil objection, Aquinas merely quotes and paraphrases Augustine, to the effect that God's omnipotence and goodness are such that good will be drawn out of all evil, so that God can legitimately "allow evil to exist." This is a straightforward appeal to authority which is dogmatically presented; and one tends to expect more of such a great philosopher as Aquinas is. (However, at the end of this chapter, we shall see, in more detail, Aquinas's treatment of the problem of evil elsewhere.) His "Reply" to the objection of naturalism is no better, begging the question outrageously. Its first sentence is predicated on the assumption in need of proof, that "nature works for a determinate end under the direction of a higher agent."[106] This is not Aquinas at his best. But it would have been far more difficult for a thirteenth-century Christian theologian to take naturalism seriously than it is for us today.

In his *Summa contra Gentiles*, Aquinas also presents a battery of "arguments in proof of the existence of God," starting with an argument from motion derived from Aristotle and similar to the first of his "five ways." Here he does try to provide some of Aristotle's justifications of the propositions "that *everything that is moved is moved by another*, and that *in movers and things moved one cannot proceed to infinity.*" Because none of this appears particularly convincing, we shall not delve into the reasoning here but merely observe that the arguments are there.[107] A curious Aristotelian argument, having some relation to the fourth of Aquinas's "five ways" is presented, based on the metaphysical axiom "that what is most true" is also most real and the thesis that there must be something "which is absolutely and supremely true," and concluding that there must be "something that is supremely being," which is God. But the premises here (the axiom and the **existential thesis**) are so dubious that it is no wonder this argument has had relatively little influence. Aquinas also presents an argument of John Damascene's "from the government of the world"; it reasons that, since "things of diverse natures" in the world regularly "come together under one order," there must be "some being by whose providence the world is governed" so that this could occur, who is God.[108] This is another version of the teleological argument (or that from design), subject to the same comments made on the last of Aquinas's "five ways."

Aquinas presents another argument for God's existence in his early work *On Being and Essence*. He says there that everything whose "act of existing is other than its nature must needs have its act of existing from something else" so that it is dependent on another for its existence. But then "there must be some being which is the cause of the existing of all things" and which itself is such that its essence is to exist ("it itself is the act of existing"). Otherwise everything would depend on other things for its existence, which, in turn, would likewise be dependent, leading to an "infinity among causes." But since there can be no such "infinity among causes," there must be a "First Being which is simply the act of existing. This is the First Cause, God."[109] This seems rather similar to the third of Aquinas's "five ways"; what was there called contingent being is here analyzed as that whose "act of existing is other than its nature," and what was there an absolutely necessary being is here analyzed as one whose nature it is to exist (which "itself is the act of existing"). This argument is therefore subject to criticisms comparable to those already indicated for the third way.

God's Essence. Thus far, we have been tracking, in some detail, Aquinas's arguments for divine existence (the fact that God is). Now we must consider, however briefly, what he says about the divine essence (what God is), and a good place to begin is with that same early work, *On Being and Essence*. There he says that, "although God is simply the act of existing, it is not necessary that He lack the other perfections or excellences."

(This assumption that existence is a perfection was to be challenged in the eighteenth century by Hume and Kant.) Quite the contrary, Aquinas contends, God "possesses all perfections of all genera of beings; so He is said to be unqualifiedly perfect." Yet the divine perfections supposedly coexist in God "in a more excellent way" than do comparable perfections in creatures, "for in Him they are one, while in other things they are diversified. The reason for this is that all these perfections are His according to His simple act of existing."[110] Another way of expressing this (easier said than understood, no doubt) is that Aquinas's God *is* all perfections in a way that does not compromise the divine simplicity.

It is this topic of "the simplicity of God" to which Aquinas turns in his *Summa*. Two sentences are noteworthy both for making a transition from existence to essence and for assigning the parameters to the discussion of the divine nature: "When the existence of a thing has been ascertained, there remains the further question of the manner of its existence, in order that we may know its essence. Now because we cannot know what God is, but rather what He is not, we have no means for considering how God is, but rather how He is not."[111] This approach in terms of a knowledge of what God is not is called "the negative way" (*via negativa*). The first characteristic Aquinas wants to rule out as belonging to the divine nature is composition, although he will proceed to argue that God's simplicity does not imply imperfection and incompleteness as does that of material things.

He argues that "God is not a body" on the grounds that God is

1. the unchanging first cause of all change,
2. having no potentiality whatsoever, and
3. the most excellent of all beings.[112]

But from this it follows logically that in God there can be no distinction between (what in old Aristotelian jargon is called) matter (a physical component) and form (its organizing structure), as there is in all things of our world: "Whatsoever is composed of matter and form is a body . . . But God is not a body . . . Therefore, He is not composed of matter and form."[113] If we grant that there is a single God (divine unity will be discussed shortly) which cannot be a body, this argument seems conclusive, since (by definition) anything containing matter is a body. But Aquinas holds that what follows from this lack of any distinction between matter and form in the divine nature is that, unlike all the things of this world, "God is the same as His essence."[114] And having argued that God is identical with the divine essence, Aquinas immediately goes on to show by a *reductio ad absurdum* argument that God's existence is identical with that essence: whenever the existence of a thing differs from its essence, that existence "must be caused either by some exterior agent or by the essential principles of the thing itself." But nothing's "essential principles" can cause its existence, "for nothing can be the sufficient cause of its own being." So any such thing, whose existence "differs from its essence, must have its being caused by another." But this could not be correctly claimed about God, whom we have (supposedly) demonstrated to be "the first efficient cause." Hence it must be false that in God existence could differ from essence.[115] If we go along with Aquinas thus far, we are logically driven to affirm the "absolute simplicity of God," which is where the argument has been heading all along. "For there is neither composition of quantitative parts in God, since He is not a body; nor composition of form and matter"; nor any distinction between God and the divine nature; nor does God's essence differ "from His being"; and so forth. "Therefore, it is clear that God is in no way composite, but is altogether simple."[116] Aquinas is such a master of logic and so patient in constructing complex argumentation that typically the only way to avoid having to grant him his conclusions is to be very cautious about accepting his premises. For example, why should we accept his claim that anything whose existence "differs from its essence" must be caused either by its own "essential properties" or by "some exterior agent"? Perhaps this is intuitively plausible on the surface, but does it bear critical scrutiny?

So, God is (allegedly) simple. Yet the divine simplicity is not like that of anything in the world of our experience (we shall discuss Aquinas's notion of analogy in the next subsection); for we identify creaturely simplicity with imperfection and incompleteness. Aquinas therefore proceeds to argue for the "perfection" and "infinity of God." In addressing the question of "whether God is perfect," Aquinas considers the etymological objection that "perfect" literally means "completely made" but that God, being uncaused, cannot properly be said "to be made" at all. Quoting the Gospels, he says, "*On the contrary*, It is written: *Be you perfect as also your heavenly Father is perfect*" (*Matt.* 5:48). Aquinas's argument, borrowing ideas from Aristotle, is that God, being "the first principle" in the order of efficient causality, must "be most actual." But, since "a thing is said to be perfect in proportion to its actuality," it must follow that God is also "most perfect." Very few people nowadays accept this Aristotelian metaphysical equating of actuality with causal primacy and perfection; for those of us who do not, this proof of God's perfection seems particularly quaint and implausible. In "Reply" to that etymological objection,

Aquinas admits that we do not call God "perfect" in the literal sense of the word but says the term "signifies by extension whatever is not wanting in actual being, whether this be "made so or not.""[117] He goes on to argue that God is not only perfect but "universally perfect," in that "All the perfections of all things are in God," who is not lacking in "any excellence which may be found in any genus" of thing.[118] But there is also no incompleteness in Aquinas's God, who is unlimited or infinite. By what could Aquinas's God, the ultimate first cause, be limited? As he says, matter and form can limit each other. But, as we have seen, in God there is no matter and thus no distinction between matter and form. Also, a thing's existence can be limited by that from which it is derived; but since the divine existence is underived and "God is His own subsistent being," it allegedly follows "that God Himself is infinite and perfect."[119] Critically, we should ask whether these are the only ways in which something can be limited. Aquinas goes on to show, by means of a neat argument drawn from Aristotle, that only God can be infinite because the infinite, by its very nature, cannot be derived from anything else and everything other than God is derived from this ultimate first cause.[120]

So far, we have traced Aquinas's argumentation for divine simplicity, perfection, and infinity. Other divine attributes for which he argues include goodness, immutability, eternity, unity, intelligence, and power. A thorough coverage of his philosophical theology would require treatment of all of these crucial divine attributes, as well as others Aquinas discusses (e.g., God's life, will, love, justice and mercy, **providence**, and personality). But, given the limits of our survey, let us confine the remainder of the analysis of this subsection to his argumentation for divine unity, since we called this into question in critically evaluating his "five ways" of proving God's existence. Having quoted the Old Testament to the effect that "*our God is one Lord*" (*Deut.* 6:4), Aquinas maintains that he has three ways of showing "that God is one. First from His simplicity." For no absolutely simple being can share its singularity with anything else. "Secondly, this is proved from the infinity of His perfection." If any other such being existed, its perfection(s) would limit God's. "Thirdly, this is shown from the unity of the world,"[121] which must have been caused by a single being. These arguments are only as convincing as are the divine simplicity, the infinity of God's perfection, and the ordered unity of our world which they presuppose. Granted any of these in the sense intended by Aquinas, divine unity might follow. Yet many of us would find it quite appropriate to doubt that any of these considerations is sufficiently conclusive to regard it as "proved" that God is one (eliminating **polytheism** as possible).

Analogy. Aquinas's discussions of analogy, miracles, and evil are related to this analysis of what we can claim to know about God. Let us consider his theory of analogy—first generally, as it is presented in *Summa Theologica*, then more carefully, as it is developed in *Summa contra Gentiles*. The *Summa* deals with theological language or "the Names of God." There, Aquinas argues that when the same words are used to speak of God as are used to describe creatures, those words cannot be employed in exactly the same sense, because of the vast dissimilarity:

> God is more distant from creatures than any creatures are from each other. But the distance of some creatures makes any univocal predication of them impossible. . . . Therefore much less can anything be predicated univocally of God and creatures.

Whenever we speak (or even think) of any attribute of any creature, we do so in such a way as to distinguish that attribute from both the creature and all its other attributes; "as, for instance, by this term *wise* applied to a man, we signify some perfection distinct from a man's essence, and distinct from his power and his being, and from all similar things. But when we apply *wise* to God, we do not mean to signify anything distinct from His essence or power or being."[122] However, the other extreme is to say that we equivocate when we use the same words of God and of creatures—that is, that the two uses have no connection or conceptual relationship. Just as the extreme of supposing that theological language is univocal had to be rejected, so now must this opposite one: "Neither, on the other hand, are names applied to God and creatures in a purely equivocal sense, as some have said. Because if that were so, it follows that from creatures nothing at all could be known or demonstrated about God." In other words, in order to argue demonstratively about God from our experience of creatures in the world, as we have seen Aquinas try to do, it must be possible accurately to make some statements about both God and creation in a manner that will connect the two logically. "Therefore it must be said that these names are said of God and creatures in an *analogous* sense, that is, according to proportion." God is not the same as any creature; yet God is the causal source of all creatures and of all their qualities. "Hence, whatever is said of God and creatures is said according as there is some relation of the creature to God as to its principle and cause, wherein all the perfections of things pre-exist excellently." This relationship of analogy, says Aquinas, is "a mean," or middle ground, between univocation and equivocation, both of which are inadequate interpretations of theological language. "For in analogies the idea is not, as in univocals, one and the same; yet it is not totally diverse as in equivocals."[123] Rather the words used signify a proportional relationship between God and creatures. Such language is derived from our experience of creatures and applies primarily to them; its application to God is secondary and indicates that relationship. There is a certain parallelism between God's wisdom and man's; we understand the former with reference to the latter but as referring to the causal source of, while devoid of the limitations of, the latter.

This ingenious theory of analogous language is perhaps even better presented in the *Summa contra Gentiles*, where Aquinas explains that because God is the efficient cause of all creatures, "some likeness must be found between them, since it belongs to the nature of action that an agent produce its like." It seems correct to say that a cause must be like its effect in at least some respects, for how could an agent produce some effect with which it has nothing in common? But how is this likeness between God and creatures to be explained? Aquinas answers that "that which is found in God perfectly is found in other things according to a certain diminished participation." We derive our qualities from God, sharing in the divine perfections, though, of course, to a limited extent. "Thus, the creature has what belongs to God and, consequently, is rightly said to be like God."[124]

Aquinas proceeds to argue that since God is the ultimate causal source of all creatures and all their perfections, the names we use to refer to the latter must also be correctly attributable to God, even if not in exactly the same manner:

> Since it is possible to find in God every perfection of creatures, but in another and more eminent way, whatever names unqualifiedly designate a perfection without defect are predicated of God and of other things: for example, goodness, wisdom, being, and the like. But when any name expresses such perfections along with a mode that is proper to a creature, it can be said of God only according to likeness and metaphor.

We say, for example, that God is omniscient to distinguish divine intelligence from man's, which is always necessarily limited. So all names apply to God in a "mode of supereminence" and can be so qualified. "Such names are the *highest good*, the *first being*, and the like." Some negative terms are designed to apply only to God," as when we say that God is *eternal* or *infinite*; and others are constructed so as to designate the special relationship God has to the world of creation, "as when He is called the *first cause* or the *highest good*."[125] Aquinas says that we must attribute a plurality of names to God. "For, since we cannot know Him naturally except by arriving at Him from His effects, the names by which we signify His perfection must be diverse, just as the perfections belonging to things are found to be diverse."[126] Yet this is merely our inadequate way of thinking and talking of God, and we should not imagine that it represents any multiplicity in God or compromises the divine simplicity.

Aquinas argues "that nothing can be predicated univocally of God and other things" in several ways, of which two will be indicated here. First, God's simplicity is such that (as was said before) God *is* all perfections, so that they are not really separate or ontologically distinguished from one another or from the divine essence. By contrast, "the things that God has made receive in a divided and particular way that which in Him is found in a simple and universal way. It is evident, then, that nothing can be said univocally of God and other things." Aquinas's second argument here goes like this: "Again, what is predicated of many things univocally is simpler than both of them, at least in concept. Now, there can be nothing simpler than God either in reality or in concept. Nothing, therefore, is predicated univocally of God and other things."[127] We should notice that both of these arguments require that God be simple in the way that Aquinas thinks he has shown God to be.

Aquinas proceeds to argue, again in several ways, "that not everything predicated of God and other things is said in a purely equivocal way." Things are conceptually related "in a purely equivocal way," he explains, whenever "there is no order or reference of one to another, but it is entirely accidental that one name is applied to diverse things." This does happen, in particular, with puns (especially where spoken rather than written)—for example, when it is said that old teachers never die, they simply lose their class and principals. "But this is not the situation with names said of God and creatures, since we note in the community of such names the order of cause and effect." A second argument maintains that "where there is pure equivocation, there is no likeness in things themselves; there is only the unity of a name. But, as is clear from what we have said, there is a certain mode of likeness of things to God." This is followed immediately by a third: "Moreover, when one name is predicated of several things in a purely equivocal way, we cannot from one of them be led to the knowledge of another." But from our experience of things of this world, "we do arrive at a knowledge of divine things, as is evident from what we have said." Aquinas continues with a similar fourth argument: If "nothing was said of God and creatures except in a purely equivocal way, no reasoning proceeding from creatures to God could take place." But, as we have seen, Aquinas's arguments for God are designed to provide precisely such reasoning. Hence, theological language cannot be used "of God and creatures in a purely equivocal way."[128] These arguments all hinge, directly or indirectly, on the adequacy of causal demonstrative arguments for God, such as the ones developed by Aquinas, which has been called into question in the previous subsection.

Aquinas presents a nice treatment of analogy as an alternative to the undesirable extremes of univocal and equivocal uses of theological language. He begins by holding "that the names said of God and creatures are predicated neither univocally nor equivocally but analogically." He explains that there are two ways in which words can be used analogically, the first of which does not apply to theological language and the second of which does. In the first way, many things are seen as referring to some one basic concept. "Thus, with reference to one *health* we say that an animal is healthy as the subject of health, medicine is healthy as its cause, food as its preserver, urine as its sign." This way does not apply to theological language because, if it did, we would "have to posit something prior to God" to which we could relate both God and things; but, of course, nothing is prior to, or more ultimate than, Aquinas's God, the first cause of all other reality. According to the second way, "the analogy can obtain" between two things in such a manner that one of them has precedence over the other or is the primary referent. "Thus, *being* is said of **substance** and **accident** according as an accident has reference to a substance, and not according as substance and accident are referred to a third thing." For example, the reality of green is parasitic on there being green things; the reality of grinning (Lewis Carroll's Cheshire Cat notwithstanding) requires persons or things doing the grinning. "In this second mode of analogical predication the order according to the name and according to reality is sometimes found to be the same and sometimes not." In the case of analogies drawn between God and creatures it is not. God is prior "according to reality" because God is the ultimate reality and the source of the reality of all creatures. But creatures have priority in "the order according to the name," which is "the order of knowledge," since we can only come to know God by way of our prior knowledge of the things of experience from which the language is taken which will be analogically applied to God, who is "named from His effects."[129]

This theory of the analogical use of theological language seems to provide a brilliant solution to the delicate problem of how we can meaningfully say (or even think) anything about God without collapsing the crucial distinction between creatures and the divine nature. However, for all the merits of this doctrine, one might object that such language, used of that which transcends all natural experience, is unable to impart or communicate rational knowledge concerning God, but can only provide belief. Yet, even with this reservation, this doctrine—along with his position on faith and reason and the argumentation for God—is one of the three most significant aspects of Aquinas's philosophical theology.

Miracles. The next topic to be discussed is that of miracles. If God is the infinite creator of all other things and governs all reality through divine providence, what are the implications for events in our world and the activities of creatures? Aquinas discusses "the Movement of God in Creatures" in the *Summa*. He holds that God is causally working in every creaturely agent, but in such a way as not to deprive the latter of true causal efficacy: "We must therefore understand that God works in things in such a manner that things have also their proper operation." This is not to say that you and God are "agents of the same order" when you perform an action. "But nothing hinders the same action from proceeding from a primary and a secondary agent."[130] Thus, God, the ultimate efficient cause of all reality, is the "primary" agent in what we call your action, while you are its "secondary agent" or immediate cause. It would take us too far afield to discuss it at this point, but this analysis does raise the critical question of whether human freedom is compromised by this theory.

Aquinas considers "whether God can do anything outside the established order of nature"—in other words, whether miracles are possible, given that the immutable (i.e., unchanging) God established that natural order and, through it, works in all creaturely agents. Aquinas argues that God, who freely created nature, "is not subject to the order of secondary causes, but, on the contrary, this order is subject to Him, as proceeding from Him, not by a natural necessity, but by the choice of His own will." God's free creative act does not bind the divine agency to the regularities of the natural order resulting from it. "Therefore God can do something outside this order created by Him, when He chooses." Nor, supposedly, does this jeopardize divine immutability:

> God fixed a certain order in things in such a way that at the same time He reserved to Himself whatever He intended to do otherwise than by a particular cause. So when He acts outside this order, He does not change.[131]

If God intended from all eternity that the burning bush of the Old Testament would blaze without being consumed, even though this is contrary to the regular order of nature, that need not threaten divine immutability.

Aquinas approvingly quotes Augustine as saying, "*Where God does anything against that order of nature which we know and are accustomed to observe, we call it a miracle.*" He traces the etymological meaning of "miracle" and explains how it can apply to events in our world: "The term *miracle* is derived from admiration, which arises when an effect is manifest, whereas its cause is hidden; as when a man sees an eclipse without knowing its cause." He goes on to say that the cause of an experienced effect may be known to some people, while others are ignorant of it.

> Hence a thing is wonderful to one man, and not at all to others; as an eclipse is to a rustic, but not to an astronomer. Now a miracle is so called as being full of wonder, in other words, as having a cause absolutely hidden from all. This cause is God. Therefore those things which God does outside the causes which we know are called miracles.[132]

In such cases the secondary or immediate causes are either unknown to all of us or what appear to be the secondary or immediate causes are ordinarily and naturally inadequate to achieve those effects.

Aquinas distinguishes three types of miracles, all of which exceed the power of the natural order, but in different ways and thus to varying degrees: "first, in the substance of the deed, for instance, if two bodies occupy the same place, or if the sun goes backward." This, says, Aquinas, is the strongest sort of exception to the natural order and therefore represents "the highest rank among miracles." A second, and lesser, order of miracle is represented by events that can occur in our world but not to this sort of **phenomena**, "as the raising of the dead, and giving sight to the blind, and the like. For nature can give life, but not to the dead, and it can give sight, but not to the blind." Whereas the strongest sort of miracle has to do with events that cannot naturally occur, and the next kind with those that can naturally occur but not to this type of phenomena, the weakest sort of miracle concerns events that can naturally occur to this type of phenomena but not in this manner, "as when a man is cured of a fever suddenly by God, without treatment or the usual process of nature."[133] This is more a conceptual analysis of what miracles are and a reconciliation of them with the nature of Aquinas's God than an attempt to argue rationally for the reality of miracles in our world, to which reality Scriptural revelation provides testimony.

The Problem of Evil. The third and final issue to be considered in connection with the kind of God for which Aquinas has argued (after those of analogical language as an instrument for referring to a transcendent, perfect being and the possibility of miracles within the natural order established by an immutable creator) is that of the problem of evil. As we have seen in relation to Aquinas's arguments for the existence of God, he adopts the Augustinian view that the divine power and goodness are such that God will draw greater good out of the evil permitted. In the *Summa contra Gentiles* we are reminded of the rational foundation of our belief in divine goodness: "From the divine perfection, which we have shown, we can conclude to the goodness of God." Beyond this, Aquinas argues that God "is good essentially" and thus is "His own goodness," since God is "a simple being," in whom existence and essence are one. And, beyond this, because "God is good essentially, while other things are good by participation" merely, it follows that "God is, therefore, the highest good." But if God is perfect and goodness itself, then "it is quite evident that there cannot be evil in God," since evil is the opposite of good and "the nature of evil consists in imperfection." It also supposedly follows from all this that "God cannot will evil," according to Aquinas, because "the will never aims at evil without some error,"[134] and a perfect being is incapable of error. How, then, can there be any evil?

This is explained in the *Summa*, where Augustine's "privation" theory is endorsed when Aquinas says that "the very nature of evil consists in the privation of good." God does not directly will evil. Yet certain sorts of evil can be willed "accidentally," and other sorts may be permitted. For example, "evil may be sought accidentally," insofar as it necessarily accompanies a greater good which is desired. "Now the evil that accompanies one good is the privation of another good. Never therefore would evil be sought after, not even accidentally, unless the good that accompanies the evil were more desired than the good of which the evil is the privation." As examples Aquinas mentions the physical evil of natural corruption, accompanying the beauty of "the preservation of the order of nature," and the evil of punishment, required of the wicked by divine justice. What is directly desired is the good.[135]

But the most important passages on Aquinas's theory of evil in the *Summa* are yet to be discussed. Since he considers all being, by its very nature, good, "it is impossible that evil signifies any being." Yet this is not to deny its reality, for "evil is found in things"—and appropriately so, since the variety of things in the universe (having greater and lesser degrees of perfection) contributes to its richness. "As was said above, evil indicates the absence of good. But not every absence of good is evil"—only the absence of that sort of good which is naturally appropriate to that which lacks it. For example, it is not evil that a tree should be unable to see, whereas it is a physical evil that a human being should be blind; after all, human beings are the sorts of things which should naturally be capable of sight, while trees are not. Even when things are evil, Aquinas says, "evil cannot wholly consume good," since there would have to be something that is evil and all being, as such, is good. Now there is evil in involuntary things—for example, the physical evil of the natural corruption in nonpersonal life—as well as in voluntary things, such as persons; and "every evil in voluntary things is to be looked upon as a pain or a fault"— for instance, we experience pain as a result of our own foolishness and fault as a result of the moral evil we choose to do. Of these two types of evil pertaining to voluntary creatures, Aquinas considers fault (*culpa*) to be worse than pain (*poena*), because "one becomes evil" through the former and not through the latter; he says, "God is the author of the evil of pain, but not of the evil of fault."[136]

Aquinas discusses "the Cause of Evil," repeating that "evil is the absence of the good which is natural and due to a thing." Now since "every evil in some way has a cause" rather than being coincidental or rationally inexplicable, and since only being (and not nonbeing) can cause anything, it must follow "that good is the cause of evil." But a central question posed by the classical problem of evil is "whether the highest good, God, is the cause of evil." Aquinas argues that God, because perfectly good, cannot cause the moral evil of fault at all. "Hence, the evil which consists in defect of action, or which is caused by defect of the agent, is not reduced to God as to its cause." God only allows or permits other intelligent beings, personal creatures, to do this kind of evil, and they are its cause. However, Aquinas admits that God is the causal source of physical evil and the evil of penalty: "But the evil which consists in the corruption of some things is reduced to God as the cause." And this is because the rich variety of "the order of the universe requires, as was said above, that there should be some things that can, and sometimes do, fail" and because our fault or moral evil-doing requires penalty or punishment, according to divine justice. Finally, Aquinas maintains that there cannot be one highest evil which is the ultimate cause of every evil, in contrast with God as the ultimate first principle of all good.[137]

There is little original in Aquinas's theory of evil, which is so heavily indebted to the enormously influential contributions of Augustine. Nor has it been particularly convincing to those who are not already committed to believing it. The answer to the question of why an absolutely perfect God would need to cause some kinds of evil and to permit others has not been significantly advanced here by Aquinas beyond those contributions of his illustrious predecessor. Nor has Aquinas provided any cogent basis for knowledge-claims regarding the traditional problem of evil with his more empirical approach. Aquinas's theory here, as in his philosophical theology generally, is vitiated by too many unjustified and crucial epistemological presuppositions: that there is an external reality to be experienced; that it is objectively knowable by us; and that this knowledge can be extended, by means of causal reasoning, from the natural order to the supernatural realm. Here is the key area of improvement, most relevant to philosophical theology, made by modern thinkers (starting with and inspired by Descartes) over not only Aquinas but the entire Middle Ages. Yet the contributions of thinkers such as Augustine, Anselm, and Aquinas have been remarkably impressive; and there is no doubt concerning the profound influence of this medieval background on subsequent philosophical theology.

Notes

1. *The Confessions of St. Augustine*, trans. John K. Ryan (Garden City, NY: Image Books, 1960), pp. 65, 67, 70, 77, 94; this book will hereafter be called "*Confessions*."

2. Ibid., pp. 80–82.   3. Ibid., p. 82.   4. Ibid., pp. 119–22.

5. Ibid., p. 126.   6. Ibid., p. 131.   7. Ibid., pp. 43, 202.

8. *The Advantage of Believing*, trans. Luanne Meagher, in *Writings of Saint Augustine*, vol. 2, ed. Ludwig Schopp (New York: CIMA, 1947), pp. 392, 396, 402; this work will hereafter be called "*Believing*."

9. Ibid., pp. 403, 409.

10. *The Soliloquies*, trans. Thomas F. Gilligan, in *Writings of Saint Augustine*, vol. 1, ed. Ludwig Schopp (New York: CIMA, 1948), pp. 350–51; this work will hereafter be called "*Soliloquies*"; cf. Augustine's *De Ordine*, trans. as *Divine Providence and the Problem of Evil* by Robert P. Russell, vol. 1, p. 324: "To philosophy pertains a twofold question: the first treats of the soul; the second, of God. The first makes us know ourselves; the second, our origin."

11. *Believing*, pp. 419–20.

12. Ibid., p. 421.

13. *The City of God*, by Augustine, trans. Marcus Dods (New York: The Modern Library, 1950), pp. 247–48, 255, 347; cf. *Against the Academicians*, by Augustine, trans. Sister Mary Patricia Garvey (Milwaukee: Marquette Univ. Press, 1957), pp. 81–82. Aquinas's verdict here is worth mentioning: "Consequently whenever Augustine, who was imbued with the doctrines of the Platonists, found in their teaching anything consistent with faith, he adopted it; and those things which he found contrary to faith he amended"—*Basic Writings of Saint Thomas Aquinas*, ed. Anton C. Pegis, vol. 1 (New York: Random House, 1945), p. 804.

14. *On Faith in Things Unseen*, trans. Roy J. Deferrari and Mary Francis McDonald, in *Writings of Saint Augustine*, vol. 2, ed. Ludwig Schopp (New York: CIMA, 1947), pp. 451–52, 454–55; this work will hereafter be called "*Faith*." Augustine makes the same point in *Believing*, pp. 422, 426–27.

15. *Faith*, pp. 456, 460, 465, 467.

16. *Believing*, pp. 423–25.

17. Ibid., p. 425.   18. Ibid., pp. 426, 437, 440.

19. *Of True Religion*, by Augustine, trans. J. H. S. Burleigh (Chicago: Henry Regnery, 1966), pp. 10, 41; cf. *De Ordine*, p. 303: "Likewise, with regard to the acquiring of knowledge, we are of necessity led in a twofold manner: by authority and by reason." For the relation between philosophy and religion, see *The City of God* (p. 243), where Augustine reflects on the concept of philosophy as "the love of wisdom" thus: "Now, if wisdom is God, who made all things, as is attested by the divine authority and truth, then the philosopher is a lover of God."

20. *Lectures or Tractates on the Gospel According to St. John*, vol. 1, trans. Rev. John Gibb, in *The Works of Aurelius Augustine*, ed. Rev. Marcus Dods, vol. 10 (Edinburgh: T. & T. Clark, 1873), p. 405 (Tractate XXIX, section 6). The imperative, "Believe so that you may understand" (*crede ut intelligas*) is used in Sermon 212—Augustine, *Sermons on the Liturgical Seasons*, trans. Sister Mary Sarah Muldowney, in *The Fathers of the Church*, vol. 38, ed. Roy Joseph Deferrari (New York: Fathers of the Church, Inc., 1959), p. 119. For a more involved treatment of the same issue, see Augustine's Letter # 120 to Consentius in *Letters*, Augustine, vol. 2 (# 83-130), trans. Sister Wilfrid Parsons, in *The Fathers of the Church*, vol. 18, ed. by Roy Joseph Deferrari (New York: Fathers of the Church, Inc., 1953), pp. 300–317.

21. *On Free Choice of the Will*, by Augustine, trans. Anna S. Benjamin and L. H. Hackstaff (Indianapolis: Bobbs-Merrill, 1964), pp. 5, 39—this work will hereafter be called "*Free Choice*"; the Scriptural reference is to *Isaiah* 7:9.

22. *Free Choice*, p. 40. Augustine's nonempirical approach to God is consistent with the interiorism expressed in his *Of True Religion* (p. 69): "Do not go abroad. Return within yourself. In the inward man dwells truth."

23. *The City of God*, p. 370.

24. *Free Choice*, pp. 40–41.

25. Ibid., pp. 41–49. In *The City of God* (p. 851) he refers to reason as "the image of God" in man.

26. *Confessions*, p. 43.

27. *Free Choice*, p. 49.

28. *On Christian Doctrine*, by Augustine, trans. D. W. Robertson, Jr. (Indianapolis: Bobbs-Merrill, 1958), pp. 11–12; see also *Confessions*, p. 161.

29. *Free Choice*, pp. 54, 66–67, 71.

30. *Confessions*, p. 45.

31. *Soliloquies*, p. 345.

32. *Free Choice*, p. 40.

33. Ibid., pp. 75–77.   34. Ibid., pp. 77–78, 80.   35. Ibid., pp. 83–84.

36. *The Enchiridion on Faith, Hope and Love*, by Augustine, trans. J. F. Shaw, ed. Henry Paolucci (Chicago: Henry Regnery, 1961), pp. 10–11; this work will hereafter be

called "*Enchiridion*." Cf. *De Ordine*, p. 299, where Augustine speaks of "the nonentity which is called evil."

37. *Enchiridion*, pp. 12–15.

38. *Confessions*, p. 172.

39. Ibid., p. 162.

40. *The City of God*, p. 811.

41. *Free Choice*, pp. 125–26.

42. *St. Anselm: Basic Writings*, trans. S. N. Deane, 2nd ed. (LaSalle: Open Court Publishing Co., 1968), p. 2. All quotations from and references to *Proslogium*, *Monologium*, and *Cur Deus Homo* use this book, which will hereafter be called "Deane."

43. Ibid., p. 36.

44. Ibid., p. 7—"*credo ut intelligam. . . . quia 'nisi credidero, non intelligam.'* "

45. Ibid., p. 178. 46. Ibid., pp. 179, 182, 265–66.

47. Ibid., p. 181. 48. Ibid., p. 128. 49. Ibid., p. 238.

50. Ibid., pp. 179, 181–82.

51. Ibid., pp. 69–70; cf. *John* 14:6.

52. *Truth, Freedom, and Evil: Three Philosophical Dialogues*, by Anselm of Canterbury, ed. and trans. Jasper Hopkins and Herbert Richardson (New York: Harper & Row, 1967), pp. 93, 110, 120.

53. Ibid., pp. 127, 143. 54. Ibid., pp. 148–49, 163.

55. Deane, pp. 129–31.

56. Ibid., pp. 132, 139, 141.

57. Ibid., pp. 37–38. 58. Ibid., pp. 38–40. 59. Ibid., p. 40.

60. Ibid., pp. 41–42. 61. Ibid., pp. 43–44. 62. Ibid., pp. 45, 35.

63. Ibid., p. 1. 64. Ibid., p. 7. 65. Ibid., p. 8.

66. Ibid., pp. 8–9. 67. Ibid., pp. 9–11. 68. Ibid., pp. 148–49.

69. Ibid., p. 167. 70. Ibid., p. 150.

71. Ibid., pp. 157–58, 169.

72. Ibid., pp. 150–51. 73. Ibid., p. 158. 74. Ibid., p. 152.

75. Ibid., pp. 158–60. 76. Ibid., p. 152. 77. Ibid., pp. 153, 170.

78. Thomas Aquinas, *On the Truth of the Catholic Faith: Summa contra Gentiles: book 1: God*, trans. Anton C. Pegis (Garden City, NY: Doubleday, 1955), p. 62; this work will hereafter be called "*God*."

79. *Basic Writings of Saint Thomas Aquinas*, ed. Anton C. Pegis, vol. 1, p. 6; this work will hereafter be called "*Basic*" (followed by volume and page numbers).

80. Ibid., pp. 7–9, 11. 81. Ibid., pp. 12–14.

82. *God*, pp. 63–64.

83. *Basic*, p. 21.

84. Thomas Aquinas, *Truth*, vol. 1, trans. Robert W. Mulligan, S.J. (Chicago: Henry Regnery, 1952), p. 13; cf. pp. 10, 33.

85. Ibid., pp. 48, 50. This empirical view that "nothing can be in the intellect which was not first in the senses" (*nihil in intellectu quod non prius fuerit in sensu*) comes from Aristotle.

86. Ibid., vol. 2, trans. James V. McGlynn, S.J. (Chicago: Henry Regnery, 1953), p. 83.

87. Ibid., pp. 220–21, 244, 250.

88. *God*, pp. 66–68.

89. Ibid., pp. 69–70.   90. Ibid., pp. 71–72.   91. Ibid., p. 74.

92. Ibid., p. 76.

93. *Basic*, vol. 2, pp. 1056–58, 1060–61; cf. p. 1080, where Aquinas says, "Science and faith cannot be in the same subject and about the same object; but what is an object of science for one can be an object of faith for another"; also, on p. 1090, he writes that "demonstrative reasons in support of the preambles of faith, but not of the articles of faith, diminish the measure of faith, since they make the thing believed to be seen."

94. Ibid., pp. 1074–77, 1087–88, 1098, 1101–2.

95. Ibid., pp. 416–17, 475–76, 478–80.

96. Ibid., vol. 1, pp. 101, 103–4, 107–8.

97. Ibid., pp. 109, 111.   98. Ibid., pp. 19–20.   99. Ibid., pp. 20–21.

100. Ibid., pp. 21–22.   101. Ibid., p. 22.   102. Ibid.

103. Ibid., pp. 22–23.   104. Ibid., p. 23.   105. Ibid.

106. Ibid., pp. 23–24.

107. *God*, pp. 86–90.

108. Ibid., pp. 95–96.

109. Thomas Aquinas, *On Being and Essence*, trans. Armand Maurer (Toronto: Pontifical Institute of Mediaeval Studies, 1949), p. 47.

110. Ibid., p. 51.

111. *Basic*, vol. 1, p. 25.

112. Ibid., p. 26.   113. Ibid., pp. 27–28.   114. Ibid., p. 29.

115. Ibid., p. 30.   116. Ibid., p. 34.   117. Ibid., pp. 37–38.

118. Ibid., pp. 38–39.

119. Ibid., p. 57; cf. p. 261. For further criticism of Aquinas's arguments for God's infinity, see "Does Reason Demand That God Be Infinite?", by Wayne P. Pomerleau, in *Sophia*, vol. 24, no. 2 (July, 1985), especially pp. 20–21.

120. *Basic*, vol. 1, p. 58.

121. Ibid., p. 89.   122. Ibid., p. 119.   123. Ibid., p. 120.

124. *God*, pp. 138–39.

125. Ibid., pp. 140–41.   126. Ibid., p. 143.   127. Ibid., pp. 143–44.

128. Ibid., pp. 145–46.   129. Ibid., pp. 147–48.

130. *Basic*, vol. 1, pp. 977–78.

131. Ibid., pp. 978–79.   132. Ibid., p. 980.   133. Ibid., p. 981.

134. *God*, pp. 150, 153, 157, 154–55, 291; cf. Thomas Aquinas, *Truth*, vol. 3, trans. Robert W. Schmidt, S.J. (Chicago: Henry Regnery, 1954), pp. 106–7.

135. *Basic*, vol. 1, pp. 150, 211; cf. *Truth*, vol. 3, pp. 38–39, 169.

136. *Basic*, vol. 1, pp. 465, 467–69, 471, 473.

137. Ibid., pp. 474, 476–78.

2

Descartes's Methodical Rationalism

Life and Writings

Descartes's life was dedicated to what his unfinished dialogue calls "The Search after Truth." René Descartes was born the third child of a noble French family on March 31, 1596. His father, Joachim Descartes, from whom he later received a legacy that allowed him to be financially independent, was a councilor of the Parliament of Brittany. He was a sickly child, having inherited from his mother the pulmonary weakness from which she died shortly after giving him birth. In 1604, he entered the recently founded **Jesuit** college of La Flèche; his studies included mathematics, logic, theology, and scholastic philosophy. After leaving La Flèche, he studied for a couple of years at the University of Poitiers, from which he received a bachelor's degree and a License in law in November of 1616.

He then amused himself for a while in Paris before deciding to travel and study as a volunteer gentleman soldier. During a period of several years, he served with the Dutch, Bavarian, and French armies. On November 10, 1619, while attached to the army of Maximilian of Bavaria, he had a succession of three dreams which he interpreted as a call to commit his life to the rational pursuit of certain truth, a vocation to which he thereafter remained faithful. Having completed these years of voluntary military service, he returned to Paris for a few years but found the social life there distracting.

In 1628, he decided to settle down in Holland, where at that time there was more intellectual freedom than in any other country in Western Europe. Despite this relatively liberal atmosphere, on learning of the Inquisition's condemnation of Galileo for teaching the Copernican theory, Descartes decided in 1633 to suppress the publication of his completed *Treatise on the World*, in which he, like Galileo, maintained that the Earth moves around the Sun, a view which the decree of the Church forbade to be taught even as a hypothesis. In Holland Descartes wrote the greatest of his philosophical works as well as a treatise in mathematics (1637), which established him as the founder of analytic geometry. (We still speak of the "Cartesian coordinate system" today, named after Descartes, whose Latin name was Cartesius.) Although he never married, in 1635 he fathered an illegitimate daughter, Francine, who died at the age of five.

His philosophy became influential in the 1640s. For example, at the University of Utrecht it was advocated by Regius, a professor of science and medicine, and condemned by Voët, the university president, who found it dangerously subversive. Later, at the University of Leyden, Descartes was accused of the **heresy** of Pelagianism. Attacks became sufficiently hostile that he feared being arrested and having his books burned, as had happened earlier to Galileo. But he also had influential friends and powerful admirers. He was invited to become a member of the courts of Charles I of England and Louis XIII of France, but he declined. He corresponded with the exiled Princess Elizabeth, a friend to whom he dedicated his *Principles of Philosophy*, as well as with Queen Christina of Sweden, who was sent a copy of his last work, *The Passions of the Soul*, a couple of years before it was published.

Except for a few visits back to France, he remained living and working in Holland for more than two decades, until September of 1649, when he accepted Queen Christina's invitation to go to Stockholm in order to instruct her in philosophy. The queen's schedule required that Descartes be at her library at five o'clock in the morning for this instruction. The bitter cold of the Swedish winter at what was, for Descartes, an abnormally early time of day broke his health; he caught pneumonia and died of a fever on February 11, 1650. Although he lived and died professing Catholicism, in 1663, the Catholic Church placed his works on its Index of Forbidden Books. But, despite opposition during his life and thereafter, his influence on intellectual history has proved so enormous that he is considered "the father of modern philosophy."

Descartes's main philosophical writings are (1) his *Rules for the Direction of the Mind*, thought to have been written just before he retired to Holland but only published posthumously in 1701, (2) his *Discourse on Method*, published in French in 1637 and in Latin in 1644, (3) his most famous work, *Meditations on First Philosophy*, published with Objections and Replies in Latin in 1641 and translated into French in 1647, (4) his *Principles of Philosophy*, published in Latin in 1644 and in French in 1647, and (5) *The Passions of the Soul*, published in French in 1649.[1] These works represent a break from the scholastic philosophy he had been taught at La Flèche, not so much in content as in method.

Three characteristics of his revolutionary approach are remarkably impressive, in contrast to the staples of scholastic philosophy. First, his entire system is based on a carefully worked out epistemological method and set of rules providing a quasi-scientific foundation for philosophizing so that the very titles of his first two philosophical works explicitly indicate a new orientation. Second, his writings which build on this methodology—especially his *Meditations*, *Principles*, and *Passions of the Soul*—develop an orderly, coherent, and relatively simple system. And, third, even though commentators often speak of Cartesian rationalism as "dogmatic," he was so open to the critical reflections of others that with his famous *Meditations* he published several sets of Objections from leading dissenting intellectuals with his considered Replies.

It should be emphasized, especially in a work on God and religion such as this, that these are all *philosophical* rather than theological writings. In the Prefatory Letter attached to the French version of his *Principles of Philosophy*, Descartes adopts the traditional view that "philosophy signifies the study of wisdom, and that by wisdom we not only understand prudence in affairs, but also a perfect knowledge of all things that man can know"; he compares "philosophy as a whole" to "a tree whose roots are metaphysics, whose trunk is physics, and whose branches, which issue from this trunk, are all the other sciences."[2] We shall concentrate our attention on Descartes's philosophical theology, which is a part of metaphysics, the very roots of the tree. Yet the distinction between philosophy and theology, which was becoming sharper in the medieval times of scholastic philosophy, is complete with Descartes.

Descartes, who devoted himself "entirely to the search after Truth," denies in his *Discourse on Method* "that by means of disputations employed by the Schools any truth has been discovered of which we were formerly ignorant." Unlike the works of scholastic philosophy, those of Descartes avoid invoking Scriptural revelation. Unlike those who constantly seek in Aristotle "the solution of many difficulties of which he says nothing, and in regard to which he possibly had not thought at all," Descartes typically avoids appeals to authority. Nor does he try to camouflage his ideas beneath a mystifying smoke screen of unclear technical terminology; indeed, he takes the scholastics to task for exploiting "the obscurity of the distinctions and principles" which allowed them "to talk of all things as boldly as though they really knew about them" and dogmatically to elude all criticisms. He compares the scholastic philosopher to "a blind man who, in order to fight on equal terms with one who sees, would have the latter to come into the bottom of a very dark cave" and compares himself to one who "threw open the windows and caused daylight to enter the cave."[3] Thus, a truly philosophical approach even to theology must avoid being merely polemical, appealing to the authority of the Scriptures or any human being other than the one philosophizing, and trading on abstract jargon. Instead, it must be anchored in clear and distinct ideas directly apprehended by the mind through intuition and in the demonstrative conclusions drawn from those intuitions by reason.

Theory of Knowledge

The First Eight Rules. Descartes's *Rules for the Direction of the Mind*, the first of his philosophical writings, is an apt text in which to seek the elements of his epistemology or theory of knowledge. (This incomplete, abandoned work was published over half a century after his death from a manuscript copy which Leibniz discovered in Holland in 1670.) Let us focus on its first eight rules.

In the first rule, he expresses his confidence in the ability of "the natural light of reason" successfully "to search out the truth of things" and warns against all diffident attempts to impose limits on the mind.[4] In the second rule, he urges us to focus our attention on those things of which "sure and indubitable knowledge" is possible, repudiating the pursuit of any "merely probable knowledge" and looking to mathematics as a model of certainty and precision.[5] He observes that we can attain factual knowledge in either of two ways, "by experience and by deduction" and that "our inferences from experience are frequently **fallacious**," while those which are carefully deduced by the rational mind "cannot be erroneous."[6] We notice here rationalism's commitment to deductive reasoning as opposed to the empiricist's (e.g., Locke's) adherence to sense experience.

His third rule advises us to rely on our own clear and distinct intuitions and deductions in our pursuit of knowledge rather than depending on "what others have thought" or "what we ourselves conjecture."[7] He explains that intuitions, in this sense, are the products of reason rather than of the senses or the imagination (again setting a distance between his own position and that of empiricism), and he defines an intuition as "the conception which an unclouded and attentive mind gives us so readily and distinctly that we are wholly freed from doubt about that which we understand." Examples of intuitions attainable by any rational person are "that he exists," "that he thinks," and "that the triangle is bounded by three lines only."[8] By contrast, deduction, defined as "all necessary inference from other facts that are known with certainty," presupposes some intuition(s), from which logical conclusions are drawn, so that it is less directly and immediately (though equally) certain.[9] Descartes holds that intuition and deduction are "the most certain routes to knowledge, and the mind should admit no others." Although other approaches to knowledge "should be rejected as suspect of error and dangerous," this does not impugn belief in divine revelation, which, unlike scientific knowledge, is an act of the will rather than of the intellect.[10]

The important fourth rule insists on the essential "need of a method for finding out the truth," maintaining that it would be "better never to think of investigating truth at all, than to do so without a method." He writes that a method requires "certain and simple rules, such that, if a man observe them accurately, he shall never assume what is false as true, and will . . . always gradually increase his knowledge and so arrive at a true understanding of all that does not surpass his powers."[11] Thus, method, for Descartes, is a necessary condition for our achieving knowledge which is both certain and comprehensive. He can call for the purely rational use of such a method, independent of sense experience and imagination, because he believes that the mind has "inborn principles," that there are "certain primary germs of truth implanted by nature in human minds." Thus, from its beginning, the mind is neither dark nor empty, as empiricists claim. The light of reason is such in even the most primitive humans that

> the same mental illumination which let them see that virtue was to be preferred to pleasure, and honour to utility, although they knew not why this was so, made them recognize true notions in Philosophy and Mathematics, although they were not yet able thoroughly to grasp these sciences.[12]

This is the core of Descartes's famous doctrine of **innate** ideas, to which Leibniz would later subscribe and which is rejected by early modern empiricists like Locke and Hume. As we shall see, Descartes will go on to say that God is one of these innate ideas. He concludes the fourth rule by resolving always systematically to follow "such an order as will require" him "to start with what is simplest and easiest" and to avoid pushing on to more complex stages until these initial ones have been dealt with completely.[13]

The fifth and sixth rules explain that we must distinguish between those truths that are relatively simple and obvious and those that are difficult and complex, try to "reduce involved and obscure propositions step by step to those that are simpler," intuitively apprehend the simplest, and then by a systematic process of deductive reasoning gradually work our way up to the knowledge of the increasingly complex.[14] In the seventh rule, Descartes prescribes that reasoning be uninterrupted and warns that its procedures must be "both adequate and methodical."[15]

The historically significant eighth rule warns us to be sensitive to the limits of our understanding, stopping short of matters of which we are incapable of reaching knowledge.[16] This requires, of course, that we conduct a kind of mental inventory whereby we examine "all the truths for the knowledge of which human reason suffices." Descartes is inspiring in his conviction that every thinking person seeking certain truth should undertake this task "at least once in his life"; otherwise he constantly runs the risks of being victimized by intellectual diffidence, of randomly flailing about in his attempts at knowledge, and of wasting time, energy, and effort pursuing matters we cannot grasp.[17] Here Descartes is establishing, against even the greatest of medieval philosophers, the primacy of the theory of knowledge as a prerequisite to attempting a philosophical theology. Even if his accomplishments here, in developing a carefully articulated theory of knowledge, are not as impressive as those of his successors, such as Locke, he is to be acclaimed for diagnosing and treating the problem of how to provide a proper epistemological foundation. From a philosophical point of view, he is correct in his confident assertion that "no more useful inquiry can be proposed than that which seeks to determine the nature and scope of human thought." Anticipating Locke, Hume, and Kant, he criticizes as "futile" his predecessors "who boldly dispute about the secrets of nature, the influence of the heavens on these lower regions, the predicting of future events and similar matters, . . . without yet having ever asked even whether human reason is adequate to the solution of these problems."[18] It is by thus resetting philosophical priorities that Descartes earned the title of "father of modern philosophy."

Experience vs. Reason. Having now analyzed those epistemological elements of the first eight of Descartes's *Rules*, which are relevant to this philosophical theology, let us observe that he is not as hostile to an experiential basis for reasoning as the traditional distinction between rationalism and empiricism would suggest. Despite the fact that he finds deductive reasoning more reliable than appeals to experience and that the intuitions he would endorse are derived from reason rather than from the senses or the imagination, rational intuitions are themselves matters of direct, immediate personal experience. Furthermore, as Descartes admits in his twelfth rule, the rational understanding is only one of the four faculties—along with sense, memory, and imagination—which can contribute to our acquisition of factual knowledge. As he writes, "The understanding is indeed alone capable of perceiving the truth, but yet it ought to be aided by imagination, sense and memory, lest perchance we omit any expedient that lies within our power."[19] Thus, he is not **categorically** opposed to the use of these other powers so long as they are subordinate and supplementary to that of the rational understanding. What allows Descartes to insist that philosophical conclusions be based on purely rational intuitions—rather than those of sensation, as for Locke— is that he (unlike Locke and other empiricists) is committed to the doctrine of innate ideas, which will be further examined.

Descartes's *Discourse on Method* connects these developing epistemological principles with reflections on the prevailing state of studies at that time—including the four of most concern here, logic, mathematics, theology, and philosophy. Although he is quite critical of academic disciplines, he does praise La Flèche as "one of the most celebrated schools in Europe."[20] Thus, his criticisms must be viewed as broadly directed at the disciplines as they existed in his day rather than at particular teachers or institutions. His criticism of logic as practiced then was that its syllogistic forms were used merely for convincingly explaining what was already known or even for enabling people "to speak without judgment" on matters of which they were ignorant, rather than for "learning what is new."[21] As we shall see, Descartes himself will make the latter, more productive use of logic. He reports that, as a student, he was especially "delighted" with mathematics because of "the certainty of its demonstrations and the evidence of its reasoning," though he could not yet discern any practical use for it;[22] later, he criticizes classical mathematics for dealing only with "matters the most abstract, such as appear to have no actual use."[23] Yet it is mathematics that was to provide Descartes with the model of rigor, precision, and certainty that would guide his philosophy. He says that he "honoured" theology but that it was taught as merely a matter of faith, "quite above our intelligence," so that he would "not have dared to submit" its revealed truths to rational consideration since that would be presumptuous for one who is not "more than a mere man."[24] Of course, in his philosophical theology, which we shall consider in detail, Descartes was confidently to subject doctrines concerning God to critical examination. He reserves his harshest comments here for philosophy, sarcastically saying that, as it is practiced, it "teaches us to speak with an appearance of truth on all things, and causes us to be admired by the less learned" and that, despite its history of two millennia, "no single thing is to be found in it which is not subject of dispute, and in consequence which is not dubious."[25] Later, he adds that, while in college, he learned "that there is nothing imaginable so strange or so little credible that it has not been maintained by one philosopher or other."[26] His methodology is designed to rehabilitate philosophy from what he considers this sad and sorry state.

By the time Descartes writes the *Discourse* (the publication of which, in 1637, best marks the birth of modern philosophy), he has conceived of a bold, new approach, developing principles contained in his *Rules*, emulating the achievements of mathematics, courageously using logic to infer new truth, and confidently converting theological beliefs into demonstrative knowledge. Even after leaving school and the tutelage of his instructors, abandoning book learning and "resolving to seek no other science than that which could be found in myself, or at least in the great book of the world," Descartes maintained his "excessive desire to learn to distinguish the true from the false."[27] But now, as he proclaims, he had discovered the tools whereby he could accomplish his project: "I have formed a Method, by whose assistance it appears to me I have the means of gradually increasing my knowledge."[28] It becomes clear that this method generalizes that of mathematics to the point where it is a tool with universal, rather than merely mathematical, applicability.[29]

Methodological Principles. His method consists of four methodological principles presented here in a personal style, using first-person pronouns to emphasize the point that this is an approach which Descartes has found works well for his own inquiries. The principle of clarity and distinctness requires me "to avoid precipitation and prejudice in judgments, and to accept in them nothing more than what was presented to my mind so clearly and distinctly that I could have no occasion to doubt it."[30] This will promote objectivity, diminish the role of bias, and maximize our chances of achieving indubitable truth. We should realize that fidelity to this first principle is compatible with Descartes's subsequent resolve to continue "adhering constantly to the religion in which by God's grace I had been instructed since my childhood";[31] for the methodological principles are theoretical, adopted for the philosophical pursuit of certain knowledge, while his allegiance to the beliefs and behavior advocated by his Christian religion is a practical matter concerned with how he will continue to live his personal life. Second, there is a principle of **analysis**, which requires that I should "divide up each of the difficulties which I examined into as many parts as possible, and as seemed requisite in order that it might be resolved." By breaking a problem up into its component elements, we increase our chances of understanding the parts and seeing how they are interrelated to comprise the problematic whole. Third, there is a principle of order, which requires that I "carry on my reflections in due order, commencing with objects that were the most simple and easy to understand, in order to rise little by little or by degrees, to knowledge of the most complex." Understanding the more easily comprehended elements of a problem can facilitate the understanding of more complex ones that are related to them. And, fourth, there is a principle of review, which requires that I "make enumerations so complete and reviews so general that I should be certain of having omitted nothing."[32] Reviewing the solution of a problem, after it has been completed, can also help us to guard against having made mistakes in what we have done and to remember better the solution. Because of his confidence in the powers of human reason and his belief that all its possible objects are interrelated, Descartes dares to hope that "there can be nothing so remote that we cannot reach to it, nor so recondite that we cannot discover it," and he is quite "pleased" with the discovery of this method which offers him that hope.[33]

Descartes briefly shows how these principles can generate philosophical conclusions that will provide the basic building blocks for a system of knowledge. The most important procedural device he uses to do this is his method of systematic doubting, which is related to the principle of clarity and distinctness. He dramatically resolves "to reject as absolutely false everything as to which I could imagine the least ground of doubt, in order to see if afterwards there remained anything in my belief that was entirely certain."[34]

This calls for some comment. Since Descartes is pursuing indubitable truth, it is important for the purposes of his critical inquiry that he treat doubtful (dubitable) beliefs as if they were false even though they might, in fact, be true. Second, this doubting is theoretical, employed for philosophical purposes; it need not affect Descartes's everyday life and common-sense beliefs, but it only limits the sort of experiences that are fair game for speculative knowledge. Third, we should not imagine that

Descartes is flirting here with skepticism. He presumably would have been familiar with the famous (or infamous) slogan of Montaigne, who died four years before Descartes was born, "*Que sais-je?*" Literally this means, "What do I know?" But, in the context of sixteenth-century French skepticism, it suggests the challenge, "What *can* I know?" Montaigne impudently presents it as if it were the slogan on his personal coat-of-arms: "I bear it as a motto along with the image of a balance."[35] But in his *Discourse*, Descartes makes it clear that his doubting is merely tactical, taking the form of a means to the higher end of certainty rather than pursued as an end in itself: "Not that indeed I imitated the sceptics, who only doubt for the sake of doubting, and pretend to be always uncertain; for, on the contrary, my design was always to provide myself with good ground for assurance."[36] Indeed, the exercise of systematic doubt does rule out some general types of beliefs, such as those derived from sense experience, as bases for philosophical knowledge. Yet this leads immediately to the first truth known with certainty, which shatters the forbidding grip of skepticism and provides the basis for Descartes's arguments for the existence of God.

Arguments concerning God

The *Cogito* As Foundation. Descartes's treatment of God in his *Discourse* is brief but adequate to show the method at work and to foreshadow the fuller discussion that was to follow four years later in his *Meditations*. In applying his process of systematic doubting, he realized "immediately" that, even if all other beliefs should be thought false, it must be undeniably true that I exist while I am thinking or doubting:

> this truth "I think, therefore I am" was so certain and so assured that all the most extravagant suppositions brought forward by the sceptics were incapable of shaking it.

This clear and distinct intuition, called Descartes's *cogito* after the Latin formulation "*cogito, ergo sum*", allows him to defeat the claim of radical skepticism that we cannot achieve certain factual knowledge and provides him with an indubitable foundation for the rest of his system; as he writes, "I came to the conclusion that I could receive it without scruple as the first principle of the Philosophy for which I was seeking."[37] This insight is not original to Descartes but is derived from Augustine's *si fallor, sum* ("if I am deceived, I am") argument in *The City of God*;[38] and in *On Free Choice of the Will* Augustine, like Descartes, uses it as an ulti-mate basis for arguing that God exists.[39] But what is remarkably special about Descartes's use of it and what leads us to associate it with his name rather that Augustine's is its place in an explicitly developed methodol-ogy. At any rate, having established his own existence, Descartes proceeds to define his essence as revealed by the *cogito*, as "a substance the whole essence or nature of which is to think."[40] Thus, through intuition, he has achieved certain knowledge of his own existence as a thinking being. This will provide him with the needed basis for knowledge of the existence and nature of God.

God's Existence. Because he experiences himself as doubting, he is limited in knowledge and, thus, imperfect, since it is "a greater perfection to know than to doubt." Yet he has an idea of something more perfect than himself. Descartes believes in and here uses an innate principle of causality, which he applies to this "idea of a Being more perfect than my own"; this principle maintains that "it is no less contradictory to say of the more perfect that it is what results from and depends on the less per-fect, than to say that there is something which proceeds from nothing." Thus, his idea of a more perfect being than himself must be the effect of something; and the idea of the more perfect supposedly cannot be the result of himself, who is less perfect. The conclusion seems demonstratively clear and certain:

> it could but follow that it had been placed in me by a Nature which was really more perfect than mine could be, and which even had within itself all the per-fections of which I could form any idea—that is to say, to put it in a word, which was God.[41]

From a critical perspective, we should begin by questioning in four ways Descartes's use of the principle of causality. First, he neither subjects it to his process of systematic doubting nor attempts to justify it (either here or in the subsequent treatment of his *Meditations*). He rather assumes it as an intuitively evident innate principle. Yet, as Hume was to argue a century later, it is questionable whether any cause-effect relationship can be anything more than highly probable (rather than indubitable, as Descartes's method requires). Second, those who subscribe to the theory of evolution, as Descartes did not, can reasonably deny his claim that the more perfect can never be the effect of a less perfect cause. Third, there is a problem involved in his saying that the idea of that more perfect Being is superior to himself. The idea is superior to his idea of himself; but how do we compare any idea to any actually existing being in terms of perfection? Indeed, if nothing existed corresponding to that idea of a more perfect Being (which is precisely the point in question), then we might say that the self is superior to that idea since the self has been shown to exist (outside the mind) and since Descartes regards existence as a perfection, as he makes clear in his *Meditations*. Fourth, Descartes has to show that there cannot be another source of his idea of "a Being more perfect," which is inferior to an infinite God but superior to himself. He was to fill in this lacuna in the more carefully detailed argumentation of his *Meditations*. But even there he does not confront the first three of these critical considerations directed against his use of the causal principle.

God's Essence. Descartes proceeds to unpack his idea of that "more perfect Being" in such a way as to reveal that it comprises the divine attributes traditionally predicated of God by the monotheistic religions—"infinite, eternal, immutable, omniscient, all-powerful." His argumentation might have seemed more cogent here if he had done this *before* his argument for God (as he later does in the *Meditations*) since this would have enabled him to avoid the fourth criticism of the preceding paragraph. But his procedure here is parallel to that used with regard to the self—first argue for the existence of a being, then analyze its essence. We might ask, then, how Descartes purportedly knows which attributes are, and which are not, to be predicated of the divine essence. Or in other words, what justification might there be for Descartes's apparently facile adoption (despite his procedure of systematic doubt) of the orthodox theological analysis? He does not pretend that he, a limited, finite, and imperfect natural being, can thoroughly comprehend the essence of God, whom he believes to be the unlimited, infinite, perfect supernatural Being. But his answer is this:

> in order to know the nature of God as far as my nature is capable of knowing it, I had only to consider in reference to all these things of which I found some idea in myself, whether it was a perfection to possess them or not. And I was assured that none of those which indicated some imperfection were in Him, but that all else was present.[42]

Again, this calls for critical evaluation. In order for this to work, Descartes's idea of God must be of a "supremely perfect Being" as he was later to say in his *Meditations*, and not merely "a Being more perfect" than himself. If he does have a clear and distinct idea of an infinite Being (as he explicitly was to claim in his *Meditations*), if infinite means having all conceivable and not merely all actual perfections and no imperfections, and if some Being must exist outside and independently of his mind corresponding to this idea, then he is correct. But, as we shall see, all three of these conditions are disputable.

The Ontological Argument. One final passage we should consider anticipates Descartes's later retrieval of Anselm's argument from *Proslogium*, which Kant would name the ontological argument and which is presented by Descartes here in the *Discourse* as a kind of argument from analogy. Just as the sum of the interior angles of any triangle, if there be any perfect triangle (and there may or may not be), must equal the sum of two right angles or 180 degrees, or just as the idea of a sphere, if anyone has such an idea, by definition involves the idea of a geometrical figure all of whose surface points "are equidistant from its centre," so the idea of "a Perfect Being," if there really is such an idea, must involve the actual existence of a Being corresponding to that idea. Descartes claims that he does have such an idea. (Notice that now he has moved from speaking merely of "a Being more perfect" than himself to "a Perfect Being.") He confidently draws his conclusion: "Consequently it is at least as certain that God, who is a Being so perfect, is, or exists, as any demonstration of geometry can possibly be."[43]

This is not Descartes's classic formulation of the ontological argument, which was to be worked out in his *Meditations* and which we shall consider later. Nevertheless, it is worthy of critical comment. First, it is questionable whether Descartes does indeed have a clear and distinct idea of a Perfect Being. Empiricists, who reject his doctrine of innate ideas, can reasonably deny it. Although it is extremely difficult, if not impossible, to show that Descartes did not have such an idea, those of us who are not aware of having it ourselves might well tend to agree with empiricists here, on the basis of our personal experience. Second, of all the forms of logical arguments, both deductive and **inductive**, the notoriously weakest form is the argument from analogy. Good analogies are illuminating and helpful for purposes of illustration, if nothing else. But even the strongest analogies are limited; if the two things being compared were exactly alike, they would be identical (this is Leibniz's principle of the **identity** of indiscernibles). So, the question is always, at what point does the analogy break down? Unfortunately, this one breaks down rather quickly. What are predicated as necessary of the geometrical figures of triangle and sphere are merely ideal qualities; in neither case is any existential claim made about reality outside the mind—the analyses start and end in the same realm of mathematical ideas. But what is predicated as necessary of the idea of a Perfect Being is its correspondence to a reality outside the mind so that the analysis moves from the realm of ideas to that of existential fact. Again, Descartes improves his presentation of this argument in the *Meditations* by subordinating the analogy in such a way that it is used merely for illustrative purposes; but what we see here is the development of his philosophical theology.

Setting Up the Causal Arguments. Descartes's arguments for God in his third meditation again build upon his knowledge of himself as a thinking thing. Earlier, he uses the principle of clarity and distinctness and the method of systematic doubting in a dramatically masterful way. He writes that reason "persuades me that I ought no less carefully to withhold my assent from matters which are not entirely certain and indubitable than from those which appear to me manifestly to be false." He detects at least three major reasons for doubting most of the beliefs to which he is accustomed to subscribe. First, the principle of analysis reveals that most of his ordinary beliefs have been acquired "either from the senses or through the senses," which at times deceive rather than accurately perceive and therefore are not yet to be trusted as a source of knowledge. Second, he worries about the problem of possible delusion because of the difficulty involved in always being able to distinguish certainly between the dream-illusions of sleep and the veridical experiences of wakefulness. And, third, he reluctantly admits the theoretical possibility that what he is used to believing about the perfectly good God of Christianity "is a fable" and that, instead, "some evil genius not less powerful than deceitful, has employed his whole energies in deceiving me." These three considerations lead him to the disturbing conclusion "that there is nothing in all that I formerly believed to be true, of which I cannot in some measure doubt."[44] Thus, the first meditation ends with the somber sense that its "task is a laborious one";[45] he is tired, frustrated, and discouraged because, while striving to achieve certain knowledge, he seems to have succumbed to insuperable doubt.

The important and justly famous second meditation starts by applying the principle of review; in remembering the meditation of the preceding day, Descartes seems to experience a panic attack, as if he were intellectually drowning in the vortex of skepticism: "just as if I had all of a sudden fallen into very deep water, I am so disconcerted that I can neither make certain of setting my feet on the bottom, nor can I swim and so support myself on the surface." Since he cannot "swim" in, or accept, the doctrine of skepticism—that the only truth of which we can be certain is "that there is nothing in the world that is certain"—he must resume the desperate effort to "touch bottom"; and the only way to do that is "to discover one thing only which is certain and indubitable." Here, as in the *Discourse*, that fundamental first truth is the *cogito*. Even though he cannot trust any beliefs derived from sense experience, even though the line between reality and illusion is not clearly demarcated, and even if there is some "evil genius" (a *malin génie*) who is "very powerful and very cunning, who ever employs his ingenuity in deceiving" Descartes, it is an experienced fact that Descartes thinks that he exists. But, even if he is mistaken with regard to all the rest of his beliefs, he could not think that he exists without actually existing. For how could a nonentity think at all or even be constantly deceived? Descartes proudly draws his conclusion "that this proposition: I am, I exist, is necessarily true each time that I pronounce it, or that I mentally conceive it."[46]

Of all the insights in the history of philosophy, this would appear to be the most reliable. As we have seen, and as the logician/theologian Antoine Arnauld points out in the fourth set of Objections,[47] its roots lie in the writings of Augustine. Remembering the third of Descartes's *Rules*, which held that intuition and deduction are different mental operations by which we are able to achieve factual knowledge, we might wonder whether the *cogito* is meant to be the product of intuition or of deduction. The language of the *Discourse*, particularly with its use of the logical indicator "therefore" (*ergo*), suggests the latter option. As Descartes admits elsewhere,[48] if it were meant to be a deductive argument, a major proposition maintaining that whatever thinks must exist would have to be "presupposed." Yet this presupposition would have to be implicit rather than explicit "because I am attending only to what I experience inside myself—for example, 'I think therefore I am': I do not pay attention in the same way to the general notion 'whatever thinks is.'" If the *cogito* is considered thus, the obvious critical question is how can Descartes clearly and distinctly justify such an implicit presupposition? It appears this could only be known through intuition. And then what if your intuition or mine fails to confirm Descartes's universal proposition? Later, in his Reply to the second set of Objections, collected by Marin Mersenne (a priest who had also attended La Flèche), Descartes seems to realize this and decides to settle for the more modest position that he is intuitively aware of a necessary connection between his own thinking, which he directly experiences, and his existence so that no deductive inference is involved at all. The passage is worth quoting in full:

But when we become aware that we are thinking beings, this is a primitive act of knowledge derived from no syllogistic reasoning. He who says, "*I think, hence I am, or exist,*" does not deduce existence from thought by a syllogism, but, by a simple act of mental vision, recognizes it as if it were a thing that is known *per se*. This is evident from the fact that if it were syllogistically deduced, the major premise, *that everything that thinks is, or exists*, would have to be known previously; but yet that has rather been learned from the experience of the individual—that unless he exists he cannot think. For our mind is so constituted by nature that general propositions are formed out of the knowledge of particulars.[49]

Even so, we might wonder whether Descartes is not assuming without critical justification the Aristotelian axiom that all functions or activities, such as those of doubting and thinking, presuppose substances (persons or things) performing them. A century later, Hume would implicitly challenge that assumption, but Descartes seems not to have done so. Secondly, as Bertrand Russell suggests, the use of the personal pronoun to affirm that "I think or I doubt" is itself problematic. Russell deliberately italicizes the first-person pronouns when he writes, " '*I* think, therefore *I* am' says rather more than is strictly certain." What I directly and immediately experience is the process or act of thinking. Even if we accept the Aristotelian assumption just mentioned, as Russell himself seems to do, this "does not of itself involve that more or less permanent person whom we call 'I.' "[50] This turns out to be particularly important since one of Descartes's key foundations for arguing God's existence in the third meditation is the allegedly certain reality of the self.

At any rate, Descartes believes he has discovered the stable foundation that will allow him to "touch bottom" in his fight against skepticism. As he writes in his *Principles*, "hence this conclusion *I think, therefore I am*, is the first and most certain of all that occurs to one who philosophises in an orderly way."[51] Here is a firm basis on which he can construct the rest of his system. Having established *that* he is, he next proceeds to define *what* he is—namely, "a thing which thinks, that is to say a mind or a soul, or an understanding, or a reason."[52] This "thinking thing" is a "substance" in the technical philosophical sense explained by Descartes in his Reply to the Objections of Arnauld: "that which can exist by itself, without the aid of any other."[53] We should observe, however, that Descartes admits to Arnauld a point Locke and Hume might appreciate—that we cannot "have immediate **cognition** of substances" but that we only give the name *substance* to that in which perceived attributes inhere.[54] So the second meditation undertakes a functional analysis of the mind, concluding, "It is a thing which doubts, understands, conceives, affirms, denies, wills, refuses, which also imagines and feels." Thus, Descartes can claim to have achieved a degree of clarity and distinctness about his essence as well as about his existence.[55] In contrast to the discouraged conclusion of his first meditation, this one ends almost jubilantly, saying he wants to pause in order to "more deeply imprint on my memory this new knowledge" of the mind.[56]

This takes us to one of the greatest passages of Descartes's philosophical theology, his third meditation. Like the second, this one also begins by applying the principle of review. What assures him of the truth of the *cogito* is the fact that it is so clearly and distinctly perceived by the mind as to be indubitable. This provides him with more than a starting place for his system; it also gives him a standard for judging the reliability of other possible truths. As he says, "I can establish as a general rule that all things which I perceive very clearly and very distinctly are true."[57] The question then is whether knowledge of anything other than the self is possible. Descartes has already moved beyond the level of radical skepticism with the *cogito*. Now he must strive to overcome **solipsism**, the view that all we can know are ourselves and our own states of consciousness. But he does not have a clear and distinct intuition of any existing thing other than himself. Hence, he must use deductive argumentation. For that argumentation to meet the requirements of his principle of clarity and distinctness, it must be based on what he intuitively knows, namely, his existing self and/or some clear and distinct idea.

Descartes conducts an inventory of his ideas, using the principle of analysis, to see whether all of them can be adequately accounted for within the parameters of solipsism, and he determines that all except the idea of God can be thus explained. So he analyzes this idea:

> By the name God I understand a substance that is infinite [eternal, immutable], independent, all-knowing, all-powerful, and by which I myself and everything else, if anything else does exist, have been created.[58]

But, in contrast to these divine attributes, he realizes that he is an imperfect, time-bound, dependent creature, subject to change and limited in knowledge and power. How could he then originate such an idea by himself?

He believes that there can be three different types of ideas distinguished by their various sources: some might be "**adventitious**," coming to us through the senses, such as sights, sounds, smells, tastes, and feelings; some might be "formed [or invented] by myself" through the imagination, such as ideas of centaurs and mermaids; and some are "innate" because we are born with them, such as my idea of myself as a thinking thing.[59] (Notice how this trichotomy connects with the distinctions introduced in the third of his *Rules* among intuitions derived from the senses, from the imagination, and from reason.) Which sort is our idea of God? As Descartes will indicate later,[60] we do not literally see, hear, smell, taste, or feel God; so it cannot be an adventitious idea. Nor does Descartes think it possible that a finite, limited, imperfect man could imagine, on his own, the Infinite, the Unlimited, the Perfect. Therefore, by a process of elimination, if Descartes's enumeration and reasoning are correct, it must be an innate idea. But, if so, it must have come from some source outside ourselves, in which case the position of solipsism is crumbling away. That is to say, there must exist some other substance or "thing capable of existing of itself,"[61] independent of myself. It must now be shown that this is God.

In his Dedication of the *Meditations* to the theology faculty at Paris, Descartes says he thinks God "ought to be demonstrated by philosophical rather than theological argument" and that the main reason "many impious persons" refuse to believe in God "is that they declare that hitherto no one has been able to demonstrate" divine existence.[62] The third meditation contains two different but associated arguments for God's existence, the first trying to find an adequate causal explanation of this special idea of God and the second trying adequately to explain the fact of my own existence as a thinking thing. Each of these bits of data with which one can supposedly work in conformity with the principle of clarity and distinctness demands a causal account. At this point Descartes invokes the causal principle that will underlie both of these arguments, presenting it as a matter of self-evident intuition:

> Now it is manifest by the natural light that there must at least be as much reality in the efficient and total cause as in its effect. . . . And from this it follows, not only that something cannot proceed from nothing, but likewise that what is more perfect—that is to say, which has more reality within itself—cannot proceed from the less perfect.[63]

This is the same principle of causality Descartes invoked in his *Discourse* and is subject to the same three criticisms mentioned: (1) it is assumed as an intuitively evident innate principle rather than justified, (2) it faces the evidence of evolution as an apparent counterexample, and (3) the reality or perfection of the idea of God, which is all we legitimately have to work with, is difficult to compare to that of the mind.

The Causal Arguments. The first argument applies this causal principle to the idea of God. Descartes states the argument rather simply: "I
should not have the idea of an infinite substance—since I am finite—if it
had not proceeded from substance which was veritably infinite."[64] We can
put this in the form of a deductive inference thus:

   a. If I am finite and my idea of an infinite substance did not come
       from a substance which is actually infinite, then I would not have
       an idea of an infinite substance.
   b. But I do have such an idea.
   c. So either I am not finite *or* my idea of an infinite substance did
       come from a substance which is actually infinite (or both).
   d. But I am indeed finite.
   e. Therefore, my idea of an infinite substance did come from a sub-
       stance which is actually infinite.

As such, this argument is perfectly valid. Thus, the only way logically
to avoid accepting the conclusion as absolutely necessary is to challenge
one or more of the premises. The last premise (*d*) seems safe enough. Like
Descartes, we can be acutely aware of the fact that we are finite beings
and could not seriously question it. He anticipates our challenging the
first premise (*a*) by objecting that our idea of the infinite is the result of
our efforts to negate our idea of the finite, which is based on personal
experience. His rebuttal to this is that "there is manifestly more reality in
infinite substance than in finite, and therefore that in some way I have in
me the notion of the infinite earlier than the finite."[65] But, unfortunately,
this is a *non sequitur*. Even if it is true that the infinite is "more real" in
the sense of more perfect than the finite, it does not follow that the former must temporally precede the latter in my mind. Descartes goes on to
ask rhetorically how we could even become aware of our own imperfections unless we had prior access to the idea of perfection against which
we could compare our deficiencies. In his *Inquiry concerning Human
Understanding* David Hume later plausibly explains that we can come to
realize our own imperfections by comparing ourselves against things we
experience as relatively more perfect, rather than against the idea of the
absolutely perfect, and indefinitely extrapolating what we experience in
our imaginations.[66] A more radical objection might take issue with
Descartes's second premise (*b*) and hold that none of us, including him,
can have a clear and distinct idea of the infinite at all. As indicated above,
this seems a powerful objection; yet how can we cogently argue the point

since, even if it were true that we are incapable of such an idea, it would not follow that Descartes was likewise, and our only access to the ideas in his mind is through his reports? So it appears that the first, hypothetical (if-then) premise (*a*) is the most vulnerable part of this argument.

To do the argument justice, we must mention two more objections which Descartes considers and handles quite nicely. First, it might be objected that he cannot truly have an idea of a "Being who is absolutely perfect and infinite" because his finite nature is such that it cannot "comprehend the infinite."[67] But a person need not thoroughly understand everything about (i.e., "comprehend") the infinite in order to have an idea of it which is adequate for philosophical reasoning. For example, even though one does not thoroughly comprehend himself, his idea of himself can be sufficiently clear and distinct for him to know that he is a different person, with a different memory and psychological history, from you. Second, a critic might demur that he might be perfect enough to originate the idea of perfection even though he does not consciously realize that he is perfect. Thus, "perhaps all those perfections which I attribute to God are in some way potentially in me, although they do not yet disclose themselves, or issue in action."[68] But, as Descartes shows, this objection should not deter us for long. To be unaware of one's perfections is itself a limitation on knowledge—an imperfection. Even if we have potentialities which are developing to actuality, that such development is needed is indicative of imperfection.

The second argument of Descartes's third meditation applies his principle of causality to the fact that he exists as a thinking thing. It is a version of what are commonly called cosmological arguments, seeking an adequate causal explanation of anything that is known to exist, and thus it is comparable to the first three of Aquinas's "five ways." Given his own reality, Descartes asks, "from whom do I then derive my existence? Perhaps from myself or from my parents, or from some other source less perfect than God."[69] He then proceeds to rule out all of these possibilities. He could not be the source of his own existence, he says, because "were I myself the author of my being, I should doubt nothing and I should desire nothing, and finally no perfection would be lacking to me; for I should have bestowed on myself every perfection of which I possessed any idea and should thus be God."[70] Nor could his parents or any other agents inferior to God be the ultimate source of his existence since, according to the causal principle, it too would have to be a thinking thing and have an idea of infinity so that we would have to "again inquire whether this cause derives its origin from itself or from some other thing."

If the former, it would be the infinite God; but if the latter, then it is not the ultimate source and the search must continue. And since an adequate causal explanation rules out any "regression into infinity," we must "finally arrive at an ultimate cause, which will be God." Next, Descartes rules out the possibility that

> several causes may have concurred in my production, and that from one I have received the idea of one of the perfections which I attribute to God, and from another the idea of some other, so that all these perfections exist somewhere in the universe, but not as complete in one unity which is God.

For if the perfections attributed to God are split up and shared by a group of gods (polytheism), then each of them is limited by what the others have so that none of them is "absolutely perfect and infinite." As Descartes expresses it, God's unity "is one of the principal perfections which I conceive to be in Him" when contemplating the idea of infinite perfection.[71] Thus, by a process of elimination, since one cannot be the source of his own existence, since no other being inferior to God (including his parents) can be his ultimate cause, and since his reality cannot be adequately explained by means of a group of gods, "we must of necessity conclude" that the existence of God, the "Being supremely perfect," is demonstrated "on the highest evidence."[72]

We may put this into logical form:

a. The ultimate source of one's own existence is either oneself *or* one's parents *or* some other source less perfect than God *or* a group of gods *or* the one infinitely perfect God.

b. But it cannot be oneself *or* one's parents *or* any other source less perfect than God *or* a group of gods.

c. Therefore, it must be the one infinitely perfect God.

This valid alternative argument appears, from a logical point of view, to be the most convincing one for God to be found in Descartes's writings. Still, in addition to the difficulties noted concerning his causal principle and its application to the idea of infinite perfection, a chief problem with this argument, as with all types of cosmological arguments, is that it rests on an unjustified and, perhaps, unjustifiable, presupposition. It presupposes that all things that exist must have a "sufficient reason" (to use Leibniz's phrase) either within or external to themselves and that nothing can exist for which there is no causal explanation, an assumption challenged by Bertrand Russell in his famous debate with Frederick Copleston (to be discussed later).

Having now critically analyzed both of Descartes's arguments in this third meditation, we should briefly consider how he explains the fact that we have an innate idea of God and how he dispels, once and for all, the possibility that God might be a deceiver or "evil genius." Descartes reviews the argument, just discussed, that the idea of God we have been considering cannot be either received through the senses or a fiction composed by the mind itself, forcing the conclusion (assuming that there are only three types of ideas) that "it is innate in me, just as the idea of myself is innate in me." He then employs a metaphor speaking of God as a divine artist, of man as God's masterpiece, and of the innate idea of God in man's mind as the artist's signature.[73] Locke and Hume were to reject this doctrine of innate ideas, whereas Leibniz would follow Descartes's lead in endorsing it. Finally, near the end of the third meditation, it becomes explicitly obvious that the "absolutely perfect" God demonstrated here, by definition, "cannot be a deceiver, since . . . fraud and deception necessarily proceed from some defect" and since absolute perfection can allow no defect.[74] To express this syllogistically, if God is perfect, then (by definition) God cannot be a deceiver, and God has been shown to exist as perfect; therefore God cannot be a deceiver. This is an obviously valid **hypothetical argument**, the controversial premise being the second. But, if Descartes is correct here, then he no longer needs to worry about the possibility of an evil genius, one which he had earlier admitted "is very slight and, so to speak, metaphysical";[75] so this doubt turns out to be hyperbolical.

The Ontological Argument Analyzed. Descartes's argument for God in his fifth meditation is, no doubt, his most famous one and the one that most influenced his immediate successors (Baruch Spinoza, Nicolas Malebranche, and G. W. Leibniz) in the line of continental rationalism. Nevertheless, this historical observation should not conceal the fact that Descartes himself in his Synopsis of the *Meditations* says that "the principal argument of which I make use in order to prove the existence of God" is to be found in the third meditation and that in the fifth "the existence of God is demonstrated by a new proof in which there may possibly be certain difficulties."[76] This "new proof" is the one originated by Anselm and called, since Immanuel Kant's time, the ontological argument. In his Reply to the Objections of Johannes Caterus, Descartes attempts at length to distinguish his own argument from the medieval one criticized by Aquinas and confesses his own reluctance to use it because of fear that it might appear "a **sophism**." But he explains that since there are two ways only of proving the existence of God, one by means of the effects due to him, the other by his essence or nature, and as I gave the former explanation in the third Meditation as well as I could, I considered that I should not afterwards omit the other proof.[77]

The argument is preceded by an analysis of how the very idea of a triangle necessarily involves "a certain determinate nature, form, or essence, which is immutable and eternal, which I have not invented, and which in no wise depends on my mind." Whether any triangles do or do not exist outside the mind, the very nature of the idea of one requires "that its three angles are equal to two right angles, that the greatest side is subtended by the greatest angle," and so forth.[78] What is the point here? Descartes is using this as an example to illustrate the "general rule" stipulated in the third meditation, and to be used as a basis for his ontological argument, "that all things which I perceive very clearly and very distinctly are true."[79] The point then is that there are certain ideas which, on mental inspection, essentially involve certain necessary truths. Descartes will argue that the very definition of his idea of God requires that "a supremely perfect Being," corresponding to that idea, must exist.

Descartes begins by invoking his principle of clarity and distinctness, which the argument applies:

> But now, if just because I can draw the idea of something from my thought, it follows that all which I know clearly and distinctly as pertaining to this object does really belong to it, may I not derive from this an argument demonstrating the existence of God?

He realizes that an argument based on this principle might "seem to present some appearance of being a sophism" and anticipates the empirical objection that "thought does not impose any necessity upon things, and just as I may imagine a winged horse although no horse with wings exists, so I could perhaps attribute existence to God, although no God existed." But his rather dogmatic response is that in the case of his idea of God, at least, there *is* a necessary connection between concept and reality: "from the fact that I cannot conceive God without existence, it follows that existence is inseparable from Him, and hence that He really exists." He explains that thought about God does not bring about any existence, but the necessity inherent in the idea itself rationally "determines me to think in this way."[80]

The idea of God utilized by this argument is that of "a supremely perfect Being."[81] This formula had been introduced, we recall, in the third meditation when God was defined as the "Being who is absolutely perfect and infinite."[82] The brief argument (less than two pages long) observes that because God is the supremely perfect Being, "it is necessary that I should attribute to Him every sort of perfection." And since "existence is a perfection," it follows that "it is not within my power to think of God without existence (that is of a supremely perfect Being devoid of a supreme perfection)." Then his "general rule" is applied to show that God must therefore really exist.[83]

We can adequately analyze this argument by reducing it to the form of a logical demonstration (as Descartes himself did not):

 a. If my idea of God is an idea of "a supremely perfect Being," then "it is necessary that I should attribute to Him every sort of perfection."

 b. My idea of God is an idea of "a supremely perfect Being."

 c. Therefore, "it is necessary that I should attribute to Him every sort of perfection."

 d. If "it is necessary that I should attribute to Him every sort of perfection" and "existence is a perfection," then "it is not within my power to think of God without existence."

 e. "Existence is a perfection."

 f. Consequently, "it is not within my power to think of God without existence."

 g. But if "it is not within my power to think of God without existence," then "it follows that existence is inseparable from Him, and hence that He really exists."

 h. Thus "it follows that existence is inseparable from Him, and hence that He really exists."

This neat but complex deductive argument, as interpreted here, is hypothetical in form. The first and second premises (*a* and *b*) logically necessitate the first conclusion (*c*); the third premise (*d*), combined with the first conclusion (*c*) and the fourth premise (*e*), necessarily yield the second conclusion (*f*), which, taken with the fifth premise (*g*), inevitably lead to the final conclusion (*h*). Since the argument as reconstructed here can be shown to be logically valid (for example, by means of the **truth-table** technique), the only way to challenge its **soundness** is to call into question the truth of one or more of its premises. Let us, then, critically assess each of its five premises.

The Ontological Argument's Premises Assessed. It does seem to be true that Descartes's conception of God requires us to attribute "every sort of perfection" to our idea of God since God is being defined as the "supremely perfect Being," which, for Descartes, means "that He possesses every sort of perfection." Notice that we are, so far, speaking only of Descartes's idea of God. If the first premise (*a*) were referring to God rather than to Descartes's idea of God, it would be a case of question-begging because whether there is a God is precisely the question to be argued. But that does not seem to be a difficulty here. What is a problem with this first premise is the possible ambiguity involved in the word "supremely." If this is to be interpreted, as Descartes no doubt intended it to be, as a being as perfect as any being can possibly be (the necessity of this interpretation will be challenged in the next paragraph), then the premise does seem to be necessarily true. On the other hand, if it is interpreted, as Descartes would not wish it to be, to mean that God is the perfect being in the sense that God has all actually existing perfections, then it would not be necessary that God have all conceivable perfections. For example, necessary existence might be a conceivable perfection which is not actually possessed by any being, including even God, who could nevertheless be "supremely perfect" in this second sense.

Descartes's second premise (*b*) is a matter of definition. What is dubious about it is that it presupposes that his is the only legitimate conception of God. Even if we happen to accept this view of God, we can conceive of (and could believe in) a finite God, such as the post-Cartesians, Hume and James, discussed, as (to paraphrase Anselm) a being than which no greater actually exists, even though a greater might be theoretically possible. Descartes seems to assume that there is no viable alternative to his conception of God and would, no doubt, have considered the notion of a finite God blasphemous, if not self-contradictory. Is such a being, we might imagine him asking, imperfectly perfect? Yet empiricists who are tempted to adopt this alternative position might reply in the negative, explaining that the concept of perfection, when applied to actually existing beings, is to be interpreted to mean complete according to its nature rather than absolutely infinite. Thus, we might speak of a "perfect" specimen of a monarch butterfly. By "supremely perfect" Descartes, no doubt, means having all conceivable perfections to an absolute degree. But this alternative interpretation, in terms of having all actually existing perfections to the highest degree to which they are, in fact, possessed, if acceptable (as it presumably would not be to Descartes), might force a new explication of certain divine attributes. For example, it may be that nothing, including God, is eternal in the sense of not being subject to the structures of time, or is immutable in the sense of not being subject to any change, or exists necessarily (which, for Descartes, is the divine attribute under consideration here). The point here is that Descartes's conception of God is not the only possible one that is legitimate. Even if nothing exists having all conceivable perfections, if there is a Being having all actually existing perfections, we should not hesitate to call that Being God and to regard that Being as the appropriate object of religion.

Descartes's third premise (*d*) can be accepted without any qualms if we accept his interpretation of the argument up to and including this premise. The necessity being discussed here is a rational necessity. We can refuse to attribute a perfection to God, in the sense that we have the ability to be irrational; but it is, according to Descartes's reasoning, impermissible to do so. On his terms, it "is not within my power" to think in certain ways and still be thinking rationally.

The fourth premise (*e*) of Descartes's argument has proved notoriously controversial. The main problem is that he provides no evidence on its behalf. Although he might have thought the statement so obvious as to render ludicrous any argumentation for it, Pierre Gassendi (a priest and philosophical skeptic) directly challenges this premise in his Objections, maintaining that "existence is a perfection neither in God nor in anything else; it is rather that in the absence of which there is no perfection." He accuses Descartes of logically begging the question by presupposing that existence is a perfection in his premise "in order to draw the conclusion that God exists."[84] Here Gassendi is clearly anticipating the more famous criticisms made by Hume and Kant a century later. In his Reply, Descartes flatly denies that this is a case of question-begging and shows his annoyance with Gassendi by remonstrating, "I do not see to what class of reality you wish to assign existence, nor do I see why it may not be said to be a property as well as omnipotence, taking the word property as equivalent to any attribute or anything which can be predicated of a thing."[85] Although this attempt to shift the burden of proof to his critic is designed to shunt the objection aside, Descartes fails to camouflage his own lack of argumentation on behalf of this crucial premise; his simple assertion that he has not begged the question of his argument is too peremptory to be convincing.

Finally, the last premise (*g*) is an application of his "general rule" that clear and distinct ideas correspond to the truth about reality. It is with this premise that Descartes's argument moves from the realm of ideas to that of fact outside the mind. Here we are urged to acknowledge that because we cannot rationally think of God except as existing, God must in fact exist independent of our thoughts. It is not that, in the words of Shakespeare's Hamlet, "thinking makes it so" but rather that it could not be rationally thought otherwise supposedly forces us to realize that it must be so. In his set of Objections, Caterus, a priest, identifies the main problem precisely in a single sentence: "Though it be conceded that an entity of the highest perfection implies its existence by its very name, yet it does not follow that that very existence is any thing actual in the real world, but merely that the concept of existence is inseparably united with the concept of highest being."[86] It is this gap between the realms of ideas and of existential fact that still requires justification. Descartes's reply seems simply to repeat his point in the form of an argument—whatever we clearly and distinctly understand to belong to a thing's nature can be truly affirmed of it; we clearly and distinctly understand that existence belongs to the nature of God; "therefore we can with truth affirm of God that He exists."[87] Descartes thinks it intuitively certain that clear and distinct *a priori* ideas (e.g., those logically prior to and independent of concrete experience) can constitute a link between the realms of conceptual thought and external reality. Yet, even when this intuition is challenged, he fails to justify it, leaving us with the impression that it is a rationalistic presupposition. The second set of Objections, collected by Marin Mersenne, anticipates Leibniz's observation that the conclusion of the argument should not be as presented here "that God actually exists, but only that He ought to exist if His nature were anything possible or not contradictory." These objections also acutely protest against Descartes "that you yourself confess that you can apprehend the infinite only inadequately. . . . How then can you have 'investigated with sufficient clearness and distinctness what God is'?"[88] Descartes's rather dogmatic reply is that even though we can only conceive of God inadequately, this does not prevent our certainty that the divine nature is "possible, or not contradictory" and that our "quite inadequate knowledge" of God can nevertheless enable us "to understand clearly and distinctly" that "necessary existence" belongs to God's nature.[89] These criticisms from the first and second sets of Objections seriously dispute Descartes's claim that our understanding of the idea of God can be sufficiently clear and distinct to justify a knowledge claim concerning the independent existence of a Being corresponding to that idea. These are telling criticisms, and Descartes's failure to refute them rigorously detracts from the credibility of his presentation of the ontological argument.

To summarize this discussion of Descartes's argument in his fifth meditation, it is perfectly valid, but there are serious problems with the first two (*a* and *b*) and the last two (*e* and *g*) of his five premises. Unlike the causal arguments in the third meditation, this one purports to demonstrate the existence of God through the analysis of the concept of a "supremely perfect Being"; as such it is arresting and provocative. Yet unless and until evidence in support of these four premises is forthcoming, Kant's verdict seems appropriate:

> The attempt to establish the existence of a supreme being by means of the famous ontological argument of Descartes is therefore merely so much labour and effort lost.[90]

The Cartesian Circle. Before completing this critical analysis of Descartes's fifth meditation, let us briefly discuss his puzzling observation, in its last two pages, concerning the paramount importance of our knowledge of God's existence: "the certainty of all other things depends on it so absolutely, that without this knowledge it is impossible ever to know anything perfectly."[91] And, indeed, in the sixth meditation Descartes was to argue that, because of the existence of a "supremely perfect Being," the nondeceiving God of monotheism, we can rationally believe in the external world of bodies and other persons. Yet before he even began to demonstrate God's existence he was certain that he existed as a thinking thing and that what we clearly and distinctly perceive must be true and, indeed, built on that certainty in his demonstrations of the third and fifth meditations. Thus, the second set of Objections and Arnauld in the fourth set of Objections raised complaints about what has come to be called "the **Cartesian circle**": our certainty of God's existence depends on prior certainty, the warrant for which is our knowledge of God's existence.[92] It seems that Descartes's reply to this accusation succeeds in breaking the "circular reasoning" Arnauld speaks of,[93] and it is perfectly **consistent** with what he says in the last two pages of the fifth meditation: before knowing that a nondeceiving God exists, I can only be certain of a truth when actively contemplating it and "the reasons that led me to it"; otherwise, "it may easily occur that I come to doubt its truth." But, having demonstrated the existence of a nondeceiving God, my certainty concerning any truth already established is safe—"although I no longer pay attention to the reasons for which I have judged this to be true, provided that I recollect having clearly and distinctly perceived it no contrary reason can be brought forward which could ever cause me to doubt of its truth." So the existence of the "supremely perfect Being" guarantees that we can be certain of any truth we remember having proved, even when we are no longer "attending to the proof."[94] This is a particularly significant safeguard for scientific knowledge, which was vulnerable to insuperable doubt as long as the "evil genius" remained even a theoretical possibility.

Other Treatments. Descartes's treatment of God elsewhere includes briefer but parallel versions of the three arguments in the *Meditations* found in his "Arguments Demonstrating the Existence of God and the Distinction between Soul and Body, Drawn up in Geometrical Fashion"[95] and his *Principles of Philosophy*.[96] The first proposition of his "Arguments" is demonstrated in the manner of the ontological argument; the second, by means of a demonstration like the first one in the third meditation; and the third, by an argument like the second demonstration in the third meditation. Similarly, the fourteenth of his *Principles* is an abbreviated version of the ontological argument, and the eighteenth and the twentieth are one-paragraph synopses of the two arguments in the third meditation. (It is unclear what significance, if any, to attach to the fact that these two later works place the ontological argument first in order, unlike the *Discourse* and *Meditations*.) But these add no new ideas to the three arguments in the *Meditations*. Finally, he briefly endorses the arguments of his third and fifth Meditations in his "Notes Directed against a Certain Programme," published in 1647.[97] Although these endorsements are not particularly interesting, what is noteworthy is his clarification of what he means by speaking of God as an innate idea. Regius, a professor at the University of Utrecht and Descartes's former friend, had tried to show "that we have no *actual* knowledge of God in our mother's womb, and accordingly that '*no actual species or idea of God is inborn in our mind.*'" In response, Descartes writes,

> By innate ideas I never understood anything other than that ... "*there is innate in us by nature a potentiality whereby we know God*"; but that these ideas are actual, or that they are some kind of species different from the faculty of thought I never wrote nor concluded.

Indeed, Descartes adds that he "cannot refrain from laughter" when he sees Regius trying "to prove that *infants have no notion of God so long as they are in their mother's womb.*"[98] This clarification is especially significant in relation to Locke's critique of the Cartesian doctrine of innate ideas.

Error and Faith

Error. Descartes's analysis of error in the fourth meditation is sandwiched between his arguments for God in the third and fifth. Perhaps the reason for this insertion is that, having established the existence of a nondeceiving God through causal arguments, he is now showing how we can rationally achieve clear and distinct ideas, apprehend truth, and avoid error. This will presumably help us to feel more confident about the "general rule," that clear and distinct ideas correspond to the truth, thus preparing for the ontological argument. At any rate, even apart from being a transitional link, this discussion of error is relevant to Descartes's philosophical theology because he must solve a problem which comes close to being one of **theodicy** (that is, the project of justifying the reality of evil in relation to a perfect God): given a nondeceiving God "of supreme perfection" and the fact that the existence of myself and everything else there may be "depends entirely on Him," why is it that "I am nevertheless subject to an infinitude of errors"?[99] In the "Synopsis" of his *Meditations*, Descartes points out that this fourth meditation is not designed to "treat of sin" primarily, that it is discussing theoretical error, "which arises in the deciding between the true and the false" rather than practical error "committed in the pursuit of good and evil."[100] So this is not a full-fledged theodicy, such as Leibniz was to develop, explaining moral and/or physical evil.

At the beginning of the first half of Descartes's six *Meditations*, the problem was how certain truth could be possible, given the unreliability of the senses, the difficulty in clearly distinguishing between illusion and reality, and the fear of an "evil genius." Now, at the beginning of the second half, Descartes faces the inverse challenge, which we might call his problem of error. In seeking a solution to it, Descartes considers Augustine's view "that error, in so far as it is such, is not a real thing depending on God, but simply a defect." God created everything that exists; but, since error is not an existing thing, on this view, there is no need to attribute it to God. Descartes, attracted by this solution, goes on to say "nevertheless this does not quite satisfy me; for error is not a pure negation [i.e. is not the simple defect or want of some perfection which ought not to be mine], but it is a lack of some knowledge which it seems I ought to possess." For example, he is not inclined to begrudge the fact that he cannot fly on his own power because that does not seem an appropriate activity for a human being; but, as a thinking thing in search of certain truth, he thinks error a deficiency contrary to his rational nature.

> And certainly there is no doubt that God could have created me so that I could never have been subject to error; it is also certain that He ever wills what is best; is it then better that I should be subject to err than that I should not?[101]

A "supremely perfect Being" is both omnipotent and all-good, able to and wanting to create what is best, the apparent logical conclusion being that it is best that error be permitted.

Descartes is struggling here with one of the great problems of philosophical theology, from which he almost backs away when he writes, "knowing that my nature is extremely feeble and limited, and that the nature of God is on the contrary immense, incomprehensible, and infinite, I have no further difficulty in recognizing that there is an infinitude of matters in His power, the causes of which transcend my knowledge." He also suggests the traditional Augustinian view that what appears imperfect from our limited perspective, abstracted from the context of all reality, may be "very perfect if regarded as part of the whole universe."[102] But, fortunately, he does not leave the matter here.

He analyzes the necessary causal conditions of his errors, his diagnosis being that "they depend on a combination of two causes, to wit, on the faculty of knowledge that rests in me, and on the power of choice or of free will—that is to say, of the understanding and at the same time of the will." My understanding is "of very small extent and extremely limited." Yet I have no reason to believe "that God should have given me a greater faculty of knowledge"; so it allegedly is not defective in the sense mentioned, of lacking in a perfection it ought to have. As for my other rational faculty, "I likewise cannot complain that God has not given me a free choice or a will which is sufficient, ample and perfect, since as a matter of fact I am conscious of a will so extended as to be subject to no limits."[103] Indeed, Descartes maintains that human freedom of choice is "so great" as to be that faculty in me whereby most obviously "I bear the image and similitude of God." This faculty, which gives us "the power of choosing to do a thing or choosing not to do it," in such a way "that we are unconscious that any outside force constrains us in doing so," is, he says, "very ample and very perfect of its kind." Therefore, it is not defective any more than is my understanding. Since God is omnipotent and all-good, all the faculties created by God are good in themselves, including these two, neither of which, by itself, is the causal source of error. But, as Descartes asks, "Whence then come my errors?"[104]

Before pursuing Descartes's answer, let us consider the problem in argument form in the context of his philosophical theology, as we have examined it:

a. If God is a supremely perfect Being and wills what is best, God gives us only good faculties.

b. God is a supremely perfect Being and wills what is best.

c. So God gives us only good faculties.

d. Now either error arises because the faculties of will and understanding are not good in themselves *or* because we misuse them.

e. But the faculties of will and understanding are (God-given and thus) good in themselves.

f. Therefore, error arises because we misuse these faculties.

This reconstruction in the form of deductive argumentation is perfectly valid; the first of the two stages (*a–c*) is hypothetical (or conditional), and the second (*d–f*) is an alternative argument. We have seen Descartes's reasoning for all the premises except the alternative (either-or) proposition (*d*), which seems to be a logical presupposition of his argument rather than explicitly stated. It seems a reasonable enough presupposition, given Descartes's conclusions thus far—that all he knows exist at this point are himself and God and that if the source of his errors were anything other than himself or God, this would compromise his freedom in and responsibility for his erroneous judgments. How then does he misuse his faculties of understanding and will in committing errors?

He explains that errors arise from the

> fact that since the will is much wider in its range and compass than the understanding, I do not restrain it within the same bounds, but extend it also to things which I do not understand: and as the will is of itself indifferent to these, it easily falls into error and sin, and chooses the evil for the good, or the false for the true.[105]

This presupposes the medieval view of a dichotomy between the two rational faculties of human nature. A more integrated conception of reason as exercising activities of understanding and choosing, dispensing with the faculty theory, could not so easily avail itself of this explanation. But because in his philosophical psychology Descartes does subscribe to the faculty theory of reason (that the mind or rational soul has various faculties or capacities), he can argue that we always have it within our power to avoid error by restricting our will within the limits of understanding in making judgments. On the other hand, if ever I exercise

> my judgment on any thing when I do not perceive it with sufficient clearness and distinctness, ... I no longer make use as I should of my free will, and if I affirm what is not true, it is evident that I deceive myself; even though I judge according to truth, this comes about only by chance, and I do not escape the blame of misusing my freedom.... And it is in the misuse of the free will that the privation which constitutes the characteristic nature of error is met with.

Privation, I say, is found in the act, in so far as it proceeds from me, but it is not found in the faculty which I have received from God, nor even in the act in so far as it depends on Him.[106]

Thus, if we misuse the good faculties God has given us, any error that results is our responsibility, not God's. Even though error be a deficiency from what ought to be, rather than "a pure negation," as Augustine might suggest, it is within our control, the clarity and distinctness of ideas being a necessary condition for the legitimate exercising of judgment.

Before completing this discussion of Descartes's analysis of error in the fourth meditation, we shall focus on one more tantalizing but disappointing passage. He claims that "God could easily have created me so that I never should err, although I still remained free, and endowed with a limited knowledge, viz. by giving to my understanding a clear and distinct intelligence of all things as to which I should ever have to deliberate; or simply by His engraving deeply in my memory the resolution never to form a judgment on anything without having a clear and distinct understanding of it, so that I could never forget it." He admits that, "in so far as I consider myself alone, . . . I should have been much more perfect than I am, if God had created me so that I could never err." What is exciting about this passage is the idea that God could have created us such that we would always freely choose to exercise our judgments in such a way that we would never err. The obvious question to raise, then, is why did God not do so? What is disappointing about this passage is Descartes's Augustinian answer:

in some sense it is a greater perfection in the whole universe that certain parts should not be exempt from error as others are than that all parts should be exactly similar. And I have no right to complain if God, having placed me in the world, has not called upon me to play a part that excels all others in distinction and perfection.[107]

This idea that greater variety significantly contributes to "the best of all possible worlds" would be later developed by Leibniz.[108] Indeed the idea is appealing to a degree. But, as Leibniz would later argue, what is needed is a balance between variety and order. Error compromises the order of the world. Furthermore, even granting Descartes's idea, the desired variety could be achieved through diverse degrees of intelligence, power, beauty, and so forth, without permitting the evil of error to contaminate the world of God's creation. If he is correct that God could have created us so that we always freely judge responsibly, his conjecture as to why God did not choose to do so seems rather lame.

Faith. Descartes's views on faith can be gleaned from an examination of several passages, mainly contained in the first part of his *Principles of Philosophy*. He warns us that, in order that we may exercise rational judgment responsibly and "with most security from error, we must recollect that God, the creator of all things, is infinite and that we are altogether finite." We should not be too presumptuous in our quest to comprehend all of reality. As he says,

> Thus if God reveals to us or to others certain things concerning Himself which surpass the range of our natural power of intelligence, such as the **mysteries** of the incarnation and the Trinity, we shall have no difficulty in believing them, although we may not clearly understand them.

He adds that we should be cautious about engaging in "disputes about the infinite,"[109] given our own finite limitations.

We may see a good example of how this applies to his attempts to philosophize in his *Principles*.[110] He argues that freedom of the will is a self-evident innate idea, directly and immediately intuited in even our most aggressive efforts to systematically doubt all of our beliefs. He points out that God's omnipotence and omniscience are such that we cannot "think ourselves ever capable of doing anything which He had not already pre-ordained." Thus, reason requires that we accept both the freedom of the human will and the divine **preordination** of all events by divine providence. But he admits that it is mysterious how we can "comprehend them both at one time." Here, it seems, for Descartes, we have reached the borderline between philosophical reason and religious faith. His advice is that

> we recollect that our thought is finite and that the omnipotence of God, whereby He has not only known from all eternity that which is or can be, but also willed and pre-ordained it, is infinite. In this way we may have intelligence enough to come clearly and distinctly to know that this power is in God, but not enough to comprehend how He leaves the free action of man indeterminate.

This may be disappointing to those of us who would rationally comprehend all truth. But, for Descartes, philosophy and theology have different, if overlapping, spheres of influence.

Can we say how he defines their relationship? He attempts to do so in his *Principles*:

> Above all we should impress on our memory as an infallible rule that what God has revealed to us is incomparably more certain than anything else; and that we ought to submit to the Divine authority rather than to our own judgment even though the light of reason may seem to suggest, with the utmost clearness and evidence, something opposite. But in things in regard to which Divine authority

reveals nothing to us, it would be unworthy of a philosopher to accept anything as true which he has not ascertained to be such.[111]

If no matters of divine revelation are at stake, we should bow to the dictates of reason. If philosophical considerations seem to conflict with divine revelation, the former must submit to the latter. (Less than half a century later, Locke was to attempt to give more autonomy to philosophical reason than this.) In his reply to the Objections of Arnauld, Descartes writes that when neither any theological consideration nor philosophical reason compels any commitment from us, "we should most readily select those beliefs that can give others no opportunity or pretext for turning aside from the truth of the faith."[112] It is ironic that one who was accused of jeopardizing the sovereignty of the Christian faith should have been so vigilant in its defense.

Perhaps a good way to end our examination of Descartes's views on faith and philosophy is to consider a couple of passages from his very long letter to Father Dinet, the head of the Jesuit province of France, who had been his teacher at La Flèche. Descartes's "new philosophy,"[113] it seems, was attacked by various critics, including Father Pierre Bourdin, a French Jesuit, who had anonymously written the seventh (and final) set of Objections, which Descartes had mistakenly assumed had been compiled by a committee of Jesuits. Descartes is anxious to insist that his "new philosophy" does not actually conflict with the doctrines of Christianity:

> As to theology, as one truth can never be contrary to another truth, it would be a kind of impiety to fear that the truths discovered in philosophy were contrary to those of the true Faith. And I even assert that our religion teaches us nothing which could not be as easily, or even more easily, explained in accordance with my principles, than with those commonly received.[114]

He is outraged by the charges raised by critics like Bourdin and writes that

> to say that anything follows from my philosophy *which clashes with the orthodox theology*, is clearly false and insulting. . . . But I have frequently protested that I did not desire to mix myself up with any theological controversies . . . I only treat in my philosophy of things clearly known by the light of nature. They cannot be contrary to the theology of anyone, unless this theology is manifestly opposed to the light of reason, which I know no one will allow of the theology professed by himself.[115]

Nevertheless, it has always been difficult for philosophers to speak of God without risking running afoul of theologians, who have a legitimate wish to protect their own area of expertise. What is sad in Descartes's case is that his philosophical system required him to include God as a most vital metaphysical component, while his religious commitments made him anxious not to give theological offense. The offense was given, though perhaps it was less significant than his impact on the history of philosophical theology. This influence was inspired by his ambitious project of constructing an entire theory of reality based on a carefully developed rationalistic methodology.

Notes

1. References to these writings will be to *The Philosophical Works of Descartes*, trans. Elizabeth S. Haldane and G. R. T. Ross, 2 vols. (New York: Cambridge Univ. Press, 1968).
2. Haldane and Ross, vol. 1, pp. 203, 211.
3. Ibid., pp. 101, 124, 125.
4. Ibid., pp. 1–2.   5. Ibid., pp. 3–4.   6. Ibid., p. 4.
7. Ibid., p. 5.   8. Ibid., p. 7.   9. Ibid., p. 8.
10. Ibid.   11. Ibid., p. 9.   12. Ibid., pp. 10, 12.
13. Ibid., p. 14.   14. Ibid., pp. 14, 17.   15. Ibid., p. 19.
16. Ibid., p. 22.   17. Ibid., pp. 24–25.   18. Ibid., p. 26.
19. Ibid., p. 35.   20. Ibid., p. 83.   21. Ibid., p. 91.
22. Ibid., p. 85.   23. Ibid., p. 91.   24. Ibid., p. 85.
25. Ibid., pp. 84, 86. 26. Ibid., p. 90.   27. Ibid., pp. 86–87.
28. Ibid., p. 82.   29. Ibid., p. 94.
30. Ibid., p. 92. In his *Principles of Philosophy*, Descartes explains (p. 237) that a "clear" idea is one "which is present and apparent to an attentive mind" and that "the distinct is that which is so precise and different from all other objects that it contains within itself nothing but what is clear."
31. Ibid., p. 95.   32. Ibid., p. 92.   33. Ibid., pp. 92, 94.
34. Ibid., p. 101.
35. Michel de Montaigne, *In Defense of Raymond Sebond*, trans. Arthur H. Beattie (New York: Frederick Ungar, 1959), p. 60. (This is the twelfth chapter of book 2 of Montaigne's *Essays*.)
36. Haldane and Ross, vol. 1, p. 99. For more on Descartes's epistemology and the metaphysical theory on which it is based, see *Twelve Great Philosophers*, by Wayne P. Pomerleau (New York: Ardsley House, 1997), especially pp. 123–33.
37. Ibid., p. 101.
38. Augustine, *The City of God*, trans. Marcus Dods (New York: Modern Library, 1950), Bk. 11, p. 370.
39. Augustine, *On Free Choice of the Will*, trans. Anna S. Benjamin and L. H. Hackstaff (Indianapolis: Bobbs-Merrill, 1964), book 2, pp. 40, 49.
40. Haldane and Ross, vol. 1, p. 101.
41. Ibid., p. 102.   42. Ibid., p. 103.   43. Ibid., pp. 103–4.

44. Ibid., pp. 145–48. 45. Ibid., p. 149. 46. Ibid., pp. 149–50.

47. Ibid., vol. 2, p. 80.

48. *Descartes' Conversation with Burman*, trans. John Cottingham (Oxford: Oxford Univ. Press, 1976), p. 4. This work will hereafter be called "*Conversation.*"

49. Haldane and Ross, vol. 2, p. 38.

50. Bertrand Russell, *The Problems of Philosophy* (New York: Oxford Univ. Press, 1959), p. 19. Cf. *Immanuel Kant's Critique of Pure Reason*, trans. Norman Kemp Smith (New York: St. Martin's Press, 1965), p. 337.

51. Haldane and Ross, vol. 1, p. 221.

52. Ibid., p. 152.

53. Ibid., vol. 2, p. 101. In his *Principles of Philosophy*, Descartes admits that the concept of substance, strictly speaking, applies only to God and "does not pertain *univoce* to God and to other things" (Haldane and Ross, vol. 1, p. 239).

54. Haldane and Ross, vol. 2, p. 98.

55. Ibid., vol. 1, p. 153. 56. Ibid., p. 157. 57. Ibid., p. 158.

58. Ibid., pp. 164–65. In the third set of Objections, the materialist Thomas Hobbes maintains that we do not have a real idea of God or, for that matter, even of substance (Haldane and Ross, vol. 2, pp. 67, 70). Descartes's reply seems to accuse Hobbes of reducing the meaning of "ideas" to "images depicted in the corporeal imagination" rather than his own broader meaning of "whatever the mind directly perceives" or "anything . . . that is in any way perceived by us" (pp. 67–68, 71).

59. Haldane and Ross, vol. 1, p. 160. In the fifth set of Objections, Gassendi argues that "all Ideas seem to be adventitious, and proceed from things existing outside the mind and falling under some sense faculty" (Haldane and Ross, vol. 2, p. 153). Descartes's reply (p. 214) is disappointingly curt and weak.

60. Haldane and Ross, vol. 1, p. 170.

61. Ibid., p. 165. 62. Ibid., pp. 133–34. 63. Ibid., p. 162.

64. Ibid., p. 166. 65. Ibid.

66. In the second set of Objections, collected by Mersenne, this critique is neatly anticipated (Haldane and Ross, vol. 2, pp. 25–26). Unfortunately, Descartes's impatient reply shows more irritation than illumination when he protests, "I really do not see what can be added to make it clearer that that idea could not be present in my consciousness unless a supreme being existed" (ibid., p. 34).

67. Haldane and Ross, vol. 1, p. 166.

68. Ibid., p. 167. 69. Ibid. 70. Ibid., p. 168.

71. Ibid., p. 169.

72. Ibid., p. 170. See Pascal's *Pensées*, trans. W. F. Trotter (New York: E. P. Dutton, 1958), #555, pp. 152–54, for a classic contemporary critique of this line of argumentation, which at best rationally leads us to merely a metaphysical principle rather than to the personal "God of Abraham, the God of Isaac, the God of Jacob, the God of Christians," who "is a God of love and of comfort, a God who fills the soul and heart of those whom He possesses"; here Pascal maintains that, even if this sort of argumentation helps us avoid atheism, it leads us to deism. Earlier in #77, p. 23, Pascal explicitly criticizes Descartes for using God as nothing more than a *deus ex*

machina explanatory principle for his system: "I cannot forgive Descartes. In all his philosophy he would have been quite willing to dispense with God. But he had to make Him give a fillip to set the world in motion; beyond this, he has no further need of God."

73. Haldane and Ross, vol. 1, p. 170.
74. Ibid., p. 171.   75. Ibid., p. 159.   76. Ibid., pp. 141–42.
77. Ibid., vol. 2, pp. 19–22.
78. Ibid., vol. 1, p. 180.   79. Ibid., p. 158.   80. Ibid., pp. 180–81.
81. Ibid., p. 180.   82. Ibid., p. 166.   83. Ibid., pp. 181–82.
84. Ibid., vol. 2, p. 186.   85. Ibid., p. 228.   86. Ibid., p. 7.
87. Ibid., p. 19.   88. Ibid., pp. 28–29.   89. Ibid., pp. 46–47.
90. *Immanuel Kant's Critique of Pure Reason*, p. 507.
91. Haldane and Ross, vol. 1, p. 183.
92. Ibid., vol. 2, pp. 26, 92.
93. Ibid., pp. 38, 114–15.
94. Ibid., vol. 1, pp. 183–84; cf. p. 224.
95. Ibid., vol. 2, pp. 57–58.
96. Ibid., vol. 1, pp. 224, 226–27.
97. Ibid., pp. 444–45.   98. Ibid., pp. 447–48; cf. *Conversation*, p. 8.
99. Ibid., p. 172.   100. Ibid., p. 142.
101. Ibid., p. 173. Descartes had raised this problem of error grippingly in the first Meditation in the form of an enthymeme with an unexpressed but arresting conclusion: "If, however, it is contrary to His goodness to have made me such that I constantly deceive myself, it would also appear to be contrary to His goodness to permit me to be sometimes deceived, and nevertheless I cannot doubt that he does permit this" (ibid., p. 147). He could not be expected to try to solve the problem there, but it is a shame that he provides no rationally adequate solution here in the fourth Meditation.
102. Ibid., pp. 173–74.   103. Ibid., p. 174.   104. Ibid., p. 175.
105. Ibid., pp. 175–76.   106. Ibid., pp. 176–77.   107. Ibid., pp. 177–78.
108. The root of Leibniz's idea of other possible worlds is to be found in Descartes's *Discourse on Method*, part 5—ibid., p. 108.
109. Haldane and Ross, vol. 1, p. 229.
110. Ibid., pp. 234–35.   111. Ibid., p. 253.   112. Ibid., vol. 2, p. 120.
113. Ibid., p. 358.   114. Ibid., p. 360.   115. Ibid., pp. 371–72.

3

Locke's Moderate Empiricism

Life and Writings

$\mathcal{L}$ocke's life began on August 29, 1632 near Bristol, England. His father was a lawyer and small landowner. As a boy, John Locke was educated at home until 1646, when he went to Westminster School in London. He received quite a strict Puritan training and acquired Parliamentarian sentiments from both his father and Westminster. In 1652, he entered Christ Church at Oxford University on a scholarship, where his sympathies shifted in the direction of the Church of England. He disliked the decadent form of scholastic philosophy taught at Oxford. After earning his bachelor's and master's degrees, he was elected in 1659 to a senior studentship at Christ Church, which was ordinarily tenable for life; he later became a lecturer in Greek, Reader in Rhetoric, and Censor of Moral Philosophy. He was elected a fellow of the Royal Society in 1668 and assisted Sir Robert Boyle in scientific experiments. He seems to have considered taking holy orders, which would have been a normal step for a university don; but his theological views had perhaps already become too liberal for him to do so comfortably, and he had become interested in studying medicine. However, he had difficulty getting a medical degree: in 1666 he applied for the degree of Doctor of Medicine and his application was denied; a second attempt to be awarded the M.D. failed in 1670. In 1674, he was made a Bachelor of

Medicine and granted a license to practice medicine, although he did not do so publicly.

Instead, he became involved in public affairs, leaving England in 1665 as secretary to a diplomatic mission to the Elector of Brandenburg. By this time he had already inherited his father's property. After returning to Oxford to resume his medical studies, Locke met Lord Ashley, who would later become the first Earl of Shaftesbury, and in 1667 entered his service as private medical advisor, tutor to Ashley's son, and sometimes political secretary. In the last of these capacities he helped Ashley prepare a constitutional charter in 1669 under which the new colony of Carolina would be governed. The document called for religious toleration; though the Church of England would receive public support, a minimum of seven persons sharing common religious persuasions would be free to establish any church of their own choosing. After Shaftesbury became Lord Chancellor in 1672, he appointed Locke to a couple of secretariat positions. But Shaftesbury alienated the king and was soon out of office. Locke returned to Oxford, where he still held his studentship at Christ Church and could enjoy an annuity received from Shaftesbury, which, combined with income from property he owned, left him financially independent.

In 1675, after being granted his medical degree and license, Locke left London for an extended stay in France because of ill health from asthma. During his graduate studies at Oxford, he had discovered the writings of Descartes, which, unlike the scholastic philosophy he found so perplexing and useless, seemed intelligible enough to make him believe that philosophical reasoning might be as productive as scientific thought. Now he was able to meet both proponents and opponents of the Cartesian philosophy, befriending, for example, Bernier, a student of Gassendi, whose work influenced Locke's own philosophy. During this time when Locke was in France, Shaftesbury spent a year imprisoned in the Tower of London. But in 1678, he returned to power as president of the privy council and requested Locke's services again. In 1679, Locke returned to England and the service of Shaftesbury, who became involved in dangerous political intrigues to prevent the succession of the king's brother, a Catholic (who would become King James II in 1685). Shaftesbury was dismissed from office later in 1679 and began supporting the Duke of Monmouth, an illegitimate son of Charles II and a Protestant, to succeed his father. In 1681, Shaftesbury was arrested in London for high treason, again imprisoned in the Tower, tried, and acquitted. The following year, Monmouth himself was arrested, and

Shaftesbury fled to refuge in Holland, where he died at the beginning of 1683. Locke, believing that his own safety was in jeopardy, destroyed many of his papers and hastily left for exile in Holland later that year. In 1684, the king had Locke's studentship at Christ Church terminated.

In 1685, the death of Charles II and the accession of his brother James II provoked the unsuccessful Monmouth's Rebellion. Though it is unclear whether or to what extent Locke had anything to do with this, he was thought to be in complicity. His name appeared on a list of eighty-five Englishmen wanted by the new government, and the Dutch government was asked to extradite him; the request was neither refused nor granted. Locke thought it prudent to go into hiding under the assumed name of Dr. Van der Linden. His friends in England managed to obtain for him the offer of a royal pardon, but Locke typically declined to accept a pardon for a crime he said he had never committed. In 1686, his name was removed from the list of wanted persons, and he could resume a normal life. His health improved and he was able to complete his *Essay concerning Human Understanding* while in Holland.

There, in 1687, he met and became friendly with Prince William and Princess Mary of Orange. Plans were under way to remove James from the British throne. Following the bloodless "Glorious Revolution" of 1688, William and Mary were installed as King and Queen of England under Whig sponsorship. Locke returned to England in the entourage of the new queen on a ship bearing the motto *Pro Religione et Libertate* ("for religion and liberty"). King William III offered Locke an ambassadorship, which he declined out of concern for his health, explaining that he wasn't up to the cold air and heavy drinking that might accompany diplomatic duties in Germany. He did accept a minor public office in London. In 1689, he met Sir Isaac ("the incomparable Mr.") Newton. But the smoke in the London air aggravated his asthma to the extent that another move seemed judicious.

In 1691, in frail health, he took up residence with Sir Francis and Lady Masham at Oates, about twenty miles from London, where he lived until his death, writing on religion and responding to his critics. For example, in 1702, Oxford University condemned his great *Essay*. He spent his last few years studying the Epistles of Paul. He died peacefully on October 28, 1704, having received the **sacraments**, while Lady Masham was reading to him from *Psalms*. He left all of his published works to the library at Oxford.

Locke's main writings appeared in the relatively short period between 1689 and 1695. These works include (1) his controversial *Letter concerning*

Toleration (1689), (2) his *Two Treatises of Government* (1690), (3) his famous *Essay concerning Human Understanding* (1690), (4) *Some Thoughts concerning Education* (1693), and (5) *The Reasonableness of Christianity* (1695). His *Discourse of Miracles*, written in 1702, was published posthumously in 1706, as was his unfinished *The Conduct of the Understanding*, which he intended to be appended as a final section to his *Essay*. His political works of 1689 and 1690—(1) and (2)—had tremendous influence in Great Britain, on the European continent, and in America. His *Two Treatises*, in particular, arguing against the divine-right theory of sovereignty, justifying the Revolution of 1688, and providing a theoretical foundation for the Whig view of government, remains a classic of liberal political thought.

Locke's greatest philosophical work, his *Essay concerning Human Understanding*, was written, off and on, for a period of almost two decades before being published in 1690. In 1671, he was discussing with "five or six friends" the principles of morality and religion, when it became clear that they could not resolve these issues without first trying "to examine our own abilities, and see what *objects* our understandings were, or were not, fitted to deal with."[1] Locke began the work on this exploration of epistemology which eventually culminated in his *Essay*, on which we shall focus. His work on this project seems to have proceeded, in fits and starts, for several years until 1684, when he began working on it in earnest in Utrecht, Holland. In its preliminary "Epistle to the Reader," Locke confesses that his "discontinued way of writing it" has led to difficulties, including the fact that it "grew insensibly" to such a massive size (about a thousand pages); he suspects that he should take the time necessary to edit and tighten it into a more compact book; yet, he wryly adds, "to confess the truth, I am now too lazy, or too busy, to make it shorter." He is typically modest in denying that his work can be compared with such "master-builders" as Boyle and Newton, claiming in this "Epistle" that "it is ambition enough to be employed as an under-labourer in clearing the ground a little, and removing some of the rubbish that lies in the way to knowledge."[2] Yet, even after 1690, Locke continued to revise and add to the *Essay* in later editions (1694, 1695, 1699) published during his lifetime. The work became quickly influential, in 1692 being recommended for students at Trinity College, Dublin (where George Berkeley enrolled eight years later). Even its condemnation at Oxford worked to its advantage, piquing the interest of eager readers. It helped establish Locke as a philosophical father of the **Enlightenment** and a seminal thinker in the tradition of British empiricism. The most comprehensive book on epistemology published before the eighteenth century, it offered a clear and distinct alternative to Cartesian rationalism, while maintaining many of the ideas and ideals of Descartes himself.

Theory of Knowledge

Cartesianism. Locke's Cartesianism in the *Essay* can be detected in its Introduction. In its very first sentence he makes it clear that he considers the understanding to be the faculty "that sets man above the rest of sensible beings, and gives him all the advantages and dominion which he has over them"; the human person is essentially as much "a rational creature" for Locke as for Descartes.[3] As we shall see, for both thinkers, the certain existential knowledge of which we are capable is achievable through reason rather than through sensation, as we might plausibly guess of an empiricist. Second, like Descartes, Locke makes it clear that theory of knowledge must precede and support metaphysical inquiry, including theological inquiry. The primary purpose of the book is epistemological, "to inquire into the original, certainty, and extent of *human knowledge*, together with the grounds and degrees of *belief, opinion,* and *assent*";[4] the metaphysical considerations that will follow in Book IV arise out of his epistemological study of the objects and limits of knowledge. Third, like Descartes, he despises the polemics, jargon, and dogmatism of scholastic philosophy and has nasty things to say about "the method of the Schools," which encourages "men to oppose and resist evident truth till they are baffled, ... without teaching the world anything but the art of wrangling."[5] By contrast, he promises to seek the truth using a "historical, plain method"—plain because it is expressed in the language of common sense and historical in the sense that it is not abstracted from the ordinary circumstances of time and space.[6]

Fourth, Locke considers human understanding, like Descartes's "natural light" of reason, to resemble a "Candle that is set up in us," which "shines bright enough" to illuminate the truths which we need to comprehend. Nor should we complain of our inability fully to understand everything or allow it as an excuse for the lazy laggard "who would not attend his business by candle light, to plead that he had not broad sunshine." Fifth, like Descartes, Locke is working to defeat the skeptics, who would have us "not set our thoughts on work at all, in despair of knowing anything" or "question everything, and disclaim all knowledge, because some things are not to be understood." He derisively compares the skeptic to one who, instead of using his legs to move about, chose to "sit still and perish, because he had no wings to fly." He believes that the failure to distinguish which inquiries are beyond our rational capacities from those which are not promotes the dangers of "perfect scepticism."[7] And, sixth, like Descartes, Locke starts with the immediate experience of "*ideas* in men's minds" of which we are all personally conscious, using the word "idea" broadly, as Descartes does, "to stand for whatsoever is the object of the understanding when a man thinks."[8] The question to be raised at this point, however, is what sort of ideas will constitute the foundation of all knowledge, including theological, of which man is capable. And it is in answering this question that Locke parts epistemological company with Descartes.

Rejection of Innate Ideas. Locke's rejection of innate ideas is established early on in the *Essay*. Without naming anyone,[9] he says,

> It is an established opinion amongst some men, that there are in the understanding certain *innate principles*; some primary notions . . . as it were stamped upon the mind of man; which the soul receives in its very first being, and brings into the world with it.[10]

As we have seen, Descartes held the idea of God to be innate. Locke argues (1) that there is no evidence that any speculative or practical principles are "universally agreed upon by all mankind" and, therefore, there is no reason to believe that any are innate,[11] (2) that even if we could find principles to which mankind does give universal assent, this would not adequately show innateness, and (3) that the doctrine of innate principles will remain implausible unless and until it can be established that there are innate ideas, which has not been done.

The speculative principles which seem the best candidates to be considered innate are the laws of logic, such as the principles of identity and contradiction: " 'Whatsoever is, is,' and 'It is impossible for the same thing to be and not to be.' " Locke's critique of the view that these laws of logic are innate principles would presumably apply equally to Descartes's causal principle. Yet it seems clear to Locke that "all children and idiots have not the least apprehension or thought of them," and it is nonsense to say that any "proposition can be said to be in the mind which it never yet knew, which it was never conscious of."[12] Thus, these principles cannot be explicitly innate in all humans. We may briefly consider two comments against Locke here: first, he assumes that because children and "idiots" do not or even cannot express these principles, they are not aware of them; and second, his argument presupposes that there cannot be any subconscious awareness of them. At any rate, proponents of this doctrine might "mean, that by the use of reason men may discover these principles,"[13] a view that they are implicit in the mind (which, it appears, Descartes and Leibniz actually held and with which Locke could agree to a point). But, Locke demands, "what is meant by a principle imprinted on the understanding implicitly, unless it be this,—that the mind is capable of understanding and assenting firmly to such propositions."[14] But if this is what is meant, that the mind has natural faculties whereby it can normally come to understand and utilize certain principles, isn't it misleading to call those principles "innate"?

This view would lead us to admit that "whatever truths reason can certainly discover to us, and make us firmly assent to, those are all naturally imprinted on the mind."[15] But, in fact, experience shows that we must learn not only the principles, but also the terms (and their meanings) comprising them.[16] Thus, the claim that these principles are innate is mistaken, if interpreted to mean explicitly so, since **counterexamples** to universal assent can easily be found, or misleading, if interpreted to mean implicitly so, since this suggests more than a natural potentiality, or is vacuous. But if this is so of speculative principles, it is even more obviously so for practical ones since "it will be hard to instance any one moral rule which can pretend to so general and ready an assent" as the basic laws of logic. Locke's challenge here is evident: "Where is that practical truth that is universally received, without doubt or question, as it must be if innate? *Justice*, and keeping of contracts, is that which most men seem to agree in."[17] Yet not only do people commonly violate these principles and/or merely "practise them as rules of convenience"; but they also disagree as to what justice requires as well as about what exceptions are allowable to the requirement that we fulfill our contracts. Again, then, if "there are no practical principles wherein all men agree," none can be considered innate.[18]

Locke goes beyond this argument that universal assent is a necessary condition of innateness yet cannot be established in the case of either speculative or practical principles. The second stage of his critique is designed to show that even "if it were true in matter of fact, that there were certain truths wherein all mankind agreed, it would not prove them innate, if there be any other way shown how men may come to that universal agreement."[19] It is conceivable that such principles were innate in one or more humans in the distant past, for example in Adam and Eve before the Fall, who taught these principles to their descendants, in whom they were not innate. Or, what might be more plausible for an empiricist, these principles could have been adventitiously discovered and passed on through education.

But, third, Locke would have us consider whether we have any reason to believe that the ideas that are essential to such principles are themselves innate:

> if the *ideas* which made up those truths were not, it was impossible that the *propositions* made up of them should be innate, or our knowledge of them to be born with us. For, if the ideas be not innate, there was a time when the mind was without those principles; and then they will not be innate, but be derived from some other original.

Locke admits that newborn children might have natural instincts, "some faint ideas of hunger, and thirst, and warmth, and some pains, which they may have felt in the womb,"[20] but he denies that these are ideas in any cognitive sense. And what about those ideas that are essential to those alleged innate principles—the ideas of identity, impossibility, justice, contracts, and so forth? Locke holds that these ideas are

> so far from being innate, or born with us, that I think it requires great care and attention to form them right in our understandings. They are so far from being brought into the world with us, so remote from the thoughts of infancy and childhood, that I believe, upon examination it will be found that many grown men want them.[21]

For Locke, as for Descartes, a test case is the idea of God. If there were any innate ideas and moral principles, the idea of God would have to be innate for two reasons: first, since God is the author of the moral law, innate moral principles would need implicitly to refer to God; and, second, if God had imprinted any innate idea on men's minds, we would "expect it should be the notion of his Maker, as a mark God set on his workmanship, to mind man of his dependence and duty."[22] However, the idea of God is obscure in some cultures rather than clear and distinct, and different people have different conceptions of God. Locke concludes "that the truest and best notions men have of God were not imprinted, but acquired by thought and meditation, and a right use of their faculties"— for example, as inferred from reflection on the extraordinary design of our world.[23] Likewise, the metaphysical idea of substance, far from being innately clear and distinct, proves on analysis to be "only an uncertain supposition of we know not what."[24]

Locke does view man as "a rational creature"; and he is willing to grant that the mind has a natural, "innate" capacity for knowing certain truths, even though the knowledge itself be "acquired."[25] He may not be as distant as he might have imagined from Descartes's explication of innate ideas as a natural potentiality for knowing. Why, then, does Locke devote one of the four books of his *Essay* to this critique of innate ideas? It seems it is because he found it a dangerous doctrine in that it could promote dogmatism (and religious fanaticism), blind acceptance of authority, and a lazy reluctance to think for oneself (what Kant, in his manifesto for the Enlightenment, would later call tutelage).[26] But, whether or not this is his primary motivation, his critique of the doctrine of innate ideas highlights an important difference between Locke and the Cartesians: he, unlike them, believes that the cognitive content of all ideas is derived from concrete experience, prior to which the mind is empty. Locke does not employ Descartes's technique of systematic doubt and never has to worry about solipsism; the fact of an external world, given as a field of experience, is never problematic for him. It is rather the primary source of our ideas. This is what characterizes Locke, and not Descartes, as an empiricist.

Empiricism. Locke's empiricism in the *Essay* begins with his tracking the origins of our ideas. Given that ideas are the direct, immediate objects of mental experience and the basic building blocks of knowledge, we are to appeal to our "own observation and experience" to determine the source of these ideas. His rejection of the doctrine of innate ideas (including that of God) leads Locke to "suppose the mind to be, as we say, white paper, void of all characters, without any ideas"; this is the **tabula rasa** ("erased tablet") theory of empiricism, according to which the mind is viewed as devoid of any cognitive content prior to the impressions gained from personal, concrete experience. Locke says that all the ideas of the mind, therefore, must be derived from the same source—"in one word, from EXPERIENCE." He goes on to explain that the two types of objects of such original experience are "external sensible objects" and "the internal operations of our minds perceived and reflected on by ourselves."[27] Through external sensation we acquire impressions of sight, sound, smell, feeling, and taste. Thus, we see the kernels of corn in the pan, hear them as they pop, smell them cooking, feel the warm pieces of popcorn in our hands, and taste them as we eat them. Locke considers sensation to be the "great source of most of the ideas we have." On the other hand, we also have ideas of our own "*perception, thinking, doubting, believing, reasoning, knowing, willing*, and all the different actings of our own minds"— ideas not derived from the sensation of any external objects but rather from what "might properly enough be called *internal sense*," that is from reflection on the operations of our own minds. Consider, for example, your idea of the feeling of anger: you cannot literally see, hear, smell, or taste the feeling; nor do you feel it by touch as you would an external object; your familiarity with the idea of anger comes from reflecting on the impressions of anger you have internally experienced. Against the Cartesians, Locke boldly draws his conclusion:

> These two, I say, viz. external material things, as the objects of SENSATION, and the operations of our own minds within, as the objects of REFLECTION, are to me the only originals from whence all our ideas take their beginnings.[28]

Locke points to the fact that we can observe children acquiring ideas in this fashion, although those derived from sensation precede those from reflection because the former normally make deeper impressions on children than the latter, which require more concentrated attention.[29] In answer to the question of when a person begins to have ideas, Locke answers,

> *when he first has any sensation.* For, since there appear not to be any ideas in the mind before the senses have conveyed any in, I conceive that ideas in the understanding are coeval with *sensation*. . . . It is about these impressions made on our senses by outward objects that the mind seems *first* to employ itself, in such operations as we call perception, remembering, consideration, reasoning, &c.

Thus, we start with impressions of sensation, which give rise to ideas of sense, which can serve as the materials for mental operations. "In time the mind comes to reflect on its own operations about the ideas got by sensation, and thereby stores itself with a new set of ideas, which I call ideas of reflection."[30]

Locke goes on to distinguish between "simple" and "complex" ideas. "Though the qualities that affect our senses are, in the things themselves, so united and blended, that there is no separation, no distance between them; yet it is plain, the ideas they produce in the mind enter by the senses simple and unmixed."[31] This is the basis of the claim of early modern empiricists that ideas are ultimately experienced in terms of isolable, discrete qualities (what Hume later called "loose and separate") rather than as intrinsically related. Locke goes on to argue that sensation and reflection are the only ways in which the human mind can achieve simple ideas, that it can neither create nor destroy them, and that it cannot even "imagine any other qualities in bodies" than those perceived through the senses.[32] He distinguishes among four types of simple ideas: (1) those perceived through a single sense alone, such as the ideas of solidity and green; (2) those perceived through more than one sense, such as the idea of flatness or that of shape; (3) those derived only from reflection, such as thought and will; and (4) those gotten through a combination of sensation and reflection, such as pleasure and existence.[33] Locke thus makes it clear that all conceiving of ideas presupposes the perceiving of objects of experience: "perception is the first operation of all our intellectual faculties, and the inlet of all knowledge in our minds."[34]

Once we have derived simple ideas from perception, we can retain them in memory, "the storehouse of our ideas"; remembering ideas need not be purely passive but can be an active matter of will.[35] Other intellectual faculties that can follow perception are discernment or distinguishing among ideas, comparing ideas with one another, compounding or combining ideas, naming ideas, and abstracting from similar ideas.[36] Locke compares the mind prior to perceptual experience to "a closet wholly shut from light" and says that external sensation and internal reflection are the only "windows by which light is let into this *dark room*."[37] But, once the light of ideas has entered the mind, it can actively work with it to bring about the illumination of knowledge.

Although "the mind is only passive" in the initial reception of simple ideas, it is active in relating them to one another, in combining them to make up complex ideas, and in abstracting them from the context of others to frame general ideas.[38] Complex ideas, which are "made up of several simple ones put together" by the mind, are of three different types: (1) modes, qualities or characteristics of things subsisting by themselves; (2) substances, "distinct *particular* things subsisting by themselves; and (3) relations of ideas to one another.[39] The complex ideas of finite and infinite are modes;[40] the complex ideas of body, spirit, and God are substances;[41] the complex ideas of cause and effect are relations.[42]

Substance-based Metaphysics. What is important for us to note is that these complex ideas, which are the materials of philosophy and theology, are not themselves the direct, immediate objects of experience. For example, we perceive the qualities of objects that give rise to simple ideas; we experience the apple as red, firm, and tart tasting, thus generating these simple ideas. Then, "not imagining how these simple ideas can subsist by themselves, we accustom ourselves to suppose some *substratum* wherein they do subsist, and from which they do result, which therefore we call substance."[43] What we experience are the qualities of things; "the substance is supposed always *something besides* the extension, figure, solidity, motion, thinking, or other observable ideas, though we know not what it is."[44] We mentally reflect on and try to account for the qualities of things as they are experienced; and,

> *because we cannot conceive how they should subsist alone, nor one in another*, we suppose them existing in and supported by some common subject; which support we denote by the name substance, though it be certain we have no clear or distinct idea of that thing we suppose a support.[45]

Given that Locke's metaphysics is (like Descartes's) substance-based and that our very idea of substance is so obscure as to be "but a supposed I know not what, to support those ideas we call accidents,"[46] we should later question how he can lay claim to metaphysical knowledge. What of our complex ideas of modes? They also are inferred rather than directly and immediately experienced. When objects of experience "affect our senses," Locke writes, they "carry with them into the mind the idea of finite."[47] Our idea of infinite is derived from that and primarily applies as a modification of expansion and duration, unlimited in space and time; as applied to God, the idea of infinite, Locke says in contrast to Descartes, is derived by **negation** so that positively "I find I cannot attain any clear comprehension of it."[48] Our complex ideas of cause and effect are also derivative, inferred rather than directly experienced. For Locke says it is through our ideas of things as beginning to exist and receiving this existence from some other source that "we get our ideas of *cause* and *effect*."[49] Thus, the idea of God as the infinite Substance who is the cause of all finite bodies and spirits cannot be the immediate object of intuition for Locke that it is for Descartes, any more than he can consider it an innate idea, as Descartes does.

Ideas and Language. Like Descartes, Locke distinguishes among ideas in relation to how they are mentally apprehended: "some are *clear* and others *obscure*; some *distinct* and others *confused*."[50] He also suggests other ways of distinguishing among ideas, as "First, either real or fantastical; Secondly, adequate or inadequate; Thirdly, true or false."[51] He maintains that both simple and complex ideas can be obscure, and complex ones "are most liable to confusion."[52] He believes that simple ideas are always real and adequate,[53] and they are the least liable to be false.[54] He does not draw the conclusion, which a skeptic like Hume might, that philosophical ideas, being complex, are most subject to error.

Locke maintains, "Some of our ideas have a *natural* correspondence and connexion one with another," while other associations of ideas are established by the mind "either **voluntarily** or by chance." These latter associations by the mind can be fixed by custom, which "settles habits of thinking in the understanding."[55] He warns us that the mistaken "connexion in our minds of ideas in themselves loose and independent of one another" must be "looked after" as a great source of error.[56]

Locke considers language as a conventional means of expressing ideas. Words, says Locke, "stand for nothing but *the ideas in the mind of him that uses them*" and perform the two functions of being memory aids and means of communication with others.[57] Although existing objects of experience are particular things, he remarks, "The far greatest part of words that make all languages are general terms: which has not been the effect of neglect or chance, but of reason and necessity." After all, it would be impossible to retain distinct names for all the particular objects of experience; second, even if it were possible, the piling up of particular names would be useless for purposes of communication; and, third, even if this problem could be overcome, the expansion of knowledge requires generalization.[58] The way in which general ideas, such as are necessary for the development of philosophical or theological knowledge, come to be is by means of "abstraction," that is, "by separating from them the circumstances of time and place, and any other ideas that may determine them to this or that particular existence"; and general words are the signs we invent to refer to such general ideas.[59] Locke's conclusion is that what are general and universal are not real, existing things at all, but only "the inventions and creatures of the understanding, made by it for its own use, and concern only signs."[60] His conceptualism then views general words as representing abstract ideas, which, in turn, can represent existing things, all of which are particular: "when general names have any connexion with particular beings, these abstract ideas are the medium that unites them."[61] As we have seen, in addition to the function of "recording our own thoughts," a second use of words is "the communicating of our thoughts to others." Locke holds that this second function also "has a double use": its "civil" purpose is to facilitate social relationships among people; and its "philosophical" purpose is "to express in general propositions certain and undoubted truths, which the mind may rest upon and be satisfied with in its search after true knowledge."[62] It is this latter purpose of language which will concern us in our examination of Locke's philosophy of religion, his argumentation for God, and his analysis of the relation between reason and religious faith.

So the mind experiences impressions which give rise to simple ideas of sensation and reflection, which can be stored in memory and recalled at will. The mind can distinguish among simple ideas, combine them to make up complex ones, abstract them from the context in which they arise, and name them. Language involves generalization and is used to aid us in remembering ideas and to express them in communication with others. This communication through language, in addition to serving a social function, can be "philosophical" in the formulation of general statements which purport to establish knowledge. What then is knowledge?

Knowledge Analyzed. Locke defines knowledge as "*the perception of the connexion of and agreement, or disagreement and repugnancy of any of our ideas.*"[63] An important implication of this definition, taken literally, is that the only objects of knowledge are our ideas—and not the objects to which those ideas supposedly correspond. Locke does not consistently hold to this view, but to the extent that he does, it may be regarded as the beginning of a strain of **subjectivism** in British empiricism. The "perception" being discussed is a mental awareness; and what the mind must be aware of are similarities and differences among ideas. Locke goes on to explain that the agreement or disagreement of which the mind must be aware can take four different forms: (1) identity or diversity—for example, the two Aristotelian laws of logic we have considered, the principles of identity and contradiction, have to do with this basic kind of relationship; (2) abstract relations—relative qualitative degrees, for example, four-legged versus eight-legged creatures; (3) necessary coexistence or non-coexistence of qualities in the same substance—for example, a certain yellowish color and malleability always coexist in solid gold; and (4) real existence as corresponding to any ideas—such as that of the paper on which these words are written.[64] Given that the objects of knowledge are only ideas, there is a problem of how we establish a correspondence between any of our ideas and real (i.e., outside the mind) existence.

This is Locke's conception of knowledge. Next he discusses the three degrees of human knowledge. He speaks of "*intuitive knowledge*" as the immediate perception by the mind of the agreement or disagreement of ideas as, for example, that a circle is not a triangle and that three is greater than two. This is the highest degree of knowledge and basic to all others: "*It is on this intuition that depends all the certainty and evidence of all our knowledge.*" He goes on to explain, agreeing with Descartes, that demonstrative knowledge, the next degree, presupposes the intuitive "connexions of the intermediate ideas."[65] Sometimes the mind can only perceive the agreement or disagreement of ideas mediately, through "*the intervention of other ideas,*" by a process of reasoning. "Those intervening ideas, which serve to show the agreement of any two others, are called *proofs*; and where the agreement and disagreement is by this means plainly and clearly perceived, it is called *demonstration*."[66] Demonstrative knowledge, though it is certain, is not as clear as intuitive knowledge because it is less immediate; and the more complex is the chain of reasoned proofs, the less clear and distinct a demonstration will be. Every step of a demonstration requires intuitive evidence and gives intuitive certainty, but it also calls for careful vigilance lest mistakes be made or steps be omitted.[67] (We might compare this to Descartes's principle of review.)

Locke seems tempted to stop his discussion of the degrees of knowledge here and not pass on to a third: "These two, viz. intuition and demonstration, are the degrees of our *knowledge*; whatever comes short of one of these, with what assurance soever embraced, is but *faith* or *opinion*, but not knowledge." Yet he does not stop here because he wishes to include a third type of mental perception, "employed about *the particular existence of finite beings without us*, which, going beyond bare probability, and yet not reaching perfectly to either of the foregoing degrees of certainty, passes under the name of *knowledge*."[68] These would be objects of sense experience. Why does Locke waver here? Perhaps it is because he is trying to meet two sets of demands: those of Cartesianism, according to which knowledge requires the highest degree of indubitable certainty, and those of common sense, which would count as knowledge whatever true beliefs are justified by empirical evidence. This is one place where Locke appears to blend his Cartesianism with a moderate empiricism. At any rate, his conclusion is straightforward:

> So that, I think, we may add to the two former sorts of knowledge this also, of the existence of particular external objects, by that perception and consciousness we have of the actual entrance of ideas from them, and allow these three degrees of knowledge, viz. *intuitive*, *demonstrative*, and *sensitive*: in each of which there are different degrees and ways of evidence and certainty.[69]

This waters down somewhat the strict standards for knowledge demanded by Descartes; and it also introduces the problem, mentioned above, of how we can establish any certainty about external objects of sensation, given that our minds have direct, immediate access only to ideas. But it also allows Locke to avoid Descartes's awkward and artificial device of appealing to the integrity of the nondeceiving God as a justification of the reliability of sense experience.

Thus, knowledge can only extend to those matters of which the mind can perceive—through intuition, rational demonstration, or sensation—the agreement or disagreement of ideas. But what we can know is more limited than the extent of our ideas, which, in turn, fall short of the reality of things.[70] Locke's conclusion here takes the form of two warnings—we should beware of dogmatic philosophical pronouncements where adequate evidence is not available; and, second, we should "discern how far our knowledge does reach" and, where it falls short, "content ourselves with faith and probability."[71] An issue of concern to us is whether, and to what extent, we can have existential knowledge, an issue on which Locke tries to be clear:

> we have an intuitive knowledge of *our own existence*, and a demonstrative knowl-
> edge of the existence of *God*; of the existence of *anything else*, we have no other
> but a sensitive knowledge; which extends not beyond the objects present to our
> senses.[72]

A problem that this poses in the age of Newton, whose great work had been published in 1687, three years before Locke's *Essay*, is that although our awareness of physical objects

> will serve us for common use and discourse, . . . we are not capable of scientif-
> ical knowledge; nor shall ever be able to discover general, instructive, unques-
> tionable truths concerning them. *Certainty* and *demonstration* are things we must
> not, in these matters, pretend to.[73]

Here Locke seems surprisingly calm about what would appear a dramatically skeptical conclusion.

The final issue of Locke's epistemology which we should consider before turning to his philosophy of religion concerns what he calls "the reality of knowledge." Given that certain knowledge extends to all mental "perception of the agreement or disagreement of our ideas," how do we distinguish between a set of ideas that is consistent and coherent but does not correspond to "the reality of things" and one which, in addition to being consistent and coherent, also corresponds to "the reality of things"? Locke diagnoses the problem very astutely:

> Our knowledge, therefore, is real only so far as there is a *conformity* between our
> ideas and the reality of things. But what shall be here the criterion? How shall
> the mind, when it perceives nothing but its own ideas, know that they agree
> with things themselves?[74]

If only Locke's answer were as satisfying as his formulation of the problem! But it is not. He says that all simple ideas "must necessarily be the product of things operating on the mind, in a natural way" and therefore really conform to the things themselves. Thus, our idea of whiteness must conform to the whiteness of objects in the physical world. This is plausible only on the assumption that the mind could not invent such simple ideas; and we cannot help asking why it could not do so. Second, he says,

> All our complex ideas, *except those of substances*, being archetypes of the mind's
> own making, not intended to be the copies of anything, nor referred to the exis-
> tence of anything, as to their originals, cannot want any conformity necessary to
> real knowledge.

Thus, mathematical knowledge is not only certain but real because it concerns only our own ideas and presupposes no corresponding actual existence.[75] But the most serious problem arises, third, in relation to our knowledge of substances, which is the kind of knowledge most crucial for metaphysics and philosophical theology. Locke writes,

> Herein, therefore, is founded the reality of our knowledge concerning substances—That all our complex idea of them must be such, and such only, as are made up of such simple ones as have been discovered to co-exist in nature. . . . Whatever simple ideas have been found to co-exist in any substance, these we may with confidence join together again, and so make abstract ideas of substances. For whatever have once had an union in nature, may be united again.[76]

Let us pose the problem bluntly. How can such coexistence be "found" or "discovered"? Locke's answer is through sensation or reflection. Through sensation we can discover the coexistence of whiteness, smoothness, flatness, and so forth in this piece of paper and thus establish our real knowledge of its existence.[77] Through reflection, or introspective intuition, we can discover the coexistence of our own states of consciousness—our thoughts, feelings, desires, pleasures, etc.—and thus establish our real knowledge of our own existence. Like Descartes, Locke observes that our very doubts confirm the certainty of our own existence, though not of the essence of the self. Indeed, he says, "In every act of sensation, reasoning, or thinking, we are conscious to ourselves of our own being; and, in this matter, come not short of the highest degree of certainty."[78] But, since we cannot discover the coexistence of simple qualities in other finite spirits, through either sensation or reflection, we cannot have real knowledge of the existence of "any other spiritual beings, but the Eternal God"; here we must fall back on faith and probability.[79] The question, though, is why God should be treated as an exception, given that we have experience of God through neither sensation nor intuitive reflection. We must examine Locke's arguments for God in hopes that an answer to this question might be indicated.

Arguments concerning God

The Cosmological Argument. Locke's cosmological argument begins with an explicit rejection of the Cartesian notion of any alleged innate idea of God; nevertheless, he asserts his confidence that a clear proof of God's existence is available whose cogency will be "equal to mathematical certainty," though he warns that it will require "thought and attention."[80]

This demonstration, comparable to Descartes's in the third meditation, does indeed begin with truths known through intuition—namely, those of our own existence and of a causal principle. Thus, although we do not have direct experience of God through sensation or reflection, we can supposedly demonstrate the existence of God from these intuitive truths. Locke builds on his Cartesian intuition of his own existence and makes it clear that he is not addressing his argument to anyone who "pretends to be so sceptical as to deny his own existence." Far more problematic is his use of a causal principle: "man knows, by an intuitive certainty, that bare *nothing can no more produce any real being, than it can be equal to two right angles.*"[81] This looks hauntingly like the sort of innate principle that he rejects and, indeed, unlike Descartes, he does not have the epistemological wherewithal to treat it that way. How then does this "intuitive certainty" come about? He does not explain. But, as we have already seen, Locke argues as a good empiricist that the complex idea of causality is derived from our empirical observations of change.[82] So, we may suppose that reflection in terms of this idea of causality suggested to some people the necessity of the causal principle, which, once discovered or learned, strikes the mind as self-evident. (Hume would call into question this alleged self-evidence a few decades later.) For, in order for it to have the "intuitive certainty" Locke requires, the causal principle cannot merely function as an empirical generalization.

At any rate, this causal principle provides the basis for Locke's argument for God, which proceeds in three stages. The first step is stated in a single sentence.

> If, therefore, we know there is some real being, and that nonentity cannot produce any real being, it is an evident demonstration, that *from eternity there has been something*; since what was not from eternity had a beginning; and what had a beginning must be produced by something else.[83]

This terse argument requires some unpacking. For it presupposes what Descartes's causal argument made explicit—that there cannot be any infinite regress of causes, each of which had a beginning. Presumably, Locke would consider this also to be an intuitively evident truth. Let us now formulate his argument more precisely:

  a. If there is some real being *and* nothing cannot produce any real being *and* there cannot be an infinite regress of noneternal causes, then an eternal Being must exist.

  b. There is some real being (since I exist).

c. Nothing cannot produce any real being (allegedly, an intuitively certain principle).

d. There cannot be an infinite regress of noneternal causes (considered a presupposition).

e. Therefore, an eternal Being must exist.

This conditional or hypothetical deductive argument is, of course, formally valid. But we have already found occasion to question all three premises, as Hume was to do in the middle of the eighteenth century.

God's Essence. The second stage of this argument concerning God tries to establish that

this eternal Being must be also the most powerful.

This step is based on still another purportedly "evident" principle,

that what had its being and beginning from another, must also have all that which is in and belongs to its being from ... the same source.[84]

Although this seems to be merely an extension of the causal principle we have just discussed, it does not seem as "evident" that the causal source of something's being must also be the source of all its powers as that everything which starts to be must be caused to be; the principle of evolution, for example, could render this extension dubious as well as superfluous, in the sense that beings with superior powers (such as humans) can evolve from those (for example, other primates) which lack them. But, again, let us formulate this second stage:

a. The causal source of anything that is caused to be must have all the powers of the effect.

b. I was caused to be by an eternal Being.

c. Therefore, that eternal Being must be the most powerful.

Now this is an **invalid** deductive argument, a *non sequitur*, in which the conclusion does not logically follow from the premises even if those premises are both true, and we have reason to doubt the necessity of both of them. Perhaps the argument could be reworked to make it logically tighter, for example, by holding that every other caused being derives its being from the same causal sources as I; but this would require considerable surgery. The point is that this stage of Locke's argument is not cogently put together. We should also notice that even if this step works, it only gives us "the most powerful" Being, not, as Locke subtly slips in a few pages later,[85] an "omnipotent Being."

In the third step in his argument Locke attempts to ascribe knowledge as well as eternity and power to God. Since one of the powers one reflectively experiences in himself is knowing, it seems that the eternal Being that is the source of his being must itself be knowing. Otherwise, the extension of the causal principle indicated in the preceding paragraph would be violated,

> it being as impossible that things wholly void of knowledge . . . should produce a knowing being, as it is impossible that a triangle should make itself three angles bigger than two right ones.[86]

This third stage can be formulated as a valid alternative syllogism:

> *a.* Either there was a time "when there was no knowing being, and when knowledge began to be; *or* else there has been also *a knowing being from eternity.*"[87]
>
> *b.* But there could not have been a time "when there was no knowing being, and when knowledge began to be" (since this would violate the causal principle).
>
> *c.* Therefore, "there has been also *a knowing being from eternity.*"

There is no new problem here. But so much, including in this case the second premise (*b*), rests on Locke's use of his unjustified, dubious, allegedly "evident" causal principle. Since it does not seem self-evident, it calls for the sort of justification Locke fails to provide; and evidence of evolution renders it doubtful.

Putting these three stages of the argument together, Locke has allegedly demonstrated the existence of an eternal, most powerful, knowing Being. He sums it up in this manner:

> Thus, from the consideration of ourselves, . . . our reason leads us to the knowledge of this certain and evident truth,—*That there is an eternal, most powerful, and most knowing Being*; which whether any one will please to call God, it matters not.[88]

You might notice how carelessly Locke seems to have slid from speaking of God as "a knowing being" to speaking of a "most knowing Being"; there is no justification for this transition in the intervening half a page. The argument taken as a whole is disappointingly loose in the context of his carefully worked out epistemology. At any rate, he goes on to say that in similar fashion "will easily be deduced all those other attributes, which we ought to ascribe to this eternal Being."[89] We might say that the first stage of the argument is designed to demonstrate God's existence, while the rest of it attempts to demonstrate God's essence.

But, speaking of God's essence, we need to return to a bit of unfinished business—to examine what Locke says about the idea of God. Remember that he said that any complex idea, in order to be the basis of "real" knowledge, must be "made up of such simple ones as have been discovered to co-exist in nature."[90] Concerning "our complex idea of God," he says that "the idea we have of the incomprehensible Supreme Being" is composed "of the simple ideas we receive from reflection," such as existence, duration, knowledge, power, and other qualities "which it is better to have than to be without" (what Descartes called perfections); "when we would frame an idea the most suitable we can to the Supreme Being, we enlarge every one of these with our idea of infinity; and so putting them together, make our complex idea of God."[91] The problem is with the extrapolation of qualities to infinity. How could our idea of God be anything but "incomprehensible" if it presupposes that of infinity? After all, Locke denies that we have any clear positive comprehension of the idea of the infinite.[92] This is crucial.

> For it is infinity, which, joined to our ideas of existence, power, knowledge, &c., makes the complex idea, whereby we represent to ourselves, the best we can, the Supreme Being.[93]

Locke ought (but fails) to recognize the unwelcome conclusion: we can have no "real" knowledge of God as the Supreme Being of the monotheistic religions. He might be able to justify claims to "real knowledge" of an original being that is extremely powerful, intelligent, etc., but not of one that is absolutely perfect because he lacks the empirical evidence to make good that claim. As he admits, "there is no idea we attribute to God, bating infinity, which is not also a part of our complex idea of other spirits."[94] As we have seen, he later denies that we have any "real" knowledge of other finite spirits,[95] relegating our belief in them to faith. On the basis of our awareness of qualities in ourselves and physical objects, he might be able successfully to argue for a causal source of all other being which was not necessarily infinite. But Locke will not settle for so little in his use of the cosmological argument and leave so much to faith.

Other Arguments for God's Existence. Locke's references to other arguments for God are brief and scattered. He seems more an empiricist than a Cartesian in his suspicions regarding the ontological argument.

The first problem is that he doubts whether any conception of God needed to make the argument work is universally accepted.[96] His rejection of the argument for God's existence based on "the idea of a most perfect being" is relatively mild for an empiricist: "it is an ill way of establishing this truth . . . to . . . take some men's having that idea of God in their minds (for it is evident some men have none, and some worse than none, and the most very different) for the only proof of a Deity." Of course, this is not what was done by Descartes, who, in fact, subordinated the ontological argument to causal arguments for God. But Locke fears that this argument might eclipse other more cogent, empirical ones. Quoting Paul's Epistle, *Romans* (1:20), he writes,

> For I judge it as certain and clear a truth as can anywhere be delivered, that "the invisible things of God are clearly seen from the creation of the world, being understood by the things that are made, even his eternal power and Godhead."[97]

There is some justification for Locke's concern here. If the ontological argument could be cogently established, it would render all others superfluous since it alone, unlike all empirical arguments for God, is designed to show not only divine existence but also divine infinity and perfection. All in all, his attitude towards this *a priori* argument is as prudently cautious as one might expect from an empiricist.

There are several texts in which Locke suggests what has come to be called the argument from design. His friend, Sir Isaac Newton, was to help make this argument scientifically respectable by endorsing it as a reasonable basis for religious faith.[98] In his critique of innate principles, one of the arguments Locke uses to show that the idea of God would not necessarily be innate even if it were universally accepted is that this could be because the idea was inspired by our experience of the world as designed:

> For the visible marks of extraordinary wisdom and power appear so plainly in all the works of the creation, that a rational creature, who will but seriously reflect on them, cannot miss the discovery of a Deity.[99]

Later, Locke appeals to design for an altogether different purpose—to argue for the unity of God and against the possibility of several "eternal, finite, cogitative beings, . . . which could never produce that order, harmony, and beauty which are to be found in nature."[100] In the first of his *Two Treatises of Government*, Locke's appeal to design, though again extremely brief, seems to be specifically an argument for God. After quoting Psalm 94:9, "Shall he that made the Eye not see?" he comments, "The Structure of that one part is sufficient to convince us of an All-wise

Contriver."[101] None of these references to divine design amounts to a fully developed, carefully argued proof. Yet they are suggestions one might reasonably expect of a philosophical theologian who was a man of common sense and a moderate empiricist.

Reason, Faith, and Religion

Reason and Probability. Locke's discussion of reason, as we have considered it thus far, has been oriented toward certain theoretical knowledge. Yet he has already warned us that human knowledge is quite limited; indeed, our reflections on his arguments for God seem to indicate that it may be even more limited than he imagines. Rational powers are needed to direct our thought and action where knowledge falls short.

> The understanding faculties being given to man, not barely for speculation, but also for the conduct of his life, man would be at a great loss if he had nothing to direct him but what has the certainty of true *knowledge*. For that being very short and scanty, as we have seen, he would be often utterly in the dark, and in most of the actions of his life, perfectly at a stand, had he nothing to guide him in the absence of clear and certain knowledge.[102]

It is judgment which takes up this epistemological slack. This is the faculty of the mind that connects or separates ideas, "when their certain agreement or disagreement is not perceived, but *presumed* to be so."[103] And Locke explains that this faculty is exercised in cases in which knowledge is not available, as well as "sometimes out of laziness, unskilfulness, or haste, even where demonstrative and certain proofs are to be had."[104]

An important object of judgment is probability, the appearance of an agreement or disagreement of ideas,

> by the intervention of proofs, whose connexion is not constant and immutable, or at least is not perceived to be so, but is, or appears for the most part to be so, . . . enough to induce the mind to judge the proposition to be true or false, rather than the contrary.[105]

This judgment of a likelihood of truth or falsehood is particularly important given the fact that we so commonly need to think and act in the absence of certainty. According to Locke, there are two foundations of probability: "First, The conformity of anything with our knowledge, observation, and experience. Secondly, The testimony of others, vouching their observation and experience." As if anticipating Hume's discussion of miracles, Locke recommends six factors for consideration in the assessment of the testimony of others: (1) the number of witnesses; (2) their integrity; (3) their skill; (4) the author's design or purposes, "where it is a testimony out of a book cited"; (5) the consistency of the various elements of testimony; and (6) any contrary testimonies.[106]

Locke goes on to explain that the propositions we rationally judge to be probable

> are of *two sorts*: either concerning some particular existence, or, as it is usually termed, matter of fact, which, falling under observation, is capable of human testimony; or else concerning things, which, being beyond the discovery of our senses, are not capable of any such testimony.[107]

He discusses three degrees of probability concerning particular observable matters of fact.

> The first, therefore, and *highest degree of probability*, is when the general consent of all men, in all ages, as far as it can be known, concurs with a man's constant and never-failing experience in like cases, to confirm the truth of any particular matter of fact attested by fair witnesses; such are all the stated constitutions and properties of bodies, and the regular proceedings of causes and effects in the ordinary course of nature.[108]

Examples of this would be that the book that dropped out of Locke's window fell to the ground below or that England froze during the winter of 1689. Concerning judgments of highest degree of probability, we can have practically certain "*assurance.*" "The *next degree of probability* is, when I find by my own experience, and the agreement of all others that mention it, a thing to be for the most part so, and that the particular instance of it is attested by many and undoubted witnesses." An example would be that if people in all cultures and historical periods, as well as within the bounds of my own experience, tend to "prefer their private advantage to the public" welfare, where there is a conflict between the two, and if all historians who write of Julius Caesar say that he also acted that way, "it is extremely probable" and we may have "*confidence*" that he did. And, third, where things might have happened one way or the other, "when any particular matter of fact is vouched by the concurrent testimony of unsuspected witnesses," it commands our "*unavoidable*" assent.[109] Most particular historical facts are of this sort—for example, the ones about Locke given at the beginning of this chapter.

The other sort of probability concerns matters that are not accessible to our senses and therefore are not subject to naturally compelling testimony—for example, that there are "finite immaterial beings," such as ghosts or angels, operating about us. Of these matters, Locke says, our judgments must be ruled by analogy in the forming of hypotheses; although this is a lower order of probability, he cautiously allows that "a wary reasoning from analogy leads us often into the discovery of truths and useful productions, which would otherwise lie concealed."[110] Thus, reason comprises these various sorts and degrees of probable judgments as well as the relating of ideas to constitute knowledge.

But what is reason? As Locke recognizes, the meaning of the word is difficult to pin down in philosophical literature. He uses it, in contrast to intuition, to refer to that faculty by which the mind infers connections among ideas in such a way as to arrive at certain knowledge or probable opinion.[111] It is "the discursive faculty" of the mind,[112] as opposed to sensation and intuition, which are limited in the scope of their objects. As Locke says, "The greatest part of our knowledge depends upon deductions and intermediate ideas," as do our probable judgments. "In both these cases, the faculty which finds out the means, and rightly applies them, to discover certainty in the one, and probability in the other, is that we call *reason*."[113] Rational knowledge is as certain, though not as immediate, as intuitive knowledge; whereas rational judgment leads to probable opinion.[114] Locke distinguishes among three types of propositions:

> those that are according to, above, and contrary to reason. 1. *According to reason* are such propositions whose truth we can discover by examining and tracing those ideas we have from sensation and reflection; and by natural deduction find to be true or probable. 2. *Above reason* are such propositions whose truth or probability we cannot by reason derive from those principles. 3. *Contrary to reason* are such propositions as are inconsistent with or irreconcilable to our clear and distinct ideas. Thus the existence of one God is according to reason; the existence of more than one God, contrary to reason; the **resurrection** of the dead, above reason.[115]

Except for that last long quote, which is rather famous, Locke's discussion of reason beyond the realm of knowledge is not particularly well-known, even by philosophers. The most celebrated parts of his epistemology are his theory of ideas and theory of knowledge. However, by contrast, his treatments of judgment, probability, and degrees of rational assent that fall short of knowledge are unfortunately neglected dimensions of his epistemology. Our interest in them is mainly for the sake of examining his ideas on the relationship between faith and reason. But it seems safe to say that this part of his epistemology is extremely well-handled by Locke and that his analysis rings true to our intellectual experience.

Analysis of Faith. Locke's discussion of faith is introduced by his admission that another use of reason, not examined yet, mistakenly contrasts it with faith. He prefers to say that "faith is nothing but a firm assent of the mind: which if it be regulated, as is our duty, cannot be afforded to anything but upon good reason; and so cannot be opposite to it."[116] Earlier, after his analysis of degrees of probable judgment, Locke had pointed out that he had not included faith in that analysis because it "is a settled and sure principle of assent and assurance, and leaves no manner of room for doubt or hesitation"; after all, as he explains, it is based on the testimony "of such an one as cannot deceive nor be deceived: and that is of God himself."[117] Let us, then, consider what sort of "assent and assurance" faith is, recognizing that it is distinguished from both knowledge and probable judgment.

Locke reminds us of what he has already established—that all knowledge is restricted to objects of which we have ideas, that all rational, as opposed to intuitive, knowledge presupposes proofs, and that even probable judgments are impossible without a basis of either our own knowledge or the testimony of other men. But if faith and reason are neither to be identified with, nor simply opposed against, one another, how are they related? Locke proposes to "lay down *the measures and boundaries between faith and reason*" and emphasizes the importance of so doing: "For till it be resolved how far we are to be guided by reason, and how far by faith, we shall in vain dispute, and endeavor to convince one another in matters of religion."[118] We may recall that the original inspiration for Locke's writing the *Essay* was his discussion with several friends in which they were unable to resolve difficulties concerning the principles of morality and religion.

Locke draws the distinction between faith and reason by defining each of them:

> *Reason*, therefore, here, as contradistinguished to *faith*, I take to be the discovery of the certainty or probability of such propositions or truths, which the mind arrives at by deduction made from such ideas, which it has got by the use of its natural faculties; viz. by sensation or reflection.

He continues,

> *Faith*, on the other side, is the assent to any proposition, not thus made out by the deductions of reason, but upon the credit of the proposer, as coming from God, in some extraordinary way of communication. This way of discovering truths to men, we call *revelation*.[119]

We should remember here that, although it is not knowledge, faith is also not reducible to probability but is certain belief in truths revealed by God. Such revealed truths must not be "according to reason," in order not to be made a matter of demonstration or probability; nor can they be "contrary to reason" since this would render them unacceptable to the mind.

Hence, they must be "above reason." The Christian doctrine of the Incarnation, for example, that God literally took on human nature in the person of Jesus without compromising or abandoning the divine nature, would be for Locke a matter of faith in this sense. However, it might be pointed out, against Locke, that it is difficult to find stable criteria for determining whether such doctrines are "contrary to" or merely "above" reason; for instance, it is easily arguable that the mystery of the Incarnation, in which Locke believes, defies the canons of reason (as even Kierkegaard was to admit) as much as does the Catholic dogma of transubstantiation, which Locke rejects as contrary to reason.[120]

Revelation As a Source of Faith. Locke distinguishes between two ways in which matters of faith may be revealed to men—through "*original revelation*" God can reveal truths directly to a man; through "*traditional revelation*" a man can communicate to others the truths directly revealed to him by God.[121] Thus, for example, Moses receiving the law directly from God on Mount Sinai (*Exodus* 20) is an example of "original revelation," whereas Moses' subsequent attempts to communicate the law to the Israelites (*Exodus* 35) is an example of "traditional revelation." Even alleged original revelation, Locke maintains, cannot "shake or overrule plain knowledge; or rationally prevail with any man to admit it for true, in a direct contradiction to the clear evidence of his own understanding."[122] Otherwise, the God-given foundations of all knowledge would be subverted, the difference between truth and falsehood would collapse, and we would be left with no stable manner of discriminating between the credible and the incredible.[123] In other words, the truths of original revelation cannot be "contrary to reason." Locke believes that original revelation affords us assurance as certain as "the natural ways of knowledge," provided that we know "that it is a revelation from God."[124] He holds that revelation should prevail against the merely "*probable conjectures of reason*" because, if it is genuine divine revelation, it is certain. But still there is the problem of how to decide whether it is indeed genuine divine revelation. All he can say here is that reason must be the arbiter in judging "of the truth of its being a revelation, and of the signification of the words wherein it is delivered."[125]

Now what about traditional revelation? Locke offers us three guidelines for judging it. First, even if a person has received original revelation, he cannot in communicating it to others convey to them "*any new simple ideas which they had not before from sensation or reflection.*" Locke uses a vivid example to get his point across:

> supposing God should discover to any one, supernaturally, a species of creatures
> inhabiting, for example, Jupiter or Saturn, . . . which had six senses; and imprint
> on his mind the ideas conveyed to theirs by that sixth sense: he could no more,
> by words, produce in the minds of other men those ideas imprinted by that sixth
> sense, than one of us could convey the idea of any colour, by the sound of words,
> into a man who, having the other four senses perfect, had always totally wanted
> the fifth, of seeing.

In other words, barring personal experience of original revelation, we are totally dependent on our natural faculties for the acquisition of all our simple ideas, none of which can be acquired through traditional revelation.[126]

Second, Locke says, although traditional revelation may disclose to us some truths that are also knowable through reason, it cannot provide the same certainty as does reason, nor can it conflict with our intuitive or demonstrative knowledge. "For the knowledge we have that this revelation came at first from God, can never be so sure as the knowledge we have from the clear and distinct perception of the agreement or disagreement of our own ideas." Even where there is no conflict, natural evidence is more certain. For example, Locke believes in the Old Testament story of Noah and his family being saved from the Deluge by means of an ark; "and yet nobody, I think, will say he has as certain and clear a knowledge of the flood as Noah, that saw it; or that he himself would have had, had he been alive and seen it."[127] Locke is a more relentless champion of reason here than Descartes was:

> In all things, therefore, where we have clear evidence from our ideas, and those
> principles of knowledge I have above mentioned, reason is the proper judge; and
> revelation, though it may, in consenting with it, confirm its dictates, yet cannot
> in such cases invalidate its decrees: nor can we be obliged, where we have the
> clear and evident sentence of reason, to quit it for the contrary opinion, under
> a pretence that it is a matter of faith.[128]

So, propositions contrary to reason must not be accepted on the basis of alleged traditional revelation, and reason itself must determine whether or not such propositions pass muster.

Third, propositions which are

> beyond the discovery of our natural faculties, and *above reason*, are, when
> revealed, *the proper matter of faith*. Thus, that part of the angels rebelled against
> God, and thereby lost their first happy state: and that the dead shall rise, and
> live again: these and the like, being beyond the discovery of reason, are purely
> matters of faith, with which reason has directly nothing to do.[129]

But, again, it is reason which must judge whether traditional revelation is divinely inspired or not.

Locke seems to be attempting (rather successfully, it seems) to strike a delicate balance. On the one hand, he makes it clear that he does not deny or even question the reliability of divine revelation when he says, "Whatever God hath revealed is certainly true: no doubt can be made of it." But, on the other hand, he staunchly defends the primacy of reason when he writes,

> There can be no evidence that any traditional revelation is of divine original, in the words we receive it, and in the sense we understand it, so clear and so certain as that of the principles of reason.[130]

It would appear that, despite Locke's wishes, this reduces our faith in traditional revelation to probable assent, rather than leaving it the certain assurance in terms of which he wants to describe all religious faith. Perhaps Locke should have admitted that faith based on traditional, as opposed to original, revelation is a matter of probable assent. Otherwise, this analysis is well-done, as helpful as Locke hoped it would be in articulating the relationship between faith and reason. We can also share the fear Locke expresses: "If the provinces of faith and reason are not kept distinct by these boundaries, there will, in matters of religion, be no room for reason at all,"[131] given that it will be edged out and exploited by fanatical zealots. Locke supplements this examination of the relationship between faith and reason in an obscure passage elsewhere:

> Thus it seems to me that God has plainly set out the boundaries of our several faculties, and showed us by which we are to conduct our lives, viz. by our senses in the cognizance of sensible objects, by reason in the deductions and discourses from perfect and clear ideas, and by faith in matters that the senses nor reason will not reach to, and though reason often helps our senses, and faith our reason, yet neither the one nor the other ever invalidates the authority, or destroys the evidence, of the inferior and subordinate faculty.[132]

Religion Considered. Locke's discussion of religion is foreshadowed by a paragraph in his *Essay*, in which he argues that religious obligations follow from our recognition of God as the source of our being:

> He also that hath the idea of an intelligent, but frail and weak being, made by and depending on another, who is eternal, omnipotent, perfectly wise and good, will as certainly know that man is to honour, fear, and obey God, as that the sun shines when he sees it. For . . . he will as certainly find that the inferior, finite, and dependent is under an obligation to obey the supreme and infinite, as he is certain to find that three, four, and seven are less than fifteen.[133]

But for the development of his ideas on religion we must turn elsewhere.

The main text here is *The Reasonableness of Christianity*, which, even though it is not critically enough argued to be truly philosophical, still contains Locke's most important treatment of religion. He explains the commitments which the Christian religion essentially requires of its adherents: "These two, faith and repentance, i.e. believing Jesus to be the Messiah, and a good life, are the indispensable conditions . . . to be performed by all those who would obtain eternal life."[134] He quotes from the Gospel, *John* (3:36), to the effect that faith in Christ is a necessary condition of eternal life; and he comments on this passage that this faith is tantamount to "believing that Jesus was the Messiah; giving credit to the miracles he did, and the profession he made of himself."[135] Locke, accepting the Scriptural testimony of traditional revelation, finds that the miracles provide ample evidence that Christ's mission was divine.[136]

That mission itself was one of moral reform, and Locke reminds us that Christ required that his followers "should be exemplary in good works" and practice the "golden rule" of behavior toward others.[137] We are reminded that a moral law can be developed in two ways: either on natural principles of reason or through divine revelation. Locke maintains that pre-Christian philosophers who attempted the first of these approaches were "unsuccessful" in producing "a true and complete morality" and that, for that purpose, natural human reason required the assistance of divine revelation.[138] This assistance was provided by the teachings of Jesus, as reported in the New Testament: "We have from him a full and sufficient rule for our direction, and conformable to that of reason."[139] (Kant, in his *Religion within the Limits of Reason Alone*, parallels Locke's discussion of this topic a century later.)

Locke reiterates a theme from his *Essay* that human reason is limited and avers that Christ's revelation of religious truths was needed, even where those truths were in accordance with reason: "The greatest part of mankind want leisure or capacity for demonstration, nor can carry a train of proofs" so that, in matters of religion, they "cannot know, and therefore they must believe."[140] In addition to teaching us what is essential for Christians to believe and what moral code they are to follow, this religion, third, communicates "the doctrine of a future state" more effectively than was ever done previously; as Locke says of this doctrine of life after death, Jesus "has given us an unquestionable assurance and pledge of it, in his own resurrection and ascension into heaven."[141] This, of course, presupposes the credibility of traditional Christian revelation. And, fourth, Locke holds that Christianity provides the religious benefit to its adherents of Jesus' "promise of assistance. If we do what we can, he will give us his Spirit to help us to do what, and how we should."[142] These are four dimensions—the essentials of faith, a moral code, the doctrine of life after death, and divine assistance—about which Locke thinks the Christian religion can and should speak authoritatively.

But beyond these fundamentals of the Christian religion, Locke shows himself to be quite tolerant. As he writes, "a great many of the truths revealed in the gospel, every one does, and must confess, a man may be ignorant of; nay, disbelieve, without danger to his salvation."[143] In these other, nonessential areas of religious faith, Locke stands firm against the kind of religious dogmatist he elsewhere calls "a creed-maker," saying,

> I allow to the makers of systems and their followers, to invent and use what dis-
> tinctions they please, and to call things by what names they see fit. But I can-
> not allow to them, or to any man, an authority to make a religion for me, or to
> alter that which God hath revealed.[144]

Here in the last decade of his life, Locke is still maintaining the advocacy of religious toleration begun much earlier with his work on the charter for the colony of Carolina.

In *A Letter concerning Toleration*, Locke defines the "business of true religion," the idea of "what a church is," and the "end of a religious society." To complete our study of his treatment of religion, then, we should briefly consider what he says there. He writes that the function of "true religion" has nothing to do with "external pomp" and power but only with "the regulating of men's lives according to the rules of virtue and piety."[145] He defines a church, rather broadly, as "a voluntary society of men, joining themselves together of their own accord in order to the public worshiping of God in such manner as they judge acceptable to Him, and effectual to the salvation of their souls." He explains that no person is naturally bound to "any particular church or sect, but everyone joins himself voluntarily to that society in which he believes he has found that profession and worship which is truly acceptable to God."[146] And he holds that the purpose of any church should be strictly religious rather than political—namely, "the public worship of God and, by means thereof, the acquisition of eternal life."[147] We shall see more about the implications of these ideas in the next section when we consider more specifically what Locke says about religious toleration.

Miracles, Toleration, and Enthusiasm

Miracles. Locke's discourse on miracles is prefigured by a single paragraph in his *Essay*, in which he argues that, although in general our "common experience and the ordinary course of things" powerfully influence our thinking, there is one sort of case in which extraordinary exceptions to these are all the more gripping and can provide justification for other truths that are above reason: "This is the proper case of *miracles*, which, well attested, do not only find credit themselves, but give it also to other truths, which need such confirmation."[148] This is not explained further or justified but leads into his claim that religious faith, based on divine revelation, transcends all probability and is as certain as, though not identical to, knowledge.

In *A Discourse of Miracles*, Locke begins by acknowledging the need for definition:

> A miracle then I take to be a sensible operation, which, being above the comprehension of the spectator, and in his opinion contrary to the established course of nature is taken by him to be divine.[149]

In analyzing this definition, we might observe, as Locke recognizes, how subjective it is. The first part of it is objective enough: a miracle must be an act or event of which people can be aware through sense experience. But the remainder is spectator-relative. It need not be altogether above all human comprehension but only that of the spectator. Whether it actually is contrary to the established course of nature is not important—only that the spectator thinks it is. And whether it be actually caused by God is not an issue but only that the spectator regards it thus. Locke admits that, on this view, "it is unavoidable that that should be a miracle to one, which is not so to another."[150] This relativizing and subjectivizing of miracles is neatly compatible with Locke's theory of knowledge as strictly related to our ideas. The problem, though, is how, on this view, Locke can hold, as he does in *The Reasonableness of Christianity*, that it is the miracles of Jesus which proclaim him to be the Messiah. The question is how miracles, whether witnessed personally or as taught through traditional revelation, can ever serve as an objective warrant for religious faith. Locke seems vague on this point.

A second possible problem with Locke's account of miracles is that he peremptorily and dogmatically asserts that miracles "have no place but upon a supposition of one only true God" and that the only three lawgivers, of whom history offers a clear account and who worked in the name of the one true God, were "Moses, Jesus, and Mahomet." He dismisses stories about miracles performed by "Brama" and Zoroaster, "not to mention all the wild stories of the religions farther east," as being "obscure" and "manifestly fabulous." Of the three mentioned lawgivers, he says, Mohammed (Mahomet) was not a miracle worker, "the only revelations that come attested by miracles, being only those of Moses and Christ, and they confirming each other."[151] Now one would need to consult a scholar of comparative religions to determine whether or not Locke's verdict here is correct. But, offhand, it seems a bit too neat that he focuses on the three lawgivers of the great monotheistic religions, snubbing the Eastern religious traditions, and that the two acclaimed as credible miracle workers are those of the Judeo-Christian tradition.

Third, the criterion that Locke offers for judging "any extraordinary operation to be a miracle" is not helpful unless we experience the alleged miracle, in the context of its historical circumstances, for ourselves. He says that what qualifies an operation to be considered a miracle is "the carrying with it the mark of a greater power than appears in opposition to it."[152] But by this analysis an astronomer in the Middle Ages who, in competition with a wizard, predicts an eclipse in the name of God (somewhat like Mark Twain's tale in *A Connecticut Yankee in King Arthur's Court*) might qualify as a miracle worker in the minds of all the spectators, although his secret is merely that he enjoys some knowledge which for that time is esoteric.

But the weakest aspect of Locke's account of miracles is that he does not critically consider how we can assess the plausibility of miracle accounts derived from traditional revelation, such as those to be found in the Judeo-Christian Scriptures—namely, the only ones available to most of us for serious consideration. What makes this omission seem particularly unfortunate is that Locke has the epistemological wherewithal, in the form of his six criteria for weighing the probability of the testimony of others, to do this as well as Hume had when he actually did it a few decades later. One cannot help supposing that the difference between them here is that Locke, unlike Hume, considers the Judeo-Christian miracle stories to be sacred, certain, and not subject to the canons for evaluating probabilities.

On the other hand, what can be said in Locke's favor here is that he does offer three sensible cautions: first, that no alleged miracles should be accepted which purportedly support propositions "inconsistent with natural religion and the rules of morality"; second, that miracle stories should not be taken seriously if they only support petty, trivial, insignificant revelations; and, third, that the only miracle stories worthy of our respect are those that support "the revelation of some supernatural truths relating to the glory of God, and some great concern of men."[153] These warnings are valuable to protect us against irrational pseudo-religious claims and foolish superstitions. Near the end of his *Discourse*, Locke summarizes the crucial significance of miracles to revealed religion by calling them "the basis on which divine mission is always established, and consequently that foundation on which the believers of any divine revelation must ultimately bottom their faith."[154]

Religious Toleration. Locke's discourse on toleration is a classic defense of religious freedom although it is not expressed in the form of a clear logical structure. Let us try, therefore, to impose a kind of order on his key points, including, as usual, some evaluative remarks concerning their strengths and weaknesses. Locke's general thesis is boldly stated in his *Letter concerning Toleration*:

> The toleration of those that differ from others in matters of religion is so agreeable to the Gospel of Jesus Christ, and to the genuine reason of mankind, that it seems monstrous for men to be so blind as not to perceive the necessity and advantage of it in so clear a light.[155]

Second, he tries to specify this general thesis, holding that

> no private person has any right in any manner to prejudice another person in his civil enjoyments because he is of another church or religion. All the rights and franchises that belong to him as a man or as a denizen are inviolably to be preserved to him. These are not the business of religion. No violence nor injury is to be offered him, whether he be Christian or pagan.

We might associate this with the concept of inalienable rights of the American Declaration of Independence and with the first amendment to the U.S. Constitution. He immediately adds that the "mutual toleration" he is prescribing for persons should also apply between different churches and religions.[156] His conclusion to this specification is straightforward:

> Nobody, therefore, in fine, neither single persons nor churches, nay, nor even commonwealths, have any just title to invade the civil rights and worldly goods of each other upon pretense of religion.[157]

Third, Locke goes even further, recommending that our attitude toward those of other religious persuasions should be one of "peace and goodwill," of "charity, meekness, and toleration."[158] Fourth, he maintains that no civil authority has any right "to enforce by law, either in his own church or much less in another, the use of any rites or ceremonies whatsoever in the worship of God" since "churches are free societies" and doing so would violate human liberty.[159] Fifth, he holds that civil authorities should not "forbid the preaching or professing of any speculative opinions in any church, because they have no manner of relation to the civil rights of the subjects." He gives as examples of teachings he considers false, but would defend the right to express, the Roman Catholic doctrine that the consecrated bread is "really the body of Christ" and the denial by a Jew that the New Testament is actually "the Word of God."[160] Finally, he pulls all this together in a concise statement reminiscent of the Golden Rule and anticipating Kant's principle of **universalizability**: "The sum of all we drive at is that every man may enjoy the same rights that are granted to others."[161]

These are admirable principles of religious toleration. The world would be a better place in which to live if they were universally followed. They are clearly formulated, historically influential, even inspiring. If only Locke had stopped at this point! But, unfortunately, being the moderate that he was, Locke saw fit to temper these liberal principles with four exceptions: (1) "no opinions contrary to human society, or to those moral rules which are necessary to the preservation of civil society, are to be tolerated"; (2) neither are those who themselves practice intolerance or who "will not own and teach the duty of tolerating all men in matters of mere religion"; (3) nor are members of a church whose allegiance is to a foreign power; and (4) nor are **atheists** "who deny the being of a God."[162] Even though it may seem unfair to criticize Locke from the perspective of social values of three centuries after his time, these exceptions do not seem worthy of a champion of religious liberty. The first one is dangerously a matter of unverifiable opinion. As for the second, a litmus test of toleration is the extent to which we are willing to tolerate even the intolerant. The third exception seems targeted against Roman Catholics, whose allegiance to Rome is nonsecular. And, regarding the final one, Locke's reason for categorically condemning atheists—that they cannot be trusted to keep their promises and fulfill their contracts—is false.

Nevertheless, let us allow that by the standards of the seventeenth century Locke's defense of religious liberty was in general a historical landmark. His brief statement of that defense in his *Essay* is a beautiful note on which to end this discussion:

> it would, methinks, become all men to maintain peace, and the common offices of humanity, and friendship, in the diversity of opinions. . . . The necessity of believing without knowledge, nay often upon very slight grounds, in this fleeting state of action and blindness we are in, should make us more busy and careful to inform ourselves than constrain others.[163]

This is the liberal spirit of Locke that renders him a lasting inspiration.

Enthusiasm. Locke's discourse on "enthusiasm" is a fitting topic with which to end our study of his thought. For it concerns those "enthusiasts" who lay claim to private divine revelation and intolerantly attempt to impose their religious beliefs on others. Today we would call such people religious fanatics (thus, the word "enthusiasm" is not being used in the more generic sense we popularly employ today of any great excitement). Locke believes that those people who are least likely to tolerate the different religious beliefs of others are those whose love of and judgments concerning truth have been compromised by their passionate, zealous partiality for their own pet beliefs: "The assuming an authority of dictating to others, and a forwardness to prescribe to their opinions, is a constant concomitant of this bias and corruption of our judgments."[164]

Locke endorses the love of truth, which everyone "in the commonwealth of learning" professes. Despite such commonplace professions, however, Locke fears that "there are very few lovers of truth, for truth's sake, even amongst those who persuade themselves that they are so." He recommends a rather stringent test we can use to determine whether we are, indeed, lovers of truth for its own sake—"viz. The not entertaining any proposition with greater assurance than the proofs it is built on will warrant." (This is the sort of view, held by William K. Clifford in the nineteenth century, that would later be criticized by William James.) One might reasonably have mixed reactions to Locke's standard here: on the one hand, it appears to be a solid, scientific standard that would help eliminate superstition; yet, on the other hand, as James would observe a couple of centuries later, it seems unrealistic in that, as human beings, we should not, and perhaps even cannot, rule out our own feelings and will, which are essential components of human nature, from the faith commitments we make. So we can admire but feel nervous about Locke's strong conclusion here:

> Whatsoever credit or authority we give to any proposition more than it receives from the principles and proofs it supports itself upon, is owing to our inclinations that way, and is so far a derogation from the love of truth as such: which, as it can receive no evidence from our passions or interests, so it should receive no tincture from them.[165]

The person who adheres to beliefs without objective evidence and merely out of an attachment to his own passions and personal interests is embracing "*a third ground of assent,*" in contrast with "either faith or reason." Knowledge and probability, as we have seen, are derived from intuition and reason; faith is derived from original and/or traditional revelation. But enthusiasm, according to Locke, discards reason and sets up alleged, but unsubstantiated, revelation in opposition to it. "Whereby in effect it takes away both reason and revelation, and substitutes in the room of them the ungrounded fancies of a man's own brain, and assumes them for a foundation both of opinion and conduct."[166] An enthusiast might declare it reasonable to follow the direction and directives of revelation; but what is unreasonable is to brook no critical inquiry concerning any evidence for the fact that it is authentic revelation. What is more difficult to understand is how enthusiasm "takes away" revelation. What Locke seems to mean here is that in dogmatically shunning rational consideration of purported revelation, enthusiasm undermines our confidence in any revelation.

We recall that Locke has already denied that faith and reason are opposed to each other, as well as that either can be legitimately reduced to the other. Now he likewise describes reason and revelation as different but complementary, saying that "*Reason is natural revelation*" and "*revelation is natural reason enlarged*." Through reason God reveals truths to man in a natural manner; whereas original and traditional revelation enlarge on the truths naturally understood through reason by means of direct divine communication. But, if this representation of the interrelationship of the two is correct, then enthusiasm jeopardizes both.

> So that he that takes away reason to make way for revelation, puts out the light of both, and does muchwhat the same as if he would persuade a man to put out his eyes, the better to receive the remote light of an invisible star by a telescope.[167]

Locke's remarkable conclusion here is a valuable one, that dogmatic, fanatical, unchallengeable claims to private revelation pose a threat for the supporter of religious revelation, even if he or she does not happen to care anything about philosophical reason.

He next adroitly explores the psychology of "enthusiasm," which makes it so dangerously alluring.

> Immediate revelation being a much easier way for men to establish their opinions and regulate their conduct, than the tedious and not always successful labour of strict reasoning, it is no wonder that some have been very apt to pretend to revelation, and to persuade themselves that they are under the peculiar guidance of heaven in their actions and opinions.[168]

This helps explain why the enthusiastic resorting to claims of private revelation can be so tempting, especially for religious people of a certain temperament, "men in whom melancholy has mixed with devotion, or whose conceit of themselves has raised them into an opinion of a greater familiarity with God, and a nearer admittance to his favour than is afforded to others." Of course, Locke is not for a moment implying a denial of God's ability to impart immediate revelation to anyone.[169] But he is severely critical of those characters for whom, "whatsoever odd action they find in themselves a strong inclination to do, that impulse is concluded to be a call or direction from heaven, and must be obeyed." It is all too easy for such a self-proclaimed prophet to fool not only others, but even himself. Often such people are dynamic and charismatic enough to impose their views effectively on followers. Thus, enthusiasm, "though founded neither on reason nor divine revelation, but rising from the conceits of a warmed or overweening brain," can exert its influence "more powerfully on the persuasions and actions of men than either of these two, or both together."[170]

This is a particular problem where piety refuses to tolerate any critical questioning and the word of the enthusiast is not allowed to be checked by rational reflection. The problem is aggravated by other psychological factors:

> the love of something extraordinary, the ease and glory it is to be inspired, and be above the common and natural ways of knowledge, so flatters many men's laziness, ignorance, and vanity, that, when once they are got into this way of immediate revelation, of illumination without search, and of certainty without proof and without examination, it is a hard matter to get them out of it. Reason is lost upon them, they are above it.

Whatever they feel strongly about "admits no doubt, needs no probation" because it is allegedly, though unverifiably and unquestionably, evident.[171] Locke is powerfully fierce in his denunciation of such people: "they are sure, because they are sure: and their persuasions are right, because they are strong in them."[172] Fervor of feeling can become a cheap and easy substitute for evidence.

Apart from these psychological considerations, the primary epistemological fault is the lack of justification. Locke observes that the entertaining "of any proposition coming into my mind, I know not how, is not a perception that it is from God. Much less is a strong persuasion that it is true, a perception that it is from God, or so much as true." It does not matter how fervently enthusiasts hold such a belief, "the proposition taken for a revelation is not such as they *know* to be true, but *take* to be true." It is not enough, epistemologically, to claim divine revelation. "The question then here is: How do I know that God is the revealer. . . . If I know not this, how great soever the assurance is that I am possessed with, it is groundless" enthusiasm.[173]

Even if one is very sympathetic to Locke's critique of enthusiasm, one cannot help recalling at this point the doubts raised earlier concerning his discussion of the "reality" of our ideas. When Locke writes, for example, "wherever we are sure those ideas agree with the reality of things, there is certain real knowledge,"[174] he fails to recognize that we have no way to confirm such correspondence, if he is correct in his view that the only objects of the mind are ideas. The failure of his theory of knowledge adequately to distinguish between subjectivity and objectivity thus poses problems for his philosophy of religion. What epistemological basis can Locke give us for discriminating between the true prophet, such as, for example, he believes Moses to have been, and the dangerous enthusiast? He maintains that instead of being illuminated by the light of genuine revelation, the minds of enthusiasts are "dazzled with . . . nothing but an *ignis fatuus*, that leads them constantly round in this circle; *It is a revelation, because they firmly believe it; and they believe it, because it is a revelation.*"[175] But what evidence is there, or can there be, on Locke's terms, to show that the same does not apply to someone he considers a true prophet?

Since God, for Locke as for Descartes, "can neither deceive nor be deceived," whatever is actually revealed by God must be so. But, given the claims people make to having experienced such revelation, what warrant can there be for their claims? As Locke neatly puts it, "The strength of our persuasions is no evidence at all of their own rectitude." Nor is it merely a matter of deliberate deception on the part of enthusiasts. Alluding to the example of Paul's persecution of the Christians before his conversion, Locke observes, "Good men are men still liable to mistakes, and are sometimes warmly engaged in errors, which they take for divine truths."[176]

This takes us back to Locke's major point, that we must not deny natural reason in the name of supernatural revelation. "God when he makes the prophet does not unmake the man. He leaves all his faculties in the natural state, to enable him to judge of his inspirations, whether they be of *divine* origin or no." Our God-given natural faculties are to be respected and used as safeguards against error. As Locke says in one of his most famous sentences,

Reason must be our last judge and guide in everything.[177]

If we fail to follow this rule, the consequences can be miserable:

> Every conceit that thoroughly warms our fancies must pass for an inspiration, if there be nothing but the strength of our persuasions, whereby to judge of our persuasions: if reason must not examine their truth by something extrinsical to the persuasions themselves, inspirations and delusions,

truth and falsehood, will have the same measure, and will not be possible to be distinguished.[178]

* * *

Thus Locke's position is that faith and knowledge, reason and revelation, are to be viewed as mutually supportive, rather than as antagonistic, that we are naturally capable of some theological knowledge and that other theological truths are given us as matters of faith, that God can and sometimes does grant us original and traditional revelation but that reason must remain the judge of whether God actually is the source of alleged truths of revelation. His sensible, moderate empiricism would base religion on concrete experience, while staunchly maintaining and defending the essential role of natural reason in our apprehending even supernatural truth.

Notes

1. John Locke, *An Essay concerning Human Understanding*, 2 vols., collated by Alexander Campbell Fraser (New York: Dover Publications, 1959), vol. 1, p. 9; this work will hereafter be called "*Essay*."

2. Ibid., pp. 10, 14.   3. Ibid., pp. 25, 31.   4. Ibid., p. 26.

5. Ibid., vol. 2, pp. 282–83.

6. Ibid., vol. 1, p. 27.   7. Ibid., pp. 30–31.

8. Ibid., pp. 33, 32. It is curious that throughout the entire long *Essay* Locke only seems to mention Descartes by name on two pages (vol. 2, pp. 37, 286); neither of these passages is relevant to or particularly interesting for our purposes.

9. Nowhere in book 1 does Locke specifically mention Descartes or the Cartesians or Cambridge Platonists such as Henry More and Ralph Cudworth (at the house of whose daughter, Lady Masham, Locke spent the last thirteen years of his life), all of whom accepted and used the doctrine of innate ideas. He does refer to Lord Herbert of Cherbury (p. 80), a contemporary of Descartes, who also did so.

10. Ibid., p. 37.   11. Ibid., p. 38.   12. Ibid., pp. 39–40.

13. Ibid., p. 42.   14. Ibid., p. 56.   15. Ibid., p. 42.

16. Ibid., pp. 56–57.   17. Ibid., pp. 64, 66.   18. Ibid., p. 91.

19. Ibid., p. 39.   20. Ibid., p. 92.   21. Ibid., p. 93.

22. Ibid., pp. 95–96, 103.

23. Ibid., pp. 105, 99.   24. Ibid., p. 107.   25. Ibid., pp. 31, 41.

26. Ibid., pp. 115–16.

27. Ibid., pp. 121–22. For more on Locke's *tabula rasa* theory, see his *Essays on the Law of Nature*, ed. W. von Leyden (Oxford: Oxford Univ. Press, 1954), p. 137; this work will hereafter be called "*Law*."

28. *Essay*, vol. 1, pp. 123–24.

29. Ibid., pp. 125–27.   30. Ibid., p. 141.   31. Ibid., p. 144.

32. Ibid., pp. 145–46.   33. Ibid., p. 148.   34. Ibid., p. 191.

35. Ibid., pp. 193, 197.   36. Ibid., pp. 202, 204–7.

37. Ibid., p. 212.   38. Ibid., pp. 213–14.   39. Ibid., pp. 215–16.

40. Ibid., p. 276.   41. Ibid., pp. 394, 418.   42. Ibid., p. 433.

43. Ibid., pp. 390–91.   44. Ibid., p. 394.   45. Ibid., p. 395.

46. Ibid., p. 406.   47. Ibid., p. 277.   48. Ibid., p. 289.

49. Ibid., p. 433.   50. Ibid., p. 486.   51. Ibid., p. 497.

52. Ibid., pp. 487–88.   53. Ibid., pp. 498, 502.   54. Ibid., p. 517.

55. Ibid., p. 529.   56. Ibid., p. 531.   57. Ibid., vol. 2, p. 9.

58. Ibid., pp. 14–15.   59. Ibid., pp. 16–17.   60. Ibid., p. 21.

61. Ibid., p. 24; cf. vol. 1, pp. 206–7.

62. Ibid., vol. 2, pp. 104–5.

63. Ibid., p. 167.   64. Ibid., pp. 168–71.   65. Ibid., pp. 176–78.

66. Ibid., pp. 178–79.   67. Ibid., pp. 179–81.   68. Ibid., p. 185.

69. Ibid., p. 188.   70. Ibid., pp. 190–91.   71. Ibid., p. 195.

72. Ibid., p. 212.   73. Ibid., p. 218.   74. Ibid., pp. 227–28.

75. Ibid., pp. 229–31.   76. Ibid., p. 237.   77. Ibid. p. 327.

78. Ibid., p. 305; cf. also p. 197.

79. Ibid., p. 337.   80. Ibid., p. 306.   81. Ibid., p. 307.

82. Ibid., vol. 1, p. 433.   83. Ibid., vol. 2., p. 308.   84. Ibid.

85. Ibid., p. 316.   86. Ibid., p. 309.   87. Ibid., pp. 308–9.

88. Ibid., p. 309.   89. Ibid.   90. Ibid., p. 237.

91. Ibid., vol. 1, p. 418.   92. Ibid., p. 289.   93. Ibid., p. 420.

94. Ibid., p. 421.   95. Ibid., vol. 2, p. 337.

96. *Law*, p. 155.

97. *Essay*, vol. 2, pp. 310–11.

98. *Newton's Philosophy of Nature: Selections from His Writings*, ed. H. S. Thayer (New York: Hafner, 1953), pp. 42–44, 65–66.

99. *Essay*, vol. 1, p. 99.

100. Ibid., vol. 2, p. 315. For more on the argument from design, see *Law*, pp. 109, 133, 153.

101. John Locke, *Two Treatises of Government*, rev. ed. Peter Laslett (New York: New American Library, 1963), p. 215.

102. *Essay*, vol. 2, p. 360.

103. Ibid., p. 362.   104. Ibid., p. 361.   105. Ibid., p. 363.

106. Ibid., pp. 365–66.   107. Ibid., pp. 374–75.   108. Ibid., p. 375.

109. Ibid., p. 376.   110. Ibid., pp. 379–80, 382.

111. Ibid., p. 387. It follows from this, as Locke explicitly says elsewhere, that "we cannot say God reasons at all," since God knows by means of a comprehensive, all-encompassing, instantaneous intuition—*An Examination of P. Malebranche's Opinion of Seeing All Things in God*, in *The Works of John Locke*, 10 vols. (London: Thomas Davidson, Whitefriars, 1823), vol. 9, p. 251. This collection of Locke's writings will hereafter be called "*Works*."

112. *Essay*, vol. 2, p. 407.

113. Ibid., p. 387.   114. Ibid., p. 409.   115. Ibid., pp. 412–13.

116. Ibid., p. 413.   117. Ibid., p. 383.   118. Ibid., p. 415.

119. Ibid., p. 416.   120. Ibid., p. 450.   121. Ibid., p. 417.

122. Ibid., p. 420.   123. Ibid., p. 421.   124. Ibid., p. 420.

125. Ibid., pp. 423–24.   126. Ibid., pp. 416–17.   127. Ibid., pp. 418–19.

128. Ibid., pp. 422–23.   129. Ibid., p. 423.

130. Ibid., p. 425. In connection with his own fidelity to the doctrines of traditional Christian revelation, consider Locke's statement to Edward Stillingfleet, Bishop of Worcester: "The holy scripture is to me, and always will be, the constant guide of my assent; and I shall always hearken to it, as containing infallible truth, relating to things of the highest concernment. And . . . I shall presently condemn and quit any opinion of mine, as soon as I am shown that it is contrary to any revelation in the holy scripture"—*Works*, vol. 4, p. 96.

131. *Essay*, vol. 2, p. 426.

132. *Law*, pp. 280–81. The intellectual historian will be interested in these journal entries from 1676, which Locke seems to have used as a basis for the chapter of his *Essay* that we have been considering.

133. *Essay*, vol. 2, p. 359.

134. *The Reasonableness of Christianity with a Discourse of Miracles and Part of a Third Letter concerning Toleration*, ed. I. T. Ramsey (Stanford: Stanford Univ. Press, 1958), pp. 44–45. This book will henceforth be called *Reasonableness*. What is controversial about Locke's treatment of Christ as Messiah is that Locke denies the doctrine of original sin in *Reasonableness* (pp. 25–28), arguing that the death brought about by the Fall of Adam is a literal (physical) one rather than a figurative (spiritual) one. As he explains, divine justice would not allow people to be "truly punished, but for their own deeds." And this requires a new interpretation of the redemptive deliverance of the Messiah: "Whereby it appears that the Life, which Jesus Christ restores to all men, is that life, which they receive again at the Resurrection."

135. Ibid., p. 32. In his *Second Vindication of the Reasonableness of Christianity*, Locke writes, "The preaching of our Saviour and his apostles has sufficiently taught us what is necessary to be proposed to every man, to make him a Christian. He that believes him to be the promised Messiah, takes Jesus for his king, and, repenting of his former sins, sincerely resolves to live, for the future, in obedience to his laws, is a subject of his kingdom, is a Christian"—*Works*, vol. 7, p. 352. He adds, "A

Christian I am sure I am, because I believe 'Jesus to be the Messiah,' the King and Saviour promised, and sent by God: and, as a subject of his kingdom, I take the rule of my faith and life from his will, declared and left upon record in the inspired writings of the apostles and evangelists in the New Testament"—ibid., p. 359.

136. *Reasonableness*, p. 57.

137. Ibid., pp. 46, 48. In *The Conduct of the Understanding* Locke writes, "Our Saviour's great rule that *we should love our neighbor as ourselves*, is such a fundamental truth for the regulating of human society that, I think, by that alone one might without difficulty determine all the cases and doubts in social morality"—*Works*, vol. 3, pp. 282–83.

138. *Reasonableness*, pp. 60–61. In Locke's *Second Vindication of the Reasonableness of Christianity*, he writes, "As men, we have God for our King, and are under the law of reason: as Christians, we have Jesus the Messiah for our King, and are under the law revealed by him in the Gospel"—*Works*, vol. 7, p. 229. Elsewhere, he says the "law of nature can be described as being the decree of the divine will discernible by the light of nature and indicating what is and what is not in conformity with rational nature, and for this very reason commanding or prohibiting"—*Law*, p. 111.

139. *Reasonableness*, p. 63. About a year later, when his friend and admirer William Molyneux recommended that Locke should write a work on morals, the latter replied, "Did the world want a rule, I confess there could be no work so necessary, nor so commendable. But the Gospel contains so perfect a body of ethics, that reason may be excused from that inquiry, since she may find man's duty clearer and easier in revelation than in herself"—*Works*, vol. 9, p. 377.

140. *Reasonableness*, p. 66.

141. Ibid., pp. 69–70.   142. Ibid., p. 70.   143. Ibid., pp. 74–75.

144. Ibid., p. 43. In his *Second Vindication* Locke writes, "I have spoken against all systems. . . . And always shall, so far as they are set up by particular men, or parties, as the just measure of every man's faith; wherein everything that is contained, is required and imposed to be believed to make a man a Christian"—*Works*, vol. 7, p. 387.

145. John Locke, *A Letter concerning Toleration* (Indianapolis: Bobbs-Merrill, 1955), p. 13. This work will hereafter be called "*Letter*."

146. Ibid., p. 20.   147. Ibid., p. 22.

148. *Essay*, vol. 2, p. 382.

149. *Reasonableness*, p. 79.

150. Ibid., p. 80.   151. Ibid., p. 81.   152. Ibid., p. 82.

153. Ibid., p. 84.   154. Ibid., p. 86.

155. *Letter*, p. 16.

156. Ibid., p. 24.   157. Ibid., p. 27.   158. Ibid., p. 28.

159. Ibid., pp. 35–36.   160. Ibid., p. 45.   161. Ibid., p. 55.

162. Ibid., pp. 50–52.

163. *Essay*, vol. 2, pp. 372–73.

164. Ibid., p. 430.   165. Ibid., pp. 428–30.

166. Ibid., p. 430. Elsewhere, he writes that "it would be a shame, nay, a contradiction too heavy for anyone's mind to lie under, for him to pretend seriously to be persuaded of the truth of any religion and yet not to be able to give any reason of his belief, or to say anything for his preference of this to any other opinion"—this is from *The Conduct of the Understanding*, in *Works*, vol. 3, p. 217.

167. *Essay*, vol. 2, p. 431.

168. Ibid.

169. Ibid.

170. Ibid., p. 432.

171. Ibid., p. 433.

172. Ibid., p. 434.

173. Ibid., pp. 434–35.

174. Ibid., pp. 242–43.

175. Ibid., p. 436.

176. Ibid., p. 437.

177. Ibid., p. 438.

178. Ibid., p. 439.

4

Leibniz's Logical Theodicy

Life and Writings

Gottfried Wilhelm Leibniz's life began in Leipzig, Germany during the Thirty Years' War, on July 1, 1646;[1] this was less than four years before Descartes's death and the year in which Locke began his studies at Westminster School. His father, already in his midsixties at the time and a professor of moral philosophy and jurisprudence at the University of Leipzig, died when the boy was six years old; his mother, who was his father's third wife and the daughter of a law professor at the same university, died before Gottfried could complete his university education. Gottfried was a precocious boy. He began learning Latin before the age of eight and became quite proficient at it by the time he was twelve. He could also read Greek, and, before his teenage years had begun, he was eagerly studying ancient and scholastic philosophy at home, making avid use of his father's private library. When he was thirteen, he turned to a serious study of logic.

At the age of fifteen he entered the University of Leipzig, where he discovered and eagerly read the works of modern thinkers, including Bacon, Galileo, Descartes, Hobbes, and Gassendi. There is a story that, during that year, he was walking in a park near Leipzig trying to decide whether to continue believing in the Aristotelian and scholastic theory of substantial forms; in fact, he abandoned the theory, falling under the influence of the moderns. However, he never reacted against scholastic philosophy as negatively as did other early moderns, including Descartes and Locke. In 1663, he spent an academic term at Jena, studying mathematics and jurisprudence. By 1664, he had completed the requirements for bachelor's and master's degrees in philosophy at Leipzig. He then began working on a doctor's degree in law but was not authorized to be examined, allegedly because he was too young. Since his mother had recently died, he no longer felt tied to Leipzig and transferred to the University of Altdorf, where he was awarded a doctorate in law in 1667. His dissertation, *On Perplexing Cases in Law*, was considered so brilliant that, despite his age, he was immediately offered a professor's chair at the university, which he declined.

Instead, he entered the diplomatic service of the Elector of Mainz at Frankfurt that same year. In 1672, he was sent on a sensitive diplomatic mission to Paris. The King of France, Louis XIV, had broken up the Triple Alliance, and it was feared that he was planning an attack on the Netherlands and Germany. In order to avert such a possibility, Leibniz devised a scheme whereby the French might, instead, make a military move against the Turks, leading to the conquest of Egypt, the trade route to the East. Nothing came of the scheme (although some historians think that Napoleon may have discovered and been influenced by it more than a century later). But what was important about Leibniz's four-year stay in Paris (from our point of view) was that it afforded him the opportunity to meet many prominent intellectuals, including Nicolas Malebranche and Antoine Arnauld. Early in 1673, he traveled to London, where he met Robert Boyle. He had hoped to visit Thomas Hobbes, who was eighty-four years old at the time; but Hobbes did not respond to Leibniz's letter, and the two never met. That same year, Leibniz was elected a fellow in the British Royal Society.

While in France, Leibniz discovered and formulated the principles of the infinitesimal calculus. As it turned out, Sir Isaac Newton had already made the same discovery, and there was an unfortunate controversy concerning the priority of discovery, in which Leibniz was accused of plagiarism. Leibniz published his findings in 1684, several years before Newton published his. It seems that Leibniz's discovery was independent and original. But in 1713, the Royal Society credited Newton, rather than Leibniz, with the founding of this new mathematical method. Moreover, Leibniz remained the target of bitter accusations by the British for the rest of his life. (Nowadays, Leibniz shares the credit for discovering calculus with Newton.)

In 1676, the Duke of Brunswick appointed Leibniz librarian and historian in Hanover. He journeyed there from Paris by way of the Netherlands, staying in Amsterdam for almost a month with one of Baruch Spinoza's friends. In November of that year, Leibniz succeeded in meeting Spinoza at the Hague and discussing philosophy with him. Leibniz was always eager to discuss philosophy with the best thinkers of his time, and his many travels afforded him an unusual opportunity to do so.

Leibniz was a universal genius. The diversity of his fields of activity is staggering. In addition to being a very important philosopher and mathematician, he was also a diplomat and historian, as well as a legal and political theorist. As a mathematician, in addition to his work in calculus, he established the foundations of modern symbolic logic, was a pioneer in statistical analysis and probability theory, and invented a calculating machine that could do the arithmetical functions of addition, subtraction, multiplication, and division, as well as extracting roots. As a diplomat, he worked for the unification of Christendom, dreaming of an alliance of Christian European states, planning for the reunion of Protestant Churches (e.g., Lutherans and Calvinists), and even hoping that Protestantism and Catholicism might one day be reunited. As a historian, he compiled an exhaustive history of the House of Brunswick. Moreover, he designed a submarine, wrote poetry, and envisioned a comprehensive encyclopedia of human knowledge, which never materialized.

Two politically influential friends of his were Sophia, the wife of the Duke of Brunswick, the granddaughter of King James I of England, and the sister of Princess Elizabeth, who had corresponded with Descartes, and Sophia's daughter, Sophia Charlotte, the wife of Frederick of Brandenburg, who in 1701 became King Frederick I of Prussia. With the assistance of Sophia Charlotte, Leibniz founded the Academy of the Sciences at Berlin (later the Prussian Academy), of which he was appointed first president (for life) in 1700. At about the age of fifty, Leibniz proposed marriage to some woman; but for some reason nothing ever came of it. In 1711, he traveled to Russia and met Czar Peter the Great, with whom he later corresponded. In 1712, Leibniz was made a baron of the Prussian Empire.

In the last few years of his life, Leibniz's fortunes changed for the worse. Queen Sophia Charlotte died in 1705, and, by the time her mother died in 1714, most of Leibniz's friends and protectors were gone. When Queen Anne of England died in 1714, the Elector of Hanover

(Leibniz's employer) was chosen to be King George I of England. But Leibniz was not invited to travel there with his court, possibly because of the lingering bitterness over the controversy with British Newtonians concerning the calculus. Leibniz remained sadly neglected until his death. He became withdrawn from his Prussian Academy and was scorned by some who parodied his name as "Lövenix," meaning "Believe nothing." He died alone and lonely in Hanover on November 14, 1716. His secretary, Eckhard, was the only mourner at his funeral. Neither the Royal Society of London, of which he was a member, nor the Prussian Academy, which he had founded, made any mention of his death, which was commemorated only in Paris on its anniversary by Bernard Fontenelle's eulogy, which is inscribed in the archives of the French Academy (of which he had also been a member). His only heir was a nephew (his sister's son), who was curé of a parish near Leipzig. A Scottish acquaintance named John Ker, who happened to be in Hanover when he died, wrote that Leibniz was buried more like a robber than like the ornament of his country that he was. Meanwhile, his prolific and prodigious works remain his greatest memorial.

Leibniz's philosophical writings constitute a frustrating treasury of ideas. Despite his diplomatic missions and responsibilities as librarian and historian for the House of Brunswick, he produced a steady stream of philosophical works, numbering in the thousands, over a period of half a century (1666–1716), almost none of which were published during his lifetime. Concerning his multifaceted brilliance, Denis Diderot, French *philosophe* and editor-in-chief of the great eighteenth-century *Encyclopedia*, remarked, When you compare yourself with Leibniz, your own lack of ability makes you want to throw your books away and sneak off to a quiet death in some forgotten corner. Most of Leibniz's works are in the form of his correspondence with over a thousand different persons, which typically involved serious discussions of ideas rather than merely social chitchat. He preferred to keep such materials rather than to throw them away. His papers were posthumously collected and stored in packing crates in the Royal Library at Hanover, including over 15,000 letters. His few books, his many essays, and his mass of letters contain innumerable brilliant insights. Yet there is no definitive *magnum opus* comparable to Descartes's *Meditations* or Locke's *Essay*.

From this wealth of material, Leibniz's philosophically most important writings include:

1. *Dissertation on the Art of Combinations*, published in 1666
2. "What Is an Idea?" (1678)

3. "Reflections on Knowledge, Truth, and Ideas," published in 1684

4. *Discourse on Metaphysics* (1686)

5. Correspondence with Arnauld (1686–90)

6. *Critical Remarks Concerning the General Part of Descartes' Principles* (1692)

7. "On the Ultimate Origin of Things" (1697)

8. *New Essays on the Human Understanding* (about 1704)

9. *Theodicy*, published in Amsterdam in 1710

10. "The Theodicy: Abridgement of the Argument Reduced to Syllogistic Form" (1710)

11. "A Vindication of God's Justice Reconciled with His Other Perfections and All His Actions" (1710)

12. "The Principles of Nature and of Grace, Based on Reason" (1714)

13. "The Monadology" (1714)

14. Correspondence with Clarke (1715–16).[2]

In spite of the extensive number of these writings and the brevity of some of them, these works all represent significant contributions to the history of Western philosophy.

What is particularly frustrating about the corpus of Leibniz's philosophical writings is not merely that it contains such an enormous mass of widely scattered works, but also that it is extremely repetitious and was never systematized by the author. Leibniz explained the redundancy of his ideas in terms of a faulty memory and the fact that he never bothered to index his works. Another factor was that these works were produced in his spare time, as it were, when he was otherwise busily occupied with his professional duties. He admitted to being confused himself about what he had written, when, and where:

> How extremely distracted I am cannot be described. . . . I receive and send letters in great number. I have, indeed, so many things in mathematics, so many thoughts in philosophy, so many other literary observations which I do not wish to have perish, that I am often bewildered as to where to begin.

Concerning the unsystematized bits-and-pieces quality of his work, Leibniz wrote, "My system . . . is not a complete body of philosophy." To make the difficult job of comprehending Leibniz's philosophy still more arduous, one cannot do justice to it by focusing exclusively on the materials he prepared for publication. He wrote in a letter of 1696, "He who knows only what I have published does not know me."[3]

Nevertheless, despite the difficulties, a systematic attempt to develop a critical study of his philosophy of religion in the light of his epistemology will be made here.

Theory of Knowledge

Logical Methodology. Leibniz's logical methodology is developed in some of his earliest philosophical works and provides a good starting point for his theory of knowledge. His early *Dissertation on the Art of Combinations*, published in 1666, envisions the ideas of a universal language and a logical calculus, which might ultimately help him verify his claim that "Perfect demonstrations are possible in all disciplines." A combination of logic and experience, he believes, will provide the solid foundation for a cognitively productive methodology:

> There are two primary propositions. The first is the principle of all theorems or necessary propositions: *what is (so) either is or is not (so)*, or **conversely**. The other is the basis of all observations or contingent propositions: *something exists.*[4]

Here we see the young Leibniz, at about the age of twenty, planning the development of a logical method which will fulfill the rationalistic dream of achieving comprehensive scientific knowledge. (Far from seeing any conflict between demonstration and experimentation, he views them as complementary operations of reason.[5]) In a letter thirty years later, he wrote about how excited he was "by the classification and order which I perceived in its principles," when he began studying logic seriously "as a lad of thirteen."[6] His new discoveries, as a teenager at the University of Leipzig, brought about a shift in intellectual commitments: "I had penetrated far into the land of the scholastics when mathematics and the modern authors made me emerge from it while I was still young." But he maintains that even after "I had freed myself from the yoke of Aristotle," he remained convinced that "there was a means to establish in philosophy something solid through clear demonstrations."[7]

Like other rationalists, including Descartes, Leibniz was inspired by the precision and rigorous certainty of mathematics. Yet, as he wrote in 1702,

> there is a calculus more important than those of arithmetic and geometry which depends on the analysis of ideas. This would be a universal characteristic, and its formation seems to me one of the most important things that can be undertaken.[8]

This is one of many ambitious projects Leibniz never completed. But the goal itself is impressive and indicative of his rationalistic epistemological commitments (anticipating such developments of symbolic logic as were later made by Bertrand Russell.) Leibniz envisioned a universal language, the "characteristic," which would employ mathematical symbols for purposes of strict logical reasoning in all the various areas of human knowledge. This new system of reasoning would involve a generalized application of a method which so far has been successfully practiced only in mathematics; but Leibniz is convinced that it could be made to bear fruit in such branches of thought as physics, metaphysics, and ethics.[9] In a now famous passage, he vividly communicates his dream:

> if we could find characters or signs appropriate for expressing all our thoughts as definitely and as exactly as arithmetic expresses numbers or geometric analysis expresses lines, we could in all subjects *in so far as they are amenable to reasoning* accomplish what is done in Arithmetic and Geometry. For all inquiries which depend on reasoning would be performed by the transposition of characters and by a calculus, which would immediately facilitate the discovery of beautiful results. . . . Moreover, we should be able to convince the world what we should have found or concluded, since it would be easy to verify the calculation either by doing it over or by trying tests. . . . And if someone would doubt my results, I should say to him: "Let us calculate, Sir," and thus by taking to pen and ink, we should soon settle the question.[10]

The first step required to realize this project is the development of the universal language using symbolic characters:

> there must be invented, I reflected, a kind of alphabet of human thoughts, and through the connection of its letters and the analysis of words which are composed out of them, everything else can be discovered and judged.

Leibniz notes that even Aristotle and Descartes failed to conceive of such a project. And Leibniz imagines that the universal calculus will provide mankind with

> a new instrument which will enhance the capabilities of the mind to a far greater extent than optical instruments strengthen the eyes, and will supersede the microscope and telescope to the same extent that reason is superior to cyesight.[11]

In his "Two Studies in the Logical Calculus" of 1679, Leibniz tries to specify and exemplify his method. He reminds us that a statement or logical proposition can be analyzed in terms of a subject term that denotes what is being talked about and a predicate term that denotes what is being said about the subject. "To every term whatever may be assigned its *characteristic number*, which we may use in calculating, as we use the term in reasoning." Terms are identical in meaning and can use the same characteristic symbol if either "can be substituted in place of the other without destroying truth, as triangle and trilateral, quadrangle and quadrilateral." A quasi-mathematical rule can be generated for the combining of terms:

> when the concept of a given term is composed directly out of the concepts of two or more other terms, then the characteristic number of the given term is to be produced by multiplying the characteristic number of the terms composing it. For example, since man is a rational animal, if the number of animal is *a*, for instance 2, and the number of rational is *r*, for instance 3, the number of man, or *b*, will be 2×3 or 6.

To the extent that they can be distinctly thought and precisely defined, Leibniz believes that all objects of experience can be represented in the calculus. The technique can be employed at the level of arguments, as well as at the propositional level. For example, if every human being is a rational animal and every animal is a substance, then every human being must be a substance.[12]

This takes us to a particularly important and controversial aspect of Leibniz's logical theory, which greatly influences his metaphysics—his belief that all predicates of any substance are contained in its very concept (or subject term). Every true, affirmative, universal proposition establishes "a certain connection between the predicate and the subject. . . . such that the predicate is said to be in the subject, or to be contained in it. . . . So when I say, 'All gold is a metal,' I mean by this only that the notion of metal is contained in the notion of gold."[13]

Leibniz boldly concludes from this that in principle every truth "may be reduced to the principle of contradiction," if ever "its terms are understood" completely. Thus, for God, who "understands everything a priori" and all at once, all truths are reducible to identities; "whereas we know hardly anything adequately, few things a priori, and most things through experience" alone, so that for us the principle of contradiction does not suffice, but "other principles and other criteria must be applied" for the attaining of knowledge.[14] (We shall soon consider these "other principles".)

Notice, however, that Leibniz is assuming here that because all truths establish a relationship between subject and predicate, that relationship is necessary, it could, in principle, be known *a priori*, and it is reducible to the **law of noncontradiction** or of identity. This seems to be the fundamental error of his philosophy. Even if it is true, for instance, that all extraterrestrial bodies are places devoid of life, this is not a logically necessary truth, since it is logically possible that some extraterrestrial body could have been inhabited by living things; it seems highly implausible that such a truth could be known *a priori* even if we fully comprehended its terms; and there is no identity of meaning between the subject term (extraterrestrial bodies) and the predicate (places devoid of life). The relationship between subject and predicate here is a contingent one that can be known only through experience, so that this is an empirical (or synthetic) truth rather than a conceptual (or analytic) one. Thus, we might challenge Leibniz's basic claim that in every true universal affirmative statement the subject term (analytically) contains the predicate.

What are those "other principles" that supposedly follow from the view that the "*complete or perfect concept of an individual substance involves all its predicates, past, present, and future,*" besides the one that all truths are theoretically reducible to identities? In his paper on "First Truths," he explains that what was later called his "Principle of Sufficient Reason" follows—namely, the "axiom that *there is nothing without a reason, or no effect without a cause.*" Otherwise, an element of irrationality would be introduced which would render it impossible, even in theory, to reduce every truth to an identity. This will turn out to be the most crucial controversial Leibnizian principle for our purposes, and we shall later consider it further. For now, we can observe that Leibniz presents it as a rationalistic "axiom" required by his equally controversial (and more basic) claim that truth "is always either expressly or implicitly identical." A second principle which supposedly follows from Leibniz's identity conception of truth is his "Identity of Indiscernibles," that "*there cannot be two individual things in nature which differ only numerically.*" If two things (i.e., clones) had exactly the same set of predicates, we should be able to characterize them by a single subject term. Leibniz appears correct here. Even if we employ different terms for things denoted by the same set of predicates (such as the planet Venus and the morning star), we should be willing to acknowledge that such things are numerically identical. A third principle that follows from Leibniz's identity view of truth is "that *there are no purely extrinsic denominations* which have no basis at all in the denominated thing itself. For the concept of the denominated subject necessarily involves the concept of the predicate."[15] The purpose of this principle might be to help us avoid the arbitrary characterizations of the **nominalists**, which might lead to subjective **relativism**.

In another of Leibniz's early papers, "On Freedom," he distinguishes between necessary and contingent statements: "A necessary proposition is one whose contrary implies a contradiction; such are all identities." He says that all such truths have a "metaphysical or geometrical necessity." It might seem that Leibniz's theory makes all truths necessary in this sense because their subject terms analytically contain their predicate terms. And, indeed, this is the case for God, whose intuition is comprehensive and instantaneous. "In contingent truths, however, though the predicate inheres in the subject, we can never demonstrate this, nor can the proposition ever be reduced to an equation or an identity" by us, because we lack insight into the essential relationship between the terms. Thus, some truths are contingent for us. These can be known in two ways—through experience or through reason. Our knowledge of contingent truths is "by experience when we perceive a thing distinctly enough by our senses; by reason, however, when we use the general principle that nothing happens without a reason."[16]

Leibniz appears mistaken in holding that the difference between necessary and contingent truths is merely relative to our way of apprehending them. To collapse this distinction from some allegedly absolute perspective, as Leibniz does, serves only to reinforce his otherwise dubious identity theory of truth. Second, Leibniz's view of necessity here appears to be too narrow. Certainly all propositions whose opposites are contradictory are logically necessary. But there might be other truths, such as Kant's "synthetic *a priori*" propositions, which could not be otherwise, even though their predicates are not analytically contained in their subject concepts, such as the claim that all deliberate attempts to deceive other persons are immoral. Third, we might observe (with Locke) that all truths which are contingent in the sense that they could be (or could have been) otherwise are knowable only through concrete experience, which is not, however, confined to that derived from external sensation. There seems no compelling reason to trust in the principle of sufficient reason as a nonempirical way of achieving knowledge of contingent truths.

One final topic to consider in connection with Leibniz's logical methodology is his treatment of probability. He maintains that even when his method cannot give us deductive certainty, it will be valuable.

> In such cases we shall attain an *infinite approximation* or, when conjectures have to be made, we shall determine by demonstrative reason the *degree of probability* which can be drawn from the data. . . . Therefore I am particularly interested in that part of logic, hitherto hardly touched, which investigates the *estimation of degrees of probability*.[17]

Here Leibniz seems closer to Locke than to Descartes. Indeed, in his critical commentary on Locke, Leibniz writes at some length on this subject. He holds that probability judgments, such as historical assertions, are deserving of the name of knowledge and that a carefully developed logic of probability is lacking and needed.[18] Leibniz is remarkable as a rationalist who appreciates the value of probability judgements in helping us to stretch beyond the limited bounds of certainty. And, despite the reservations about his methodology expressed in this subsection, he was a more capable logician than either Descartes or Locke and used logical argumentation more effectively than either of them typically did.

On Descartes. Leibniz's analysis of Descartes is mainly to be found in his *Critical Remarks Concerning the General Part of Descartes' Principles* (1692). We recall that soon after entering the University of Leipzig, he was exposed to the new philosophies of modern thinkers, including Descartes, and turned away from an allegiance to Aristotle and scholasticism. Because he is a modern rationalist who was significantly influenced by Descartes, it is tempting to think of Leibniz as a Cartesian. Nevertheless, in a letter to Jacob Thomasius, one of his professors at Leipzig, written a few years after finishing his schooling, Leibniz emphatically asserts, "I am anything but a Cartesian," and that even in that era of scientific genius "I approve of more things in Aristotle's books on physics than in the meditations of Descartes; so far am I from being a Cartesian."[19]

In a letter to Malebranche (1679), who was then perhaps the most famous living Cartesian, he expresses mixed opinions:

> Descartes has said some fine things; his was a most penetrating and judicious mind. But it is impossible to do everything at once, and he has given us only some beautiful beginnings, without getting to the bottom of things. It seems to me that he is still far from the true analysis and the general art of discovery.

A few paragraphs later he explains that the underlying problem is a yet inadequate methodology: "In short, I could write a scholarly work . . . on what no Cartesian, whoever he may be, can succeed in doing without discovering some method which goes further than that of Descartes."[20] In later works, Leibniz makes it clear that the weakness of Descartes's methodology is most conspicuous in argumentation that fails to be sufficiently rigorous and cogent.[21] Near the end of the letter to Malebranche, he writes, "If I have the leisure, I hope some day to show, by some effective evidence, how far Descartes was from giving us the foundations of the true method."[22] But the closest he ever comes to fulfilling this hope is in his *Critical Remarks* of 1692, to which we now turn.

This work is a systematic evaluation of Descartes's *Principles of Philosophy* and quite effectively discriminates between its strengths and its weaknesses. Leibniz indicates that he is unimpressed with Descartes's ideal of "doubting anything in which there is the slightest uncertainty," preferring to admit shades of gray between the black and white extremes of ignorance and certainty—"The degree of assent or dissent which any proposition deserves must be considered"; and he questions whether there is any serious "advantage in considering as false what is doubtful." He praises Descartes's commitment to the *cogito* as a primary truth as "excellent" but denies that it is unique as a primary truth, since another is that "Various things are thought by me." In other words, we can look to the object pole of mental experience for a primary truth as well as to its subject pole. Leibniz dismisses the appeal to God's character as a warrant for all knowledge as "a sort of theatrical effect," explaining that we can know some basic truths whether or not there is a God and that fallibility and imperfection are quite compatible with God's existence.[23]

He comments that Descartes seems to have borrowed Anselm's argument for God's existence by way of the writings of Aquinas, who criticized it. Leibniz does a good job of drawing out a logical structure from the argument and says it is "valid, provided it is taken for granted that the most perfect Being or the necessary Being is possible and does not imply contradiction, or, which comes to the same, that an essence from which existence would follow is possible." Without a proof of God's possibility, he writes, God's existence "cannot be admitted as perfectly demonstrated by such an argument. . . . Nevertheless, this argument reveals the exalted privilege of the divine nature, that He need only to be possible in order to exist." He claims that Descartes's argument that God must exist as the only adequate cause of "the idea of the most perfect Being" is "still more doubtful" than the ontological argument, because it presupposes without justification that we have such a clear and distinct idea of a most perfect Being, without, for example, showing that it is even a consistent notion. And the cosmological argument, from our existence as finite beings to God's existence as ultimate cause, contains "the same defect," as used by Descartes, because it makes the same unjustified assumption.[24]

Leibniz takes Descartes to task for failing to struggle productively with the problem of human freedom in the light of divine preordination. Instead of untying the knot with a plausible solution, Descartes resorts "to cutting the knot" by weakly protesting "that our minds are finite and unable to understand such things." He writes that truths—whether of faith or of nature—cannot contradict each other. "Hence, if you want to think philosophically, it will be necessary that you take up again any reasoning which has some justification and yet seems to involve contradiction and that you find out where the mistake lies."[25] Descartes has failed to make a serious effort to do this regarding the issue of human freedom and divine preordination.

Leibniz repudiates Descartes's principle of clarity and distinctness. To say that "Only what is clear and distinct ought to be accepted as true," for Leibniz, "has no value unless better criteria of clearness and distinctness than those given by Descartes are established." But, even then, the principle leaves us with the black-and-white dichotomy mentioned earlier, ignoring valuable degrees of probable belief. Leibniz admits that "the part of logic so very useful in life, which deals with the estimation of degrees of probability" had not been developed in Descartes's time and reminds us that he himself has done work in this area.[26] Leibniz suggests that Descartes, in his effort to philosophize from scratch, does not give sufficient credit to his predecessors:

> It would be fair, I think, to attribute to the ancients what is due to them and not to obfuscate their merits by a silence which is spiteful and harmful to ourselves. What Aristotle taught in his Logic may not be sufficient to discover truth, yet it usually suffices to judge correctly where we only deal with necessary consequences.[27]

Leibniz seems to have been more sensitive than either Descartes or Locke to Newton's idea that in our thinking we stand on the shoulders of giants.

Finally, Leibniz expresses a reservation about Descartes's attempt to appeal only to mathematical principles in the area of physics. This seems to ignore or minimize the vital role played by God in the workings of physical nature and to reduce God to a "*deus ex machina.*" Leibniz sounds almost like Pascal in his scolding in the following passage:

> We ought to recognize in God not only the architect of the material world, but also and even more the king of minds, whose intelligence has ordained everything for the best and who has created the world as the most perfect of all possible states, ruled by the wisest and most powerful monarch.[28]

Of all the passages from the *Critical Remarks* considered here (and, of course, it is necessary to be quite selective for lack of space and time), this is the only one that seems to be off the mark. Descartes could and would willingly agree with the last quoted sentence from Leibniz. Yet Descartes would be right to object that the divine nature and activity are not appropriate considerations for the explanations of physical science. Apart from this point, the aspects of Leibniz's critique discussed here are remarkably insightful, even-handed, and fair-minded. He has learned much from Descartes's mistakes, assimilated his more valuable contributions, and rendered himself ready to move on beyond him.

On Locke. Leibniz's critique of Locke is contained in a very long but often brilliant dialogue, *New Essays on the Human Understanding*, in which the character Philalethes represents Locke, while Theophilus expresses the views of Leibniz, with which we shall be concerned. In his Preface Leibniz begins with a tribute: "The essay on the human Understanding by an illustrious Englishman is one of the most beautiful and esteemed works of the time." He recognizes that their "systems differ very much," Locke's being empirical and thus more Aristotelian, whereas Leibniz's own is rationalistic and thus more Platonic; and he admits that Locke's is "more popular," while he has been "forced at times to be a little more esoteric and more abstract,"[29] a contrast which he fears is to his disadvantage.

The first point of substantive disagreement and the part of the *New Essays* that is most well-known concerns Locke's rejection of innate ideas.

> The question is to know whether the soul in itself is entirely empty, like the tablet on which nothing has yet been written (*tabula rasa*) according to Aristotle and the author of the *Essay*, and whether all that is traced thereon comes solely from the senses and from experience; or whether the soul contains originally the principles of several notions and doctrines which external objects merely awaken on occasions, as I believe, with Plato.

Leibniz recognizes that sense experience is "necessary for all our actual knowledge" but denies that it is "sufficient to give us the whole of it, since the senses never give anything except examples, that is to say, particular or individual truths." As he explains, no matter how many examples are drawn from sense experience to support a general truth, they will never "suffice to establish the universal necessity of this same truth; for it does not follow that what has happened will happen in the same way." (A few decades later Hume drove home this lesson relentlessly.) Thus, the necessary and universal truths of mathematics, logic, metaphysics, and **ethics** "can only come from internal principles which are called innate,"[30] unless they are to be dismissed as contingent and merely probable.

Leibniz suspects that he and Locke may not be as far apart on this issue as the language of innate ideas might suggest. Although Locke explicitly rejects innate knowledge, he admits that we get ideas from reflection as well as from sensation. Leibniz maintains that "reflection is nothing else than attention to what is in us" already without input from the senses and concludes that Locke should not then deny "that there is much that is innate in our mind."[31] Leibniz seems either to miss or to gloss over Locke's point here. Prior to sense experience, for Locke, the mind is devoid of cognitive content, so that there is nothing on which it can reflect. After it has experienced objects through sensation, there is mental activity on which it can reflect.

Leibniz plays with the *tabula rasa* metaphor somewhat to illustrate his claim: If the mind or soul is originally a blank tablet, then at first it contains truths only potentially, "as the figure of Hercules is in marble when the marble is entirely indifferent toward receiving this figure or some other" such as that of Venus. On the other hand, if, as Leibniz believes, the mind or soul is already conditioned to know certain truths, it would be as if "there were veins in the block which should mark out the figure of Hercules rather than other figures," even though, of course, we might need to do some work in order to discover those veins and expose them by polishing and removing obstacles blocking them from clear view. This is not an argument so much as a figure of speech. Yet Leibniz concludes, "It is thus that ideas and truths are innate in us, as inclinations, dispositions, habits, or natural capacities." He mistakenly imagines that "our able author claims that there is nothing *virtual* in us."[32] But, in fact, Locke not only admits the "natural capacities" championed by Leibniz but also explicitly claims that "nobody, I think, ever denied that the mind was capable of knowing several truths. The capacity . . . is innate; the knowledge acquired."[33] Yet, as if unaware of this passage, Leibniz asks and answers a rhetorical question:

> Is our soul then such a blank that, besides the images imprinted from without, it is nothing? This is not an opinion (I am sure) which our judicious author can approve.

He concludes,

> Thus I am led to believe that at bottom his opinion on this point is not different from mine.[34]

Leibniz's suspicion is correct. Although there might be disagreement between them as to whether the mind can reflect prior to and independent of sense experience, their agreement regarding innate "natural capacities" is much stronger than might appear at first blush.

Leibniz says (through his spokesman, Theophilus),

> I have always favored, as I do still, the innate idea of God, which M. Descartes maintained, and consequently other innate ideas which cannot come to us from the senses. . . . there are ideas and principles which do not come to us from the senses, and which we find in us without forming them, although the senses give us occasion to become conscious of them.

His key illustration of such innate ideas and principles other than what concerns God is drawn from mathematics:

> In a sense it must be said that all arithmetic and all geometry are innate and are in us virtually, so that they may be found there if we consider attentively and arrange what is already in the mind, without making use of any truth learned by experience.[35]

Leibniz seems only partly correct here. We do normally have a natural capacity to discover mathematical ideas and principles, which can therefore be said to be virtually (or potentially) "in" the mind. But they are not innate in the sense of being there prior to concrete experience (except as potential). It seems false or misleading (or both) to say that we can grasp them "without making use of any truth learned by experience." It would be better to say, using Leibniz's own previous terminology, that concrete experience "gives us occasion to become conscious of them." On the occasion of such experience, the mind reasons to the truths of mathematics. But this is compatible with Locke's version of the *tabula rasa* theory.

In one of the most famous paragraphs from the *New Essays*, Leibniz writes, "This *tabula rasa*, of which so much is said, is, in my opinion, only a fiction." He claims that even if we interpret the theory to mean "that the soul has naturally and originally only bare faculties," it is inadequate. The view of mental faculties "without some act," he holds, is a fiction identical to "the pure powers" of scholastic philosophers. Although he repudiates the *tabula rasa* theory as "a fiction," there is more dogmatic assertion here than argumentation. In response to this view and Locke's comparison of the mind to a dark closet before the light of experience is let in through the senses, Leibniz protests:

> Has the soul windows? does it resemble tablets? is it like wax? It is evident that all who think of the soul thus, make it at bottom corporeal. This axiom received among the philosophers will be opposed by me, *that there is nothing in the soul which does not come from the senses.* But the soul itself and its affections must be excepted.

Thus, for Leibniz, the mind, or rational soul, can be aware of itself prior to and independent of external experience. Furthermore, through reflection on itself, the mind can become aware of certain innate ideas contained within: "Now the soul comprises being, substance, unity, identity, cause, perception, reason, and many other notions which the senses cannot give." Through these innate ideas the knowing mind can establish the correlation between itself and external reality on which rationalism traditionally insists. So Leibniz claims, "The nature of things and the nature of the mind agree."[36] At this point Leibniz has sided with Descartes against Locke and Hume, and the battle is joined between rationalism and empiricism.

Leibniz disapproves of Locke's treatment of such important ideas as those of infinity and substance. The idea of infinity or the absolute, he maintains, "is in us internally, like that of being." Therefore, against Locke, he contends that it is "a positive idea."[37] Unfortunately, he does not provide convincing argumentation to substantiate the claim. He thinks Locke's stripping things of all their predicates and then asking for detailed knowledge of substance "is to demand the impossible," since any details specified would have to be in terms of predicates. To admit that we cannot specify our knowledge of a substance except in terms of its predicates is not tantamount to confessing that substance is "*something, I know not what*." His conclusion, then, is that our "consideration of substance, very inconsiderable as it seems to be, is not so void and sterile as is thought."[38] Here again, Locke's view appears closer to being correct. The reason our idea of substance is "inconsiderable" (to use Leibniz's own word) is that it cannot be known in itself, apart from the way it appears through its "attributes or predicates." And what is at stake here is the claim of **phenomenalism**, that all we can know of things are their appearances.

So far, Leibniz's theory of ideas does not seem to be as successful as that of Locke. But it is in his theory of knowledge that Locke has the most problems. Let us consider three points in connection with these epistemological problems. First, Leibniz is correct in observing that Locke's account of knowledge as our perception of the agreement or disagreement of ideas is "taking *knowledge* in a narrower meaning, that is, for knowledge of truth" and that the concept "is employed still more generally, in such a way that it is found also in ideas or terms, before we come to propositions or truths." For example, when one knows about triangles, that knowledge involves a relationship between his mind, as the subject of experience, and the idea, as the object of experience. Second, Leibniz acutely suggests how we can avoid Locke's problem of establishing a correspondence between our ideas of external objects, to which we have access, and "things outside of us," to which we do not—by shifting from the traditional correspondence theory to something like what later evolved as the coherence theory:

> I believe that the true *criterion* as regards the objects of the senses is the *connection* of phenomena, that is, the connection of that which takes place in different places and times, and in the experience of different men, who are themselves, each to the others, very important phenomena on this score.

Although he does not develop this into a full-blown theory, the valuable germ of the coherence theory can be detected here. Third, on the topic of the "reality" of human knowledge, where Locke has particular trouble, Leibniz is not tough enough. He does protest that empiricism is ill-equipped to establish the "reality" of knowledge: "Our certainty would be slight or rather none, if it had no other foundation for simple ideas than that which comes from the senses." He also repeats his claim that "the ground of our certainty in regard to universal and eternal truths lies in the ideas themselves, independently of the senses."[39] But he fails to point out that existential knowledge of things other than the self cannot be established as "real" on Locke's view that we only have direct, immediate access to our own ideas and knowledge therefore consists merely in the awareness of relationships among our ideas.

Leibniz is considerably more sympathetic to Descartes's ontological argument than Locke was. Unlike Hume and Kant, Leibniz agrees with the view that existence is a predicate "when it is said that a thing exists or that it has real existence" because such a judgment establishes a "connection between these two notions" of the thing and existence. He denies that the argument is merely a trick of reason ("a **paralogism**") but concedes that "it is an imperfect demonstration" because it presupposes "that this idea of the all-great or all-perfect being is possible" and implies no contradiction. But he adds that the causal argument used by Descartes is subject to the very same "defect . . . that it supposes that there is in us such an idea, that is, that God is possible." Yet, even if we did have an adequate idea of God, it would not follow, as Descartes maintains, that that idea must ultimately come from God. "And, secondly, this same argument does not sufficiently prove that the idea of God, if we have it, must come from the original."[40] Although this critique is directed explicitly against Descartes rather than Locke, it seems apparent that it calls into question Locke's cosmological argument as well (so that it is appropriate for Leibniz to include it in his analysis of Locke). Given Locke's empiricism, it is difficult to substantiate even the claim that we have an adequate idea of infinity or perfection, let alone that something exists corresponding to such an idea.

Leibniz holds, despite these critical reservations, that "almost all the means which have been employed to prove the existence of God are good, and might serve, if they were perfected." He particularly praises Locke's reasoning from the existence of finite knowing beings, such as myself, to that of God as their only adequate cause. But he also endorses an argument from design ("drawn from the order of things") and reminds us that he has discovered a related argument from "Pre-established Harmony," which "furnishes a new and incontestable means" of proving God's existence. Whereas the popular argument from design leads only to a "moral certainty," he claims that his new argument (which we shall examine in the next section) produces "a necessity altogether metaphysical."[41]

In general, Leibniz's critique of Locke is uneven. He makes some valuable points and effectively draws the contrast between rationalism and empiricism. But more than anything else from our point of view, the *New Essays* is useful as an introduction to Leibniz's own epistemology, which is developed in other works and to which we now turn.

Epistemology and Metaphysical Implications. Leibniz's epistemology and its metaphysical implications were not presented in a sustained and systematic manner in any one or two works comparable to Descartes's *Rules* and *Discourse* or Locke's *Essay*. Instead, they are developed in bits and pieces through many works written over a forty-year period, from "What Is an Idea?" (1676) to his correspondence with Samuel Clarke (1715–16). To the extent that it seems productive to do so, we shall try to focus on his *Discourse on Metaphysics* (1686), "Principles of Nature and of Grace" (1714), and "Monadology" (1714) in this subsection because they are nowadays the most studied of his philosophical works. But first we need briefly to consider the groundwork previously laid in a couple of shorter papers.

In "What Is an Idea?" he defines an idea, the object of mental experience, as "*something which is in our mind.*" He goes on to explain that an idea can be "in" our mind even when we are not consciously aware of it— "we have an idea of a thing even if we are not actually thinking it but know that we can think it when the occasion arises." Thus, one's idea of a right triangle is "in" his mind even when it is not in his thoughts. Leibniz seems to anticipate **pragmatists** like William James when he writes that the function of an idea is that it "*not only leads to the thing but also expresses it.*" But he is clearly pre-Kantian in specifying that it is the thing represented by the idea that sets the conditions to which the idea and its expression must correspond. He is not a naive correspondence theorist (or representationalist) and realizes that ideas do not perfectly resemble their objects. Yet adequate ideas lead us to experientially satisfying objects: "although the idea of a circle is not exactly like a circle, we may yet infer from the idea truths which experience would undoubtedly confirm concerning the true circle."[42] This early two-page paper succinctly articulates the core of Leibniz's theory of ideas.

The first published paper in which he formulates his mature thoughts on epistemology is "Reflections on Knowledge, Truth, and Ideas" (1684), which is important for setting out his basic epistemological terminology. An idea can be either *obscure* ("when it does not suffice for the recognition of things after they have been experienced") or *clear* ("when it is sufficient to enable me to recognize the things represented"). Clear ideas can be "either *indistinct* or *distinct*; distinct ideas are either *adequate* or *inadequate*, *symbolic* or *intuitive*; perfect knowledge, finally, is that which is both *adequate* and *intuitive*." He explains that an idea of something is indistinct when "I am not able to enumerate separately the characteristics required to distinguish the thing from others, even though such characteristics and distinctions are really in the thing itself and in the data which enable us to analyze the notion." For example, even though people have experienced both birch trees and aspens and heard them properly identified, their ideas of them are "indistinct" if they cannot distinguish between a birch and an aspen. Leibniz's standards for adequacy in ideas are very high:

> if every element included in a distinct concept is again distinctly known, and if the analysis is carried through to the end, then the knowledge is *adequate*. Of course, our human knowledge reveals perhaps no perfect example of this kind of knowledge, but the knowledge of numbers comes pretty close to it.

To the extent that we are incapable of having adequate ideas, perfect knowledge is impossible. Finally, our ideas are "intuitive" when we can "perceive all at once the whole nature of the objects" and "symbolic" when we cannot do this but have to "substitute for the objects themselves defined signs." And he warns that "we can have only symbolic knowledge of complex ideas,"[43] such as kingdoms and philosophical systems. Here it seems that Leibniz is even more exacting than Descartes was about what will qualify as certain knowledge (although, as we have seen, he also pays more attention than Descartes did to probable knowledge).

So much for the early foundations of Leibniz's epistemology. For the mature treatments we can look to works written in the last thirty years of his life, especially his most famous ones, *Discourse on Metaphysics*, "The Principles of Nature and of Grace," and "The Monadology," three works which overlap a great deal in content. Leibniz's first great work is an untitled essay, which he sent to a count in 1686 to pass on to Arnauld for critical review and which Leibniz's accompanying letter described as a "discourse on metaphysics." (It seems that the entire work was not forwarded to Arnauld but only Leibniz's synopsis of its conclusions; this led to four years of correspondence between Leibniz and Arnauld, with the count acting as intermediary, between 1686 and 1690.) The *Discourse* is a wide-ranging work, both philosophical and theological. For now, however, we shall be especially concerned with its epistemological principles and the metaphysical doctrines to which they lead.

As we have seen, Leibniz rejects the *tabula rasa* theory of the empiricists. In the *Discourse* he notes that "Aristotle preferred to compare our souls to blank tablets prepared for writing, and he maintained that nothing is in the understanding which does not come through the senses." Although he admits that Aristotle's view conforms to popular thinking here, as usual, he asserts that "Plato thinks more profoundly" and that there are ideas "in the soul whether one is conceiving of them or not" which "come from an inner experience," including "those conceptions which I have of myself and of my thoughts, and consequently of being, of substance, of action, of identity, and of many others."[44]

As he points out in "Monadology," we are not always consciously aware of all our ideas and must distinguish between perception and **apperception**. In his "Principles" he explains that a perception is the internal state of the mind in representing objects while apperception is the *"consciousness* or the reflective knowledge of this inner state." So apperception requires, in addition to having ideas, that we be consciously aware of having ideas—or, in other words, it requires an element of self-consciousness or reflective awareness. Thus, we may have innate ideas without realizing it and be mistakenly led to presume a *tabula rasa* theory of mental experience.[45] And if we do have innate ideas, then universal and necessary knowledge is possible for us; otherwise, it is problematic.

The mere having and contemplating of ideas does not constitute knowledge, as Leibniz argues in the *Discourse*. We can mistakenly assume that we understand an idea, whereas it lacks coherence because "it is an impossible truth or at least is incompatible with others" to which we try to relate it.[46] As we have seen, in order to lead to knowledge, an idea must be not only clear and distinct, but adequate and intuitively apprehended; Leibniz briefly reviews these criteria here. An idea that meets these requirements will "afford a conception so complete that the concept shall be sufficient for the understanding of it and for the deduction of all the predicates" of which it is the subject. We might well ask whether this requirement, from the *Discourse*,[47] is not too stringent to be practically useful. Thus, a true knowledge of Alexander the Great, to use Leibniz's own example, comprehends all the qualities and claims "which can be truly uttered regarding him." But only God can have this kind of knowledge; we cannot know any existing being, including ourselves, so comprehensively.

A principle that follows from this is that of the identity of indiscernibles, which holds that "it is not true that two substances may be exactly alike and differ only numerically."[48] If we had a thoroughgoing knowledge of any two things, we would recognize that what prevents them from being identical is that there are some predicates which they do not commonly share. As Leibniz makes clear in "Monadology," this principle is important in defense of **pluralism**, for preserving the ontological (or metaphysical) uniqueness of every existing thing.[49]

Another crucial Leibnizian principle that follows from the axiom that the perfect knowledge of anything must involve a comprehension of all its predicates is that of sufficient reason. As he writes in his "Principles," "*nothing happens without a sufficient reason*; that is to say, that nothing happens without its being possible for him who should sufficiently understand things, to give a reason sufficient to determine why it is so and not otherwise." This legitimacy of demanding and expecting rational explanation for everything extends even to the ultimate such question, "*Why is there something rather than nothing?*"[50]

But this principle of sufficient reason, in turn, provides Leibniz with his own unique argument for God. Not only must there be sufficient reason for something to exist in general and for individual things to exist in particular. But the universe as a whole requires a sufficient reason for being, which could only be God.[51] We shall analyze this argument in detail in the next section. For now, we should observe the important metaphysical implication of this principle to which Leibniz's epistemology has led him. A second such metaphysical implication is that this is the best of all possible worlds. As Leibniz writes in the *Discourse*, "God acts always in the most perfect and most desirable manner possible" and "does nothing out of order." Therefore, he concludes, among the worlds that might have been created, God "has chosen the most perfect, that is to say the one which is at the same time the simplest in hypotheses and the richest in phenomena."[52] So what Leibniz means by his Platonic claim that this is the best possible world (as he clearly explains in "Monadology") is that it contains "as great a variety as possible, but with the greatest order."[53] A third metaphysical implication is that the world is designed according to a system of preestablished harmony. Because the principle of sufficient reason universally applies and God created the best of all possible worlds, reality is shot through with intelligible order. In "Monadology" Leibniz speaks of "the *pre-established harmony* between all substances, since they are all representations of one and the same universe"; and he writes that this "perfect harmony" relates "the physical kingdom of nature" and "the moral kingdom of grace" to one another in an orderly way, so that spiritual progress can occur through natural means.[54]

Now that we have considered three important metaphysical implications of the principle of sufficient reason, let us return to Leibniz's epistemology. Thinking by means of ideas can produce knowledge of necessary and contingent truths. As he says in "Monadology," "Truths of reasoning are necessary and their opposite is impossible, and those of fact are contingent and their opposite is possible." These two kinds of truth depend on two different epistemological principles. Necessary truths of reasoning are founded on the principle of "*contradiction*, in virtue of which we judge that to be *false* which involves contradiction, and that *true*, which is opposed or contradictory to the false." Thus, without interviewing the man, one can know *a priori* that you cannot possibly live next door to a married bachelor, since logical reasoning dictates that it must be true (by definition) that no bachelors are married. By contrast, contingent truths of fact, whose opposites are not logically contradictory, appeal to the principle of "*sufficient reason*, in virtue of which we hold that no fact can be real or existent, no statement true, unless there be a sufficient reason why it is so and not otherwise, although most often these reasons cannot be known to us."[55] Thus, there is a reason why this critical analysis of Leibniz's philosophy has been written, and that reason is at least theoretically knowable. Mathematical truths are rationally necessary, while those dependent on sense experience have to do with contingent matters of fact.[56] Notice that by analyzing all truth in this manner and making it rest on one or the other of these two principles, Leibniz eliminates any possibility of irrationality or absurdity from the world.

Monadic Theory of Substances. Like Descartes and Locke, Leibniz subscribes to a substance-based metaphysics—that is to say, his view of reality is built on an analysis of different kinds of substances and their various interrelationships. Since metaphysics is a study of ultimate reality, any substance-based metaphysics will focus on the centrality of substance, which must be viewed as "the most real thing."[57] In *New Essays* Leibniz says, "I believe that the consideration of substance is a point of philosophy of the greatest importance and of the greatest fruitfulness."[58]

We humans, God, and the Pacific Ocean are all substances. In "Principles," Leibniz analyzes this central metaphysical concept:

> *Substance* is a being capable of action. It is simple or compound. *Simple substance* is that which has no parts. *Compound* substance is the collection of simple substances or **monads**.

He notes that the term comes from the Greek *Monas*, meaning indivisible unity.[59] In "Monadology" (which thus means the study of monads) he writes,

> The *monad* of which we shall speak is merely a simple substance, which enters into composites; *simple*, that is to say, without parts. And there must be simple substances, since there are composites; for the composite is only a collection or *aggregatum* of simple substances.... And these monads are the true atoms of nature, and, in a word, the elements of all things.[60]

He goes on to say in both his "Principles" and his "Monadology" that monads, because they are simple, "cannot be formed or decomposed" but "can only begin by creation and end by annihilation." In "Monadology," he avers, "The monads have no windows through which anything can enter or depart." This picturesque metaphor of monads as "windowless" connotes that they cannot be naturally affected from outside themselves; as Leibniz writes, all natural changes they undergo "proceed from an *internal principle*, since an external cause could not influence their inner being."[61]

In the *Discourse* Leibniz pushes the point even further: "In the strictly metaphysical sense no external cause acts upon us excepting God alone."[62] Thus, as he says in "Monadology,"

> in simple substances the influence of one monad upon another is purely *ideal* and it can have its effect only through the intervention of God.[63]

And again in the *Discourse*:

> We may say, therefore, that God is for us the only immediate external object, and that we see things through him.... Thus God alone constitutes the relation or communication between substances. It is through him that the phenomena of the one meet and accord with the phenomena of the others, so that there may be a reality in our perceptions.[64]

This is surely counterintuitive. If we ask what accounts for this conveniently orderly arrangement, Leibniz's handy answer is that it is due to God's preestablished harmony for this best of all possible worlds, that is, it is the result of divine providence.

In "On the Improvement of Metaphysics and on the Concept of Substance" (published in 1694), Leibniz develops his dynamic view of substance in terms of "the concept of force." In the spirit of the Newtonian age, he writes, "This force of action, I affirm, is inherent in all substances, and always engenders some action; that is, corporeal substance itself—and the same is true of spiritual substance—is never inactive." He criticizes Descartes and the Cartesians who present a static view of physical substance as merely passive extension or impenetrability.[65] Despite this generic view of substances as monadic centers of active force, Leibniz recognizes, of course, that there are different types or kinds of substances. As he says in his *New Essays*, "It is essential to substances to act, to created substances to be acted on, to minds to think, to bodies to have extension and motion."[66] The divine substance, God, is pure act, while all created substances are passive as well as active. Near the end of his life, he was still maintaining and explaining his monadic theory of substance. In a letter to the Jesuit des Bosses, written about a year before he died, Leibniz says,

> I do not see how we can maintain the substance of a composite being. . . . I should prefer to say that there are no substances over and above monads, but only appearances, but that these are not illusory, like a dream, . . . but that they are true phenomena, that is, in the sense that a rainbow or parhelion is an appearance. . . . It can be said that composite beings which are not a unity per se or are not held together by a substantial chain or . . . by one spirit are semientities. Aggregates of simple substances such as an army or a pile of stones are semientities.[67]

On this view, then, metaphysics, the study of ultimate reality, is essentially a monadology.

Panpsychism and Spirits. In "Monadology," Leibniz suggests that all things that exist, down to "the smallest particle of matter" are alive—a theory of **panpsychism**. He had earlier attributed "*perceptions* and *desires* in the general sense" to "all simple substances or created monads," although, of course, not all are self-conscious or have apperception. Among monads, those that are capable of feeling and "whose perception is more distinct and is accompanied by memory" are called "*souls*" in the stricter sense. Thus, for example, dogs that are struck feel pain distinctly and can remember the experience, so that subsequently "if we show dogs a stick, they remember the pain it has caused them and whine and run." So dogs have souls as surely as we do. Indeed, insofar as we live merely at the level of perception, feeling, and memory, we "act like the brutes . . . and we are simple empirics in three-fourths of our actions." We all expect the sun to rise tomorrow—most of us, "as empirics," do so on the basis of memory and habit, but the astronomical scientist "judges of this by reason," understanding the principles involved. Leibniz concludes that "the knowledge of necessary and eternal truths is what distinguishes us from mere animals and furnishes us with *reason* and the sciences, raising us to a knowledge of ourselves and of God." So, unlike the dog's soul, your soul is rational, a "*spirit*."[68] Leibniz shows why spirits are special as against all other monads. They are obviously made in God's image and "are capable of entering into a sort of society with God"; they inhabit a moral realm of grace as well as the physical realm of nature and are accountable for their actions in terms of reward and punishment.[69]

This assumes that spirits or rational souls are free in (at least some of) their actions—a topic which will be crucial for Leibniz's theodicy. But there is a tension between this assumption and his basic doctrine that the concept of every substance contains all its predicates. He addresses this tension in *Discourse*, holding that although for someone like God who can thoroughly comprehend the essential nature of Julius Caesar, all his attributes and actions will be known as certain, nevertheless this certain knowledge would not necessitate those attributes and actions. In creating this world, God foresees that Julius Caesar will cross the Rubicon in defiance of the orders of the Senate, that he "will become perpetual Dictator and master of the Republic and will overthrow the liberty of Rome," because these future actions are "contained in his concept," which God comprehends. However, it is Caesar's nature, character, and personality which immediately cause Caesar's actions; they are not simply determined by anything external to Caesar, including the will of God. There do remain problems of divine complicity here which Leibniz will need to consider more painstakingly in his works on theodicy, since, in creating this world with that Julius Caesar who has a particular character, God seems to be the ultimate cause (or "sufficient reason") of Caesar's actions. Leibniz's treatment of this thorny issue is foreshadowed here in the *Discourse*.[70] A large part of his answer is that it was better for God to create than not to create and that of all the possible worlds God might have created, this one, including Julius Caesar and all his attributes and actions, was the best possible.

Because we are creatures, we are limited in perfection—if only insofar as we are not self-sufficient. By definition, then, it was impossible for God to create an absolutely perfect world, despite the fact that "God is absolutely perfect, *perfection* being only the magnitude of positive reality." Here, in "Monadology," Leibniz continues, "And where there are no limits, that is, in God, perfection is absolutely infinite." But this is not the case in creatures, who "have their perfections from" God but whose "imperfections arise from their own nature, incapable of existing without limits. For it is by this that they are distinguished from God."[71]

* * *

We cannot explore Leibniz's fascinating metaphysical theory any further here. But this will suffice to show what worldview he connected with his epistemology and to provide the relevant background for our discussion of his philosophy of religion. Unlike Locke's, his theory of knowledge is rationalistic rather than empirical, built on a defense of innate ideas. And it is far more obviously derived from a fresh rethinking of logical methodology than was Descartes's. His most famous and most controversial doctrines—the identity of indiscernibles, the principle of sufficient reason, that this is the best of all possible worlds, that of preestablished harmony, and the monadic theory of substances—all directly or indirectly stem from his view that all the predicates of anything are already contained in its concept, of which we have seen reason to be suspicious. Given his extremely strict standards of knowledge, in terms of a conception of ideas that is clear, distinct, adequate, and intuitive, we might wonder how he will be able to deduce any metaphysical knowledge of God. And we have already been alerted to a tension between his belief in human freedom and responsibility, on the one hand, and his claim that all the possible actions of any substance are implicitly contained in its essential nature, on the other. But let us now turn to his philosophy of religion proper.

Arguments for God's Existence

The Cosmological Argument. Leibniz's use of the cosmological argument assumes different forms in different works, going back to his first publication, the *Dissertation*, of 1666. What is most impressive in the demonstration there is an early illustration of Leibniz's more explicitly rigorous use of logic than was made by either Descartes or Locke. In a letter thirty years later, he makes it clear that this is deliberate, when he says that "in important matters such as theological controversies . . . we do well to analyze matters most industriously and reduce everything to the simplest and most easily grasped inferences."[72]

The complex cosmological demonstration of the *Dissertation* (which we shall simplify somewhat) begins with three definitions: (1) of *God* as "an incorporeal substance of infinite power"; (2) of *substance* as "whatever moves or is moved"; and (3) of *infinite power* as "an original capacity to move the infinite." He next invokes three axioms: (4) "If anything is moved, there is a mover"; (5) "Every moving body is being moved"; and (6) "If all its parts are moved, the whole is moved." Finally, he makes a single simple observation statement, (7) "There is a moving body." Then comes his proof:

8. Some thing must move that moving body (by 4).

9. This something is a substance (by 2), which is either incorporeal or a body.

10. If it is an incorporeal substance, it is God (by 1).

11. But if it is a body, it is also moved (by 5).

12. *Either* this second body would be moved by an incorporeal substance, which is God (by 1).

13. *Or* there is an infinite whole of bodies moving each other.

14. But if all the parts of this infinite whole are moved, then the infinite whole itself must be moved (by 6).

15. This infinite whole would be moved by some other mover (by 4).

16. That mover of the whole would be an incorporeal being, since all bodies are included in the infinite whole.

17. This incorporeal mover must have infinite power (by 3), since it moves an infinite whole.

18. And it must be a substance (by 2).

19. In which case, it is God (by 1).

20. Therefore, God must exist (by 12 and 19).[73]

Even this slightly simplified version of Leibniz's demonstration reveals its geometrical form and makes manifest his logical virtuosity. It is structurally the most stunningly impressive argument for God's existence we are considering in this book (indeed, it borders on the work of a genius showing off). But what can we say about it critically?

First of all, we might call into question two of his three definitions. To say that God must, by definition, have "infinite power" seems to presume too much in favor of orthodox monotheistic theology. Even if nothing were infinite or had infinite power, there might still be an original first cause that could be considered God—that is, an object of religious concern. But even if Leibniz wants to insist on God's infinite power for the sake of orthodoxy, infinite power might be the ultimate source of motion that is not limited by anything external to itself, without its object being the infinite, as his definition requires. If Leibniz were to drop the whole notion of infinite power by changing his definition of God and eliminating the need for his third definition altogether, he would not need to presume (in 13) that the complex whole of mutually affecting bodies is an "infinite whole"—a presumption that introduces a structural weakness in the demonstration.

Second, given the first two of his axioms (4 and 5), Leibniz fails to show that a moving body cannot be self-moved. This failure introduces a loophole into his argument. Also his third axiom (6) seems dubious. It is a logical fallacy (called "composition") to presume that because all the parts of a whole have a certain quality, the whole of which they are parts must also have that quality. Yet Leibniz needs this unsubstantiated axiom to establish a key premise (14) of his proof.

Third, this causal argument probably seemed more plausible in the eighteenth century than it would to people of the last two centuries who have studied the critiques of causal reasoning developed by Hume (who challenges our knowledge of any necessary connection between events called causes and others called effects) and Kant (who admits that there is a necessary relationship between phenomenal causes and effects but denies that we are justified in predicating such a necessary relationship of realities transcending phenomena of experience, such as the world as an "infinite whole"). Even though Leibniz changed the language of causal reasoning, he could not anticipate these critical developments of the next century. He rejects scholastic philosophy's manner of characterizing causal reasoning: "It is very improbable that the term *cause* expresses an unequivocal concept to cover efficient, material, formal, and final causes."[74] In 1667, Leibniz admits that "we cannot explain the method of causality" thus; but he substitutes his own "remarkable principle" for this Aristotelian terminology.[75] This is, of course, his crucial but problematic principle of sufficient reason, which we have already examined and which he considers crucial to an adequate demonstration of God's existence.[76]

A better known (but logically less striking) Leibnizian version of the cosmological argument is the *a posteriori* argument from contingent matters of fact to the metaphysically necessary being, contained at the beginning of his essay "On the Ultimate Origin of Things" (1697). This argument explicitly uses Leibniz's controversial principle in its very first premise: in the world of finite things, "the sufficient reason of existence can not be found either in any particular thing or in the whole aggregate or series." As he goes on to explain, no matter how long a string of antecedent conditions may be considered, "to whatever anterior state you may go back you will never find there a complete reason why there is any world at all, and why this world rather than some other." The adequate explanation of anything requires an ultimate sufficient reason, even if there is nothing temporally prior to the thing to be explained: "For in eternal things even where there is no cause there must be a reason which, in permanent things, is necessity itself." His second premise is a simple existential assertion, that experience reveals "that something exists rather than nothing." His conclusion is,

> The reasons of the world, therefore, lie hidden in something extramundane different from the chain of states or series of things, the aggregate of which constitutes the world. . . . there must exist some one being metaphysically necessary, or whose essence is existence.[77]

This is a far simpler version of the cosmological argument than the *tour de force* from the *Dissertation* we have just considered. Indeed, without much effort, we can put it in the form of a valid conditional syllogism:

If anything exists, then a metaphysically necessary being must exist.

Something does exist.

Consequently a metaphysically necessary being must exist.

The problem is with the first premise, the hypothetical (if . . . then) statement. Why should we accept it? The appeal is supposedly to the principle of sufficient reason. Whatever is experienced as existing (mentioned in the second premise), assuming it is not itself metaphysically necessary, could only be adequately explained ultimately in terms of something else that is. Leibniz's argument (which, apart from the language of "sufficient reason" rather than that of efficient causality, is hauntingly similar to the proof from contingency in Aquinas's third way) is only convincing for those who accept his principle of sufficient reason, which (in the preceding section) has already been called into question.

But this is only one of several arguments for God's existence which Leibniz uses. As we have seen, he wrote in his *New Essays*, "almost all the means which have been employed to prove the existence of God are good, and might serve, if they were perfected."[78] An interesting variation is his argument from eternal truths indicated in both "On the Ultimate Origin of Things" and "The Monadology." The argument runs like this: essences and eternal truths are not fictions, but "they exist in a certain region of ideas"; but "since that which exists can only come from that which exists, . . . eternal truths must have their existence in a certain subject, absolutely and metaphysically necessary, that is in God"; and "therefore, we have the ultimate reason of the reality of essences as well as of existences in one Being."[79] There is a new problem here to which we have not yet adverted—with his assumption that "essences and eternal truths" do, in fact, "exist in a certain region of ideas." It does not appear that Leibniz ever justifies this assumption, which seems to be a prime example of his Platonism. If such a realm of ideas does exist outside the mind of man, then it is plausible to identify it, as Augustine did before him, with the mind of an eternal thinker and to say with Leibniz that "the understanding of God is the region of eternal truths."[80] But a great deal of argumentation would be needed to substantiate this great and controversial supposition.

The Ontological Argument. Leibniz's use of the ontological argument, as has been indicated in the last section, builds on that of Descartes but adds the dimension of critically considering (rather than merely assuming) the very possibility of God's existence. One of the best known passages in which he considers this argument is in the *Discourse*, where he analyzes its traditional use by others in the standard way:

> It must be, they say, that I have an idea of God, or of a perfect being, since I think of him and we cannot think without having ideas; now the idea of this being includes all perfections and since existence is one of these perfections, it follows that he exists.

As thus traditionally formulated, Leibniz considers the argument "imperfect"; because "we often think of impossible chimeras," he says, "such reasoning is not sufficient" unless and until we can be "assured of the possibility" of God. "Therefore, the aforesaid argument proves that God exists, if he is possible."[81] We might observe here that Leibniz never critically questions (as Hume and Kant were to do) whether existence is a perfection; on the contrary, he explicitly says, in *New Essays*, "when it is said that a thing exists or that it has real existence, this existence itself is the predicate."[82]

At any rate, his is an interesting addition to the old ontological argument. But how can Leibniz prove the possibility of something whose existence is in question? He obviously cannot do so empirically. The key passage here is in "Monadology":

> Hence God alone (or the necessary being) has this prerogative, that he must exist if he is possible. And since nothing can hinder the possibility of that which possesses no limitations, no negation, and, consequently, no contradiction, this alone is sufficient to establish the existence of God *a priori*.[83]

This reasoning is very similar to that used by Spinoza (in the eleventh proposition of his *Ethics*); and one of the subjects for discussion between Spinoza and Leibniz when they met in 1676 was an argument the latter had devised "to show that *all perfections are compatible with each other* or can be in the same subject."[84]

From a critical perspective, the argument for the possibility of God (or the compossibility of all perfections) seems specious. The question is not so much whether anything could prevent an all-perfect Being from existing as whether the idea of a Being having all perfections is coherent—is it a clear and distinct, intuitively adequate idea? For example, can we know that absolute simplicity, eternity, and immutability are compatible (or compossible) with God's entering into interpersonal relationships with rational creatures? We can accept this as a matter of faith, as Leibniz presumably does; but this is not tantamount to the sort of logical understanding that will serve his argumentative purposes. We might wish to raise against Leibniz the objection he raised against Descartes (in a letter to Malebranche, 1679):

> I consider it certain that the proofs which he produces for the existence of God are imperfect as long as he does not prove that we have an idea of God or of the greatest of all beings. You may reply that, if we did not, we could not reason about him. But one can also reason about the greatest of all numbers, an idea which nevertheless implies a contradiction.[85]

Leibniz clearly believes that "the innate idea of God" is clear, distinct, and intuitively adequate.[86] But one of the hazards of thinking something self-evident is that one then tends not to wish to argue the point for others.

The Argument from Design. Leibniz's use of the argument from design employs his principle of preestablished harmony. In *New Essays* he wrote, "*Pre-established Harmony* itself furnishes a new and incontestable means" of proving God's existence; after acknowledging merit in "almost all" the traditional arguments, he adds, "and I am not at all of the opinion that the one which is drawn from the order of things is to be neglected."[87] Even as a very young man, Leibniz was impressed with this. In a letter of 1669 to his teacher Jacob Thomasius, he wrote that "though there is in fact no wisdom in nature and no appetite . . . a beautiful order arises in it because it is the timepiece of God."[88]

In reflecting on our observations of the systematic interrelationships among independent objects of experience, we are struck with the belief that "they could never produce that *order*, that *harmony*, that *beauty*, which we observe in nature." This is the traditional (teleological) argument from design (comparable to Aquinas's fifth way and referred to by Locke). But so far Leibniz considers it "to be only of moral certainty"[89]; and it requires his principle to strengthen it further:

> My system of Pre-established Harmony furnishes a new proof, hitherto unknown, of the existence of God, since it is quite manifest that the agreement of so many substances, of which the one has no influence upon the other, could only come from a general cause, on which all of them depend, and that this must have infinite power and wisdom to pre-establish all these harmonies.[90]

If the natural order is "the timepiece of God" that Leibniz thinks it is, what could account for the apparent harmony among its parts? Leibniz claims that there are three possible explanations.[91] First, they might exert "a mutual influence" on each other. But his theory of substances as "windowless" monads rules out this option of two things in nature mutually affecting one another. Second, they might be constantly made to harmonize by "a skillful worker" determined to "adjust them and keep them in agreement." But this would require continuous divine intervention that would forever disrupt the natural order and require an endless string of miracles. Third, they could have been designed from the very beginning "with so much art and accuracy that their agreement is guaranteed thereafter." By a process of elimination, this third option is the one with which Leibniz would leave us. However, let us observe that the facile exclusion of his first option, of different things in the natural order harmoniously influencing each other, is only as convincing as is his monadic theory of substances, which is not cogently established and of the correctness of which very few people have been convinced (though, of course, this last fact does not disprove his theory).

Leibniz believes that one of the greatest advantages of his theory of preestablished harmony is that it "removes any notion of miracles from purely natural actions, and makes things run their course regulated in an intelligible manner."[92] What is allegedly eliminated here is the need for violations of or exceptions to the general design of divine providence. Leibniz discusses this at some length in *Discourse*. Because "God is an absolutely perfect being," we can be certain that "God does nothing out of order. Therefore, that which passes for extraordinary is so only with regard to a particular order established among the created things, for as regards the universal order, everything conforms to it." It would supposedly violate God's perfection for anything in the world of divine creation and providence to be irregular. According to this view, although events may occur because God "has particular intentions which are exceptions to the subordinate regulations" governing particular things, we can still maintain that "the most universal" of God's laws, "i.e., that which rules the whole course of the universe, is without exceptions." Thus, he concludes, we can admit miracles but should recognize that they "always conform to the universal law of the general order, although they may contravene the subordinate regulations."[93]

This is at least a clever solution to the problem of how an eternally immutable, omniscient, and omnipotent God would intervene in temporal history to change an already divinely established order. Leibniz says that exceptions to subordinate natural rules were part of God's general providential order from all eternity. To the extent that miracles contravene laws of nature, the latter are, after all, only generalizations of customary but limited applicability. There are allegedly no exceptions to the universal order of divine providence, although it is beyond our comprehension and a matter of faith. As he writes in a letter of 1702 to Queen Sophia Charlotte,

> The natural light of reason does not suffice for knowing the detail thereof, and our experiences are still too limited to catch a glimpse of the laws of this order. The revealed light guides us meanwhile through faith.[94]

This takes us to our next topic.

Faith, Reason, and Religion

Faith and Reason. Leibniz's analysis of "the conformity of faith with reason" is given at the beginning of *Theodicy* (1710). In this book he tries to answer the **fideism** and skeptical critique of rationalism which the French *philosophe* Pierre Bayle had articulated in his very popular *Historical and Critical Dictionary* of 1697. (It is historically curious that Leibniz responded at length, either directly or indirectly, to the three men who may be called the fathers of the European Enlightenment: his *New Essays* was a critique of Locke; his correspondence with Clarke was indirectly a debate with Newton, since Clarke represented the Newtonian position; and his *Theodicy* was an extended answer to Bayle.) In 1698, Leibniz published a paper which courteously responded to some of the points Bayle made in the *Dictionary*; and in 1702 Leibniz wrote another paper responding to the second edition of Bayle's *Dictionary*, published that same year.[95] Let us briefly consider what Bayle's position was, relative to those aspects of Leibniz's thought that we are examining.

Bayle, whose father was a Calvinist pastor and who himself had converted to Catholicism when he was young and then quickly returned to his former faith, was deeply suspicious of all philosophical theology. He holds that Catholics and Protestants alike believe that Descartes's philosophy, for example, would "undermine all the foundations" of Christian faith. He says that "the Cartesians are suspected of irreligion; and their philosophy is believed to be very dangerous to Christendom." (Bayle seems very close to Pascal in this respect.) More generally, he writes, "Man's understanding must be made a captive of faith and must submit to it." For Bayle, the problem of evil is a prime case in point. He believes that reason is impotent to refute objections against the compatibility of evil and an all-good God:

> Human reason is too feeble for this. It is a principle of destruction and not of edification. It is only proper for raising doubts, and for turning things on all sides in order to make disputes endless.

Thus, against Descartes, Locke, and Leibniz, he advocates, "the doctrine of the *elevation of faith and the abasement of reason.*" The article of the *Dictionary* on "Rorarius" is directed largely, though politely, against "Leibniz, one of the greatest minds in Europe."[96] Although Bayle's remarks are not directed against Leibniz's philosophy of religion, as such, they were sufficient to elicit the more general response of *Theodicy*.

The part of *Theodicy* which Leibniz calls "Preliminary Dissertation on the Conformity of Faith with Reason" deals with our general topic here, "the use of philosophy in theology," which Bayle had challenged. Against critics like Bayle, Leibniz notes that such a "divorce between faith and reason was . . . condemned in the last Lateran Council under Leo X. On that occasion also, scholars were urged to work for the removal of the difficulties that appeared to set theology and philosophy at variance."[97] So he sees his philosophical activity here as serving, rather than as threatening, religious faith.

Leibniz begins by stating his presupposition that all truths are complementary and therefore cannot be mutually inconsistent:

> I assume that two truths cannot contradict each other; that the object of faith is the truth God has revealed in an extraordinary way; and that reason is the linking together of truths, but especially (when it is compared with faith) of those whereto the human mind can attain naturally without being aided by the light of faith.

He reminds us of what he maintained in his theory of knowledge, that there are two general types of truths—those that "are altogether necessary, so that the opposite implies contradiction," and those that are consequences of "the laws which it has pleased God to give to Nature." The first kind is that "whose necessity is logical, metaphysical or geometrical, which one cannot deny without being led into absurdities"; the second must be learned "either by experience, that is, *a posteriori*, or by reason and *a priori*, that is, by considerations of the fitness of things which have caused their choice" by God. There can be a tension between truths of the second sort because "the laws of Nature are subject to be dispensed from by the Law-giver; whereas the eternal verities, as for instance those of geometry, admit no dispensation, and faith cannot contradict them."

Thus, it is not logically necessary that a person who has died should permanently remain dead, although "once dead, forever dead" is true as a general rule. If an alleged doctrine of faith were clearly and certainly opposed to logically necessary truths, it would have to be rejected as false. On the other hand, if a doctrine of faith is only in tension with truths of the second sort, "the objection is not conclusive" and "has no force against faith, since it is agreed that the Mysteries of religion are contrary to appearances" of ordinary experience.[98]

Thus, one may show that "the necessary truths and the conclusive results of philosophy cannot be contrary to revelation." But though we may explain how mysteries of the faith are compatible with the logically necessary truths that might threaten their credibility, "one cannot *comprehend* them, nor give understanding of how they come to pass. . . . Nor is it possible for us, either, to prove Mysteries by reason." But a role that reason can perform is that of defending doctrines of faith against objections that they are incompatible with necessary truth. And this is an important service. "Without that our belief in them would have no firm foundation; for all that which can be refuted in a sound and conclusive manner cannot but be false."[99] Doctrines of faith, even if they are Mysteries, cannot be irrational, in the sense of violating logically necessary truth.

Leibniz is confident that all theologians except those who are fanatics will "agree at least that no article of faith must imply contradiction." If it could ever be shown that religion was abandoning "the necessary and eternal truths for the sake of upholding Mysteries," its enemies would have ample ammunition for their opposition. Leibniz relates the traditional distinction between truths that are "*above* reason" and beliefs that are "*against* reason" to this discussion:

> For what is contrary to reason is contrary to the absolutely certain and inevitable truths; and what is above reason is in opposition only to what one is wont to experience or to understand.

Mysteries, such as that of "the Holy Trinity" are "above reason" in the sense that we cannot naturally comprehend them. But they are not "against reason" in the sense of violating logically necessary truths. For example, even though we may never have experienced three different persons sharing the nature of a single being and cannot understand how that could possibly ever be the case, we do not therefore have any reason to call it logically impossible. In this way Leibniz denies Bayle's claim that a truth, such as that concerning the existence of an all-good God, "can admit of irrefutable objections," such as those based on the fact of evil. More generally, Leibniz concludes "that when an objection is put forward against some truth, it is always possible to answer it satisfactorily."[100]

But this is a solution to only half of the problem of relating religious faith to philosophical reason. Even if there is no logical incompatibility, how do we weigh the *probabilities* favoring a doctrine of faith against those derived from general experience and our understanding of the laws of nature? This is a more difficult part of the problem to solve. Leibniz reminds us of a point he made in his logical writings, that

> the art of judging from probable reasons is not yet well established; so that our logic in this connexion is still very imperfect, and to this very day we have little beyond the art of judging from demonstrations.

Referring to Arnauld, Malebranche, and Locke (in that order), he denies that any of the post-Cartesian thinkers has significantly altered this deplorable state:

> The most excellent philosophers of our time, such as the authors of *The Art of Thinking*, of *The Search for Truth* and of the *Essay concerning Human Understanding*, have been very far from indicating to us the true means fitted to assist the faculty whose business it is to make us weigh the probabilities of the true and the false.[101]

What we must try to do as best we can, according to Leibniz, is reckon the reasons we have for believing a doctrine of faith versus those on which are based our empirical generalizations and the laws of nature, mindful all the while of the existence and nature of God, as well as the universal harmony whereby the world was providentially created and ordered.

> Thus faith triumphs over false reasons by means of sound and superior reasons that have made us embrace it; but it would not triumph if the contrary opinion had for it reasons as strong as or even stronger than those which form the foundation of faith, that is, if there were invincible and conclusive objections against faith.

In this way reason is an arbiter for Leibniz, as it was for Locke; it complements and supports religious faith rather than opposing it:

> For reason, far from being contrary to Christianity, serves as a foundation for this religion, and will bring about its acceptance by those who can achieve the examination of it. But, as few people are capable of this, the heavenly gift of plain faith tending towards good suffices for men in general.[102]

Leibniz criticizes Bayle for confounding the legitimate role of philosophical reason vis-à-vis religious faith:

> I have marvelled many times that a writer so precise and so shrewd as M. Bayle
> so often here confuses things where so much difference exists as between these
> three acts of reason: to comprehend, to prove, and to answer objections.

When Bayle says that reason is "too feeble" adequately to deal with challenges raised against religious faith to which it should simply "submit," he sells reason short. Human reason cannot comprehend all the truths of faith; nor can it prove them all. But it can always answer objections in such a way as to show that there is no logical incompatibility between faith and reason, that though the truths of the former may be "above" the latter, they are not "against" it. But we should not be too quick to give up on reason's capacity to comprehend and prove. Here Leibniz takes Descartes to task for presuming that there is no rational solution to the problem of how the human will can be free when all events have been foreordained by God: "Not content with saying that, as for him, he sees no way of reconciling the two dogmas, he puts the whole human race, and even all rational creatures, in the same case." Leibniz tries to show in *Theodicy* that although "our mind is finite and cannot comprehend the infinite, of the infinite nevertheless it has proofs whose strength or weakness it comprehends."[103] In this respect, he might turn out to be an even more thoroughgoing rationalist than was Descartes. But first let us briefly consider what he says about religion.

Religion. Leibniz's remarks concerning religion are typically scattered. In a little-known satirical dialogue on religion written about 1678, Leibniz has two characters discuss the relationship between faith and practice in religion. Poliander is described as "an apostolic missionary" who "had grown old in controversy" and who is quick to engage others in arguments and to make full use of rhetoric and disputatious devices. Theophile (the name of Leibniz's spokesman here) is described as "a very honorable man" capable of defending himself "with a certain self-effacement and simplicity which gave ample evidence of great resources and an enlightened and tranquil soul." Poliander is a hell-and-brimstone sort of character who believes that the love of God and a life of good works are not enough and that non-Christians will be damned. By contrast, Theophile (literally "the lover of God") maintains that "God does not deny his grace to those who do their part." Poliander agrees that the love of God is of primary importance but holds that fear of God can be an adequate substitute and that another essential requirement is that we "search for the true church," whether this search be motivated by love or fear. Theophile (as spokesman for

Leibniz) raises the following criticism of militant evangelicals: "But you make no mention of charity or justice, and I do not see many reformers who take up these things and still fewer who succeed with them." Poliander scornfully dismisses this rebuke:

> Justice and charity are things which we can have in common with pagans; it takes other pious practices to please God. That is, we need fastings, **hair shirts**, disciplines, **gratings**, books of **hours**, the **Ave Maria**, and similar things; as for the **Lord's Prayer**, I see nothing in it which a pagan cannot say. This is why we make much more of a case for the Ave Maria.

Theophile upbraids Poliander for forgetting the teaching of Jesus that what the law requires is that "we must love God above all things and our neighbor as ourselves" and for being too concerned about superstitions and ecclesiastical rituals:

> You wish us to be convinced of a great number of new and doubtful things and to condemn absolutely all who dare to doubt them. Besides, you are too ceremonious, and you engage souls with so many superfluous cares that they turn away from him who ought to be their chief care. All this hurts this universal charity, it seems to me.[104]

Leibniz does believe in the supernatural efficacy of prayer and good works, even though he thinks our eternal destinies are foreseen by divine providence: "Despite the certainty of the events in this universe, our prayers and labors are not useless for the obtaining of those future goods which we desire."[105] In the *Discourse* Leibniz holds that God "demands only the right intentions" from us; our actions should be motivated by love whether or not our "good designs succeed."[106] Near the end of "Principles," Leibniz reminds us that, as spirits, we humans can enter "into a sort of society with God," so that we "are members of the City of God," to borrow Augustine's memorable phrase. For Leibniz love is not merely a means to ultimate **beatitude**, but even now

> the *love of God* makes us enjoy a foretaste of future felicity. . . . And besides the present pleasure, nothing can be more useful for the future; for the love of God fulfills also our hopes, and leads us in the road of supreme happiness.[107]

In "Monadology," he writes that "under this perfect government" of the City of God "there will be no good action unrewarded, no bad action unpunished; and everything must result in the well-being of the good."[108] This is a statement of Leibniz's religious faith. If pressed to justify it rationally, he could appeal to God's justice, to the principle of sufficient reason, and to his thesis that things ultimately work out in the best way possible in a world governed by divine providence.

Theodicy

The Problem of Evil. Leibniz's treatment of the problem of evil in general is anticipated in a couple of his late seventeenth-century works. In *Discourse* he reminds us that God's nature is such that all things are for the best but warns us that we cannot reasonably expect to comprehend thoroughly the sufficient reason motivating God's providential ways:

> To know in particular, however, the reasons which have moved him to choose this order of the universe, to permit sin, to dispense his salutary grace in a certain manner—this passes the capacity of a finite mind, above all when such a mind has not come into the joy of the vision of God.

He maintains that to the extent that we do try to explain things that are bad in the world,

> we must say that God permits the evil, and not that he desired it, although he has co-operated by means of the laws of nature which he has established. He knows how to produce the greatest good from them.[109]

In "On the Ultimate Origin of Things" (1697) he acknowledges that there is a problem of evil in the context of a harmonious, best possible world created by an infinite, perfectly good God:

> for often good people are very unhappy, . . . innocent men are afflicted and even put to death with torture . . ., the world, if you regard especially the government of the human race, resembles a sort of confused chaos rather than the well ordered work of a supreme wisdom.

He warns us that "it is not proper to judge before having examined the whole" and complains that "from an experience so short we dare to judge of the immense and of the eternal." He also employs an aesthetic metaphor to signify that we must experience things that are bad in order to enjoy the good more fully: "He who has not tasted bitter things has not merited sweet things and, indeed, will not appreciate them." But, most boldly, he asserts that

> we may affirm, generally, that afflictions, temporarily evil, are in effect good, since they are short cuts to greater perfections. . . . And we might say of this that it is retreating in order the better to leap forward.[110]

These comments on the problem of evil do not appear to be any more impressive than were those of Descartes a few decades earlier. But they do show that Leibniz was sensitive to the need to use his philosophical skills, in the words of his older contemporary John Milton (near the beginning of *Paradise Lost*), to "justify the ways of God to men." This is literally what "theodicy" is: an attempted justification or vindication of God. But in order to consider the works of Leibniz on theodicy which are impressive and for which he was and remains celebrated, we must turn to three of his writings of 1710: his book, *Theodicy: Essays on the Goodness of God, the Freedom of Man, and the Origin of Evil*; his paper, "A Vindication of God's Justice Reconciled with His Other Perfections and All His Actions"; and his brief synopsis, "The Theodicy: Abridgement of the Argument Reduced to Syllogistic Form." In *Theodicy* Leibniz provides a distinction which is convenient for organizational purposes, saying that the problem of evil comprises two great types of difficulties:

> The one kind springs from man's freedom, which appears incompatible with the divine nature; and nevertheless freedom is deemed necessary, in order that man may be deemed guilty and open to punishment. The other kind concerns the conduct of God, and seems to make him participate also therein. And this conduct appears contrary to the goodness, the holiness and the justice of God, since God co-operates in evil as well physical as moral.[111]

The first step, then, is to show that man is truly free; otherwise, moral responsibility is lost, and evil becomes either illusory or unavoidable. The second step is to show that God is not to blame for evil and that it does not derogate from divine perfection.

Our Freedom to Do Evil. Leibniz's defense of man's freedom to do evil should be considered in the context of what he has said about all the predicates of any substance being contained in its concept and about God's **foreknowledge** of all future actions. In the *Discourse* he writes that "future contingencies are assured since God foresees them, but we do not say just because of that that they are necessary."[112] The obvious objection here is that if a person's very concept implicitly contains all his future actions, all of which are infallibly known in advance by God, then his doing those actions is necessary rather than free. In his "Vindication" Leibniz answers this objection by defining freedom and then making a vital distinction. He writes that freedom "consists in this: that the voluntary action be spontaneous and deliberate, and therefore exclude that necessity which suppresses deliberation. Freedom excludes *metaphysical necessity*, the opposite of which is impossible, that is, implies contradiction. However, it does not exclude *moral* necessity, the opposite of which is unfit."[113]

For example, it would have been logically possible (i.e., not contradictory) for God to create a world in which there were no rumors of people participating in poison plots against members of their own families. But this would have been a world in which there was no Lucrezia Borgia because her nature is such that she would be implicated in such rumors. This would also preclude the existence of Pope Alexander VI, her father, since his having Lucrezia for a daughter is required by his very nature. And so it goes—changes in the history of the papacy, of the Catholic Church, of Christendom, of Western civilization, etc. We are considering here a possible world that is quite different from the one we actually live in. God chose to create our actual world because it was better than any alternative possibility. That is to say, God chose to create a world in which Alexander VI would choose to act in such a way that Lucrezia would be born and in which Lucrezia would choose to live in such a manner that rumors of her involvement in poison plots would abound. However, God does not make Alexander father a child utterly against his will or force Lucrezia to lead the sort of life she lived. They make their own choices, although God knows from all eternity what those choices are to be and has chosen to create the world in which they would make those choices.

In *Theodicy* Leibniz writes,

> When we act freely we are not being forced, as would happen if we were pushed on to a precipice and thrown from top to bottom. . . . It is not to be imagined, however, that our freedom consists in an indetermination or an indifference of equipoise, as if one must needs be inclined equally

to both sides of a set of alternatives. Assuming it is true "that I shall write tomorrow," God foresees that truth about me "because it is true; but it is not true because it is foreseen." If there had not been a best possible world, God would not have created; and if this had not been the best possible world, God would have chosen to create the other that was, since, by nature, God "cannot but have created the best."[114] In creating this world, divine providence determined everything that would ever be true of it. Yet, for Leibniz, this does not nullify the fact that we are free agents who cause things to happen and are morally responsible. We are ignorant of what God has determined for the future and unaware of what divine providence foresees.

> The whole future is doubtless determined: but since we know not what it is, nor what is foreseen or resolved, we must do our duty, according to the reason that God has given us and according to the rules that he has prescribed for us; and thereafter we must have a quiet mind, and leave to God himself the care for the outcome.[115]

It does not seem that Leibniz has justified his analysis of God's nature sufficiently to show that God must be omniscient in his sense.[116]

And we have already called into question his doctrine that the concept of every substance implicitly contains all its predicates. Yet we may agree that his conception of divine omniscience combined with this doctrine will require that God must infallibly foresee all future events, including human actions. And, although it seems a more debatable issue, we can accept Leibniz's point of view that God's foreknowledge of our future actions is logically compatible with their being freely chosen actions. But we should deny his view that they can be our freely chosen actions (for which we are morally responsible) if they are determined by our natures, insofar as we could not be the persons God created us to be without those actions. It is in choosing to create the persons whose natures require the performance of those actions (and not merely in foreseeing that they will occur) that Leibniz's God determines our future and takes away from us the spontaneity that Leibniz says is essential to freedom. So it seems his mistake here is in holding the logical doctrine that all the predicates of any substance are necessarily contained in its concept and are therefore, in principle, knowable *a priori*.

God and Evil. Leibniz's vindication of God in regard to evil builds on this view that man is free and thus can be a sufficient reason for evil in our world. Leibniz endorses Augustine's Neoplatonic theory that "evil is a privation of being,"[117] rather than any really existing thing. Thus, the fact that God created all existing things does not make God the creator of evil. As Leibniz puts it, "properly speaking, the formal character of evil has no *efficient* cause, for it consists in privation." He goes on to explain that evil may be considered in three different ways—"metaphysically, physically, and morally. *Metaphysical evil* consists in mere imperfection, *physical evil* in suffering, and *moral evil* in sin."[118] Creatures, by their very nature, must be imperfect, since anything that owes its being to another and thus is not self-sufficient is imperfect.[119] Therefore, in creating at all, God must produce a world containing metaphysical evil. Although it was best that God create, doing so required that God permit metaphysical evil. In this sense it is allegedly best that God will metaphysical evil. But, as Leibniz says, "God wills moral evil not at all, and physical evil or suffering he does not will absolutely," but only "as a penalty owing to guilt" or as a means to a greater good. After all, Leibniz assures us, "often an evil brings forth a good whereto one would not have attained without that evil."[120] This view presupposes, of course, controversial claims we have already considered—that God would only create the best of all possible worlds and that our actual world is, in fact, the best possible—which, in turn, rest on Leibniz's principle of sufficient reason, which has been critically discussed above.

Leibniz nicely crystallizes the charge of divine complicity in evil in his "Vindication": "God, it is said, *concurs too much in moral evil*, both physically and morally." Critics object that God "morally" allows ("permits or does not prevent") evil and "physically" provides the power and occasions whereby sin arises.

> This is the reason why certain authors even dare to infer that God is morally and physically, or certainly in at least one of the two ways, an accomplice, even the author, of sin. By this means they destroy the divine holiness as well as his justice and goodness. Others prefer to tear down the divine omniscience and omnipotence or, in one word, his greatness. According to them, God either does not foresee the evil, or is not concerned with it at all, or is unable to resist its torrential flood.[121]

Thus, an alleged divine complicity in evil might call into question God's metaphysical and/or moral attributes.

In *Theodicy*, Leibniz sets the stage for his answer by admitting

> that God co-operates in moral evil, and in physical evil, and in each of them both morally and physically; and that man co-operates therein also morally and physically in a free and active way, becoming in consequence subject to blame and punishment.[122]

The question, then, is whether God's cooperation, like man's, entails guilt and might derogate from the divine perfection. A large part of the answer is that it does not so long as it is for the best that God should so cooperate.

Regarding physical evil, which God does will (though not "absolutely" or for its own sake), Leibniz avers that "the happiness of intelligent creatures is the principal part of God's design, for they are most like him; but nevertheless I do not see how one can prove that to be his sole aim"— and later he adds, "nor even his final aim." So the unhappiness and suffering constituting physical evil might appropriately befall humans as rational creatures. Like Descartes, Leibniz maintains that human reason, as a God-given faculty, is "a great good," although, being endowed with free choice, it can directly and indirectly cause evil.

> But even though it should prove that reason did more harm than good to men (which, however, I do not admit), . . . it might still be the case that it was more in accordance with the perfection of the universe to give reason to men, notwithstanding all the evil consequences which it might have with reference to them. Consequently, . . . far from being subject to blame for this, he would be blameworthy if he did not so.

The point to stress is that reason, with its capacity for free choice, "is always a good in itself," despite the fact that it can be abused in such a way that it causes evil results. And, for Leibniz, "the best possible plan of the universe" requires its inclusion. As he rhetorically asks,

> Must God spoil his system, must there be less beauty, perfection and reason in the universe, because there are people who misuse reason?[123]

Regarding moral evil, which God never wills but merely permits, Leibniz's solution is along similar lines. If the perfection of the universe requires that there be rational creatures and if the capacity for free choice is essential to rational creatures, then God has a morally sufficient reason for permitting the abuse of that freedom. Leibniz suggests that in permitting this abuse God respects man's rational freedom, while remaining concerned for human welfare:

> God has care for men, he loves the human race, he wishes it well, nothing so true. Yet he allows men to fall, he often allows them to perish, he gives them goods that tend towards their destruction.

Leibniz answers Bayle's concern that God's permitting moral evil which divine omnipotence could prevent makes it appear as if God does not care about, or even wills, the evil. Leibniz reminds us that at times good human beings also "permit evils which they could prevent." For example, parents allow their children's broken arms to be reset painfully in order that they might regain proper form and efficient use; we tend to regard such a permission of the physical evil of pain as more praiseworthy than blameworthy. Why could we not say something comparable about God's permission of moral evil?

> God has a far stronger reason, and one far more worthy of him, for tolerating evils. Not only does he derive from them greater goods, but he finds them connected with the greatest goods of all those that are possible.

These greater goods include the exercising of reason and free choice and the personal commitment to love and virtue. Thus, Leibniz explains

> that God loves virtue supremely and hates vice supremely, and that nevertheless some vice is to be permitted.[124]

Nowadays, a theodicy such as Leibniz's, which locates "*the origin of evil in the freedom of creatures*" is sometimes called a "free will defence." The roots of this sort of theodicy lie in the thought of Augustine. Leibniz says that apart from a few points (such as "the damnation of unregenerate children" and "damnation resulting from **original sin** alone") on which "St. Augustine appears obscure or even repellent, it seems as though one can conform to his system."[125] Of the traditional (i.e., precontemporary) theories we are considering, this seems the most effective approach to reconciling the fact of evil with the orthodox conception of divine perfection. Nevertheless, there are plausible objections to be raised against it. And it is to Leibniz's credit that he anticipated and answered eight of the most powerful and important ones in a masterful manner. In this way he could complete his efforts, as Alexander Pope puts it in the first few lines of his "Essay on Man," to "vindicate the ways of God to man."

Objections to Theodicy Addressed. Leibniz's logical response to eight objections to theodicy is found in "The Theodicy: Abridgement of the Argument Reduced to Syllogistic Form," a paper containing a *tour de force* display of argumentation. The first objection holds that God must be "lacking in power, or in knowledge, or in goodness" because anyone who fails to choose the best is so lacking and "God did not choose the best in creating this world." Leibniz denies the second premise, which the opponent of theodicy proves by means of the following premises: "Whoever makes things in which there is evil, which could have been made without any evil, or the making of which could have been omitted, does not choose the best," and God has made the world thus. Here Leibniz concedes the second premise but denies the first one. He explains that "*the evil is accompanied by a greater good*," and he acknowledges that he is following the lead of Augustine and Aquinas here.[126] It seems Leibniz is correct on this point—a state of affairs containing some evil may be better than one with none under the condition specified, and therefore the mere fact that there is evil is not logically incompatible with divine perfection.

The second objection holds that there must be more evil than good in all of creation because this would be so if there is more evil than good in intelligent creatures, and there is. Here Leibniz denies both premises. The first one commits the fallacy of illicitly generalizing from a part to the whole of creation. The second premise is unfounded. Even if more humans were miserable than are happy, the quality of happiness in the fortunate might outweigh that of misery in the unfortunate. And even if there were more evil than good in humans, it would not follow that this is the case among intelligent creatures in general (of whatever kinds and however many they might be).[127] Again, Leibniz is correct. It has not been (and could not easily be) shown that evil outweighs good in all of creation.

The third objection holds that it would always be unjust for God to punish because it is unjust to punish sins that are necessary, and "every sin is necessary." The second premise is the one Leibniz denies, and it is argued for on the basis that everything "that is **predetermined** is necessary" and every event is predetermined. Leibniz denies that everything "that is predetermined is necessary" in the absolute sense that "destroys the morality of an action and the justice of punishments."[128] He seems unconvincing here. While accepting his distinction between "absolute" necessity, which would require the logical impossibility of the contrary of an action, and "conditional or hypothetical" necessity, which applies on condition that there be certain subjects, we may hold that moral responsibility is compromised, if not eradicated, by the fact that a subject's very nature requires (in the sense of logically implies) certain actions.

The fourth objection maintains that God must be an accessory to sin because anyone who "can prevent the sin of another and does not do so, but rather contributes to it although he is well informed of it, is accessory to it," and this is the case with God. Leibniz denies the first premise, pointing out that a person who could prevent a sin only by committing one or "performing an unreasonable action" is not blameworthy for failing to prevent it. So God would be vindicated here if in a situation comparable to one that is common to us: "We do not desire these evils; but we are willing to permit them for the sake of a greater good."[129] However, there are two problems with Leibniz's position here. First his God, unlike us, is allegedly infinite in knowledge and power as well as in goodness. A large part of the reason we must compromise in permitting evil is that we are so limited in what we can do. Leibniz's God is only limited by the impossible (what violates the principle of contradiction) and the divine nature (e.g., God would not choose less than the best). It may be that Leibniz's analogy is well-founded; but the fact that it involves a relationship between the perfect, unlimited, infinite God of Christianity and imperfect, limited, finite human beings certainly does place a strain on it. Second, there are certain types of evil which seem so repugnant as to be morally intolerable, from the point of view that it is difficult, if not impossible, to see how they could be adequately compensated or justified by good future consequences. The gripping, famous illustration that comes to mind is from Dostoyevsky's *Brothers Karamazov*, where Ivan tells of a five-year-old girl who is tortured in an unspeakably horrible way and later poses the problem most forcefully and personally:

> Imagine that you are creating a fabric of human destiny with the object of making men happy in the end, giving them peace and rest at last. Imagine that you are doing this but that it is essential and inevitable to torture to death only one tiny creature . . . Would you consent to be the architect on those conditions?[130]

We may be no more able to answer that question in the affirmative than was Alyosha, Ivan's pious brother. Yet our world is one in which there have been and continue to be an untold number of instances of tortured innocents comparable to Ivan's example. And Leibniz's theodicy would push us to say that all of them are justified.

The fifth objection holds that God must be the cause of sin because anything that "produces all that is real in a thing, is its cause," and "God produces all that is real in sin." Leibniz says he would deny either premise, depending on how the term "real" is interpreted. If "real" refers to "that which is positive only," then Leibniz admits the second premise but denies the first one. For "God is the cause of all . . . realities considered as purely positive." But the cause of sin is the "imperfection of creatures," which is a negative kind of reality termed "privation" by Augustine; and this is "a defective cause." As we have seen, the metaphysical evil of imperfection is necessary if there are to be creatures at all. On the other hand, if "real," in addition to positive beings, "includes also privative beings," then Leibniz admits the first premise while denying the second one. For sin is privation; and, on this interpretation, we, rather than God, produce the privative reality of sin by misusing the good (positive) faculties God gave us. We might want to protest here that God gave us those faculties knowing we would abuse them and is thus our accomplice in (if not the ultimate cause of) our sins. Leibniz invokes an aesthetic metaphor to justify God's implication here: "There are certain disorders in the parts which marvelously enhance the beauty of the whole; just as certain dissonances, when properly used, render harmony more beautiful."[131] Yet this analogy is quite unconvincing. It is one thing to justify the ugliness of a part by showing that it does "enhance the beauty of the whole." But it is something altogether different to try justifying an evil means with reference to a desirable end.

The sixth objection maintains that God is unjust because anyone who "punishes those who have done as well as it was in their power to do, is unjust," and God does this. As we might expect, Leibniz denies the second premise, while conceding the first one. He maintains that "God always gives sufficient aid and grace to those who have a good will, that is, to those who do not reject this grace by new sin."[132] But the problem with this is that, according to Leibniz, their natures require people to accept or reject God's grace, and each person's nature was created by God.

The seventh objection holds that God's goodness must be deficient because anyone who "gives only to some, and not to all, the means which produces in them effectively a good will and salutary final truth, has not sufficient goodness," and "God does this." Here Leibniz denies only the first premise. He does not deny that God elects to confer more grace on some than on others. And he admits that

> God could overcome the greatest resistance of the human heart: and does it, too, sometimes, either by internal grace, or by external circumstances which have a great effect on souls; but he does not always do this.

His explanation is that it would be inappropriate for God to be disrupting "the connection of things" by constant miraculous intervention. And if we ask why the preestablished harmony is such that this sort of intervention might be needed for the salvation of intelligent creatures, Leibniz assures us that it is for the best, but he falls back on the disappointing answer we have seen before (for example, in Descartes's fourth Meditation):

> The reasons of this connection, by means of which one is placed in more favorable circumstances than another, are hidden in the depths of the wisdom of God.[133]

What makes this so disappointing is that a theodicy should explain, whereas here Leibniz retreats into the inexplicable and mysterious.

The eighth objection maintains that God cannot be free, since anyone who "cannot fail to choose the best, is not free," and "God cannot fail to choose the best." Leibniz denies the first premise, holding that true freedom involves consistently using one's will to do what is best. Because God is perfectly good, it is morally necessary that God always choose what is best. Thus, the sufficient reason that guarantees that God will always choose the best lies in the divine nature itself. This is not a matter of external compulsion; nor is it logically impossible that God would choose less than the best. "This necessity is called moral" and allegedly is not the absolute sort "which destroys morality" and is inconsistent with freedom. This is clearly not the sort of "freedom" that involves a capacity to want anything *and* to do what one wants. Leibniz would view any conception of freedom as arbitrary caprice as a caricature which "perverts" the very idea of freedom.[134] The critical question is whether being able to do what one wants is freedom, if one's nature only permits wanting what is both possible and best. It would be hard to answer this question except by saying that if this is freedom, it is merely analogous to any freedom of which we have personal experience.

* * *

Even though some of the aspects of this theodicy seem dubious, it is a fine discussion with which to conclude our consideration of Leibniz's thought. It shows Leibniz near the end of his life using logic as impressively as he did in his youth. His use of argumentation in philosophical theology is generally more effective than that of either Descartes or Locke. His inferences are consistently correct, the conclusions reliably following from his premises. The problems with his reasoning suggested here have to do with his basic principles, which serve as either premises or the foundations of premises in his arguments. His philosophy is in the tradition of Cartesian rationalism but developed in the context of an explicit critique of Lockean empiricism. Thus it can be seen as a provocative stimulus to the more radical empiricism of Hume.

Notes

1. Leibniz's birthdate is frequently listed as June 21 because until 1700, Leipzig did not adopt our Gregorian calendar, according to which the correct date is ten days later.

2. English translations of many of these works—especially (3), (4), (7), (12), and (13)—are widely reprinted; yet there is no convenient collection which includes them all. Whenever possible, textual references will be made to *Leibniz Selections*, Philip P. Wiener, ed. (New York: Charles Scribner's Sons, 1951), identified hereafter as "Wiener." A second choice for textual sources will be *Monadology and Other Philosophical Essays*, by Gottfried Wilhelm von Leibniz, trans. Paul Schrecker and Anne Martin Schrecker (Indianapolis: Bobbs-Merrill, 1965), hereafter called "Schrecker." Many references to works that are in neither Wiener's nor Schrecker's anthologies will be to *Philosophical Papers and Letters*, by Gottfried Wilhelm Leibniz, ed. and trans. Leroy E. Loemker, 2nd ed. (Dordrecht: D. Reidel, 1970), identified hereafter as "Loemker." We shall also make many references to *Theodicy: Essays on the Goodness of God, the Freedom of Man and the Origin of Evil*, by G. W. Leibniz, trans. E. M. Huggard, ed. Austin Farrer (London: Routledge & Kegan Paul, 1951), referring to it as "*Theodicy*." Abbreviated references to many of Leibniz's works will be used. For example, "*Dissertation*" will refer to his *Dissertation on the Art of Combinations*; "*Discourse*" will refer to his *Discourse on Metaphysics*; "*New Essays*" will refer to his *New Essays on the Human Understanding*; "Vindication" will refer to his "Vindication of God's Justice Reconciled with His Other Perfections and All His Actions"; "Principles" will refer to his "Principles of Nature and of Grace, Based on Reason"; and "Monadology" will refer to "The Monadology."

3. Loemker, pp. 12–13.

4. Ibid., p. 74; cf. Schrecker, p. 13.

5. Schrecker, p. 11.

6. Loemker, p. 463.

7. Wiener, p. 107.

8. Loemker, p. 585; cf. Wiener, p. 16.

9. Wiener, pp. 12–13.

10. Ibid., p. 15; cf. p. 51 and Schrecker, p. 14.

11. Ibid., pp. 20–21, 23; cf. Schrecker, pp. 12, 16.

12. Loemker, pp. 235, 241.

13. Ibid., p. 236.   14. Ibid., p. 232.   15. Ibid., p. 268.

16. Ibid., pp. 264–65. In a letter written almost three decades later, Leibniz seems more correct, saying, "A truth is *necessary* when the opposite implies contradiction, and when it is not necessary it is called *contingent*"—Wiener, p. 480.

17. Schrecker, p. 15.

18. Wiener, pp. 82, 87. In his "Abstract of *A Treatise of Human Nature*," Hume pays him tribute for taking seriously the logic of probability: "The celebrated Monsieur Leibniz has observed it to be a defect in the common systems of logic that they are very copious when they explain the operations of the understanding in the forming of demonstrations, but are too concise when they treat of probabilities and those other measures of evidence on which life and action entirely depend, and which are our guides even in most of our philosophical speculations"—David Hume, *An Inquiry concerning Human Understanding*, ed. Charles W. Hendel (Indianapolis: Bobbs-Merrill, 1955), p. 184.

19. Loemker, p. 94.

20. Ibid., pp. 209–10.

21. Wiener, pp. 54, 60, 89.

22. Loemker, p. 210.

23. Schrecker, pp. 22, 24–27.

24. Ibid., pp. 28–30.   25. Ibid., pp. 34–35.

26. Ibid., pp. 35–36; cf. Wiener, p. 288.

27. Ibid., p. 40. Likewise in his *Discourse on Metaphysics*, he cautiously says that "the opinions . . . of the so-called scholastic philosophers are not to be wholly despised," that "our moderns do not do sufficient justice to Saint Thomas and to the other great men of that period and that there is in the theories of the scholastic philosophers and theologians far more solidity than is imagined"—Wiener, pp. 303–4. See Wiener, p. 553, for a comparable criticism.

28. Schrecker, p. 80.

29. Wiener, pp. 367–68. As a historical note it might be observed that Locke was at least somewhat familiar with Leibniz's critique of his ideas. In 1696, Leibniz sent a brief critique to a Scottish friend, Thomas Burnett, to pass on to Locke, who did receive and read it. In a letter of April 10, 1697, Locke expressed his disappointment with the remarks of Leibniz, whose reputation had preceded him: "I must confess to you that Mr. L—'s great name had raised in me an expectation which the sight of his paper did not answer"—*The Works of John Locke* (London: Thomas Davidson, Whitefriars, 1823), vol. 9, p. 407.

30. Wiener, pp. 369–70.

31. Ibid., p. 372.   32. Ibid., p. 373.

33. John Locke, *An Essay concerning Human Understanding*, collated by Alexander Campbell Fraser (New York: Dover Publications, 1959), vol. 1, p. 41.

34. Wiener, p. 374.

35. Ibid., pp. 397–98, 400; cf. p. 406.

36. Ibid., pp. 408–10, 405.

37. Ibid., p. 424.   38. Ibid., p. 440.

39. Ibid., pp. 460, 463, 465–66.

40. Ibid., pp. 461, 472–73.   41. Ibid., pp. 473–74.   42. Ibid., pp. 281, 283.

43. Ibid., pp. 283–85.   44. Ibid., pp. 328–29; cf. pp. 289–90.

45. Ibid., pp. 535, 525. For further analysis of the sensible and the intelligible dimensions of knowledge, see Leibniz's letter to Queen Sophia Charlotte (1702)— pp. 355–61.

46. Ibid., pp. 326–27. In a rather unknown, undated paper, "On the Method of Distinguishing Real from Imaginary Phenomena," Leibniz suggests four criteria of coherence for knowledge of empirical phenomena: they should be rationally explicable, be consistent with past experience, conform to the experience of others, and be fruitful for predicting future phenomena—Loemker, p. 364.

47. Wiener, p. 300; cf. "Monadology," no. 22, Wiener, p. 537. In two letters to Arnauld, written a few months after the *Discourse*, Leibniz explained this idea in more detail—George R. Montgomery, trans., *Leibniz: Discourse on Metaphysics, Correspondence with Arnauld, and Monadology* (La Salle: Open Court, 1968), pp. 107, 113, 117, 126, 132; this work will hereafter be called "Montgomery."

48. Wiener, p. 301.

49. Ibid., p. 534; cf. pp. 96, 243–44, 380, 441–42; also letters to Arnauld, Montgomery, pp. 111, 129.

50. Wiener, p. 527. Statements and uses of this principle permeate Leibniz's philosophical writings. See "Monadology," Wiener, p. 540; also Wiener, pp. 92–96, 218, 225, 228–29, 242, 278–79, 346, 436, 482; also letters to Arnauld, Montgomery, pp. 132, 218.

51. Wiener, pp. 527–28, 540–41.

52. Ibid., pp. 294, 297.

53. Ibid., p. 544 ("Monadology," section 58); cf. "Principles," p. 528. In 1759, Voltaire caustically satirized this Leibnizian doctrine by attributing it to the ridiculous Dr. Pangloss, who, in the midst of horrible devastation, insists that "all is for the best" in this "best of all possible worlds," leading the frantic Candide to ask himself, "If this is the best of all possible worlds, what are the others like?"—Voltaire, *Candide*, trans. Lowell Bair (New York: Bantam Books, 1959), pp. 18, 31.

54. Wiener, pp. 549, 551; cf. "Principles," p. 524; also letter to Arnauld, Montgomery, p. 188.

55. Wiener, p. 539; cf. letter to Arnauld, Montgomery, p. 141.

56. Wiener, pp. 360–61.

57. Ibid., p. 163.   58. Ibid., p. 422.

59. Ibid., p. 522. This is a more dynamic conception than Leibniz used in his *Dissertation* of 1666, where he asserted, "I call *substance* whatever moves or is moved" —Loemker, p. 73.

60. Ibid., p. 533.   61. Ibid., p. 534.   62. Ibid., p. 330.

63. Ibid., p. 543.   64. Ibid., pp. 330, 337.

65. Schrecker, p. 83.

66. Wiener, p. 453.

67. Loemker, p. 614.

68. Wiener, pp. 547, 536–39.

69. Ibid., pp. 550–52; cf. pp. 305, 339–44 (*Discourse*); also letter to Arnauld, Montgomery, pp. 155–56; also Wiener, pp. 108–10, 371, 419, 504–7.

70. Ibid., pp. 331–34.   71. Ibid., p. 541.

72. Loemker, p. 466.

73. Ibid., pp. 73–74.   74. Ibid., p. 75.   75. Ibid., p. 89.

76. Wiener, p. 436.

77. Ibid., pp. 345–47. Compare the argument from sufficient reason in sections 7–8 of "Principles" (Wiener, pp. 527–28), as well as sections 36–38 of "Monadology" (Wiener, p. 540). In both of these passages Leibniz explains that God, as "a necessary being," has "the reason of his existence in himself." The sufficient reason of God's existence is to be found in the divine nature itself.

78. Ibid., p. 473.

79. Ibid., pp. 349–50; cf. "Monadology," sections 43–44, Wiener, p. 541.

80. Ibid., p. 541.

81. Ibid., p. 324. As a historical note, we might point out that this is not an entirely original idea on Leibniz's part. In his reply to the second set of Objections, collected by Mersenne, Descartes considers adding to his rule "*that which we clearly understand to belong to the nature of anything, can truthfully be asserted to belong to its nature*" the proviso as long as "*the nature of that thing be possible, or not contradictory.*" But he immediately dismisses this idea by observing "how little value this exception has"— *The Philosophical Works of Descartes*, translated by Elizabeth S. Haldane and G.R.T. Ross (Cambridge Univ. Press, 1968), vol. 2, p. 45.

82. Wiener, p. 461.

83. Ibid., pp. 541–42; cf. pp. 286–87; also Loemker, p. 231.

84. Loemker, p. 167.

85. Ibid., p. 211.

86. Wiener, p. 397.

87. Ibid., p. 473.

88. Loemker, p. 101; cf. pp. 217–18, 565–66.

89. Wiener, pp. 473–74.

90. Ibid., pp. 192–93.   91. Ibid., p. 118; cf. Loemker, p. 494.

92. Wiener, p. 192; cf. Preface to *New Essays*, Wiener, pp. 384, 391; also *Theodicy*, p. 257.

93. Wiener, pp. 290, 297–98, 313; cf. correspondence with Clarke, Wiener, pp. 235, 268, 274–75.

94. Ibid., p. 366.

95. Loemker, pp. 492–97, 574–85.

96. Pierre Bayle, *Historical and Critical Dictionary: Selections*, trans. Richard H. Popkin (Indianapolis: Bobbs-Merrill, 1965), pp. 340–41, 186, 151, 177, 218.

97. *Theodicy*, pp. 73, 80.

98. Ibid., pp. 73–75.   99. Ibid., pp. 75–76.   100. Ibid., pp. 87–90.

101. Ibid., pp. 90–92.

102. Ibid., pp. 98, 102; cf. Leibniz's claim in "On True Method in Philosophy and Theology": "It is a wise saying of that distinguished man Francis Bacon: a little philosophy 'inclineth man's mind to atheism, but depth in philosophy bringeth men's minds about to religion'"—Wiener, p. 62.

103. *Theodicy*, pp. 105, 111–12.

104. Loemker, pp. 213–16.

105. Schrecker, p. 123.

106. Wiener, p. 295; cf. section 36, p. 344.

107. Ibid., pp. 531–32.   108. Ibid., p. 552.

109. Ibid., pp. 295, 299; cf. Paul's Epistle, *Romans* (5:20)—"But where sin abounded, grace did much more abound."

110. Wiener, pp. 351–54.

111. *Theodicy*, p. 123.

112. Wiener, p. 306.

113. Schrecker, p. 117.

114. *Theodicy*, pp. 143–44, 128. A problem evident here is this: What if (1) there were two equally good (but different) possible worlds, (2) all other possible worlds were less good than either of these two, and (3) it would be better for God to create either of these possible worlds than not to create at all? According to Leibniz, God would have no sufficient reason to choose either of these possible worlds over the other. In this way there seems to be a conflict between saying that God will always do what is best and the possibility that two possible worlds might be equally good.

115. Ibid., p. 154; cf. Schrecker, p. 136.

116. Schrecker, p. 116.

117. *Theodicy*, p. 140.

118. Ibid., p. 136; cf. Schrecker, p. 120.

119. *Theodicy*, pp. 141–42; cf. Schrecker, p. 129.

120. *Theodicy*, pp. 137, 129.

121. Schrecker, p. 127.

122. *Theodicy*, p. 182.

123. Ibid., pp. 188–91.   124. Ibid., pp. 192, 196, 200, 266.

125. Ibid., p. 300.

126. Wiener, pp. 509–10.

127. Ibid., pp. 510–12.   128. Ibid., pp. 512–13.   129. Ibid., pp. 515–16.

130. Fyodor Dostoyevsky, *The Brothers Karamazov*, trans. Constance Garnett, ed. Manuel Komroff (New York: New American Library, 1957), pp. 223, 226.

131. Wiener, pp. 517–18.

132. Ibid., pp. 518–19.   133. Ibid., p. 519.

134. Ibid., pp. 520–22; cf. *Theodicy*, p. 299.

5

Hume's Skeptical Deism

Life and Writings

Hume's life began in Edinburgh, Scotland on April 26, 1711 (six and a half years after Locke died and five and a half years before the death of Leibniz). David Hume was the youngest child of Joseph Home, pronounced "Hume," a lawyer and landowner, who died in 1713. David's mother, Katherine Falconer, the daughter of a president of the College of Justice, did not remarry but committed herself to bringing up her three children, John, Katherine, and David. They grew up, under her tutelage, in the pleasant but not luxurious environment of the family estate at Ninewells. The elder son, John, was legal heir to the family estate. There seems to have been a considerable amount of warmth and affection in the family while the children were growing up. The family was Presbyterian, members of the established Calvinist Church of Scotland, and David seems to have been quite pious as a small boy.

The Hume children were educated at home, while young, and had access to the Ninewells library. Although he was no precocious genius (like Leibniz), David seems to have had a quick and eager mind. In a letter of 1734, he provides "a kind of History of my Life," in which he says that from "earliest Infancy" he had "a strong Inclination to Books & Letters." Before he was twelve, David was sent up to Edinburgh University to begin college with his brother John (who was two years older). There is extremely little information about the undergraduate education of its most famous alumnus either from Edinburgh University's official records or from the man himself. Perhaps the best comment is from that same letter of 1734, where Hume writes,

> As our college education in Scotland, extending little further than the Languages, ends commonly when we are about 14 or 15 Years of Age, I was after that left to my own Choice in my Reading, & found it encline me almost equally to Books of Reasoning & Philosophy, & to Poetry.[1]

The normal course of studies at Edinburgh at the time was such that it is reasonable to suppose that Hume took classes in Greek, mathematics, logic and metaphysics, ethics, and natural philosophy. And it is likely that he was exposed there to the thought of Newton and Locke. It is also probable that his orthodox Christian religious beliefs were crumbling during these college years.

As the preceding quotation indicates, Hume left Edinburgh at about the age of fourteen or fifteen. He did not take any academic degree. This was certainly not for lack of ability or interest in learning. In the year in which he died, he wrote a very brief autobiography, "My Own Life," in which he said, "I passed through the ordinary course of education with success, and was seized very early with a passion for literature, which has been the ruling passion of my life, and the great source of my enjoyments." His family encouraged him to make a profession of the law, which would have been in keeping with family tradition as well as his own abilities and character. But, as he says, "I found an unsurmountable aversion to every thing but the pursuits of philosophy and general learning."[2] Most of his time between about 1726 and 1734 was spent on private studies; the first three of those years included the learning of law, which gave him access to the Advocates' Library at Edinburgh.

Not being in a formal course of studies, Hume could happily direct his own learning. In the earliest letter of his that we have (1727), he writes,

> just now I am entirely confined to my self & Library for Diversion.... I take no more of them than I please, for I hate task-reading, & I diversify them at my Pleasure; sometimes a Philosopher, sometimes a Poet.... I live like a King pretty much by my self.

He expresses here his special passion for philosophy, saying, "tis a subject I think much on & could talk all day long" about. During these years he also gained a facility in the French language. By early 1729, he had abandoned his (rather half-hearted) commitment to legal studies: "The Law, which was the Business I design'd to follow, appear'd nauseous to me, & I cou'd think of no other way of pushing my Fortune in the World, but that of a Scholar & Philosopher." For several months he pursued philosophical studies "with an Ardor natural to young men" and was "infinitely happy" doing so.[3]

But when he was eighteen, he suffered a period of what today is called "burnout." As he says, "about the beginning of Sept 1729, all my Ardor seem'd in a moment to be extinguisht, & I cou'd no longer raise my Mind to that pitch, which formerly gave me such excessive Pleasure." He attributed this insouciance to "a Laziness of Temper, which must be overcome by redoubling my Application. In this Condition I remain'd for nine Months, very uneasy to myself."[4] He suffered a bout of scurvy during this period and underwent medical treatment (which included antihysteric pills and claret wine). He gradually recovered his health and energy. During the next few years, he continued to alternate between staying in Edinburgh and residing at Ninewells.

One of the works Hume was probably studying during the period following his recovery was Bayle's *Dictionary*. It is exciting to think of Hume, at twenty-one years of age, having been schooled in the ancients and relatively orthodox moderns such as Newton and Locke, trying to assimilate the critique of rationalism to be found in Bayle's work. One cannot help wondering how great a stimulus this was to the development of Hume's own skeptical philosophy. Sometime between 1732 and 1734, Hume says, "I began to consider seriously, how I should proceed in my Philosophical Enquiries." He was becoming critical of philosophies, including those "transmitted to us by Antiquity," that are guilty "of being entirely Hypothetical, and depending more upon Invention than Experience. . . . without regarding human Nature."[5] It was during this time that Hume was planning his own approach to doing philosophy.

By the spring of 1734, Hume says, "I resolved to seek out a more active Life, & tho' I cou'd not quit my Pretensions to Learning, but with my last Breath, to lay them aside for some time, in order the more effectually to resume them." He decided to try the life of a merchant and set off for Bristol, England to work for a reputable businessman.[6] (Very soon after he left Scotland, he was accused by an Agnes Galbraith of fathering her illegitimate child. But her sexual history was a shady one, and Hume was not present to answer the charges. At any rate, the Presbytery to which the accusation was made was not convinced of her story, and we have no way of knowing whether it was true.) Hume found his job as a clerk in a Bristol trading firm quite unsatisfying and "in a few months found that scene totally unsuitable to me."[7] He quarrelled with his supervisor over matters of grammatical style and decided to leave the world of commerce. (It was while he was in Bristol that he changed the spelling of his name from "Home" to "Hume" in order that it might conform to its pronunciation.) In the summer of 1734, he retired to France, where he was to stay for three years.

Most of these three years were pleasantly spent in La Flèche, which was notable mainly for its Jesuit College, of which Descartes had been an alumnus. Hume's French was good enough that he could study the works of Descartes, Malebranche, and Arnauld, thus getting a direct familiarity with the modern rationalism against which he would write. His relationships with the Jesuits there seem to have been quite cordial. (In a letter he tells of an argument he had with one of them about "some nonsensical miracle performed in their convent."[8]) Most importantly, during this time at La Flèche, Hume composed his philosophical masterpiece, *A Treatise of Human Nature*. It is one of the ironies in the history of philosophy that the strongest alternative to modern rationalism of that time was written at what, in a sense, its birthplace. In the second half of 1737, his mission in France accomplished, Hume returned to London.

Between September of 1737 and February of 1739, he was in London trying to engage a publisher for his *Treatise*. He indicates in a letter of 1737 that he was excited, anxious, and perhaps a bit irritable in this pursuit:

> I began to feel some Passages weaker for the Style & Diction than I cou'd have wisht. The Nearness & Greatness of the Event rouz'd up my Attention, & made me more difficult to please than when I was alone in perfect Tranquillity in France.

With that letter Hume enclosed "some Reasonings concerning Miracles," which he had decided against publishing with the *Treatise* for fear of giving "too much Offence" and which he asks his friend to burn after reading. He admits with some embarrassment that he has decided to excise some of the more controversial sections of what he wrote in France:

> I am at present castrating my Work, that is, cutting off its noble Parts, that is, endeavouring it shall give as little Offence as possible. . . . This is a Piece of Cowardice, for which I blame myself; tho I believe none of my Friends will blame me. But I was resolv'd not to be an Enthusiast, in Philosophy, while I was blaming other Enthusiasms.[9]

In 1738, Hume did secure a publisher for a first edition of one thousand copies of the *Treatise*. In January of 1739, the first two books of the

Treatise were published; the third book, which needed further revision, was not printed until November of 1740. The critical notices and reviews (in English, German, and French) were generally bad and occasionally nasty. The now famous words of his autobiography vividly express Hume's acute disappointment with the cold reception his masterpiece received: "Never literary attempt was more unfortunate than my Treatise of Human Nature. It fell *dead-born from the press*, without reaching such distinction, as even to excite a murmur among the zealots." This is probably an exaggeration on his part. But one can understand and sympathize with his crushed feelings after investing the bulk of his time, effort, and energy between 1734 and 1740 into the producing of a remarkably original and painstakingly developed work (which is arguably the most important and provocative book of philosophy ever written in the English language). He immediately proceeds to say that he quickly rebounded from his disappointment: "But being naturally of a cheerful and sanguine temper, I very soon recovered the blow, and prosecuted with great ardour my studies in the country."[10]

He set to work on a series of twenty-seven essays, published in two volumes in Edinburgh in 1741–42 under the title of *Essays Moral and Political*. This effort, unlike the earlier *Treatise*, proved fortunately successful. In "My Own Life" he writes that "the work was favourably received, and soon made me entirely forget my former disappointment."[11] He proudly boasts in a 1742 letter to a friend, "The Essays are all sold in London. . . . There is a Demand for them; & . . . Innys the great Bookseller in Paul's Church Yard wonders there is not a new Edition, for that he cannot find Copies for his Customers"; and he even expresses the hope that this success might "bring forward the rest of my Philosophy."[12] Meanwhile, he continued to reside at Ninewells with his mother and brother, improving his facility in Greek.

In 1744, he applied to fill a vacant chair in ethics and spiritual philosophy at the University of Edinburgh, his *alma mater*. The duties of that position required that its holder give instructions in the truths of the Christian religion. There were delays in the making of an appointment. Hume was attacked, accused of "Heresy, **Deism**, Scepticism, Atheism,"[13] and denied the position.

In 1745, he took a position as private tutor to the Marquis of Annandale, who turned out to be insane. The job was lucrative but very trying. Hume had to act as keeper to the mad marquis, whose behavior was erratic and sometimes violent. To make matters worse, Hume's mother died that same year, while he was away in England. He was extremely attached to her and, in a letter written at that time, describes her death as leaving "an immense void in our Family."[14] He was dismissed in 1746 from his position with the marquis and immediately accepted another as secretary to General James St. Clair, a distant relation, who was planning a military expedition against the French in Canada. Hume was willing to accompany the general, but the expedition failed to materialize. However, the general had Hume commissioned as a judge-advocate of his forces, which unsuccessfully attempted to invade the coast of Brittany. In 1747, Hume accompanied the general on a secret mission to the courts of Vienna and Turin. He seems to have become infatuated with a countess in Turin, but she did not reciprocate his affections. His years with the general were otherwise profitable and pleasant; as he put it, "I passed them agreeably and in good company; and my appointments, with my frugality, had made me reach a fortune."[15]

While in the general's employ, Hume ate well and became quite fat. At about six feet, he was tall for the time—but his newly acquired bulk made his appearance something of a laughingstock. There is a wonderful description of him by James Caulfield (later Lord Charlemont), who met him in Turin and emphasizes the striking disparity between his personality and his physical appearance:

> Nature, I believe, never formed any man more unlike his real character than David Hume. . . . His face was broad and fat, his mouth wide, and without any other expression than that of imbecility. His eyes vacant and spiritless, and the corpulence of his whole person was far better fitted to communicate the idea of a turtle-eating alderman than of a refined philosopher.[16]

Meanwhile, Hume had not abandoned his literary pursuits. Encouraged by the popularity of his *Essays*, he worked on revising Book I of the *Treatise*:

> I had always entertained a notion, that my want of success in publishing the Treatise of Human Nature, had proceeded more from the manner than the matter, and that I had been guilty of a very usual indiscretion, in going to the press too early. I, therefore, cast the first part of that work anew in the Enquiry concerning Human Understanding, which was published while I was at Turin

—that is, in 1748. As he adds, "this piece was at first little more successful than the Treatise." In 1749, he resumed living with his brother at Ninewells for a couple of years until the latter married. While there, he was informed by his bookseller that his "former publications (all but the unfortunate Treatise) were beginning to be the subject of conversation; that the sale of them was gradually increasing, and that new editions were demanded." In 1751, he moved to Edinburgh, where his sister lived, "the true scene for a man of letters." His *Enquiry concerning the Principles of Morals*, which was a revised version of Book III of the *Treatise* and which Hume himself considered his best writing, was published that same year. But like his first two hard-core works of philosophy, this one "came unnoticed and unobserved into the world." By contrast, in 1752, "were published at Edinburgh, where I then lived, my Political Discourses, the only work of mine that was successful on the first publication. It was well received abroad and at home."[17] Favorable reviews of his works were appearing in print. By 1753, collected editions of his writings (again except for the *Treatise*) were being published. French and German translations of his works were printed. His literary ambitions were being fulfilled. In 1751, he was elected secretary of the Philosophical Society of Edinburgh.

He applied for a chair in logic at Glasgow University in 1752 but again failed to get the academic position. (The man who was appointed proved to be as obscure a philosopher as the one preferred to Hume by the University of Edinburgh eight years earlier. But in each case acceptable mediocrity prevailed over controversial talent.) That same year, he was appointed Keeper of the Advocates' Library in Edinburgh. As librarian, he had access to the thousands of printed materials that could facilitate his writing of a history of Great Britain. He held this position until the beginning of 1757, when he resigned. His *History of England* was published in six volumes between 1754 and 1762. Its reception was initially discouraging, but it became popular in Hume's lifetime and ultimately contributed to both his fame and his fortune. In France Voltaire wrote (in 1764) that it was possibly the best history ever written in any language.

Animosity against Hume's philosophical writings increased, especially against his first *Enquiry* (which had originally been called *Philosophical Essays concerning Human Understanding*) and which he had published against the advice of friends. As he wrote to one of them, "I won't justify the prudence of this step, any other way than by expressing my indifference about all the consequences that may follow."[18] The essay "Of Miracles," which appeared as section X (and which we shall examine later) proved to be as offensive as Hume had anticipated. "Of a Particular Providence and of a Future State," the eleventh section, also generated opposition, although it was diplomatically couched in the form of a dialogue. As if to add fuel to the fire, in 1757, he published his *Four Dissertations*, including the controversial "Natural History of Religion," written several years earlier.

Unlike the proverbial prophet of the Gospels, Hume was not "without honor in his own country." But he was far more warmly appreciated in France, especially by the *philosophes*. Madame de Boufflers, a French countess who was the patron of Rousseau, had read him and wrote to him in 1761 expressing her admiration and the hope that he might go to France. The following year, she appealed to him to help Jean-Jacques Rousseau, who had gotten into difficulties and needed to flee from France, by serving as his protector. Hume eagerly agreed to do so. But Rousseau politely declined to accept his hospitality at that time.

In 1763, Hume accepted the invitation of Francis Conway, the Earl of Hertford and British ambassador to France, to accompany him there as his personal secretary. It was as if Hume's reputation had been washed pure. As he wryly says in a letter of that time, "I was now a Person clean & white as the driven Snow."[19] His welcome to France was magnificent. He writes in his autobiography, "Those who have not seen the strange effects of modes, will never imagine the reception I met with at Paris, from men and women of all ranks and stations. The more I resiled from their excessive civilities, the more I was loaded with them."[20] His popularity with the French, far from being a momentary sensation, persisted for the twenty-six months he was there. He became a particularly close friend of Jean d'Alembert and Denis Diderot, the editors of the *Encyclopedia*; Hume's favorite *philosophe* was d'Alembert, to whom he bequeathed a legacy in his will.

Hume's relationship with Madame de Boufflers intensified while he was in France. She and her husband had been estranged and living apart for well over a decade before she actually met Hume. For a while, she had been the mistress of a widowed Prince de Conti, with whom she remained friends after the ardor of their love affair had passed. When they first met in France, Hume was fifty-two and she was thirty-eight. She must have been quite attractive in both physical appearance and personality. She was very warm and gracious toward Hume, calling him her "Master of philosophy and ethics." From his point of view, the relationship had developed from friendship into romantic love by the summer of 1764. Some of his letters of that season reveal that he was suffering "the inquietudes of the most unfortunate passion." A letter written in early August is particularly pathetic. But, of course, from Hume's point of view there was a problem in that she had a living husband. It seems clear that Hume's infatuation was apparent to others. His friend Gilbert Elliot visited him in France and in September wrote Hume strongly urging caution, appealing to him "in friendship" to realize that he was standing "upon the very brink of a precipice." What is not clear is how she felt about Hume. Did she regard him merely as a friend and confidant, with a combination of flirtation and respect? Did she encourage his romantic inclinations? Did she reciprocate such feelings? We do not know. The event that brought the strained relationship to an ironic climax was the death of her husband that autumn. Whatever she had felt for and said to Hume, she "grew obsessed with one ambition—to marry her former lover, the Prince de Conti. This, it seems, helped to cure Hume of his infatuation, as well it might. For she now shamelessly made use of him as go-between" with the Prince.[21] It is a mark of his character and loyalty, however, that he remained constant in his friendship for her, one of the last letters he wrote (five days before his death) being to her.

Hume's official appointment as secretary to the French Embassy came in the summer of 1765. Considering all the accusations that had been raised against him over the years, Hume was proud to have received the commission, as he put it, "in spite of Atheism & Deism, of Whiggism & Toryism, of Scoticism & Philosophy."[22] The Earl of Hertford, the British Ambassador there, was appointed the Lord Lieutenant of Ireland that same summer. So for a few months, as Hume writes, he "was *chargé d'affaires* till the arrival of the Duke of Richmond," the new Ambassador.[23]

The man the French lovingly called "le bon David" left Paris for London at the beginning of 1766, taking with him the beleaguered Rousseau, whom he had met and liked in December of the preceding year. Hume had been warned that he was a very difficult, quarrelsome person; but the warm-hearted Hume nevertheless helped to get Rousseau settled in England. Given the personality differences between the warm, affable Hume and the distrustful, moody Rousseau, friction was inevitable. The latter suspiciously imagined Hume to be hypocritically leading an international conspiracy against him. Hume tried to defend himself against Rousseau's public accusations of treachery, but to no avail. Rousseau never realized that his sense of persecution and betrayal by the man who had shown him only kindness and solicitude was no more than a fabrication of his own imagination. As Hume wrote Mme. de Boufflers in December of 1766, "Thanks to God, my affair with Rousseau is now finally and totally at an end."[24]

In 1767, Hume was appointed an under secretary of state, an honor to which no official salary was attached, although he was not anxious to stay on in England. As he wrote to a friend a few months before the appointment, "London at least can appear very little tempting to one who believes he is there hated as a Scotsman and despised as a Man of Letters."[25] Hume's politics were suspect. His sympathies were with the Whigs, with republicanism, and with the American Colonies in their struggle for more freedom from England. (In a letter of 1775 he wrote, "I am an American in my Principles, and wish we would let them alone to govern or misgovern themselves as they think proper"; in another letter that same year, written to his nephew, David Hume, he wrote "that the Republican Form of [Government] is by far the best."[26]) Nevertheless, Hume stayed in office in London until August of 1769, when he retired to Edinburgh, where he spent the rest of his life.

Although he was nearing sixty, Hume seems to have considered marrying; but caution prevailed, and he did not do so. He had a house built in St. Andrews Square in Edinburgh, where he lived with his sister Katherine (who also never married) and his dog, Foxey. (One of his first house-guests there was Benjamin Franklin from America.) He remained attached to his married brother John's large family at Ninewells and was particularly partial to his nephew, David, paying to have him educated at Glasgow.

In his autobiography Hume writes, "In spring 1775, I was struck with a disorder in my bowels, which at first gave me no alarm, but has since, as I apprehend it, become mortal and incurable."[27] (The disease may have been intestinal cancer or colitis.) His suffering and prospect of death did not mar his characteristic good nature. He was especially eager to work on revising and seeing to the eventual publication of his *Dialogues concerning Natural Religion*, which he had written in the early 1750s and had sporadically worked at over a period of about a quarter of a century. He asked his friend Adam Smith, the economist, to have them published, but Smith did not wish to do so. In a codicil to his will, with his *Dialogues* and brief autobiography in mind, Hume wrote, "if my Dialogues, from whatever cause, be not published within two years and a half after my Death, as also the account of my Life, the Property shall return to my Nephew, David, whose Duty, in publishing them as the last Request of his Uncle, must be approved of by all the World."[28] Hume died on August 25, 1776 and was buried four days later, a large crowd gathering in the rain to watch his coffin pass.

At the end of his autobiography Hume gives what seems to be an accurate assessment of his own character:

> I was, I say, a man of mild dispositions, of command of temper, of an open, social, and cheerful humour, capable of attachment, but little susceptible of enmity, and of great moderation in all my passions. Even my love of literary

fame, my ruling passion, never soured my temper, notwithstanding my frequent disappointments.[29]

A movingly beautiful tribute was made by Adam Smith in a letter to another of Hume's friends later that year and followed a description of his dying:

> Thus died our most excellent, and never-to-be-forgotten friend; concerning whose philosophical opinions men will no doubt judge variously, every one approving or condemning them according as they happen to coincide or disagree with his own; but concerning whose character and conduct there can scarce be a difference of opinion. His temper, indeed, seemed to be more happily balanced, if I may be allowed such an expression, than that perhaps of any other man I have ever known. . . . The extreme gentleness of his nature never weakened either the firmness of his mind, or the steadiness of his resolutions. His constant pleasantry was the genuine effusion of good nature and good humour, tempered with delicacy and modesty, and without even the slightest tincture of malignity, so frequently the disagreeable source of what is called wit in other men. . . . Upon the whole, I have always considered him, both in his lifetime, and since his death, as approaching as nearly to the idea of a perfectly wise and virtuous man, as perhaps the nature of human frailty will admit.[30]

Of all the thinkers discussed here, Hume would probably have been the most pleasant to meet and engage in conversation.

Hume's main philosophical writings are his (1) *Treatise of Human Nature*,[31] which was published anonymously in 1739–40; (2) "Abstract of a Treatise of Human Nature,"[32] published anonymously in 1740; (3) *Enquiry concerning Human Understanding*,[33] published in 1748; (4) *Enquiry concerning the Principles of Morals*,[34] published in 1751; (5) essays "On Suicide" and "On the **Immortality** of the Soul,"[35] written in the early 1750s and printed shortly thereafter, though Hume suppressed their distribution; however, copies were passed around, smuggled abroad, and the essays were published posthumously in London in 1777; and (6) *Dialogues concerning Natural Religion*,[36] published posthumously (by his nephew) in 1779. Although this list is rather short (in comparison, for example, with that for Leibniz), these are all important contributions to the history of philosophy; and, it would seem, the four books, (1), (3), (4), and (6), should be included in any list of the greatest works of philosophy ever written in any language. Two other writings that will be important for our purposes deal more with the psychology of religion than philosophy: his essay "Of Superstition and Enthusiasm,"[37] which appeared in the first volume of *Essays Moral and Political*, was published in 1741; and his *Natural History of Religion*,[38] one of his *Four Dissertations*, was published in 1757.

Theory of Knowledge

On Descartes, Leibniz, and Locke. Hume's treatment of his predecessors and innate ideas is to be found in his first three philosophical works, (1), (2), and (3). He was far more an original thinker than a historian of philosophy, and his discussions of Descartes, Leibniz, and Locke are few, scattered, and cursory. He also has relatively little to say about the issue of innate ideas. Nevertheless, his considerations here will provide us with a context in which we can situate his theory of knowledge.

In 1737, when Hume had left La Flèche, where Descartes had gone to school, and was on his way to London, he wrote to a friend with whom he hoped to discuss the *Treatise* he had composed while in France. He suggested that Descartes's *Meditations* would be useful background material for a critical consideration of parts of his own ideas. In his *Enquiry concerning Human Understanding*,[39] Hume rejects the "*antecedent*" skepticism represented by Descartes's method of systematic doubt "as a sovereign preservative against error and precipitate judgement" on the grounds that it is not feasible to carry it out, that it will not reveal an "original principle" on which all commitments can be indubitably based, and will therefore prove to be insuperable.

> The Cartesian doubt, therefore, were it ever possible to be attained by any human creature (as it plainly is not), would be entirely incurable, and no reasoning could ever bring us to a state of assurance and conviction upon any subject.

In Hume's "Abstract" he takes him to task for his abstract, unfounded conception of mental substance:

> Descartes maintained that thought was the essence of the mind—not this thought or that thought, but thought in general. This seems to be absolutely unintelligible, since everything that exists is particular.[40]

In the *Treatise* he likewise criticizes "the *Cartesians*" for imagining that we have a clear and distinct idea of physical substance as essentially extended but inert, "endow'd with no efficacy" and unable "to communicate motion."[41] Yet, in trying to account for the motion of bodies,

> *Cartesians*, proceeding upon their principle of innate ideas, have had recourse to a supreme spirit or deity, whom they consider as the only active being in the universe, and as the immediate cause of every alteration in matter. But the principle of innate ideas being allow'd to be false, it follows, that the supposition of a deity can serve us in no stead, in accounting for that idea of agency.

Now this critique may be more obviously directed against Malebranche than Descartes himself, as Hume acknowledges in a footnote to the *Enquiry*; but he also says there that "Descartes insinuated that doctrine of the universal and sole efficacy of the Deity, without insisting on it."[42]

Hume rarely refers to Leibniz by name. In his "Abstract" he praises Leibniz for recognizing, as earlier Cartesians seem not to have done, the importance of a logic of probabilities to those of our reasonings "on which life and action entirely depend, and which are our guides even in most of our philosophical speculations."[43] There is another mention of Leibniz by name in the *Dialogues*,[44] where he is (mistakenly) accused of having denied the reality of evil. Perhaps Hume so seldom speaks of Leibniz because he did not have a good first-hand knowledge of his writings.

The references to Locke, as one might expect, are more frequent. Hume was almost surely exposed to Locke's ideas when he was a student at Edinburgh; and we know that one of the first philosophers he studied after arriving in France in 1734 was Locke. In the "Introduction" to his *Treatise*,[45] as well as in his "Abstract,"[46] Hume mentions Locke by name, praising him as one of a group of English philosophers who had worked at establishing a science of human nature on empirical foundations (as opposed to the abstract speculations of the rationalists). And later in the *Treatise* he refers to Locke as "a great philosopher," calling him that in the first *Enquiry* as well.[47] On the other hand, in a note to the *Treatise*, he accuses Locke of having "perverted" the concept of an idea by using it too broadly to "stand for all our perceptions" of the mind.[48] In the *Treatise*,[49] as well as the first *Enquiry*,[50] he criticizes Locke's supposition that reason can discover the idea of power as a result of reflecting on the experience of change. In a footnote in the first *Enquiry*,[51] Hume expands Locke's dichotomy between demonstrative and probable arguments into a trichotomy, saying that "we ought to divide arguments into *demonstrations*, *proofs*, and *probabilities*," where proofs are different from demonstrations because they are based on concrete experience rather than abstract reasoning and different from probabilities because they "leave no room for doubt or opposition." In Hume's *Dialogues* his character Cleanthes credits Locke with being "the first Christian, who ventured openly to assert, that *faith* was nothing but a species of *reason*, that religion was only a branch of philosophy."[52]

Innate Ideas. Hume does not seem to feel a need to discuss innate ideas, such as God, at any great length because Locke and Berkeley (both of whom he was reading on first arriving in France), in his opinion, had "already refuted" that rationalistic doctrine. In the *Treatise* he indicates that he has studied the dispute as to "whether there be any *innate ideas*, or whether all ideas be derived from sensation and reflexion" (to put the matter in Lockean words). In a section "Of Abstract Ideas," he calls the empirical theory that all general ideas are derived from concrete particular experience "one of the greatest and most valuable discoveries that has been made of late years in the republic of letters."[53]

Yet elsewhere Hume somewhat complicates the matter. In the "Abstract" he says that on Locke's broad interpretation of the concept of "idea" (which Hume calls "an inaccuracy of that famous philosopher"), we do have innate impressions and feelings, such as our "love of virtue, resentment, and all the other passions" that "arise immediately from nature."[54] And in a footnote to the first *Enquiry*, he indicates that whether there are innate ideas depends on "what is meant" by "innate." If "innate" means "natural," says Hume, all our ideas are natural rather than artificial, supernatural, or miraculous. Second, if "innate" means "contemporary to our birth," we have no innate ideas, and (from the point of view of the *tabula rasa* theory, which Hume accepts) "the dispute seems to be frivolous." And, third, if "innate" means "original or copied from no precedent perception, then may we assert that all our impressions are innate, and our ideas are not innate."[55] His rejection of the rationalists' theory of innate ideas agrees with the perspective of Locke (and Berkeley); but, as we shall see, his is a more radical empiricism.

Ideas and Impressions. Hume's treatment of ideas is the starting point for his own epistemology (as Locke's was for his) in both the *Treatise* and the first *Enquiry*. In the latter book he acknowledges that theoretical speculation can be frustrating and obscure: "But this obscurity, in the profound and abstract philosophy, is objected to, not only as painful and fatiguing, but as the inevitable source of uncertainty and error." It seems he especially has in mind here the "metaphysical" approach of rationalists such as Descartes and Leibniz. He goes on to say,

> The only method of freeing learning at once from these abstruse questions is to inquire seriously into the nature of human understanding and show, from an exact analysis of its powers and capacity, that it is by no means fitted for such remote and abstruse subjects.[56]

So he proposes to analyze critically the powers of the mind in order to define its capabilities and thus to liberate us from useless pursuits.

But how should we proceed in developing this theory of knowledge? In the Introduction to the *Treatise*, he gives the empiricist's answer, that "the only solid foundation we can give to this science itself must be laid on experience and observation."[57] And what "experience and observation" reveal to be the direct, immediate objects of our minds are perceptions. In the *Treatise,* as well as the first *Enquiry,*[58] Hume says that all mental perceptions are of two types, impressions and ideas, distinguished from one another in terms of the different "degrees of force and liveliness with which they strike upon the mind." He goes on to elucidate this distinction:

> Those perceptions, which enter with most force and violence, we may name *impressions*; and under this name I comprehend all our sensations, passions and emotions, as they make their first appearance in the soul. By *ideas* I mean the faint images of these in thinking and reasoning; such as, for instance, are all the perceptions excited by the present discourse, excepting only those which arise from the sight and touch, and excepting the immediate pleasure or uneasiness it may occasion.

So the distinction is quantitative, one of degree rather than of kind. And Hume does admit that ideas (e.g., those of a nightmare) may be so powerful as to resemble impressions and that impressions may be "so faint and low, that we cannot distinguish them from ideas." He next divides both types of perceptions "into Simple and Complex," depending on whether they can be further analyzed into component parts. He then goes on to say that there is a "great resemblance betwixt our impressions and ideas in every other particular, except their degree of force and vivacity. The one seem to be in a manner the reflexion of the other."[59]

Yet, apart from resemblance, what is the relationship between the two types of perceptions? A tempting response easily comes to mind—"Ideas and impressions appear always to correspond to each other." But this answer, in terms of a straightforward one-to-one correspondence, fails to pass critical muster. For I have ideas of "the *New Jerusalem,* whose pavement is gold and walls are rubies, tho' I never saw any such" and of "a golden mountain," although I have never beheld any.[60] So *complex* impressions and ideas, at least, cannot be simply considered "exact copies of each other." We have directly experienced gold (for example, in wedding rings) and mountains (when we visit Mt. Rainier or see it from a distance). By combining the two ideas, which are derived from experience, we form the complex idea of "a golden mountain." It is therefore only of "our *simple* perceptions" that the rule "holds without any exception," according to Hume, "*that all our simple ideas in their first appearance are deriv'd from simple impressions, which are correspondent to them, and which they exactly represent.*" And since there are no innate ideas and all simple impressions originate in the concrete experiences of external and internal sensation (what Locke called sensation and reflection), Hume can nail down his empirical conclusion:

> In short, all the materials of thinking are derived either from our outward or inward sentiment: the mixture and composition of these belongs alone to the mind and will. Or, to express myself in philosophical language, all our ideas or more feeble perceptions are copies of our impressions or more lively ones.

As our understanding of the four tastes (sweet, sour, salty, and bitter) is derived from our concrete experience of corresponding impressions, so it is, for Hume, that all genuine ideas must (at least ultimately) be derived from concrete impressions. But what about one of the rationalists' favorite counterexamples to such an empirical generalization? Hume's answer is similar to Locke's and to the one Descartes tried to ward off with a pre-emptive strike:

> The idea of God, as meaning an infinitely intelligent, wise, and good Being, arises from reflecting on the operations of our own mind and augmenting, with-out limit, those qualities of goodness and wisdom.

He challenges anyone who would disagree with his empirical position here to come up with a telling counterexample, and then the burden will be on him to respond as he did with the idea of God.[61]

But, as if meeting his own challenge, he proceeds to provide "one con-tradictory phenomenon, which may prove that it is not absolutely impos-sible for ideas to arise, independent of their correspondent impressions." This is Hume's missing "shade of blue" counterexample:

> Suppose, therefore, a person to have enjoyed his sight for thirty years and to have become perfectly acquainted with colors of all kinds, except one particular shade of blue, for instance, which it never has been his fortune to meet with; let all the different shades of that color, except that single one, be placed before him, descending gradually from the deepest to the lightest, it is plain that he will perceive a blank where that shade is wanting

and be able to imagine what the intermediate shade will look like (i.e., slightly lighter than the one on this side and slightly darker than the one on that side). Hume's response to this counterexample seems a bit too cavalier. He admits that

> this may serve as a proof that the simple ideas are not always, in every instance, derived from the correspondent impressions, though this instance is so singular that it is scarcely worth our observing, and does not merit that for it alone we should alter our general maxim.[62]

This is fairly inadequate. Any generalization (of the form "all x's are y's" or "no x's are y's") can be destroyed by a single compelling counterexample, so that it needs to be abandoned or modified. A satisfactory answer should have been obvious to Hume. Just as he can empirically account for our idea of God by extrapolating from experience, so he could account for the missing shade of blue by interpolating between experiences. In each case the resulting idea is a product of the imagination reflecting on concrete experience (although the idea of God is complex, whereas that of a shade of blue is simple).

This theory of ideas, as developed thus far, leads, in the *Enquiry*, to what we may call "Hume's empirical test":

> When we entertain, therefore, any suspicion that a philosophical term is employed without any meaning or idea (as is but too frequent), we need but inquire, *from what impression is that supposed idea derived?* And if it be impossible to assign any, this will serve to confirm our suspicion.[63]

Hume himself applies the test to the ideas of substance, causality, freedom, self, and God.

Association of Ideas and Abstraction. So far, according to Hume, the mind receives simple and complex impressions from without and within itself, copies impressions with corresponding ideas, and combines simple ideas to form complex ones. But it also connects ideas by association. In his "Abstract" Hume points with pride at his original use of "the principles of the association of ideas."[64] Both the *Treatise* and the *Enquiry* deal with this topic. We experience ourselves as mentally associating ideas and thus reacting to "three principles of connection among ideas, namely, *Resemblance*, *Contiguity* in time or place, and *Cause* or *Effect*." Hume provides an example of each: (1) the idea or experience of a "picture naturally leads our thoughts to the original" that the picture is designed to resemble; (2) the "mention of one apartment in a building naturally introduces an inquiry or discourse concerning the others" that are contiguous—i.e., near to it in time and space; and (3) "if we think of a wound, we can scarcely forbear reflecting on the pain which follows it" as an effect or the blow which caused it.[65] These principles of association keep ideas from being "entirely loose and unconnected," as we experience them and provide "some bond of union among them" such that "one idea naturally introduces another." We should not imagine that such a psychological relationship is always determinatively compelling, "but we are only to regard it as a gentle force, which commonly prevails."[66]

In addition to being able to associate ideas, the mind also has the power to abstract from particular aspects or features of them. Like Locke (and Berkeley), in the *Treatise*, Hume maintains that all our ideas, as mental images, are particular but that the mind has the capacity to allow some such particulars to represent others, by ignoring certain specific differences:

> Abstract ideas are therefore in themselves individual, however they may become general in their representation. The image in the mind is only that of a particular object, tho' the application of it in our reasoning be the same as if it were universal.

For example, a person who grew up watching old Western movies might associate the idea of "dog" with Roy Rogers's German shepherd, Bullet; another might think of a collie such as Lassie. But in each case, by ignoring the attributes peculiar to that sort of dog, we can let our own mental image of what a dog is like stand for all the other objects of experience to which we would apply the concept of "dog." As Hume says, "They are not really and in fact present to the mind, but only in power; nor do we draw them all out distinctly in the imagination, but keep ourselves in a readiness to survey any of them." So if you say to the two persons mentioned above, "No, I mean a bulldog," they can both shift their paradigm images. Thus it is, says Hume,

> *that some ideas are particular in their nature, but general in their representation.* A particular idea becomes general by being annex'd to a general term; that is, to a term, which from a customary **conjunction**, has a relation to many other particular ideas, and readily recalls them in the imagination.[67]

Reasoning. The mind uses its ideas, including general ones, to reason. In *Enquiry* Hume considers the two types of objects of human reasoning (roughly corresponding to Leibniz's distinction between truths of reason and of fact). "Relations of ideas," he says, "are discoverable by the mere operation of thought, without dependence on what is anywhere existent in the universe" and are therefore "either intuitively or demonstratively certain." His examples here are mathematical: "*That three times five is equal to the half of thirty*" is an arithmetical necessary and universal truth; the Pythagorean theorem, that the square of the hypotenuse of any right triangle is equal to the sum of the squares of the two legs, is a geometrical universal and necessary truth. Notice that there can also be "relations of ideas" that are universally and necessarily false—for example, the idea of a virgin who has engaged in sexual intercourse—because self-contradictory.

> Matters of fact, which are the second objects of human reason, are not ascertained in the same manner, nor is our evidence of their truth, however great, of a like nature with the foregoing. The contrary of every matter of fact is still possible, because it can never imply a contradiction.

Hume presents us with the following thought-provoking example to illustrate his point:

> *That the sun will not rise tomorrow* is no less intelligible a proposition and implies no more contradiction than the affirmation *that it will rise*. We should in vain, therefore, attempt to demonstrate its falsehood

in a strict sense of the word demonstration.[68] We could, however, show that the experience of the past makes it unreasonable to believe that the sun will not rise tomorrow. We can always achieve absolute demonstrative certainty regarding "relations of ideas," but they do not necessarily have anything to do with the world of fact and existence. By contrast, "matters of fact" are intimately related to the world of existence, but of them we can never achieve absolute demonstrative certainty by reasoning. We shall see the repercussions of this epistemological theory on the attempt to prove God.

One particularly important philosophical idea about which we try to reason is that of substance. It looks like an abstract idea. But does it represent any thing of which we have concrete experience, either external or internal, as a matter of fact? Hume applies his empirical test to the alleged idea in the *Treatise*, asking "whether the idea of *substance* be deriv'd from the impressions of sensation or reflexion." Not of sensation, since what we see, hear, smell, touch, and taste are qualities of a thing rather than its substance. Nor do we internally feel our own substance, "our passions and emotions" being directed rather at our states of consciousness. His inference is even stronger than Locke's view that it is a useful "something I know not what." As he concludes,

> We have therefore no idea of substance, distinct from that of a collection of particular qualities. . . . The idea of a substance . . . is nothing but a collection of simple ideas, that are united by the imagination.

Later, he casts his position into the form of a syllogism:

> We have no . . . idea of any thing but of a perception. A substance is entirely different from a perception. We have, therefore, no idea of a substance.[69]

The first premise is the controversial one of modern empiricism. Hume's position here is that of a full-blown phenomenalism. All objects of experience are reduced to phenomena or appearances. We know nothing about, and have no experiential basis for any claims concerning, things as they are in themselves, apart from the way they appear. Thus, metaphysics, traditionally interpreted as the study of ultimate reality, must be either radically reformed or eliminated altogether. The alleged philosophical idea of substance has supposedly failed Hume's empirical test.

The second of three crucial philosophical ideas Hume considers is that of existence, discussed in the *Treatise* in such a way as to add to his phenomenalism. This idea, like that of substance, allegedly fails Hume's empirical test—"tho' every impression and idea we remember be consider'd as existent, the idea of existence is not deriv'd from any particular impression." We attribute existence to objects of experience rather than finding it already in them. "The idea of existence, then, is the very same with the idea of what we conceive to be existent. To reflect on any thing simply, and to reflect on it as existent, are nothing different from each other. That idea, when conjoin'd with the idea of any object, makes no addition to it."[70] This analysis rules out the legitimacy of ontological argumentation, such as Anselm and Descartes used.

Cause and Effect. The most famous of his analyses is of the idea of causality or necessary connection, which appears in the *Treatise*, the "Abstract," and the *Enquiry*. The principle of cause-effect relationship is, for Hume, one of the three principles of the association of ideas. More importantly, he says,

> All reasonings concerning matter of fact seem to be founded on the relation of *cause* and *effect*. By means of that relation alone we can go beyond the evidence of our memory and senses.[71]

Again, Hume applies his empirical test to determine on what impression or set of impressions the alleged idea of causality is based. If we consider any two events which we think of as causally related, we can ask what we actually experience that could account for our conceiving of them in that way. Hume's famous example is of billiard balls. We can experience one event of a billiard ball moving toward and colliding with a stationary ball and a second event in which "the ball which was formerly at rest now acquires a motion." If we analyze the relationship between such events, what do we actually experience? Hume says three things: (1) we experience the events as contiguous, or near to one another, in time and place; (2) we experience the first event as prior to the second in time; and (3) we experience a regular or constant conjunction between events like the first and others like the second. What, then, is there in the first that we regard as the "cause" of the second? Hume answers, "Beyond these three circumstances of contiguity, priority, and constant conjunction I can discover nothing in this cause."[72]

Yet we *think* of causes and their effects as necessarily connected, so that from a future event like the first we can reasonably infer an event like the second. We cannot do so in terms of an abstract demonstration, since there is nothing in the concept, for example, of a billiard ball moving toward another that is stationary which logically requires the second event. As Hume says, "there can be no *demonstrative* arguments to prove, *that those instances, of which we have had no experience, resemble those, of which we have had experience.*"[73] So we have no basis for the relationship independent of experience: "In a word, then, every effect is a distinct event from its cause. It could not, therefore, be discovered in the cause, and the first invention or conception of it, *a priori*, must be entirely arbitrary." Can we perhaps find an empirical proof of a necessary connection between causes and effects? No, we cannot, because to do so would involve presupposing the uniformity of nature:

> For all inferences from experience suppose, as their foundation, that the future will resemble the past and that similar powers will be conjoined with similar sensible qualities. If there be any suspicion that the course of nature may change, and that the past may be no rule for the future, all experience becomes useless and can give rise to no inference or conclusion. It is impossible, therefore, that any arguments from experience can prove this resemblance of the past to the future, since all these arguments are founded on the supposition of that resemblance.[74]

Thus, the best we can achieve for all our causal reasonings would appear to be probability.

And where can we profitably seek a warrant for this inferred probability? Not in the world of phenomena out there, which only reveals the here and now, which we try to connect with a remembered set of past experiences, and which is mute concerning the future. The answer must be in here, in the psychological realm of our own mental states. We remember having experienced the first sort of event being followed by the second, and

> we are determined by custom alone to expect the one from the appearance of the other. . . . Custom, then, is the great guide of human life. It is that principle alone which renders our experience useful to us and makes us expect, for the future, a similar train of events with those which have appeared in the past. Without the influence of custom we should be entirely ignorant of every matter of fact beyond what is immediately present to the memory and senses. We should never know how to adjust means to ends or to employ our natural powers in the production of any effect. There would be an end at once of all action as well as of the chief part of speculation.[75]

Hume's phenomenalism is here complete, the result of a far more radical empiricism than Locke (or Berkeley, for that matter) would have tolerated.

> All events seem entirely loose and separate. One event follows another, but we never can observe any tie between them. They seem *conjoined* but never *connected*.

To put the matter bluntly, we never experience a necessary connection in the phenomena we observe, but we only establish such connections in our own minds.

> This connection, therefore, which we feel in the mind, this customary transition of the imagination from one object to its usual attendant, is the sentiment or impression from which we form the idea of power or necessary connection.[76]

Thus, we do have an idea of causality. But it is produced by the imagination, which is motivated by a habitual pattern of remembered past experiences. For Hume, then, unlike Descartes and Leibniz, it is psychological custom, rather than scientific reason, which rules our speculative and practical lives. This view will severely undermine causal demonstrations of God's existence.

If Hume's analysis of causality is correct, then it seems that all we human beings can know for certain are abstract conceptual relationships, phenomenal objects of immediate experience, and our memories of past states of consciousness. But in that case we could know nothing of the world of fact and existence as it is in itself, and science is either fraudulent or reduced to a system of generalized probabilities. It must be admitted that Hume never explicitly draws this conclusion himself. But it was due to his realization of such skeptical implications of Hume's theory that Immanuel Kant later felt his "dogmatic slumber" interrupted by the critical nudging of Hume, so that he was driven to seek an adequate response, which assumed the form of the radically new epistemology that would be a kind of synthesis of early modern rationalism and early modern empiricism, which we consider in our next chapter.

A Critique of Hume's Empiricism. What are we critically to make of Hume's very powerful antithesis to Cartesian rationalism, as represented by this empirical theory of ideas? It seems Hume (like Locke) was right to deny innate ideas in the sense of a cognitive content prior to any experience, although this is not how Descartes and Leibniz meant their doctrine of innate ideas to be interpreted. Hume seems correct in holding that all human ideas must start with concrete experience (whether internal or external) but mistaken in supposing that they are all derived from particular impressions in some manner of representationalist correspondence. Finally, he may have looked in the wrong "place" for the basis of our ideas of substance, existence, and causality; rather than being derived from impressions of objects out there in the world of phenomena or in here among our own contingent feelings and psychological propensities, they may be, as Kant was to argue, *a priori* structures, concepts of the human understanding which are universally and necessarily applied to data of experience for the achieving of knowledge.

Belief. Hume's treatment of belief builds on this theory of ideas. In the *Treatise* he writes: "The idea of an object is an essential part of the belief of it, but not the whole. We conceive many things, which we do not believe." For example, a person who has studied Greek mythology can have an idea of Pegasus, a winged horse, without believing that any such creature actually exists apart from the realm of the imagination. Hume goes on to say that the difference between entertaining or conceiving of an idea and believing in it "lies not in the parts or composition of the idea, which we conceive; it follows, that it must lie in the *manner*, in which we conceive it." It is the psychological way in which the mind apprehends an idea that constitutes a believing attitude.

> So that as belief does nothing but vary the manner, in which we conceive any object, it can only bestow on our ideas an additional force and vivacity. An opinion, therefore, or belief may be most accurately defin'd, A lively idea related to or associated with a present impression.[77]

If you have an audio-visual impression of a man stomping toward you with clenched fists and screaming obscenities at you, you are liable to believe in (and not merely entertain the idea of) his threatening to clobber you; then the idea of his clobbering you assumes great psychological force in your mind and constitutes a belief that he is about to do so.

Similarly, in the *Enquiry*, Hume is anxious to distinguish between fiction and belief (again consider the idea of Pegasus), leading to his definition there: "I say that belief is nothing but a more vivid, lively, forcible, firm, steady conception of an object, than what the imagination alone is ever able to attain." This, in turn, leads to the distinction he seeks—

> the sentiment of belief is nothing but a conception more intense and steady than what attends the mere fictions of the imagination, and that this *manner* of conception arises from a customary conjunction of the object with something present to the memory or senses.[78]

Hume tries to show how beliefs, prompted by impressions, are conceived by the mind as related to existence by principles of association. "The influence of the picture" of a dead friend on us "supposes that we *believe* our friend to have once existed and to have resembled the picture." Contiguity to home can never excite our ideas of home unless we *believe* that it really exists "in fact." When a woman throws a piece of dry wood into a fire, her mind is immediately carried "to believe that this event will cause an augmentation of the fire." Thus all three of Hume's principles of association can contribute to belief; but in every case, belief is related to the world of fact and existence. And the "transition of thought" that psychologically constitutes belief "derives its origin altogether from custom and experience."[79] Conversely, the weakening of these principles of association can detract from belief, and their loss can destroy it altogether. For example, Hume says of the first of these principles,

> As belief is an act of the mind arising from custom, 'tis not strange the want of resemblance shou'd overthrow what custom has establish'd, and diminish the force of the idea, as much as that latter principle encreases it.[80]

Hume fears that this psychological analysis of belief will be rejected as too subjective. Given "that the far greatest part of our reasonings, with all our actions and passions" stem from beliefs, he expects that few will admit that our beliefs "can be deriv'd from nothing but custom and habit." This position would make belief more a matter of feeling than of reasoning—"more properly an act of the sensitive, than of the cogitative part of our natures." He also seems to anticipate the objection that the analysis is too vague to be helpful. If the distinction between impressions and ideas is merely a matter of degree and therefore difficult to draw clearly, does not the theory of belief as so strong an idea as to be like an impression make the matter even fuzzier? And yet this is what Hume says in the *Treatise*:

> The effect, then, of belief is to raise up a simple idea to an equality with our impressions, and bestow on it a like influence on the passions. This effect it can only have by making an idea approach an impression in force and vivacity. . . . Belief, therefore, since it causes an idea to imitate the effects of the impressions, must make it resemble them in these qualities, and is nothing but *a more vivid and intense conception of any idea.*[81]

Hume's analysis of belief is, in fact, somewhat lacking in clarity here. And he seems to acknowledge as much in the Appendix to the *Treatise*, when he writes, "I confess, that 'tis impossible to explain perfectly this feeling or manner of conception," but he adds that *belief* "is a term that every one sufficiently understands in common life."[82] Perhaps this is simply a common-sense concept that defies precise analysis. Nevertheless, even if it is unavoidably so, Hume's theory of impressions, ideas, and beliefs might seem, to this extent, a bit of a muddle. The stability and reliability of the beliefs of religious faith are implicated here.

Knowledge and Probability. Hume's treatment of knowledge and probability contributes to his image as a philosophical skeptic. In terms of the strictest criteria of precision and certainty, mathematics is as much a paradigm of scientific knowledge for Hume as it was for the Cartesian rationalists. In the *Treatise*, he identifies

> algebra and arithmetic as the only sciences, in which we can carry on a chain of reasoning to any degree of intricacy, and yet preserve a perfect exactness and certainty. We are possest of a precise standard, by which we can judge of the equality and proportion of numbers; and according as they correspond or not to that standard, we determine their relations, without any possibility of error.

He goes on to say that although "it excels the imperfect judgments of our senses and imagination," nevertheless "geometry falls short of that perfect precision and certainty, . . . because its original and fundamental principles are deriv'd merely from appearances."[83] So it is only in the realm of abstract relations of ideas, divorced from the world of empirical fact and existential appearances, that our reasoning can achieve demonstrative knowledge.

It is in this sense that Hume distinguishes demonstrative knowledge from proofs and probabilities:

> By knowledge, I mean the assurance arising from the comparison of ideas. By proofs, those arguments, which are deriv'd from the relation of cause and effect, and which are entirely free from doubt and uncertainty. By probability, that evidence, which is still attended with uncertainty.

Thus, one can have demonstrative knowledge that $x = 4$ in the algebraic formula $20x = 80$; and it is conceptually impossible that this is wrong. We can have empirical proof that the deaths of both John and Robert Kennedy were caused by gunshot wounds; we are practically certain that this is so, although, conceivably, it is otherwise. It is probable that few engineering students enjoy reading Hume's *Dialogues* as much as philosophy majors do, although there is very little evidence to that effect and it would be an extremely difficult matter to quantify even if one wanted to try to do so. These, then, are three different results of human reasoning: demonstrative knowledge, empirical proofs, and probabilities "or reasoning from conjecture."[84] We should also remember, however, that some knowledge is not dependent on reasoning—namely, that of direct, immediate objects of present experience and that of remembered past experience. When we look at (what we call) chalk marks on the chalkboard in our classrooms, we know we see (i.e., phenomenally experience) white on green; and we know we sometimes feel pain when a dentist drills and fills cavities in our molars.

In a section of the *Treatise*, entitled "Of Knowledge," Hume reminds us that he has already analyzed the "seven different kinds of philosophical relation, *viz. resemblance, identity, relations of time and place, proportion in quantity or number, degrees in any quality, contrariety, and causation.*" Now Hume holds that identity and spatio-temporal relations are relative and that causal relations are based on psychological habits rather than reasoning. So he maintains

> that of these seven philosophical relations, there remain only four, which depending solely upon ideas, can be the objects of knowledge and certainty. These four are *resemblance, contrariety, degrees in quality, and proportions in quantity or number*. Three of these relations are discoverable at first sight, and fall more properly under the province of intuition than demonstration.[85]

For resemblance, contrariety, and degrees of quality are immediately apparent to the perceiving mind—for example, that two fluorescent light fixtures look alike, that a person looks different when he is bearded from when he is clean-shaven, and that one shade of green is darker than another. It is only the relation of proportions in quantity or number that is strictly a matter of demonstrative knowledge. That the square root of 1,024 is an even number greater than three cubed is not intuitively obvious but can be mathematically demonstrated.

For our purposes, the important thing to observe here is how narrow are the limits of absolutely certain knowledge—limited to our intuitive experience of resemblance, contrariety, and qualitative degrees and the mathematically demonstrative matters of quantitative or numerical proportions. Empirical proofs depend on the relation of cause and effect, which may give us psychological conviction but cannot impart the objective certainty of intuition or demonstration. Also, to the extent that a proof involves a "multitude of connected arguments," it "degenerates insensibly" to the level of probability.[86] In the *Treatise* Hume adds a reminder of "our fallible and uncertain faculties" and "the inconstancy of our mental powers." So, everything that is left must be reduced to probability. Hume expresses the point in what should be one of the most alarming sentences written in the history of philosophy:

> By this means all knowledge degenerates into probability; and this probability is greater or less, according to our experience of the veracity or deceitfulness of our understanding, and according to the simplicity or intricacy of the question.[87]

According to Hume, there are two types of probability which "are receiv'd by philosophers, and allow'd to be reasonable foundations of belief and opinion," although he speaks of "unphilosophical probability" as well. "Probability or reasoning from conjecture may be divided into two kinds, viz. that which is founded on *chance*, and that which arises from *causes*.[88] The first sort occurs when there is no adequately experienced causal relation but there is a greater likelihood of chances one way than another. If we toss a normally marked six-sided die, there is a greater likelihood, or "probability of chances," that the number that comes up will be greater than two than that it will be less than three. The second sort of probability arises from associating a present or future event with other similar events of the past which have been experienced as related in terms of cause and effect. For example, imagine a college professor who, over the years, invariably sees row after row of blank faces when she mentions the Enlightenment at the beginning of her freshman class; she attributes this ignorance to poor and unenthusiastic history teaching at the secondary school level and to the fact that our mass media emphasize the transient present and immediate future to the exclusion of any serious historical concern. She reasonably considers it probable that if she tries to speak of the Enlightenment in her next freshman class, she will meet with similar results; the causal conditions will not have significantly changed, and therefore the effects are not likely to be different. "All our reasonings concerning the probability of causes are founded on the transferring of past to future,"[89] where there is an experienced resemblance between the two.

"But beside these two species of probability"—of chances and of causes—Hume adds that "there is a third arising from Analogy." The difference between this type and the first two is that here there is a slight or imperfect resemblance between the experienced past and the present or future being reasoned about. There must be, even in reasonings from analogy, "some degree of resemblance"; otherwise, says Hume,

> 'tis impossible there can be any reasoning: but as this resemblance admits of many different degrees, the reasoning becomes proportionably more or less firm and certain. An experiment loses of its force, when transferr'd to instances, which are not exactly resembling; tho' 'tis evident it may still retain as much as may be the foundation of probability, as long as there is any resemblance remaining.[90]

Probability will be a particularly important sort of reasoning for Hume's philosophy of religion. Since we have no direct, immediate experience of God (for Hume), intuition is unavailable; nor does God admit of demonstration, being outside the realm of mathematics and abstract relations of ideas. Causal reasoning, leading to proofs, will not strictly apply, because God allegedly does not exactly resemble anything of this world which we directly experience. Thus, all that is left in reasoning about God will be probability—and that must be of the third kind, from analogy, since only a slight and distant sort of resemblance between God and the things of this world can be plausibly supposed. But before moving on to consider Hume's philosophy of religion proper, we should address the issue of his skepticism.

Skepticism. Hume's skepticism follows from this position on knowledge and probability. "Since therefore all knowledge," apart from intuition and the demonstration of mathematical relations of ideas, "resolves itself into probability, and becomes at last of the same nature with that evidence, which we employ in common life," we should recognize that that latter sort of evidence does point the way to theoretical (if not practical) skepticism. Hume's theoretical skepticism is a result of his being willing to "bite the bullet" and accept the logical implications (as Locke was not willing to do) of the empirical doctrine that "nothing is ever really present to the mind, besides its own perceptions." This leads to the phenomenalistic view that we can only know things' appearances:

> The only existences, of which we are certain, are perceptions, which being immediately present to us by consciousness, command our strongest assent, and are the first foundations of all our conclusions.

Even ordinary causal beliefs, such as "that fire warms, or water refreshes," should be held as practically useful rather than as strictly knowable. Such beliefs work for us at the level of common sense, yet we should not fool ourselves that they are philosophically demonstrable or provable. "Nay if we are philosophers, it ought only to be upon sceptical principles."[91]

The final section of the *Enquiry* is explicitly devoted to skepticism. As we have seen, Hume repudiates the "species of skepticism" which is affiliated with "Cartesian doubt" and is *"antecedent* to all study and philosophy," as a game that will either not be seriously undertaken or will prove to be "entirely incurable," failing to produce the certain knowledge at which it aims.

> There is another species of skepticism, *consequent* to science and inquiry, when men are supposed to have discovered either the absolute fallaciousness of their mental faculties or their unfitness to reach any fixed determination in all those curious subjects of speculation about which they are commonly employed.

Here philosophical reflection on our experience leads us to be skeptical of reason and the senses. Hume is sympathetic to this form as long as it remains theoretical: "This is a topic, therefore, in which the profounder and more philosophical skeptics will always triumph when they endeavor to introduce a universal doubt into all subjects of human knowledge and inquiry."[92] From the point of view of theoretical philosophy, our experience, and therefore our knowledge, of matters of existential fact is so limited and our powers of perceiving and conceiving so fallible as to give good grounds for consequent skepticism.

Nevertheless, Hume warns against "*excessive* skepticism," which is practically applied as well as theoretically considered. If we consistently practiced in our everyday lives what the extreme skeptic preaches, the results would be disastrous. As Hume writes,

> all human life must perish were his principles universally and steadily to prevail. All discourse, all action would immediately cease, and men remain in a total lethargy till the necessities of nature, unsatisfied, put an end to their miserable existence.

(One is reminded of the ancient Greek philospher Cratylus, who became so convinced that everything is constantly changing that he would not commit himself to any linguistic assertions, since the things to be discussed and the meanings of our words would not remain stable enough for communication to be possible.) Hume immediately adds, however, that the practical necessities of life prevent this calamity from actually occurring to ordinary human beings: "It is true, so fatal an event is very little to be dreaded. Nature is always too strong for principles." The philosophical objections of excessive skepticism or "Pyrrhonism," as Hume also calls it, do not easily or comfortably translate into practical application:

> The great subverter of Pyrrhonism, or the excessive principles of skepticism, is action, and employment, and the occupations of common life. These principles may flourish and triumph in the schools, where it is indeed difficult, if not impossible, to refute them.

But in the everyday world of practical activity "they vanish like smoke and leave the most determined skeptic in the same condition as other mortals."[93]

There is a wonderful passage in the *Treatise* in which Hume personalizes this point quite effectively. He compares himself to a sailor who, on countless occasions, has "narrowly escap'd ship-wreck" on the shoals of skepticism, who "has yet the temerity to put out to sea" philosophically "in the same leaky weather-beaten vessel" of radical empiricism, "and even carries his ambition so far as to think of compassing the globe" of human understanding "under these disadvantageous circumstances." He admits,

"My memory of past errors and perplexities, makes me diffident for the future" and that at times he feels so overwhelmed by skepticism "that I am ready to reject all belief and reasoning, and can look upon no opinion even as more probable or likely than another." It is at moments such as those that he is in danger of succumbing to excessive skepticism.

> Most fortunately it happens, that since reason is incapable of dispelling these clouds, nature herself suffices to that purpose, and cures me of this philosophical melancholy and delirium, either by relaxing this bent of mind, or by some avocation, and lively impression of my senses, which obliterate all these chimeras. I dine, I play a game of back-gammon, I converse, and am merry with my friends; and when after three or four hours' amusement, I wou'd return to these speculations, they appear so cold, and strain'd, and ridiculous, that I cannot find in my heart to enter into them any further.

He continues,

> Here then I find myself absolutely and necessarily determin'd to live, and talk, and act like other people in the common affairs of life. . . . I am ready to throw all my books and papers into the fire, and resolve never more to renounce the pleasures of life for the sake of reasoning and philosophy.

Of course, Hume never gave in to this inclination. He rather kept returning to philosophy, driven by a combination of intellectual curiosity and "an ambition . . . of contributing to the instruction of mankind." Given his skepticism, Hume's approach to philosophy is critical rather than speculative and is based on both a keen awareness of the limitations of human reason and a faith-commitment to employing it as best we can. He puts the point nicely in the *Treatise*: "Thus the sceptic still continues to reason and believe, even tho' he asserts that he cannot defend his reason by reason."[94]

Hume advocates "a more *mitigated* skepticism or *academical* philosophy which may be both durable and useful." This is "*excessive* skepticism" mitigated or "corrected by common sense and reflection." He sees it as a healthy corrective to a fanatical dogmatism and philosophical "haughtiness and obstinacy," which makes people sensitive to the limits of human knowledge, more aware of "the imperfection of those faculties which they employ, their narrow reach, and their inaccurate operations."[95]

If we do manage to restrict our studies to "the proper subjects of science and inquiry," our investigations will tend to be either mathematical or empirical. Hume says,

> It seems to me that the only objects of the abstract sciences, or of demonstration, are quantity and number, and that all attempts to extend this more perfect species of knowledge beyond these bounds are mere sophistry and illusion.

It is the mathematical sciences, then, that are "the only proper objects of knowledge and demonstration," according to Hume, because they deal with relations of ideas and are independent of the contingencies of existential fact.

> All other inquiries of men regard only matter of fact and existence, and these are evidently incapable of demonstration. Whatever *is* may *not be*. No negation of a fact can involve a contradiction. The nonexistence of any being, without exception, is as clear and distinct an idea as its existence. The proposition which affirms it not to be, however false, is no less conceivable and intelligible than that which affirms it to be.

Therefore, only causal arguments, "founded entirely on experience," can establish any matter of fact or the existence of any being. All such empirical arguments are inductive (rather than deductive), generating degrees of probability for their conclusions, and subject to the qualifications concerning causal reasoning which we have considered. This is true for the existence of God as well as for any other's existence. Hume's famous (some would say infamous) inflammatory conclusion is that any subject, such as "Divinity or Theology" and metaphysics, which is neither mathematical nor subject to empirical observation, is "neither fish nor fowl," an illegitimate hodgepodge which is scientifically disreputable. Hence the well-known final paragraph of the *Enquiry*:

> When we run over libraries, persuaded of these principles, what havoc must we make? If we take in our hand any volume—of divinity or school metaphysics, for instance—let us ask, *Does it contain any abstract reasoning concerning quantity or number?* No. *Does it contain any experimental reasoning concerning matter of fact and existence?* No. Commit it then to the flames, for it can contain nothing but sophistry and illusion.[96]

With this ominous warning as background, let us turn to Hume's philosophy of religion.

Critique of Arguments for God's Existence

The Argument from General Consensus. Hume's views on the **argument from general consensus** are indicated in his *Natural History of Religion*, in which he treats of popular religion from the perspective of a social scientist. Thus, he makes clear what he had written in the Introduction to his *Treatise*, that natural religion must be viewed in the context of "the science of Man" and "is not content with instructing us in the nature of superior powers, but carries its views farther, to their disposition towards us, and our duties towards them."[97] It is a practical matter, not merely theoretical, affecting our whole person, rather than simply our speculative intellect. He makes a similar point in his essay on "The Sceptic," when he writes that

> an abstract, invisible object, like that which *natural* religion alone presents to us, cannot long actuate the mind, or be of any moment in life. To render the passion of continuance, we must find some method of affecting the senses and imagination, and must embrace some *historical* as well as *philosophical* account of the Divinity.[98]

This is particularly true of the popular religion treated in the *Natural History*, as opposed to "the philosophical and rational kind" of religion discussed in the *Dialogues*.

Popular religion is based on social custom and the traditional handing down of beliefs from one generation to another. Pressure to conform to the views of one's fellows tends to reinforce and extend the scope of popular religion. There is a sense that "we all share these beliefs, so why shouldn't you?" The argument from general consensus is ancient and can be found, for example, in Book X of Plato's *Laws*. There Clinias bases his "case for the existence of gods" on "the fact that all mankind, Greeks and non-Greeks alike, believe in the existence of gods."[99] We might formulate the argument thus: If there is a general consensus of mankind about the existence of God (or the gods), then God (or the gods) must in fact exist. There is such a general consensus of mankind. Therefore, God (or the gods) must in fact exist. Given the validity of this hypothetical (or conditional) argument, its criticism must consist of a challenge against either or both of the premises.

Hume is not as tough as one might expect on the first premise. It seems reasonable to assert that Hume would maintain that its "then" clause (the consequent) does not follow from its "if" clause (the antecedent). In order to justify such a connection, we would have to be prepared to show that human judgment is so trustworthy that universal agreement is a warrant for truth—a claim that would run counter to Hume's skepticism. The observation he actually makes in connection with this premise, however, is a psychological one, rather than logical or epistemological, and seems ironically expressed:

> The universal propensity to believe in invisible, intelligent power, if not an original instinct, being at least a general attendant of human nature, may be considered as a kind of mark or stamp, which the divine workman has set upon his work.[100]

Apart from the metaphor that is reminiscent of Descartes's comparison of our innate idea of God to the signature of the divine Artist on his

masterpiece of creation, the key words here are "may be considered"—
that is to say, people can conceive of things in this way if they like. In
fact, we do tend to assume that views in which we are commonly
inclined to believe are true. Yet this is no assurance that such an uncritical assumption is, or ever could be, justified.

What about the second premise? A good deal depends on how it is
interpreted. If the "general consensus of mankind" is interpreted to mean
that all people, in all circumstances, in all cultures, in all ages have agreed
(even in general) about religion, then Hume the historian is sure the
premise is false:

> Some nations have been discovered, who entertained no sentiments of Religion,
> if travellers and historians may be credited; and no two nations, and scarce any
> two men, have ever agreed precisely in the same sentiments. It would appear,
> therefore, that this preconception springs not from an original instinct.

On the other hand, if we limit our interpretation to speaking of the vast
majority of people from vastly different societies in diverse periods of history, Hume is willing to admit consensus on one rather carefully limited
religious issue:

> The only point of theology, in which we shall find a consent of mankind almost
> universal, is, that there is invisible, intelligent power in the world: But whether
> this power be supreme or subordinate, whether confined to one being, or dis-
> tributed among several, what attributes, qualities, connexions, or principles of
> action ought to be ascribed to those beings; concerning all these points, there is
> the widest difference in the popular systems of theology.[101]

So, interpreted this way, Hume does think there is a general consensus of
mankind about some "invisible, intelligent power in the world." What this
would indicate is neither atheism nor **agnosticism**, but some form of **theism** or, at least, deism. Nevertheless, Hume was not the sort of thinker to
base his own beliefs on those of others.

Even if we were to accept the argument from the general consensus
of mankind as a foundation for popular religion, historical facts in connection with it could prove embarrassing. Hume makes several factual
claims. First, popular religion is derived from "hope and fear" and the
instinct to anthropomorphism; second, the original form taken by popular religion is "polytheism or **idolatry**"; third, monotheism's evolution is
no more rational, but is based on a consolidation of religious "exaggeration" and "panegyric"; fourth, there is no finality to monotheism, but
rather "a natural tendency" to fluctuate with polytheistic idolatry
throughout history; and, fifth, the behavior and interpersonal conduct
fostered by popular religion, far from being moral, tend to be "barbarous

or corrupted," with "intolerance" particularly characteristic of monotheism.[102] We should not imagine that Christianity, the popular religion in which Hume grew up, would escape his censure here. Whether or not we read the history of the Judeo-Christian tradition as Hume would, there is ample ammunition therein for his harsh judgements. At any rate, the argument from general consensus, he would have us conclude, (1) is not logically compelling because of dubious premises, (2) to the extent that it has psychological force leads to an extremely limited conclusion, and (3) fails to establish popular religion as rational or stable or admirable or beneficial.

The Argument from Design. Hume's views on the argument from design are more complex and more thoroughly worked out. In a note in his "Appendix" to the *Treatise*, Hume rather incautiously writes, "The order of the universe proves an omnipotent mind. . . . Nothing more is requisite to give a foundation to all the articles of religion."[103] In his essay "On Suicide" he maintains that the "sympathy, harmony, and proportion" of "inanimate bodies and living creatures" in the natural order are collectively what "affords the surest argument of Supreme Wisdom."[104] Here he is no longer calling this a "proof," and what sort of "argument" it is to be is not specified.

The Introduction of the *Natural History* contains a strong (but more cautiously worded) statement of this argument:

> The whole frame of nature bespeaks an intelligent author; and no rational enquirer can, after serious reflection, suspend his belief a moment with regard to the primary principles of genuine Theism and Religion.

Later, he writes that "a contemplation of the works of nature" leads us to the idea "of one single being, who bestowed existence and order on this vast machine, and adjusted all its parts, according to one regular plan or connected system." He speaks of those who "reason from the admirable contrivance of natural objects, and must suppose the world to be the workmanship of that divine being, the original cause of all things." He says that the "regularity and uniformity" of the natural order constitute "the strongest proof of design and of a supreme intelligence." Near the end of the book, he writes,

> A purpose, an intention, a design is evident in everything; and . . . we must adopt, with the strongest conviction, the idea of some intelligent cause or author. The uniform maxims, too, which prevail throughout the whole frame of the universe, naturally, if not necessarily, lead us to conceive this intelligence as single and undivided.[105]

Hume seems to be saying here that our experience of the natural world as ordered or designed psychologically leads us to entertain the idea of and to believe in a single intelligent causal source of that order or design. This would be the God of either deism or monotheism. Although he is willing to accept this as a psychologically natural belief, he is not presenting it as a logically necessary one.

One section of Hume's *Enquiry* (originally called "Of the Practical Consequences of Natural Religion" but now entitled "Of a particular Providence and of a future State") contains an imaginary dialogue between Hume and "a friend who loves sceptical paradoxes" and (taking on the part of Epicurus) develops some critical objections against the argument from design. It is worth noting, however, that the design and general providence of the natural order are *not* called into question. As the skeptical friend says, "We shall not here dispute concerning the origin and government of worlds. . . . the chief or sole argument for a divine existence (which I never questioned) is derived from the order of nature."[106]

Perhaps the argument from design can be framed in such a way that Hume's skeptical friend will not find it objectionable; the catch is that it will then have little import: If we experience the natural order as comparable to effects of intelligent design, then it is reasonable to regard it as (probably) caused by some intelligent Designer(s), since all other effects of intelligent design we have experienced are caused by intelligent designers. We do experience the natural order as comparable to effects of intelligent design. Hence it is reasonable to regard the natural order as (probably) caused by some intelligent Designer(s).

This argument, based on "experience and observation and analogy," establishes what Hume calls "the religious **hypothesis**." But it establishes it as

> both uncertain and useless. It is uncertain; because the subject lies entirely beyond the reach of human experience. It is useless; because our knowledge of this cause being derived entirely from the course of nature, we can never, according to the rules of just reasoning, return back from the cause with any new inference, or making additions to the common and experienced course of nature, establish any new principles of conduct and behaviour.[107]

In other words, because the analogy compares objects of "experience and observation" to that which, as a whole, transcends "experience and observation," the best we can reasonably hope for is some degree of probability, so that theoretical certainty is impossible. Because the analogy yields no imperatives regarding human action, it is practically useless.

The main problem with this is that religious believers who appeal to the argument from design will never be satisfied with such pitifully paltry results. Thus, the major criticism presented by Hume's skeptical friend is that extravagant, unwarrantable assertions are made concerning the intelligent Designer(s) to which the argument points. If we accept the argument as carefully presented, it gives us (at best) probable grounds for believing in God or gods.

> Allowing, therefore, the gods to be the authors of the existence or order of the universe; it follows, that they possess that precise degree of power, intelligence, and benevolence, which appears in their workmanship; but nothing further can ever be proved, except we call in the assistance of exaggeration and flattery to supply the defects of argument and reasoning . . . The supposition of farther attributes is mere hypothesis. . . . The knowledge of the cause being derived solely from the effect, they must be exactly adjusted to each other; and the one can never refer to anything farther, or be the foundation of any new inference and conclusion.[108]

Thus, our probable knowledge of the intelligent Designer(s) of the natural order might indicate a certain amount of power, "wisdom and goodness." But to puff this up into the claim that this is an omnipotent, omniscient, omnibenevolent God would be to violate the "rules of just reasoning" by analogy. And then to infer that this God requires or expects specifiable modes of conduct of us is an even worse case of extracting wild suppositions from unjustified assumptions. Although analogous reasoning can lead us to probable conclusions (especially where the things compared have actually been experienced), the argument from design stretches matters considerably by comparing common objects of experience (such as "a half-finished building" constructed by a human architect) to what is unique and eludes our experience (such as the natural order as a whole and the powerful intelligence that caused it). Yet to try to derive an infinitely perfect Cause from finite, imperfect effects is absolutely illegitimate. For,

> this method of reasoning can never have place with regard to a Being, so remote and incomprehensible, who bears much less analogy to any other being in the universe than the sun to a waxen taper, and who discovers himself only by some faint traces or outlines, beyond which we have no authority to ascribe to him any attribute or perfection.[109]

Through the skeptical friend, Hume can admit that we can believe that the source of intelligent design in the universe might be an absolutely perfect God:

> That the divinity may *possibly* be endowed with attributes, which we have never seen exerted; may be governed by principles of action, which we cannot

discover to be satisfied: all this will be freely allowed. But still this is mere *possibility* and hypothesis. We never have reason to *infer* any attributes, or any principles of action in him, but so far as we know them to have been exerted and satisfied.

Weak and tentative as analogous reasoning is, we should not make the mistake of deriving causal conclusions that have no reasonable proportion to experienced effects. Further, it is hopeless to try to squeeze practical conclusions concerning human "conduct and behaviour" from the argument from design alone:

> No new fact can ever be inferred from the religious hypothesis; no event foreseen or foretold; no reward or punishment expected or dreaded, beyond what is already known by practice and observation.[110]

The most thorough, comprehensive, exhaustive critique of the argument from design which Hume presents is in *Dialogues*, narrated by Pamphilus to Hermippus. The three main interlocutors are Demea, representing the position of dogmatic rationalism, who might be viewed as a caricature of Descartes or Leibniz; Cleanthes, representing the position of empirical theism, who might be considered somewhat similar to Locke; and Philo, the skeptical deist, who most obviously speaks for Hume (but who is also comparable to Bayle). These are arguably the finest philosophical dialogues written after Plato in terms of both argued content and dramatic style. This is due to a careful, distinctive delineation of the three major characters and Hume's conscientious effort properly to establish "a spirit of dialogue" by means of "a tolerable equality maintained among the speakers."[111]

In an important letter of March 10, 1751, Hume writes his friend Gilbert Elliot of Minto about his *Dialogues*, suggesting that he has a natural affinity for the views of Philo and appealing to Elliot for help in strengthening the case of "Cleanthes the Hero of the Dialogue." Hume is particularly anxious that "that vulgar Error" should "be avoided, of putting nothing but Nonsense into the Mouth of the Adversary." He is speaking of the argument from design when he writes,

> I cou'd wish that Cleanthes' Argument coud be so analys'd, as to be render'd quite formal & regular. The Propensity of the Mind towards it, unless that Propensity were as strong & universal as that to believe in our Senses & Experience, will still, I am afraid, be esteem'd a suspicious Foundation.

Whether or not Elliot tried to comply with this request, Hume continued to postpone publishing the *Dialogues* during his life, revising and trying to improve them, concerned that he not repeat the mistake he made with the *Treatise*, of being "carry'd away by the Heat of Youth & Invention to publish too precipitately."[112]

Hume's prudence was clearly a factor here. Another important letter, written in the last year of his life, to his publisher, William Strahan, speaks of the *Dialogues* thus:

> Some of my Friends flatter me, that it is the best thing I ever wrote. I have hith-erto forborne to publish it, because I was of late desirous to live quietly, and keep remote from all Clamour. . . . I there introduce a Sceptic, who is indeed refuted, and at last gives up the Argument, nay confesses that he was only amusing him-self by all his Cavils.

In the *Dialogues* Hume contrives to make it superficially appear that Cleanthes, rather than Philo, emerges the winner. Yet this contrivance seems to fool few people, even though, as Hume wrote to Adam Smith ten days before he died, "nothing can be more cautiously and more art-fully written" than the *Dialogues*,[113] which thus lend themselves to vari-ous interpretations. Indeed, it is difficult to think of a non-Platonic philosophical dialogue that is less "cut-and-dried" than Hume's.

All three major characters sometimes seem to speak for Hume: Philo is the primary spokesman for expressing Hume's skepticism; Cleanthes speaks for Hume in refuting the *a priori* argument of Demea; and even Demea (Hume's least likely spokesman) might plausibly be seen as expressing Humean views at the beginning of Part II. Yet none of the characters always represents Hume: Demea uses the despised *a priori* approach to argumentation; Cleanthes tries to present the argument from design as a logical proof; and even Philo vacillates about whether or not to adopt the view of "**mystics**" that God is altogether incomprehensible. It is an indication of Hume's literary artistry that, in the clash of differ-ent perspectives, illuminating sparks can fly from all participants, with none of them so disproportionately superior as to emerge completely unscathed. Natural religion attempts to justify religious beliefs on the basis of reason, human nature, and natural experience. As such, it is rad-ically different from revealed religion. And there is no reason to suppose that it admits of any one infallible, final interpretation.

In the Introduction to the *Dialogues*, Pamphilus, the narrator, indi-cates that he is a student of Cleanthes, which may explain his bias in con-trasting "the accurate philosophical turn of Cleanthes to the careless scepticism of Philo" and "the rigid inflexible orthodoxy of Demea." He also warns us that the topic for discussion is not a "truth so obvious, so certain, as the being of a God" but rather "the nature of that divine being." Demea and Philo agree with Cleanthes' pupil on this point, with the latter even calling the *being* of the Deity an "unquestionable and self-evident" truth (which may indeed sound like a "careless scepticism"). At any rate, Hume does not obviously consider the positions of atheism or agnosticism here. Second, all three of the major characters accept some sort of causal reasoning in connection with natural religion. Even the skeptical Philo admits, "Nothing exists without a cause" and that there must be some "original cause of this universe," its nature being the issue for debate. But he poses the challenge strongly in the form of an **enthymeme**—a deductive argument, one proposition (in this case the conclusion) of which is implied rather than explicitly stated: "Our ideas reach no farther than our experience: We have no experience of divine attributes and operations: I need not conclude my syllogism: You can draw the inference yourself."[114] The logical conclusion, which would serve as a major obstacle to natural theology, is that we have no ideas of divine attributes and operations—that the nature of God is unknowable. It is to this challenge that Cleanthes and Demea will attempt to respond.

Cleanthes' initial presentation of the argument from design assumes the form of an empirical proof from analogy:

> Look round the world: contemplate the whole and every part of it: You will find it to be nothing but one great machine, subdivided into an infinite number of lesser machines ... All these various machines, and even their most minute parts, are adjusted to each other with an accuracy, which ravishes into admiration all men, who have ever contemplated them. The curious adapting of means to ends, throughout all nature, resembles exactly, though it much exceeds, the productions of human contrivance; of human designs, thought, wisdom, and intelligence. Since therefore the effects resemble each other, we are led to infer, by all the rules of analogy, that the causes also resemble; and that the Author of Nature is somewhat similar to the mind of man; though possessed of much larger faculties, proportioned to the grandeur of the work, which he has executed. By this argument *a posteriori*, and by this argument alone, do we prove at once the existence of a Deity, and his similarity to human mind and intelligence.[115]

We might frame Cleanthes' attempted proof thus: We experience the world as an extremely complex but harmoniously ordered machine, whose design exactly (but more impressively) resembles the products of human design. But since the world and products of human design are so strikingly similar as effects, the Author of nature must be similar to (though greater than) human intelligence as a cause.

The immediate reactions of Demea and Philo are revealing. Demea, wanting an argument that yields absolute logical necessity and is not dependent on contingent experience, protests against the argument in exclamatory fashion because it is only an empirical proof and not an *a priori* demonstration. Philo's first objection is quite different—an experiential argument, although "inferior" in rigor to a demonstration, is the appropriate sort to use, but "all religious arguments" which draw an analogy between the world as a whole and human artifacts "appear not to be even the most certain and irrefragable" of empirical arguments.[116] Philo also objects that, however useful the argument from design may be shown to be, it cannot successfully work as a logical proof because our experience of the world as a whole (not to mention its origin) is so limited (even nonexistent) as to give us no sufficient foundation for analogous reasoning. Philo correctly points out that the stronger (quantitatively and qualitatively) the similarities experienced between the terms of an analogy, the more reliable is the inference.

> But where-ever you depart, in the least, from the similarity of the cases, you diminish proportionably the evidence; and may at last bring it to a very weak *analogy*, which is confessedly liable to error and uncertainty.

We may experience certain parts or aspects of the universe to be similar, for example, to a building, and thus be led to postulate "an architect or builder" to explain the resemblance.

> But surely you will not affirm, that the universe bears such a resemblance to a house, that we can with the same certainty infer a similar cause, or that the analogy is here entire and perfect. The dissimilitude is so striking, that the utmost you can pretend to is a guess, a conjecture, a presumption concerning a similar cause.[117]

Philo's point is well-taken. A critical consideration of an argument from analogy that is presented as a logical proof must focus on the number and strength of experienced similarities and the number and strength of experienced dissimilarities. We can experience both similarities and dissimilarities between parts or aspects of the natural order and human artifacts. But we cannot experience the world as a whole at all and have no direct empirical access, even in principle, to its designing.

Cleanthes does not retreat in reaction to this critique by Philo and clearly refuses to admit "that the proofs of a Deity amounted to no more than a guess or conjecture." So, after another brief emotional outburst from Demea, Philo resumes his refutation. He firmly rejects the abstract demonstrative approach favored by Demea, endorsing the empirical one of Cleanthes:

> order, arrangement, or the adjustment of final causes is not, of itself, any proof of design; but only so far as it has been experienced to proceed from

that principle. For ought we can know *a priori*, matter may contain the source or spring of order originally, within itself, as well as mind does.

It is only experience that could serve as a basis for adequate argumentation here, as Cleanthes believes. But what, in fact, does our experience disclose?

> Thought, design, intelligence, such as we discover in men and other animals, is no more than one of the springs and principles of the universe, as well as heat or cold, attraction or repulsion, and a hundred others, which fall under daily observation. It is an active cause, by which some particular parts of nature, we find, produce alterations on other parts. But can a conclusion, with any propriety, be transferred from parts to the whole? Does not the great disproportion bar all comparison and inference?

This passage nicely captures the problem with treating the argument from design as if it could be a logically coercive proof. Philo acutely warns us against both assuming "that the operations of a part can afford us any just conclusion concerning the origin of the whole" and allowing "any one part to form a rule for another part, if the latter be very remote from the former." But thought and intelligent design are experienced as causes only in the animal "part" of the universe, and not in the more vast vegetable or mineral "parts." The proponent of the argument from design, used as a logical proof, should take to heart Philo's rhetorical question: "A very small part of this great system, during a very short time, is very imperfectly discovered to us: and do we then pronounce decisively concerning the origin of the whole?"[118]

Hume is not opposed to analogous reasoning. The point here is rather that we lack experiential grounds for establishing similarity and a lack of dissimilarity in a case like this one:

> When two *species* of objects have always been observed to be conjoined together, I can *infer*, by custom, the existence of one where-ever I see the existence of the other: and this I call an argument from experience. But how this argument can have place, where the objects, as in the present case, are single, individual, without parallel, or specific resemblance, may be difficult to explain.

The universe is unique and not an instance of any species of objects, and we have no experience of it as a whole. Philo concludes his refutation of the argument from design as a logical proof by telling Cleanthes that

> the subject in which you are engaged exceeds all human reason and enquiry. Can you pretend to show any such similarity between the fabric of a house, and the generation of a universe? . . . Have worlds ever been formed under your eye?[119]

The obvious answers are negative, which presents a serious problem for an avowed empiricist like Cleanthes. In this respect Cleanthes is typical of proponents of the argument from design.

This takes us to a subtle shift executed by Cleanthes. He asks Philo to imagine that "an articulate voice were heard in the clouds, much louder and more melodious than any which human art could ever reach," by people in all societies, in such a way that each could hear the voice "in its own language and dialect," and that the words not only made sense but conveyed "instruction altogether worthy of a benevolent being, superior to mankind." If that were to happen, Cleanthes asks Philo, "could you possibly hesitate a moment concerning the cause of this voice? and must you not instantly ascribe it to some design or purpose?" Now, in fact, we have not experienced this. But Cleanthes' point is that the combination of complexity and harmonious organization in the natural order is a comparable experience and that whatever difference there is "between this supposed case and the real one of the universe, it is all to the advantage of the latter."[120]

Cleanthes reminds Philo that even a "reasonable sceptic" will try "to adhere to common sense and the plain instincts of nature; and to assent, where-ever any reasons strike him with so full a force, that he cannot, without the greatest of violence, prevent it." He then encourages Philo to analyze a single part of the natural order as an object of reflective experience:

> Consider, anatomize the eye; Survey its structure and contrivance; and tell me, from your own feeling, if the idea of a contriver does not immediately flow in upon you with a force like that of sensation. The most obvious conclusion surely is in favour of design.[121]

Analyzing the text, we notice that Cleanthes has dropped the language of logical argumentation in favor of that of psychological persuasion and instinctive reactions ("could you possibly hesitate a moment"; "must you not instantly ascribe it"; "tell me, from your own feeling"; "the idea" will "immediately flow in upon you with a force like that of sensation"). The clearest indication Cleanthes gives us of this shift follows his revised use of the argument from design:

> And if the argument for Theism be, as you pretend, contradictory to the principles of logic; its universal, its irresistible influence proves clearly, that there may be arguments of a like irregular nature.[122]

The formal logical argument (with which Gilbert Elliot failed to help Hume) has been found wanting; now, in its place, an informal, "irregular," psychological argument is substituted.

As a literary way of signaling such a shift of form for the argument from design, Hume has Pamphilus, the narrator, interject that Philo was (uncharacteristically, we might observe) "a little embarrassed and confounded" and "hesitated in delivering an answer." Now why should Philo be at such a loss except that he is surprised that Cleanthes has been sufficiently swayed by his objections as to change the thrust of the argument? While Philo was attempting to respond to this new tack, we are told, "Demea broke in upon the discourse, and saved his countenance." Demea's point echoes Hume's *Natural History*, that the Deity's "ways are not our ways. His attributes are perfect, but incomprehensible. And this volume of Nature contains a great and inexplicable riddle, more than any intelligible discourse or reasoning."[123]

Cleanthes attacks this emphasis on "the mysterious, incomprehensible nature of the Deity" as rationally undermining "the cause of religion" and compares "mystics" who advocate it to "Sceptics or Atheists." Demea responds that Cleanthes' anthropomorphism is what subverts religion. To analyze divine intelligence is inevitably to reduce God to (at least) the level of man. Hume would agree with Demea's point that the only sort of intelligence of which we have experience is incompatible "with that perfect immutability and simplicity, which all true Theists ascribe to the Deity." Cleanthes' reply continues the spate of name-calling. Since the ideas of "perfect immutability and simplicity" transcend all experience, those who ascribe them to the Deity "are complete mystics," who fail to affirm anything intelligible or positive about the Deity and are, therefore, "atheists, without knowing it."[124] (James will later present a more favorable empirical analysis of mysticism.)

By now Philo is ready to return to the action of the dialogue. Religion typically seeks a causal source of the world as we know it which is not itself causally dependent. Thus, Philo challenges Cleanthes' revised argument from design for not being able to show that the sequence of causal explanation will stop with the intelligent Designer:

> How therefore shall we satisfy ourselves concerning the cause of that Being, whom you suppose the Author of Nature, or . . . the ideal world, into which you trace the material? Have we not the same reason to trace that ideal world into another ideal world, or new intelligent principle? But if we stop, and go no farther, why go so far? Why not stop at the material world?

Cleanthes' reply, in effect, is that we need not causally explain everything in order causally to explain something:

> Even in common life, if I assign a cause for any event; is it any objection, Philo, that I cannot assign the cause of that cause, and answer every new question, which may incessantly be started?

Thus, for Cleanthes, the psychological argument for the intelligent designer is a sufficient achievement of natural religion, whether or not it is also the effect of something beyond itself. As Cleanthes impatiently puts it,

> You ask me, what is the cause of this cause? I know not; I care not; that concerns not me. I have found a Deity; and here I stop my enquiry. Let those go farther, who are wiser or more enterprising.

Philo answers that this attitude is acceptable when we are explaining particular effects in terms of more general causes, which themselves are inexplicable, but that it is scientifically irresponsible "to explain a particular effect" (like the universe or the eye) "by a particular cause" (God or the intelligent Designer) when the latter is "no more to be accounted for than the effect itself."[125] Is religion content to relate to an inferior, intermediate causal source of our experience? If so, then Cleanthes' attitude is warranted. Or does religion attempt to deal with the ultimate condition of all experience? If this is so, then Philo's critique is well-taken.

Philo tries to show that analogous reasoning used in the psychologically persuasive manner advocated by Cleanthes could just as easily lead us to conclusions which are startlingly different from that of "an intelligent cause or author." What should be initially noticed here is that Philo—a "mitigated" or "reasonable sceptic," rather than an "excessive" one—does accept causal reasoning. He is the character who says,

> *Like effects prove like causes.* This is the experimental argument. . . . the liker the effects are, which are seen, and the liker the causes, which are inferred, the stronger is the argument. Every departure on either side diminishes the probability, and renders the experiment less conclusive.

It is precisely because the argument from design compares causes and effects that we have not experienced as extremely similar (to the extent that we have experienced them at all) that critical thinking should leave us suspicious of the "hypothesis of experimental Theism" to which it leads. At the very least, we should be honest enough to admit that the argument can provide no grounds for ascribing "infinity" or "perfection to the Deity,"[126] since such attributes transcend all human experience.

But, worse, several other hypotheses arise which are as experientially possible as (though anthropomorphically less attractive than) that of theism. Seven such alternative hypotheses are mentioned: (1) the world as we know it might be the result of an architectural blunderer using a trial-and-error method; (2) there might have been a committee of collaborating demiurges; (3) a plurality of deities might be corporeal humanoids like the gods and goddesses of ancient polytheism; (4) there might be an animal-like world-soul responsible for the life and actions of our universe; (5) our world might be more like a vegetable than any sort of animal, the product of a seed cast off by some other world; (6) the Eastern worldview could be correct, regarding the universe in terms of the cosmic spinnings of an infinite spider; or (7) the Epicurean materialists might have accurately described reality in terms of eternal atomic particles perpetually moving through space. This last alternative, in particular, strikes us today as plausible. Hume, a century before Charles Darwin, suggests something like the idea of natural selection to explain the relative stability of the world as we know it:

> Is there a system, an order, an oeconomy of things, by which matter can pre-serve that perpetual agitation, which seems essential to it, and yet maintain a constancy in the forms, which it produces? There certainly is such an oeconomy: for this is actually the case with the present world. . . . by its very nature, that order, when once established, supports itself, for many ages, if not to eternity. But where-ever matter is so poized, arranged, and adjusted as to continue in per-petual motion, and yet preserve a constancy in the forms, its situation must, of necessity, have all the same appearance of art and contrivance, which we observe at present.[127]

It would be missing the point to try to figure out which of these alternative hypotheses would be the most plausible to Philo (or Hume), i.e., which he would wish to encourage us to take most seriously. The truth is that no sustained and serious case is being made for any of them. Cleanthes is correct when he comments, "These suppositions" all involve "the hypothesis of design in the universe."[128] They differ in their descriptions of the nature of the principle which accounts for that design. Philo has no trouble admitting that all these hypotheses could be shown to be "subject to great and insuperable difficulties" and that a critical competition among them would only "prepare a complete triumph for the Sceptic." Although he does not deny the existence of some causal source of design in the world, which can be considered a Deity (or more than one deities), the issue which eludes our knowledge concerns its (or their) nature. "A total suspense of judgment is here our only reasonable resource."[129] Up to this point Philo seems to be in agreement with Demea's "mystical" view of divine incomprehensibility and to be thoroughly opposed to the anthropomorphism of Cleanthes.

Perhaps the most famous portion of the *Dialogues* is its penultimate paragraph, in which Philo appears to undergo a reversal after Demea has abandoned the dialogue. Yet this shift on Philo's part is not as extreme as it might superficially seem. He consistently rejects the argument from design when it is presented as a logical proof. Like Cleanthes, however, he is willing to speak of its psychological force:

> A purpose, an intention, a design strikes everywhere the most careless, the most stupid thinker; and no man can be so hardened in absurd systems, as at all times to reject it.

At this level (of psychologically persuasive rather than logically cogent arguments) he too adopts an empirical attitude which agrees with Cleanthes' view that "all the sciences almost lead us insensibly to acknowledge a first intelligent Author." Indeed, it is Philo rather than Cleanthes who asks "to what pitch of pertinacious obstinacy must a philosopher in this age have attained, who can now doubt of a Supreme Intelligence?"[130]

By this last part of the *Dialogues* Philo seems to have abandoned the solidarity which he appeared (was it merely a ruse?) to share with Demea regarding the utter incomprehensibility of the cosmic Designer and to be accepting a limited degree of Cleanthes' anthropomorphism. Having held that alternative hypotheses are as possible as the hypothesis for which Cleanthes was arguing, Philo can nevertheless acknowledge different degrees of probability among them, with the likeliest (or most appealing) being that of an intelligent Designer. And this is all he seems to be saying in the cautiously worded, famous penultimate paragraph—

> *That the cause or causes of order in the universe probably bear some remote analogy to human intelligence.*[131]

Because of the heavily qualified language ("probably ... some remote analogy"), this is not granting Cleanthes a great deal more than was allowed earlier on.

Actually, Philo's most strongly stated agreement with Cleanthes, and the one that poses the most serious threat to the consistency of his position, appears earlier. Three long sentences there are especially worth quoting:

> That the works of Nature bear a great analogy to the productions of art is evident: and according to all the rules of good reasoning, we ought to infer, if we argue at all concerning them, that their causes have a proportional analogy. But as there are also considerable differences, we have reason to suppose a proportional difference in the causes; and in particular ought to attribute a much higher degree of power and energy to the supreme cause than any we have ever observed in mankind. . . . And if we are not contented with calling the first and supreme cause a God or Deity, but desire to vary the expression; what can we call him but mind or thought, to which he is justly supposed to bear a considerable resemblance?[132]

Philo's saying here that "a great analogy" between "the works of Nature" and "the productions of art is evident" seems a significant departure from before. His claim that "we have reason to suppose a proportional difference" between the Deity and man and "to attribute a much higher degree of power and energy to the supreme cause than any we have ever observed in mankind" is, for Philo, a relatively strong one. And his use of personal pronouns in connection with his willingness to accept divine intelligence moves him closer to Cleanthes' position than one might have expected.

What are we to make of the apparent shift in Philo's stance? It seems that earlier, with Demea present, Philo was more playing the role of "devil's advocate" in the dialogue and that after Demea's departure Philo is willing to confess his own position to Cleanthes, with whom he says he lives "in unreserved intimacy." Thus, in the course of the *Dialogues*, a middle ground emerges between utter skepticism of belief and the view that the argument from design can work as a logical proof. This interpretation dovetails with Hume's apparent acceptance, in other works, of the argument from design as psychologically persuasive, though not logically coercive. But what it discloses about the nature of the Deity is consistently far too limited to serve well the interests of theism.

The *A Priori* Argument. Hume's views on the *a priori* argument are most powerfully expressed in the *Dialogues*. In light of Philo's many reservations concerning the argument from design, Demea presents what he calls a "simple and sublime argument *a priori*, which, by offering to us infallible demonstration, cuts off at once all doubt and difficulty" as well as allegedly being able to "prove the infinity of the divine attributes." It is a causal argument comparable to the cosmological one used by Leibniz:

> Whatever exists must have a cause or reason of its existence; it being absolutely impossible for anything to produce itself, or be the cause of its own existence. In mounting up, therefore, from effects to causes, we must either go on in tracing an infinite succession, without any ultimate cause at all; or must at last have recourse to some ultimate cause, that is *necessarily* existent: Now that the first supposition is absurd may be . . . proved. . . . We must, therefore, have recourse to a necessarily-existent Being, who carries the reason of his existence in himself; and who cannot be supposed not to exist without an express contradiction. There is consequently such a Being, that is, there is a Deity.

The first sentence of this passage is a statement of Leibniz's principle of sufficient reason. From Hume's point of view it need not be considered self-evident. Why could something not exist which is uncaused, although it is contingent in the sense that it might not have been, so that its necessity is not to be found in its own nature? The way Demea eliminates the alternative of "an infinite succession" of causes, "without any ultimate cause at all," is quite Leibnizian, demanding that there be a sufficient reason for "the whole eternal chain or succession, taken together" as there must be for "any particular object, which begins to exist in time."[133] Thus, given the plausible presupposition that something does exist, we are supposedly led to the Deity as "a necessarily-existent Being."

Without challenging the logical validity of this *a priori* demonstration, Hume (through Cleanthes) offers four critical objections against it. First, the idea of any demonstrable being, such as the Deity is here conceived to be, is logically problematic:

> Nothing is demonstrable, unless the contrary implies a contradiction. Nothing, that is distinctly conceivable, implies a contradiction. Whatever we conceive as existent, we can also conceive as non-existent. There is no being, therefore, whose non-existence implies a contradiction. Consequently there is no being, whose existence is demonstrable.

Second, the idea of "necessary existence" is epistemologically unfounded, because, "while our faculties remain the same as at present," we cannot perceive the impossibility of anything's (including the Deity's) nonexistence:

> It will still be possible for us, at any time, to conceive the non-existence of what we formerly conceived to exist ... The words, therefore, *necessary existence*, have no meaning; or, which is the same thing, none that is consistent,

since the phrase fails to pass Hume's empirical test. Third, Cleanthes points out, even if, for the sake of argument, we disregard these objections, "why may not the material universe be the necessarily-existent Being, according to this pretended explication of necessity?" Since the sum total of "the qualities of matter" is "altogether unknown and inconceivable" to us, we have no adequate basis for ruling out this possibility. And, fourth, the very idea of the world as a whole, in need of a causal explanation, may be produced "merely by an arbitrary act of the mind" in such a way that it "has no influence on the nature of things." Although they are expressed by Cleanthes rather than Philo, these four dimensions of a critique of the *a priori* argument are typically Humean. Philo can only add insult to the injury Cleanthes has done when he comments that this sort of argument could only appeal "to people of a metaphysical head, who have accustomed themselves to abstract reasoning" and will always be found deficient by ordinary people of common sense.[134]

Hume does not explicitly consider the (*a priori*) ontological argument in his *Dialogues*—and for good reason, since it eschews all contact with the realm of empirical fact. Any argument based on an analysis of the greatest conceivable Being or the absolutely perfect Being or infinite Being is doomed from the outset from Hume's perspective of radical empiricism. Finally, any modern (Cartesian) version of the ontological

argument that involves the premise that existence is a predicate (or perfection) is subject to the objection that we have already seen Hume raise
in the *Treatise*:

> To reflect on anything simply, and to reflect on it as existent, are nothing dif-
> ferent from each other. That idea, when conjoin'd with the idea of any object,
> makes no addition to it.

(This neatly anticipates Kant's later critique.) Hume explicitly applies it
to the idea of God:

> Thus when we affirm, that God is existent, we simply form the idea of such a
> being, as he is represented to us; nor is the existence, which we attribute to him,
> conceiv'd by a particular idea, which we join to the idea of his other qualities,
> and can again separate and distinguish from them.

Against the rationalists, Hume concludes,

> When I think of God, when I think of him as existent, and when I believe him
> to be existent, my idea of him neither encreases nor diminishes.[135]

Indeed, it seems reasonable to generalize that no *a priori* argument purporting to establish (even divine) existence can pass muster in the context
of Hume's epistemology.

Miracles, Evil, and Religion

Miracles. Hume's analysis of miracles is chiefly in his *Enquiry*. Those
who wish to justify religious faith by means of traditional revelation will
find even less support in Hume's writings than advocates of natural religion. In his *Natural History* Hume sarcastically indicates that the believer
in miracles appeals to the disruptions in the very natural order with which
the argument from design is so impressed, when he says that "such events,
as with good reasoners, are the chief difficulties in admitting a supreme
intelligence, are with him the sole arguments for it."[136] But in "Of
Miracles" Hume turns from the flip backhanded slap to a sustained critical treatment. He brags,

> I flatter myself, that I have discovered an argument . . . which, if just, will, with
> the wise and learned, be an everlasting check to all kinds of superstitious delu-
> sion, and consequently, will be useful as long as the world endures. For so long,
> I presume, will the accounts of miracles and prodigies be found in all history,
> sacred and profane.[137]

As an empiricist, Hume must insist that concrete experience of all
kinds is "our only guide in reasoning concerning matters of fact."

Nevertheless, now he warns us "that this guide is not altogether infallible, but in some cases is apt to lead us into errors." Of the various kinds of experience beyond the first-hand sort (both immediate and remembered), Hume says, "there is no species of reasoning more common, more useful, and even necessary to human life, than that which is derived from the testimony of men, and the reports of eye-witnesses and spectators." Like all evidence "founded on past experience," testimonial evidence varies in reliability

> and is regarded either as a *proof* or a *probability*, according as the conjunction between any particular kind of report and any kind of object has been found to be constant or variable. . . . and the ultimate standard, by which we determine all disputes, that may arise concerning them, is always derived from experience and observation.

Hume considers the example of a prince, who has never left India, refusing to believe what would seem "extraordinary" and "marvellous" tales of snow and frost, because they fail to conform to his own "constant and uniform experience."[138] Hume regards his refusal in such circumstances as reasonable, even though his judgment turns out to be false.

"But in order to encrease the probability against the testimony of witnesses, let us suppose, that the fact, which they affirm, instead of being only marvellous, is really miraculous." What would this mean? "A miracle is a violation of the laws of nature," says Hume. Or, again, "A Miracle may be accurately defined, *a transgression of a law of nature by a particular volition of the Deity*, or by the interposition of some invisible agent," such as an angel. Although he does not define the phrase, Hume initially seems to regard a "law of nature" as a pattern of past experience to which there has never been an exception. Thus, he can rather summarily dismiss any miracle claim:

> There must, therefore, be a uniform experience against every miraculous event, otherwise the event would not merit that appellation. And as a uniform experience amounts to a proof, there is here a direct and full *proof*, from the nature of the fact, against the existence of any miracle.[139]

Suppose we consider it a law of nature (as, indeed, it is) that all water heated to 212 degrees Fahrenheit under standard pressure vaporizes into steam. Then this must have always been the case in the past, as far as experience can reveal. But if we have criteria for identifying water which are independent of boiling point and tomorrow come upon water heated to 215 degrees under standard pressure not even beginning to vaporize into steam, we must reject that as a law of nature. There cannot be a precedent set for violations of a law of nature since the first contrary experience establishes that it was not a law of nature after all. Yet this is too slick. Hume's way of understanding a law of nature here seems to rule out exceptions as *a priori* impossible. It becomes merely a matter of definition that no law of nature can admit of exceptions. To put it in Hume's epistemological terminology, we are in the realm of relations of ideas rather than of matters of fact, and the question of whether there might be miracles in his sense of violations of laws of nature ceases to be an empirical one at all. A preferable alternative interpretation of a law of nature might specify what must happen if merely physical (or natural) conditions are causally involved. This would leave open for empirical determination whether there are or ever have been miracles as Hume defines them. It would also make more valuable the comments of the second part of his essay "Of Miracles," to which we now turn.

So far Hume has not impugned the trustworthiness of the witnesses on whose testimony belief in miracles supposedly rests. By contrast, this now becomes the focus of attention. As a historian who has had to wrestle professionally with the believability of traditional testimony, Hume is in a strong position to bring out the reservations appropriate to assessing the testimony of those who make claims on behalf of miracles. First, human beings commonly are deceived, deceive themselves, and deceive others;

> there is not to be found, in all history, any miracle attested by a sufficient number of men, of such unquestioned good-sense, education, and learning, as to secure us against all delusion in themselves; of such undoubted integrity, as to place them beyond all suspicion of any design to deceive others.

Second, we all tend to relish tall tales:

> The passion of *surprise* and *wonder*, arising from miracles, being an agreeable emotion, gives a sensible tendency towards the belief of those events, from which it is derived.

Third, miracle stories thrive among the least credible peoples and those who have been directly influenced by them:

> It forms a strong presumption against all supernatural and miraculous relations, that they are observed chiefly to abound among ignorant and barbarous nations

or those who accept on authority what they have handed down. Fourth, miracle stories are inevitably countered by conflicting evidence; thus, Hume says

> that there is no testimony for any . . . that is not opposed by an infinite number of witnesses.

In connection with this last point, he observes that "in matters of religion, whatever is different is contrary," so that the miracle stories of any one religious tradition threaten the plausibility of those of all competing religious traditions. Finally, Hume encourages us to consider the vested interests of those who start or spread such stories, asking

> what greater temptation than to appear a missionary, a prophet, an ambassador from heaven? Who would not encounter many dangers and difficulties in order to attain so sublime a character?[140]

Hume's conclusion regarding reports of miracles is first overstated: "Upon the whole, then, it appears, that no testimony, for any kind of miracle has ever amounted to a probability, much less to a proof." But then, a few lines further, it is more moderately expressed, to the effect "that no human testimony can have such force as to prove a miracle, and make it a just foundation for any such system of religion." We might agree that Hume offers us valuable critical considerations to bring to bear in weighing the plausibility of traditional revelation and that they are all the more important if the above alternative to his conception of a law of nature be accepted, leaving open the possibility of miracles. It should also be noted that this affects only traditional (and not original or personal) revelation (to invoke Locke's distinction). Notice the cautious way in which Hume then assesses the import of his own argument:

> I beg the limitations here made may be remarked, when I say, that a miracle can never be proved, so as to be the foundation of a system of religion. For I own, that otherwise, there may possibly be miracles, or violations of the usual course of nature, of such a kind as to admit of proof from human testimony; though, perhaps, it will be impossible to find any such in all the records of history.

Here, then, he does allow for both the possibility of miracles and their "proof from human testimony," as we too might wish to do, while expressing doubt that adequate evidence would ever be naturally forthcoming. He also points out in the last paragraph of the essay, "What we have said of miracles may be applied, without any variation, to prophecies."[141] All in all, this essay ranks among the most celebrated and most provocative critiques of traditional revelation in the history of philosophy.

The Problem of Evil. Hume's analysis of the problem of evil leads to his lack of commitment concerning God's moral attributes and ongoing relation to human beings, which is characteristic of deism and at odds with popular religion. In his *Enquiry*, he touches upon the problem of evil in connection with human freedom and moral guilt. He writes that since God is the original causal source of all other reality, the "ultimate Author of all our volitions is the Creator of the world." But this leads us to a **dilemma**:

> Human actions, therefore, either can have no moral turpitude at all, as proceeding from so good a cause, or if they have any turpitude, they must involve our Creator in the same guilt, while he is acknowledged to be their ultimate cause and Author.

Both horns of this dilemma seem unacceptable, which might compel us to question the underlying "doctrine from which they are deduced"—namely, Hume's position of **determinism**. Hume considers the Leibnizians' answer to the dilemma, which would make God responsible but not to blame—

> that the *whole*, considered as one system, is, in every period of its existence, ordered with perfect benevolence; and that the utmost possible happiness will, in the end, result . . . Every physical ill, say they, makes an essential part of this benevolent system, and could not possibly be removed, by even the Deity himself, considered as a wise agent, without giving entrance to greater ill or excluding greater good which will result from it.

But Hume rejects this "solution" as "specious," ultimately unconvincing, "remote and uncertain speculations." Finally, Hume dodges the problem as one that is philosophically unsolvable and rationally impenetrable:

> These are mysteries which mere natural and unassisted reason is very unfit to handle; and whatever system she embraces, she must find herself involved in inextricable difficulties, and even contradictions, at every step which she takes with regard to such subjects.[142]

But to consider Hume's most well-known and most extensive treatment of the problem of evil, we must again turn to his *Dialogues*. Demea presents a parody of Cleanthes' earlier "Look round the world" endorsement of the argument from design, emphasizing the disharmony of things as the flip side of that coin:

> Look round this library of Cleanthes. I shall venture to affirm that, except authors of particular sciences, such as chymistry or botany, who have no occasion to treat of human life, there is scarce one of those innumerable writers, from whom the sense of human misery has not, in some passage or other, extorted a complaint and confession of it. . . . and no one author has ever, so far as I can recollect, been so extravagant as to deny it.

Philo mistakenly responds,

> Leibnitz has denied it; and is perhaps the first, who ventured upon so bold and paradoxical an opinion; at least, the first, who made it essential to his philosophical system.

For the next few pages Philo and Demea try to outdo each other in their graphic descriptions of the evils and miseries of our world. Cleanthes, who earlier had characterized the world in terms of "a benevolent design," is quite reluctant to admit that things are anywhere near as bad as the others assert.[143]

It is Philo who crystallizes the problem which evil poses for Cleanthes' anthropomorphism, challenging him, in this context, to "assert the moral attributes of the Deity, his justice, benevolence, mercy, and rectitude, to be of the same nature with these virtues in human creatures." Philo's succinct summary of the problem of evil (attributed to the influence of Epicurus) still remains its classic formulation. Referring to the Deity, Philo asks,

> Is he willing to prevent evil, but not able? then is he impotent. Is he able, but not willing? then is he malevolent. Is he both able and willing? whence then is evil?

Traditionally orthodox philosophical monotheism (at least since the time of Augustine) has wanted to affirm God's metaphysical attribute of omnipotence (including the power to know what is best and to do what is best) and God's moral attribute of benevolence (the will to do good and prevent evil). But the dilemma is such that affirming these divine attributes seems logically to push a person to deny evil in some way. On the other hand, the common-sense acceptance of evil in the world appears to militate against the orthodox conception of divine attributes, so that God's metaphysical or moral nature is compromised. The argument from design, by focusing on the order and beauty of the world, rather than its disorder and ugliness, typically ignores the fact that we live in an environment in which the good and the evil, pleasure and pain, are mixed. Philo mockingly jeers at Cleanthes, "None but we Mystics, as you were pleased to call us, can account for this strange mixture of phenomena, by deriving it from attributes, infinitely perfect, but incomprehensible." This is, of course, the position that Demea has been advocating, and Philo has thus far been pretending to be allied with him. Cleanthes, unlike Demea, sees through Philo's ruse as well as recognizing the threat Philo presents against all popular religion. As he rhetorically asks, "For to what purpose establish the natural attributes of the Deity, while the moral are still doubtful and uncertain?"[144] Popular religion typically invokes a personal Deity, with moral attributes, that cares about and can have a relationship with mankind.

Demea espouses the traditional (for example, that of Augustine and/or Leibniz) response to the problem of evil:

> Have not all pious divines and preachers ... given a solution of any difficulties, which may attend it? This world is but a point in comparison of the universe: this life but a moment in comparison of eternity. The present evil phenomena, therefore, are rectified in other regions, and in some future period of existence.[145]

We might express this position in the form of an argument: If the present evil phenomena are rectified elsewhere, then there can be sufficient reason for a perfect God's permitting them. Indeed, the present evil phenomena are rectified (supernaturally). Therefore, there can be sufficient reason for a perfect God's permitting them. Both of the premises of this valid conditional syllogism stand in need of careful justification, and Demea makes no serious effort to justify them, which Hume might consider typical of a dogmatic rationalist.

Cleanthes, the empirical theist, immediately protests,

> No! These arbitrary suppositions can never be admitted, contrary to matters of fact, visible and uncontroverted. Whence can any cause be known but from its known effects? Whence can any hypothesis be proved but from the apparent phenomena? To establish one hypothesis upon another, is building entirely in the air.

He prefers to defend the orthodox conception of God by the more radical strategy of refusing altogether to admit the reality of evil:

> The only method of supporting divine benevolence (and it is what I willingly embrace) is to deny absolutely the misery and wickedness of man.

His view can be formulated thus: If we absolutely deny physical and moral evil (misery and wickedness), then we can consistently defend the traditional conception of the divine nature. I do absolutely deny physical and moral evil (misery and wickedness). Therefore, I can consistently defend the traditional conception of the divine nature. Again, we have a valid, conditional syllogism; and this time the first premise seems safe enough. The glaring problem is with the second premise, especially for an empiricist like Cleanthes, because it appears to fly in the face of everyday experience. Cleanthes could try to adopt the privation theory of evil, denying it in that way (in the manner of Augustine and Leibniz); but this would be an awkwardly artificial and speculative solution for an empiricist to advocate. In fact, before the paragraph has been completed, Cleanthes is already contradicting himself by implicitly admitting that experience does reveal at least some evil:

> Health is more common than sickness: Pleasure than pain: Happiness than misery. And for one vexation, which we meet with, we attain, upon computation, a hundred enjoyments.[146]

It would seem that Cleanthes' empiricism has prevailed over his consistency in this passage.

Philo justifiably takes to task Cleanthes' attempt to dismiss the evil of our world: "But this is contrary to every one's feeling and experience: It is contrary to an authority so established as nothing can subvert." He goes on to suggest that as Cleanthes' stronger position is at loggerheads with everyday experience, so his weaker position (that good far outweighs evil in the world), even if correct, is logically irrelevant:

> Why is there any misery at all in the world? Not by chance surely. From some cause then. Is it from the intention of the Deity? But he is perfectly benevolent. Is it contrary to his intention? But he is almighty. Nothing can shake the solidity of this reasoning, so short, so clear, so decisive; except we assert, that these subjects exceed all human capacity, and that our common measures of truth and falsehood are not applicable to them.[147]

In other words, philosophical reason has no way of adequately solving the problem of evil as a matter of logical compatibility, and it remains a mystery of religious faith.

Philo next shifts ground a bit for the purpose of advancing the discussion. He says he is willing to grant, for the sake of argument, that we might logically accept both the reality of evil and the orthodox monotheistic conception of God:

> I will allow, that pain and misery in man is *compatible* with infinite power and goodness in the Deity, even in your sense of these attributes: What are you advanced by all these concessions? A mere possible compatibility is not sufficient. You must prove these pure, unmixt, and uncontrollable attributes from the present mixed and confused phenomena, and from these alone. A hopeful undertaking!

This is an acute move on Philo's (Hume's) part. Even if we overlook the extremely severe problem of establishing that an infinitely perfect God *might* allow evil in the world, from an empirical point of view, the evil of the world does count against the belief that its designer or creator is infinitely perfect. On nonphilosophical grounds, we may wish to believe in such a God.

> But there is no view of human life or of the condition of mankind, from which, without the greatest violence, we can infer the moral attributes, or learn that infinite benevolence, conjoined with infinite power and infinite wisdom, which we must discover by the eyes of faith alone.[148]

An empiricist cannot rationally prove an infinite, absolutely good cause on the basis of finite effects which comprise a mixture of good and bad.

Cleanthes makes a major concession, to the effect that Philo's last point is well taken:

> I have been apt to suspect the frequent repetition of the word, *infinite*, which
> we meet with in all theological writers, to savour more of panegyric than of
> philosophy.... But supposing the Author of Nature to be finitely perfect,
> though far exceeding mankind; a satisfactory account may then be given of nat-
> ural and moral evil, and every untoward phenomenon be explained and
> adjusted. A less evil may then be chosen, in order to avoid a greater;
> Inconveniences be submitted to, in order to reach a desirable end: And in a
> word, benevolence, regulated by wisdom, and limited by necessity, may produce
> just such a world as the present.[149]

This concept of a finite God makes a philosophical solution to the problem of evil more defensible. From this perspective—"finitely perfect" in
the sense of more perfect than anything else in fact is, though not
absolutely infinite—God can be extremely intelligent, powerful, and
benevolent, but there are limits to one or more of the relevant divine
attributes, accounting for the fact of evil in the world.

Yet Philo is not content to let Cleanthes off the hook so easily but
repeats his objection

> that, however consistent the world may be, allowing certain suppositions and
> conjectures, with the idea of such a Deity, it can never afford us an inference
> concerning his existence.

After several more pages, it becomes clear that the point Philo is pressing is that we have no empirical grounds for predicating any moral attributes of the Deity. As Demea earlier parodied Cleanthes' "Look round the
world" speech, so Philo does now:

> Look round this universe. What an immense profusion of beings, animated and
> organized, sensible and active. You admire this prodigious variety and fecundity.
> But inspect a little more narrowly these living existences ... How hostile and
> destructive to each other! ... The whole presents nothing but the idea of a blind
> Nature ... pouring forth from her lap, without discernment or parental care her
> maimed and abortive children![150]

Philo delineates the four logical alternatives we might consider regarding divine attributes:

> There may *four* hypotheses be framed concerning the first causes of the universe;
> *that* they are endowed with perfect goodness, *that* they have perfect malice, *that*
> they are opposite and have both goodness and malice, *that* they have neither
> goodness nor malice.

Philo eliminates the first and second alternatives by saying, "Mixt phenomena can never prove the two former unmixt principles." He likewise
holds that our experiences of "the uniformity and steadiness of general
laws seem to oppose the third." By a process of elimination, he maintains,
"The fourth, therefore, seems by far the most probable." His conclusion

is that, based on our experience of the natural order as an alleged effect of the Deity's activity, we should "exclude from him moral sentiments, such as we feel them."[151] Philo's conclusions here are hasty. It is at least as plausible that God has "perfect goodness" but limited power to act on the divine benevolence as that a God that is neither good nor evil designed (or created) a world containing both good and evil.

Demea feels betrayed and is appalled at the conclusions to which his supposed ally has driven the argument. He exclaims in protest and is chided by Cleanthes for being so slow to detect Philo's point of view. We are told that a disgusted Demea "took occasion soon after, on some pretence or other, to leave the company";[152] and he does not figure into the final dialogue at all. Meanwhile, he has contributed to Hume's development of what may be the most important philosophical critique ever written of the orthodox monotheistic conception of God in light of the problem of evil. What emerges from this critique is the bold question of whether the world, as we experience it, does not point to a finite God, even if an absolutely infinite God is logically compatible with its evil.

Religion. Hume's analysis of religion is indicated by Philo in the twelfth dialogue. He accepts the argument from design as one of empirical analogous reasoning, psychologically persuasive (rather than logically coercive), pointing to a Deity with sufficient power and intelligence to design the world as we experience it. But he remains deeply skeptical about the Deity's having any identifiable moral attributes; as he says, "we have reason to infer that the natural attributes of the Deity have a greater resemblance to those of man, than his moral have to human virtues." He contrasts this intellectual attitude towards God, which he calls religion of "the philosophical and rational kind," to popular religion, by saying that "in proportion to my veneration for true religion, is my abhorrence of vulgar superstitions."[153]

Unlike Cleanthes, who maintains that religion should influence our practical conduct, Philo wishes to restrict "true religion" to "that speculative tenet" indicated in the preceding paragraph. He holds that popular religion is typically built on "both fear and hope" and breeds "superstition or enthusiasm" as well as mean-spirited habits.

> Factions, civil wars, persecutions, subversions of government, oppression . . . are the dismal consequences which always attend its prevalency over the minds of men. If the religious spirit be ever mentioned in any historical narration, we are sure to meet afterwards with a detail of the miseries, which attend it.

Although this is an exaggeration of the practical damage caused by popular religion, history does reveal a checkered record of good and bad effects. It appears that Cleanthes (rather than Philo) is more reasonable in maintaining that a "proper office of religion is to regulate the heart of men, humanize their conduct, infuse the spirit of temperance" and other virtues,[154] even if historically it has too often failed to do so.

Nevertheless, despite this observation, it seems clear from Hume's other writings that Philo rather than Cleanthes is his principal spokesman in this last disagreement between them. In a letter to William Mure of June 30, 1743, Hume raises an "Objection both to Devotion & Prayer, & indeed to every thing we commonly call Religion, except the Practice of Morality, & the Assent of the Understanding to the Proposition *that God exists*" and expresses his belief that the Deity "is not the natural Object of any Passion or Affection." In another letter to Henry Home, written four years later, he writes that "the Church is my Aversion."[155]

Another case in point is Hume's essay "Of Superstition and Enthusiasm," in which he analyses the negative psychology of popular religion.[156] Hume's *Natural History*, as we have seen, is permeated with similar reservations about the psychological roots and dangerous consequences of popular religion.[157] Near the end of this work he seems to condemn both kinds of popular religion, polytheism (including that of the ancient Greeks and Romans) and monotheism (including Judaism and Christianity):

> Examine the religious principles, which have, in fact, prevailed in the world. You will scarcely be persuaded, that they are any thing but sick men's dreams: Or perhaps will regard them more as the playsome whimsies of monkeys in human shape, than the serious, positive, dogmatical asseverations of a being, who dignifies himself with the name of rational.[158]

Although such sarcastic personal attacks against believers in popular religion do not show them to be mistaken, they do clearly demonstrate Hume's contempt.

The penultimate paragraph of the *Dialogues* was supposedly one of the last bits of philosophical work Hume did before he died. Philo is advocating what can be called a position of skeptical deism. He believes, on the basis of apparent design, in a Deity comparable to, though greater than, human beings in some respects and suggests that

> the whole of Natural Theology . . . resolves itself into one simple, though somewhat ambiguous, at least undefined proposition, *That the cause or causes of order in the universe probably bear some remote analogy to human intelligence.*

The unity of design leads him to believe in a single Deity rather than a plurality of deities (polytheism). He doubts that this single speculative tenet has any particular practical implications, saying that "it affords no inference that affects human life, or can be the source of any action or forbearance."[159] Reason and experience do not establish divine infinity, anything about God's moral attributes, or any ongoing relationship between the Deity and man. For all we know, the Deity designed our world and then left it to operate independently. This is deism rather than orthodox theism, despite the fact that Hume preferred to identify his position as one of "genuine Theism,"[160] rather than to adopt the label of "Deism," which was so closely associated with atheism and heresy.[161]

For Philo and Hume, reason and experience can only adequately establish a form of deism. The skepticism advocated by both leaves open the possibility of religious faith-commitments, which transcend reason and experience. The last words uttered by Philo (and probably some of the last words written by Hume before he died) make this point:

> But believe me, Cleanthes, the most natural sentiment, which a well-disposed mind will feel on this occasion, is a longing desire and expectation, that heaven would be pleased to dissipate, at least alleviate this profound ignorance, by affording some particular revelation to mankind, and making discoveries of the nature, attributes, and operations of the divine Object of our faith. A person, seasoned with a just sense of the imperfections of natural reason, will fly to revealed truth with the greatest avidity.

Thus, near the end we see confirmed the suspicions raised by Cleanthes near the beginning: "You propose, then, Philo, said Cleanthes, to erect religious faith on philosophical scepticism." That this is precisely what Philo purports to do is, in effect, admitted near the end of his final speech, when he says,

> To be a philosophical Sceptic is, in a man of letters, the first and most essential step toward being a sound, believing Christian.[162]

Some might interpret this as merely an ironic contrivance of the dialogue form. But it would seem that a close look at other works of Hume's that are not dialogues will indicate that such an interpretation is rash.

In a footnote at the end of his essay "On Suicide," Hume speaks of Scripture in a manner that cuts against the grain of his reputation, when he calls it "That great and infallible rule of faith and practice which must control all philosophy and human reasoning."[163] The first and final paragraphs of his essay "On the Immortality of the Soul" read like endorsements of the possibility of religious faith based on revelation rather than reason:

> By the mere light of reason it seems difficult to prove the immortality of the soul . . . But in reality it is the gospel, and the gospel alone, that has brought *life and immortality to light.*

The body of the essay comprises a critique of attempted rational arguments on behalf of immortality, leading to the last sentence:

> Nothing could set in a fuller light the infinite obligation which mankind have to Divine revelation, since we find that no other medium could ascertain this great and important truth.[164]

By far the most well-known text along these lines is one of the most frequently quoted sentences in the entire corpus of Hume's writings, from his essay "Of Miracles." There he is warning us of the dangers of attempting to base religion on the shaky and limited pillar of reason alone:

> Our most holy religion is founded on *Faith*, not on reason; and it is a sure method of exposing it to put it to such a trial as it is, by no means, fitted to endure.[165]

This is admittedly a tricky point of controversial interpretation, and one cannot rule out the possibility that all of these Humean statements are dripping with ironic sarcasm. Yet it seems that Hume has a good deal of respect for and tolerance of honest belief—for example, faith which does not pretend to be knowledge or to be rationally established—as long as it is open to new experience and avoids fanaticism. He is certainly opposed to the exaggerated theological claims of philosophical rationalists such as Descartes and Leibniz and finds even the empiricism of a thinker like Locke insufficiently radical. But he also reflects the fideism of Bayle, by whom he was clearly influenced, and Kierkegaard, whose thought, in many ways, he surprisingly anticipates. Although his philosophical skepticism will not allow him to move from deism to theism, he leaves the way free to make that religious shift at the level of belief. It is as if he, like Kant a few years later, by circumscribing the legitimate bounds of knowledge, had left room for faith.

Notes

1. *The Letters of David Hume*, ed. J. Y. T. Grieg, vol. 1 (Oxford: Oxford Univ. Press, 1932), p. 13. This work will hereafter be called "Grieg," followed by volume and page numbers.
2. "My Own Life," by David Hume, in *Hume on Religion*, ed. Richard Wollheim (Cleveland: World Publishing Co., 1969), p. 271. This work will hereafter be called "Wollheim."

3. Grieg, 1, pp. 9–10, 13.

4. Ibid., p. 13. 5. Ibid., pp. 12, 16. 6. Ibid., pp. 17–18.

7. Wollheim, p. 272.

8. Grieg, 1, p. 361.

9. *New Letters of David Hume*, Raymond Klibansky and Ernest C. Mossner, eds. (Oxford: Oxford Univ. Press, 1954), pp. 1–3. This work will hereafter be called "Klibansky and Mossner."

10. Wollheim, p. 272.

11. Ibid.

12. Klibansky and Mossner, p. 10.

13. Grieg, 1, p. 57.

14. Klibansky and Mossner, p. 17.

15. Wollheim, p. 273.

16. *Letters of David Hume to William Strahan*, G. Birkbeck Hill, ed. (Oxford: Oxford Univ. Press, 1888), p. xxii, note.

17. Wollheim, pp. 273–75.

18. Grieg, 1, p. 111.

19. Ibid., p. 393.

20. Wollheim, p. 277.

21. Grieg, 1, pp. 455–59, 469, xxv.

22. Ibid., p. 510.

23. Wollheim, p. 277.

24. Grieg, 2, p. 114.

25. Klibansky and Mossner, p. 155.

26. Grieg, 2, pp. 303, 306.

27. Wollheim, p. 278.

28. Grieg, 2, p. 334n.

29. Wollheim, pp. 278–79.

30. Grieg, 2, p. 452.

31. *A Treatise of Human Nature*, by David Hume, L. A. Selby-Bigge, ed. (Oxford: Oxford Univ. Press, 1888)—hereafter called "*Treatise.*"

32. "An Abstract of a Treatise of Human Nature," by David Hume, bound with *An Inquiry concerning Human Understanding*, by David Hume, Charles W. Hendel, ed. (Indianapolis: Bobbs-Merrill, 1955). This work will hereafter be called "Abstract," and Hendel's book will be referred to as "Hendel."

33. *An Inquiry concerning Human Understanding*, bound with "An Abstract of a Treatise of Human Nature," by David Hume, in Hendel—hereafter called "*Enquiry.*"

34. *An Enquiry concerning the Principles of Morals*, by David Hume, J. B. Schneewind, ed. (Indianapolis: Hackett Publishing Co., 1983).

35. "On Suicide" and "On the Immortality of the Soul," both by David Hume, included in Wollheim.

36. *Dialogues concerning Natural Religion*, by David Hume, included in Wollheim.

37. "Of Superstition and Enthusiasm," by David Hume, included in Wollheim.

38. *The Natural History of Religion*, by David Hume, included in Wollheim—referred to as *Natural History*.

39. Hendel, pp. 158–59. In the spring of 1751, Hume wrote his friend Gilbert Elliot of Minto to promote the reading of his first *Enquiry* (then called *Philosophical Essays*) rather than the *Treatise*: "I believe the philosophical Essays contain every thing of Consequence relating to the Understanding, which you woud meet with in the Treatise; & I give you my Advice against reading the latter. By shortening & simplifying the Questions, I really render them much more complete. *Addo dum minuo*. The philosophical Principles are the same in both: But I was carry'd away by the Heat of Youth & Invention to publish too precipitately. So vast an Undertaking, plan'd before I was one and twenty, & compos'd before twenty five, must necessarily be very defective. I have repented of my Haste a hundred, & a hundred times"—Grieg, 1, p. 158.

40. Hendel, p. 194.

41. *Treatise*, pp. 159–60.

42. Hendel, p. 84n.

43. Ibid., p. 184.

44. Wollheim, p. 167.

45. *Treatise*, p. xxi.

46. Hendel, p. 184.

47. *Treatise*, p. 35, Hendel, p. 17n.

48. *Treatise*, p. 2n; cf. Hendel, p. 31n.

49. *Treatise*, p. 157.

50. Hendel, p. 75n.

51. Ibid., p. 85n.

52. Wollheim, p. 111.

53. *Treatise*, pp. 158, 7, 17.

54. Hendel, p. 185.

55. Ibid., pp. 30–31n.   56. Ibid., pp. 20–21.

57. *Treatise*, p. xx.

58. Ibid., p. 1, and Hendel, pp. 26–28.

59. *Treatise*, p. 2.

60. Ibid., p. 3, and Hendel, p. 27.

61. *Treatise*, pp. 3–4, and Hendel, pp. 27–28.

62. *Treatise*, pp. 5–6, and Hendel, pp. 29–30.

63. Hendel, p. 30.

64. Ibid., p. 198.

65. Hendel, p. 32, and *Treatise*, p. 11.

66. Hendel, p. 32, and *Treatise*, pp. 10–11.

67. *Treatise*, pp. 20, 22.

68. Hendel, p. 40.

69. *Treatise*, pp. 15–16, 234.

70. Ibid., pp. 66–67.

71. Hendel, p. 41.

72. Ibid., pp. 186–87.

73. *Treatise*, p. 89.

74. Hendel, pp. 44, 51.

75. Ibid., pp. 57–59.   76. Ibid., pp. 85–86.

77. *Treatise*, pp. 94–96; cf. pp. 101, 103, 629.

78. Hendel, pp. 61–63.

79. Ibid., p. 67; cf. *Treatise*, pp. 102, 107.

80. *Treatise*, p. 114.

81. Ibid., pp. 118, 183, 119–20.

82. Ibid., p. 629.   83. Ibid., p. 71.

84. Ibid., p. 124; cf. Hendel, p. 69n.

85. *Treatise*, pp. 69–70; cf. pp. 14–15.

86. Ibid., p. 144; cf. p. 131.

87. Ibid., p. 180.   88. Ibid., pp. 143, 124–25.   89. Ibid., p. 137.

90. Ibid., p. 142.   91. Ibid., pp. 181, 197, 212, 270.

92. Hendel, pp. 158–59, 162.

93. Ibid., pp. 168, 167; cf. *Treatise*, p. 183.

94. *Treatise*, pp. 263–64, 268–69, 271, 187.

95. Hendel, pp. 169–70. Elsewhere (*Treatise*, p. 224) Hume speaks of "moderate scepticism."

96. Hendel, pp. 171–73. For more on Hume's epistemology and views on metaphysics, see *Twelve Great Philosophers*, by Wayne P. Pomerleau (New York: Ardsley House, 1997), pp. 190–202.

97. *Treatise*, p. xix.

98. *Of the Standard of Taste and Other Essays*, by David Hume, John W. Lenz, ed. (Indianapolis: Bobbs-Merrill, 1965), pp. 126–27. This work will hereafter be called "Lenz."

99. *The Collected Dialogues of Plato*, Edith Hamilton and Huntington Cairns, eds. (New York: Pantheon Books, 1961), p. 1441.

100. Wollheim, p. 97.

101. Ibid., pp. 31, 44.   102. Ibid., pp. 40–41, 33, 85–86, 62, 64, 66.

103. *Treatise*, p. 633n.

104. Wollheim, p. 254.

105. Ibid., pp. 31, 37, 51, 56, 96.

106. Ibid., pp. 230, 232–33.   107. Ibid., pp. 245, 239–40.

108. Ibid., pp. 234–35.   109. Ibid., pp. 242–43.   110. Ibid., pp. 239, 244.

111. Lenz, p. 176; this is a note to Hume's essay "Of the Rise and Progress of the Arts and Sciences."

112. Grieg, 1, pp. 153–58.

113. Ibid., 2, pp. 323, 334.
114. Wollheim, pp. 100–101, 113–15.
115. Ibid., pp. 115–16.   116. Ibid., p. 116.   117. Ibid., pp. 116–17.
118. Ibid., pp. 117, 119–22.
119. Ibid., pp. 123, 125.   120. Ibid., pp. 126–27.   121. Ibid., p. 128.
122. Ibid., p. 129.   123. Ibid., pp. 129–30.
124. Ibid., pp. 131–33; cf. *Treatise*, p. 240.
125. Wollheim, pp. 135–37.
126. Ibid., pp. 138–39.   127. Ibid., pp. 140–56.   128. Ibid., pp. 142–43.
129. Ibid., p. 160.   130. Ibid., pp. 189–91.   131. Ibid., p. 203.
132. Ibid., p. 192.
133. Ibid., pp. 161–62; elsewhere, Hume critically considers the foundation of the causal principle "that whatever begins to exist, must have a cause of existence," arguing that it "is not intuitively certain"—*Treatise*, pp. 78–79.
134. Wollheim, pp. 162–65.
135. *Treatise*, pp. 66–67, 94.
136. Wollheim, p. 56.
137. Ibid., p. 206.   138. Ibid., pp. 206–9.   139. Ibid., pp. 210–11.
140. Ibid., pp. 212–13, 215, 217, 221.
141. Ibid., pp. 222–23, 226. See the discussion of arguments from miracles in "Does Reason Demand That God Be Infinite?" by Wayne P. Pomerleau, *Sophia*, vol. 24, no. 2 (July, 1985), pp. 21–22.
142. Hendel, pp. 108–11.
143. Wollheim, pp. 166–67, 159.
144. Ibid., pp. 171–73.   145. Ibid., p. 173.   146. Ibid., pp. 173–74.
147. Ibid., p. 175.
148. Ibid., pp. 175–76; see "Does Reason Demand That God Be Infinite?" by Wayne P. Pomerleau, *Sophia*, vol. 24, no. 2 (July, 1985), pp. 21–22.
149. Wollheim, pp. 176–77.
150. Ibid., pp. 179, 186.   151. Ibid., pp. 186–87.   152. Ibid., p. 188.
153. Ibid., pp. 194–96.   154. Ibid., pp. 195–96, 198, 200–202.
155. Klibansky and Mossner, pp. 12–13, 26.
156. Wollheim, pp. 246–50.
157. Ibid., pp. 64, 66–67, 85–87, 91, 94.
158. Ibid., pp. 97–98.   159. Ibid., p. 203.   160. Ibid., p. 31; cf. p. 200.
161. Ibid., p. 112.   162. Ibid., pp. 204, 104, 204.
163. Ibid., p. 262n.   164. Ibid., p. 270.   165. Ibid., p. 225.

6

Kant's Critical Moralism

Life and Writings

*I*mmanuel Kant's life was relatively uneventful, being spent entirely in and near Königsberg, the provincial capital of East Prussia (now Kaliningrad, part of Russia). He never married or traveled more than seventy miles from that city of about 54,000 people, and his life was simply that of student, teacher, and philosopher. Nevertheless, the German poet Heinrich Heine's famous quip that there could be no history of Kant's life since he had neither life nor history is as unfair as it is clever.[1] In one of his later letters Kant writes that his paternal grandfather emigrated from Scotland toward the end of the seventeenth century.[2] The philosopher's father, Johann Georg Cant, a harness-maker by trade, married Anna Regina Reuter in 1715. Immanuel was born on April 22, 1724, their fourth child of nine (only Immanuel, three sisters, and a younger brother were to survive childhood); and he was baptized the following day.

The Kant family subscribed to the **Pietist** movement in German Lutheranism. Pietism had been founded in the seventeenth century by Philipp Jakob Spener (1635–1705), whose *Pia Desideria* of 1675 emphasized Biblical study for personal devotion (as opposed to academic expertise), active participation of the laity in the governing of the church, the revival of Christian ethics as a matter of practical (and not merely intellectual) faith, a less polemical form of apologetics designed to appeal to the whole person, a reform of theological education to focus on practical values (rather than abstract speculation), and a renewal of preaching as a means to the nurturing of sincere piety. Not only was Immanuel reared in this faith at home; but at the age of eight, in 1732, he was sent to the Pietist school in Königsberg, the Collegium Fredericianum; the Kant family's pastor, Franz Albert Schultz, whom Immanuel greatly respected, was its capable director. There the boy became well trained in the Latin language and its literature. In 1740, at the age of sixteen, the boy entered Albertus University of Königsberg, which had been founded in 1544 as a Lutheran school by Albert I, Duke of Prussia.

By this time, the eighteenth-century cultural and intellectual movement of the Enlightenment was becoming quite influential in Prussia. There as elsewhere in Europe (and, for that matter, in North America as well) the movement (called *Aufklärung* in German) was committed to the ideals of reason, experience, nature, freedom, and progress (all of which were to become Kantian ideals). The same year in which Kant entered the University of Königsberg, 1740, Frederick II became King of Prussia. The king was enamored of French culture and literature and admired the thought of Voltaire and Bayle, as well as that of Locke and Leibniz. He came to be called "Frederick the Great" and "the Enlightenment King" because of his commitment to learning and policies of toleration toward the open discussion and publication of even unorthodox ideas. Rationalism flourished, and even expressions of skepticism were permitted. In his essay, "What Is Enlightenment?" (published in 1784, two years before the death of the Enlightenment King), Kant writes that "this is the age of enlightenment, or the century of Frederick" and praises the king for encouraging argumentation.[3]

Curiously, the themes of Kant's education, Pietism, rationalism, Enlightenment thought, and Frederick the Great are all related to the most important link in German philosophy between Leibniz, its first great thinker, and Kant. Christian Wolff (1679–1754), who had studied theology at Jena, was appointed professor of mathematics at the Pietist University of Halle (founded in 1694) on the recommendation of Leibniz himself. Wolff was a rationalist who adopted the Leibnizian philosophy and spent much of his professional life trying to systematize it. In 1711, again on Leibniz's recommendation, Wolff was elected to the Berlin Academy. But his rationalism offended anti-intellectual Pietists, who in 1723 had him removed from his chair at Halle and convinced King Frederick William I to exile him. He was appointed professor of mathematics and philosophy at the Calvinist university in Marburg, where he became increasingly famous. In 1728, Wolff's *Preliminary Discourse on*

Philosophy in General was published, distinguishing among three types of human knowledge—historical (factual), mathematical (quantitative), and philosophical (concerning "the reason of things which are or can be"). Following Descartes and Leibniz, Wolff says that the three types of "beings which we can know are God, human souls, and bodies or material things"; corresponding to these, three areas of metaphysics are philosophical theology, philosophical psychology, and philosophical cosmology. In accordance with the ideals of the Enlightenment, he defends "the freedom to philosophize," denying that there could ever be any real conflict between philosophical truth and revealed truth.[4] As a Leibnizian rationalist, he believed that nothing is without a sufficient reason for so being. After Frederick the Great became King of Prussia in 1740, one of the first things he did was reinstate Wolff at Halle. Within three years, Wolff had been appointed university chancellor, and in 1745 he was named a baron of the Holy Roman Empire. By 1754, when he died at Halle, Wolff's synthesis of Leibnizian rationalism had emerged as a serious alternative to Aristotelian scholasticism in German universities.

Kant's mentor, Pastor Schultz, had studied with Wolff at Halle and become a Wolffian. Also, at the University of Königsberg, Kant came under the influence of Martin Knutzen (1713–51), extraordinary professor of logic and metaphysics, a Pietist follower of the Leibnizian-Wolffian philosophy. Knutzen not only converted Kant to this philosophy, but he also exposed Kant to the scientific work of Newton and then opened up his extensive library to his eager student. Although Schultz tried to persuade Kant to enter the ministry, the young man was more inclined to follow Knutzen's lead. This was evident from his first published work, *Thoughts on the True Estimation of Living Forces*, presented in 1746, which dealt with modern philosophical and scientific theory, with particular reference to Descartes and Leibniz.

But that same year, Kant's father died (his mother had already passed away in 1637, when Kant was thirteen), leaving him poor and in need of supporting himself. So he left the university to work as a tutor (outside the city walls of Königsberg) in the province of East Prussia. This period as tutor in several families lasted from 1747 through 1754. We do not know much about these years of Kant's life, but it appears that he acquired a refined taste for fashion and manners during this time.

In 1755, Kant returned to Königsberg and presented a scientific dissertation, *On Fire (De Igne)*, for his graduate degree. That same year, he qualified for an appointment as *Privatdozent* (private lecturer) with another Latin treatise, *A New Exposition of the First Principles of*

Metaphysical Knowledge (the *Nova Dilucidatio*). Later that year, a still larger scientific work was published, his *Universal Natural History and Theory of the Heavens*, dedicated to Frederick the Great and written from a Newtonian perspective. Other scientific works of less importance followed in the late 1750s.

Kant's fifteen years as *Privatdozent* were marked by poverty and hard work. He received no salary, so that his income was dependent on the number of students he could attract to his lectures. Fortunately, he was an engaging lecturer, and the lectures were quite well attended. There is a story that during this period his one coat became so worn that some friends wanted to help him purchase a new one, but he declined the gift. He lectured on logic, metaphysics, ethics, physics, mathematics, geography, and anthropology for between sixteen and twenty-eight hours a week. During this time, there were about thirty-eight professors in the university, with only eight ordinary (or regular) professors on the philosophy faculty—plus some extraordinary ones such as Knutzen. In 1756, Kant unsuccessfully applied for the professorial chair at the university that had been left vacant by Knutzen's death; but the vacancy was not filled. Again in 1758, he applied for a chair in logic and metaphysics at Königsberg, but another man got the appointment. In 1764, he was considered for a chair in poetry, which he declined. In early 1766, he was appointed assistant librarian, a position which he held until 1772; the salary supplemented the meager earnings from his teaching. While he was *Privatdozent* he was offered at least a couple of professorships, at Erlangen in 1769 and at Jena in 1770, which he declined. Despite its remote geography, he liked the place of his birth and felt no need to wander. As he wrote much later,

> A large city like Königsberg on the river Pregel, the capital of a state, where the representative National Assembly of the government resides, a city with a university (for the cultivation of the sciences), a city also favored by its location for maritime commerce, and which, by way of rivers, has the advantages of commerce both with the interior of the country as well as with neighboring countries of different languages and customs, can well be taken as an appropriate place for enlarging one's knowledge of people as well as of the world at large, where such knowledge can be acquired even without travel.[5]

During the 1760s—perhaps under the influence of Rousseau and Hume—the focus of Kant's writings shifted from science to philosophy. Indeed, it is a mistake to imagine that Kant's work as an author (or even as a philosopher) begins at the age of fifty-seven with his first *Critique*, although it is true that his most important work was published in the twenty years from 1781 to 1800. In 1763, his *Enquiry concerning the Clarity of the Principles of Natural Theology and Ethics* and *One Possible Basis for a Demonstration of the Existence of God* were published. These works were followed in 1764 by *Observations on the Feeling of the Beautiful and Sublime* and in 1766 by *Dreams of a Spirit Seer*. By the turn of the decade, when he received the offers from Erlangen and Jena, he had established a reputation.

Finally in 1770, he was appointed to the ordinary professorship in logic and metaphysics at the University of Königsberg. His Inaugural Dissertation, *On the Form and Principles of the Sensible and Intelligible World*, marks a turning-point in his philosophical career, separating his pre-critical phase from that of his critical philosophy. The 1770s are sometimes called Kant's silent decade; between his Inaugural Dissertation and the publication of his first *Critique* Kant wrote nothing else of philosophical importance. Yet he was busy trying to create his own new system. There is some evidence that he was starting to think his way to the critical philosophy as early as 1765 (the year in which Leibniz's *New Essays* was posthumously published); for that year he writes in a letter, "What I am working on is mainly a book on the proper method of metaphysics (and thereby also the proper method for the whole of philosophy)." A few days after he assumed his long awaited chair in philosophy, he writes,

> For perhaps a year now, I believe I have arrived at a position that, I flatter myself, I shall never have to change, even though extensions will be needed, a position from which all sorts of metaphysical questions can be examined according to wholly certain and easy criteria.[6]

In the often quoted letter of February 21, 1772 to his former student and faithful disciple Marcus Herz, Kant delineates the plan "for a work that might perhaps have the title, "The Limits of Sense and Reason," comprising a theoretical part, made up of "two sections, (1) general **phenomenology** and (2) metaphysics," and a practical part, made up of "two sections, (1) the universal principles of feeling, taste, and sensuous desire and (2) the basic principles of morality." Here we have the blueprint for his entire critical philosophy. In that same letter Kant proceeds to say that "the pure concepts of the understanding must not be abstracted from sense perceptions" and that "sensuous representations present things as they appear," rather than "as they are"—the seeds of his critical idealism; and he claims to have systematically classified categories of the understanding on which to build a "**transcendental** philosophy"—so that he feels he is "in a position to bring out a 'Critique of Pure Reason.' " Yet he is struggling with the problem of how such categories, which neither create their objects nor are the products of their objects, can have objective validity.[7] By 1777, he is complaining to Herz about "the problem of presenting these ideas with total clarity," which is seen as "an obstacle to the completion of my 'Critique of Pure Reason.' "[8] By May of 1781, the first *Critique* was printed in Halle, dedicated to Baron von Zedlitz, Frederick the Great's liberal minister of justice and education. Kant makes it clear that "the book is the product of nearly twelve years of reflection," although he "completed it hastily, in perhaps four or five months, with the greatest attentiveness to its content but less care about its style and ease of comprehension."[9] Consequently, the work was not much read, understood, or appreciated at first; it was not until 1782 that the first review of it was published, and it was not particularly favorable. But that should not be too surprising. In the Preface to his *Prolegomena* Kant admits (what generations of students have found to be true) that "the book is dry, obscure, opposed to all ordinary notions, and moreover long-winded."[10] But it was also a revolutionary work which did not fall into the established pigeonholes of scholastic philosophy, Cartesian rationalism, and British empiricism. As Kant wrote to that first reviewer, he was creating "a whole new science, never before attempted, namely, the critique of *an a priori judging* reason," a project never before systematically tackled by anyone and only "touched on" by a few of his predecessors, "for instance, Locke and Leibnitz."[11] At any rate, though appreciative reviews were not quickly forthcoming, the book that many professional philosophers consider the greatest volume of philosophy ever written was in print, and the development of the critical philosophy that for two centuries has been identified as the Kantian system was under way.

Before chronicling Kant's achievements in the astoundingly productive decade from the publication of his first *Critique* in 1781 to that of his third *Critique* in 1790, let us briefly consider his appearance, character, habits, and teaching at about this time of his life. He was a physically small man, never more than five feet, two inches in height or more than one hundred pounds in weight, narrow-chested, frail, with one shoulder somewhat higher than the other. He assumed the dress of a gentleman and was even a bit of a dandy in his appearance: frock-coat, frilled front, silk stockings, wig, three-cornered hat, and cane (in his earlier days, when it was fashionable, even wearing a sword).

He was prudent, cautious, deliberate, frugal, punctual, earnest, and conscientious. He was resolutely careful not to speak rashly, though consistently and reliably honest; as he writes to an intellectual who was offended by the jocular, ironic tone of his *Dreams of a Spirit Seer*, "I shall certainly never become a fickle or fraudulent person. . . . Although I am absolutely convinced of many things that I shall never have the courage to say, I shall never say anything I do not believe."[12] He was a hypochondriac; and his letters are riddled with nagging complaints and worries about his own health. He laments his "sensitive nerves" and low tolerance for "all medicines," which "are without exception poison for me," as well as "an irregular pulse." He frets over "heartburn," his digestion, and a "cloudy brain." By the beginning of the 1790s, he was losing his appetite and the energy needed for philosophizing and lecturing—attributing this to "nothing but old age."[13]

Kant was known for his regular routine. Just before five each morning, his servant Martin Lampe (whom he employed from 1762 to 1802) woke him with the words, "It is time." Between five and six Kant would drink tea and smoke one bowl of pipe tobacco. Then he would prepare and deliver his lectures and after that write in the mornings. He dined at one in the afternoon, typically with two to five guests. Although the writings Kant prepared for publication give the impression of a cold stuffiness, he appears to have been a charming host, a lively conversationalist, and a kindly friend. He regarded that midday meal as a social occasion, and it would commonly last from two to three hours. He preferred to talk politics rather than philosophy with his friends. After dinner he walked for an hour eight times up and down the avenue which came to be called, in his honor, the Philosopher's Walk. Legend has it that this walk was so measured and regular that some citizens of Königsberg used to set their clocks by it. (He allegedly neglected his daily walk on only two occasions before he became infirm: once in order to read a copy of Jean-Jacques Rousseau's *Émile* that had just arrived and another time while awaiting further news of the French Revolution.) After his walk, he spent time reading and thinking before going to bed at ten in the evening.

Although he was a life-long bachelor, he is thought to have considered marrying a couple of women, both of whom moved on before he could make up his mind. His relations with his siblings and their children seem to have been rather distant and formal. We have a short letter of 1792 which Kant wrote his brother Johann Heinrich, who was eleven years his junior, had attended his lectures at the university, became a village pastor, and died in 1800. It says, "Despite my apparent indifference, I have thought of you often and fraternally—not only for the time we are both living but also for after my death, which, since I am 68, cannot be far off." The purpose of the letter seems to be to inform his brother of his recently made will's provisions for the family.[14] Kant went many years without any contact with his brother and apparently never even met his sister-in-law at all.

Kant seems to have been a great success as a teacher, offering a staggeringly wide variety of courses over the years. For the three main philosophical courses he taught repeatedly he conformed to the requirement that Wolffian texts should be used—G. F. Maier's *Theory of Reason* for logic and books by Alexander Baumgarten for metaphysics and ethics. His public lectures reached audiences of up to one hundred, whereas his private lectures were to twenty or fewer people. Kant's purpose as a teacher was to promote right opinion and to inculcate sound principles in his students (rather than to try to make philosophers of them). He deliberately chose to deliver popular lectures on the empirical subjects of anthropology and physical geography, designed to impart to his students "knowledge of the world."[15] Like so many other teachers before and since his time, he wished for a greater number of good students. He complains to Marcus Herz, one of his most gifted disciples, that "it is a matter of luck whether one has attentive and capable students during a period of time" and that the students who scribble the greatest quantity of notes "are seldom capable of distinguishing the important from the unimportant."[16] Nevertheless, he seemed especially proud of being able to work effectively with average students, on the view that the brilliant ones did not really need him, whereas the stupid ones were hopeless despite anyone's efforts. He tried to challenge them to develop and exercise the skills of philosophical analysis and evaluation.

The verbal portrait of Kant by Johann Gottfried Herder, who had been his pupil from 1762 to 1764 and then achieved fame as a German man of letters, is so beautiful and moving that it is worth quoting, despite its length:

> I have had the good fortune to know a philosopher. He was my teacher. In his prime he had the happy sprightliness of a youth; he continued to have it, I believe, even as a very old man. His broad forehead, built for thinking, was the seat of an imperturbable cheerfulness and joy. Speech, the richest in thought, flowed from his lips. Playfulness, wit, and humor were at his command. His lectures were the most entertaining talks. His mind . . . comprehended equally the newest works of Rousseau . . . and the latest discoveries in science. He weighed them all, and always came back to the unbiased knowledge of nature and to the moral worth of man. The history of men and peoples, natural history and science, enlivened his lectures and conversation. He was indifferent to nothing worth knowing. No cabal, no sect, no prejudice, no desire for fame could ever

tempt him in the slightest away from broadening and illuminating the truth. He incited and gently forced others to think for themselves; despotism was foreign to his mind. This man, whom I name with the greatest gratitude and respect, was Immanuel Kant.[17]

Kant's productivity in the decade following the publication of his first *Critique* was astonishing. If he had never written anything but that book, he would probably remain the greatest philosopher of modern times. But while continuing to meet his responsibilities as full-time professor at the university, he developed his critical philosophy in one great work after another. Undaunted by the initially unenthusiastic reception of his first *Critique*, in 1783, he published his *Prolegomena to Any Future Metaphysics*; in 1784, there appeared "What Is Enlightenment?" and "Idea for a Universal History from a Cosmopolitan Point of View." In 1785, his *Grounding for the Metaphysics of Morals* was published. In 1786, there appeared "Conjectural Beginning of Human History" and *Metaphysical Foundations of Natural Science*. In 1787, the second edition of his first *Critique*, which he had extensively revised, was published. In 1788, the *Critique of Practical Reason* appeared, and, in 1790, the *Critique of Judgment*. As he became increasingly famous, opportunities became available to him which might have proved attractive except for the time they would require (as he says), "which I must rather use to complete my project."[18] By the middle of the 1780s, the Kantian critical philosophy was being enthusiastically received and taught in various parts of Germany by younger professors, including some of Kant's former students. Baron von Zedlitz, the minister of education, was a supporter. (Indeed, in 1778, he unsuccessfully urged Kant to take a more prestigious professorship at Halle.)

Then, in 1786, Frederick the Great died, after four and a half decades as the Enlightenment King. He was succeeded by his illiberal nephew, Frederick William II, whose coronation took place in Königsberg, at a time when Kant was university rector (i.e., vice-chancellor). In July of 1788, the new king replaced the liberal von Zedlitz with Johann Christoff Wollner, a former preacher and champion of orthodox theology, an enemy of the Enlightenment, whom Frederick the Great had dismissed as "a deceitful, scheming priest and nothing more." Six days after his appointment, Wollner's religious edict appeared, forbidding any deviation from Biblical doctrines. Within half a year after that, another edict was promulgated requiring that all works dealing with religion must be approved by official state censors prior to publication. Wollner planted a spy among the audience attending the lectures on Kant's philosophy by one of his disciples. Even near the end of 1786, Kant learned from another of his followers that a "Cabinets Order" had been issued temporarily forbidding any lecturing on Kant's philosophy at Marburg, which later came to be a center of Kantian scholarship; this injunction was reversed about a year later, although lectures on the Kantian philosophy were ordered to be restricted to advanced students.[19] This was the climate in which Kant's most distressing confrontation with established authorities arose.

Although advancing age was slowing his momentum, Kant did want to write on religion in the 1790s. His work "On the Failure of All Attempted Philosophical Theodicies" was published in 1791. And he was working on *Religion within the Limits of Reason Alone*, the book that was to get him into trouble. A friend of his warned him in 1791 that Wollner was not to be trusted, that the new king was behaving like a religious fanatic, and that it was feared that a new religious edict might be forthcoming, calling for mandatory church attendance and reception of the sacraments.[20] Although he remained privately reverential, during the last few decades of his life, Kant did not attend church services or engage in public religious practices and seemed to find all external shows of piety distasteful. In 1792, Kant published "On the Radical Evil in Human Nature," which was to become Book One of his *Religion* and which was accepted by one of Wollner's censors in Berlin. But Berlin denied Kant permission to publish Book Two, which was deemed contrary to Biblical teachings. As a champion of the Enlightenment, Kant had insisted on the right of a scholar to disseminate his ideas. In his "What Is Enlightenment?" he had proclaimed, "*Sapere aude!* 'Have courage to use your own reason!'—that is the motto of enlightenment."[21] Would he practice what he had preached or timidly submit? Complicating matters was the fact that Kant always deeply respected the authority of the state. Yet he decided to skirt the censorship of Berlin by getting permission to publish the last three books of his *Religion* from the philosophical faculty at Jena (which also had that authority) and then having all four books published together in Königsberg in 1793. As Kant explained to a theology professor (to whom he later dedicated his *Conflict of the Faculties*) when sending him a copy of *Religion* that year, his philosophy was designed to solve certain problems:

> (1) What can I know? (metaphysics). (2) What ought I to do? (moral philosophy). (3) What may I hope? (philosophy of religion). A fourth question ought to follow, finally: What is man? (anthropology . . .). With the enclosed work, *Religion within the Limits* [*of Reason Alone*], I have tried to complete the third part of my plan.[22]

So this book, *Religion within the Limits of Reason Alone*, was important for the development of Kant's system.

But it also incurred the wrath of Wollner, the villain of Kant's life story. In October of 1794, Wollner wrote and signed a document in which he censured Kant for misusing his philosophy "to distort and disparage many of the cardinal and basic teachings of the Holy Scriptures and of Christianity . . . particularly in your book *Religion within the Limits of Reason Alone*," demanding that he "give at once a most conscientious account" of himself, and enjoining him, with a threat of unspecified "unpleasant measures," from incurring further disfavor. Kant wrote a letter to the king in reply saying, "I have done no harm to the public *religion of the land*," denying that his *Religion* even appraises Christianity, let alone disparages it, claiming, "I have evidenced my great respect for Christianity in many ways" in *Religion*, and promising the king, "*as Your Majesty's most loyal subject*, that I will hereafter refrain altogether from discoursing publicly, in lectures or writings, on religion, whether natural or revealed." Because of that last italicized qualifying phrase, Kant felt released from his promise with the death of Frederick William II. As he later writes in a footnote, "This expression, too, I chose carefully, so that I would not renounce my freedom to judge in this religious suit *forever*, but only during His Majesty's lifetime."[23]

From then until the king died in 1797, Kant kept his promise. During that time he published on nonreligious matters: *Perpetual Peace* in 1795 and both parts of his *Metaphysics of Morals* in 1797. The new king, Frederick William III, dismissed Wollner and abolished the program of censorship. In 1798, Kant published *The Conflict of the Faculties*, which deals with religion, and his *Anthropology from a Pragmatic Point of View*.

By the 1790s books on Kant's critical philosophy were being written by others, and his ideas were being introduced into France, England, and the Netherlands. We have letters from two Benedictine philosophers at the Catholic university at Wurzburg, attesting to the popularity of Kant's philosophy (to which they are both sympathetic) there in 1796.[24] But he was aging and failing physically. In 1795, he cut back his lecturing to the daily public presentations on logic and metaphysics, and, in 1797, he gave up lecturing at the university altogether. In late 1798, he writes that his lifestyle seems to be reducing itself to "not that of a scholar but of a vegetable—eating, seeing, sleeping."[25]

By the turn of the century, his memory was failing and he was losing his vision. By the end of 1801, a friend and former student of his had to assume control of the keys to Kant's household and assist Kant in performing everyday activities. In early 1802, after four decades of service,

Kant's old servant Lampe had to be dismissed with a pension and replaced with an abler man. By the fall of 1803, Kant could no longer be safely left alone, and his youngest (widowed) sister moved in to take care of him. By the beginning of 1804, he was unable to recognize his friends. Finally, on February 12, 1804, he died, his last words being, "*Es ist gut*" ("It is good"). For sixteen days, large crowds of admirers paid their respects, and his funeral, on February 28th, was well attended. On April 23, 1804 (the day after what would have been his eightieth birthday), a university convocation solemnly assembled to hear a memorial address honoring Königsberg's greatest philosopher; and in 1810, a white marble bust of Kant was erected.

Kant's philosophical writings are customarily classified as pre-critical and critical works, the Inaugural Dissertation of 1770 being the dividing point. Kant has provided some foundation for this distinction in a letter of 1797, agreeing that a collection of his works might be published with this proviso: "I would not want you to start the collection with anything before 1770, that is, my dissertation on the sensible world and the intelligible world."[26]

The pre-critical works include his *New Exposition of the First Principles of Metaphysical Knowledge* (1755),[27] his *One Possible Basis for a Demonstration of the Existence of God* (1763),[28] his *Enquiry concerning the Clarity of the Principles of Natural Theology and Ethics* (1763),[29] his *Observations on the Feeling of the Beautiful and Sublime* (1764),[30] and his *Dreams of a Spirit Seer* (1766).[31] The watershed Inaugural Dissertation of 1770 is *On the Form and Principles of the Sensible and Intelligible World.*[32] His monumental first *Critique*, the *Critique of Pure Reason*, was published in 1781. Later works he published include *Prolegomena to Any Future Metaphysics* (1783), *Grounding for the Metaphysics of Morals* (1785),[33] *Metaphysical Foundations of Natural Science* (1786),[34] his second *Critique*, the *Critique of Practical Reason* (1788), his third *Critique*, the *Critique of Judgment* (1790),[35] various essays from the 1780s and 90s now available in English translations as a collection *On History*, his essay "On the Failure of All Attempted Philosophical Theodicies" (1791),[36] *Religion within the Limits of Reason Alone* (1793),[37] the two parts of *Metaphysics of Morals* (1797), *The Metaphysical Elements of Justice*,[38] as well as *The Doctrine of Virtue*,[39] *The Conflict of the Faculties* (1798), and *Anthropology from a Pragmatic Point of View* (1798). Works of his that were edited for publication by others include *Logic* (1800), *Education* (1803),[40] *What Real Progress Has Metaphysics Made in Germany Since the Time of Leibniz and Wolff?* (1804),[41] *Lectures on Philosophical Theology* (1817),[42] and *Lectures on Ethics* (1924).[43] Two fine anthologies of Kant's philosophical writings,

Kant Selections, edited by Theodore M. Greene, and *The Philosophy of Kant*, edited by Carl J. Friedrich, contain important material from Kant's theory of knowledge and philosophy of God and religion.

Theory of Knowledge

Toward the Critical Philosophy. Kant's development toward the critical philosophy was lengthy and labored. His *New Exposition* of 1755, as the title specifies, deals with "the First Principles of Metaphysical Knowledge." For someone working in the Leibnizian-Wolffian tradition, as Kant was, such a study called for a treatment of the principles of contradiction and of sufficient reason—the topics of his first two sections. Even at this formative stage of his career, he was not a blind follower of the prevailing school of German philosophy. He denies that the principle of contradiction can be the single foundation of all knowledge, claiming that it is, in fact, merely "a definition of the impossible." He maintains, further, "that there cannot be one sole, ultimate, universal principle of all truths," as that of contradiction is alleged to be by the Leibnizian-Wolffians. Instead, he says,

> There are two absolutely first principles of all truths: the one of affirmative truths, the proposition, viz., *Whatever is is*; the other of negative truths, the proposition, viz., *Whatever is not is not*. Taken together these are jointly called the principle of Identity.

Kant is likewise critical of the established conception of the principle of sufficient reason:

> The illustrious definition of Wolff (for it has great renown) here seems to me to need correction. For he defines a reason as that by which it is understood why a thing is rather than is not.

Kant shows that "why" here means "for what reason," establishing the circularity of the Wolffian analysis. He also criticizes the concept of "sufficient" as being vague "since it is not on the face of it clear how much suffices." Kant prefers to speak of "a determining reason" instead of a sufficient reason; "seeing that to determine means to affirm in such a way that every opposite is excluded, it denotes that which certainly suffices for conceiving a thing thus and not otherwise." These quarrels show that Kant, even at this early stage of his professional life, has a critical mind and is prepared to use it. Nevertheless, he proceeds to elaborate a series of propositions, which are fairly typical of dogmatic rationalists after Descartes:

"Nothing is true without a determining reason"; "It is impossible that anything should have the reason of its own existence in itself"; and "There is a being whose existence is prior to the very possibility both of itself and of all things; this being, therefore, is said to exist absolutely necessarily." He is talking here, of course, about God and is concerned with argumentation for God's necessary existence, rejecting "the Cartesian argument" he later calls "ontological" as successful only in the realm of ideas, "and not in the real order." His own argument at this point is that God must necessarily exist as the ultimate "determining reason" of all that is real or possible:

> It is clear, therefore, that if you take away God, not only all existence of things but even the internal possibility of them is also absolutely abolished.[44]

This is capable work in the Leibnizian-Wolffian tradition, although it is dogmatic in Kant's later sense of not being based on a prior critique of the powers of reason.

In his *Basis*, a few years later, Kant more systematically considers the project of demonstrating the existence of God. Here we see Kant becoming a bit more skeptical (he may have read some Hume by the early 1760s), saying that human fulfillment does not require the pursuit of rational argumentation, although it is natural for reason to strive for it. "Achievement of this goal, however, requires that one venture into the fathomless abyss of metaphysics. This is a dark ocean without coasts and without lighthouses." This is a metaphorical warning worthy of a David Hume. Nevertheless, Kant proceeds to develop the same proof for God's necessary existence which he had indicated in his *New Exposition*. He admits, from a purely logical perspective, "There is, to be sure, no internal contradiction in the denial of all existence." Yet he observes that "if nothing exists, nothing conceivable is given and one would contradict himself in nevertheless pretending something to be possible." In other words, in the very act of thinking, we implicitly conceive that things either are or are possible. "Consequently, it is absolutely impossible that nothing at all exist" to the extent that we think at all. This leads to the conclusion of Kant's argument:

> All possibility presupposes something actual in which and through which everything conceivable is given. Accordingly there is a certain actuality whose annulment itself would totally annul all internal possibility. But that whose annulment or negation eradicates all possibility is absolutely necessary. Accordingly something exists in an absolutely necessary fashion.

Kant goes on to argue that this absolutely necessary being is unitary, simple, immutable, eternal, the highest reality, and a spirit. His line of reasoning here will be familiar to those of us who have studied the philosophical theology of medieval and early modern times. Kant divides all of the possible proofs for God's existence into four types, two derived "from rational concepts of the merely possible" and the other two "from the empirical concepts of the *existent*." Of the two derived from possibility, one moves "from the possible as a *ground*" to "the existence of God as a consequence," whereas the other proceeds "from the possible as a *consequence*" to the "divine existence as a ground." The second of these proofs from possibility is Kant's own, as has been indicated. He rejects the first argument from possibility (which he identifies with the "Cartesian" proof and will later label the "ontological" argument) because it involves a type of "logical analysis" presupposing that "existence must be contained as a predicate in the possibility" regarded as the ground of argumentation. Yet Kant maintains here (as, more famously, in his first *Critique*, published eighteen years later) that existence is never a predicate or determination of anything, but rather is the positing of a thing with all its predicates, so that "in an existent thing nothing more is posited than in a merely possible one." Of the two empirical proofs, the first infers "the existence of an ultimate and *independent cause*" from experienced existence, whereas the second infers "not only the existence, but also the *properties* of this ultimate cause" of reality "from what experience teaches." The first of these empirical arguments (which Kant later calls "cosmological" and here says "has gained much attention through the Wolffian school of philosophy") fails to show that only God can be identified with "the absolutely necessary being" (the same objection might be raised against the argument from possibility which Kant favors here). Finally, the second empirical proof (which Kant later calls the "**physico-theological**" and which is similar to the argument from design) seems more to Kant's liking:

> Things of the world which our senses reveal to us give clear signs of their contingency as well as evidence of a rational creator of great wisdom, power and goodness through the magnitude, order, and purposive arrangement which one is aware of everywhere. The vast unity in such an extensive totality allows the conclusion that there can be only one single creator of all things.

However, that experience "gives clear signs" and "allows the conclusion" desired by natural theology does not suffice for a philosophical demonstration; and Kant criticizes the argument by saying that "geometric rigor does not appear in all of these conclusions." Kant ends his *Basis* by making the same point expressed near its beginning: "It is thoroughly necessary that one be convinced of God's existence; but it is not nearly so necessary that it be demonstrated."[45] Again this is a competent contribution to rationalistic philosophical theology but lacks the epistemological groundwork needed to be quite cogent.

Kant's *Enquiry* also indicates what could be the influence of Hume. At any rate, it is clear that Kant is struggling to assess the procedures of traditional rationalistic philosophy, which tends to adopt a mathematical model of methodology. He, on the other hand, contrasts the difficulty and complexity of philosophy with the clarity and simplicity of mathematics, pointing out that, among all the areas of philosophy, "Metaphysics is without doubt the most difficult of all human enquiries; but one has never yet been written." Of course, works had been written (for example, by Leibniz and his followers) which were *called* metaphysics. But they fail to prove cogent, because based on an inappropriate methodology. "Metaphysics is nothing other than a philosophy of the first principles of our knowledge." But its appropriate methodology is empirical rather than mathematical: "The true method of metaphysics is basically the same as that introduced by *Newton* into natural science and which had such useful consequences in that field." But in metaphysics, as opposed to physics, the experience to be appealed to is "inner" rather than external; so if you wish to pursue metaphysical knowledge, then "by means of an immediate evident consciousness, you ought to seek out those characteristics which certainly lie in the concept of any general condition." (Although this is abstract, it could anticipate Kant's later notion of the transcendental method of inquiry.) A bit later he says that "in metaphysics one must proceed entirely by analysis" designed to help us move "towards clearly and fully understood concepts." Although metaphysical explanations thus far have turned out to be "far more uncertain" than mathematical ones, Kant insists that "we can in many cases be perfectly certain, to the extent of conviction, by means of rational argument." On the one hand, he warns us that we should not mistake "the feeling of conviction" for a demonstrative argument; on the other hand, he claims, "Metaphysics is as much capable of the certainty necessary for conviction as mathematics; only the latter is easier and partakes of greater intuition." This may be a foreshadowing of Kant's later distinction between the subjective validity of rational faith and the objective validity of scientific knowledge. The last major section of Kant's *Enquiry* expresses his views that the greatest clarity and most certain conviction are achievable in the area of natural theology and that ethics is based on *feeling*, which is "the faculty of perceiving what is good," as opposed to science, based on *knowledge*, which is "the faculty of representing what is true."[46] On the first of these points, we see Kant disagreeing with Humean skepticism, whereas on the second we see him in agreement with Hume (in his critical writings he would change his position on both points).

It is in *Dreams* that Kant comes closest to a position of skepticism, writing sarcastically of "the Wonderland of Metaphysics," where "Folly and wisdom are separated by such indistinct borderlines that one can hardly walk for any length of time on the path of one without straying a little into the path of the other." (This seems a very remarkable comment for an untenured professor of metaphysics to make!) Like Leibniz, who distinguished between "truths of reason" and "truths of fact," and Hume, who contrasted "relations of ideas" with "matters of fact," Kant says, "We should realize that there are two methods by which we obtain knowledge: *a priori* and *a posteriori*"; and he points out the difficulties involved in trying to do metaphysics from either perspective. He has yet to work out the doctrine of synthetic *a priori* knowledge as a third possible approach. Thus, he can caustically write that "the principles of reason, on the one side, and the facts of experience . . . , on the other side, kept running next to each other like a pair of parallel lines which never meet, right into the (realm of the) unthinkable." Kant inserts a personal and whimsical reference of the sort that is unusual in writings he prepared for publication, when he speaks of metaphysics, "with whom destiny made me fall in love hopelessly though I can but rarely pride myself on any reciprocated favours on her part." And he seems to anticipate a reformed conception of it when he writes that "metaphysics becomes a true science tracing the limits of human understanding." He is probably influenced by the skepticism of Hume when he says,

> We can never know by reasoning alone how a thing can be a cause or can possess a force; such relations must be ascertained exclusively from experience. . . . In so far as something is regarded as a cause, something else is just being assumed.

By the end of *Dreams*, Kant is acknowledging that we can do quite well without the sort of metaphysical knowledge traditionally promised by dogmatic rationalism:

> If we begin to realize in the course of further investigations that a convincing philosophical insight in the case examined is an impossibility, we shall have no more difficulty in admitting that such a kind of knowledge is quite useless and unnecessary in any case.

Even if metaphysical knowledge should turn out to be illusory, "moral faith leads man without deviation to his true purpose." He alludes to that "true purpose" when he urges that we devote ourselves to living well in this life and patiently wait until a life hereafter allows us to understand the supernatural realm:

> Human reason was not meant to try and part the highest clouds in heaven or lift from our eyes the curtains in order to reveal to us the secrets of the other world.[47]

Although Kant never fully embraces skepticism, he comes closest to following Hume's lead in this pre-critical work.

The last important work of Kant's before the first *Critique* is his Inaugural Dissertation (dedicated to Frederick the Great). He distinguishes between two types of knowledge:

> Cognition in so far as it is subject to the laws of sensuality is *sensitive*, in so far as it is subject to the laws of the intelligence is *intellectual* or rational.

Each type of knowledge requires the representation of objects; for sensitive knowledge, we need "representations of things *as they appear*," whereas intellectual knowledge involves "representations of things *as they are*." Representations of appearances can be analyzed in terms of their *matter* ("namely the *sensation*") and their *form* ("namely space and time"). The forms of sensible intuition, space and time, are not "objective and real" nor substantial, accidental or relational, but are rather ideal subjective conditions for the human mind's interrelating of objects of its experience. Against the tradition of dogmatic rationalism, Kant says, "There is not given (to man) an *intuition* of things intellectual, but only a *symbolic cognition*," so that our knowledge is always discursive, achieved through abstraction and the use of "universal concepts," rather than immediately comprehensive, as God's would be. "Indeed the *intuition* of our mind is always *passive*. And so it is only possible to the extent that something can affect our senses." He defines metaphysics as the area of philosophy "which contains the *first principles* of the use of the *pure intellect*," and he holds that its concepts are neither given by the senses nor innate, but rather are derived through the mind's abstract reflection on its own activity. Such "acquired concepts" include those of "possibility, existence, necessity, substance, cause etc." The final section of the Inaugural Dissertation deals with the establishing of a proper methodology as a condition for doing metaphysics. Unlike sciences, such as physics and mathematics, "whose principles are given intuitively" and whose method can be developed after they have generated results, in metaphysics, which is more subject to illusions and errors because of our lack of pure intelligible intuitions, *it is the method which comes before all science,* and everything which is attempted before the precepts of this method have been properly hammered out and firmly established is seen to have been rashly conceived and such that it must be rejected as among the vain playthings of the mind.

Although Kant does not systematically elaborate upon this method, it seems clear to us today that what it was to be is the transcendental method of his critical philosophy. An epistemological critique of the powers of human reason needed to be developed as a necessary condition for any work in metaphysics, including in the area of natural theology. Kant issues a methodological warning that would turn out to be an important plank in the structure of his critical philosophy: "great care must be taken *lest the domestic principles of sensitive cognition transgress their boundaries and affect things intellectual.*"[48] What is still needed, however, is the systematic development of the critical epistemology that is thus anticipated.

There is a well-known paragraph in the first *Critique*, in which Kant traces the evolution of philosophical methodology through three stages:

> The first step in matters of pure reason, marking its infancy, is *dogmatic.* The second step is *sceptical* . . . But a third step. . . . is not the censorship but the *criticism* of reason.

This subsection has traced Kant's own philosophical odyssey from his attachment to the dogmatic rationalism of Leibnizian-Wolffian thought through its increasingly skeptical rejection, which seems to have been influenced by Hume, to the entryway of his own critical philosophy. Never in his professional career was Kant an uncritical adherent of the views of Leibniz and Wolff. But he was clearly committed to the problems, principles, and terminology of the rationalistic tradition. And he was "dogmatic" in his own special sense of basing his work on "the presumption that it is possible to make progress with pure knowledge, according to principles, from concepts alone . . . without having first investigated in what way and by what right reason has come into possession of these concepts." His own first *Critique* was to provide a devastating blow against future attempts of reason to generate metaphysical (and, thus, theological) knowledge claims "*without previous criticism of its own powers.*"[49] Second, Kant was never an out-and-out skeptic, and we do not know exactly when or to what extent he fell under the influence of Hume. But he makes it clear in the Preface to *Prolegomena* that he considers Hume's attack on metaphysics to have been the most decisive event in its history; and he explicitly writes,

> I openly confess that my remembering David Hume was the very thing which many years ago first interrupted my dogmatic slumber and gave my investigations in the field of speculative philosophy a new direction,

"is sufficient both subjectively and objectively."[58] In other words, in knowledge, the mind assents to the truth of a true judgment on the basis of evidence that is adequate to justify that person or anyone else in giving such assent. Although the wording is, perhaps, unfamiliar, this is basically the classical conception of knowledge (going back to the ancient Greeks) as justified true belief; one who knows has adequate reason for holding a belief which corresponds to reality.

Next, we should consider the component elements of knowledge, which can again be analyzed in terms of its matter (or content) and its form (or structures).

> Our knowledge springs from two fundamental sources of the mind; the first is the capacity of receiving representations (receptivity for impressions), the second is the power of knowing an object through these representations.

Like the empiricists, Kant affirms that we can only know objects that are given to us in the context of experience; like the rationalists, he emphasizes the vital contributions of the knowing mind. The mind must be characterized by both a passive receptivity and a dynamic activity.

> Through the first an object is *given* to us, through the second the object is *thought* . . . Intuition and concepts constitute, therefore, the elements of all our knowledge, so that neither concepts without an intuition in some way corresponding to them, nor intuition without concepts, can yield knowledge.

Thus, the work of the understanding is seen as presupposing and building upon the representations of sensibility, both being necessary conditions of human knowledge.

> Without sensibility no object would be given to us, without understanding no object would be thought. Thoughts without content are empty, intuitions without concepts are blind.

Furthermore, it is impossible to switch these contributions of the mind:

> These two powers or capacities cannot exchange their functions. The understanding can intuit nothing, the senses can think nothing. Only through their union can knowledge arise.[59]

What, then, are the concepts of the understanding that provide the structural forms of human knowing? The quick answer is that they are Kant's twelve logical categories. As might be expected, Kant presents this answer in far more depth and detail than we can afford to consider here. But, briefly put, he analyzes judgments as to their quantity (universal, particular, or singular), their quality (affirmative, negative, or infinite), their relation or logical type (categorical, hypothetical, or disjunctive), and their modality (problematic, assertoric, or **apodeictic**). Without getting into the specifics of these distinctions, we can note that Kant presents a systematically organized "Table of Categories"—three of quantity (unity, plurality, and totality), three of quality (reality, negation, and limitation), three of relation (of inherence and subsistence, of causality and dependence, and of community or reciprocity), and three of modality (of possibility-impossibility, of existence-nonexistence, and of necessity-contingency). In order for anything to be known, and not merely conceived of or thought about, it must be subsumed under one or more of these categories. For example, one knows his own copy of the first *Critique* as one real, contingently existing, subsisting thing produced (or caused) by Kant for the sake of establishing a relationship (or community) between his ideas and the minds of his readers. Because these categories can be applied to the object of intuition that we call the book by you or the pope or anyone else, and not merely by that person, there is a universality attached to them; because that object cannot be known by you or the pope or anyone else, any more than by that person, except under the structures of such categories, there is a necessity connected with them. By applying the categories, the understanding can synthesize or unify the data of experience in such a way as to constitute knowledge. This synthesis through the application of categories is judgment. "Judgment is therefore the mediate knowledge of an object, that is, the representation of a representation of it. In every judgment there is a concept which holds of many representations." Thus, for example, when you express a knowledge claim by saying, "This is a philosophy book," the concepts being employed represent a manifold of phenomenal experiences in a synthetic or unifying manner. "Accordingly, all judgments are functions of unity among our representations."[60]

A "judgment of perception," having only subjective validity because it is operative merely at the level of sensibility, can be converted into a "judgment of experience," which is objectively valid, only through the application of one or more of the categories, such as that of substance.

> Before, therefore, a judgment of perception can become a judgment of experience, it is requisite that the perception should be subsumed under some such concept of the understanding.

Kant provides a helpful example. We can observe a spatio-temporal relation between sunshine and increasing temperature expressed in the statement, "when the sun shines on the stone, it grows warm." Such "a mere judgment of perception" explains nothing at all, merely associating two particular phenomenal representations in a contingent manner.

> But if I say: the sun warms the stone, I add to the perception a concept of the understanding, viz., that of cause, which necessarily connects with the concept of sunshine that of heat, and the synthetic judgment becomes of necessity universally valid, viz., objective, and is converted from a perception into experience.[61]

And all knowledge must be characterized by a similar "objective validity"—that is universality and necessity.

Now let us consider the legitimate limits of this work of the understanding and therefore of knowledge itself, since for Kant all human knowing must occur at the level of the understanding. He warns that we should not presume or claim to know that the categories, or concepts of the understanding, legitimately apply to "things *in themselves*," independently of their appearances, even if, in fact, they might.

> This nobody can prove, because such a synthetic connection from mere concepts, without any reference to sensuous intuition on the one side or connection of such intuition in a possible experience on the other, is absolutely impossible. The essential limitation of the concepts . . . , then, is that all things stand necessarily *a priori* under the aforementioned conditions only *as objects of experience*.

We do have ideas of things in themselves (more of this in the next subsection), and we tend to think of them, for example, as substantial realities causally affecting the world of appearances to which they are thus related. But Kant warns us that we can have no knowledge "of such a connection of things in themselves, how they can either exist as substances, or act as causes, or stand in community with others." Without objects of experience to which they can refer—i.e., the appearances of intuition—the categories are devoid of cognitive sense: "Hence if the pure concepts of the understanding try to go beyond objects of experience and be referred to things in themselves (**noumena**), they have no meaning whatever." Their cognitively legitimate function is therefore restricted "for use in experience. Beyond this they are arbitrary combinations without objective reality." As we shall see, this is a central problem with the pursuit of metaphysical (and theological) knowledge. Nevertheless, Kant maintains, in thinking through the implications of our experience, we must postulate things in themselves, although they are unknowable:

> And we indeed, rightly considering objects of sense as mere appearances, confess thereby that they are based upon a thing in itself, though we know not this thing as it is in itself but only know its appearances.

This seems reasonable—how can we regard the objects of our experience as phenomenal appearances without imagining that they are appearances of *something*? Thus, we form ideas of things in themselves (which Kant calls *noumena*) which, because they transcend our experience, must remain unknowable.

> The understanding therefore, by assuming appearances, grants also the existence of things in themselves, and thus far we may say that the representations of such things as are the basis of appearances, consequently of mere beings of the understanding, is not only admissible but unavoidable.

Of course, we find ourselves constantly tempted to conceptualize these transcendent ideas by means of the categories of the understanding. Hence, Kant insists that we should observe a

> rule which admits of no exception: that we neither know nor can know anything determinate whatever about these pure beings of the understanding, because our pure concepts of the understanding as well as our pure intuitions extend to nothing but objects of possible experience, consequently to mere things of sense, and as soon as we leave this sphere, these concepts retain no meaning whatever.[62]

Again, we might note that this casts the notion of mystical knowledge into serious doubt. Mystics speak of their experiences as "ineffable," meaning that they cannot be clearly articulated because they defy the ordinary conceptual categories of thought and language. But, then, on Kant's grounds, they are essentially unknowable.

As Kant himself was the first to note, there is something revolutionary in this theory of knowledge. Whereas earlier epistemologies were built on the traditional correspondence theory, according to which the ideas of the mind must meet the requirements of the objects and laws of nature, here we are told that in order for an object to be an object of human experience or knowledge, it must meet the requirements of the knowing mind. This is what Kant means when he writes

> that we must not seek the universal laws of nature in nature by means of experience, but conversely must seek nature, as to its universal conformity to law, in the conditions of the possibility of experience, which lie in our sensibility and in our understanding.

In this respect Kant's is an idealistic epistemology, viewing the mind and its ideas as the basis of all cognitive experience. Because the established view before 1781 held that the world of objects is the independent variable, while the mind is the dependent variable, in human knowledge, Kant says that

> it seems at first strange, but is not the less certain, to say: *the understanding does not derive its laws (a priori) from, but prescribes them to, nature.*[63]

This is a far more dynamic, **autonomous** view of the mind than was otherwise available in Kant's day.

> Thus the order and regularity in the appearances, which we entitle nature, we ourselves introduce. We could never find them in appearances, had not we ourselves, or the nature of our mind, originally set them there.

The reason for this is that the "unity of the connection of appearances" must be necessary if it is to be a (transcendental) condition of knowledge; if we simply discovered that unity already given in nature, it would be contingent and fortuitous. It is in the subjectivity of the mind itself that all representations become synthesized in knowledge. Kant calls this the "transcendental unity of apperception," meaning that the representations of consciousness are unified in relation to self-consciousness, this unity being a necessary condition of cognitive experience:

> It must be possible for the "I think" to accompany all my representations. . . . In other words, only in so far as I can grasp the manifold of the representations in one consciousness, do I call them one and all *mine*.

Kant writes of revolutions in mathematics (in ancient times) and natural science (in the early seventeenth century) which transformed those disciplines, making them intellectually respectable.

> The examples of mathematics and natural science, which by a single and sudden revolution have become what they now are, seem to me sufficiently remarkable to. . . . incline us, at least by way of experiment, to imitate their procedure.

Kant's "**Copernican revolution**" would have us turn upside down our ordinary way of conceiving the relationship between our knowing and what we know:

> Hitherto it has been assumed that all our knowledge must conform to objects. But all attempts to extend our knowledge of objects by establishing something in regard to them *a priori*, by means of concepts, have, on this assumption, ended in failure. We must therefore make trial whether we may not have more success in the tasks of metaphysics, if we suppose that objects must conform to our knowledge.[64]

Before Copernicus, it was assumed that the Earth is the fixed center of the universe, with all other heavenly bodies, including the Sun, moving around it; Copernicus's revolutionary model viewed the Sun as the center of our planetary system, with all other bodies in the system, including the Earth, moving around it. Similarly Kant would replace the objects known with the knowing mind as the central focus of epistemology.

We have already identified this as an idealistic epistemology, and so it is. But it is a new kind of idealism, never previously conceived in the history of philosophy. Kant was rightly upset when he was accused of adopting an old-fashioned type of idealism. In both the second edition of the first *Critique* and the *Prolegomena* he is anxious to distinguish his own form of idealism from earlier kinds. In his "Refutation of Idealism" he attacks "material idealism," which is

> the theory which declares the existence of objects in space outside us to be merely doubtful and indemonstrable or to be false and impossible. The former is the *problematic* idealism of Descartes, which holds that there is only one empirical assertion that is indubitably certain, namely, that "I am."

The second type he labels "*dogmatic* idealism," viewing all physical objects "as merely imaginary entities." In the *Prolegomena* Kant contrasts his own "transcendental idealism," as he calls it, "or better, *critical* idealism," with these traditional forms which he rejects:

> My idealism concerns not the existence of things (the doubting of which, how-ever, constitutes idealism in the ordinary sense), since it never came into my head to doubt it; but it concerns the sensuous representations of things,

holding that all appearances (and space and time) "are neither things (but are mere modes of representation) nor are they determinations belonging to things in themselves."[65] Before Kant, it was normal to view all philoso-phers as basically either Platonists (for example, rationalists such as Augustine, Anselm, Descartes, and Leibniz) or Aristotelians (for example, empiricists such as Aquinas, Locke, and Hume). We can classify philoso-phers of the last couple of centuries as generally Kantians (for example, Kierkegaard and William James) or non-Kantians (for example, Hegel) in their epistemologies. Kant's critics can deny that sensibility is our only source of intuition *or* that we intuit only appearances rather than things in themselves *or* that objects of experience must conform to the require-ments of the knowing mind rather than the other way around *or* that all knowledge must be filtered through the categories of the understanding *or* that these categories legitimately apply only to phenomena.

Let us conclude this subsection with an explicit answer to the ques-tion raised earlier, "How are *a priori* synthetic judgments possible?" This is equivalent to the question of how scientific knowledge is possible. The answer is that the mind is capable of receiving data through sensible intu-ition, organizing those data by means of the forms of space and time, and then subsuming them under the categories, or concepts of the under-standing, in such a way as to constitute judgments. These judgments are synthetic, or factually informative, because they connect data of experience; but the application of *a priori* categories to them can confer the universal-ity and necessity needed to qualify as knowledge. Such judgments can be objectively (and not just subjectively) valid because they are confirmable by other minds than mine, so long as they are restricted within the bounds of possible human experience and do not attempt to deal with things in themselves, which, as such, transcend experience. This leads us to our final subsection on Kant's epistemology, its implications for metaphysics.

Critique of Metaphysical Reason. Kant's critique of metaphysical reason is of a piece with the limitations emphasized in his treatments of the forms of sensibility and the concepts of the understanding. It is the failure to mind those limitations that leads to the baffling discord of metaphysical thought. Thus, in the first *Critique*, Kant writes,

> Human reason has this peculiar fate that in one species of its knowledge it is burdened by questions which, as prescribed by the very nature of reason itself, it is not able to ignore, but which, as transcending all its powers, it is also not able to answer.

These are, of course, metaphysical questions. As a professor of metaphysics, Kant laments the loss of reputation of this area of philosophy:

> Time was when metaphysics was entitled the Queen of all the sciences.... Now, however, the changed fashion of the time brings her only scorn; a matron outcast and forsaken, she mourns like Hecuba.

The eighteenth century is an age of science. Metaphysics pretends to offer a loftier form of knowledge than we can find in mathematics or physics.

> But though it is older than all other sciences, and would survive even if all the rest were swallowed up in the abyss of an all-destroying barbarism, it has not yet had the good fortune to enter upon the secure path of a science.[66]

The problem is how we can explain the lack of progress in metaphysics over a period of more than two millennia.

> It seems almost ridiculous, while every other science is continually advancing, that in this, which pretends to be wisdom incarnate, for whose oracle everyone inquires, we should constantly move round the same spot, without gaining a single step.

Kant's solution is to explain that metaphysics has failed because it has dogmatically presumed to apply the concepts of the understanding (for example, unity, reality, substance, causality, etc.) to ideas of things which, by their nature, transcend all natural experience, "without investigating the basis of their objective validity." Against this dogmatic presumption, Kant insists

> that critique must exist as a science, systematic and complete as to its smallest parts, before we can think of letting metaphysics appear on the scene, or even have the most distant hope of so doing.[67]

And, of course, it is the construction of this critical science, which we call epistemology or the theory of knowledge, at which he is working.

As there is "a logic of truth," Kant observes, "which deals with the elements of the pure knowledge yielded by understanding," so there is also a *"logic of illusion,"* which Kant calls "dialectic," involving the extension of knowledge beyond its legitimate bounds. The third level of the mind, transcending sensibility and the understanding, is pure speculative reason. As time and space are the forms of sensibility and the twelve categories are the concepts of the understanding, so there are three ideas of pure reason, those of the soul, of the cosmos, and of God, providing the subject-matter for the three areas of metaphysics, philosophical psychology, philosophical cosmology, and philosophical theology (the last of which will be of greatest concern to us). Each of these ideas of pure reason lures us into the domain of *"transcendental illusion,"* which tempts us to strive to know the unknowable. "In defiance of all the warnings of criticism, it carries us altogether beyond the empirical employment of categories and puts us off with a merely deceptive extension of *pure understanding*." There is a natural but dangerous progression from one level of the mind to another:

> All our knowledge starts with the senses, proceeds from thence to understanding, and ends with reason, beyond which there is no higher faculty to be found in us for elaborating the matter of intuition and bringing it under the highest unity of thought.

It is natural for reason to strive to know the determining conditions of objects of (psychological, scientific, and religious) experience. This natural pursuit drives reason to the metaphysical ideas of unconditional conditions. Yet we have—and naturally can have—no experience of anything to which such ideas refer. Kant says, "I understand by idea a necessary concept of reason to which no corresponding object can be given in sense-experience." On the one hand, these ideas "are not arbitrarily invented; they are imposed by the very nature of reason itself." On the other hand, "they are transcendent and overstep the limits of all experience." They cannot constitute knowledge but are useful for regulating our thought and action:

> Although we must say of the transcendental concepts of reason that *they are only ideas*, this is not by any means to be taken as signifying that they are superfluous and void. For even if they cannot determine any object, they may yet . . . be of service to the understanding as a canon for its extended and consistent employment.[68]

As we have seen, there are three ideas of pure reason, each representing an attempt to grasp a unified ground of all conditioned experience—"the *first* containing the absolute (unconditioned) *unity of the thinking subject*, the *second* the absolute *unity of the series of conditions of appearance*, the *third* the absolute *unity of the condition of all objects of thought in general*." Corresponding to each of these ideas is a particular area of metaphysics:

> The thinking subject is the object of *psychology*, the sum-total of all appearances (the world) is the object of *cosmology*, and the thing which contains the highest condition of the possibility of all that can be thought (the being of all beings) the object of *theology*.[69]

In concluding this section on Kant's theory of knowledge, let us briefly consider his critique of each of these three ideas of metaphysical reason.

Not only do we experience physical objects (including our own bodies) through the external senses; but we also experience ourselves through internal sense. As the predicates we use to describe physical objects all allegedly define them, so the psychological predicates we ascribe to ourselves are designed to characterize our subjectivity. Thus, Kant says that "all the predicates of an internal sense refer to the *ego*, as a subject, and I cannot conceive myself as the predicate of any other subject." This realization of one's own separate identity and integrity as a person, not reducible to characteristics of any other subject, leads to the idea of the soul or "*absolute subject*," which, of course, is not an object of intuition. We naturally tend to want to characterize this absolute subject and can only do so by means of concepts of the understanding, which Kantian critique tells us do not legitimately apply to such transcendent ideas. We want to ask, for example, whether the soul is a unitary, substantial, simple reality, which is necessarily related to possible objects. "But though we may call this thinking self (the soul) substance, as being the ultimate subject of thinking which cannot be further represented as the predicate of another thing, it remains quite empty and inconsequential" from the perspective of possible knowledge, because it "falls quite without the complex of experience." Nevertheless, it is useful in that it "serves very well as a regulative principle totally to destroy all materialistic explanations of the internal phenomena of the soul."[70] This psychological idea guides our thoughts and actions beyond the **reductionistic** view that all reality is merely physical.

Second, "the cosmological idea extends the connection of the conditioned" phenomena of experience with "the absolute completeness of the series of the conditions" that would account for them—this is the idea of the cosmos or world as an organized whole. But when we try to characterize the cosmos, we find ourselves led into the dialectical traps which

Kant calls the **antinomies**; each metaphysical antinomy involves two principles that appear mutually contradictory. The logic of scientific understanding would lead us to maintain that the world either has a spatio-temporal beginning or is infinite in time and space. Yet both of these **antitheses** are false because it is illegitimate to apply the categories of limitation and infinity to such a transcendent idea. Second, we want to say that the cosmos is ultimately simple or composite. Yet this is again the logic of illusion. Third, we cannot help imagining that either there is free causality or the world is characterized only by natural causality. Yet Kant holds that this is a **false dilemma**—that freedom is characteristic of noumenal (i.e., spiritual) action, whereas everything in the phenomenal world is naturally determined. And, fourth, it would seem either that there is an absolutely necessary being or that everything in the world is contingent. Yet again, Kant holds that both theses can be true, if they apply to different levels of reality (the noumenal and the phenomenal, respectively). Metaphysical theories have never managed to lead to the scientific resolution of these antinomies because they have not been built upon a prior critique of reason that could reveal "the dialectical illusion of pure reason, which would otherwise forever remain concealed." It is Kant's critique which not only exposes the problem but explains it and shows to what extent it is unavoidable when he says that "it is quite impossible to prevent this conflict of reason with itself—so long as the objects of the sensible world are taken for things in themselves and not for mere appearances, which they are in fact."[71] The way to protect ourselves is to heed the limitations of the Kantian critique and not allow ourselves to be led to apply the categories of the understanding (or, for that matter, the forms of intuition) to our ideas of things in themselves transcending all possible phenomenal experience. Meanwhile, the value of the cosmological idea is that it leads us beyond a potentially chaotic naturalism to the view of reality as an ordered whole that will provide us with an incentive for continued scientific investigation.

Finally, the theological idea of God, which Kant also calls "the ideal of pure reason," is that of "a most perfect primal being" totally transcending all possible experiences of inner or external sense. Here reason is led beyond the bounds of experience "for the sake of conceiving its connection, order and unity."[72] Whatever we say (or even think) about God will inevitably require the illegitimate application of mental structures to that which inevitably transcends all natural experience. The value of philosophical theology, however, is that it opens up the spiritual possibilities of religious faith. But here, as in the other areas of metaphysics, we run into trouble "if we regard that which is merely *regulative* to be *constitutive*." The theological idea, like the other two ideas of metaphysical reason, is useful as a heuristic guide for regulating our thought and action (this may anticipate the pragmatism of James); yet we fall into the swamp of dialectical illusion to the extent that we imagine it can constitute knowledge. Needless to say, we shall consider Kant's discussion of philosophical theology in much greater depth now.

Rational Theology

On Speculative Arguments for God's Existence. Kant's refutations of speculative arguments for God have come to be regarded as a classic critique of what were traditionally crucial planks in the edifice of philosophical theology. The idea of God, as Kant conceives it, is that of the most real being (**ens realissimum**), which is regarded under "the concept of an unconditionally necessary being" and as the "supreme cause" of the world as we know it. Corresponding to these three conceptions of God are what Kant, in the first *Critique*, thinks are the three traditional ways of trying to prove divine existence. We can attempt such a proof on the basis of "determinate experience and the specific constitution of the world" or, second, of "experience which is purely indeterminate, that is, from experience of existence in general," or, third, of "mere concepts" of pure reason. "The first proof is the *physico-theological*, the second the *cosmological*, the third the *ontological*. There are, and there can be, no others."[73] Aquinas's fifth way and the argument from design attacked by Hume are famous examples of what Kant calls the "physico-theological" argument; the first three of Aquinas's five ways, the argumentation of Descartes's third meditation, Locke's causal demonstration, and Leibniz's proof from sufficient reason are famous examples of the "cosmological" argument; and Anselm's argument, that of Descartes's fifth meditation, and Leibniz's proof from the idea of a perfect being are famous examples of the "ontological" argument.

Is Kant correct that these three are the only possible speculative approaches? What about the medieval argument from degrees of perfection used by Anselm and representing the fourth of Aquinas's five ways? Kant would probably view it as a variation of the physico-theological proof since it is based on the determinate constitution of the world of our concrete experience. But what of the argument from possibility which Kant himself advocated in his pre-critical works? By 1781, Kant might regard it as a variant of the cosmological proof since it is based on the most general admission of some reality. But even if we grant Kant the benefit of the doubt on such matters, we might well be cautious about accepting his dogmatic assertion, "There are, and there can be, no others." For as long as God's existence is even possible, we must admit that a new kind of speculative proof may be developed in the future.

Theology, for Kant, "is the system of our knowledge of the highest being." Yet his theory of knowledge rules out the natural knowledge of any reality transcending our experience. Thus, the object it would leave for theology's systematic consideration is the *idea* of God. In *Theology*, Kant analyzes "the idea of a highest Being" as one "which *excludes every deficiency,*" one "which contains all realities in itself," and one that "can be considered as the highest good, to which wisdom and morality belong." As he comments, these are three dimensions of divine perfection. We are concerned here with Kant's "rational theology," as opposed to the "empirical theology" of religious studies, which is based on revelation. The former, in turn, is distinguished into two parts (to be emphasized in this and the next subsection, respectively): "Rational theology is either *speculative* (with theoretical science as its ground) or *moral* (with practical knowledge as its object)." Speculative theology is likewise divided into two types since it can be "either (1) *transcendental*, taking its origin merely from pure understanding and reason independent of all experience, or (2) *natural*," based on our experience of our world. Thus, we have analyzed rational theology into three types—transcendental, natural, and moral.

> In the first I think of God solely in terms of transcendental concepts. In the second I think of him in terms of physical concepts, and in the last I think of God in terms of concepts drawn from morals.

All three of them view God "as the *ens originarium* [original being]." Transcendental theology specifies this "as the *ens summum* [highest being]," which is infinite; natural theology specifies it "as the *summa intelligentia* [highest intelligence]," knowing and free; and moral theology specifies it "as the ***summum bonum***, as the *highest good*." The first speculative argument to be considered is that of transcendental theology (or "*ontotheology*"), which Kant names the "ontological proof," because it rests on an analysis of the mere concept of God as the most real being (an *ens realissimum*). "Anselm was the first to try to establish the necessity of a highest being from mere concepts, proceeding from the concept of an *entis realissimi*." Yet it is the modern Cartesian version that Kant attacks:

> Descartes argued that a being containing every reality in itself must *necessarily* exist, since existence is also a reality.... In this way he derived the necessary existence of such a being merely out of a pure concept of the understanding.[74]

But why, we might wonder, should we start with this most abstract of all the arguments?

Kant begins with the ontological proof because he is convinced that the other two types of speculative arguments, the cosmological and the teleological, surreptitiously utilize the reasoning of this one in order to deliver the kind of God that measures up to the requirements of the highest being and is thus worthy of religious devotion. (We shall see how these arguments supposedly incorporate ontological reasoning later in this subsection.) The ontological argument is unique in asserting a necessary connection between the *idea* of God as a perfect being (i.e., having all perfections) and the *existence* of God (i.e., existence being such a perfection or positive predicate). Let us analyze Kant's critique of the argument in terms of three specific objections.

The first is that, unless we can grasp the conditions that make God's existence necessary, the very concept of "*absolutely necessary* being" may be neither coherent nor determinable. Unlike Leibniz, who maintained that God's existence must be viewed as necessary unless there be some power sufficient to prevent it, Kant demands that we be able to determine some positive condition that will ensure God's existence as necessary before claiming to know that it is so. Of course, we can say that the divine reality is "*unconditioned*," but the word, by itself, "is very far from sufficing to show whether I am still thinking anything in the concept of the unconditionally necessary, or perhaps rather nothing at all."[75] Given the Kantian epistemology, this seems correct. If experience must be the touchstone of what is legitimately accounted real and our experience can provide us no access to unconditioned, necessary being, then we have no grounds for knowledge of any such idea. We might also recall that reality, existence, and necessity have been analyzed as concepts of the human understanding (rather than objects of experience), legitimately applicable only within the phenomenal realm. On this view we can have no cognitive foundation for any knowledge claims applying such concepts to the idea of that which transcends all natural experience.

But even if we could somehow make the idea of God determinate and assure ourselves that it is coherent, a second objection arises. Kant protests that all analogies (such as Descartes's example comparing the existence of God to the triangularity of a triangle) are misleading failures because any subject, whatever its predicates, can be thought away. Such analogies are failures because they only succeed by showing that God is *unlike* the examples used in one important respect—i.e., that unlike all other cases, in the case of God's existence, any denial of the subject with all its predicates will land us in self-contradiction; but this *dis*similarity can only be justified by assuming of God a *necessary* existence which we can predicate of nothing else—and this involves begging the question. Such analogies are deceptive in that they pack the notion of existence (or necessary existence) into our alleged concept of God, and then, under the guise of an analytical demonstration, extract it as a predicate already contained in the original concept. Ultimately we fall back on the question whether any existential proposition (including "God exists") is analytic or synthetic. "If it is analytic, the assertion of the existence of a thing adds nothing to the thought of the thing," so that the statement "is nothing but a miserable **tautology**," trivially true, an exercise in conceptual analysis.

> But if, on the other hand, we admit, as every reasonable person must, that all existential propositions are synthetic, how can we profess to maintain that the predicate of existence cannot be rejected without contradiction? This is a feature which is found only in analytic propositions.[76]

Kant seems correct here, that the attempt to show that denying God's existence is tantamount to self-contradiction is, indeed, fruitless. On the other hand, what he does not consider here is whether "God exists" might be a synthetic *a priori* judgment, not conceptually guaranteed, to be sure, but universally and necessarily assured on other grounds. For example, one might wonder, can God's existence be shown to be a transcendental condition of man's knowing or doing anything? Kant would surely have tried to answer this in the negative, but he does not consider the matter here. At any rate, this second of Kant's three objections to the ontological argument seems to be the clearest and most convincing, although it is not the one that has come to be the most famous.

That distinction is reserved for the third objection, that, in fact, existence is "not a real predicate" at all. Since "exists" grammatically functions as a predicate in our language, Kant is willing to admit that it is "a logical predicate." Yet, he insists, it is not "a real predicate" or a *"determining* predicate" which "is added to the concept of the subject and enlarges it." Rather, existence merely posits such a concept as subject to real predication.

> The proposition, "God is omnipotent," contains two concepts, each of which has its object—God and omnipotence. The small word "is" adds no new predicate, but only serves to posit the predicate *in its relation* to the subject.

In grammar we say that this is the "copula" of a judgment, linking its subject and predicate terms.

> If, now, we take the subject (God) with all its predicates (among which is omnipotence), and say "God is," or "There is a God," we attach no new predicate to the concept of God, but only posit the subject in itself with all its predicates, and indeed posit it as being an *object* that stands in relation to my *concept*.

Kant presents a famous but unfortunate example to illustrate his point that "the real contains no more than the merely possible." He writes, "A hundred real thalers do not contain the least coin more than a hundred possible thalers." The example is confusingly paradoxical. Since "a hundred possible thalers" (or, as we would say, dollars) count as no real coins whatsoever, there surely is a quantitative difference between the possible thalers and the real ones. There is also, of course, a practical difference since, on the one hand, real coins can be used to purchase commodities which merely possible ones will not afford. Yet even if this is an infelicitous example, it does not wreck the main point of Kant's third objection, that existence (let alone necessary existence) is not a "real" predicate. The three objections combined undermine the ontological argument's attempt to span the gap between the conceptual and existential realms. "When, therefore, I think a being as the supreme reality, without any defect, the question still remains whether it exists or not." In defiance of the proponents of the ontological argument, Kant adds, "Whatever, therefore, and however much, our concept of an object may contain, we must go outside it, if we are to ascribe existence to the object."[77]

Against the first of Kant's three objections, we might note that Leibniz tried to determine the possibility of God's existence, thus defending the idea of a most real being. Yet because "Leibniz confused the possibility of this concept with the possibility of the thing itself" (namely, God), he succeeded in showing "only that my idea of such a thing is possible." Yet this is not equivalent to demonstrating that God might exist as a reality outside the mind. "And thus the celebrated Leibniz is far from having succeeded in what he plumed himself on achieving—the comprehension *a priori* of the possibility of this sublime ideal being." Regarding the third of Kant's objections, we might observe that only the modern Cartesian versions of the ontological argument explicitly use the "existence is a perfection" premise, so that this objection, even if well-founded, is not fatal to the original Anselmian version of the argument. It is the second objection, however, which is most damaging. All versions of the ontological argument try to define God into existence through conceptual analysis, which is impossible unless "God exists" be an analytic proposition. Although divine existence may be factually necessary, it is not conceptually necessary. Kant's final judgment here appears well taken:

> The attempt to establish the existence of a supreme being by means of the famous ontological argument of Descartes is therefore merely so much labour and effort lost.[78]

In contrast to the ontological argument of transcendental theology, the cosmological proof of natural theology has the apparent advantage of beginning with an accepted fact—i.e., the contingency of the experienced world—rather than with pure concepts. However, this advantage, at best, suffices only to demonstrate the existence of a necessary cause.

> Leibniz, and later Wolff, called this proof *a contingentia mundi* [from the contingency of the world]. It says that if something exists, then an absolutely necessary being must also exist. But at the very least, I myself exist. Therefore, an absolutely necessary being exists.

In order to identify this metaphysical principle as a religiously adequate God, Kant believes that a second stage of argumentation, employing ontological reasoning, is required:

> But the cosmological proof argues further from the existence of an absolutely necessary being to the conclusion that this being must also be an *ens realissimum*.[79]

The first stage of this proof is causal, seeking in necessary reality the only final, adequate, synthesizing causal condition of the contingent being which is given as object of our experience. Kant boasts "that in this cosmological argument there lies hidden a whole nest of dialectical assumptions, which the transcendental critique can easily detect and destroy." Three of these seem particularly important: (1) that the principle of causality is applicable beyond the spatio-temporal world as well as within it; (2) that an infinite series of causes is impossible; and (3) that there must be some existent principle which synthesizes all reality. The first of these presuppositions violates a basic principle of Kantian epistemology, that the categories of the understanding can be legitimately applied only to the data of sensible intuition.

> The principle of causality has no meaning and no criterion for its application save only in the sensible world. But in the cosmological proof it is precisely in order to enable us to advance beyond the sensible world that it is employed.

The second of these presuppositions seems to function as a time-honored axiom, never justified and apparently unjustifiable. It might have been derived as a probable inductive conclusion from our reflections on past phenomenal experience, but how could it ever be certainly established? "The principles of the employment of reason do not justify this conclusion even within the world of experience, still less beyond this world in a realm into which this series can never be extended." The third of these presuppositions seems the most presumptuous of all. Despite "the logical possibility of a concept of all reality united into one" and despite what may be a "need on the part of reason to complete all synthetic unity by means of it," it does not follow that there must actually exist a being which would serve as ultimate explanatory principle for all contingent reality. Reality may constitute a multitude of causal series, each of them terminating in its own ultimate, irreducible principle.

> We may indeed be allowed to *postulate* the existence of an all-sufficient being, as the cause of all possible effects. . . . But in presuming so far as to say that such a being *necessarily exists*, we are no longer giving modest expression to an admissible hypothesis, but are confidently laying claim to apodeictic certainty.[80]

These three presuppositions all seem to underlie the initial (hypothetical) premise of the first stage of the cosmological proof.

Taken by itself, that first stage is a complete, though dubious, logical argument and does not involve anything like ontological reasoning. But, if it is accepted (i.e., if we can swallow its presuppositions), all it succeeds in demonstrating is the existence of a metaphysical principle, a necessary first cause. It does *not* provide us with a God that is obviously worthy of religious veneration. Thus, Kant holds that a second stage of argumentation, involving ontological reasoning, must be added to show that the necessary first cause is the *ens realissimum*. Kant points out that this second stage must show us "that every absolutely necessary being is likewise the most real of all beings." But, if this were so, granting (for the sake of argument) that the first stage of the cosmological proof has shown at least one necessary being to exist, then it would follow logically by conversion that some (i.e., at least one) most real being is absolutely necessary. But then, since "one *ens realissimum* is in no respect different from another, and what is true of *some* under this concept is true of *all*," we could logically conclude "that every *ens realissimum* is a necessary being." And that is precisely the claim of the ontological argument, of which we have already denied that knowledge is possible. Unfortunately, although the cosmological proof starts with an empirical premise, it offers us no solid evidence that its allegedly demonstrated necessary being must be an *ens realissimum* and is "deceptive" in that it "covertly" attempts to smuggle in the sort of ontological reasoning that has already been discredited.[81]

Although Kant's reasoning here may be too slick and subtle for comfort, his basic point is well-taken and may be posed as a rhetorical challenge: even if we could accept all the presuppositions on which the proof of a necessary being is based, how could we possibly determine the nature of that necessary being as perfect, infinite, a most real being, a personal God, an adequate object of religious experience? In other words, to what extent can natural theology ever demonstrate the God of monotheistic faith?

The teleological or "physico-theological" argument is the oldest and has always been the most popular of the arguments for the existence of God, predating the entire history of philosophy (see *Psalms* 19:1 and 94:9), and Kant is rather respectful toward it. Although he raises logical objections against it, he is never as strong in his denunciation of it as Hume was. Indeed, he pays tribute to Hume's critique of it in the *Dialogues*,[82] and he does not add anything substantively new to what can be found there. Of all the traditional speculative arguments for God's existence, the teleological is held in highest regard by Kant, who says,

> This proof always deserves to be mentioned with respect. It is the oldest, the clearest, and the most accordant with the common reason of mankind. It enlivens the study of nature.... It suggests ends and purposes, where our observation would not have detected them by itself.

Like Hume, Kant indicates that, though the argument from design may offer subjectively persuasive psychological motives for believing, it does not offer logically compelling grounds for any knowledge claims.[83]

Kant's critique of the argument is less concerned with its validity or soundness than with its abuse. He finds that its proponents have exaggerated its achievements in two ways: by claiming without justification to reach "apodeictic certainty" of what is, at best, merely probable and by purporting to "establish the existence of a supreme being." Thus, both the cogency and the conclusion of the argument are commonly inflated by those who use it. As an argument from analogy, it is inductive and can give us only probable grounds for its conclusion. And, to the extent that it works at all, it cannot give us the *ens realissimum* or even the necessary causal source of all other reality.

> The utmost, therefore, that the argument can prove is an *architect* of the world who is always very much hampered by the adaptability of the material in which he works, not a *creator* of the world to whose idea everything is subject.[84]

In order to identify the cosmic architect with the God of the Judeo-Christian religious tradition, we might have to smuggle in the cosmological argument to show that the architect is a necessary causal creator, and then the ontological argument to reveal a perfect being.

The most curious feature of Kant's generally unremarkable critique of this argument is in terms of what it does *not* do. Given the dominant emphasis of his epistemology on the distinction between phenomenal appearances and our ideas of noumenal reality, it is strange that Kant does not challenge the reliability of the apparent order of the world. In light of the prior 500 pages of his first *Critique*, one would expect Kant to suggest that the order and apparent design of the phenomenal world are the products of man's subjective structuring of his field of perceptual experience. Yet he does not thus take to task the argument at its core. Nor is it at all clear whether this was an oversight on his part. It may well be that he was reluctant to scotch an approach to God which he found attractive and which he would want to employ in his own fashion in the future (more of this in the next subsection). Kant was always a **teleological** thinker, even when his critical epistemology protected him against making exaggerated knowledge claims.

Thus, Kant repudiates all three of the traditional avenues of speculative theology. The part of rational theology we will consider in the next subsection is moral theology. But even if all rational theology were to be found groundless, there would still be theology based on revelation. "Whoever assumes no theology at all is an *atheist*. Whoever assumes only transcendental theology is a *deist*." The God of deism, disclosed by transcendental theology, is conceived as most real substance, one, simple, immutable, transcendent, eternal, omnipresent, and omnipotent. This is an abstract metaphysical principle, not necessarily a personal God. By contrast, natural theology discloses the God of theism, characterized by knowledge and free will. "*Theism* consists in believing not merely in a God, but in a *living* God who has produced the world through knowledge and by means of his free will." It is moral theology that regards God as the highest good. In moral theism "God is thought of as the author of our moral laws. And this is the real theology which serves as the foundation of religion."[85]

Kant's critique of speculative theology is meant to show that knowledge of God is impossible, a theme which is consistent with his epistemology. The idea of God cannot serve the "constitutive" function of referring to a necessarily existing corresponding reality. But, by helping us to think of the world as the work of a rationally purposeful intelligence, the idea of God does serve the important "regulative" function of guiding further investigation by encouraging belief in reality as an organized, intelligible, unified system. Therefore, we can achieve a basis in rational faith for acting "as if such connection had its source in one single all-embracing being, as the supreme and all-sufficient cause."[86] Thus, we can acquire a coherent teleology drawn from rational faith.

In a key sentence of his first *Critique*, Kant writes:

> I have therefore found it necessary to deny *knowledge*, in order to make room for *faith* (*Ich musste also das Wissen aufheben, um zum Glauben Platz zu bekommen*).

Kant, of course, is no skeptic. He affirms human knowledge and shows how and to what extent it is possible. But in the area of theology he does deny that we have any knowledge, thus clearing the way for faith as all the more vitally important. In demolishing the pretensions of speculative theology, Kant renders a kind of negative service. We shall see in the next subsection how he goes on to advance his own positive contribution, which seeks to justify religious belief as necessarily presupposed in the operations of practical or moral reason.

> So far, therefore, as our Critique limits speculative reason, it is indeed *negative*; but since it thereby removes an obstacle which stands in the way of the employment of practical reason, nay threatens to destroy it, it has in reality a *positive* and very important use. At least this is so, immediately we are convinced that there is an absolutely necessary *practical* employment of pure reason—the *moral*—in which it inevitably goes beyond the limits of sensibility.

If Kant is correct, our faith in God, without ever constituting knowledge, may be shown to be rational by other means than those of the theoretical demonstrations of speculative theology. It would be based on subjectively rational grounds rather than being either groundless opinion or objectively certain knowledge.

> The holding of a thing to be true ... has the following three degrees: *opining*, *believing*, and *knowing* (*das Furwahrhalten ... hat folgende drei Stufen: Meinen, Glauben und Wissen*).

These are three ways of entertaining judgments—through *opinion* (which is "consciously insufficient, not only objectively, but also subjectively"), through *belief* (which is subjectively sufficient but objectively insufficient), and through *knowledge* (which is "sufficient both subjectively and objectively"). Kant explains that "subjective sufficiency is termed *conviction* (for myself), the objective sufficiency is termed *certainty* (for everyone)."[87] One crucial contribution of the Kantian philosophy is the doctrine that subjective conviction, no matter how deep and passionate it may be, is not equivalent to objective certainty. But equally important is Kant's doctrine that some human beliefs are anchored in the universal and necessary demands of reason. To unfold this second doctrine we must turn to his moral theology.

Moral Argument for God's Existence. Kant's moral argumentation for God is the basis of his attempted justification of a rational religious faith (his "positive" contribution), which is contained in his second *Critique* and the appendix to his third *Critique*, as well as in *Theology*. As it was necessary to consider his epistemology as background for his critique of speculative theology, so we must briefly discuss his ethical theory in order to analyze his moral theology. Philosophically, Kant claims,

> All the interests of my reason, speculative as well as practical, combine in the three following questions: 1. What can I know? 2. What ought I to do? 3. What may I hope?

The first one is the epistemological, or theoretical, problem of his first *Critique* and *Prolegomena*; the second is the practical or moral problem of his *Grounding* and second *Critique*; the third is the problem of Kantian philosophy of religion and "is at once practical and theoretical."[88] Of the three, we have already seriously considered Kant's answer to the first question and must now briefly turn to his answer to the second, in preparation for our study of his answer to the third.

As we experience the phenomenal world as spatio-temporally structured, we also find our own existence, as rational agents, to be structured in such a way that we have a sense of moral obligation. Kant holds that this awareness is an essential fact of our lives as rational beings and moral agents. He sees us all as bound to obey the universal requirements of moral law, which can be ascertained by means of a criterion called the "categorical imperative." Although there is only one such criterion, it can be expressed by means of various formulations, some of which may prove to be more useful than others in certain circumstances, and which he illustrates by means of moral examples.[89] But Kant never allows the utilitarian consideration of happy or unhappy consequences to count as a criterion of moral judgment.

Then in the second *Critique*, we see Kant going even further, maintaining that it is man's duty to strive to realize "the highest good" that is possible, which he characterizes as the ultimate "connection of virtue with happiness." There seems no reason to believe that this perfect conformity ever has been or ever will be achieved in this world. Yet "ought implies can," so that if we should strive for this goal it must be achievable. God's existence is demanded (postulated) in order to render possible this high-est good, only a moral governor of the universe being adequate to guar-antee this ideal conformity of virtue and happiness, which we must attempt to help bring about. In speaking of a "highest good," Kant admits, there is an ambiguity of meaning: "The 'highest' can mean the 'supreme' (*supremum*) or the 'perfect' (*consummatum*)." In connection with the first of these, he says that "virtue (as the worthiness to be happy) is the supreme condition of whatever appears to us to be desirable and thus of all our pursuit of happiness." The "perfect" or complete good is the cor-relation of virtue and happiness. It is in the latter sense of the perfect or complete good that Kant proceeds to use the ambiguous phrase when he writes that "happiness and morality are two specifically different elements of the highest good" and that the "highest good is a *synthesis* of concepts." And it is in this sense also that he says, "It is a priori (morally) necessary to bring forth the highest good." Yet a more characteristic statement of Kantian ethics (especially in passages where he is not building up to the moral argument for God) comes a few pages earlier: "The moral law is the sole determining ground of the pure will."[90] In other words, only virtue or the moral law (the "highest good" in the first sense, or only one of the two components of the "highest good" in the second sense) should determine the will. Exactly where, we might ask, does our obligation lie?

To say that man has a moral obligation to strive to realize virtue and follow the moral law is one thing, and to say that he has a moral obli-gation to strive to realize the connection of virtue with happiness is quite another. Nor is the former obligation sufficient grounds for the latter. What connection is established between the two elements of the highest good—virtue and happiness? It seems that the only relationship Kant establishes between them is in terms of his stipulative analysis of virtue as a "worthiness to be happy." But, given the fragility of this connection, it is no wonder that the moral argument, built on the more complex inter-pretation of the "highest good," should prove so unconvincing. Even if we grant Kant an obligation to pursue the complete or perfect good (and not merely the supreme good of virtue), as well as his claim that "ought" implies "can" (meaning that if we have an obligation to do something, it must at least be possible), the duty in question, it seems, is one of *attempt-ing* to promote the highest good "as far as it lies within our power to do so,"[91] and not that of actually realizing the ideal itself.

In the interest of clarification, let us distinguish among six diff-erent possible duties. It might be said that we have a moral obligation to: (1) strive to achieve virtue; (2) strive for perfect virtue; (3) strive for the complete good (as the perfect correlation between virtue and happiness); (4) actually be virtuous; (5) actually be perfectly virtuous; and (6) actually bring about the complete good. Now, using Kant's "ought" implies "can" principle as a two-edged sword that cuts both ways, we can say that since (1), (2), (3), and, perhaps, (4) are possible for us as human beings, they might qualify as legitimate moral duties; but since (5) and (6) are not possible for us, they clearly do not so qualify. The logic of Kant's moral argument, however, is to *assume* (5) and (6) as moral obligations and try to justify the assumptions by postulating the immortality of the soul, to serve as a warrant for the possibility of (5), and the existence of God, to serve to guarantee the possibility of (6). This is Kant at his least convincing. As science tries to account for observed and objectively observable facts about the phenomenal world in terms of testable hypotheses, he tries to justify claims of moral facts (which are only subjectively observable, if at all) by means of scientifically unverifiable (because they are transphenomenal) assumptions.

The most famous source for Kant's moral argument is his second *Critique*. Let us crystallize the argumentation there: (1) The *summum bonum*, as perfect good, is "happiness proportional to that morality" identified with virtue; (2) "we *should* seek to further the highest good (which therefore must at least be possible)," since "ought" logically implies "can"; (3) yet by our own efforts in this life we can never hope to bring about this perfect correlation.

> Therefore, the highest good is possible in the world only on the supposition of a supreme cause of nature which has a causality corresponding to the moral intention

of a being of "understanding and will" who is the "highest original good" of all.

> Therefore, it is morally necessary to assume the existence of God (*es ist moralisch nothwendig, das Daseyn Gottes anzunehmen*).

We have already challenged the first premise and its peculiar interpretation of the "highest good" we are obliged to strive to realize. Kant immediately proceeds to emphasize that this is not meant to be another theoretical proof of speculative reason such as the ones he refuted in the first *Critique*: "It is well to notice here that this moral necessity is subjective, . . . and not objective." He is making no knowledge claims here. In regard to our theoretical reason, the God assumed by the moral argument "is a hypothesis, i.e., a ground of explanation" of how the perfect good can be achieved. But from a practical point of view, it is a matter of "*faith* and even pure *rational faith*." (Finally, Kant tries to stifle the misinterpretation that would portray God as the source or foundation of moral duty, when he writes, "It is also not to be understood that the assumption of the existence of God is necessary as a ground of all obligation in general." For Kant, morality is independent of theology rather than built upon it.)[92]

In a curious paragraph in *Theology*, Kant suggests that the moral argument is not logical but practical:

> Our moral faith is a practical postulate, in that anyone who denies it is brought *ad absurdum practicum*. An *absurdum logicum* is an absurdity in judgments; but there is an *absurdum practicum* when it is shown that anyone who denies this or that would have to be a scoundrel. And this is the case with moral faith.

But is Kant correct? Would the virtuous man who follows the moral law and tries to do what he thinks is his duty nevertheless be a scoundrel if he did not believe that the complete or perfect good is realizable and did not assume the existence of (Kant's kind of) God? He need not be, even on the ordinary terms of Kantian ethics. Near the end of this same paragraph, though, Kant makes another striking statement:

> Hence our faith is not scientific knowledge, and thank heaven it is not! For God's wisdom is apparent in the fact that we do not *know* that God exists, but should *believe* that God exists.

Kant believes that moral virtue requires that we should try to do what is right through a pure desire to do our duty, rather than because of selfish motives. But if man had scientific knowledge of God, he thinks, such disinterested virtuous action would become impossible. "In his every action, man would represent God to himself as a rewarder or avenger . . . , and his hope for reward and fear of punishment would take the place of moral motives," to the detriment of moral worth.[93] This seems to anticipate a Kierkegaardian analysis of the value of religious faith as opposed to religious knowledge.

Let us now consider the last few sections of the appendix to Kant's third *Critique*, which are concerned with the philosophy of religion, in general, and with the teleological and moral arguments, in particular. Kant distinguishes between the domains of the teleological and moral arguments:

> *Physicotheology* is the endeavor of reason to infer the supreme cause of nature and its properties from the *purposes* of nature (which can only be empirically known). *Moral theology* (ethico-theology) would be the endeavor to infer that cause and its properties from the moral purpose of rational beings in nature (which can be known *a priori*).

The teleological argument, which Kant has criticized, considers natural purposes and seeks their ultimate causal condition, which it can suggest but properly leaves indeterminate; and the moral argument, which he advocates, considers moral purpose and seeks its ultimate causal condition, which it can render determinate. Whereas the physico-theological argument points to God as the intelligent designer of the world of sense experience, the moral argument determines God as "a moral world cause." As Kant says, "Physical teleology impels us, it is true, to seek a theology, but it cannot produce one," and is "only serviceable as a preparation (propaedeutic) for theology," because the concepts of experience cannot be legitimately applied to that which transcends all natural experience. By contrast, "*moral teleology* supplies the deficiency in *physical teleology* and first establishes a *theology*,"[94] which is a matter of practical faith rather than of scientific knowledge.

In the third *Critique*, Kant reconsiders the question of whether any theoretical proof of God might be feasible. He analyzes all theoretical grounds of proof into four types: (1) those given "by logically strict *syllogisms of reason*"; (2) those "according to *analogy*"; (3) those of "*probable opinion*; or finally, which has the least weight, (4) assumption of a merely possible ground of explanation, i.e. *hypothesis*." He considers each of these four kinds of theoretical proofs, finds each inadequate to produce conviction regarding the existence of God, and concludes that "absolutely no proof in a theoretical point of view is possible for the human reason which can bring about even the least degree of belief."[95] Thus, even the teleological argument is still considered inconclusive as a theoretical proof and does not constitute knowledge of any determinable object. Yet it does encourage us to seek the way of moral theology, which, Kant maintains, can provide us with a rational faith.

Rational Faith. Kant's view of rational faith is well-developed in his third *Critique*, in a discussion of "the kind of belief produced by a practical faith." We have already considered Kant's distinction among opinion, belief, and knowledge made in the first *Critique*. Here again, we see the same distinction, expressed in a single sentence: "*Cognizable* things are of three kinds: *things of opinion* (*opinabile*); *things of fact* (*scibile*); and *things of faith* (*mere credibile*)." The existence of God, as a postulate of practical reason, is classified as a matter of "moral faith." (Interestingly, Kant here includes "the *highest good*" among "mere *things of faith*," saying that, although it "cannot be established as regards its objective reality in any experience possible for us," it nevertheless "must be assumed possible." This admission might support the objection that the moral argument for God's existence is merely founded on an assumption and might call into question the alleged universality and necessity of the highest good as an object of moral obligation.) Unlike earlier philosophers (for example, Locke), who distinguished between faith and reason, Kant insists that faith is essentially rational and distinguishes it from knowledge. Yet, unlike Hume, who might allow faith some rational grounds while reducing it to mere opinion, Kant emphasizes the subjective sufficiency distinguishing faith from opinion. Also, though clearly distinguishing rational faith from both knowledge and mere opinion, Kant does not regard it (in the manner, for example, of Augustine) as consisting in a submission to an external authority. It is rather "a free belief," an autonomous, relatively stable response of reason to the practical sense of ethical duty.

> Faith (as *habitus*, not as *actus*) is the moral attitude of reason as to belief in that which is unattainable by theoretical cognition. It is therefore the permanent principle of the mind to assume as true, on account of the obligation in reference to it, that which is necessary to presuppose as condition of the possibility of the highest moral final purpose.

By contrast, Kierkegaard will see faith as radically impermanent, an act having validity only for the instant in which it is achieved and calling for perpetual renewal. The element on which both Kant and Kierkegaard could agree, however, is that of hope or trust:

> Faith (absolutely so called) is trust in the attainment of a design, the promotion of which is a duty, but the possibility of the fulfillment of which . . . is not to be *comprehended* by us.

Like Kierkegaard, Kant can speak of "a *doubtful faith*."[96]

But also like Kierkegaard, Kant views moral faith as practical conviction which, because it is not theoretical, is not even a matter of probability. Because it deals with that which transcends the entire world of experience, he says, "no probability can apply to it."[97] The demands of practical reason are seen as logically prior to the contents of faith. It is as if roles were reversed from medieval times so that now theology is the "handmaid" of moral philosophy. And even then it is moral theology, rather than speculative theology, that is relevant to religion. Kant addresses this issue in his *Lectures on Ethics* (delivered in the late 1770s, when he was working out his first *Critique*):

> Speculation concerning God . . . does not appertain to the sphere of religion, for religion must be practical. Theology, indeed, can contain speculative elements, but to religion these must remain foreign.

Theological subtleties are dismissed as "obstacles to religion." Kant is insistent that we respect the distinction between religion and speculation:

> But how are we to judge whether a particular question is religious or speculative? Here is our criterion; if, whatever the answer, it will make no difference to our actions, the question is not religious but speculative; if the rule of our conduct is unaffected by it, the problem is not religious but speculative.

We shall consider Kant's treatment of religion in more depth in the final section of this chapter; but for now the point is the practical thrust of his conception of faith (which shall also be heavily emphasized by William James). The trust in God that is essential to faith is not a passive one:

> Of course, we have reason to leave ourselves entirely in God's hands, to let His will hold sway; but this does not imply that we ought to do nothing, leaving Him to do all. We must do what is in our power; we must do what we ought; the rest we should leave to God. That is true submission to the divine will.

So, an emphasis on practical effort is packed into Kant's analysis:

> Faith, then, denotes trust in God that He will supply our deficiency in things beyond our power, provided we have done all within our power.

He explains this further,

> Practical faith does not consist in saying: "If only I trust implicitly in God He will do what I want"; but rather in saying: "I will myself do all I can, and if I then leave myself in God's hands, He will strengthen my weaknesses and make up my shortcomings as He knows best."[98]

Of course, the most strikingly characteristic aspect of Kant's view of faith is its derivation in morality. It is tempting but historically inaccurate to suppose that he was the first important thinker to conceive of religious faith as essentially moral. We know that Kant was profoundly impressed and influenced by Rousseau. In *The Creed of a Priest of Savoy*, Rousseau's cleric says,

> I seek to know only what is important for my conduct. As for those dogmas which affect neither actions nor morals, and over which so many people torment themselves, I do not worry about them in the least.

He insists, in his own religious creed,

> that there is no religion which frees one from the duties of morality, that there are no really essential duties other than those, that worship within your own heart is the first of those duties, and that without faith no true virtue exists.

So far this sounds proto-Kantian. But Rousseau's priest is capable of a self-effacing disavowal of reason, which is quite alien to Kant, as when, admitting that the "Gospel is full of unbelievable things, of things which repel the reason, and which it is impossible for any reasonable man to imagine or to admit," he nevertheless recognizes a need to "respect in silence what one could neither reject nor understand, and humble yourself before the great Being who alone knows the truth." It is hard to imagine Kant saying with Rousseau's cleric, "I try to eliminate my reason before the supreme Intelligence."[99] So, although Rousseau also bases religious faith on morality rather than on theoretical speculations, his (like Kierkegaard's) is too nonrational a view of faith to be comfortably identified with Kant's.

The uniqueness of Kant's conception of faith lies in its complexity. Like Hume, Kierkegaard, and the fideists (and unlike Hegel), he denies any theoretical grounds of faith adequate to provide knowledge; but like the rationalists, he holds that there is a rational basis for faith, which provides more or less stable conviction. Like Rousseau, he sees morality as the basis of religious faith; but Kant, unlike Rousseau (and Hume too, for that matter), thinks morality is itself a practical necessity of reason. It is this synthesis of faith as both moral and rational that sets apart the Kantian position.

Analogous Theological Language. Kant's doctrine of analogous theological language, although not so original, is useful for blocking an obvious objection against his own rational theology. Since we can only express ideas by means of categories of the understanding, and since the latter can be legitimately applied only to the data of phenomenal experience, how is it possible to speak or even think of God? How is any cognition—whether at the level of theoretical knowledge or of practical faith or of mere opinion—possible except through the use of our concepts? It might seem as if Kant were ceremoniously booting cognition of the **supersensible** out the front door of epistemology only to sneak it in again surreptitiously through the back door of philosophical theology. It is to Kant's credit that he himself anticipates this objection near the end of his third *Critique*; and his response is in terms of a theory of analogy comparable to that developed by Aquinas five centuries earlier. For example, he says that "the great purposiveness in the world compels us to *think* a supreme cause of it and to *think* its causality as that of an understanding, but we are not therefore entitled to *ascribe* this to it." In other words, of course, we have no basis for any knowledge claims about the divine understanding or its causality. Indeed, we have no experience of any sort of understanding other than our own discursive one, anchored in sensible intuition.

> However, according to the analogy of an understanding, I can in a certain other aspect think a supersensible being without at the same time meaning thereby to cognize it theoretically.

The "certain other aspect" referred to here is the practical function of reason. The concepts of the understanding (including causality) remain incoherent or meaningless when applied to the supersensible, only if this application is taken literally. We should rather interpret theological language analogically.

> For then a cognition of God and of His Being (theology) is possible by means of properties and determinations of His causality merely thought in Him according to analogy, which has all requisite reality in a practical reference, though *only in respect of this* (as moral). An ethical theology is therefore possible.

This will be a theology that is moral rather than theoretical, "a theology which shall determine the concept of God adequately for the highest practical use of reason, but it cannot develop this and base it satisfactorily on its proofs,"[100] as speculative theology traditionally would do.

Kant develops the theory of analogy in the conclusion of his *Prolegomena* in a passage in which he is coming to grips with Hume's devastating assault on anthropomorphism. He admits that Hume's objections against theism are "very strong," to the extent that it is inextricably bound up with the literal use of concepts:

> All his dangerous arguments refer to anthropomorphism, which he holds to be inseparable from theism . . . ; but if the former can be abandoned, the latter must vanish with it and nothing remain but deism, of which nothing can come, which is of no value and which cannot serve as any foundation to religion or morals,

from the Humean perspective. Hume posed the challenge beautifully: how is it possible for human beings to steer a middle path between the Scylla of anthropomorphic literalism and the Charybdis of a mystical incomprehensibility? Kant feels the pinch of the problem acutely, knowing all too well that the only concepts with which we can work must be drawn from our finite experience of the natural world. He certainly will not settle for silence, regarding the most real being. But neither is he willing to use language that reduces the infinite, perfect Creator to the level of finite, imperfect creatures. His solution is to distinguish two different sorts of anthropomorphism, only one of which is vicious in this blasphemous way, the other of which talks of God not as a thing in itself but only in relation to us.

> For we then do not attribute to the Supreme Being any of the properties in themselves by which we represent objects of experience, and thereby avoid

> *dogmatic* anthropomorphism; but we attribute them to his relation to the world and allow ourselves a *symbolic* anthropomorphism, which in fact concerns language only and not the object itself.

Thus, the divine nature remains unknowable, and I focus on a cluster of ideas "which I do not hereby cognize as it is in itself but as it is for me, i.e., in relation to the world of which I am a part." This is not a speculative cognition which constitutes knowledge of its object but rather a practical one of our own ideas as illuminating our own experience. "Such a cognition is one of analogy and does not signify (as is commonly understood) an imperfect similarity of two things, but a perfect similarity of relations between two quite dissimilar things." In a footnote Kant illustrates his point: we have no natural knowledge of what we call God's love for man; but we can express our idea of this analogically, saying that as the welfare of their children is to the love of human parents, so is the welfare of humans to what we refer to as God's love for man.

> By means of this analogy, however, there remains a concept of the Supreme Being sufficiently determined *for us*, though we have left out everything that could determine it absolutely and *in itself*; for we determine it as regards the world and therefore as regards ourselves, and more do we not require.

Kant is confident that this sort of "*symbolic* anthropomorphism," using analogical language, is not vicious, escapes the "attacks which Hume makes," and remains quite compatible with the critical epistemology. Similarly, when we speak of God's rational plan for the phenomena of creation, "reason is thereby not transferred as a property to the First Being in itself, but only to its relation to the world of sense." In this way, "reason is attributed to the Supreme Being so far as it contains the ground of this rational form in the world, but according to analogy only." We strive to remember that knowledge of God is impossible for us in this life. "We thereby acknowledge that the Supreme Being is quite inscrutable and even unthinkable in any determinate way as to what it is in itself." Nevertheless, we can use analogical language to express connections between our phenomenal realm of experience and our theological ideas. "The expression suited to our feeble concepts is that we conceive the world *as if* it came, regarding its existence and its inner determination, from a Supreme Reason."[101] Thus, rational theology can involve a legitimate communication of ideas.

In conclusion, let us ask what moral theism, making an analogous use of theological language, discloses about the divine nature in relation to us. Kant assures us "that the moral theist can have a wholly precise and determinate concept of God," based on the requirements of moral theology.

He will have to think of this being as most perfect, for otherwise his morality could not obtain reality through it. It must be *omniscient* if it is to know even the smallest stirrings of his innermost heart and all the motives and intentions of his actions.

Further, he says, "This being must also be *omnipotent* if it is to arrange the whole of nature." Then Kant adds three specifically moral attributes:

Any being who is to give objective reality to moral duties must possess without limit the moral perfections of *holiness*, *benevolence*, and *justice*. These three attributes constitute the whole moral concept of God. In God they belong together, but of course in our representation of them, they have to be distinguished from one another. Thus through morality we know God as a *holy lawgiver*, a *benevolent sustainer of the world*, and a *just judge*.[102]

This is the remarkably orthodox concept of God to which Kant's rational theology leads him.

Religion and Evil

Religion. Kant's conception of religion is most known from its presentation in his *Religion within the Limits of Reason Alone*, which comprises four books. In his preface to the first edition, Kant contends that "for its own sake morality does not need religion at all" but that, in order to establish hope that virtue and happiness will be properly harmonized, "we must postulate a higher, moral, most holy, and omnipotent Being which alone can unite the two elements of this highest good." In this way Kant says, "Morality thus leads ineluctably to religion." Here Kant is not discussing religion from the perspective of "Biblical theology," and his "philosophical theology remains within the limits of reason alone." In his preface to the second edition, Kant expresses his confidence that the reader can understand his *Religion* "without meddling with the *Critique of Practical Reason*, still less with the theoretical Critique."[103] Although this is true, a background knowledge of his critical philosophy does provide a context in which we can better interpret this later work.

The first book of *Religion* deals with man's alleged innate predispositions to good and evil. Man is naturally both good (in his animality, humanity, and personality) and evil (in his frailty, impurity, and wickedness), his praiseworthiness and blameworthiness being functions of his free will, rather than of his sensuous nature or theoretical reason. This free will is naturally oriented toward evil as well as toward good. This is purportedly the demythologized truth in the theological doctrine of original sin, although "the most inept" interpretation of that doctrine is the childish one "which describes it as descending to us as an inheritance from our first parents." At any rate, on this view, man does have a natural propensity to evil, to which religion is a beneficial response. There are two general types of religion. The debased kind is a religion of "mere worship," which is nothing more than a series of "*endeavors to win favor.*" The genuine kind is "the moral religion" of "*good life-conduct.*" We may legitimately hope for God's grace in helping us to overcome our propensity to evil. But to approach religion merely as worship designed to solicit that grace without the believer doing "as much as lies in his power to become a better man" is a dangerous "fanaticism."[104]

The second book of *Religion* depicts a conflict between the principles of good and evil for sovereignty over man, where virtue and vice are viewed as functions of conformity and opposition to the moral law. In this book (which was denied publication permission by the Berlin censor) Jesus is characterized as a symbol of our capacity to resist evil and "to elevate ourselves to this ideal of moral perfection" represented by virtue. In Jesus we personify this ideal and metaphorically say "that this archetype has *come down* to us from heaven and has assumed our humanity." Thus, Jesus is a moral model, "an *example*" for us to strive to follow. "This is not, to be sure, absolutely to deny that he might be a man supernaturally begotten. But to suppose the latter can in no way benefit us practically inasmuch as the archetype which we find embodied in this manifestation must, after all, be sought in ourselves (even though we are but natural men)." Even if Jesus were uniquely and literally divine (which Kant leaves an open question), we are not and must imitate his moral example as mere human beings. Jesus presented himself, according to Kant, as a human being who was "also an envoy from heaven" showing us how to break the power of evil over the human will. Kant is very careful not to deny the divinity and supernatural power of Jesus, whose personality, he says, "may indeed be a mystery" and whose deeds "may all be nothing but miracles." Yet it is Jesus' moral message and example that are important, rather than the alleged mystery of his nature or the miracles of his actions. Kant defines miracles as "events in the world the operating laws of whose causes are, and must remain, absolutely unknown to us" and classifies them as "either *theistic* or *demonic*," the latter kind being either "*angelic*" (performed by good spirits) or "*devilish*" (performed by bad spirits). Again, Kant is careful not to deny them altogether:

> As for miracles in general, it appears that sensible men, while not disposed to renounce belief in them, never want to allow such belief to appear in practice;

that is to say, they believe *in theory* that there are such things as miracles but they do not warrant them *in the affairs of life*.

From a practical point of view, "it is impossible for us to count on miracles" without becoming superstitious; and to imagine that we can, by our own efforts, do anything to effect their performance is "a senseless conceit."[105]

The third book of *Religion* envisions the victory of good over evil and the establishment of "an *ethical* commonwealth," united under "a higher moral Being." God is here conceived as "law-giver" and "moral ruler of the world." Only God can ultimately establish this moral order, yet man must strive to help bring about its realization. "An ethical commonwealth under divine moral legislation is a *church*." Kant distinguishes between "the *church invisible*," which is an ideal "of the union of all the righteous under direct and moral divine world-government," and the "*visible church*," which is "the actual union of men into a whole which harmonizes with that ideal." A particular society of people within the visible church, operating "under public laws," is "a *congregation* under authorities," who should be regarded as "teachers" and "*servants* of the church." By contrast with "statutory religion," which focuses on an obedience to (external) divine and human legislation, "true religion" requires our obedience to the moral law "engraved in our hearts." Likewise, the cultic "*religion of divine worship*," which "rests upon arbitrary precepts," should never be allowed to replace the pursuit of "the best life-conduct." Particular ecclesiastical sects typically cherish their own ritualistic practices. "All these observances are at bottom morally indifferent actions." Kant holds that there is a single universal moral religion: "There is only *one* (true) *religion*; but there can be *faiths* of several kinds." He objects to saying that people are of different religions, as if more than one were genuinely possible:

> It is therefore more fitting (as it is more customary in actual practice) to say: This man is of this or that *faith* (Jewish, Mohammedan, Christian, Catholic, Lutheran), than: He is of this or that religion.

However, some faiths can be relatively more adequate expressions of "the pure religion of reason" than are others. Some faiths claim access to a special sort of illumination regarding alleged mysteries "which may indeed be *known* by each single individual but cannot be *made known* publicly, that is, shared universally." Kant again adopts a cautious attitude toward such claims: "It is impossible to settle, *a priori* and objectively, whether there are such mysteries or not." Familiar examples are the mysteries of the divine Trinity, of the atonement, and of divine election.[106] But in all such cases the practical significance of such doctrines depends on whether and to what extent moral meaning can be read into them.

The fourth (and final) book of *Religion* distinguishes between genuine religious service and the pseudo-service of clericalism. The genuine service of God consists in leading a life of moral virtue.

> Religion is (subjectively regarded) the recognition of all duties as divine commands. That religion in which I must know in advance that something is a divine command in order to recognize it as my duty, is the *revealed* religion . . . ; in contrast, that religion in which I must first know that something is my duty before I can accept it as a divine injunction is the *natural* religion.

(At one extreme is "the pure *supernaturalist*," who maintains that belief in revelation is necessary; at the other extreme is the "*naturalist*," who "denies the reality of all supernatural divine revelation; in between is "the *rationalist*," who regards only natural religion as morally necessary; Kant himself seems to be "a *pure rationalist*," in that he "recognizes revelation, but asserts that to know and accept it as real is not a necessary requisite to religion.") Christianity is depicted as both a natural religion and a revealed religion. Kant devotes three paragraphs to showing how the Gospel of Matthew can be interpreted as expressive of Kantian ethics, revealing Jesus as the wise moral Teacher. Christianity, in addition to being "a pure *rational faith*," is also "a *revealed faith*" to be *learned*. Yet insofar as it is genuine religion, its ultimate ends remain those of the moral order.

> This is the *true service* of the church under the dominion of the good principle; whereas that in which revealed faith is to precede religion is *pseudo-service*. In it the moral order is wholly reversed and what is merely means is commanded unconditionally (as an end).

What sort of cultic, ritualistic pseudo-service can supplant the pursuit of a moral life, amounting to "*religious illusion*"? As examples, Kant mentions sacrifices, religious festivals, penances, castigations, and pilgrimages. He emphasizes his point, lest we miss its import:

> *Whatever, over and above good life-conduct, man fancies that he can do to become well-pleasing to God is mere religious illusion and pseudo-service of God.*

Kant distinguishes two such dangers:

> The illusion of being able to accomplish anything in the way of justifying ourselves before God through religious acts of worship is religious *superstition*, just as the illusion of wishing to accomplish this by striving for what is supposed to be communion with God is religious *fanaticism*.

Kant contends that only "moral service" is "well-pleasing to God" and that any superficial, ritualistic substitute for that is mere "*fetishism*." As religious individuals must strive to avoid superstition and fanaticism, a church must beware of a dangerous institutionalized fetishism:

> *Clericalism*, therefore, is the constitution of a church to the extent to which a *fetish-worship* dominates it; and this condition is always found wherever, instead of principles of morality, statutory commands, rules of faith, and observances constitute the basis and essence of the church.

If we are not to resort to personal or collective flattery of God, what is a proper religious attitude for humans to have toward the divine? It is with his *"doctrine of godliness"* that Kant answers this:

> Godliness comprises two determinations of the moral disposition in relation to God: *fear* of God is this disposition in obedience to His commands from *bounden* duty (the duty of a subject), i.e., from respect for the law; *love* of God, on the other hand, is the disposition to obedience from one's own *free choice* and from approval of the law (the duty of a son).

Finally, Kant discusses certain religious practices—including praying, church-going, and sacramental participation—which can be either beneficial, edifying expressions of devotion, binding members of a church together as a group, or forms of religious illusion if conceived of as *"means of grace"* whereby we may win God over. He warns that the latter can lead to the loss of our religious autonomy:

> *Clericalism* in general would therefore be the dominion of the clergy over men's hearts, usurped by dint of arrogating to themselves the prestige attached to exclusive possession of means of grace.[107]

If religion be analyzed in terms of creed, code, and cult, it is clear that Kant sees a moral code as its core. He is not opposed to cultic dimensions of ritual but warns against their abuses. He expresses the essence of his creed in terms of three articles of faith:

> I believe in one God, original source of all good in the world, as its ultimate end;—I believe in the possibility of harmonizing this ultimate end with the highest good in the world, as far as it pertains to men;—I believe in a future eternal life as the condition of the perpetual approach of the world to the highest good possible in it.[108]

But for Kant the heart of true religion is its relating of a moral code to the idea of God. This is why the title of this chapter characterizes Kant's position as one of "critical moralism." It is founded on his critical philosophy and essentially involves a system of ethical principles governing conduct. We might do well to consider again Kant's often used definition of religion as "the recognition of all duties as divine commands" (*Erkenntniss aller Pflichten als gottlicher Gebote*). He himself points out two advantages of this definition over more orthodox conceptions of religion: it assumes no theoretical knowledge ("even of God's existence"), resting as it does on practical faith, and it "obviates the erroneous representation of religion as an aggregate of *special* duties having reference directly to God," focusing as it does on morality.[109] Thus, Kant's conception of religion essentially militates against both dogmatism and superstitious ritual and accentuates the crucial importance of moral commitment.

The Problem of Evil. Kant's analysis of the problem of evil changed between the 1780s and the 1790s. In his *Lectures on Philosophical Theology*, from the earlier decade, he says, "Against the moral perfection of God, reason raises many objections which are strong enough to lead many men astray and plunge them into despair." He mentions that Leibniz, in his *Theodicy*, tried to answer those objections, and Kant announces that he intends to present his own defense of God's three moral attributes in the face of the problem of evil.

> The first objection is against God's *holiness*. If God is holy and hates evil, then whence comes this *evil*, which is an object of abhorrence to all rational beings and the ground of all intellectual abhorrence?

In response, Kant speculates that God created man good "both in his nature and as regards his predispositions," but that, as created, man was "still crude and uncultivated. Man himself had to be responsible for this development, through the cultivation of his talents and the goodness of his will." The idea, then, is that it is better for us to use our own free will to achieve moral improvement but that, in the process, we shall make mistakes and do wrong. Adopting the traditional Augustinian view, Kant says,

> Evil . . . is only a negation, and consists only in a limitation of what is good. It is nothing but the incomplete development of the seed of goodness out of its uncultivated condition.

It is only through trial and error that we can grow. "Evil, therefore, is inevitable" and is permitted, though not willed, by God. What Kant fails to answer, however, is why it is better that man should develop himself in a manner that necessitates evil.

> The second objection is against God's benevolence. If God is benevolent and wills that men be happy, then whence comes all the *ill* in the world, which is an object of abhorrence to everyone who meets with it and constitutes the ground of physical abhorrence?

In other words, how can a truly benevolent God allow suffering? Kant answers that we cannot legitimately gauge happiness from our limited, momentary point of view and that what matters is "the happiness of creatures throughout the whole duration of their existence. *Ill* is only a special arrangement for leading man toward happiness." It provides us with an incentive for progressive improvement and for striving to make ourselves worthy of happiness. Again, though, Kant fails to indicate why a perfect God would need to utilize suffering as a means to move us to happiness and the worthiness to achieve it.

> The third objection is against God's *justice*, and has this question as its object: Why in this world is there no proportion between good conduct and well-being?

Here Kant's response is, perhaps, weakest of all. He first assures us that the disproportion between virtue and happiness "is not really so large, and in the end *honesty* is the best attitude." But then he does admit that sometimes "even the most righteous man" is liable to find himself the victim of a harsh fate. Yet self-sacrifice, he avers, can be tantamount to "true virtue, and worthy of future recompense." The problem is that self-sacrifice is necessary in circumstances established by persons of limited abilities and/or resources, unlike Kant's infinite God, and that compensation is necessitated to rectify the very sort of injustice Kant wishes to deny. He concludes the section with the implausible claim, "If there were no disproportion at all between morality and well-being here in this world, there would be no opportunity for us to be truly virtuous."[110] It is dubious that true virtue could not exist in a world so perfect that everyone received his just deserts. This exercise in theodicy does not represent Kant at his best, being neither original nor convincing.

His essay of 1791 "On the Failure of All Attempted Philosophical Theodicies" is far more impressive. He begins with a definition: "By theodicies, one means defences of the highest wisdom of the Creator against the complaints which reason makes by pointing to the existence of things in the world which contradict the wise purpose." He says there are three possible strategies a theodicy might use in dealing with the problem of evil: (1) it can try to show that there is no genuine contrariety, that what we think evil is not really so; (2) it can try to show that the contrariety or evil that exists is necessary; or (3) it can try to show that the contrariety or evil that exists is the work of someone other than God. Kant's own exercise in theodicy, in his lectures of the 1780s, combines (2) and (3). If a theodicy is to be philosophical, it is necessary "that the case be tried before the tribunal of reason," the theodicist serving as "an attorney" for the defense and being unwilling to give it all up as an incomprehensible mystery. Moral evil can be viewed as contrary to "the *holiness* of the Creator as *legislator*"; second, the physical evils of pain and suffering can be regarded as contrary to "the goodness of the Creator as *governor* (or sustainer)"; and, third, the scandalous "disproportion between the impunity of the guilty and the gravity of their crimes" can be considered contrary to "the *justice* of the Creator as *judge*."[111] In each case, then, the challenge is raised against one of God's three moral attributes.

Against the first sort of challenge (to God's holiness), if the defense is (*a*) that there is no absolute opposition but that moral evils are merely "stumbling blocks" from our limited perspective, Kant holds that "the response is worse than the charge," because it trivializes our rational sense of morality; if the defense is (*b*) that the moral evil of the world "is inevitable since it rests on the limitations of the nature of men as finite beings," then guilt could no longer be associated with it and "we should stop calling it a moral evil"; and if the defense is (*c*) that moral evil is only a man-made misfortune tolerated, but not approved, by God, then its roots lie "in the necessary limits of humanity as finite being, and thereby mankind cannot really be made responsible for it."[112] All three of these defenses fail to take seriously enough moral evil and moral responsibility.

Against the second sort of challenge (to God's goodness), if the defense is (*d*) that suffering cannot really outweigh happiness, since "everyone prefers life to death," Kant considers this a *non sequitur* and points out that, though people might fear death and wish to postpone or avoid it, few would choose to repeat this life, if given a choice; if the defense is (*e*) that our animal nature requires a preponderance of pain over pleasure, the question to be raised in cross-examination is, "why has the Author of our existence called us into this life when this life, rightly evaluated, is not desirable?"; and if the defense is (*f*) that suffering is caused by our own actions and is a necessary means to future blessedness, it fails to explain why (a perfect) God would need to allow such means to our "future joy."[113] These three defenses fail to show that our present suffering is necessary or justified.

Against the third sort of challenge (to God's justice), if the defense is (*g*) that the wicked really do suffer as they deserve to, despite appearances to the contrary, because of their "inner reproaches of conscience," this mistakenly imputes to the vicious the conscience of the virtuous; if the defense is (*h*) that things simply are as they are because of "the nature of things" without being willed so by anyone and that vice is needed "to heighten the worth of virtue," then the rebuttal is that, far from enhancing virtue, unjust suffering sometimes seems to result from (and detract from) its practice; and if the defense is (*i*) that the injustice experienced here and now is man's doing but will be rectified in the hereafter by God, the obvious retort demands what justification we have for such a supposition.[114] Thus, each of the three possible defenses of divine justice seems unlikely to guarantee an acquittal.

So, Kant renders his negative verdict: "The result of this trial before the tribunal of philosophy is that no theodicy proposed so far has kept its promise" to reconcile the infinite "moral wisdom" of God and the evil experienced in our world. On the other hand, he quickly adds, "these doubts cannot disprove such moral wisdom either." Thus, we are merely led to the "negative wisdom" that this is an area in which we run up against "the necessary limits of our reflections on the subjects which are beyond our reach." Kant recommends that we follow the example of Job, who "did not base his morality on his faith but his faith upon his morality." We must strive to live a morally good life and not get hung up on trying to know the unknowable. And if the problem of evil cannot be conclusively solved by philosophy, we can approach it from the perspective of belief, so that "theodicy is not a task of science but is a matter of faith."[115]

In this area, as in others we have considered, Kant can say, "my conviction is not *logical*, but *moral* certainty." Here, as elsewhere, Kant avoids both dogmatism and skepticism. As he indicates in the final paragraph of his pivotal first *Critique*, his predecessors chose between these extremes: "I may cite the celebrated Wolff as a representative of the former mode of procedure, and David Hume as a representative of the latter." Both approaches have proved unsatisfactory. Kant adds, "The *critical* path alone is still open."[116] This is the route his own philosophy has carefully taken.

Notes

1. *Kant Selections*, ed. Theodore M. Greene (New York: Charles Scribner's Sons, 1957), p. xvii; this work will hereafter be called "Greene."

2. *Kant—Philosophical Correspondence: 1759–99*, ed. and trans. Arnulf Zweig (Chicago: The Univ. of Chicago Press, 1967), p. 237; this book will hereafter be called "*Correspondence*."

3. *On History*, by Immanuel Kant, ed. Lewis White Beck, trans. Lewis White Beck, Robert E. Anchor, and Emil L. Fackenheim (Indianapolis: Bobbs-Merrill, 1963), pp. 9–10; this book will hereafter be called "*History*." See also *The Philosophy of Kant*, ed. Carl J. Friedrich (New York: Modern Library, 1949), pp. 138–39; this work will hereafter be called "Friedrich."

4. *Preliminary Discourse on Philosophy in General*, by Christian Wolff, trans. Richard J. Blackwell (Indianapolis: Bobbs-Merrill, 1963), pp. 4, 10, 17, 33, 50–51, 88–89, 103–4.

5. *Anthropology from a Pragmatic Point of View*, by Immanuel Kant, trans. Victor Lyle Dowdell (Carbondale, IL: Southern Illinois Univ. Press, 1978), pp. 4–5n.; this book will hereafter be called "*Anthropology*." For much of the fifteen years in which Kant was a *Privatdozent*, Prussia opposed Russia in the Seven Years' War (1756–63); during part of this time Russian troops occupied Königsberg.

6. *Correspondence*, pp. 48, 56, 58.

7. Ibid., pp. 71–73.   8. Ibid., p. 89.

9. Ibid., pp. 105–6; see also p. 100.

10. *Prolegomena to Any Future Metaphysics That Will Be Able to Come Forward As Science*, by Immanuel Kant, trans. Paul Carus and revised by James W. Ellington (Indianapolis: Hackett Publishing Co., 1977), p. 6; this work will hereafter be called "*Prolegomena*." See also Friedrich, p. 46.

11. *Correspondence*, p. 102.

12. Ibid., p. 54.   13. Ibid., pp. 77, 88, 177–78.

14. Ibid., p. 185.   15. Ibid., pp. 78–79; cf. *Anthropology*, p. 6n.

16. *Correspondence*, pp. 89, 91.

17. *Critique of Practical Reason*, by Immanuel Kant, trans. Lewis White Beck (Indianapolis: Bobbs-Merrill, 1956), p. xxii; this work will hereafter be called "second *Critique*." See also *History*, p. xxviii.

18. *Correspondence*, p. 150.

19. Ibid., pp. 163–64n., 122.

20. Ibid., p. 173.

21. *History*, pp. 3–5; cf. Friedrich, pp. 132–34.

22. *Correspondence*, p. 205. See *Logic*, by Immanuel Kant, trans. Robert S. Hartman and Wolfgang Schwarz (Indianapolis: Bobbs-Merrill, 1974), p. 29; this book will hereafter be called "*Logic*." See also *Immanuel Kant's Critique of Pure Reason*, trans. Norman Kemp Smith (New York: St. Martin's Press, 1965), pp. 635–36; this work will hereafter be called "first *Critique*."

23. *The Conflict of the Faculties*, by Immanuel Kant, trans. Mary J. Gregor and Robert E. Anchor (New York: Abaris Books, 1979), pp. 11–19; this work will hereafter be called "*Conflict*." See also *Correspondence*, pp. 217–20.

24. *Correspondence*, pp. 223–25.

25. Ibid., p. 251.   26. Ibid., p. 239.

27. *A New Exposition of the First Principles of Metaphysical Knowledge*, by Immanuel Kant, trans. F. E. England as an appendix to his book, *Kant's Conception of God* (New York: Humanities Press, 1968); this work will hereafter be called "*New Exposition*."

28. *The One Possible Basis for a Demonstration of the Existence of God*, by Immanuel Kant, trans. Gordon Treash (New York: Abaris Books, 1979); this work will hereafter be called "*Basis*."

29. *Enquiry concerning the Clarity of the Principles of Natural Theology and Ethics*, by Immanuel Kant, trans. D. E. Walford, in *Kant: Selected Pre-Critical Writings*

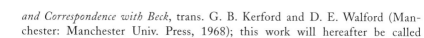

and Correspondence with Beck, trans. G. B. Kerford and D. E. Walford (Manchester: Manchester Univ. Press, 1968); this work will hereafter be called *"Enquiry."*

30. *Observations on the Feeling of the Beautiful and Sublime*, by Immanuel Kant, trans. John T. Goldthwait (Berkeley: Univ. of California Press, 1965).

31. *Dreams of a Spirit Seer*, by Immanuel Kant, trans. John Manolesco (New York: Vantage Press, 1969); this work will hereafter be called *Dreams.*

32. *On the Form and Principles of the Sensible and Intelligible World*, by Immanuel Kant, trans. G. B. Kerford, in *Kant: Selected Pre-Critical Writings and Correspondence with Beck*, trans. G. B. Kerford and D. E. Walford (Manchester: Manchester Univ. Press, 1968); this work will hereafter be called "Inaugural Dissertation."

33. *Grounding for the Metaphysics of Morals*, by Immanuel Kant, trans. James W. Ellington (Indianapolis: Hackett Publishing Co., 1981); this work will hereafter be called *"Grounding."*

34. *Metaphysical Foundations of Natural Science*, by Immanuel Kant, trans. James Ellington (Indianapolis: Bobbs-Merrill, 1970).

35. *Critique of Judgment*, by Immanuel Kant, trans. J. H. Bernard (New York: Hafner Publishing Co., 1968); this book will hereafter be called "third *Critique."*

36. "On the Failure of All Attempted Philosophical Theodicies," Immanuel Kant, trans. Michel Despland as an appendix to his book, *Kant on History and Religion* (Montreal: McGill-Queen's Univ. Press, 1973); this book will hereafter be called "Theodicies."

37. *Religion within the Limits of Reason Alone*, by Immanuel Kant, trans. Theodore M. Greene and Hoyt H. Hudson (New York: Harper & Row, 1960); this work will hereafter be called *"Religion."*

38. *The Metaphysical Elements of Justice: Part 1 of The Metaphysics of Morals*, by Immanuel Kant, trans. John Ladd (Indianapolis: Bobbs-Merrill, 1965).

39. *The Doctrine of Virtue: Part 2 of The Metaphysics of Morals*, by Immanuel Kant, trans. Mary J. Gregor (New York: Harper & Row, 1964).

40. *Education*, by Immanuel Kant, trans. Annette Churton (Ann Arbor: Univ. of Michigan Press, 1960).

41. *What Real Progress Has Metaphysics Made in Germany Since the Time of Leibniz and Wolff?*, by Immanuel Kant, trans. Ted Humphrey (New York: Abaris Books, 1983); this work will hereafter be called *"Metaphysics."*

42. *Lectures on Philosophical Theology*, by Immanuel Kant, trans. Allen W. Wood and Gertrude M. Clark (Ithaca: Cornell Univ. Press, 1978); this book will hereafter be called *"Theology."*

43. *Lectures on Ethics*, by Immanuel Kant, trans. Louis Infield (New York: Harper & Row, 1963); this book will hereafter be called *"Ethics."*

44. *New Exposition*, pp. 215–18, 221–25.

45. *Basis*, pp. 43–45, 69, 71, 79, 81, 83, 87, 223, 225, 57, 59, 63, 225, 227, 229, 231, 239.

46. *Enquiry*, pp. 13–14, 17–18, 21–23, 25, 28–30, 33.

47. *Dreams*, pp. 76–77, 79–80, 90–91, 94, 96–98; cf. Friedrich, pp. 19, 21–23.

48. Inaugural Dissertation, pp. 54–55, 63, 65–66, 70, 60–61, 58–59, 79–81.

49. First *Critique*, pp. 607, 32 (A671/B789 and Bxxxv); we shall adopt the usual practice of providing "A" and "B" references corresponding to the original numbering of passages in the first and second editions of the first *Critique*; cf. Greene, p. 25. See also *Metaphysics*, p. 61.

50. *Prolegomena*, pp. 3, 5, 19, 100; cf. Friedrich, pp. 42, 45, 60.

51. *Prolegomena*, pp. 26–27.

52. First *Critique*, pp. 65–66 (A19–20/B34); cf. Greene, pp. 43–44.

53. First *Critique*, pp. 66–68 (A20–24/B35–39), 71–72 (A26–28/B42–44), 74–78 (A30–36/B46–52); cf. Greene, pp. 44–46, 48–50.

54. First *Critique*, pp. 82 (A42/B59), 90 (B72); cf. Greene, p. 56.

55. *Prolegomena*, pp. 41, 47; cf. Friedrich, p. 71.

56. First *Critique*, pp. 41 (B1), 43–44 (B2–4); cf. Greene, pp. 26, 28–29.

57. First *Critique*, pp. 48 (A7/B11), 55 (B19); cf. Greene, pp. 33, 39.

58. First *Critique*, p. 646 (A822/B850).

59. Ibid., pp. 92–93 (A50–51/B74–75); cf. Greene, pp. 56–58.

60. First *Critique*, pp. 107 (A70/B95), 113 (A80/B106), 105–6 (A68–69/B93); cf. Greene, pp. 63, 66.

61. *Prolegomena*, p. 44 (including note); cf. Friedrich, pp. 73–74.

62. *Prolegomena*, pp. 51, 54–55, 57–58; cf. Friedrich, pp. 80, 83–85, 87.

63. *Prolegomena*, pp. 61–62; cf. Friedrich, pp. 90–91.

64. First *Critique*, pp. 147 (A125), 152–54 (B131–34), 19–22 (Bxi–xvi); cf. Greene, pp. 11–14.

65. First *Critique*, p. 244 (B274); cf. Greene, p. 139. *Prolegomena*, p. 37.

66. First *Critique*, pp. 7–8 (Avii–viii), 21 (Bxiv); cf. Greene, pp. 1–2, 13.

67. *Prolegomena*, pp. 1–2, 6–7; cf. Friedrich, pp. 41, 46–47.

68. First *Critique*, pp. 99–100 (A61–62/B85–87), 298 (A295/B352), 300 (A298/B355), 318–20 (A327–29/B383–85); cf. Greene, pp. 60, 156, 162–63.

69. First *Critique*, p. 323 (A334/B391); cf. Greene, p. 164.

70. *Prolegomena*, pp. 75–76.

71. Ibid., pp. 79–81, 88.

72. Ibid., pp. 88–90. For more on Kant's epistemology and views on metaphysics, see *Twelve Great Philosophers*, by Wayne P. Pomerleau (New York: Ardsley House, 1997), pp. 230–44.

73. First *Critique*, pp. 497 (A586/B614), 499–500 (A590–91/B618–19); cf. Greene, pp. 242–43. See also *Theology*, pp. 31–38. In cases such as this, where passages in *Theology* make much the same point as material in one of the three critiques, the latter will usually be quoted, despite the fact that *Theology* is generally more readable. This is done for two reasons: first, *Theology* is far less famous than any of the critiques; and, second, each critique, unlike *Theology*, was prepared for publication by Kant himself. (Kant assesses his own pre-critical proof of God's existence in *Theology*, pp. 66–68.)

74. *Theology*, pp. 23, 28–29, 32, 34.

75. First *Critique*, p. 501 (A592–93/B620–21); cf. Greene, p. 244.

76. First *Critique*, pp. 501–4 (A593–98/B621–26); cf. Greene, pp. 245–48.

77. First *Critique*, pp. 504–6 (A598–601/B626–29); cf. Greene, pp. 248–50. See also *Theology*, pp. 46–47.

78. *Theology*, pp. 55–56; first *Critique*, p. 507 (A602/B630); cf. Greene, p. 251.

79. *Theology*, pp. 60–61.

80. First *Critique*, pp. 511–14 (A609–14/B637–42); cf. Greene, pp. 254–56.

81. First *Critique*, pp. 510–11 (A607–9/B635–37).

82. *Theology*, pp. 99–101.

83. First *Critique*, p. 520 (A623–24/B651–52); cf. Greene, pp. 259–60.

84. First *Critique*, pp. 520–22 (A624–27/B652–55); cf. Greene, pp. 260–62.

85. *Theology*, pp. 29, 69–71, 76, 78, 83, 95, 30.

86. First *Critique*, pp. 533, 550–51, 558–60 (A644, 671–73, 684–86/B672, 699–701, 712–14).

87. Ibid., pp. 29, 26–27, 646 (Bxxx,xxv; A822/B850); cf. Greene, pp. 22, 18.

88. First *Critique*, pp. 635–36 (A804–5/B832–33).

89. *Grounding*, pp. 30–32, 36–40, 43–44; cf. Friedrich, pp. 170–72, 178–82, 186–87.

90. Second *Critique*, pp. 113–17; cf. Greene, pp. 350–52.

91. Second *Critique*, p. 149n.; see *Religion*, pp. 43, 45–46, for the "ought" implies "can" principle.

92. Second *Critique*, pp. 129–30; cf. Greene, pp. 361–62.

93. *Theology*, pp. 122–23; cf. second *Critique*, pp. 152–53.

94. Third *Critique*, pp. 286–87, 291–92, 295, 301; cf. Greene, pp. 502, 505–6, 509, 514.

95. Third *Critique*, pp. 315, 318.

96. Ibid., pp. 318–19, 321–22, 324–25; cf. Greene, pp. 524–26.

97. *Theology*, pp. 121–22; cf. *Metaphysics*, p. 133.

98. *Ethics*, pp. 93–96.

99. *The Creed of a Priest of Savoy*, by Jean-Jacques Rousseau, trans. Arthur H. Beattie, 2nd ed. (New York: Frederick Ungar Publishing Co., 1968), pp. 75, 80, 74–76.

100. Third *Critique*, pp. 336–39; cf. Greene, pp. 521–24. For Kant's technical discussion of analogy, see *Logic*, pp. 136–37.

101. *Prolegomena*, pp. 96–99; cf. Friedrich, pp. 104–6. See also *Religion*, pp. 58–59n. (Friedrich, p. 401n.).

102. *Theology*, pp. 41, 111–12.

103. *Religion*, pp. 3–5, 8, 12.

104. Ibid., pp. 21–25, 30, 32, 35, 47–48; cf. Friedrich, pp. 372–77, 382, 384, 388.

105. *Religion*, pp. 51, 54, 57, 74, 77, 79–83; cf. Friedrich, pp. 394, 396, 399–400. See also *Conflict*, p. 67, for more on the Incarnation.

106. *Religion*, pp. 86, 89–92, 95, 97–98, 113, 129, 133–34; cf. Friedrich, pp. 404, 407–10. See also *Conflict*, pp. 61–67.

107. *Religion*, pp. 142–43, 147–53, 156–58, 162, 165, 167–68, 170, 182–88; cf. *Ethics*, pp. 78–116, for ten sections in which Kant discusses religion. See also *Education*, pp. 111–14, for his comments on proper religious pedagogy.

108. *Metaphysics*, p. 131.

109. Second *Critique*, p. 134 (Greene, p. 365); third *Critique*, p. 334 (Greene, pp. 519–20); and *Religion*, pp. 79, 100, 142.

110. *Theology*, pp. 115–21.

111. "Theodicies," pp. 283, 285.

112. Ibid., p. 286.   113. Ibid., p. 287.   114. Ibid., pp. 288–89.

115. Ibid., pp. 290, 293.

116. First *Critique*, pp. 650 (A829/B857), 668 (A856/B884).

7

Hegel's Dialectical Idealism

Life and Writings

$\mathcal{H}$egel's life began in 1770, the year in which Kant was appointed professor at the University of Königsberg. Born on August 27, 1770, in Stuttgart (in southwest Germany), the son of a civil servant of the department of finance in the Duchy of Wurttemberg, Georg Wilhelm Friedrich Hegel seems to have been a diligent but otherwise undistinguished student in his boyhood. He did develop an early appreciation of Greek poetry, and as a teenager he kept a bilingual journal in German and Latin. He had a brother and a sister, and his mother died in 1781 (the year in which Kant's first *Critique* was published).

In 1788, he graduated from his local *gymnasium*, where he did well academically, and enrolled in the Protestant theological seminary at Tübingen, as his father wished, presumably with the idea of entering the Lutheran ministry. It was an exciting time in Europe, with the French Revolution coming to a head. In the middle of June, 1789 the Bastille was stormed and taken. Hegel and a number of his friends at the seminary (including the younger but more precocious future philosopher Schelling and the poet Hölderlin) were enthusiastic supporters of the revolution. There is an apocryphal story that they planted a "liberty tree" to commemorate the occasion.

In 1790, Hegel received his master of philosophy degree. He continued to study for his theology examinations, which he passed in 1793. (During that same year, he wrote his "Tübingen essay.") His graduation certificate described him as of good character and well-versed in theology and philology, but of little philosophical ability. He was poor when he left the seminary. Avoiding entry into parish work, he accepted a position as tutor for a rich family in Berne, Switzerland, where he wrote the "Berne Fragments" on religion, as well as (in 1795) his "Life of Jesus" and *The Positivity of the Christian Religion*. He ended this job in 1796 and, in 1797, accepted a similar position with a family in Frankfurt, Germany. In 1798, he wrote *The Spirit of Christianity and Its Fate*. Although these writings from his years at Tübingen, Berne, and Frankfurt are not spectacular in themselves, they reveal a young thinker struggling to come to grips with the intellectual legacy of Kant, especially as it impacts on theology.

In 1799, his father died, leaving Hegel an inheritance sufficient to allow him to change his life. He quit private tutoring and wrote to his friend Schelling, asking where he might go to find "inexpensive provisions, a good beer for the sake of my physical condition, [and] a few acquaintances."[1] On Schelling's recommendation, he moved to the University of Jena (in eastern Germany) in 1801, where he became a *Privatdozent*, lecturing on logic and metaphysics. (Fichte had taught at Jena until 1799, when he moved to Berlin; Schelling had been given a chair at Jena in 1798, at the age of twenty-three.) Hegel's first published work, *The Difference between Fichte's and Schelling's Systems of Philosophy*, appeared in 1801, defending Schelling's views against Fichte's. By 1802, Hegel was coediting with Schelling *The Critical Journal of Philosophy*, in which his own essay on *Natural Law* and his *Faith and Knowledge* were published in 1803 (the same year Schelling left Jena to lecture at Wurzburg). By 1804 (the year Kant died), Hegel had thirty students (he had only eleven in 1801). In 1805, he was promoted to extraordinary professor and began lecturing on the history of philosophy.

At this time, he was also working on his "voyage of discovery," *Phenomenology of Spirit*. Although he now had a regular salary, he had depleted the legacy from his father during those years as *Privatdozent* and needed money. So he signed a contract to have his *Phenomenology* published. The good news was that it gave him an advance cash payment; the bad news was that it contained severe penalty clauses for his failure to get the completed manuscript to the publisher by October 18, 1806, and he was advised to have it in the mail by October 13th. In a letter of 1805, Hegel wrote that as "Luther made the Bible speak German," so he would "try to teach philosophy to speak German,"[2] as if Kant had not already done so. The trouble was that war was brewing between Napoleon's French troops and the Prussians, who were occupying Jena. On October 12, 1806, Napoleon bombarded Jena and entered it the following day, which was to be Hegel's deadline for mailing the complete manuscript. In a letter written that very day, he said, "I saw the Emperor—this world-soul—riding. . . . It is indeed a wonderful sensation to see such an individual, who, . . . astride a horse, reaches out over the world and masters it."[3] Hegel missed his deadline, though his legal advisor assured him that he would not be liable for what was the consequence of acts of war.[4] A couple of weeks later Napoleon had capped this victory over the Prussians at Jena by taking Berlin.

It is not surprising, under the circumstances, that Hegel was less than satisfied with the finished product. As he wrote to his friend Schelling a few months later, "Make allowances for the greater want of form in the last sections by recalling that I actually completed the draft in its entirety in the middle of the night before the Battle of Jena."[5] In that same letter he warns that in the preface to the *Phenomenology* he takes to task "the shallowness" of some of Schelling's followers. For example, he criticizes the Schellingian philosophy for trying "to palm off its **Absolute** as the night in which, as the saying goes, all cows are black."[6] After the *Phenomenology* was published in 1807, Schelling was predictably concerned about what he called "the polemical part of the Preface,"[7] and their friendship came to an end.

In Jena Hegel fathered an illegitimate son, Ludwig, in 1807, the mother being Hegel's landlady. But the war had so disrupted operations at the University of Jena that Hegel moved to Bamberg, where he became the editor of a French-controlled newspaper. The following year, 1808, Hegel became director and philosophy professor at the *gymnasium* at Nuremberg. The school was dedicated to classical studies; in an address to the school in 1809, Hegel defends its curriculum: "The spirit and purpose of our foundation is preparation for learned study, a preparation grounded on Greece and Rome." He boasts that the study of language and grammar "constitutes the beginning of logical training" and "can be looked on as a preliminary instruction in philosophy."[8]

In 1811, at the age of forty-one, Hegel married Marie von Tucher, a lady of about half his age, from an established Nuremberg family. He had courted her with poetry in April of that year.[9] They appear to have had a good marriage. Their first child, a girl, died in infancy in 1812; their sons, Karl and Immanuel, were born in 1813 and 1814. In 1816, after the death of his mother, Hegel's illegitimate son, Ludwig, joined their household. During these years, 1812–16, Hegel's most carefully completed book, his *Science of Logic*, was published in installments.

This led to his being offered three academic positions, at Erlangen, at Heidelberg, and at Berlin. In 1816, he accepted the offer of a professorship of philosophy from the University of Heidelberg, where he added lectures on **aesthetics** to his repertoire. His growing reputation was enhanced the following year with the publication of his *Encyclopaedia of the Philosophical Sciences*, in three parts (a logic, a philosophy of nature, and a philosophy of mind). This, in turn, led to his being named to succeed Fichte in a philosophy professorship at the University of Berlin, where he stayed from 1818 until his death. Berlin had recently become the cultural and academic bastion of Germany, and Hegel quickly emerged as its most prominent intellectual.

In 1821, his *Philosophy of Right* was published and he began lecturing on the philosophy of religion.[10] His lectures at the university were attracting large audiences from all over Germany. In 1822, he made holiday tours of Belgium and Holland and began lecturing on the philosophy of history. In 1824, he traveled to Prague and Vienna. Three years later, he visited Paris and revised and published a second edition of his *Encyclopaedia*. In 1829 he was elected rector of the University of Berlin but had to defend himself against charges of **pantheism**. In letters of 1826 he had asserted, "I am a Lutheran, and through philosophy have been at once completely confirmed in Lutheranism"; and he described himself as "a professor who prides himself on having been baptized and raised a Lutheran, which he still is and shall remain."[11] Hegel acknowledged that "all speculative philosophizing on religion permits of being led to atheism" and resolved to write Hermann Friedrich Henrichs to warn him of this. (After studying with Hegel at Heidelberg, Henrichs had become a *Privatdozent* there in 1819 and was teaching Hegelianism.) Hegel also wrote to Georg Andreas Gabler (who had been his student at Jena and would succeed him at Berlin, becoming a leading figure in right-wing Hegelianism) concerning "the twaddle about pantheism."[12]

The Berlin years were a happy time for Hegel, characterized by professional popularity and family stability. He seemed pleased to be able to write that "my philosophy has now gained more widespread currency" and that "more and more universities are offering lectures according to my ideas."[13] He allied himself with the Prussian government and became recognized as its official philosopher. But he was also starting to show his age, becoming absent-minded; there is a story that he once entered his lecture hall wearing only one shoe, not having noticed that he had left the other stuck in the mud outside. When the cholera epidemic of 1831 hit Berlin, he was one of its first victims, dying in his sleep on November 14th, the day after he became ill (and the anniversary of Leibniz's death).

As Gabler, his successor at Berlin, was a representative of right-wing Hegelianism, interpreting his thought in a politically and theologically conservative manner, so there was a left-wing Hegelianism, which was politically radical and tended towards atheistic naturalism, represented, for example, by Ludwig Feuerbach, who had attended Hegel's lectures for two years in Berlin before completing his doctorate at Erlangen.[14] Feuerbach, whose critique of religion, *The Essence of Christianity*, was published in 1841, exerted considerable influence on Karl Marx, who regarded religion as the opiate of the masses. Thus, in the conflict between these two factions of German philosophy following Hegel's death, his powerful influence endured.

Hegel's writings include "The Tübingen Essay" of 1793, the "Berne Fragments" of 1793–94, and his "Life of Jesus" of 1795,[15] as well as *The Positivity of the Christian Religion* (1795) and *The Spirit of Christianity and Its Fate* (1798).[16] *Faith and Knowledge* was published in 1803,[17] as was *Natural Law*.[18] In 1807, the *Phenomenology of Spirit* was published. His *Science of Logic* appeared between 1812 and 1816.[19] In 1817, the three parts of his *Encyclopaedia of the Philosophical Sciences*, the *Logic*,[20] the *Philosophy of Nature*,[21] and the *Philosophy of Mind*,[22] were published. In 1821, the *Philosophy of Right* appeared.[23] His four great lecture series were published posthumously: these are on the *Philosophy of History* (in one volume),[24] on the *Philosophy of Fine Art* (in four volumes),[25] *Lectures on the History of Philosophy* (three volumes),[26] and, most important for our purposes, *Lectures on the Philosophy of Religion* (in three volumes).[27] Cross-references will frequently be made here to *The Philosophy of Hegel*,[28] a good general anthology edited by Carl J. Friedrich, and *On Art, Religion, Philosophy*,[29] a collection of the introductions to Hegel's lecture series on fine art, the philosophy of religion, and the history of philosophy, edited by J. Glenn Gray.

Knowledge and Reality

Early Religious Essays. Hegel's early religious essays represent a series of attempts he made (between 1793, his final year at the Tübingen theological seminary, and 1800, just before moving to Jena) to appropriate the doctrines of Christianity in the light of Kant's philosophy and the rise of German Romanticism. These works of Hegel's twenties fail to be philosophical because they lack any systematically developed epistemological foundation. But they are genetically important in that they expose the matrix within which his great system would emerge a decade later.

The first of these early works for us to consider is Hegel's "Tübingen Essay" of 1793 (the year in which Kant's *Religion* was published). His lifelong fascination with the subject is nicely indicated by its opening words, "Religion is one of our greatest concerns in life" (*Religion ist eine der michtigsten Ungelegenheiten unseres Lebens*). Later in that initial paragraph he adds that "indeed for some the whole circuit of their thoughts and aspirations is unified by religion in the way that a wheel's outer rim is linked to the hub." Against the focus of the Enlightenment, he insists that religion cannot be adequately reduced to the theoretical, that

> religion is not merely a systematic investigation of God, his attributes, the relation of the world and ourselves to him. . . . Rather religion engages the heart. It influences our feelings and the determination of our will.

What Hegel calls "objective religion" is merely a matter of abstract doctrine: "understanding and memory are the powers that do the work, investigating facts, thinking them through, retaining and even believing them. . . . Subjective religion on the other hand expresses itself only in feelings and actions" and is therefore personal and "individual." This corresponds to the contrast between theology and religion, and it is clear on which side of the distinction Hegel would place his emphasis at this point: "Everything depends on subjective religion; this is what has inherent and true worth." Enlightenment is inadequate insofar as it cultivates mere reflective understanding and fails to lead to wisdom, which must "be practical and not merely a complacent and boastful intellectualism" and which must "endow mankind with morality," with "goodness and purity of heart." At this point Hegel introduces a fundamental concept of his early essays, that of love, which, like reason, establishes a relationship between self and others.

> Forgetting about itself, love is able to step outside of a given individual's existence and live, feel, and act no less fully in others—just as reason, the principle of universally valid laws, recognizes its own self in the shared citizenship each rational being has in an intelligible world.

Here he reveals the influence of Kantian ideas. But Hegel also yearns for the development of "a folk religion" which might be compatible with the demands of "the universal reason of mankind." As a man of the Romantic period he nostalgically reflects on the folk religion of the ancient Greeks, which, on the one hand, did justice to the "profoundly moral demand of reason" and, on the other, engaged "the heart and imagination" of its adherents. In contrast to a folk religion, such as that of the ancient Greeks, which nurtured individual freedom, Hegel savagely condemns "our religion" of Christianity for "making our most human feelings seem alien."[30] There is a good deal of critical insight in this early essay, although it is unphilosophical in the sense of not being based on argumentation and fails to show adequately how the theoretical and the practical, reflection and feeling, theology and religion, should be synthesized.

After Hegel left Tübingen to work as a tutor in Switzerland, he made a series of efforts to develop his ideas on religion, the "Berne Fragments," most of which seem to have been written in 1794. Here the influence of Kant has become intensified since the previous year. There are passages in which Christ is unfavorably contrasted with Socrates and in which suspicions are cast on the self-serving motives of priests and the need of a religious people to protect itself against the manipulations of "phrases and pictures which were intelligible and appropriate only several thousand years ago in Syria." Whereas the essence of religion "is to better man morally and make him more pleasing to God," Hegel assails Christianity for having "burgeoned into the most shocking profusion of repressive institutions and ways of deluding mankind: oral confession, excommunication, penances, and a whole array of disgraceful monuments to self-abasement." Christianity, with its promise of an eternal carrot and threat of the eternal stick, can erode the rational autonomy (and dignity) of its adherents.

> For reason leads us irresistibly to the great principle that duty and virtue are self-sufficient—a principle whose sanctity is surely being undermined when the motives calling for duty and virtue are any more circuitous or heterogeneous than the merest association with the idea of God.

Here we see ideas that are strikingly similar to Kant's warnings against the "pseudo-service of God in statutory religion"; but Hegel's protests are worded more strongly, perhaps because, unlike Kant, he did not intend his for publication. Hegel includes Kant's name in a list of important thinkers "whose souls have rendered highest tribute to virtue and moral greatness," and whose increasing reverence for "morality and the moral character of Christ's teaching" was accompanied by a growing suspicion of the external trappings of institutionalized religion as "irrelevant and superfluous." Like Kant, Hegel is convinced at this point that the admirable essence of Christianity is its morality, which even its detractors accept as rational and in accordance with universal law:

A great many of those who generally oppose everything Christian have nonetheless shown the greatest respect for the morality of the Christian religion. For all the ridicule and other weapons they have loosed upon the doctrines of the Trinity, Atonement, and Original Sin, they have nonetheless become enchanted with the morality of Christendom and have extolled it as a great boon to the human race. . . . as a whole the spirit of Christ's moral teaching can be brought into harmony with the most sublime morality.

Like Kant, Hegel asserts that the "proper task" of religion

is to strengthen, by means of the idea of God as moral lawgiver, what impels us to act ethically and to enhance the satisfaction we derive from performing what our practical reason demands, specifically with regard to the ultimate end that reason posits: the highest good.

In a Kantian manner this "highest good" is analyzed in terms of "morality and a form of happiness commensurate with it." Meanwhile, Hegel adds, "Belief in the historical person of Christ is not based on any requirement of practical reason, but rests on the testimony of others," the docile acceptance of which, he sarcastically comments, "is far easier than cultivating the habit of thinking for ourselves," which Kant had so fostered. Near the end of the "Fragments," Hegel somewhat mysteriously writes, "Faith in Christ is faith in a personified ideal."[31] At this stage of Hegel's development, it is difficult to specify what this statement is intended to assert and what it is meant to deny. At any rate, in these "Fragments" we see a follower of Kant attempting to undertake a radical critique of the orthodox views of religion he had been taught.

In 1795, Hegel wrote a "Life of Jesus," which is a strikingly humanistic portrayal, stripping away the miracles and all traces of mystery and presenting a view of Christ as an admirable moral teacher preaching and practicing the Kantian ethic. Its opening sentence uses language that harks back to Kant and communicates an idea on which Hegel's later philosophy of history would be based: "Pure reason, transcending all limits, is divinity itself—whereby and in accordance with which the very plan of the world is ordered (*John* 1)." Hegel's Jesus, "born to Mary and Joseph," teaches that man is a rational spirit who "has received as his inheritance a spark of the divine essence" and whose natural impulses should be governed and subordinated to "the higher demands of reason," which "imposes morality as a matter of duty." He enjoins us to "at least respect the humanity in" our enemies if we cannot actually love them. He dissuades us from misusing prayer to request the satisfaction of our own needs or wants or to "curry favor with God." Echoing Kant's discussions of the kingdom of ends and of virtue as that by which we deserve to be

happy, he says, "The highest goal of your endeavors should be the kingdom of God, and the morality by means of which alone you may become
worthy of being its citizens." He even preaches Kant's categorical imperative in urging us to "act only on principles that you can will to become
universal laws among men, laws no less binding on you than on them."
In contrast to certain "miracle-makers" who "are not citizens" of his realm,
Jesus teaches that "morality alone is the criterion of what is pleasing to
God" and is said merely to have "performed an act of kindness for a poor
and sick person." He considers the view of "ecclesiastical statutes and positive precepts as the highest law given to mankind" to be in conflict with
"man's dignity and his capacity to derive from his own self the concept of
divinity." Hegel's Jesus advocates Kantian autonomy when he says,

> I cling only to the untainted voice of my heart and conscience. . . . And all I
> ask of my disciples is that they heed this voice too. This inner law is a law of
> freedom to which a person submits voluntarily, as though he had imposed it
> on himself.

The Kantian tension between self-serving inclinations and moral behavior is indicated by the words of this Jesus:

> A life spent in pursuit of one's own advantage can never be reconciled with a
> life in the service of virtue. . . . Anyone who cannot sacrifice everything for the
> sake of his duty by that very fact becomes unworthy of the kingdom of God.

He proclaims his message clearly:

> Respect for yourselves, belief in the sacred law of your own reason, and atten-
> tiveness to the judge residing within your own heart—your conscience, the
> very standard that is the criterion of divinity—this is what I have sought to
> awaken in you.

The emphasis on love as a reconciling force is prominent here, Jesus
telling his disciples, "What I leave you is the commandment to love one
another and the example of my love for you. Only through this mutual
love are you to distinguish yourselves as my friends." The divinity of
Christ is curiously handled here. Although Hegel's Jesus addresses God
as "My father," he does not, of his own initiative, profess to be God. Near
the end, the high priest commands, "Then in the name of the living God
I order you to tell us whether you are a holy man, a son of the Deity."
Jesus answers, "Yes, that is what I am." Then we are told that "in the eyes
of the Jews Jesus' declaration" that he was a son of God was considered
blasphemy. But, of course, it is a matter of interpretation. Hegel seems to
be moving toward the view that we are all children of God and, in some
sense, divine, so that there is nothing ontologically unique about Christ,

although he remains a most obvious exemplar of the unity of God and man. Finally, Hegel's "Life of Jesus" is striking for ending with the burial and making no mention of any resurrection.[32] All in all, it is a remarkably humanistic portrayal for an eighteenth-century graduate of a prominent German theological institute.

That same year, while still in Berne, Hegel wrote the sometimes scathing essay, *The Positivity of the Christian Religion*, which is another strikingly Kantian work, as is evident in its very first section, where he says that

> the aim and essence of all true religion, our religion included, is human morality, and that all the more detailed doctrines of Christianity . . . have their worth and their sanctity appraised according to their close or distant connection with that aim.

Jesus is praised as someone who "undertook to raise religion and virtue to morality and to restore to morality the freedom which is its essence." This moral religion advocated by Hegel is contrasted with Judaism as "a positive religion, i.e., a religion which is grounded in authority and puts man's worth not at all, or at least not wholly in morals." Hegel's Kantianism at this stage of his life renders him quite hostile to religious authority. The Gospel perspective is depicted as rejecting any ideal of "virtue grounded on authority," in favor of "a free virtue" rationally chosen by autonomous individuals. "Jesus, on this view, was the teacher of a purely moral religion, not a positive one." The issue of his divinity is again gingerly handled: "He may have been conscious of a tie between himself and God, or he may merely have held that the law hidden in our hearts was an immediate revelation of God or a divine spark." Jesus is now acknowledged as having performed remarkable actions; whether or not they were miracles in any sense denoting actual supernatural power,

> these deeds of Jesus were miracles in the eyes of his pupils and friends. Nothing has contributed so much as these miracles to making the religion of Jesus positive, to basing the whole of it, even its teaching about virtue, on authority.

And this led to the subsequent exaggerated emphasis on the trappings of institutionalized churches, so that

> just as the Jews made sacrifices, ceremonies, and a compulsory faith into the essence of religion, so the Christians made its essence consist in lip service, external actions, inner feelings, and a historical faith.

This, in turn, detracted from the value of Christian ethics:

> Even moral doctrines, now made obligatory in a positive sense, i.e., not on their own account, but as commanded by Jesus, lost the inner criterion whereby their necessity is established.

When morality is reduced to a submission to external authority, so that autonomy is destroyed, we have a perversion of religion, as understood by Kant and the early Hegel, from

> the essence of any true religion, the Christian religion included, i.e., ... the establishment of human duties and their underlying motives in their purity and the use of the idea of God to show the possibility of the *summum bonum*.

Hegel takes Christianity to task for becoming as authoritarian and "positive" as Judaism:

> It has also directly prescribed laws for our mode of thinking, feeling, and willing, and Christians have thus reverted to the position of the Jews. The special characteristic of the Jewish religion—that bondage to law from which Christians so heartily congratulate themselves on being free—turns up once more in the Christian church.

Indeed, whereas Judaism only commanded the conformity of our external actions, "the Christian church goes farther and commands feelings, a contradiction in terms," since feelings can only be existentially genuine if autonomous. In some respects these seem to be *anti*-theological writings, protesting against the rigid, illiberal tendencies of established religion as being opposed to right and reason. Not only does positive religion fail to advance the progressive realization of human reason, but it is built upon a basic disrespect for it. The embracing of positive religion is seen as accomplished only through the unnatural prostitution of human autonomy. "Christianity has emptied Valhalla, felled the sacred groves," destroying the natural values of folk religion and introducing alien and alienating values in their place. By contrast with "The Positivity of the Christian Religion," Hegel writes that "Greek and Roman religion was a religion for free peoples only." Whereas Jesus had emphasized the relationship between the divine and the human, positive Christianity introduced an alienating dichotomy:

> The spirit of the age was revealed in its objective conception of God when he was no longer regarded as like ourselves, though infinitely greater, but was put into another world in whose confines we had no part, to which we can contribute nothing by our activity, but into which, at best, we could beg or conjure our way.

Thus, Hegel warns us against the unwholesome tendencies to "positivity" which any religion, including Christianity, can have

> if human nature is absolutely severed from the divine, if no mediation between the two is conceded except in one isolated individual, if all man's consciousness of the good and the divine is degraded to the dull and killing belief in a superior Being altogether alien to man.

Again, Hegel can be criticized for not providing any constructive solution. Yet by now he recognizes the prerequisite for such a solution and admits,

> It is obvious that an examination of this question cannot be thoughtfully and thoroughly pursued without becoming in the end a metaphysical treatment of the relation between the finite and the infinite.[33]

This is the very sort of metaphysical inquiry Kant denied can ever lead to knowledge. Before he can fruitfully undertake it, Hegel must abandon the Kantian perspective and formulate his own theory of knowledge.

In a fragment on "Love," written in Frankfurt late in 1797 or near the beginning of 1798, Hegel seems to begin weaning himself from his tutelage to Kant, viewing love as an emotional synthesis, which subjectively "excludes all oppositions" and which transcends the limitations of the understanding and reason. "Love neither restricts nor is restricted; it is not finite at all. It is a feeling, yet not a single feeling," representing only a part of life, such as desire or jealousy. Kantian sensibility can experience only particular objects; Kantian understanding categorizes objects of experience in such a way as to discriminate; and Kantian reason hurls us in the direction of irresolvable antinomies. All of these are man's intellectual instruments for dealing with objectivity. But love, Hegel says,

> completely destroys objectivity and thereby annuls and transcends reflection, deprives man's opposite of all foreign character, and discovers life itself without any further defect. In love the separate does still remain, but as something united and no longer as something separate.[34]

Here, it seems, we find the germ of the dialectical method, with its analysis of distinction-in-unity, which would constitute Hegel's great contribution to the theory of knowledge.

But it is in *The Spirit of Christianity and Its Fate* that we can find more obvious examples of Hegel's early criticisms of Kant's moral religion and the intimations of a distinctively Hegelian position. Here the moral teachings of Jesus are contrasted, rather than identified, with the ethical system of Kant, which is now rejected as being based on a theory of necessarily conflicting elements in human nature. Kant's subordination of natural inclinations to the rule of reason makes for as alienating a division as positive religion's subjection of human behavior to external authority. Kant is accused of "wrongly" restricting and reducing even love to the level of a command, whereas Hegel asserts that "in love all thought of duties vanishes." Kant is accused of setting up an opposition between the moral law (in its universality) and human inclination (in its particularity)—an opposition which admits of subordination, but not of reconciliation: "the expression 'correspondence of inclination with the law' is therefore wholly unsatisfactory because it implies that law and inclination are still particulars, still opposites." But Hegel points to love as "the 'fulfillment' of both the laws and duty," a force whereby opposition can be overcome and reconciliation achieved. And it is Christ, the religious teacher, rather than Kant, the philosopher, who shows us how to transcend "law and duty in love, which Jesus signalizes as the highest morality," as opposed to the abstract theoretical principle of the categorical imperative. Where the Kantian ethic tries to subordinate natural inclinations to rational duty, the moral message of Jesus is integrative: "The opposition of duty to inclination has found its unification in the modifications of love, i.e., in the virtues." We can also detect here glimmerings of the mature Hegel's position on faith and knowledge and of its basis, the relationship between finite and infinite spirit. Where Kant had contrasted faith and knowledge, Hegel assimilates them; where Kant had emphasized the radical difference between finite man and the infinite God, Hegel tends to focus on a kinship between them which is most conspicuous in Christ:

> Faith in Jesus means more than knowing his real personality, feeling one's own reality as inferior to his in might and strength, and being his servant. Faith is a knowledge of spirit through spirit, and only like spirits can know and understand one another; unlike ones can know only that they are not what the other is.

Thus, the identification of faith and knowledge is linked to that between finite and infinite spirit. If the "objectivity" of (for example, Kantian) reflective thought seems to underscore the unbridgeable difference between God and man, it is through love that they are rejoined: "To love God is to feel one's self in the 'all' of life, with no restrictions, in the infinite. . . . Only through love is the might of objectivity broken." Here we see strong traces of Romanticism in the emphasis on unity with all of life and on the capacity of emotion to overcome the limitations of intellect. Jesus is viewed as historical witness to the identity of the human and the divine: "The son of God is also son of man; the divine in a particular shape appears as a man." It is philosophy of the Kantian sort which threatens to lure us away from the truth of this identity.

> Reflective thinking, which partitions life, can distinguish it into infinite and finite, and then it is only the restriction, the finite regarded by itself, which affords the concept of man as opposed to the divine. But outside reflective thinking, and in truth, there is no such restriction.

How could we have any relationship—in love, in faith, in knowledge—to that which is radically other?

> Faith in the divine is only possible if in the believer himself there is a divine element which rediscovers itself, its own nature, in that on which it believes, even if it be unconscious that what it has found is its own nature.

Although Hegel is groping admirably towards his own distinctive contribution to philosophy, all of this is still prephilosophical in that it offers no attempt at rational justification. At any rate, we are assured that we are capable of a faith which *is* a knowledge of the infinite, and from this assertion is drawn a startling conclusion regarding the relationship of man to God: "Hence faith in the divine grows out of the divinity of the believer's own nature; only a modification of the Godhead can know the Godhead." It seems that Hegel is moving away from Christian orthodoxy when he concludes, "All thought of a difference in essence between Jesus and those in whom faith in him has become life, in whom the divine is present, must be eliminated."[35] Hegel's theological **panentheism** is beginning to emerge from his efforts to relate the finite and the infinite.

The final piece of Hegel's prephilosophical writings to be considered here is his "Fragment of a System," written in 1800, which indicates his struggle to cast his theological ideas into more systematic form. The human individual is seen as different from but unified with that which transcends him: "The concept of individuality includes opposition to infinite variety and also inner association with it." God is now conceived as "spirit," as the "all-living and all-powerful infinite life." It is religion, rather than philosophy, which realizes the "self-elevation of man . . . from finite life to infinite life"—and, as we shall see, this was to remain his sense of "religion" for the duration of his intellectual career. Yet even here man's rational thought is acknowledged as limited in its capacity to grasp reality conceptually as a unified whole, so that "what has been called a union of synthesis and antithesis is not something propounded by the understanding or by reflection but has a character of its own, namely, that of being a reality beyond all reflection." Although he is using what will become the language of his dialectical logic, Hegel has not figured out how we can achieve rational knowledge of God despite Kant's critical admonitions. Only his own epistemological critique can enable him to overcome the forbidding dichotomies of Kant. He has to conclude by subordinating philosophical reflection to the "self-elevation" of religious worship:

> Philosophy therefore has to stop short of religion because it is a process of thinking and, as such a process, implies an opposition with nonthinking [processes] as well as the opposition between the thinking mind and the object of thought.

Thus, philosophy finds itself forced "to place the true infinite outside its confines."[36] By this stage of his development, Hegel is breaking from Kant. However, in order to argue convincingly against the latter, he must shift from theological ruminations to philosophical critique. In a letter to Schelling written just a few weeks after this fragment, he describes himself as "inevitably driven toward science" and needing to cast his ideas into "the form of reflection and thus at once of a system."[37] In short, he must commit his time and efforts to a religious epistemology.

Faith and Knowledge. Hegel's *Faith and Knowledge* represents a significant link between his prephilosophical religious writings and his original system. It was written after his move to Jena in 1801 (published in 1803) and arose in the context of his first job as a philosophy lecturer in the university and of his association with the philosophically established Schelling. Although this essay is more a polemic (against Kant, Jacobi, and Fichte) than the formulation of an original position, it is philosophical in a way that none of the previous *Early Theological Writings* discussed above can be said to be. For our purposes, three of its elements, all of which are pertinent to Hegel's theory of knowledge, can be fruitfully discussed (in the next three paragraphs): (1) his positioning himself against the dominant philosophy of modern times; (2) his critique of the Kantian philosophy in particular; and (3) his indications of a possible unity between faith and knowledge.

The subtitle of the work, *Reflective Philosophy of Subjectivity*, provides valuable insight into Hegel's characterization of modern philosophy in general. It reflects on the objects of experience, rather than speculating about transcendent reality; and it ends up with the subject of that experience as its ultimate reference point. In the process, it has moved from the medieval conception of "the handmaid of faith" and "has irresistibly affirmed its absolute autonomy," setting up a strict "opposition of faith and knowledge." Knowledge is restricted to the contingent, finite arena of phenomena. "Enlightened Reason," on this view, becomes "mere intellect, acknowledges its own nothingness by placing that which is better than it in a *faith outside and above* itself, as a *beyond* [to be believed in]." This orientation of modern philosophy is pronounced in Kant's writings, which are so obviously designed to limit knowledge in order to make room for belief, which must then be justified as rational. Thus, says Hegel, "Philosophy has made itself the handmaid of a faith once more," only this time one which is autonomously constituted rather than one externally imposed. Hegel laments the tendency of modern philosophy to view the

Absolute as being "beyond Reason." Especially in the last half of the eighteenth century, according to thinkers such as Hume, Kant, and Fichte, "God is something incomprehensible and unthinkable. Knowledge knows nothing save that it knows nothing; it must take refuge in faith." If we can know only phenomenal appearances, if our only access to objective reality is necessarily filtered through the representations of subjectivity, then everything is in itself unknowable and merely an object of possible belief. But Reason requires the truth, which can only be of reality, for its survival; and to deny itself access to that is an act of intellectual suicide:

> Thus what used to be regarded as the death of philosophy, that Reason should renounce its existence in the Absolute, excluding itself totally from it and relating itself to it only negatively, became now the zenith of philosophy.

Reflective thought has become so mired in "the empirical world" because its "fixed point of departure" is "the empirical subject," which is seen as conditioning and limiting all its possible objects. This, for Hegel, is "the dogmatism of the Enlightenment." Thus, it follows, on this view, that "the sphere of the eternal is the incalculable, the inconceivable, the empty—an incognizable God beyond the boundary stakes of Reason." By the time modern philosophy gets to Locke, empirical subjectivity has allegedly established limits such that transcendent reality represents "a sphere that is nothing for intuition since intuition is only allowed to be sensuous and limited." It was Locke and his followers, Hegel says, who "transformed philosophy into empirical psychology. They raised the standpoint of the subject, the standpoint of absolutely existing finitude, to the first and highest place." Hegel condemns this perspective as a "realism of finitude," not acknowledging that Locke's metaphysics raises him to a demonstrative knowledge of infinity or that his famous Irish disciple, George Berkeley, generates an idealism from this starting point. More recently, Hegel complains,

> The philosophies of Kant, Jacobi, and Fichte are the completion and idealization of this empirical psychology; they consist in coming to understand that the infinite concept is strictly opposed to the empirical. They understood the sphere of this antithesis, a finite and an infinite, to be absolute: but [they did not see that] if infinity is thus set up against finitude, each is as finite as the other.

Although Hegel is correct that Kant sees no cognitive synthesis of the finite and the infinite to be possible, it does not follow that this necessarily represents a limitation of the infinite in such a way that it becomes finite—for Kant it only signifies the limits of the finite knower. Even though this perspective rises above realism, Hegel condemns it as "an idealism of the finite." Such a truncated conception of Reason does not allow us legitimately to "aim at the cognition of God, but only of what is called the cognition of man. This so-called man and his humanity conceived as a rigidly, insuperably finite sort of Reason form philosophy's absolute standpoint."[38] What sort of philosophical theology worthy of the name, Hegel wonders, can result from a phenomenalistic theory rooted in the finite subject and doomed to remain reflective because of its utter denial of speculative knowledge of reality?

Hegel's critique of Kant is consistent with this general analysis. Hegel praises his departure from empirical realism: "The Kantian philosophy has the merit of being idealism." At the same time, however, he attacks it for its strict dichotomy between the finite and the infinite, for denying rational knowledge of the latter, and thus for reducing metaphysics to epistemology:

> In so doing, it falls back into absolute finitude and subjectivity, and the whole task and content of this philosophy is, not the cognition of the Absolute, but the cognition of this subjectivity. In other words, it is a critique of the cognitive faculties.

To this extent, despite its status as an idealism, the Kantian philosophy "confines itself to Locke's goal, that is, to an investigation of the finite intellect." And even though "Kant reproaches Hume" for his failure to rise to the universal and prides himself on constructively addressing the issue of how synthetic *a priori* judgments are possible, Hegel objects that "like Hume he stopped at the *subjective* and external meaning of this question and believed he had established that rational cognition is impossible." But this seems unfair to Kant, who does achieve the sort of universality in his theory of knowledge (and ethical theory) that allows him to avoid Hume's skepticism, who strives for and, one might say, achieves an objective point of view which far surpasses Humean relativism, and who is anything but superficial in his treatment of the possibility of synthetic *a priori* judgments. It is true that Kant thought he had established the impossibility of rational cognition of the sort the mature Hegel will try to justify. But he does not attempt to do this, and does not succeed in doing so, in the Humean manner. Hegel acknowledges that Kant offers us a "synthesis" of sorts in addition to the "antithesis" of the manifold of intuition. Yet this synthetic "unity of apperception" only "appears in consciousness as judgment." This is a limited synthesis imposed on the given manifold by consciousness itself in the constituting of its judgments and falls woefully short of a real, "absolute synthesis" which is given to the mind as discoverable and knowable. "The absolute synthesis is absolute insofar as it is not an aggregate of manifolds which are first picked up, and then the synthesis supervenes upon them afterwards." Kant's limited synthesis allegedly fails to overcome the antithesis between subjectivity and objectivity, merely absorbing the latter into the former, and is utterly incapable of reconciling the finite and the infinite. "It would seem, then, as if critical idealism consisted in nothing but the formal knowledge that the subject and the things or the non-Ego exist each for itself." The dichotomy of subject and object is dealt with here only by characterizing them as conceptually correlative in the matrix of human experience: "The absolute identity of the subject and the object has passed into this formal or more properly, psychological idealism." Hegel shrewdly identifies the crux of what he takes to be Kant's problem: "Cognition of appearances is dogmatically regarded as the only kind of cognition there is, and rational cognition is denied." Denying any rational knowledge of reality which might make possible an absolute synthesis, Kant is left with "a dualism" of subject and object, of our finite experience and our idea of the infinite. Even his idealism, Hegel somewhat strangely remarks, "is nothing but an extension of Locke's view," although he praises Kant for the "infinite gain" of that extension. Even when Kant achieves "the speculative Idea" of Reason, it is so devoid of content that it must be presented as "a merely regulative and not a constitutive principle."[39] From Hegel's perspective, such a theory is doomed to regard faith and knowledge as irreconcilably opposed.

What indications, then, is he prepared to offer of his own alternative? They are relatively few and fall short of systematic development. But they include the insight that the experienced antithesis between subjective unity and objective manifold must be genuinely synthesized and not merely "in a formal way, as something alien." What is needed to accomplish this is "the middle term" adequate for such a synthesis, "which is Reason." Hegel hopes that, if stripped of "some of the popular and unphilosophical garments in which it is decked," Kant's philosophy might yet expose "the Idea that Reason does have absolute reality, . . . that infinite thought is at the same time absolute reality—or in short we shall find the absolute identity of thought and being." It is this "Idea of the absolute identity of thought and being," which Hegel says is the truth of the ontological argument, that constitutes the fundamental claim of the absolute idealism he would go on to construct. We must establish a "philosophy of the Absolute" which overcomes the antithetical dualism between the unknowable idea of an abstract infinite and the finite reality experienced. "In [truly philosophical] cognition, infinity as this negative significance of the Absolute is conditioned by the positive Idea that being is strictly nothing outside of the infinite, or apart from the Ego and thought. Both being and thought are one." In the final paragraph of *Faith and Knowledge*, Hegel observes that the Christianity of his day finds itself distressed by "the feeling that 'God Himself is dead.'" This **alienation** can only be transcended by means of a higher synthesis. He concludes somewhat mysteriously by saying that what is needed is a "speculative Good Friday," since "the highest totality can and must achieve its resurrection."[40] We might interpret this strange remark as signifying that the death of "the Reflective Philosophy of Subjectivity" must be endured in order that the speculative philosophy of Absolute Idealism might arise. But then two things must be accomplished: that death-blow must be completed, and a new philosophy must be systematically developed. The more thorough and cogent achievement of both of these objectives would require a radically original contribution to intellectual history.

Dialectical Logic. Hegel's dialectical logic constitutes the core of his theory of knowledge; it is utilized in his masterpiece, the *Phenomenology of Spirit*, and is expounded in both his larger and lesser works on logic (the *Science of Logic* and the *Encyclopaedia Logic*, respectively). Its presentation is typically made in the context of his critique of Kant for three reasons, as he explains in a footnote: first, however severely Kantian philosophy is to be criticized, "it constitutes the base and the starting-point of recent German philosophy"; second, even more recent philosophizing "does *not* go beyond the Kantian results, that reason cannot acquire knowledge of any true content or subject-matter and in regard to absolute truth must be directed to faith"; and, third, because it denies the very possibility of knowledge through metaphysical (including theological) speculation, the "Kantian philosophy thus serves as a cushion for intellectual indolence."[41] Kant had provided an all-too-convenient excuse for not bothering to attempt any such speculation, and that excuse was too eagerly accepted by Hegel's generation. If Kant's epistemology, with its logic of the understanding, were allowed to thrive unchallenged, philosophy would be cut off from what Hegel (in the *Phenomenology*) takes to be its primary concern, "the actual cognition of what truly is."[42] Consequently, the restriction of knowledge to the realm of sense experience, made by Kant and other proponents of "*reflective* understanding" (as opposed to speculative reason), is repudiated as the irrational

> view that truth rests on sensuous reality, . . . that reason left to its own resources engenders only figments of the brain. In this self-renunciation on the part of

reason, the Notion of truth is lost; it is limited to knowing only subjective truth, only phenomena, appearances, only something to which the nature of the object itself does not correspond: knowing has lapsed into opinion.

Then Hegel sarcastically adds,

This is like attributing to someone a correct perception, with the rider that nevertheless he is incapable of perceiving what is true but only what is false. Absurd as this would be, it would not be more so than a true knowledge which did not know the object as it is in itself.[43]

Kant goes wrong, in Hegel's view, in his insistence that philosophy must be based on a merely reflective epistemology, that "Thought must itself investigate its own capacity of knowledge." To be sure, this may sound like a reasonable demand, that we should "become acquainted with the instrument, before we undertake the work for which it is to be employed; for if the instrument be insufficient, all our trouble will be spent in vain." But, despite the initial plausibility of this view, Hegel thinks that the project is doomed to failure from the start. He subjects the requirement to heavy ridicule, saying that an examination of the so-called instrument of knowledge presupposes our already knowing something: "But to seek to know before we know is as absurd as the wise resolution of Scholasticus, not to venture into the water until he had learned to swim."[44] A second problem with reflective philosophy's analogy of knowledge to an instrument which must be critically investigated before it can be securely utilized is that the employment of any instrument necessarily modifies the subject matter on which it is used. This view of knowledge as "the instrument for getting hold of absolute being" allegedly is self-defeating and predetermines Kant's problematic restriction of knowledge to phenomena, i.e., to reality only as it appears to us after being affected by the instrument. Hegel also notes that another analogy frequently used, regarding knowledge as "a more or less passive medium through which the light of truth reaches us," is subject to fundamentally the same criticism, that knowledge distorts its object.[45] However, it is not clear that the Kantian project depends on such admittedly limited analogies as Hegel supposes. For Kant knowledge is an undisputed fact of human experience, his task being the transcendental one of determining its necessary conditions and limits. Whatever analogies might prove to be relatively useful for conceiving of it, for Kant as for Hegel, knowledge is both reflective and self-reflective and may be both critical and self-critical; and to this extent, of course, descriptive analogies do break down. Second, even if a critical investigation such as Kant proposes is not a presupposition of any knowledge whatsoever, it *is* necessary for an epistemological understanding of our own cognitive faculties.

Whereas Kant presents a logic of the understanding, whose object is the finite and conditioned, Hegel will develop a logic of reason, which aims at the infinite and unconditioned. Hegel praises Kant for clearly distinguishing "between Reason and Understanding" and for pointing up the limits of the latter. "But his mistake was to stop at the purely negative point of view" and to restrict knowledge to the bounds legitimate for the understanding, viewing the object of reason as beyond the pale of possible human knowledge. The identification of reason with a transgression of the legitimate limits of understanding involves the degradation of reason to something finite, whereas Hegel would have it acknowledged as infinite. "The real infinite, far from being a mere transcendence of the finite, always involves the absorption of the finite into its own fuller nature." Against "the subjective idealism of the Critical philosophy," Hegel is constructing an "absolute idealism," which can justify theological knowledge.[46] Hegel's infinite Reason will absorb, and not merely transcend, the finite understanding. But because he is stuck on the level of the understanding, which he assumes sets all the rules for cognition, Kant thinks in terms of contrasts and oppositions, failing (or refusing) to see more inclusive syntheses, such as that represented by the idea of the "real infinite," which can be grasped only by reason.

> This Idea is equally something beyond the grasp of the Understanding and is for it a secret, for it is the very nature of the Understanding to hold fast by and keep unchangeably to the idea that the categories of thought are absolutely exclusive and different.[47]

Hegel has no doubt that knowledge of the finite world, achieved through the understanding, is possible and valuable. The question is whether, as Kant maintained, this is the only sort of knowledge humanly possible. Hegel's claim is that knowledge is also possible at the level of reason, knowledge of the infinite and unconditioned. Whereas Kant's logic of the understanding distinguishes particular objects of experience by categorizing them, Hegel maintains that it is "in the grasping of opposites in their unity or of the positive in the negative, that speculative thought consists." This is the level of reason, which requires its own logic to supplant the categorical logic of the understanding. Hegel mocks the limited view "that reason is incapable of knowing the infinite; a strange result for—since the infinite is the Reasonable—it asserts that reason is incapable of knowing the Reasonable."[48] Hegel's speculative knowledge differs from Kant's reflective knowledge in not being necessarily based on sensible intuition; for Hegel, intellectual intuition, which Kant thought the privilege of God alone, is possible for man. Hegel does not deny the claim (common to empiricism and Kant's critical idealism) that "experience affords the one sole foundation for cognitions." But what he finds objectionable is the narrow restriction of all experience to sense experience. It is as if, through Kant, German philosophy has capitulated to the demands of British empiricism, abdicating its speculative function (evident, for example, in Leibniz) and concentrating attention on its critical function alone, as if it "can furnish only a *criticism* of knowledge, not a *doctrine* of the infinite."[49] Hegel's final verdict concerning this aspect of Kant's thought is that it constitutes "a complete philosophy of the Understanding, which renounces Reason," that it is only "a good introduction to Philosophy." It is Kant's reductionistic analysis of reason and its powers that makes him an enemy dangerous enough to be worthy of attack:

> The man who speaks of the *merely* finite, of *merely* human reason, and of the limits to mere reason, lies against the spirit, for the spirit as infinite and universal, as self-comprehension, comprehends itself not in a "merely" nor in limits, nor in the finite as such. It has nothing to do with this, for it comprehends itself within itself alone, in its infinitude.[50]

Hegel holds that "the proper problem of logic" is the "study of truth." This makes his conception of logic different from the traditional Aristotelian view (embraced by Kant) that logic is a system of formal relationships divorced from metaphysical content. "*Logic therefore coincides with metaphysics, the science of things set and held in thoughts*—thoughts accredited able to express the essential reality of things."[51] Thus, it must have content rather than being purely formal. In an often quoted passage, Hegel says that logic exhibits "truth as it is without veil," that it "is the exposition of God as he is in his eternal essence before the creation of nature and a finite mind."[52] This metaphysical truth, which Hegel says must be the object of logic, will have to be pursued at the level of speculative reason, since Kant has shown that the understanding can grasp only partial truths. This truth, writes Hegel, "is the Idea, or the Absolute. The science of this Idea must form a system." What is needed here is the synthesis of all partial truths: "Truth, then, is only possible as a universe or totality of thought."[53] He expresses the same point more famously in his *Phenomenology*: "The True is the whole" (*Das Wahre ist das Ganze*). This Truth is not merely an abstract metaphysical principle; "everything turns on grasping and expressing the True, not only as *Substance*, but equally as *Subject*." The highest, all-inclusive reality must be of the nature of Spirit.

But spiritual life is not static; it must be viewed as dynamic **process**, as "in truth actual only in so far as it is the movement of positing itself. . . . It is the process of its own becoming."[54] This dynamic Spirit, which is the Truth sought by the logic of speculative reason, is also God.

If the Truth of Hegelian logic, metaphysical theology, and philosophy of religion is to be conceived as a process of becoming, a new logical method must be devised, one that rises above the oppositions of the Understanding and reveals the unity-in-difference that Hegel thinks characteristic of all thought and being; this new logical method is, of course, the dialectic. Hegel believes that it will provide us access to knowledge at the level of reason: "It is in this dialectic . . . , in the grasping of opposites in their unity or of the positive in the negative, that speculative thought consists." It must encompass and overcome antitheses by means of "forms of consciousness each of which in realizing itself at the same time resolves itself, has for its result its own negation—and so passes into a higher form." If this seems to violate the law of noncontradiction of Aristotelian logic, so much the worse for that law and that logic, which have held us back for too long. "All that is necessary to achieve scientific progress . . . is the recognition of the logical principle that the negative is just as much positive, or that what is self-contradictory does not resolve itself into a nullity." Out of the relationship between any particular thesis and its antithesis ought to emerge a new synthetic idea, which is not reducible to either of them or to their opposition. "It is a fresh Notion but higher and richer than its predecessor; for it is richer by the negation or opposite of the latter, therefore contains it, but also something more, and is the unity" of that thesis and its antithesis.[55] Thus, dialectical logic incorporates the limited truth of opposition but builds higher (for example, more adequate, more comprehensive) truth on that.

Only such a method, which recognizes and transcends "disparity" and "the negative," is adequate for comprehending the Absolute, with its "restless process of superseding itself." Because thought and reality interlock, and because reality is a unified whole, the understanding—which holds the principles of noncontradiction and excluded middle as ultimate—will not suffice. As a process, it is already implicitly reasonable. But it cannot provide what is needed, to overcome "the antithesis of being and knowing" by means of a metaphysical "*Logic* or *speculative* philosophy."[56] As Hegel writes in his lesser *Logic*,

> To see that thought in its very nature is dialectical, and that, as understanding, it must fall into contradiction—the negative of itself—will form one of the main lessons of logic.

The dialectical principle, reaching beyond mere contradiction to grasp the unity of opposites, is allegedly inherent in all thought and reality.

> Wherever there is movement, wherever there is life, wherever anything is carried into effect in the actual world, there Dialectic is at work. It is also the soul of all knowledge which is truly scientific. . . . Everything that surrounds us may be viewed as an instance of Dialectic.

It is the method of dialectical logic which cancels the deficiencies and inadequacies of every limited, provisional definition of the Truth, while maintaining its accuracies and raising them to a higher level. Hegel has the ideal concept for such an appropriation of Truth. He bids us "note the double meaning of the German word *aufheben* (to put by, or set aside). We mean by it (1) to clear away, or annul . . . (2) to keep, or preserve"; and he comments that the word indicates "the speculative spirit of our language rising above the mere 'either-or' of understanding."[57] Unfortunately, we have no adequate English translation of the word in common usage, and it is usually translated as "to sublate" or "to supersede" (with the corresponding substantive forms, **"sublation"** and "supersession").

Absolute Idealism. Hegel's system of absolute idealism is a metaphysical extension of his theory of knowledge and is developed by means of this dialectical logic. Nowhere is this clearer than in his masterpiece, the *Phenomenology*, where he argues for "the identity of Thought and Being." This involves two dimensions: "the fact that Being is Thought" and its converse, that "Reason is the certainty of consciousness that it is all reality." This principle, in both its dimensions, underlies the Absolute Idealism which views all thought and reality as in the Spirit of the Absolute. The heart of Hegel's metaphysics is concisely expressed in his idealistic statement, "The spiritual alone is the *actual.*" If all reality is one and spiritual, how is it to be described? "Spirit is thus self-supporting, absolute, real being."[58] This is a philosophical way of saying that it is divine.

> The objects of philosophy, it is true, are upon the whole the same as those of religion. In both the object is Truth, in that supreme sense in which God and God only is the Truth. Both in like manner go on to treat of the finite worlds of nature and the human Mind, with their relation to each other and to their truth in God.[59]

But to say that all reality is spiritual is not a naive denial of matter, of physical reality, the existence of which is as undeniable as the stone at the tip of Dr. Samuel Johnson's boot. It is rather an assertion that spirit is "the truth" of matter, its ontological source and teleological end. It is not that matter does not "really" exist, but that even matter is essentially spiritual.

One of the most famous of Hegel's expressions of idealism holds,

> What is rational is actual and what is actual is rational.

The point is not that reality as it exists in fact is already fully rational; what is held to be rational is "actuality"—that is, reality insofar as it conforms to its ideal essence. Although Hegel tries to make this conviction more palatable by ascribing it to "the plain man" as well as to "the philosopher,"[60] he later faces up to the common prejudice against such a thesis:

> The actuality of the rational stands opposed by the popular fancy that Ideas and ideals are nothing but chimeras, and philosophy a mere system of such phantasms. It is also opposed by the very different fancy that Ideas and ideals are something far too excellent to have actuality, or something too impotent to procure it for themselves.

But it is because things are the expression of Spirit that thought is capable of expressing their essential reality. To claim that actuality is spiritual does not amount to saying that all things "really" are—or have—ideas or minds; this assertion would surely fly in the face of common experience, as Hegel would prefer not to do. In calling thought "the heart and soul of the world," he does not mean to characterize the things of material nature, for example, as actually conscious. Indeed, he admits to "a certain repugnance against making thought the inward function of things, especially as we speak of thought as marking the divergence of man from nature." Hegel's thesis is rather that all things are derived from Mind, that Spirit is their ultimate source. But this is not to say that things are the products of any finite (for example, human) mind: "nothing can be more obvious than that anything we only think or conceive is not on that account actual." This was allegedly the implicit mistake of Kant's "subjective idealism," which placed the locus of truth in the human "subject-mind." Because Kant offers no higher perspective than that of the subjective thinker, "The divorce between thought and thing is mainly the work of the Critical Philosophy." But if finite mind cannot ground the ideal intelligibility of reality, it is also true that the things of this world are not self-explanatory or self-sufficient;

> and the true and proper case of these things, finite as they are, is to have their existence founded not in themselves but in the universal divine Idea. This view of things, it is true, is as idealist as Kant's; but in contradistinction to the subjective idealism of the Critical philosophy should be termed absolute idealism.[61]

Does Hegel offer any argument to support this insight that constitutes the core of his system? In the sense of a concise proof he does not. The only "demonstration" seems to be the Hegelian system itself. If, having studied it, we are left unconvinced, then presumably we have failed to comprehend it—perhaps because we are still squinting through the spectacles of the understanding. One might object that Hegel, in effect, has set his principle of the identification of thought and being above criticism by making it a rational insight which the understanding cannot comprehend. Despite Hegel's aversion to presuppositions, this is as much a postulate of the Hegelian system as freedom, immortality, and God are postulates of Kant's ethical theory. If the postulate renders intelligible reality as we experience it (a subjective judgment for each of us to make), then it is reasonable for us to accept it "as if" it were (objectively) true. It is only in this sense, perhaps, that the Hegelian system can be said to provide an "argument" on behalf of the identification of thought and being. The postulate (if it now can be so called) of this identity is to propel us towards the ultimate vision of the Absolute as the "unity of the Subjective and Objective Idea,"[62] in which the system culminates.

Hegel's second metaphysical identification, of finite and infinite reason, may seem as provocative, as shocking, and as unacceptable as his first. God or the Absolute is characterized as "*infinite thought.*" In religion and in philosophy man is to be related to this "*infinite thought.*" But this requires that man—weak, limited, and evil as he often is—should also be of a spiritual nature, alive and with the capacity for thought. Yet, if it is "the very essence of thought to be infinite,"[63] as Hegel claims, and if man—who is spiritual and, thus, like God—is capable of thought, then he must participate in the divine life. The most difficult principle of Hegel's system for most of us is that we, finite and evil though we be, share in the life of infinite reason. He means neither to deny human finitude nor to dismiss it as an illusion although it

> must be regarded not as a fixed determination, but must be recognized as a mere moment. . . . Mind *qua* mind *is* not finite, it *has* finitude within itself, but only as a finitude which is to be, and has been, reduced to a moment.

It is only the understanding with its rigid "either-or" abstractions that is stuck on man's finitude, insisting on a gulf between it and the Infinite,

> maintaining that mind is *either* limited *or* unlimited. Finitude, truly comprehended, is as we have said, contained in infinitude, limitation in the unlimited. Mind is, therefore, *as well* infinite as finite, and *neither* merely the one *nor* merely the other.[64]

This doctrine of the union of the infinite and the finite is more familiar to most of us as applied to Jesus: "The individual man grasped as also in unity with the divine essence is the object of the Christian religion."[65] This is "the dogma revealed through Christ to men, of the unity of the divine and human nature, according to which the subjective and the objective Idea—man and God—are one."[66] The truth of religion—a truth which is fully explicated and comprehended by philosophy—is that the otherness of God and man is to be "sublated" or "superseded" in their union. God, as the "true infinite," is not what is other than the finite (for this, says Hegel, is only another-larger-finite), but what *includes* the finite. At the level of Absolute Mind (that of art, religion, and philosophy), our consciousness "relates itself no longer to something that is other than itself, and that is limited, but to the unlimited and infinite, and this is an infinite relation." If this is, indeed, the case, then religious awareness and self-awareness would seem to be mutually implicative.

> All knowledge, all conviction, all piety, regarded from the point of view which we are considering, is based on the principle that in the spirit, as such, the consciousness of God exists immediately with the consciousness of its self.

Hegel acknowledges the need to prove the union of finite spirit and the infinite Spirit and tries to do so in two ways. He first argues that reason is one and should not be fragmented:

> there cannot be a Divine reason and a human, there cannot be a Divine Spirit and a human, which are *absolutely different*. Human reason . . . is the divine in man. . . . God is present, omnipresent, and exists as Spirit in all spirits.[67]

What this argument presumes, and what is quite controversial, is the existence and all-inclusiveness of infinite reason. Although we are told repeatedly that "there is no gulf between the Infinite and the finite,"[68] this alleged unity rests upon the idealist's identification of thought and being, which we have already considered.

Hegel's second way of arguing for the union of the finite and the Infinite is based on the alleged limits of our finite reason. His argument is that, even in considering these supposed boundaries, reason transcends and, in effect, annuls them. "No one knows, or even feels, that anything is a limit or defect, until he is at the same time above and beyond it."[69] In acknowledging our own finitude, we supposedly comprehend the apparent limit between ourselves and the Infinite. "Thus the limitation of finiteness only exists for us in so far as we are above and beyond it." Yet the recognition of something does *not* entail its comprehension. The recognition of a limit involves the intimation of something beyond it; but that "something beyond" may well remain what Locke called a "something I know not what." In short, what is being criticized here is Hegel's assumption that we do comprehend our own finitude; to use a Kantian distinction, we seem to be dealing with a boundary-concept that can be thought but not known (by us). Hegel himself, it is interesting to note, foresaw this criticism; for he imagines his critics admitting that a looking beyond the limit is involved while maintaining that "this going out of ourselves is, however, merely something attempted, a mere yearning which does not attain to what it seeks."[70] At any rate, this second argument for the unity of the finite and the infinite seems no more cogent and conclusive than the first.

The identification of finite and infinite reason—like that of thought and being—is a principle which is fundamental to Hegel's philosophy of religion. Yet it, like that other basic principle, is not conclusively demonstrated and seems to function as a postulate requiring an act of faith. It has been necessary to spend so much time and space critically analyzing these twin identifications of Hegel's because the whole of his mature philosophy of religion is founded on them. If we grant Hegel these two basic principles of identity, it becomes necessary to concede to him (at least in substance) his entire basic system.

If Hegel is correct, all of reality is essentially one (this is his "monism"), so that the experience, awareness, and knowledge of anything at least implicitly involves its relation to God; ultimately everything is God, and whatever exists as finite has its reality in God (this is his "panentheism"). All the objects of our experience are expressions of God. The self-manifestation of God is to be found in nature and in history. The nature of the divine Idea is "to disclose itself, to posit this Other outside itself and to take it back again into itself, in order to be subjectivity and Spirit." God, as self-revealed in space, is the natural order: "Nature is Spirit estranged from itself; in Nature, Spirit lets itself go."[71] This self-alienation of God is overcome through the dialectically developing process of knowledge represented by history. Hegel holds that Reason rules the world and that "the history of the world, therefore, presents us with a rational process." Hegel sees this process presenting itself in three main phases: the Oriental, the Greco-Roman, and the Germanic Christian. The Orientals represent an extremely limited thesis, in that they allegedly "only know that *one is free*," namely the ruler. Against this limited conception supposedly emerges the broader, more adequate truth underlying the contradictory of that thesis, not only one is free. The Greco-Roman consciousness became aware "that *some* are free," namely the citizens. Finally, says Hegel, "The German nations, under the influence of Christianity, were the first to attain the consciousness, that man, as man, is free." On this view (seen, for example, in Kantian ethics), each person is an autonomous ruler, morally speaking, *and* a citizen in a spiritual commonwealth; yet both the Oriental thesis and the Greco-Roman antithesis are denied as inadequate in this synthesis. "The History of the world is none other than the progress of the consciousness of Freedom";[72] here is the conclusion to which our study of history supposedly leads us.

The object of knowledge must be Truth. The object of Truth must be reality. And the only complete Truth must deal with the whole of reality. Man's pilgrimage towards this Absolute is gradual, often tedious, sometimes discouraging. This course, dramatically and brilliantly analyzed in the *Phenomenology*, is "the way of the Soul which journeys through the series of its own configurations as though they were the stations appointed for it by its own nature." The odyssey involves consciousness coming to grips with its lack of knowledge and potentially demoralizing misconceptions. "The road can therefore be regarded as the pathway of *doubt*, or more precisely as the way of despair." It carries us from the most extreme rudimentary experience of "sense-certainty," which "appears to be the *truest* knowledge" but is exposed as highly misleading and most inadequate, to the highest level of "absolute knowing," in which "it is Spirit that knows itself in the shape of Spirit." Along the way there are passages in which Hegel exhibits his dialectical reasoning, in magnificent fashion, such as those on "Lordship and Bondage" and "**Stoicism**, Scepticism, and the Unhappy Consciousness." But we cannot trace the many steps up the rungs of "the ladder" of knowledge. We shall rather focus on the highest rungs of art, religion, and philosophy constituting what Hegel calls Absolute Mind. "The *goal*, Absolute knowing, or Spirit that knows itself as Spirit,"[73] calls for further analysis here. And the only adequate object of Absolute knowing is the Absolute or God.

God

Approach to God. Hegel's approach to God is neatly summarized in the concluding section of his *Encyclopaedia*, dealing with "Absolute Mind." If reality and truth constitute one, coherent, rational Whole, as we have seen Hegel assert, it is not surprising that we should be able to apprehend this Whole in different ways, that it should admit of a variety of more or less adequate perspectives. "The subjective consciousness of the absolute spirit is essentially and intrinsically a process" in which truth is progressively achieved at the levels of art, religion, and philosophy. Aesthetic intuition, religious belief, and philosophical knowledge are viewed as different forms of man's attempts to grasp the Absolute; there is an ultimate identification of the Beautiful, the Holy, and the True as their common object. Man's "consciousness of the Absolute first takes shape," in its most immediate form, "in Art," representing it in "the shape or form of *Beauty*." Hegel analyzes various types of aesthetic experience: "*Romantic art*" is distinguished in form from "*symbolic art*" and "*classical art*." By contrast with the "sensuous externality attaching to the beautiful" found in artistic creation, religion "essentially" must "be *revealed*, and, what is more, revealed *by God*"; and this revelation must be internally appropriated in faith. Parallel to Hegel's three main phases of world history are the Oriental religions of nature, the Greco-Roman religions of individuality, and the absolute religion of Christianity. Whereas art provides an immediate, external representation of the Absolute, in religion God is revealed through the medium of pictorial thought as the object of internal belief. It is philosophy, according to Hegel, that "is the unity of Art and Religion. Whereas the vision-method of Art, external in point of form, is but subjective production" and religion, internalized in faith, is objective revelation,

> Philosophy not merely keeps them together to make a totality, but even unifies them into the simple spiritual vision, and then in that raises them to self-conscious thought. Such consciousness is thus the intelligible unity (cognized by thought) of art and religion, in which the diverse elements in the content are cognized as necessary.

To put this into the language of the dialectic, philosophy synthesizes the external beauty of subjective production and the internalized belief in the holy as objectively revealed to achieve truth as both constituted by and eternally beyond human knowing. "The eternal Idea," which is the content of philosophical speculation, presents itself to our consciousness "as absolute Mind," while requiring our awareness for its self-realization. However, heterodox and even blasphemous this last point might sound, Hegel is explicit in holding that the self-revelation of the Absolute requires the awareness of us to whom that revelation is made: "God is God only so far as he knows himself: his self-knowledge is, further, a self-consciousness in man and man's knowledge of God, which proceeds to man's self-knowledge *in* God."[74] Our awareness is ultimately oriented toward the Absolute, and the Absolute can only be Absolute in relation to our awareness. The relationship between God and man is therefore mutual and necessary.

We shall not consider art's approach to God much here, although, of course, Hegel has a great deal to say about it in his lectures on fine art. Its kinship with the other two realms of Absolute Mind is emphasized early on in the Introduction to these lectures:

> Fine art is not art in the true sense of the term until . . . it has established itself in a sphere which it shares with religion and philosophy, becoming thereby merely one mode and form through which the *Divine*

is expressed. This orientation to God as its object "is an attribute which art shares in common with religion and philosophy"; its differentiating characteristic is that it expresses this divine object "in sensuous form." Hegel analyzes "the symbolic type of art" that is architecture, "the classical type of art" that is sculpture, and the "romantic type of art" represented by painting, music, and poetry. In its various forms art creatively presents "the self-unfolding Idea of beauty."[75] We shall focus on religion's approach to God in the final section of this chapter and on that of philosophy in this one.

The relationship between religion and philosophy is of particular concern to us here, and the continuum between them must be emphasized.

> The object of religion as well as of philosophy is eternal truth in its objectivity, God and nothing but God, and the explication of God. Philosophy is not a wisdom of the world, but is knowledge of what is not of the world; it is . . . knowledge of that which is eternal, of what God is, and what flows out of His nature.

Philosophy, in Hegel's sense of the word, although it is higher (because more adequate) than religion, cannot be independent of it. "Philosophy, therefore, only unfolds itself when it unfolds religion, and in unfolding itself it unfolds religion." This follows from the fact that they share the same content.

> Thus religion and philosophy come to be one. Philosophy is itself, in fact, worship; it is religion, for in the same way it renounces subjective notions and opinions in order to occupy itself with God. Philosophy is thus identical with religion

in relation to its objective content. "It is in the peculiar way in which they both occupy themselves with God that the distinction comes out."[76] Where religious faith assumes the form of pictorial thought, philosophical knowledge requires conceptual thought.

"Thus Religion has a content in common with Philosophy, the forms alone being different." Although he stresses the continuity between religion and philosophy and identifies their common content, Hegel does not ignore their differences, contrasting the intuitive symbols of religion with the more precise concepts of philosophy. We can analyze the contrast point by point. First, unlike religion, philosophy recognizes an obligation to be presuppositionless. "It is required by Philosophy that it should justify its beginning and its manner of knowledge, and Philosophy has thus placed itself in opposition to Religion." Second, whereas philosophy is purely conceptual, a matter of thought, religion is fundamentally a matter of feeling—"that in which it reveals itself is the heart." Third, there is "the mythical aspect of Religion"; by contrast, "Mythology must remain excluded from our history of Philosophy." Whereas philosophy is concerned "with thoughts which are explicit," it is true that "all Religion is thinking,"[77] and not mere feeling, but this is implicit thought, veiled in mythical or symbolic imagery. Fourth, whereas religious faith remains subjective, the approach of philosophy is objective: "It is the science of thinking Reason, just as religious faith is the consciousness and the absolute conviction of the truth of Reason presented in the form of picture-thinking."[78] Fifth, as was shown in the *Phenomenology*, religion is a necessary and logically prior evolutionary stage in the rise of consciousness to philosophy. Hegel writes in his *Encyclopaedia* that "religion may well exist without philosophy, but philosophy not without religion—which it rather includes."[79] Thus, although religion and philosophy share a common content, they are different in form; and it is the form of the latter that makes it more adequate in expressing that content.

Despite the extreme rationalism of Hegel's absolute idealism, he regards faith, with its pictorial symbols, as a necessary step on the road to knowledge, which is never simply superseded.

> For, though philosophy must not allow herself to be overawed by religion, . . . she cannot afford to neglect these popular conceptions. The tales and allegories of religion, which have enjoyed for thousands of years the veneration of nations, are not to be set aside as antiquated even now.

Hegel warns us against the intuitionist position (of Jacobi) which confuses faith and knowledge while trying to distinguish between them. "Thus, we often find knowledge contrasted with faith, and faith at the same time explained to be an underivative or intuitive knowledge."[80] Rather than viewing faith as opposed to knowledge, Hegel sees it dialectically as a lower order of knowledge: "belief or faith is not opposite to consciousness or knowledge, but rather . . . belief is only a particular form of the latter."[81] Although this might seem vague, it becomes intelligible when we recall Hegel's distinction between categorical knowledge at the level of the understanding (the only kind Kant thought humanly possible) and speculative knowledge at the level of reason (which Hegel thinks available in metaphysical philosophy). Faith is opposed to the knowledge of the understanding; and, as Kant showed, it becomes necessary, due to the limitations of this kind of knowledge; but, like the knowledge of the understanding, faith is an inferior mode of knowing what can be apprehended adequately only by speculative reason.

In 1822, Hegel wrote a still neglected essay (from which we have already considered a quotation) on "Reason and Religious Truth" as a foreword to a book by one of his followers. There he says that the alleged "opposition between faith and reason," which has been discussed for centuries,

> is such that the human spirit cannot turn its back on either faith or reason; each shows itself to be so deeply rooted in man's innermost self-consciousness that when they come into conflict, he is shaken to the depths of his being and his inner disharmony makes his condition one of utter wretchedness.

So, a reconciliation must be sought by any serious philosopher of religion. But Hegel warns against the sort of "superficial, barren peace" between faith and reason, which would either gloss over their difference or virtually exclude one in favor of the other, and his criticism can be directed against both Kierkegaard after him and Kant before him:

> It would be an unsatisfactory peace if, on the one hand, faith has lost all substantial meaning, only the empty husk of subjective conviction remaining, or, on the other hand, reason had renounced all claim to a knowledge of the Truth, the human spirit being left with only appearances and feelings for its sustenance.

What is called for is rather a synthesis of existential commitment and cognitive content.

> For I understand by faith neither the merely subjective state of belief which is restricted to the form of certainty, leaving untouched the nature of the content, if any, of the belief, nor on the other hand only the *credo*, the church's confession of faith which can be recited and learnt by rote without communicating itself to man's innermost self.

He wants to emphasize equally both elements of faith—an objective content and subjective feeling relating the whole self to that content. "I hold that faith, in the true, ancient sense of the word, is a unity of both these meanings, including the one no less than the other." Feelings are indeed crucial to religious faith, but they should not be emphasized to such an extent that they leave no place for objective thought, which is likewise essential to—if only implicit in—religious faith. The Enlightenment thinker, restricting knowledge to the sphere of phenomena, "has emptied Truth of all content whatever so that nothing remains for it except, on the one hand, the pure negative, the *caput mortuum* of a merely abstract *Being*, and, on the other hand, a finite material." Thus, having consigned God to a transcendent Beyond to which knowledge is denied access, Kant leaves us only a faith which, although nominally "rational," easily degenerates into mere subjective conviction. "But the Understanding, having dissipated all this content, has again veiled God from human knowledge and reduced Him to the status of something merely yearned for." This can lead to religious emotivism, devoid of any cognitive content. "The only way now in which this need can still be satisfied is for spirit to fall back on *feelings*." Man's feelings in relation to God, if severed from rational knowledge, are likely to take the form of subservience.

> If religion in man is based only on a feeling, then the nature of that feeling can be none other than the *feeling of his dependence*, and so a dog would be the best Christian for it possesses this in the highest degree and lives mainly in this feeling.

Despite this mockery (of Friedrich Schleiermacher, his theological colleague at Berlin), Hegel does not want to suggest that feelings do not play an important role in religious faith. But because "the essential nature of feeling as such is to be a *mere form*, indeterminate on its own account and capable of holding any content whatever," it cannot constitute a criterion of legitimacy for its object.

> Religion, like duty and right, also becomes and should become a matter of feeling and dwell in one's heart. . . . Only, it is quite another matter whether such a content as God, Truth, freedom, as simply felt, is supposed to have its warrant in feeling.

If the only adequate object of knowledge is the Truth, and this Truth is a trans-phenomenal Whole identified with God, as Hegel has maintained, then those (like Kant) who deny knowledge of God subvert philosophy as well as theology.

> What is a theology without a knowledge of God? Precisely what a philosophy is without that knowledge, sounding brass and a tinkling cymbal![82]

Hegel's critique of Kant is not convincing here. The rational faith of Kant is supposedly certified by objective, universal demands of reason. To this extent, it does not seem that his denial of theological knowledge inevitably leads to either subjective intuitionism (as in Jacobi) or subjective emotivism (as in Schleiermacher)—either of which, as Hegel indicates, would prove objectionable. Hegel's critique is more effective against the radical fideism of someone like Kierkegaard. Any faith which is systematically divorced from all rational justification is blind and in danger of collapsing into fanaticism (what Locke called "enthusiasm"). Indeed (though this will sound anachronistic), as Kierkegaard is the greatest philosophical critic of Hegel, the reverse relationship may also apply.

Absolute Spirit. Hegel's view of Absolute Spirit is neither thoroughly nor systematically developed but can be reconstructed from scattered passages. When we strive to comprehend it, we may be initially drawn to the very abstract conception of pure being. But this analysis of the Absolute must be viewed as merely "the beginning of philosophy"; unless and until further "determination" is provided, it is "only an empty word."[83] The concept, although not wholly inappropriate, fails to do justice to the nature of the Absolute. Kant's "Ideal of Reason," the *ens realissimum*, fares no better for the same reason.

> Accordingly God, when he is defined to be the sum of all realities, the most real of beings, turns into a *mere abstract*. And the only term under which that most real of real things can be defined is that of Being—itself the height of abstraction.

Such a vapid view is similar to that which Hegel attributes to the

> modern "enlightenment" and abstract understanding, which is content to say *Il y a un être suprême*: and there lets the matter rest. . . . If God be the abstract supersensible Being, outside whom therefore lies all difference and all specific character, he is only a bare name, a mere *caput mortuum* of abstracting understanding.

Since indeterminate being is no more concrete a notion than that of nothing, Hegel claims, this is "a definition not a whit better than that of the **Buddhists**, who make God to be Nought, and who from that principle draw the further conclusion that self-annihilation is the means by which man becomes God."[84] This is not to deny that Being should characterize the Absolute Idea: "Being is the poorest of all abstractions; but the Notion is not so poor as not to contain this determination in it." However, that abstract determination does not exhaust the richness of the divine Idea: "Being is not the entire Notion, but is only one of its characteristics."[85]

As we have seen, Hegel holds that "everything turns on grasping and expressing the True, not only as *Substance*, but equally as *Subject*." This is the view of the Absolute as "living Substance," dynamic rather than static, determinate rather than merely abstract. So, as thought makes the conception of the Absolute concrete, it becomes clear that God is not merely Being but Life. Yet even this is not the most concrete determination of

God. As the antitheses of abstract Being and Nothing are synthesized in the richer concept of Becoming, so those of Substance and Subject are synthesized in the idea of Spirit.[86]

> God is more than life: he is Spirit. And therefore if the thought of the Absolute takes a starting-point . . . , the most true and adequate starting-point will be found in the nature of spirit alone.[87]

Here, finally, is a conception of God which is rich enough to pass muster.

> *The Absolute is Mind* (Spirit)—this is the supreme definition of the Absolute. To find this definition and to grasp its meaning and burden was, we may say, the ultimate purpose of all education and all philosophy.[88]

Yet even this perspective is inadequate without a recognition of the all-inclusive nature of the Absolute, in general, and of our ontological participation in it, in particular. We are told that "the Idea of Spirit means the unity of divine and human nature" and that "it is just the unity of divine and human nature which is itself the Absolute Spirit." By the time Hegel is writing these *Lectures on the Philosophy of Religion*, he seems to have resolved the problem with which he wrestled as a young man, of how to relate the finite and the infinite. These antitheses are now synthesized in God: "Spirit is accordingly the living Process by which the implicit unity of the divine and human natures becomes actual and comes to have a definite existence."[89] We shall soon consider the panentheistic implications of this unity.

Meanwhile, what are we to make of this grand, majestic vision? That art, religion, and philosophy all have ultimate reality as at least their implicit object, that the quest for that object must be rational, and that the Absolute thus pursued by reason is to be viewed as all-inclusive Spirit constitute a powerful worldview. It is of a piece with the Hegelian identifications we considered in the last section of this chapter: of final Truth as "the Whole," of Thought and Being, and of finite and infinite Reason. These identifications seem to function as fundamental postulates underlying Hegel's system, in the light of which what we have been considering here makes sense. But it does not seem that he is prepared to demonstrate them in the form of traditional deductive argumentation. Let us turn our attention now to his novel way of dealing with the old proofs of philosophical theology.

Proofs of God's Existence. Hegel's treatment of the proofs for God is quite different from that employed by pre-Kantian rational theologians. Hegel acknowledges that any attempt to prove the existence of God logically by syllogistic arguments must assume the finite, human perspective as its starting point and is, therefore, from its very beginning, inadequate:

> God, the absolute, the unconditioned, cannot . . . be proved. For proof, comprehension, means to discover conditions for something, to derive from conditions; but a derived absolute, God, &c., would thus not be absolute at all, would not be unconditioned, would not be God.[90]

Hegel does not, for the most part, try to refute Kant's devastating critique of the arguments for God (although, as we shall soon see, he does attempt to answer a specific reservation about the ontological argument) or to defend the proofs in their traditional form.

He rather tries to reinterpret the proofs as particular intellectual expressions of the need of finite spirit to elevate itself to a realization of oneness with God.

> When the exaltation is exhibited in a syllogistic process, in the shape of what we call *proofs* of the being of God. . . . The rise of thought beyond the world of sense, its passage from the finite to the infinite, the leap into the supersensible which it takes when it snaps asunder the chain of sense, all this transition is thought and nothing but thought.

(It is this "leap" that Kierkegaard will maintain is *rationally* unjustified.) As conceptual expressions of the mind's attempts to elevate itself to an identification with God, the various proofs are different in content (i.e., express different aspects of the God with whom we wish to be identified), and these contents are all equally legitimate—"though it may be that, in their ordinary form, these proofs have not their correct and adequate expression." On this view, the traditional interpretation of "proofs" must give way; they are now to be viewed as "ways of describing and analyzing" the mind's self-elevation to God rather than as logical demonstrations.[91]

Man does (historically) try to identify himself with his God. In religion this is done primarily at the level of feeling. But a key theme of Hegel's mature philosophy is that man does not live by feeling alone, that, as spirit, he is essentially oriented to thought. When religion evolves into philosophy, man's attempts to identify himself with God assume conceptual form—and these are the proofs. On this view each "proof of the existence of God is nothing but the description of that act of rising up to the infinite." This is not, of course, to rule out or downgrade the role of feeling. Even though philosophy should not pretend to be edifying, the whole person should be affected by a knowledge of God. Like Pascal before him and Kierkegaard after him, Hegel is sensitive to the dangers of overintellectualizing man's approach to God: "Such a process of thought, it is said, is too objective; it is cold conviction; this kind of insight is not in the heart, and it is in the heart and its feelings that convictions must exist." But granting this point, Hegel sets out to rehabilitate the old proofs by freeing them from the deficient form in which unfortunate interpretations have cast them: "What has to be done, therefore, is to restore the proofs of the existence of God to their place of honour, by divesting them of what is inadequate in them."[92]

Hegel begins his *Lectures on the Proofs of the Existence of God* by noting that, thanks largely to Kant, the proofs have so

> fallen into discredit that they pass for something antiquated, belonging to the metaphysics of days gone by; a barren desert, out of which we have escaped and brought ourselves back to a living faith; the region of arid Understanding, out of which we have once more raised ourselves to the warm feeling of religion.

The artificial interpretation of the proofs as abstract demonstrations has been exploded by that great critic of the understanding, Kant. On this level the proofs are indefensible, and Hegel forswears any "attempt to renovate, by means of new applications and artifices of an acute understanding, those rotten props of our belief that there is a God, which have passed for proofs." Syllogistic exercises have never had the traditionally intended effect, anyway. The necessity of these proofs, as reinterpreted by Hegel, is psychological rather than narrowly logical, grounded in man's natural need, as a limited, finite being, to identify his entire spiritual self with unlimited, infinite Being. The

> proofs of the existence of God.... ought to comprise the elevation of the human spirit to God, and express it for thought.... Therefore we have not to prove this elevation from the outside; it ... is by its very nature necessary.[93]

Thus, it is the relationship between the religious believer and God that the proofs, on this new interpretation, are designed to express. This is the novel twist Hegel gives to our understanding of how properly to regard a proof: "for, speaking generally, to prove simply means to become conscious of the connection, and consequently of the necessity of things." What is no longer to be demonstrated is the mere existence of a Being. On the old view of the proofs, all of them were seeking to demonstrate the same thing by different conceptual routes. But now "it comes about that the different proofs of the existence of God result in giving different characteristics or aspects of God. This is opposed to ... the opinion that in the proofs of the existence of God the interest centres in the fact of existence only, and that this one abstract characteristic or determination ought to represent the common result of all the different proofs." Hegel does not pretend that the proofs will give us conceptual access to all of God's attributes.[94] But the more we thus can grasp, the greater will be our knowledge of God and our recognition of the necessary connection between God and ourselves. Let us, then, consider each of the three traditional proofs to see what they allegedly express about God and this relationship.

In his logical writings Hegel does attempt to refute a specific point Kant raised against the ontological argument—that being or existence can never be legitimately deduced from a mere concept. He admits that such an inference would be illegitimate in the case of any finite thing. But, if it is true that the concept of, for example, one hundred dollars is not the same as their reality, "there is a still greater difference between God and the hundred dollars and other finite things." Hegel's claim is that it is only in the case of the Absolute that "his Notion and his being are *unseparated* and *inseparable*."[95] On this analysis, Kant is seen as having begged the question of whether the deducing of reality from a concept is ever permissible. But, from his side, Kant could just as easily accuse Hegel of begging the question in assuming that there is this exception to the rule. Indeed, Hegel seems to recognize that the ontological argument is built on the assumption of the identity of thought and being. "This unity of Notion and Being is hypothetical, and its defect consists just in the very fact of its being hypothetical" in previous philosophies. "What is presupposed is that the pure Notion, the Notion-in-and-for-itself, the Notion of God, is, involves Being also." This unjustified presupposition is what admittedly exposes all earlier versions of the argument, going all the way back to that "given by Anselm," as "unsatisfactory."[96] But Hegel believes that his own logical writings have justified it and rendered it fit for service.

The ontological argument gives conceptual expression to the fact that finite man strives to achieve union with "the Infinite or God." Man, who recognizes in himself a gap between what he actually is and what he might become, desires elevation to an identity with "the Being of God, as absolutely concrete Being" which is perfectly adequate to its own Notion. Man, who discovers himself to be a spirit alienated in a world of others, seeks reconciliation with an all-inclusive, self-differentiating, self-revealing Spirit.[97] Thus the ontological argument expresses man's aspiration to realize, in fact, the ideal identification of himself and infinite Spirit, which identity is supposedly established by Hegelian logic.

The cosmological argument gives conceptual expression to the fact that man, acknowledging himself as one of a myriad of contingent things, longs to identify himself with a unified "absolutely necessary Cause"—as a rational source of meaning for his otherwise inexplicable being. Man, who is constantly reminded of his own frail and limited power, strives to ally himself with "the absolute power of the Infinite." According to Hegel, Kant's critique of the cosmological arguments missed the point, precisely because he failed to recognize that, despite their deceptive logical form, they should not be regarded as purely theoretical attempts at demonstrative proof. Kant, following the tradition of European rational theology since medieval times, allegedly made the mistake of viewing the cosmological argument as a single isolable logical unit, whereas, in fact, it "is of use solely in connection with the effort to bring into consciousness what . . . , regarded in its subjective aspect, is called religious elevation." The argument should be understood as the intellectual expression of a fundamentally religious act, rather than as a matter of purely abstract theorizing. Understood in this light, the cosmological argument is seen to be conceptually independent, rather than as parasitic on the ontological.

> We must therefore hold that Kant is in error in asserting that the Cosmological Proof rests on the Ontological, and we must regard it as a mistake even to maintain that it requires this latter to complete it, that is, in regard to what it has in general to accomplish.[98]

The two types of "proofs" independently express different sorts of divine attributes (infinite perfection versus absolute necessity) and different dimensions of the relationship between God and man (that of all-inclusive Whole to finite determination versus that of determining ontological matrix to dependent phenomenon).

Finally, the teleological argument gives conceptual expression to the fact that man, so often the victim of his own folly and irrational vacillations, looks for a definite purposive end determined by "a wise author." Man, who sees his own life as oriented towards death, needs to associate himself with "the essence of life itself." And man, whose particular ends are often at loggerheads with what is good and righteous, desires the moral exaltation necessary to identify himself with "the Good, the general final-end of the world." Thus, through the intellectual negating of his own limitations, man strives to overcome his own alienation. Hegel concludes, "By means of this negation Man's spirit raises itself to God, brings itself into harmony with God."[99]

These, then, are the divine attributes and the aspects of the relationship between God and man given conceptual expression by the various kinds of "proofs." On this view mere existence, a lesser category in

Hegelian logic deemed "too low for the Absolute Idea, and unworthy of God,"[100] is not the crucial issue at all. For Hegel the entire order of thought and being (and the coherence of the two) demands the view *that* God is; what is at stake in the proofs is the divine nature, *what* God is. This is alleged to be the true significance of the proofs, reinterpreted by Hegel as descriptive expressions of spirit's religious ascent to union with absolute Spirit. On this view, it can be admitted that none of the "proofs"—nor any combination of them—will suffice as a logical demonstration. Thus, they are purportedly immune to the logical refutations of thinkers such as Hume, Kant, and Kierkegaard. Nevertheless, even as thus reinterpreted, they remain rationalistic—i.e., derived from reason and oriented toward knowledge (of the divine nature and of man's relationship to God).

However, Hegel's rationalism should not be confused with that of Descartes and his followers, who represented a rationalism of the understanding, failing to achieve knowledge at the level of dialectical reason. This "Metaphysic of the past" has been refuted by empiricism (for example, Hume) and the critical philosophy (of Kant). The old rationalism, with its inability to transcend the dichotomies of the understanding, was inadequate to the content of religion and speculative philosophy. Not only does it utilize a misguided conception of proofs of God; but it also misconceives the divine nature. According to its "either-or" mentality, an infinite God cannot also be finite, an eternal God cannot be temporal, an immutable God can admit of no development, and that which is truly God must remain radically other to man. But, as we have seen, the thrust of Hegel's dialectical logic is designed to overcome these dichotomies.

> The metaphysic of understanding is dogmatic, because it maintains half-truths in their isolation: whereas the idealism of speculative philosophy carries out the principle of totality and shows that it can reach beyond the inadequate formularies of abstract thought.

A facile identification of Hegel's philosophy with that of pre-Kantian rationalists would not do justice to the antagonism (pressed by Hegel himself) between a rationalism of the understanding and that of speculative reason: "The battle of reason is the struggle to break up the rigidity to which the understanding has reduced everything." Rationalistic attempts to deal with God before Hegel terminated in "the lifeless product of modern 'Deism'" represented by Hume or the crude "Pantheism" sometimes (perhaps unfairly) associated with Spinoza or the irresolvable "Dualism"[101] of Descartes, Locke, Leibniz, and Kant—all three of which positions are religiously inadequate.

Thus, it is not surprising that this brand of rationalism should be seen as antagonistic to religion whereas, by contrast, Hegel's version is presented as harmonious with religion:

> If the spirit yields to this finite reflection, which has usurped the title of reason and philosophy—("Rationalism")—it strips religious truth of its infinity and makes it in reality nought. Religion in that case is completely in the right in guarding herself against such reason and philosophy and treating them as enemies.

Matters are different with Hegelian rationalism:

> But it is another thing when religion sets herself against comprehending reason, and against philosophy in general, and specifically against a philosophy of which the doctrine is speculative, and so religious.[102]

Hegelian rationalism not only is supposed to do justice to the proofs for God in a way that pre-Kantian rationalism cannot; but it also allegedly comprehends the true relationship between God and man in a manner of which no previous rationalism was capable.

Panentheism. Hegel's panentheism is the articulation of this relationship. He dismisses *deism*, which sets an unbridgeable chasm between the human and the divine, as "merely the mode in which the understanding thinks God." What is needed is a perspective that dialectically synthesizes the antithesis between human subject and divine object.

> As absolute object, however, God does not therefore take up the position of a dark and hostile power over against subjectivity. He rather involves it as a vital element in himself.... The salvation and the blessedness of men are attained when they come to feel themselves at one with God, so that God ... ceases to be for them mere object.[103]

The philosophical conception that specifies this essential relationship of God and man is that of *immanence*. Hegel would take more literally than most of us the Scriptural statement of the relationship between us and God, to the effect that "in him we live, and move, and have our being" (*Acts* 17:28).

But if the infinite is, indeed, immanent in the finite, then *theism*—even that of Christianity—cannot provide an adequate knowledge of the relationship between God and man. For theism provides an image of a transcendent God "out there," in a realm different from that of man and nature, as if there were an ontological gap between the finite and the infinite. For Hegel, such a transcendent conception of God would be one of a merely finite reality, the "false infinite," only another particular. God must not be viewed as set over against, or outside of, finite spirit and nature;

otherwise true infinity becomes compromised. Instead of being the absolute Spirit who created Nature as something other, "God, we are entitled to say, is that Being in whom Spirit and Nature are united."[104] Thus, theism, even as developed by Christianity, the "absolute religion," distorts the dialectical truth of the relationship of difference-in-unity between God and man and can comprehend the truth discovered by Hegelian philosophy only through the imagery of the Incarnation of Christ.

Yet *pantheism* goes too far in the other direction, absorbing all things into God to the point where they lose their identity. Hegel sees pantheism as a crude oversimplification, "to which everything is God and God everything."[105] Pantheism wants to claim that all the infinitely many finite things of the world, as they exist empirically, are God. This is a view which Hegel dismisses as never having been seriously believed by anyone (including Spinoza).[106] Indeed Hegel believes that the true pantheist (if he exists at all) "could only be a narrow and ordinary or rather scholastic kind of mind" seriously to hold the "absurd idea" that "every existing thing in its finitude and particularity, is held to be possessed of Being as God."[107] Since Hegel was himself accused of pantheism, it is not surprising that he should strive to establish a clear-cut distance between it and his own position.

The truth of Hegelian *panentheism* is rather that finite spirits and the world of nature are, in their essential (or ideal) actuality, moments in the self-differentiation of the one, infinite Being. As Hegel says, speaking of objects of experience in our world,

> These things are not only natural things, but also include Spirit.... They are contingent things. Further, they are distinct from absolute necessity itself.

Yet their relationship to absolute Spirit is essential, since

> they have no independent Being as against it, and neither has it, consequently, against them. There is only one Being, . . . and things by their very nature form part of it.

He concludes,

> Everything is thus included in it, and it is immediately present in everything.[108]

This is Hegel's definitive statement of the relationship between God and the things of our world.

There are at least three problems with Hegel's panentheism. The first is one of clarity. In what respect are finite things to be identified with God? It is not finite things as they are in fact that are God—for this is the crude misconception of pantheism. But if what are identified with

God are things as they *essentially* (or *ideally*) are, what is left out of account is the relationship of all this to things in their "facticity" or "brute givenness" (the relevant terminology here tends to be drawn from the literature of **existentialism**, which began in opposition to idealism)—i.e., to things as they are accessible to us in sense experience and as they are knowable by the human understanding. The facticity of things constitutes their estrangement from—rather than their identification with—God. But to deny this (or to try to overcome it) in the name of a dubious ideal essence is to repudiate human experience and to strain the bounds of credibility.

Second, even if we could render intelligible this position, the question would remain as to whether this is, indeed, true (let alone "the truth of") religion. Can an ideal Absolute, of which we are supposed to be finite determinations, be an adequate object of religious worship? Or is not more of an ontological separation needed between the subject and the object of religious worship?

A third problem is that Hegel's Absolute, the philosophical "truth" of the God of religion, although it (somehow) "involves" our subjectivity, is not a personal Being. It is true that Hegel sometimes speaks of God as "the absolute Person." But he is then employing the symbolic language of religion. He characterizes "the personality of God" as universal rather than as individual: "Such personality is a thought, and falls within the province of thought only."[109] Hegel's Absolute, as an all-encompassing Whole, must involve personality; but it includes personality without being a person. (Since it cannot be adequately called impersonal, it is probably safest to call it transpersonal.) Hegel wisely calls for a spiritual (as opposed to a purely intellectual) commitment to God. But it seems that such a relationship satisfactorily obtains only between persons, so that a God to whom we are so related would have to be a person. Although Hegel tries to present his Absolute as concrete Spirit, so long as it is conceived of as Idea, rather than as Person, it may seem too abstract to enter into a fully spiritual relationship worthy of being termed "religious." But this takes us to the topic of his complex idea of the religious.

Analysis of Religion

Phenomenology of Religions. Hegel's phenomenology of religions runs the gamut from primitive religions of nature to the "absolute religion" of Christianity. Although his development is far more extensive and detailed in the *Lectures on the Philosophy of Religion* (including, for example, a section on Chinese religion and even a brief discussion of Eskimo religion), our focus here will be on the simpler treatment in his *Phenomenology of Spirit* for several reasons: first, its length (of about eighty pages) lends itself to better analysis, given the constraints of this section; second, there is no problem of how much of it is Hegel's own words, as opposed to those of his students, transcribed from their lecture notes; and, third, Hegel did prepare this, unlike the *Lectures*, for publication, so that it has the form of a finished product (even if it is not his last word on the subject).

The structure of the *Phenomenology* prior to the section on "Religion" has broken down into treatments of "Consciousness, Self-consciousness, Reason, and Spirit," in all of which, Hegel says, "religion, too, as consciousness of *absolute Being* as such, has indeed made its appearance," though only implicitly and from our nebulous point of view. Phenomenology is the systematic study of the forms or shapes of consciousness. And until the passage on "Religion" it seems that "absolute Being in and for itself, the self-consciousness of Spirit, has not appeared in those 'shapes' " in any explicit way. Yet these previous "moments" in the evolution of consciousness must now be used as necessary foundations for the dialectical development of religious awareness: "Religion presupposes that these have run their full course and is their *simple* totality or absolute self." What religion comes to recognize is that God has been operative in all those earlier phenomenological stages. Hegel announces that he will trace the development of religious consciousness in three stages: first, "as *immediate*, and therefore Natural Religion"; second, "in the shape of a *superseded* natural existence," as "the Religion of Art"; and, third, in its absolute form, as "the Revealed Religion." He identifies the natural religions of Oriental cultures with "the form of consciousness," the aesthetic religions of Greek culture with "that of self-consciousness," and the absolute revealed religion of Christianity with "the form of the unity of both" consciousness and self-consciousness,[110] each later phase allegedly being more adequate than its predecessor.

The section on "Natural Religion" comprises treatments of Persian Zoroastrianism, which sees God as Light, of Indian animism, which views God as Life, and of Egyptian expressionism, which depicts God as Artificer. This "series of different religions" can be viewed as "only the different aspects of a *single* religion," which tends to characterize God as Substance. The Zoroastrianism of ancient Persia conceives of the Absolute as "the pure all-embracing and all-pervading *essential light* of

sunrise. . . . Its otherness is the equally simple negative, *darkness*." Here
we have a cosmic dualism (comparable to the Manicheanism which mes-
merized Augustine for a while) between supernatural forces of good
and evil which continually struggle for dominance, the things of this
world being their pawns. At a higher level, in the **animism** of ancient
India, this crude dichotomy "falls apart into the numberless multiplicity
of weaker and stronger, richer and poorer Spirits." Here we find a
panpsychism, in which everything is perceived as if alive and sacred,
lending itself to a *"flower religion"* and to *"animal religions."* The conflict
now is no longer between two great cosmic forces but, Hegel avers, is
suffered among a staggering multiplicity, "a host of separate, antagonistic
national Spirits who hate and fight each other to the death" and seem
utterly "unconscious of their universality." In the religion of ancient
Egypt, Spirit appears "as an *artificer*," and becomes more obviously self-
expressive, though performing "an instinctive operation," produced "without having yet grasped the thought of itself" (as will be done in the
aesthetic religion of the Greeks). The initial, immediate form of this activity is to be found in the "rigid," lifeless "crystals of pyramids and obelisks."
Gradually these abstract shapes become supplemented by representations
of deities that mix animal characteristics "with the human form." Yet this
imaginative production still "lacks speech," even the moaning statues of
Memnon emitting "merely noise and not speech," revealing "only an outer,
not the inner self" of Spirit. With the construction of the Sphinx, riddles
emerge, articulating "the language of a profound, but scarcely intelligible
wisdom." At this highest form of natural religion it becomes increasingly
evident that "Spirit is Artist" (*Der Geist ist Künstler*),[111] self-expressive
Subject, and not merely objective Substance.

In the aesthetic religion of the ancient Greeks, religious consciousness
becomes more dynamically involved with the divine Substance, which, for
its part, becomes more "individualized" and somehow acknowledged by
religious believers "as their own essence and their own work." (Hegel's fascination with and admiration of the Greeks is reflected in the fact that
his treatment of their religion gets more than three times the amount of
coverage given the natural religions of Oriental cultures.) "The first work
of art, as immediate, is abstract and individual." The art of sculpture produces statues of gods and goddesses which have "the distinction of individuality" and each of which "bears within it the shape of the self." But
the expression of self-consciousness requires more. "This higher element
is Language," says Hegel. "Devotion" is expressed in the lyrics of "the
hymn" of Greek religion. "This language is distinct from another language

of the god which is not that of universal self-consciousness. The *Oracle"* emerges as the "form of the god's utterance." But more is needed to pull together worshippers and gods. "The movement of the two sides constitutes the Cult." In this way the feeling of interpersonal relationship is established: "In the Cult, the self gives itself the consciousness of the divine Being descending to it from its remoteness." The believer strives to render himself worthy of communion with a god, becomes "a soul that cleanses its exterior by washing it, and puts on white robes, while its inward being traverses the imaginatively conceived path of works, punishments, and rewards, the path of spiritual training in general." Religious ritual calls for "sacrifice" and "renunciation," but also for consumption (and "enjoyment") of a portion of what is given up. Architecture constructs a temple, "produces a dwelling and adornments for the glory of the god." Yet, because of the religious identity between man and the object of his worship, Hegel points out,

> The dwellings and halls of the god are for the use of man, the treasures preserved therein are his own in case of need; the honour and glory enjoyed by the god in his adornment are the honour and glory of the nation, great in soul and in artistic achievement.

Yet this is still what Hegel calls the "abstract work of art."[112]

The second phase of the aesthetic religion of the Greeks is that of the "living work of art." The satisfaction produced by abstract art makes possible higher and richer insight, and "enjoyment is the mystery of its being. For the mystical is not concealment of a secret, or ignorance, but consists in the self knowing itself to be one with the divine Being." The dynamic involvement of the worshipper takes the form of "a crowd of frenzied females, the untamed revelry" of the mysteries, with its "enthusiasm" and ecstasy. It is difficult to say whether "man celebrates in his own honour" or that of the gods "the festival" of ancient Greek worship—for example, that "of bread and wine, of Ceres and Bacchus." But an individual human (athlete) can be seen as taking on the god's persona. "He is an inspired and living work of art that matches strength with its beauty; and on him is bestowed . . . the honour of being, in place of the god in stone, the highest bodily representation among his people of their essence."[113]

The third and final phase of the aesthetic religion of the Greeks is that of the "spiritual work of art." As abstract art had to take on the form of life, so living art must assume a higher level of spiritual self-expression. The scattered variety of "national Spirits" representing diverse city-states and social groups also requires some sort of consolidation. "Thus it is that the separate beautiful national Spirits unite into a single **pantheon**, the element and habitation of which is language." The aesthetic language created here, binding the Greeks together in a collective culture, is that of poetry—for example, the epics of Homer, the tragedies of Sophocles and Aeschylus, and the comedies of Aristophanes. The "picture-thinking" of "the Epic" is communicated through songs of "the Minstrel." The "higher" art of Tragedy improves upon the scattered events of the Epic by providing more dramatic unity and probing spiritual motivation; it "gathers closer together the dispersed moments of the inner essential world and the world of action." Meanwhile, Greek polytheism crystallizes into a **henotheism**, in which one of the gods is seen as sovereign: "The self-consciousness that is represented in Tragedy knows and acknowledges, therefore, only one supreme power," Zeus. In Comedy the "pretensions of universal essentiality are uncovered in the self; it shows itself to be entangled in an actual existence" of human individuality through all these attempts at transcendence.[114]

But it is in the "Revealed Religion" of Christianity that God is manifest as Absolute. "Through the religion of Art, Spirit has advanced from the form of *Substance* to assume that of *Subject*." Now it must take a further step. "In Spirit that is completely certain of itself in the individuality of consciousness," it becomes evident that the proposition "The Self is absolute Being" is inadequate. The "Unhappy Consciousness" of religious man must suffer "the tragic fate of the certainty of self that aims to be absolute" and must suffer the destruction of the old static, transcendent God. "It is the consciousness of the loss of all *essential* being" that must be borne—"the loss of substance as well as of the Self, it is the grief which expresses itself in the hard saying that 'God is dead.'" This formula from one of Luther's hymns expresses the ultimate religious tragedy. But Christianity expresses this truth concerning the obsolescence of the old conception of God by means of picture-thinking. In order for religion to make sense of the death of God, the divine must become incarnate in a mortal being. The Absolute is thus seen as assuming human personality:

> Of this Spirit, which has abandoned the form of Substance and enters existence in the shape of self-consciousness, it may therefore be said—if we wish to employ relationships derived from natural generation—that it has an *actual* mother but an *implicit* father.

That is to say, Christ, the Son of God, has a human mother, Mary. In the person of Christ, God becomes self-aware, as man.

> This incarnation of the divine Being, or the fact that it essentially and directly has the shape of self-consciousness, is the simple content of the absolute religion.

> In this religion the divine Being is known as Spirit, or this religion is the consciousness of the divine Being that it is Spirit.

But the Incarnation of God in man is also the ultimate revelation. "Consequently, in this religion the divine Being is *revealed*." From this point of view God is seen as self-revealing Spirit, establishing the identity of the divine and the human: "The divine nature is the same as the human, and it is this unity that is beheld" in the person of Christ, who embodies the central truth of Hegel's system; "for this unity of Being and Thought is *self*-consciousness" and not merely an abstract idea. This truth must await the emergence of speculative philosophy for its rational comprehension, and even Christianity—as religion—can only grasp it in the "*form of picture-thinking*," which is, by its very nature, necessarily "defective." So it also is with other truths revealed by the Christian religion. Our thought of our relation to God "is still burdened with an unreconciled split into a Here and a Beyond. The content is the true content," but religion's "picture-thinking" form proves inadequate.[115]

Likewise, the doctrine of the Trinity is a representation of the truth (made manifest in Hegelian philosophy) that God is "Substance" and "Subject" and "the rich life of Spirit." Again, the myth of creation is religion's way of expressing the Absolute Spirit's self-estrangement in nature and history. "This 'creating' is picture-thinking's word for the Notion itself in its absolute movement." The limitation of this idea is that it fosters an ultimate dichotomy between God and the world and conceals the fact that the Absolute Spirit "is equally present in the world." Similarly, man's alienation from self is characterized in terms of an internal struggle between

> Good and Evil. Man is pictorially thought of in this way: that it once *happened*, without any necessity, that he lost the form of being at one with himself through plucking the fruit of the tree of the knowledge of Good and Evil, and was expelled from the state of innocence . . . and from Paradise.

This, of course, is the *Genesis* myth of the Fall. The reconciliation of all self-estrangement in the Absolute is represented by the doctrine of the atonement by the God-man. "In this picture-thought there is depicted the reconciliation of the divine Being with its 'other' in general, and specifically with the *thought* of it—*Evil*." The more adequate interpretation of philosophy is religiously regarded as blasphemous and dangerous:

> If this reconciliation is *notionally* expressed by saying that it consists in the fact that Evil is *in itself* the same as Goodness, or again that the divine Being is the same as Nature in its whole extent, or that Nature separated from the divine

> Being is simply nothing—we must regard this as an unspiritual way of talking
> and one that is necessarily bound to give rise to misunderstandings.

In terms of any logic but that of dialectical reason, it will appear that self-contradiction is rearing its ugly head. "For the consciousness that thinks in pictures the world has *actually* become, and is, evil, and the propitiation of the absolute Being was a real event" in history rather than an image of a truth that is eternal. Christ's resurrection symbolizes the overcoming of the particularity of death and the ultimate affirmation of eternal universality. Thus, the doctrine of Christ's resurrection represents "the supersession of his objective existence or his particular being-for-self: this *particular* being-for-self has become a universal self-consciousness"—not merely Jesus, the God-man, but the all-encompassing Absolute Spirit. The very idea of Jesus as the God-man must be overcome in favor of the truth of monism, that we are all identified with the Absolute. "The death of this picture-thought contains, therefore, at the same time the death of the *abstraction of the divine Being* which is not posited as Self." Hegel comments that our rising above the limited imagery of Christianity's pictorial thinking of the Mediator can involve "the painful feeling of the Unhappy Consciousness that *God Himself is dead*," admitting that this is a "hard saying."[116]

But only philosophy can adequately grasp these conceptual truths expressed by the picture-thinking of the Christian religion, which deals with them in the manner appropriate to faith and worship. "The world is indeed *implicitly* reconciled with the divine Being; and regarding the divine Being it is known, of course, that it recognizes the object as no longer alienated from it but as identical with it in its love". The "it" here refers to "religious consciousness," which is aware of a kind of community with God. "But for self-consciousness, this immediate presence still has not the shape of Spirit,"[117] because God is still regarded as transcendent other. It is only at philosophy's level of "Absolute Knowing" that religion's form is finally superseded and its content (allegedly) comprehended.

We have already questioned whether this rational knowledge is ever achieved by Hegelian philosophy. But, beyond this, what can be said of Hegel's phenomenology of religions, or study of its various forms? It does not offer us a fair or complete profile of Eastern religions but presents a brilliant and rather affectionate view of Greek religion. One must turn to the more extensive treatment in his *Lectures on the Philosophy of Religion* for serious mention of Buddhism, Chinese religion, Judaism, and Islam. On the other hand, Hegel is significantly important as an early nineteenth-century European who did try to relate Christianity to other religious traditions. His dialectical method provides him with a remarkable technique for doing this. At the same time, he uses it as a Procrustean bed, on which Greek religion is stretched and **Hinduism** is truncated to serve his dialectical purposes. The entire passage is ingeniously contrived to tie in neatly with his view of world-history as comprising the three stages of Oriental, Greco-Roman, and Christian development of consciousness. Yet what a brilliant contribution to religious demythologizing is his interpretation of the symbolism of Christianity! Hegel challenges us to think of religion as a relationship to that which is *not* radically other.

Religion As Man's Self-Elevation. Hegel's notion of religion as man's self-elevation is this alternative perspective. He describes it as "the act of rising up to the True" and says that by means of religion "I lift myself up to the Absolute above all that is finite, and am infinite consciousness, while I am at the same time finite consciousness." The realization of a true unity with God transcends even religious community. It is "partaking in this Absolute, and making unity with it actually one's own," requiring an "abolition of the dualism" between God and man, "which constitutes the sphere of worship." Far from being a relation to a transcendent other, the worship of Hegelian panentheism is a "process by which the subject posits itself as identical with its essential being,"[118] which is that of infinite Spirit.

We might note that this analysis of religion and religious worship is applicable within any of the various traditions treated in Hegel's phenomenology of religions. After all, he believes that all the particular religions are oriented toward the Truth. Although he sees them as relatively more or less adequate to the Truth, none of them is to be rejected outright, for all of them provide for this self-elevation to God:

> Even in the worst religions—those that is in which servitude, and with it superstition, is most powerful—it is when man lifts himself up to God that he feels, intuits and enjoys his freedom, his infinitude and universality, that is, his higher nature.[119]

Although we might attribute to ethnocentrism Hegel's characterization of his own religious tradition as "absolute," he is never so parochial as merely to disdain or patronize those of others. On the contrary, he says, "These definite religions are not indeed *our* religion, yet they are included in ours as essential. . . . Therefore in them we have not to do with what is foreign to us, but with what is our own." A bit later, he adds,

> They are human beings who have hit upon such religions, therefore there must be *reason* in them, and amidst all that is accidental in them a higher necessity. We must do them this justice, for what is human, rational in them, is *our own* too.[120]

386 ■ *Hegel's Dialectical Idealism*

There is something refreshing in Hegel's cosmopolitan attitude toward other cultures and worldviews. As in his phenomenology of conscious experience, in general, so in his phenomenology of religions, in particular: nothing is utterly wasted; no efforts go for naught; even the lesser forms have their necessary place in the dialectical progress of spirit in its crusade to reestablish union with its divine Source and End. All religious attempts are sacred, as is man himself, because they are ultimately the workings of infinite, Absolute Spirit.

Against Hume and Kant, Hegel has argued for the legitimacy of man's speculative knowledge of God and for the ultimate coalescence of religious faith and philosophical reason. His radical rationalism holds "that religion consists just in this, that man has immediate knowledge of God. This immediate knowing is called reason, and also faith." He shrewdly anticipates a reaction which "takes up a directly polemical attitude to philosophical knowledge, and directs its attacks especially against the philosophical knowledge and comprehension of God." This is not merely Hume and Kant worrying Hegel, but the proponent of the principle of immediate knowledge of God, such as Kierkegaard would prove to be.

> Not only does it teach that we are to believe and to know in an immediate manner, not only is it maintained that the consciousness of God is bound up with the consciousness of self, but that the relation to God is *only* an immediate one.

This point of view will threaten to kill philosophical theology, insofar as it holds "that we can only know our relation to God, not what God Himself is; and that it is only our relation to God which is embraced in what is generally called religion." Hegel assumes that this denial of philosophical (mediated) knowledge would succumb to an affirmation of "an essential relation" between God and man,[121] comprehensible through speculative reason. What he perhaps could not foresee was the fact that the objections raised by the proponent of immediacy might be based on the claim that the relation between God and man, as it appears in religion, should be conceived as *existential*, rather than as "essential" or metaphysical.

Notes

1. *Hegel: The Letters*, trans. Clark Butler and Christiane Seiler (Bloomington: Indiana Univ. Press, 1984), p. 64; this work will hereafter be called "*Letters*."

2. Ibid., p. 107.   3. Ibid., p. 114.   4.   Ibid., p. 115.

5. Ibid., p. 80.

6. *Phenomenology of Spirit*, by G. W. F. Hegel, trans. A. V. Miller (New York: Oxford Univ. Press, 1979), p. 9; this work will hereafter be called "*Phenomenology*."

7. *Letters*, p. 80.

8. *Early Theological Writings*, by G. W. F. Hegel, trans. T. M. Knox (Philadelphia: Univ. of Pennsylvania Press, 1971), pp. 321, 328–29; this book will hereafter be called "*Writings*."

9. *Letters*, pp. 236–38.

10. Ibid., p. 460.

11. Ibid., pp. 520, 532; cf. *Hegel's Lectures on the History of Philosophy*, trans. E. S. Haldane (New York: The Humanities Press, Inc., 1955), vol. 1, p. 73—this three-volume work will hereafter be called "*Philosophy*."

12. *Letters*, pp. 467, 535.

13. Ibid., p. 556.

14. See *Letters*, pp. 547–50, for an 1828 correspondence from Feuerbach to Hegel, to which the latter apparently never replied.

15. These comprise *Three Essays, 1793–1795*, by G. W. F. Hegel, ed. and trans. Peter Fuss and John Dobbins (Notre Dame: Univ. of Notre Dame Press, 1984); this work will hereafter be called "*Essays*."

16. These are contained in *Writings*.

17. *Faith and Knowledge*, by G. W. F. Hegel, trans. Walter Cerf and H. S. Harris (Albany: State Univ. of New York Press, 1977); this work will hereafter be called "*Faith*."

18. *Natural Law*, by G. W. F. Hegel, trans. T. M. Knox (Philadelphia: Univ. of Pennsylvania Press, 1975).

19. *Hegel's Science of Logic*, trans. A. V. Miller (London: George Allen & Unwin, Ltd., 1969)—hereafter called "*Science*."

20. *Hegel's Logic*, trans. William Wallace (Oxford: Oxford Univ. Press, 1975)—hereafter called "*Logic*."

21. *Hegel's Philosophy of Nature*, trans. A. V. Miller (Oxford: Oxford Univ. Press, 1970)—hereafter called "*Nature*."

22. *Hegel's Philosophy of Mind*, trans. A. V. Miller (Oxford: Oxford Univ. Press, 1971)—hereafter called "*Mind*."

23. *Hegel's Philosophy of Right*, trans. T. M. Knox (New York: Oxford Univ. Press, 1967)—hereafter called "*Right*."

24. *Philosophy of History*, by G. W. F. Hegel, trans. J. Sibree (New York: P. F. Collier and Son, 1900)—hereafter called "*History*"; Hegel's *Vorlesungen über die Philosophie der Geschichte* was first published in 1837, with a second edition in 1840.

25. *The Philosophy of Fine Art*, by G. W. F. Hegel, trans. F. P. B. Osmaston (London: G. Bell and Sons, Ltd., 1920)—hereafter called "*Art*"; Hegel's *Vorlesungen über die Aesthetik* was first published in 1835–38, with a second edition in 1840–43.

26. Hegel's *Vorlesungen über die Geschichte der Philosophie* was first published in 1833–36, with a second edition in 1842.

27. *Lectures on the Philosophy of Religion Together with a Work on the Proofs of the Existence of God*, by Georg Wilhelm Friedrich Hegel, trans. E. B. Speirs and

J. Burdon Sanderson (London: Routledge & Kegan Paul, 1968)—hereafter called "*Religion*"; Hegel's *Vorlesungen über die Philosophie der Religion* was first published in 1832, with a second edition in 1840.

28. *The Philosophy of Hegel*, ed. Carl J. Friedrich (New York: Modern Library, 1953)—hereafter called "Friedrich."

29. *On Art, Religion, Philosophy: Introductory Lectures to the Realm of Absolute Spirit*, by G. W. F. Hegel, ed. J. Glenn Gray (New York: Harper & Row, 1970)—hereafter called "Gray."

30. *Essays*, pp. 30, 32–36, 43–44, 46, 49, 51–52, 56. For a good expression of Hegel's romanticism during this period, see his poem "Eleusis," which in 1796 he sent to his friend Hölderlin, whom he joined in Frankfurt a few months later: *Letters*, pp. 46–50.

31. *Essays*, pp. 61–63, 68, 70, 72, 81–82, 90, 93–94, 96, 98–99.

32. Ibid., pp. 104, 108, 112–13, 115–18, 127, 140–42, 148–49, 151, 154–55, 157, 159–60, 165.

33. *Writings*, pp. 68–69, 71, 76, 78–79, 85–86, 139–40, 143–46, 154, 163, 176.

34. Ibid., pp. 304–5.   35. Ibid., pp. 211–15, 223, 225, 239, 247, 262, 266, 268.

36. Ibid., pp. 310–13.

37. *Letters*, p. 64.

38. *Faith*, pp. 55–56, 59–60, 63–65.

39. Ibid., pp. 68–69, 71, 75, 77–78, 80.

40. Ibid., pp. 94, 190–91.

41. *Science*, pp. 61–62n; Friedrich, p. 200n. (Friedrich is using the older translation by W. H. Johnston and L. G. Struthers here).

42. *Phenomenology*, p. 46.

43. *Science*, pp. 45–46; Friedrich, pp. 180–82.

44. *Logic*, pp. 67, 14.

45. *Phenomenology*, p. 46.

46. *Logic*, p. 73; cf. also pp. 113, 115. See also *Mind*, p. 226, and *Philosophy*, vol. 3, p. 444.

47. *Religion*, vol. 3, p. 18; this whole section, pp. 17–23, is an extensive analysis of the limits of the understanding.

48. *Science*, p. 56; Friedrich, p. 194.

49. *Logic*, pp. 65, 86.

50. *Philosophy*, vol. 3, pp. 476, 478, and vol. 1, p. 74; Gray, pp. 278–79.

51. *Logic*, pp. 41, 36; cf. *Letters*, p. 277.

52. *Science*, pp. 44, 50; Friedrich, pp. 178, 186.

53. *Logic*, pp. 19–20.

54. *Phenomenology*, pp. 10–11; cf. *Mind*, p. 3.

55. *Science*, pp. 56, 54; Friedrich, pp. 194, 190–91. See also *Science*, pp. 438–43.

56. *Phenomenology*, pp. 23, 491, 34, 22.

57. *Logic*, pp. 15, 116, 118, 142.

58. *Phenomenology*, pp. 33, 140, 142, 14, 264.

59. *Logic*, p. 3.

60. *Right*, p. 10.

61. *Logic*, pp. 9, 37, 84, 70, 35, 73.

62. Ibid., p. 292.   63. Ibid., p. 49.

64. *Mind*, pp. 1, 23–24.

65. *Nature*, p. 14.

66. *Philosophy*, vol. 1, p. 105.

67. *Religion*, vol. 1, pp. 2, 42–43, 325, 33.

68. Ibid., vol. 3, p. 348.

69. *Logic*, pp. 91–92.

70. *Religion*, vol. 1, pp. 174, 176.

71. *Nature*, p. 14.

72. *History*, pp. 52, 62–64; Friedrich, pp. 4, 12.

73. *Phenomenology*, pp. 49, 58, 485, 111–28, 14, 493; Friedrich, pp. 399–410. For more on Hegel's epistemology and metaphysical theory, see *Twelve Great Philosophers*, by Wayne P. Pomerleau (New York: Ardsley House, 1997), pp. 290–306.

74. *Mind*, pp. 292–93, 295, 297, 302, 315, 298. In the introduction to his lectures on the *Philosophy of History* (p. 99), Hegel says, "But the True is the object not only of conception and feeling, as in Religion—and of intuition, as in Art—but also of the thinking faculty; and this gives us the third form of the union in question—*Philosophy*"; cf. p. 103.

75. *Art*, vol. 1, pp. 8–9, 103–22; Gray, pp. 29, 110–27.

76. *Religion*, vol. 1, pp. 19–20; Gray, p. 145.

77. *Philosophy*, vol. 1, pp. 79, 65, 69, 64, 83, 94; Gray, pp. 283, 269, 274, 269, 286, 297.

78. "Reason and Religious Truth," by G. W. F. Hegel, trans. A. V. Miller, included as an appendix to *Beyond Epistemology: New Studies in the Philosophy of Hegel*, ed. Frederick G. Weiss (the Hague: Martinus Nijhoff, 1974), p. 233; this essay will hereafter be called "Reason."

79. *Logic*, p. xl. For more on Hegel's theory concerning the relationship between religion and philosophy, see "The Accession and Dismissal of an Upstart Handmaid," by Wayne P. Pomerleau, in *The Monist*, vol. 60, no. 2 (April, 1977), pp. 213–20.

80. Ibid., pp. 42, 97.

81. *Mind*, p. 292.

82. "Reason," pp. 227–28, 232, 238–40, 243.

83. *Science*, p. 78; Friedrich, p. 217.

84. *Logic*, pp. 79–80, 164, 128.

85. *Religion*, vol. 3, pp. 365, 356.

86. *Phenomenology*, pp. 10, 490.

87. *Logic*, p. 84.

88. *Mind*, p. 18.

89. *Religion*, vol. 2, p. 349; cf. *History*, pp. 414–15.

90. *Philosophy*, vol. 3, p. 417; see also *Religion*, vol. 1, p. 170, and vol. 3, pp. 282–83.
91. *Logic*, pp. 81, 104.
92. *Religion*, vol. 1, pp. 171, 168.
93. Ibid., vol. 3, pp. 156, 164, 231–32, 237, 239.
94. Ibid., pp. 188, 216, 229, 234.
95. *Science*, pp. 89–90; cf. *Logic*, p. 84.
96. *Religion*, vol. 3, pp. 357, 363–64.
97. Ibid., pp. 363, 365–66.
98. Ibid., vol. 2, p. 144; vol. 3, pp. 260–61, 264, 246.
99. Ibid., vol. 3, pp. 227, 329, 331, 342–43, 345, 359.
100. *Logic*, p. 49.
101. Ibid., pp. 49, 52–53, 56.
102. *Mind*, p. 303; cf. "Reason," pp. 231–32, *Philosophy*, vol. 1, p. 80, and *Religion*, vol. 1, pp. 31, 34; Gray, pp. 283–84, 156, 158–59.
103. *Logic*, pp. 246, 260.
104. *Nature*, pp. 13, 8.
105. *Mind*, p. 307.
106. *Religion*, vol. 1, pp. 96–97; cf. vol. 2, pp. 55–56, and *Logic*, pp. 213–14.
107. *Religion*, vol. 3, p. 319.
108. Ibid., pp. 315–16.
109. *Logic*, pp. 214, 98.
110. *Phenomenology*, pp. 410, 413, 416; Friedrich, pp. 461, 467.
111. Ibid., pp. 417, 419–21, 423–24; Friedrich, pp. 467, 469–72, 474–76.
112. Ibid., pp. 424, 427, 430, 432–35; Friedrich, pp. 476, 478, 481, 483–87.
113. Ibid., pp. 437–38; Friedrich, pp. 487–90.
114. Ibid., pp. 439–41, 443, 449–50; Friedrich, pp. 490–91, 494, 499–500.
115. Ibid., pp. 453, 455, 457, 459–61, 463; Friedrich, pp. 503–4, 506, 508, 510–13, 516.
116. Ibid., pp. 463, 467–68, 472, 474–76; Friedrich, pp. 516–17.
117. Ibid., p. 478.
118. *Religion*, vol. 1, pp. 61, 63, 66–67, 70; Gray, pp. 184, 186, 189, 192.
119. "Reason," p. 239.
120. *Religion*, vol. 1, pp. 76–78; Gray, pp. 198, 200.
121. Ibid., pp. 42, 44–46; Gray, pp. 167–69.

8

Kierkegaard's Existential Fideism

Life and Writings

*K*ierkegaard's life was psychologically more eccentric than that of almost any other thinker considered here. Søren Aabye Kierkegaard was born in Copenhagen, Denmark on May 5, 1813, the seventh (and last) child of Michael Pedersen Kierkegaard (then fifty-six years old) and his second wife, Anne Sørensdatter Lund (then forty-five). The baby was baptized on June 3, 1813 in the Church of the Holy Ghost. This was a time of terrible inflation, due to the Danish government's issuing a blizzard of bank notes to support its involvement in the Napoleonic Wars. Later, Kierkegaard humorously writes in his *Journals*: "I was born in 1813, in that mad year when so many other mad bank-notes were put into circulation."[1]

His father, Michael, one of the two most important figures in his personal life, came from West Jutland. As an unhappy child, he had secretly raised his fist against heaven. Almost eighty years later, his son Søren is brooding over the significance of this blasphemous act of defiance in his *Journals*:

> How terrible about the man who once as a little boy, while herding sheep on the heaths of Jutland, suffering greatly, in hunger and in want, stood upon a hill and cursed God—and the man who was unable to forget it even when he was eighty-two years old.[2]

Paradoxically, the father's fortunes changed for the better soon thereafter. About a year later (at the age of twelve) he was released from the life of a serf and brought to Copenhagen by a prosperous uncle to help in his clothing business (using Jutland wool). After the uncle died, Michael went into business for himself, doing so well financially (by a combination of capable effort and lucky investments) that he retired at the age of forty (leaving the business to his nephew).

Just prior to the retirement, Michael's wife of two years died, leaving him childless. Before the end of the customary year of mourning, in 1797, he had to marry her servant, Anne, whom he had gotten pregnant and who gave birth to a daughter less than four and a half months after the wedding. Two more daughters and then four sons followed. The mother, who seems to have been a cheerful, simple (and illiterate) woman, appears not to have had a prominent role in Søren's psychological development.

By contrast, the influence of the father was profound. He was a melancholic, deeply religious man, racked by guilt feelings over his childhood cursing of God and sexual liaison with his first wife's maid. He had a shrewd and imaginative mind and was self-educated; after retiring, he devoted himself to theology and German philosophy (including that of the Leibnizian Wolff, whom he particularly admired). In his *Journals* his son reflects on the "terrible," gloomy atmosphere of his home, "which, from the very earliest time, was part of my life. The dread with which my father filled my soul, his own frightful melancholy," and the communication of religious scrupulosity left its mark. The father pessimistically imagined that his family was doomed to divine vengeance for his own transgressions. Two of the seven children died in childhood (a twelve-year-old son in 1819 and a fourteen-year-old daughter in 1822). Between 1832 and the end of 1834, another son, the other two daughters, and the mother all died, leaving only the father, Søren, and his older brother Peter (who would become a bishop). In his mid-thirties, Kierkegaard writes, "I owe everything, from the beginning, to my father," from whom he inherited a morbid religious melancholy. "The greatest danger for a child, where religion is concerned," he writes, is not that the father should be "a free-thinker" or even "a hypocrite," but that he should be "a pious, God-fearing man," deeply affecting a sensitive child whose soul is troubled by a turbulence which "not even the fear of God and piety could calm."[3]

As a motto for his own childhood, Kierkegaard chose a passage from Goethe's *Faust*: "*Halb Kinderspiel, Halb Gott im Herzen*," meaning, "Half child-play, half God in the heart." He seems to have been a very quick and clever child, nicknamed "the fork" for his sharp and penetrating wit.

He played elaborate imagination games with his father. He was physically frail, with a curved spine and uneven legs, viewing his intelligence as his saving strength without which he would have been "quite defenceless."⁴ He learned to hide his "prodigious melancholy" with "an apparent gaiety and *joie de vivre*" from childhood. But through it all, he writes later, "I suffered the pain of not being like the others—which naturally at that period I would have given everything to be able to be, if only for a short time."⁵

In 1821, the eight-year-old Søren entered the School of Civic Virtue, whose rector described him as intelligent but superficial and lacking in seriousness. In April, 1828 he was confirmed by J. P. Mynster, his father's friend and pastor, who would be Bishop of Copenhagen and Primate of the Danish Church from 1834 to 1854.⁶

In 1830 (the year before Hegel's death), at the age of seventeen, Søren entered the University of Copenhagen. As his father wished, he enrolled as a theology student (his brother Peter had already completed his own theological studies at Copenhagen and was in Germany doing graduate work in philosophy). He did well in his preliminary examinations in languages (Danish, Greek, French, Latin, Hebrew, and German), history, philosophical theory, physics, and mathematics, becoming a candidate in theology. In 1834, he took as his theological tutor Hans L. Martensen, a young Hegelian, who was only five years older than Kierkegaard himself. But he soon ceased to apply himself conscientiously to his theological studies, preferring to dabble in literature and philosophy. In June of 1835, he writes in a letter, "It is perhaps my misfortune that I am interested in far too much and not decisively in any one thing; my interests are not subordinated to one but instead all stand coordinate." He proceeds to say, "I am starting to study for the theological examination, a pursuit that does not interest me in the least and that therefore does not get done very fast"; he goes on to explain that he prefers free and unstructured studies to a systematically prescribed curriculum but intends to "dig in" and get through the degree program in order "to enter into the scholarly pastures" and to "make my father happy."⁷ In fact, however, he spent the next three years more or less drifting.

In August of 1835, he admits to himself,

> What I really lack is to be clear in my mind *what I am to do*, not what I am to know, except in so far as a certain understanding must precede every action. The thing is to understand myself, to see what God really wishes *me* to do; the thing is to find a truth which is true *for me*, to find *the idea for which I can live and die*.⁸

This passage neatly captures the quest for an existential identity and personal commitment which was to characterize the last twenty years of his life. What did he do during these aimless years? He attended the theater, frequented restaurants, indulged his fancies in fashionable clothing and drink. He may have visited a prostitute while in an inebriated condition, although his brief description of such an episode is ambiguous, suggesting a tortured remorse.[9] His analysis of his own reputation during this period of his life is merciless:

> If Copenhagen ever has been of one opinion about anybody, I venture to say that it was of one opinion about me, that I was an idler, a dawdler, a *flaneur*, a frivolous bird, intelligent, perhaps brilliant, witty, &c.—but as for "seriousness," I lacked it utterly.[10]

Why was he behaving in such an irresponsible manner as must have mortified his sober-minded father? Again the details are not very clear. In 1835, he writes, "the great earthquake occurred, the terrible revolution which suddenly forced upon me a new and infallible law of interpretation of all the facts." Remember that by this time "the facts" included the deaths of his mother and five of his six siblings. There seems little doubt that "the great earthquake" that left him so shaken had to do with one or more discoveries about his father, whom he had previously idolized. He probably learned that his father had cursed God in childhood or impregnated his mother before they had married or both. At any rate, he started viewing his father's advanced age as "not a divine blessing but rather a curse" and to regard his "whole family" as tainted with a sinful guilt for which "the punishment of God must be on it." He describes himself during this period as "torn asunder" and "in desperate despair." One part of him ("my real self") yearned to overcome the anguish, while another part ("my reflective self") found it fascinating. In 1836, he appears to have considered suicide:

> I have just returned from a party of which I was the life and soul; wit poured from my lips, everyone laughed and admired me—but I went away—and the dash should be as long as the earth's orbit—and wanted to shoot myself.

Still, in public, he played the part of the happy-go-lucky dilettante: "I am a Janus bifrons; I laugh with one face, I weep with the other."[11] In 1837, this life of the aesthete was partially mitigated by his teaching a Latin class at his childhood school.

In May of 1838, he seems to have had a religious experience which filled him with "an indescribable joy." His self-indulgent profligacy ended, and he was reconciled with his father. Unfortunately, less than three months later, his father died, and Kierkegaard writes regretfully, "I had so very much wished that he might live a few years longer"—presumably to see his son Søren complete his theology program. He felt driven to do so anyway, writing, "I can only presume that it is God's will that I should read for my exam." He worked at this for almost two years, describing this period of his life as "the longest parenthesis I have known."[12] On June 2, 1840, he formally petitioned the theology faculty for examination, admitting in his letter that he had drifted "farther and farther away from theology and in the course of time with all sails set slipped into the study of philosophy" and that it was his father's death which occasioned his resumption of theological studies.[13] Then, on July 3, 1840, he successfully completed his final examination in theology, almost ten years after he had entered the university. Thanks to his father's leaving him the family house and a considerable fortune, he would be financially secure for years to come.

In addition to his father, the other most important person in his life was Regina Olsen. He met her in 1837, when she was fourteen years of age (and he twenty-four). She was the youngest daughter of Terkel Olsen, a state councilor and official in the ministry of finance. Kierkegaard fell in love with her; and, although it has come to be a cliché, she would prove to be the love of his life. He waited for her to grow up. But an entry from his *Journals*, dated Feb. 2, 1839, indicates the force of his passion for her:

> Thou sovereign of my heart ("Regina") treasured in the deepest fastness of my breast, in the fullness of my thought. . . . Everywhere, in the face of every girl I see traces of your beauty, but it seems to me that I should have to possess the beauty of all of them in order to draw out a beauty equal to yours.

The month he completed his theology degree (July 1840), he left for a trip to Jutland to visit his father's birthplace. Even the sight of two mismatched "cows harnessed together . . . , the one jogging gaily along and swinging its tail with a fine dash, the other . . . depressed at having to take part in such emotions," was associated in his mind with his relationship to Regina, leading him to wonder, "Are not most marriages like that?" He was obsessed with thoughts of her: "During the whole of that time I let her being penetrate mine." He returned from the trip in early August. "The period from August 9 till the beginning of September I used in the strict sense to approach her." On the 8th of September, he passionately and dramatically proposed marriage to her, and she accepted a couple of days later. But he was flooded with doubts, for "the next day I saw that I had made a false step."[14]

In November, he entered the Royal Pastoral Seminary, which trained future clergymen, as if in pursuit of a profession (though he was never ordained). He was also at work at the university on his academic dissertation, *The Concept of Irony*. In January of 1841, he preached his first sermon. He submitted his dissertation for the degree of Master of Arts in June; it was accepted by the faculty of philosophy the following month, and in September he defended it orally for over seven hours.

In October of 1841, Kierkegaard performed the most painful act of his life, breaking off his engagement to Regina. The way in which he did this was peculiar. Not wanting her to feel rejected, he tried to engineer her rejecting him. As he writes, "I constrained my whole nature so as to repel her." But the ruse was unsuccessful, for "she answered passionately that she would bear anything rather than let me go." There can be no doubt that he loved her. He says that if he had been of a less melancholic nature, their marriage might have made him happier than he could ever dream of being. "But there was a divine protest, that is how I understand it." It appears that he did not believe it possible truly to commit himself to another human being and simultaneously to love God fully. Her father (whom he deeply respected) implored him to reconsider; but he feigned indifference even in the face of her appeal to Christ and his dead father's memory. He later writes, "It was a time of terrible suffering: to have to be so cruel and at the same time to love as I did. She fought like a tigress. If I had not believed that God had lodged a veto she would have been victorious." As they were parting, she asked him to promise to remember her, and he did. She asked that he kiss her goodbye; he says, "I did so but without passion." Then he left her; and, he says, "I spent the whole night crying on my bed."[15]

Almost two years later he recalled being in fear of "losing my mind in those days" because of grief. And he wistfully writes, "Had I had faith I should have remained with Regine." Is this faith in God's allowing him to commit to marriage or faith in his own ability to do so while continuing to love God fully? A third alternative is that he lacked faith in her capacity to stand his honest confessions concerning his own past and personality. He was unwilling to conceal existentially important truths from a wife. "But if I had had to explain myself then I would have had to initiate her into terrible things: my relation to my father, his melancholy, the eternal darkness that broods within, my going astray . . ."[16]

Two weeks later, Kierkegaard went to Berlin for a few months. He attended classes of the sixty-seven year old philosopher Schelling. In a letter, dated Feb. 27, 1842, to his brother Peter, he writes, "Schelling drivels on quite intolerably. . . . I am too old to attend lectures and Schelling is too old to give them." He cut short his visit to Berlin and returned to

Copenhagen a week later. Then began a prodigious output of writings. He was working on *Either/Or*, which was published in two volumes in February 1843. Before that time, he writes, "I began my little essay: *de omnibus dubitandum est* in which I made my first attempt at a bit of philosophical writing";[17] it, however, was left unfinished and was only published posthumously.[18]

In 1843, in addition to *Either/Or*,[19] Kierkegaard published *Fear and Trembling*,[20] as well as *Repetition*,[21] another "esthetic book." The following year, he published *Philosophical Fragments*,[22] as well as *The Concept of Dread.*[23] In 1845, his *Stages on Life's Way* was published. By the end of the year, he had delivered to the printer his *Concluding Unscientific Postscript*;[24] this work (which is arguably the finest anti-Hegelian book of philosophy) was published on Feb. 27, 1846. Its title has turned out to be ironic: (1) although Kierkegaard thought of ending his literary work and becoming a pastor, he, in fact, went on to write many more works; (2) it is proudly unsystematic, avoiding any pretense of being "scientific" in anything like the sense of Hegelian philosophy; and (3) this "postscript" to his earlier *Philosophical Fragments* turns out to be some 550 pages long. All of the works referred to thus far in these last two paragraphs were written under a variety of pseudonyms (more about the problem this poses later), which Kierkegaard acknowledged as his own in "A First and Last Declaration," attached as an appendix to the *Postscript*. But meanwhile, he was also writing and publishing many so-called *Edifying Discourses* under his own name. His literary output in this three-year period from February 1843 to February 1846 was astonishing.

During the last decade of his life, Kierkegaard became involved in polemics—with the press and with the Danish Church. *The Corsair* was a comic newspaper in Copenhagen that was founded and edited by Aaron Goldschmidt, who admired Kierkegaard. The paper dealt in caricature and gossip and was eagerly read, to the point of having the largest circulation in Denmark. While ridiculing everyone else, *The Corsair* lavished praise on the pseudonymous esthetic works of Kierkegaard. Far from being pleased, the latter is perversely provoked to write,

> Finally, one wish: if only I might appear in *The Corsair* soon. It is very difficult for an author to stand singled out in Danish literature as the only one (assuming that we pseudonyms are one) who is not abused there.[25]

The newspaper granted his wish with a vengeance. Almost every week for almost a year, *The Corsair* caricatured Kierkegaard in articles and cartoon drawings, making fun of his misshapen physique, his foppish style of dress, his personal habits, even his unfortunate love affair. Children in the streets took to taunting him as "old Either/Or." In 1846, he writes, "Even the butcher's boy almost thinks himself justified in being offensive to me at the behest of *The Corsair.* Undergraduates grin and giggle and are delighted that someone prominent should be trodden down." And indeed he had already become the most famous Danish intellectual, although he himself pokes fun at this status: "To be the greatest philosopher in Denmark is on the very border line of satire."[26] By the end of 1846, perhaps out of a sense of shame, Goldschmidt gave up on *The Corsair.* But out of this painful episode in Kierkegaard's life flowed his contempt for both the press and the crowd, as expressed, for example in his fierce denunciation of *The Present Age,* first published in 1846.

From the beginning of 1847 through the end of 1853 (that is, between the end of *The Corsair* affair and the beginning of his "Attack upon Christendom"), he returned to writing. Almost every year during this interval religious works were published under his own name, including *Works of Love.* In addition, he published *Two Minor Ethico-Religious Essays* and *Sickness unto Death* in 1849;[27] the following year, he published *Training in Christianity*;[28] both were published under pseudonyms. Thus Kierkegaard, instead of "concluding" his authorship with the *Postscript,* as he had intended, came to view that book as its "turning-point," which philosophically "set the problem . . . of the whole authorship, namely, 'how to become a Christian.'"[29] The religious works referred to in this paragraph were designed to address that problem.

An even more trying relationship than that with *The Corsair* was that generated by Kierkegaard's critique of the established Danish Church. Most of the documents of this critique have been gathered under the title *Attack upon "Christendom."*[30] As early as 1853, he felt driven by conscience to launch this critique, although he held back out of concern for Bishop J. P. Mynster, his father's friend and pastor. In Kierkegaard's mind the bishop personified the smug, stolid, self-satisfied religion of the official Christianity which Kierkegaard labeled "Christendom." Yet Kierkegaard hoped the bishop would come to realize the inadequacy of his attitude, without being subjected to public criticism, and adopt a more rigorous sense of what Christianity demands of the believer. This did not, in fact, happen, and the bishop died in January of 1854. On March 1, Kierkegaard writes in his *Journals,* "So now he is dead. If only it had been possible to persuade him to end his life with the admission that what he represented was not really Christianity." Now that reformation of the bishop was no longer possible, Kierkegaard adds, "everything is altered," including obligations connected with "my melancholy devotion to my father's priest." Given that Christianity requires a conscientious effort at "self-denial," it seems as "ridiculous" to Kierkegaard that the established Danish Church should call itself "Christian" as that someone should imagine a cow to be a horse. He regards his critique as "a battle against lies." Although it seems harsh to accuse the Church of systematic deception, "fundamentally that is the condition in Christendom, particularly in Protestantism, particularly in Denmark." He is convinced that reform is inevitable, "and it will be a frightful reformation compared with which the Lutheran reformation will be almost a joke." What is horrible to Kierkegaard is the self-deception of Christendom;

> for the thing is that Christianity really no longer exists, and it is terrible when a generation which has been molly-coddled by a childish Christianity, fooled into thinking it is Christianity, when it has to receive the death blow of learning once again what it means to be Christian.[31]

From Kierkegaard's point of view, Mynster had nurtured this awful illusion. Now that he was dead, Christendom could be openly attacked. What brought the need for such an assault to a head was a eulogy of Mynster by Hans Martensen (Kierkegaard's former theology tutor at the university), who in mid-April would succeed Mynster as bishop. Martensen praised Mynster as a model Christian in "the holy chain of witnesses to the truth which stretches through the ages from the days of the Apostles." Kierkegaard's response is strong: "Against this I must protest— and now that Bishop Mynster is dead, I can speak willingly." Christendom continues to follow his bad example insofar as it "soft-pedals, slurs over, suppresses, omits something decisively Christian . . . , which would make our life strenuous . . . , that part of Christianity which has to do with dying from this world, by voluntary renunciation."[32] Kierkegaard suffered a series of counterattacks and was vilified as anti-Christian. As a matter of fact, what he denied was that official Christendom was truly Christian. Comparisons with the Reformation continue: "O Luther, you had ninety-five theses; in our present situation there is only one thesis: Christianity does not exist at all."[33] Most of the last two years of his life were consumed by the polemics of this controversy.

During the last months of his life, Kierkegaard stopped his habitual attendance at church services. Meanwhile, the legacy he had inherited from his father was dwindling away. On October 2, 1855, he withdrew the last of his money from his bank; while returning home, he lost consciousness and fell to the street, paralyzed in the legs. He was taken to the Frederick's Hospital, where he allowed few visitors; he admitted some friends and relatives (but not his brother Peter). Urged to receive Holy Communion, he answered that he would not take it from any priest, but only from a layman. He died in the hospital on November 11.

There was only enough money left to pay for his hospital and funeral expenses. (His possessions—the most important being his personal library of over 2,000 volumes, most of which were religious, philosophical, and literary works—were auctioned off.) The funeral service was held in the cathedral, where his brother Peter delivered the eulogy. He was buried in the family plot next to his father. But there was an embarrassing scene at the cemetery, when his nephew, Henrik Lund, a young physician, protested against the Church's dishonest attempts to claim as its own a man who had vigorously and conscientiously denounced it. At any rate, his legacy was to have started what would become the existential movement in Western philosophy. As Kierkegaard was the first religious existentialist, a few decades later the German Friedrich Nietzsche, who invents a madman to proclaim that "God is dead," began the atheistic branch of existentialism.

Kierkegaard's writings have, for the most part, been mentioned in the previous subsection. We shall continue to consider his *Journals*, posthumously published *Papers*, and *Point of View*, all of which provide direct insight into his thought, as well as his *Attack upon "Christendom"* and *The Present Age*.[34] Occasional references will be made to his *Edifying Discourses*,[35] *Christian Discourses*,[36] and *Works of Love*.[37] But most of our attention will be focused upon such pseudonymous works as *Either/Or*, *Fear and Trembling*, *The Concept of Dread*, *Sickness unto Death*, and *Training in Christianity*—and, especially, on the three philosophical works identified with the pseudonym of Johannes Climacus, *De Omnibus Dubitandum Est*, *Philosophical Fragments*, and the *Postscript*. (Citations will often be cross-referenced with the selections included in *A Kierkegaard Anthology*, edited by Robert Bretall.)

This leads us to the problem of how to relate Kierkegaard's thought to the words expressed pseudonymously. He anticipated that scholars would wish to study him,[38] and he deliberately made the task difficult. In his "First and Last Declaration," appended to the *Postscript*, he insists that "in the pseudonymous works there is not a single word which is mine," despite the fact that the pseudonymous characters are admittedly his creations. He adds, "My wish, my prayer, is that, if it might occur to anyone to quote a particular saying from the books, he would do me the favor to cite the name of the respective pseudonymous author." He concludes with the hope that no would-be scholars "would lay a dialectic hand upon this work, but would let it stand as it now stands!"[39] However, in analyzing and interpreting his work and in attributing the words of his pseudonymous characters to him, this chapter will contravene his request. After all, he is the author of their words, and they do represent at least perspectives on his thought.

Yet, even given this decision to try to analyze Kierkegaard's thought and to identify the words expressed pseudonymously as his own, three further difficulties remain that do not beset other thinkers considered here. First, there will be a problem of interrelating works written under different pseudonyms to each other, as well as to Kierkegaard's non-pseudonymous works; this will call for careful interpretation, and we must beware of cheap accusations of inconsistency. Second, even within individual works, Kierkegaard's writing is notoriously and deliberately unsystematic; he self-consciously avoids imposing any artificial logical structure on his ideas, which leaves them somewhat resistant to the usual methods of philosophical analysis. Third, even individual sentences of Kierkegaard's writings cannot always be taken literally; it was not merely because of the title of his dissertation that he was called "the Master of Irony," and his works are permeated by an irrepressible wit and a sometimes savage sarcasm. However, there is no need to regard these difficulties as insuperable, as we proceed to study Kierkegaard's philosophical and religious ideas.

Existential Philosophy

Human Existence. Kierkegaard's analysis of human existence provides the backdrop against which his philosophy, in general, and his philosophy of religion, in particular, are developed. He builds on the traditional Christian theory of human nature as involving a combination of body and soul: "Man is a synthesis of the soulish and the bodily. But a synthesis is unthinkable if the two are not united in a third factor." As Kant had maintained that there is a phenomenal dimension to human nature existing in time and a noumenal dimension to human nature that transcends time, Kierkegaard says (in what sounds like Hegelian language) that man is "*a synthesis of the temporal and the eternal.*"[40] This synthesizing element constitutes the human essence.

> Man is spirit. But what is spirit? Spirit is the self. But what is the self? The self is a relation which relates itself to its own self.

His analysis here becomes even more tortuous, to the point where one wonders whether the pseudonymous character (called Anti-Climacus) is producing a parody of Hegelian language. Yet what is striking is the definition of the human person as essentially relational:

> Man is a synthesis of the infinite and the finite, of the temporal and the eternal, of freedom and necessity.

This is a more dynamic conception of man than was prevalent before Hegel, holding that "a self, every instant it exists, is in process of becoming."[41] Human existence, unlike the static being of other finite things, is a perpetual coming-to-be.

Kierkegaard is regarded as the father of existentialism. What sets him apart from earlier modern philosophers and connects him with later existentialists is his emphasis on individuality, free choice and personal commitment, and certain emotions which are uniquely characteristic of the human person.

The concept of individuality is essential not only to his philosophical perspective but also to his conception of religion. In *Journals*, he writes, "The whole development of the world tends to the importance of the individual; that and nothing else, is the principle of Christianity." He says that if he were to select an inscription for his own tombstone, he "would ask for none other than 'the individual.'" Monistic theories, such as those of Spinoza and Hegel, which subordinate individuality to some ideal, all-encompassing Absolute, pose a danger: "'The individual'; now that the world has gone so far along the road of reflection Christianity stands and falls with that category. But for that category Pantheism would have triumphed." Yet, he complains, in the history of philosophy, only Socrates has done justice to that category.[42] This notion of individuality suggests to Kierkegaard what it connotes to us—a uniqueness which radically distinguishes one person from all others. Although Hegel and Kierkegaard both view man as essentially spiritual, it is difficult to imagine the former saying with the latter, "Spirit precisely is this: not to be like others."[43]

For a couple of millennia philosophers had speculated about free will. What is wrong with this tradition, from Kierkegaard's perspective, is that the discussion usually tends to be hopelessly abstract and theoretical. We have already seen his own need for decisive action and personal commitment to "*what I am to do*" as opposed to "what I am to know" for its own sake. Later in the *Journals* he protests that "scientific" or objective speculation concerning the "phantom" of "freedom of choice" leads a person to become "doubtful whether he is free or not," until finally "he loses his freedom of choice." And he denies that it can ever be recovered "by the use of thought alone"—but only through the active practice of "choosing."

(A generation later, William James arrived at a similar conclusion.) Man cannot and should not live by abstract thought alone. "The most tremendous thing which has been granted to man is: the choice, freedom."[44]

Kierkegard, in addition to emphasizing individuality and free choice, focuses on certain existential emotions which previous philosophers ignored. Unlike most philosophers before him, especially the rationalists up to and including Hegel, he does not focus on the intellectual dimension as constituting the human essence. Rather, as he says in his *Journals*, "Passion is the real thing, the real measure of man's power." His dominant criticism of his own culture is for its lack of passion: "What the age needs is *pathos*."[45] This critique is developed at length in *The Present Age*, beginning with its famous first sentence: "Our age is essentially one of understanding and reflection, without passion, momentarily bursting into enthusiasm, and shrewdly relapsing into repose."[46]

Three existential emotions on which he focuses are melancholy, dread, and despair. We have already considered his reflections on his own melancholy and that of his father. He analyzes it more objectively in *Either/Or* as "hysteria of the spirit." It should not be confused with "sorrow," in that it is normal for a person to understand "why he is sorrowful"—because his brother died or his marriage has fallen apart, etc. By contrast, it is useless to ask the melancholic person "what it is that weighs upon him" so. If we do so, the "correct" response is, "I know not, I cannot explain it." Kierkegaard refers to this inexplicability as "the infinity of melancholy." He warns us that it is not susceptible to extrinsic cure, that "the physicians cannot relieve it. Only spirit can relieve ... a spiritual ailment."[47] Its source is internal, and its object is the self. Whereas I am sorrowful about some event or condition in my environment, I am melancholic about the condition of my own spirit.

Kierkegaard wrote a whole book on *The Concept of Dread*, a second existential emotion. He says that nothing—that is, no particular thing—"begets dread." He adds that "it is different from fear," which has a specific object (for example, that bear attacking me or the threat of nuclear war), "whereas dread is freedom's reality as possibility." Then a paradoxical definition is provided: "Dread is a *sympathetic antipathy and an antipathetic sympathy*." Thus, it is an emotional ambivalence (a physical analogue would be that of simultaneous attraction and repulsion), provoking anguish, whereby I yearn for that which I would avoid. But what is that? He illustrates by means of the Old Testament story of Adam being forbidden to eat of the tree of the knowledge of good and evil. Adam experiences dread insofar as "the prohibition awakens in him the possibility of freedom." So for us too dread is "the alarming possibility of *being able*." He uses an analogy of a person walking along a precipice "whose eye chances to look down into the yawning abyss" and who "becomes dizzy." Part of his problem is the realization that he might let himself fall or even throw himself headlong. "Thus dread is the dizziness of freedom." To be incapable of dread would be humanly unfortunate, since it would indicate a lack of spirit and of the awareness of freedom's possibilities.[48]

In *The Sickness unto Death*, Kierkegaard's pseudonymous Anti-Climacus explains that three different forms of "despair" can arise from the kind of synthesis that the human self is: first, there is "Despair at Not Being Conscious of Having a Self (Despair Improperly So Called);" second, there is "Despair at Not Willing to Be Oneself;" and, third, there is "Despair at Willing to Be Oneself." The last two forms are genuine—wishing to deny one's own self, on the one hand, and defiantly wishing to assert one's identity in absolute independence, on the other. Kierkegaard maintains (rather dogmatically) that the self one is has not been one's own creation merely but "is grounded transparently in the Power which posited it." This, of course, is an allusion to God and distinguishes Kierkegaard's Christian existentialism from the atheistic brand of, say, Nietzsche. Despair is held to be both "an advantage" (insofar as it is spiritual and makes man qualitatively superior to "the beast") and "a drawback" (insofar as it involves "the greatest misfortune and misery"). Despair is a "sickness unto death" in that it robs us of the hope of spiritual life without affording us the relief of death; "no, the hopelessness in this case is that even the last hope, death, is not available." Thus, far from actually destroying us, "the sickness unto death" or "despair is the disconsolateness of not being able to die."[49] The human spiritual self can experience despair because it is conscious and free to choose existential possibilities in relation to the necessity of its own existence.

In one of his most original and extensively developed contributions to psychological theory, Kierkegaard charts the course of human development through several spheres of existence. *Either/Or* is structured in such a way as to contrast two such spheres, the aesthetic sphere of immediacy, which is essentially oriented towards feelings of pleasure or enjoyment (which may be intellectual as well as physical), and the ethico-religious, which is rooted in personal commitment to values: "What is it, then, that I distinguish in my either/or? Is it good and evil? No, ... one either has to live aesthetically or one has to live ethically." The aesthetic life precedes all moral action. "My either/or does not in the first instance denote the choice between good and evil; it denotes the choice whereby one chooses good *and* evil/or excludes them." Prior to ethical commitment, one drifts amorally. "It is, therefore, not so much a question of choosing between willing the good or the evil, as of choosing to will, but by this in turn the good and the evil are posited."[50] Once one has entered the ethical sphere, then the choice between good and evil becomes meaningful.

Stages on Life's Way (two years later) presents a more complex scheme: "There are three existence-spheres: the aesthetic, the ethical, the religious." Here the ethical is described as "only a transitional sphere" between the first and the third. "The aesthetic sphere is that of immediacy, the ethical is that of requirement . . . , the religious sphere is that of fulfillment." It is significant that there is no separate philosophical stage. Kierkegaard seems to reject Hegel's highest level of spiritual development when he writes, "The metaphysical is abstraction, there is no man who exists metaphysically."[51]

The *Postscript* (one year later still) recalls the "tripartite division" of *Stages*, identifying the aesthetic sphere with "enjoyment," the ethical with "action," and the religious with "suffering." Kierkegaard's pseudonymous Johannes Climacus admits that its scheme is different from the earlier dichotomy. "But in spite of this triple division the book is nevertheless an either-or. The ethical and the religious stages have in fact an essential relationship to one another." In the *Postscript* there emerges a greater refinement of this psychological schema:

> There are thus three spheres of existence: the aesthetic, the ethical, the religious. Two boundary zones correspond to these three: irony, constituting the boundary between the aesthetic and the ethical; humor, as the boundary that separates the ethical from the religious.

Irony arises from the juxtaposition of the finite particularities of transient aesthetic interest and the universal commitments of ethical responsibility; humor consists in the contrast between the actively involved ethical hero and the equally committed "knight of hidden inwardness," who is "incognito" as "a religious individual." Kierkegaard now differentiates between two kinds of religiousness—the religion of immanence and that of paradox: "*The religiousness A,*" as he calls the former, strives to absorb (Hegel might say "sublate") the contradiction between transcendence and existential inwardness. "*The paradoxical religiousness* breaks with immanence and makes the fact of existing the absolute contradiction," not to be absorbed or overcome at all. It is debatable whether Kierkegaard means to present his doctrine of existential spheres as a hierarchy, but it appears that he does. Human existence is always originally at the level of the aesthetic, and a person must choose to rise above this level and live within the ethical. One can become religious only by passing through (and never entirely abandoning—remember the "either-or") the ethical; and, similarly, one must pass through the religion of immanence to reach the paradoxical religiousness. Kierkegaard rejects the Hegelian notion that we can move by means of any dialectical "transition of speculative philosophy" as "a chimera, an illusion," emphasizing precisely the lack of continuity in progressing from one sphere to the next, that can only be accomplished by means of "a *leap*."[52] This psychological analysis of human existence provides a context for Kierkegaard's ambivalence toward philosophy in general and repudiation of Hegelian philosophy in particular.

Attitude toward Philosophy. Kierkegaard's attitude toward philosophy is, indeed, ambivalent. Although he exhibited a special interest in philosophy even when he was supposed to be studying theology, and despite the fact that his graduate degree was in philosophy, he does not typically pass himself off as a philosopher. On the contrary, he repeatedly denies—at least pseudonymously—that he is any such thing.[53] Nor does he pretend to comprehend the Hegelian system, the prevailing philosophy of his time and therefore of special concern to him (more of this in the next subsection). As one of his pseudonymous characters says, "I for my part have devoted a good deal of time to the understanding of the Hegelian philosophy, I believe also that I understand it tolerably well, but . . . there are certain passages I cannot understand."[54] The pseudonymous character with whom his most philosophical works are identified, Johannes Climacus, is presented as a student of philosophy who is in love with reflective thinking, although uncertain of his chances of success at it: "Whether he would ever become a philosopher he did not know, but he would try his best."[55]

Not only does Kierkegaard shy away from claiming to be a philosopher, but he also refuses to call himself a Christian, acknowledges his imperfections as a Christian, and goes so far as to aver, "I have not seen a single Christian existence in the more rigorous sense, and this applies to me."[56] Yet he does claim to "know what Christianity is" and defends the possibility of even a non-Christian's knowing this; even the dialectical Climacus "does not raise the question of the truth of Christianity" but "merely deals with the question of the individual's relationship to Christianity."[57]

If Kierkegaard is reluctant to identify himself as either a philosopher or a Christian (let alone as a Christian philosopher), he does claim to be a poet and a religious author. He wants to provide "what may be called a 'corrective' " to philosophy and for Christianity. He realizes that, in order to be effective, it is sometimes necessary to exaggerate his case and admits that he leaves himself open to the accusation (which will be raised here) that that corrective is too "one-sided." Presumably, he would have held that the one-sidedness is necessary in order "to introduce Christianity into Christendom."[58] The purpose of his authorship is to provide a critique—sometimes using a philosophical methodology—of philosophy relative to Christianity and of Christendom itself. His polemic against philosophy is designed to defend Christianity against rationalizations which he sees as diluting it and threatening to make it comfortably bland because it systematically avoids all controversy.

It is particularly modern philosophy that provides Kierkegaard with his philosophical target. Following Descartes, it purports to have been born in systematic, disinterested doubt. This is the main topic of *De Omnibus Dubitandum Est* (literally meaning, "Everything Must Be Doubted"), which is about Climacus; this sort of Cartesian doubt is later (in the *Postscript*) dismissed by Climacus as "an impossibility for an existing individual." Kierkegaard suspects that modern philosophy views doubt and wonder as opposites and prefers to side with Plato and Aristotle in the view that philosophy should begin with a concerned wonder. He complains that his own age has become so blasé as to have neglected "this thing of wondering"—and, correlatively, "the thing of believing"—in its quest for indubitable knowledge born of methodical doubting. Kierkegaard's preference ties in with his reluctance to analyze human existence in terms of a purely intellectual dimension. Wonder affects the human spirit in a global manner, as do two existential conditions previously discussed, dread and despair. Not that he takes doubt lightly—on the contrary, he takes it so seriously that he finds it ridiculous that philosophers should make an intellectual game of it for their own self-aggrandizement, insincerely bragging that they have doubted everything. He experiences a less artificial doubt, which is neither abstractly theoretical nor self-imposed, "a cursed hunger" which afflicts him willy-nilly: "My doubt is terrible.—Nothing can withstand it." This existential doubt, so different from what Kierkegaard regards as the phony doubt of Descartes and his followers, is comparable to despair: "Doubt is a despair of thought, despair is a doubt of the personality." Genuine doubt, far from being disinterested, is not a matter of abstract speculation at all. As Kierkegaard writes in his discourse on "The Expectation of Faith," "Doubt is a profound and cunning passion, but he whose soul it did not grip so intensely that he became speechless, only falsely imputes this passion to himself." Thus, Kierkegaard finds deceptive not only the Cartesian doubting exercise, but also the entire set of philosophical worldviews built upon it. One might suppose that this is the point of the cryptic, but charming, allegory contained among his "Diapsalmata": "What the philosophers say about Reality is often as disappointing as a sign you see in a shop window, which reads: Pressing Done Here. If you brought your clothes to be pressed, you would be fooled; for the sign is only for sale."[59]

On this view, modern philosophy's quest for indubitable knowledge and its claims to have achieved certainty from the starting point of skeptical doubt strike Kierkegaard as a fatuous sham. Is this fair to the tradition stretching from Descartes through Locke, Leibniz, Hume, and Kant to Hegel? Probably it is not. Despite the dubious methods and conclusions of some of them, all these philosophers seriously and sincerely probe the foundations and limits of human knowledge, including that which would be theological. Here is an example of where Kierkegaard's "corrective" seems too "one-sided."

Critique of Hegel. Kierkegaard's critique of Hegel is particularly well focused and adroitly executed because in Denmark, during the former's lifetime, Hegel was hailed as the apotheosis of modern philosophy. The contrast between these two thinkers is glaring. Where Hegel sought the idea, which is true independently of my acknowledging it, Kierkegaard, as we have seen, sought "a truth which is true *for me*, to find *the idea for which I can live and die*," an existential "Archimedean point," as he so frequently puts it.[60] Where Hegel delights in abstract thought, Kierkegaard denies that he, as an existing human, can ever abstract from his own self; where Hegel forswears the edifying (as nonphilosophical), the first important book of Kierkegaard's official authorship concludes with the claim that "only the truth which edifies is truth for you," and a large percentage of his writings are labeled "Edifying Discourses"; where Hegel sees philosophical knowledge as the highest achievement of the human spirit, Kierkegaard seeks the "total transformation" of the personality which religion rather than philosophy provides.[61] Where Hegel follows the age-old tradition of seeking self-knowledge as the upshot of reflective thought, Kierkegaard "deliberately preferred to use the expression 'choose oneself' instead of know oneself."[62]

Because Hegel serves as the takeoff point for most of Kierkegaard's critical observations about philosophy, it should come as no surprise that the position of faith and reason which will be attributed to the latter in the next section will be sharply antithetical to Hegel's own. But before turning to that, let us examine six objections Kierkegaard raises against Hegel.

First, although Hegel's comprehensive system is an impressive construction, an admirably consistent and ingenious mass of theory, where it fails is in its practical application to individual human beings—one can marvel at it and strive to comprehend it intellectually. But one cannot live by it. Kierkegaard humorously compares the Hegelian thinker to an architect who builds an elaborate palace in which he cannot live, but who is forced to reside in an adjoining shack.[63]

Second, Kierkegaard finds it annoying that the Hegelian system is never quite finished (since, after all, history remains an ongoing process). The critic who complains that the system is not quite clear or convincing is only given the promissory note that clarity and conviction will come at the end of the exposition when the entire system can be comprehended as a whole. But, as Kierkegaard points out, a system must be characterized by finality; one that is unfinished is not truly (or, at least, not yet) a system. He admits that reality as a whole "is a system—for God; but it cannot be a system for any existing spirit,"[64] such as we are, who cannot step outside the flux of becoming to comprehend it.

Third, Kierkegaard accuses Hegel of having omitted from his system an ethics. He does not mean, of course, that Hegel has neglected to discuss ethical matters; certainly, the system includes social theory and political philosophy. But the essential ingredient of ethical theory, the existing, individual human subject, is either ignored or absorbed into the cosmic, historical process. For Kierkegaard, the individual's place in ethical theory is its most important part; its omission makes a meaningful "life view" impossible,[65] and it renders the system personally irrelevant to both the speculative thinker and his reader or student.

Fourth, Kierkegaard objects that the Hegelian philosophy, with its method of dialectical mediation, blurs real distinctions which life affirms: "The systematic Idea is the identity of subject and object, the unity of thought and being. Existence, on the other hand, is their separation." A favorite example is the distinction between inner and outer. Surely they are correlative categories, but Kierkegaard points to the religious believer as a concrete example of the fact that "there is an inwardness which is incommensurable for the outward," because his external behavior may reveal nothing of his internal faith-commitment. The alleged identity of most importance for Kierkegaard is that of reality and ideality: things which have "real" being are immediate objects that might be encountered in direct experience, whereas speech and thought have an "ideal" being in the mind; these two spheres are ontologically opposed to one another and are related only by consciousness, which itself is neither reality nor ideality, but is rather the relationship between the two.[66] Thought and being are identical only for a consciousness which mistakenly interprets both of them ideally, as Hegel purportedly does.

Fifth, Kierkegaard holds that existence necessarily resists all attempts at dialectical mediation. Much of the *Postscript* is devoted to showing that an existential system is humanly impossible, that the "either-or" of existence (Hamlet's dichotomy, "to be or not to be") cannot be abrogated.[67] Although the essential function of consciousness is to relate reality and thought, existence eludes attempts at scientific definition and objective knowledge; absolute certainty for human beings is to be found in the abstract realms of logic and mathematics, neither of which successfully encompasses existence.

Sixth, Kierkegaard rejects the notion that the Hegelian system was— or could be—presuppositionless. In fact, he notes, it assumes at least three possible points of departure:

> There is (1) The *absolute* beginning, i.e. the concept of Absolute Spirit or Mind which is also the goal and end of the System. (2) The *objective* beginning, i.e. the absolute undefined concept of Pure Being ... (3) The *subjective* beginning, i.e. the work of consciousness.[68]

Each of these three possible beginnings (the first most relevant to the philosophy of religion and the philosophy of history, the second to the logic, and the last to the phenomenology of mind) is based on its own presupposition. Kierkegaard's point, then, seems to be that, however we choose to begin philosophizing, we do so on the basis of some presupposition(s)—whether it be the Absolute, Pure Being, Consciousness, or whatever—and that the only way to avoid theoretical presuppositions altogether is to refuse to begin philosophizing at all.

These, then, are six recurrent objections that Kierkegaard marshals against Hegelian philosophy, although he never systematically organizes them as has been done here. What they all have in common is a rejection of any attempt to absorb the existential dimensions of reality into a logical system with its neat and sterile **triadic** schema. Such an attempt is seen as little more than philosophical legerdemain, to be accomplished with the distracting bombast of a magical formula—*"ein zwei drei kokolorum"* ("one, two, three, abracadabra," as we might say). Despite its failures, the Hegelian project remains impressive, and Kierkegaard promises that, as an "opponent" of Hegel, he "will always know how to hold him in honor, as one who has willed something great, though without having achieved it." If, as Kierkegaard maintains, existential reality is a system only for God, who transcends the constant flux of existence, the systematic thinker who presumptuously pretends to share in the divine prerogative is like a deluded dancer—admirable in that he outleaps all other dancers, but ridiculous in thinking he can fly.[69]

We should realize the extent to which Kierkegaard respects Hegel as "a great, an outstanding logician," expresses his admiration for Hegel's "philosophical knowledge, his amazing learning, the insight of his genius," and is confident that he will continue to be "willing to learn from him" in the future. All this is important in the light of Kierkegaard's savage attacks, as when he calls him "a repulsive professor" and expresses appreciation for Schopenhauer's description of Hegel as "a windbag." But perhaps the best summary of his own critical view is this:

> If Hegel had written his whole logic and had written in the preface that it was only a thought-experiment, in which at many points he still steered clear of some things, he undoubtedly would have been the greatest thinker who has ever lived. As it is he is comic.[70]

Kierkegaard has arguably presented the most penetrating critique of Hegel in the history of Western philosophy. Apart from the sarcasm and unkind personal attacks, this critique seems generally correct. We might agree with Kierkegaard, for example, on all six of the preceding objections. Yet what is most important for our purposes is that this critique is the takeoff point for Kierkegaard's philosophy of religion, which is staunchly opposed to the Hegelian one that was so dominant in the first half of the nineteenth century. Kierkegaard realizes how unfashionable it is to attack Hegel and that the easy way to a speculative coronation would be to have "extolled most beautifully the praises of the deceased king" (as Martensen did Mynster). But he hopes that the turmoil of opposition may provide the stimulus necessary to establish the truth concerning man's religious relationship to God—"one always fishes best in troubled waters." To achieve this end, he is fully prepared to be an outsider in the realm of thought—"like a sparrow at a dance of cranes."[71]

Religious Epistemology

Faith and Knowledge. Kierkegaard's distinction between faith and knowledge is crucial to his religious epistemology. Even more than Kant had done, he denies knowledge in order to make room for faith. Nevertheless, he does *not* deny the validity of objective thought, even if he does restrict its scope (for example, to the areas of science, mathematics, and historical knowledge). His words on this point are clear, though they do not stand out in such a way as to arrest the attention of his reader: "It is not denied that objective thought has validity; but in connection with all thinking where subjectivity must be accentuated, it is a misunderstanding." It is specifically ethico-religious knowledge, which is value-oriented and calls for personal commitment, that cannot be objective, disinterested, and impersonal:

> All essential knowledge relates to existence. . . . has a relationship to the knower, who is essentially an existing individual. . . . Only ethical and ethico-religious knowledge has an essential relationship to the existence of the knower.

Kierkegaard's story of the lunatic who has escaped from the asylum and tries to convince everyone that he is sane by repeating the datum of objective knowledge that "the earth is round" establishes the point. There is no problem with the reality, accuracy, validity, or importance of such objective knowledge, but only with its relevance to our lives, to our values, and to our personal convictions. By contrast, Kierkegaard says of ethico-religious truth that "its decisive characterization as edifying for you, i.e. for the subject, constitutes its essential difference from all objective knowledge, in that the subjectivity itself becomes the mark of the truth."[72] So, objective knowledge has its uses; yet not all knowledge need be reduced to it.

Kierkegaard has his pseudonymous Climacus push this point by distinguishing between objective truth (as in matters of scientific fact) and subjective truth (appropriate to ethico-religious relationships). "In the ethico-religious sphere" (this qualification is important and too easily overlooked) truth is to be located in the authenticity of the relationship between a person and the object of his attention, rather than in the nature of the content to which the person is related: "*The objective accent falls on WHAT is said, the subjective accent on HOW it is said.*" In subjective truth what is emphasized—as against the validity of knowledge—is the authenticity (i.e., the sincerity and intensity of commitment) of the believer. Kierkegaard even invents a definition of subjective truth, which, if taken seriously, seems to demand the absence of (objective) knowledge: "Here is such a definition of truth: *An objective uncertainty held fast in an appropriation-process of the most passionate inwardness is the truth*, the highest truth attainable for an *existing* individual." He adds that this conception of subjective truth (the sort relevant to ethical and religious values) "is an equivalent expression for faith."[73] The dialectical tension between the two component elements of this definition—the "objective uncertainty" of its content, on the one hand, and "the most passionate inwardness" of its appropriation, on the other—renders it strikingly paradoxical.

The simplest recourse is to dismiss it as a joke, a parody of philosophical definitions; and, indeed, it must be admitted that one is rarely sure when dealing with Kierkegaard's pseudonymous characters. But if this is to be understood as foundational to a philosophy of religion which is to have rational import, it must be taken seriously and critically analyzed. Thus interpreted, the definition is a novel one which flies in the face of all traditional analyses of (objective) truth. One might acknowledge a certain brilliance of psychological insight here while objecting to the unconventional use of the word "truth." It seems perverse to call this "appropriation-process" by the name of "truth" while denying that it has anything to do with the established canons of truth. It can only generate confusion to say of religion, for example, that "objectively there is no truth; for an objective knowledge of the truth of Christianity, or of its truths, is precisely untruth." Or consider the famous six word slogan, "Subjectivity is truth, subjectivity is reality."[74] Even if we restrict its application to ethico-religious matters as we should (to ward off charges of irresponsible irrationalism), the formula is at loggerheads with ordinary opinion, rendering it suspect (though, of course, not necessarily false).

Although this may seem a bit artificial, let us consider the formula by emphasizing, in turn, each of its six component words. First, it is not *subjectivity*, but objectivity which is generally understood to be related to truth; what is normally considered true is so independently of any particular perceiving or conceiving subject. Second, subjectivity is not itself understood to be what *is* the truth; at most it is thought to be a manner in which truth might (perhaps sometimes should) be appropriated or a condition of the acceptance of truth. Third, subjectivity—far from being *truth*—is commonly considered a prejudicial obstacle in the way to establishing truth. Fourth, it is not *subjectivity* but the objective realm of fact that is commonly taken to constitute reality. Fifth, subjectivity *is* not itself reality but that which relates itself to reality. And, sixth, subjectivity is usually understood, not as *reality*, but rather as a contrasting ideality. (All of this, of course, does not refute the slogan but only emphasizes its deviation from ordinary conceptual usage.)

Beyond these misgivings about the concept of "subjective truth" presented in the *Postscript* is Kierkegaard's rejection of any assimilation of religious faith to reflective knowledge: "Faith is not a form of knowledge. . . .

belief is not a form of knowledge, but a free act, an expression of will."[75] This thesis can be analyzed as a threefold denial regarding faith:

1. Faith can never be a matter of objective certainty.[76]
2. Faith should never involve the reckoning of probabilities.[77]
3. Faith is not any sort of intellectual acceptance of doctrine at all.[78]

The next four paragraphs will consider these three points in inverse order.

Because Christianity, in Kierkegaard's opinion, is not any sort of intellectual doctrine, it is (as Anti-Climacus puts it) "extraordinarily stupid" even to attempt to defend it rationally. Although we are not given any argument to support this strong (and dubious) thesis, it seems that Kierkegaard has it in mind when he accuses Hegel of being one of the greatest enemies of Christianity: whereas others have attacked it without distortion, Hegel perverts it into an intellectual doctrine to be intellectually appropriated. For Hegel, faith is only a steppingstone on the highway of speculative knowledge, whereas, for Kierkegaard, Christian faith originates in a submission of the intellect and an acknowledgment of the lack of any possible knowledge. Against the view that religious faith prepares the way for philosophical knowledge, he writes, "Christianity begins about where Hegel ends; the misunderstanding is only that Hegel thought that he was through with Christianity *at that point*—had even gone beyond it."[79]

If religious faith does not essentially involve matters of intellectual doctrine, it follows that it cannot rest on the calculation of probabilities that Kierkegaard calls an "approximation-process." One might imagine, for example, that Christianity, being a historical religion, could find historical data relevant to its confirmation or falsification. Yet Kierkegaard insists that historical knowledge is always merely an inductive approximation, a matter of probabilities, and that historical certainty is impossible:

> Nothing historical can become infinitely certain for me except the fact of my own existence (which again cannot become infinitely certain for any other individual, who has infinite certainty only of his own existence), and this is not something historical.

But if historical certainty is impossible, probability is inadequate because, in relation to an eternal happiness, even an iota of uncertainty or improbability is significant.[80]

It may be granted that religious faith cannot be reasonably "regarded merely as knowledge of historical matters" and also that it is foolish to demand documentary proof of the essence of the Christian faith, in particular of the Incarnation. But what seems unreasonable is Kierkegaard's view that all this "makes every historic support meaningless," that historical knowledge is completely irrelevant to the validity of Christianity, that the "religious seeks no support in the historic."[81] The fact of the historical existence or nonexistence of Christ is clearly relevant, if not critical. Likewise, much of what we might learn about the sort of person he was and the kind of things he did is relevant—it matters whether the evidence shows him to have been kind or cruel, loving or sadistic, a benefactor or a ne'er-do-well. Historical records may not be conclusive here, but they are relevant.

Kierkegaard is on safer ground (with Kant and against Hegel) in his denial that religious faith can ever be "elevated" to the status of objective certainty. His very definition of faith in terms of "objective uncertainty" (analyzed previously) makes his point strongly. But he perhaps goes too far in implying that proof and conviction are inversely related.[82] Personal commitment to a demonstrable fact may be a distasteful perversion of inwardness; we might think that this is not a proper object of intense concern. Yet it is not generally true to the psychological facts to say that the more (objective) certainty there is, the less (subjective) conviction there can be; and it seems arbitrary to demand that we should assume it true in the case of religious faith. Since so much of rational theology, in the history of Christian philosophy, has revolved around the project of speculative arguments for God, let us briefly consider what Kierkegaard says about them.

God's Existence. Kierkegaard's rejection of proofs of God is contained in his *Philosophical Fragments*, in one of the few sustained arguments in his entire authorship. Climacus puts the challenge in the form of a dilemma. Either God does or does not exist. But if "God does not exist it would of course be impossible to prove it; and if he does exist it would be folly to attempt it. For at the very outset, in beginning my proof, I would have presupposed it." Kierkegaard realizes that this last point is most vulnerable to attack. Can we demonstrate existence without (somehow) presupposing it in the process? "Generally speaking, it is a difficult matter to prove that anything exists," he maintains. "I do not, for example, prove that a stone exists, but that some existing thing is a stone." In other words, existence must be experienced; only properties of existing things are provable. Thus, existence "is never subject to demonstration." For example, Napoleon's "existence does indeed explain his deeds, but the deeds do not prove *his* existence, unless I have already understood the word 'his' so as thereby to have assumed his existence." Nor will it do to say that this sort of argument from someone's deeds to his existence only works in the case of God, whose essence, unlike Napoleon's, necessarily involves existence. This invokes the ontological argument, which mistakenly blurs the "distinction between factual being and ideal being." If we nevertheless try to argue to God's existence from God's deeds, where do we start? "The wisdom in nature, the goodness, the wisdom in the governance of the world—are all these manifest, perhaps, upon the very face of things?" No, they are rather interpretations attached to my experience of my world.

> From what works then do I propose to derive the proof? From the works as apprehended through an ideal interpretation. . . . But in that case it is not from the works that I make the proof; I merely develop the ideality I have presupposed.

The moment I presuppose that ideal interpretation I must make what Kierkegaard calls "a *leap*" in logic. Such proof can only be called "demonstration by a leap."[83]

This is a philosophically competent critique of the traditional proofs of God, and it seems plausible, although it does not present anything strikingly new. The point made against the ontological argument goes back to medieval times; the point that our experience of the world must be subjectively interpreted before it can be used in a proof would be familiar to Hume; and the denial that existence can be demonstrated is a restatement of Kant's claim that existence is not a predicate. (Nor does Kierkegaard seem to take into account Hegel's attempt to rework the proofs.) Against Hegel, Kierkegaard is correct in emphasizing the difference between logical demonstration and religious worship: "To stand on one foot and prove the existence of God is altogether different from falling on one's knees and thanking him";[84] but this is a distinction also stressed by another of his predecessors, Pascal, who noted that the god of philosophers and scientists is not necessarily identical with the religious God of Abraham, Isaac, and Jacob. So, on the one hand, Kierkegaard's views here are well taken; but, on the other hand, there is not much here that is original.

Faith and Reason. Kierkegaard's fideistic deflation of reason goes beyond his refusal to assimilate religious faith to reflective knowledge. Here his analysis will constitute an attack on the very possibility of any rational theology—so that he offers a philosophy of religion to end all positive philosophies of religion. Yet this will also provide his own idea of what faith is as a complement to the negative characterization we considered earlier (that it is not intellectual, not a matter of probability calculation, and not a matter of speculative proof). His view, which we shall carefully analyze here, portrays faith as essentially a matter of passion and inwardness, of willed immediacy after reflection, of a submission to authority, of interpersonal trust, and of risk, as "a leap" willed in grace. Putting false modesty aside, he claims in his *Journals*, "It is clear that in my writings I have given a further definition of the concept faith, which did not exist until now."[85] This may or may not be so. But no one, at least, had previously developed, with such keen acuity as Kierkegaard, the dialectical tension, for the person of faith, between subjective certitude and objective uncertainty; and this is the feature of his philosophy of religion which is most famous and most controversial.

In the *Postscript*, Kierkegaard has Climacus define faith as the act of holding fast the improbable (indeed the absurd) "in the passion of inwardness."[86] Although there can be no doubt that this is the view attributed to Climacus, can we reasonably attribute it to Kierkegaard himself? Yes, because it is compatible with analyses made under four other pseudonyms, as well as material he wrote under his own name. In *Either/Or* faith is called "an inwardness of the entire being"; *Fear and Trembling* tells us that "faith is the highest passion in a man" which "begins precisely there where thinking leaves off"; in *The Concept of Dread* faith is described as "the inward certainty which anticipates infinity"; and in *Training in Christianity* Anti-Climacus holds that faith is an acceptance of subjective truth in inwardness—no mere intellectual opinion, but an acceptance of the paradoxical in the face of intellectual offense. And in his *Christian Discourses*, which is not written under any pseudonym, Kierkegaard explains faith as a matter of "personal concern" held in "fear and trembling" in the face of "all doubt about the truth of the doctrine."[87]

Assuming, then, that this is Kierkegaard's own conception of faith, he has performed a valuable service in distinguishing between a mere intellectual assent to a collection of rational truths, understood in an objective manner, and a personal commitment to a relationship of subjects. The problem with the analysis is not that it aims at going beyond the findings of objective thought, but that faith is presented as if it were at loggerheads with objective thought.[88] The antithesis between subjective faith (as personal passion) and objective thought (as reflective reason) is too radically uncompromising. Although faith be incompatible with a purely objective attitude, the "passionate inwardness" might itself (at least in part) be achieved as a result of, or be supported by, rational considerations. Attempts to show the reasonableness of belief in God, so long as these do not purport to be logically conclusive, far from destroying the possibility of faith, may well support it. Despite Kierkegaard, there could be findings of reason which incline toward belief without coercing it, so that the subjective relationship which is faith is (at least somewhat) motivated by objective considerations, such as the acknowledgement of factual probabilities.

The movement of faith is an act of will rather than of the intellect. In one of the earliest of all the entries in his *Papers* (from 1834), Kierkegaard writes, "Faith certainly requires an expression of will"—and the reason for his conviction here is the New Testament teaching (probably a reference to the last clause of *Romans* 14) "which says that he who does not have faith shall be punished." He speaks of faith as a higher form of immediacy than spontaneous prereflective intuition, as "immediacy or spontaneity after reflection." It is interesting to contrast with Climacus's intellectually oriented analysis of faith, in the *Postscript*, the more voluntaristic definition provided here:

> What is it to believe? It is to will (what one *ought* and because one *ought*), God-fearingly and unconditionally obediently, to defend oneself against the vain thought of wanting to comprehend and against the vain imagination of being able to comprehend.

This **voluntaristic** definition of faith incorporates an element of irrationalism. Sometimes, Kierkegaard suggests that an adequately determined "will to believe" (to use James's subsequent phrase) will suffice for the attaining of religious faith. Commenting on a famous Scriptural passage (*Matthew* 7:7), he writes that—although the door will be opened to us when we knock—it may be that "the difficulty for us human beings is simply that we are afraid to go—and knock."[89] When we see to what extent a denial of reason and its methods and findings is demanded as a prerequisite for the "knocking" of Kierkegaardian faith, this reluctance may be understandable.

We have already referred to what may be the most important of his *Edifying Discourses*, the one on "The Expectation of Faith," which this paragraph will consider more carefully. First, if faith is a matter of will, rather than of intellect, then "it is a good in which all can share," and not merely the clever. Second, he tries to distinguish between idly and passively wishing one could believe and making a deliberate, active commitment of the will. Third, he presents a fourfold analysis of faith as *incommunicable* ("no man can give it to another"), *intrinsic* ("it is inherent" in the believer), *deliberate* ("every man has it if he wills to have it"), and *transient* ("it can only be had through being constantly acquired, and can only be acquired through being constantly developed"). Finally, there is the theme that the person who lacks faith is responsible for "his failure—that he did not will it."[90]

Next (in addition to being a matter of passion and inwardness and of willed immediacy after reflection), faith is also seen as a submission to authority and interpersonal trust. Unlike scientific and philosophical points of view, which regard the submission to authority as indicating a lack of intellectual strength, integrity, and autonomy, genuine Christian faith, for Kierkegaard, rests on an acceptance of authority. He upbraids his culture for its lack of humility, its resistance to obedience, and its rebelling against all authority. Interpersonal trust is involved, such that I accept faith "because I believe the person who asserts it." (The Latin word for faith, *fides*, is etymologically related to *fidelitas*, meaning loyalty or fidelity, and *fiducia*, meaning trust or confidence.) In contrast to the impersonal, intellectual account of religious belief given by Hegel, Kierkegaard deliberately focuses on the personal quality of the Christian's faith in the word of Jesus:

> it is infinitely important that it is Christ who has spoken it, and when it is spoken to an individual it is precisely to *him* that it is spoken . . . , even if it is in a sense spoken to all individuals. . . . it constrains the person addressed to see who is talking with him and then fastens its piercing look on him and says with this glance, "It is you to whom this is said."[91]

What can be said of these characteristics of submission to authority and interpersonal trust? They are important elements of religious faith—elements rightly emphasized by religious thinkers like Augustine, but perhaps ignored or even dismissed by much of modern philosophy. So, again, the Kierkegaardian "corrective" is in order. But once more it goes too far in excluding all considerations of reason. Belief in the absence of knowledge is reasonable, but the repudiation of knowledge is not. So long as we do not deny knowledge, its value, and its relevance, it remains a possibility. But, by giving it up as hopeless and/or useless and by ceasing to desire it, we rule it out as a practical possibility.

For Kierkegaard faith essentially involves risk and calls for "a leap" of personal commitment. It is conceived as a venture against all rational odds. "Without risk there is no faith." The reason for the necessary involvement of risk in any commitment of religious faith "is precisely the contradiction between the infinite passion of the individual's inwardness and the objective uncertainty" of what is believed. Faith demands from finite, limited man an absolute relationship to the Absolute, to which all other, relative relationships are to be subordinated.[92] In relation to this absolute relationship, human knowledge and understanding, which are necessarily finite and relative, are disproportionately inadequate, so that the venture itself is absolute.

Hence there is a need for what Kierkegaard calls "a leap" of faith. This analogy of the movement of faith to a leap is employed primarily, but not exclusively, in the *Postscript* and serves as a contrast to the sort of Hegelian "approximation-process" which Kierkegaard thinks so ill-suited to the disparate relationship between God and man.[93] The analogy suggests that faith is an action, a movement initiated by a human being (with God's grace), and not something passively received. However, Kierkegaard does not mean to imply any license for whimsy. He does not think we can or should arbitrarily jump into any set of beliefs that might strike our fancy. The concept of the leap must relate to one's vital human concerns, for genuine faith only arises within a concrete existential situation. You seriously contemplate the possibility of religious commitment, according to Kierkegaard, only in the context of a sense that

> the abyss of eternity opens before you, the sharp scythe of the leveller makes it possible for every one individually to leap over the blade—and behold, it is God who waits. Leap, then, into the arms of God.[94]

So far, Kierkegaardian faith seems anti-intellectual and nonrational. But is it also irrational? It is in the discussion of religious faith as involving paradox and "the absurd" that an affirmative answer seems warranted. He repeatedly identifies religious faith with "paradox, inaccessible to thought." The word "paradox" is used here in the strong sense, referring not merely to a contravention of ordinary opinion but to that which flies in the face of human reason. What is paradoxical is the juxtaposition of "the eternal truth and existence," the fact that any relationship might obtain between the infinite God and finite man; "the eternal essential truth is by no means in its own nature paradoxical, but only in its relationship to an existing individual."[95]

The paradox of religious faith is especially characteristic of Christianity. For that religion essentially involves what Kierkegaard calls "the absolute paradox" of the Incarnation: "That God has existed in human form, has been born, grown up, and so forth, is surely the paradox *sensu strictissimo*, the absolute paradox." Nor can the contradiction involved here be explained away as an illusion, as if the lowly human servant-form assumed by God were only a disguise, for this would entail divine deception.[96]

Given Kierkegaard's conviction that there is an infinite qualitative difference between the eternal, infinite God and temporal, finite man, the mystery of the Incarnation cannot be rationally solved or dissolved. Yet this is simply the most extreme particular instance of his general characterization of all religious faith as a movement made "by virtue of the absurd, not by virtue of human understanding."[97]

As we have already seen, Kierkegaard often minimizes the importance of faith's content, subordinating its "what" to its "how." Yet when he does speak of the content of faith, he characterizes it as intellectually preposterous, foolishness, an offense to reason, in defiance of all possible conceptualization, etc. His entire authorship—published and unpublished writings alike, the "edifying" works as well as the pseudonymous—are shot through with this sort of characterization of faith's content.

In *Fear and Trembling*, Abraham is presented as a paradigm of religious faith (although, of course, he was not a Christian). The content of his faith is described as "preposterous," as "the paradox which keeps him upon the sheer edge and which he cannot make clear to any other man," as an incommunicable matter about which he "absolutely cannot make himself intelligible to anybody." These qualities of religious faith make it so painful that it is necessarily experienced in "fear and trembling."[98]

Kierkegaard's pseudonymous Climacus, whose persistent theme is that Christian faith cannot be rationally apprehended, repeatedly quotes Paul's description (*I Corinthians* 1:23) of the content of faith as "a stumbling block" or "an offense to the Jews and a folly to the Greeks—and an absurdity to the understanding." He speaks of "faith's crucifixion of the understanding," and he also maintains that the believer necessarily "gives up his understanding for faith and believes against the understanding."[99]

But, again, it is not merely Climacus who speaks this way of religious faith. Anti-Climacus, who represents a radically different dimension of Kierkegaard's thought (as his name suggests), classifies the content of Christian faith as "insane" and "self-contradiction." And in his unpublished writings as well as in *Fear and Trembling*, Kierkegaard identifies faith with "what the Greeks called the divine madness."[100]

Many more references might be cited. But the preceding should suffice to justify the claim that, for Kierkegaard, the content of religious faith is irrational as well as nonintellectual, contrary to reason as well as above reason, against reason as well as against the understanding. If this interpretation is accurate and adequate, his position is one of radical fideism.

Where Hegel had inflated the role of reason to the point where it is held to rule the world, Kierkegaard deflates that role as regards existential (i.e., ethico-religious) commitments.

A problem with this view should now be faced: if the content of faith transcends the bounds of knowledge and the findings of reason, why can it not be anything whatever, such that it becomes impossible to distinguish between Kierkegaardian faith and religious fanaticism? Kierkegaard seems to be aware of the problem and tries to ward off the objection:

> In all that is usually said about Johannes Climacus being purely subjective and so on, people have forgotten . . . that there is a "how" which has this quality, that if it is truly given, then the "what" is also given; and that it is the "how" of "faith."[101]

In other words, he is trying to assure us that, given sufficiently intense inwardness on the part of the believer, the proper content of faith will follow. But how convincing is this?

It is dogmatically stated, with no attempt at justification, as if it too must be accepted on faith. Second, no criterion is furnished whereby a manner of belief which is "truly given" can be distinguished from others which are not. In the absence of such a criterion, it seems arbitrary to hold, for example, that the faith of the adherent of Islam cannot be as "truly given" as that of the most authentic Christian. But then, if we could conceive of an absolute force of evil as positive reality (against the Augustinian-Leibnizian view of evil as mere privation), why could we not admit that the faith of the Satanist might be as authentic as that of the Christian?

If Hegel made the mistake of emphasizing the content of faith over the manner in which it is appropriated, Kierkegaard makes the opposite error. A balance between these extremes would be more adequate, a position which recognizes the equal importance of the content and the manner of religious faith, without attempting to subordinate either to the other.

The danger of Kierkegaard's conception of faith is that it offers no protection against fanaticism—that is, an excessive zeal or irrational enthusiasm (of the sort that Locke opposed). Kierkegaard might protest that the charge cannot apply to Christian faith because one's commitment to the Absolute should itself be absolute and cannot be excessive. But this would again be merely a dogmatic assertion with no criteria for validation.

If the accusation of potential fanaticism raised here seems unfair to Kierkegaard, his own words and those of his pseudonymous characters (and again not just Climacus) lend themselves to it. In at least three different works he explicitly compares religious faith to "what the Greeks called the divine madness." He rules out objective rational considerations and admits, "In a merely subjective determination of the truth, madness and truth become in the last analysis indistinguishable."[102]

Most of us want nothing to do with madness, even if it be glorified with the adjective "divine," nor are we willing to deny or disregard our own intellects to achieve a more passionate "inwardness." The danger of fanaticism should be faced squarely. Once the moorings of reason have been cast away, religious faith may haphazardly carry us in any direction whatever, and stability becomes an illusion thrust upon us by chance.

Although the content of faith is irrational, for Kierkegaard, he does indicate that the "leap" is rationally motivated, at least from the subjective perspective of the believer. That is to say, there are good subjective reasons for making the act of faith:

> Only when a person has become so unhappy or has penetrated the wretchedness of this existence so deeply that he must truly say: For me life has no value—only then can he make a bid for Christianity.[103]

Thus, Kierkegaard's paradoxical thesis seems to be that it is subjectively reasonable for some people to believe in that which is objectively irrational.

Unlike Hegel, Kierkegaard does not conceive of faith as a way station on the road to rational knowledge. Nor does he, like Kant, attempt to cast it in the dress of reason, while divorcing it from knowledge. He writes, "The Christian thesis is not: *intelligere ut credam*, nor is it *credere, ut intelligam*. . . . Christianity in no way lies in the sphere of intellectuality."[104] But then, it seems, it must be divorced from philosophy; the only contribution to it the latter supposedly makes is the negative one of criticizing the intellect when it oversteps its legitimate bounds.

Perhaps rational theology, particularly in modern times, has been too one-sided in its emphases, tending to characterize the object of religious faith as an abstract explanatory principle rather than as a divine Subject with whom man can attain a personal relationship and stressing the propositional contents of the doctrines of faith over the quality of the religious relationship between God and man. To this extent, Kierkegaard's "corrective" has been valuable in pointing this out. But his weakness consists in his one-sided emphasis on the contrary position. Neither he nor traditional rational theology is wholly right or entirely wrong in this controversy. Both offer valuable perspectives. The findings of reason are relevant to religious faith, although the latter also transcends the former. If the causal principle revealed by the philosophical theologian need not also be the appropriate object of religious devotion, the two may be identified as the same God. But this is to say, against Kierkegaard, that rational understanding is both relevant to and compatible with—without being equivalent to—religious faith.

God and Religion

God's Nature. Kierkegaard's characterizations of God's nature are few and scattered. Having severed direct relations between human reason and the content of religious faith, he is rightly reluctant to commit himself to much that is specific along those lines. In *Philosophical Fragments*, Climacus pointedly refers to God as "the Unknown," defining this as "the limit to which the Reason repeatedly comes" and maintaining that "because it is absolutely different, there is no mark by which it could be distinguished . . . for the Reason cannot even conceive an absolute unlikeness." This view of God as eluding all human efforts at conceptual analysis carries over into the nonpseudonymous works as well. For example, in his discourse (on *I John* 3:20), "God Is Greater than Our Heart," Kierkegaard admits that we must either refrain altogether from talking about God or use the admittedly inadequate language appropriate for describing human beings, mindful that "God and man resemble one another only inversely."[105]

Yet Kierkegaard does not restrict himself to the use of "God" or "the Unknown" as names or indeterminate concepts that obliquely refer to his religious Absolute. There are two descriptive phrases, in particular, which he employs to define God in relation to man: God is referred to as the Power that has posited the human self and as the One "for whom all things are possible."[106] Furthermore, Kierkegaard's God (like Kant's Transcendental Idea) is conceived as ultimate ontological source and as ground of all existential possibility (both of which are surprisingly metaphysical-sounding conceptions, given his religious epistemology). Of course, these characterizations are subject to the proviso indicated above, that our human language is only analogically applicable to God—for example, God is *not* a cause in the same way as are human agents, and God's omnipotence can *not* be weighed against the relative power of the human person.

In deliberate opposition to Hegel, Kierkegaard repeatedly emphasizes the "infinite, radical, qualitative difference between God and man." He is occasionally willing to specify this difference: "God does not think, he creates; God does not exist, He is eternal. Man thinks and exists, and existence separates thought and being." He also insists, still against Hegel, that God is absolutely independent of man and of all creation, the divine self-realization being in no way a function of finite, temporal processes. In keeping with the Judeo-Christian tradition, Kierkegaard's God is transcendent, present everywhere in creation, but only indirectly. To this extent, Kierkegaard sides with "honest Kant" in defending divine transcendence: "In the relation between Kant and Hegel it is already apparent how inadequate immanence is."[107]

It is not necessary to say much more about Kierkegaard's conception of God. Not only did he avoid lengthy analyses of the divine nature, but his idea of God is already familiar to those reared in Judeo-Christian cultures. Against Hegel, he asserts that "God is certainly personal," but he qualifies this by saying that God is free to choose which human individuals to engage in a personal relationship, and that, far from being a religious panacea, a personal relationship with God is a fearful responsibility. As against Kant's stern, authoritarian, divine Lawgiver, Kierkegaard emphasizes the Christian conception of God as Love. On his view, God relates to the world of creation through an infinite concern for even the least significant of creatures and occurrences.[108]

Religion. Kierkegaard's view of religion, as might be expected, is far more personal than was Hegel's. He seems opposed to any mediation between God and the individual—whether it be in the form of the state or an established church or the whole human race. God engages a particular human being in an immediate I-thou relation: "He speaks directly to every separate individual." Kierkegaard frequently warns that one's religious relationship to God should not be taken for granted, that it should not be allowed to become merely an object for disinterested reflection.[109]

He is particularly opposed to the notion that Christian faith is an easy route to eternal happiness, emphasizing that "religious existence is essentially suffering." Why should this be the case? Because of the radical difference between God and man, who are related in a demanding faith, and because of sin, as a result of which man is always "in the wrong before God" and necessarily in despair. The only antidote to the despair of the spirit, is religious faith—"the opposite of being in despair is believing"; for in faith, "by willing to be itself, the self is grounded transparently in the Power which constituted it."[110]

The religious life of the believer supposedly includes but transcends the characteristic modes of existing in the aesthetic and ethical spheres.

Like the aesthete, the person of faith is capable of relishing the moment and relating himself to the particulars of everyday life—but they are not his highest values. Like the ethical man, he respects and is generally obedient to the directives of universal laws—though these are not, for him, the highest authority. The person of faith must be resigned to giving up all creaturely attachments, if need be, and the last stage achieved prior to that of religious faith is the ethical one of "infinite resignation." Yet he does not need to be a sackcloth-and-ashes ascetic, and his resignation, Kierkegaard believes, should be tempered with the confidence (like Abraham's) that somehow the things loved in this life will be restored. It is to this tension between resignation and confidence that he seems to refer with the striking phrase, "the dying away from the life of immediacy while still remaining in the finite."[111]

Just as the person of faith combines ethical resignation with religious confidence, he also combines ethical obedience to the rule of law with a higher respect for the authority of the personal God to whom he is related in religious faith. So it is allegedly possible to conceive of a "teleological suspension of the ethical," because for the person of faith, although the laws of morality commonly apply, "the particular is higher than the universal";[112] that is, God, the particular Person to whom he is related in faith, is a higher authority than the impersonal rule of universal law. Kierkegaard does not say that the ethical is cancelled or abolished for the person of faith, but only that it can be suspended, temporarily set aside in submission to particular divine commands accepted by the believer as more ultimately binding.

Kierkegaard speaks of "the Exceptional" as a category which applies only to the religious sphere and never to the ethical, which "has nothing to do with ethically fulfilling what is demanded, but is a particular relation to God."[113] The contrast here with Kant's moral religion should be apparent. No such possibility of a religious exception to the ethical could be tolerated by Kant's legalistic **universalism**.

Nevertheless, Kierkegaard insists that the difference between the man of faith and other persons is not remarkable in terms of visible appearances or behavioral characteristics. Thus he makes what might seem a striking statement:

> I have not found any reliable example of the knight of faith, though I would not therefore deny that every second man may be such an example.

Unlike the ethical hero, the "knight of infinite resignation," whose grace, nobility, and self-assurance identify him as someone special, the religious exception is externally inconspicuous, a "knight of hidden inwardness."[114] This individual, who has made the commitment to religious belief despite the lack of objective evidence, best personifies the human ideal indicated by Kierkegaard's challenging position of existential fideism.

Notes

1. *The Journals of Kierkegaard*, trans. and ed. Alexander Dru (New York: Harper & Row, 1959), p. 90; this book will hereafter be called "*Journals.*"

2. Ibid., p. 96.   3. Ibid., pp. 149, 145, 190.

4. Ibid., pp. 39, 80–81, 243; the couplet quoted from Goethe also appears in *Either/Or*, by Søren Kierkegaard, vol. 1, trans. David F. Swenson and Lillian Marvin Swenson (Garden City, NY: Doubleday & Co., 1959), p. 203.

5. *The Point of View for My Work as an Author*, by Søren Kierkegaard, trans. Walter Lowrie (New York: Harper & Row, 1962), pp. 76, 81; this work will hereafter be called "*View.*"

6. *Letters and Documents*, by Kierkegaard, trans. Henrik Rosenmeier (Princeton: Princeton Univ. Press, 1978), p. 4; this work will hereafter be called "*Documents.*"

7. *Søren Kierkegaard's Journals and Papers*, ed. and trans. Howard V. Hong and Edna H. Hong, vol. 5 (Bloomington: Indiana Univ. Press, 1978), pp. 21, 23–24. This collection, published in seven volumes between 1967 and 1978, will hereafter be called "*Papers,*" followed by volume numbers.

8. *Journals*, p. 44. This passage can also be found in *A Kierkegaard Anthology*, ed. Robert Bretall (Princeton: Princeton Univ. Press, 1946), pp. 4–5; cross-references will frequently be made to this book, hereafter called "Bretall."

9. *Journals*, p. 85.

10. *View*, p. 50; a *flaneur* is what we call "a loafer."

11. *Journals*, pp. 39–41, 50–51, 55; Bretall, pp. 7–8, 11.

12. *Journals*, pp. 59–60, 62, 64; Bretall, pp. 10, 13.

13. *Documents*, p. 10.

14. *Journals*, pp. 61–62, 67, 69–70; Bretall, pp. 14–15.

15. *Journals*, pp. 72–73; Bretall, pp. 16–18.

16. *Journals*, pp. 86–87. A long series of brooding reflections on the Regina Olsen relationship can be found in Kierkegaard's *Stages on Life's Way*, trans. Walter Lowrie (New York: Schocken Books, 1967). Regina later married Fritz Schlegel, a former suitor, who became governor of the Danish West Indies, and she lived until 1904. In his will Kierkegaard left her his belongings, saying that he believed "an engagement was and is just as binding as a marriage, and that therefore my estate is her due, exactly as if I had been married to her"—*Documents*, p. 33. This translation of *Stages on Life's Way* will hereafter be called "*Stages.*"

17. *Journals*, pp. 79, 91.

18. *Johannes Climacus or, De Omnibus Dubitandum Est and A Sermon*, by Søren Kierkegaard, trans. T. H. Croxall (Stanford: Stanford Univ. Press, 1958); this work will hereafter be called "*Dubitandum.*"

19. *Either/Or*, by Søren Kierkegaard (Garden City, NY: Doubleday & Co., 1959), published in two volumes. Volume 1 is translated by David F. Swenson and Lillian Marvin Swenson, and volume 2 is translated by Walter Lowrie; both volumes have revisions by Howard A. Johnson. This work will hereafter be called "*Either/Or.*"

20. *Fear and Trembling* and *The Sickness unto Death*, by Søren Kierkegaard, trans. Walter Lowrie (Garden City, NY: Doubleday & Co., 1954); *Fear and Trembling* will hereafter be called "*Fear.*"

21. *Repetition*, by Søren Kierkegaard, trans. Walter Lowrie (New York: Harper & Row, 1964).

22. *Philosophical Fragments or A Fragment of Philosophy*, by Søren Kierkegaard, trans. David F. Swenson and revised by Howard V. Hong (Princeton: Princeton Univ. Press, 1967); this work will hereafter be called "*Fragments.*"

23. *Kierkegaard's The Concept of Dread*, trans. Walter Lowrie (Princeton: Princeton Univ. Press, 1957); this work will hereafter be called "*Dread.*"

24. *Kierkegaard's Concluding Unscientific Postscript*, trans. David F. Swenson and completed by Walter Lowrie (Princeton: Princeton Univ. Press, 1941); this work will hereafter be called "*Postscript.*"

25. *Papers*, vol. 5, p. 300.

26. *Journals*, pp. 103, 105.

27. *The Sickness after Death* will hereafter be called "*Sickness.*"

28. *Training in Christianity and the Edifying Discourse Which 'Accompanied' It*, by Søren Kierkegaard, trans. Walter Lowrie (Princeton: Princeton Univ. Press, 1944); this work will hereafter be called "*Training.*"

29. *View*, pp. 97, 145.

30. *Kierkegaard's Attack upon "Christendom" 1854–1855*, trans. Walter Lowrie (Princeton: Princeton Univ. Press, 1968); this work will hereafter be called "*Attack.*"

31. *Journals*, pp. 231, 241, 246, 253.

32. *Attack*, p. 5.

33. *Papers*, vol. 6, p. 558.

34. *The Present Age* and *Of the Difference between a Genius and an Apostle*, by Søren Kierkegaard, trans. Alexander Dru (New York: Harper & Row, 1962); this work will hereafter be called "*Present.*"

35. *Edifying Discourses: A Selection*, by Søren Kierkegaard, ed. Paul L. Holmer, trans. David F. and Lillian Marvin Swenson (New York: Harper & Row, 1958); this work will hereafter be called "*Edifying.*"

36. *Christian Discourses*, by Søren Kierkegaard, trans. Walter Lowrie (Princeton: Princeton Univ. Press, 1971); this work will hereafter be called "*Christian.*"

37. *Works of Love: Some Christian Reflections in the Form of Discourses*, by Søren Kierkegaard, trans. Howard and Edna Hong (New York: Harper & Row, 1964); this work will hereafter be called "*Love.*"

38. *Papers*, vol. 5, p. 419.

39. *Postscript*, pp. 551–52.

40. *Dread*, pp. 39, 76.

41. *Sickness*, pp. 146, 163; Bretall, p. 340.

42. *Journals*, pp. 116–17, 133–35; Bretall, p. 258.

43. *Attack*, p. 286; Bretall, p. 467.

44. *Journals*, pp. 44, 188–89; Bretall, pp. 4, 428.

45. *Journals*, pp. 77, 120.

46. *Present*, p. 33; Bretall, p. 260.

47. *Either/Or*, vol. 2, pp. 193–94.

48. *Dread*, pp. 38, 40, 55, 141.

49. *Sickness*, pp. 146–48, 150–51; Bretall, pp. 341–42.

50. *Either/Or*, vol. 2, pp. 172–73; Bretall, pp. 106–7.

51. *Stages*, p. 430.

52. *Postscript*, pp. 261, 448, 452–53, 507, 473n., 262.

53. *Either/Or*, vol. 2, p. 215; *Fear*, pp. 23–24; *Stages*, p. 99; and *Postscript*, p. 548. For details on Kierkegaard's relationship to other modern philosophers, see "Kierkegaard's Existential Critique of Modern Rationalists," by Wayne P. Pomerleau, in *Explorations*, vol. 8, no. 2 (Winter, 1989), pp. 27–38.

54. *Fear*, pp. 43–44; cf. *Postscript*, p. 276.

55. *Dubitandum*, pp. 103, 116. In *Postscript*, pp. 545–46, Climacus describes himself as "a humorist," whose sole opinion is "that it must be the most difficult of all things to become a Christian"; cf. *Fragments*, pp. 5–6, where Climacus describes his work as "a sort of nimble dancing in the service of Thought, so far as possible also to the honor of God, and for my own satisfaction."

56. *Attack*, pp. 282–83; *View*, p. 153; *Papers*, vol. 1, p. 158.

57. *View*, p. 153; *Postscript*, pp. 332, 18–19.

58. *Journals*, p. 217; *Papers*, vol. 2, p. 538; View, pp. 155, 5, 21, 156; *Journals*, p. 200; *Attack*, p. 90; *Training*, p. 39; and *Papers*, vol. 1, p. 160; Bretall, pp. 329, 397.

59. *Postscript*, p. 228; *Dread*, p. 130; *Journals*, p. 68; *Stages*, pp. 457–58, 462; *Papers*, vol. 2, p. 534; *Christian*, p. 111; *Either/Or*, vol. 2, p. 215; *Edifying*, p. 21; *Either/Or*, vol. 1, p. 31; Bretall, p. 14.

60. *Journals*, pp. 44, 66, 145; *Either/Or*, vol. 1, p. 291; *Either/Or*, vol. 2, p. 270; Bretall, pp. 5, 28.

61. *Journals*, p. 51; *Either/Or*, vol. 2, p. 356; *Attack*, p. 221; Bretall, p. 457.

62. *Either/Or*, vol. 2, p. 263; *Stages*, p. 124.

63. *Postscript*, p. 109; *Sickness*, pp. 176–77; Bretall, pp. 202–3, 346.

64. *Postscript*, pp. 16, 98, 107; Bretall, pp. 195–96, 221.

65. *Postscript*, pp. 108, 110, 119, 275, 309, 450n; *Either/Or*, vol. 2, p. 326; Bretall, pp. 202–3.

66. *Postscript*, pp. 112, 263n; *Either/Or*, vol. 1, p. 3; *Fear*, p. 79; *Dubitandum*, pp. 148–50, 153; Bretall, p. 205.

67. *Postscript*, pp. 357, 99, 107, 275, 292, 270–71; *Papers*, vol. 2, p. 210; Bretall, pp. 196, 201.

68. *Postscript*, pp. 18, 49, 101; *Dread*, p. 73; *Dubitandum*, p. 132; Bretall, p. 197.

69. *Postscript*, pp. 107, 177, 100n., and 112–13; Bretall, pp. 200, 206–7.

70. *Papers*, vol. 2, pp. 218, 221, 227, 217.

71. *Either/Or*, vol. 1, pp. 284, 318, and vol. 2, p. 282; Bretall, p. 43.

72. *Postscript*, pp. 85–86, 176–77, 174, 226.

73. Ibid., pp. 178–82, 540; Bretall, pp. 210–15, 255.

74. *Postscript*, pp. 201, 306; Bretall, p. 231.

75. *Fragments*, pp. 76, 103. It might be objected that this is still only Climacus's view; but see also *Training*, pp. 36, 38, and *Love*, pp. 218, 221; Bretall, pp. 394, 396.

76. *Postscript*, pp. 30, 32, 380–81, 407; *Papers*, vol. 2, p. 538.

77. *Postscript*, pp. 179–80, 189, 208–9; *Papers*, vol. 2, p. 533; Bretall, pp. 212, 220–21.

78. *Postscript*, pp. 290–91; *Training*, pp. 108–9; *Edifying*, p. 23; *Papers*, vol. 2, p. 15; Bretall, pp. 230–31.

79. *Sickness*, pp. 218, 235; *Papers*, vol. 2, pp. 225–26.

80. *Postscript*, pp. 189, 25, 31, 509–10, 75, 28; Bretall, pp. 220–21. Kierkegaard accepts Lessing's view on this matter: "If no historical truth can be demonstrated, then nothing can be demonstrated by means of historical truths"—Gotthold Lessing, "On the Proof of the Spirit and of Power," in *Lessing's Theological Writings*, ed. and trans. Henry Chadwick (Stanford: Stanford Univ. Press, 1957), p. 53. In words that were later to inspire Kierkegaard, Lessing wrote (p. 55) that this inability to substantiate Christianity historically "is the ugly, broad ditch which I cannot get across, however often and however earnestly I have tried to make the leap."

81. *Papers*, vol. 2, p. 6, and vol. 1, p. 123; *Stages*, p. 403.

82. *Dread*, p. 125; *Edifying*, pp. 26–27; *Papers*, vol. 2, p. 536.

83. *Fragments*, pp. 49–54.

84. *Papers*, vol. 2, p. 531; cf. *Christian*, p. 200.

85. *Journals*, p. 201.

86. *Postscript*, pp. 188, 209; see also pp. 33, 42, 251, 313, 538; Bretall, pp. 219–20, 253.

87. *Either/Or*, vol. 2, p. 204; *Fear*, pp. 131, 64; *Dread*, pp. 140–41; *Training*, pp. 87, 140–41; *Christian*, p. 198. In his writings, Kierkegaard uses about nineteen different pseudonyms. Rather than bothering the reader with this bewildering variety of personae, the two that best typify the poles of Kierkegaard's own thought are named here. As he says in his *Journals* (p. 175), "To me there is something so inexplicably happy in the antithesis Climacus–Anti-Climacus, I recognise myself, and my nature so entirely in it that if someone else had discovered it I should have thought he had spied upon me."

88. *Postscript*, pp. 193, 67–68.

89. *Papers*, vol. 2, pp. 3, 12, 14, 20, 22; Bretall, p. 2.

90. *Edifying*, pp. 5, 9–10, 12.

91. *Journals*, p. 179; *Papers*, vol. 1, pp. 78, 359; *Papers*, vol. 2, pp. 13–14; *Dubitandum*, p. 137; and *Love*, p. 104.

92. *Postscript*, pp. 182, 364–65, 377–78; Bretall, p. 214.

93. *Postscript*, pp. 96, 105, 231, 327; *Papers*, vol. 3, pp. 16, 20, 22; Bretall, p. 200. Note that in these works the notion of "the leap" is attributed to Lessing.

94. *Papers*, vol. 2, p. 20; *Present*, p. 82; Bretall, p. 269.

95. *Fear*, p. 58, 64, 66; *Fragments*, pp. 46–67; *Postscript*, pp. 183–88; Bretall, pp. 126, 130, 215–20.

96. *Sickness*, p. 231; *Postscript*, pp. 38, 95, 188, 194–95, 206, 480, 512, 515; *Fragments*, pp. 40–42, 68; Bretall, pp. 220, 169–70.

97. *Papers*, vol. 1, p. 4; see also *Fear*, pp. 46–48, 51, 59–60, 67; Bretall, pp. 118, 120–21, 128.

98. *Fear*, pp. 35, 72, 81, 90.

99. *Postscript*, pp. 191, 196, 260, 530, 535, 500–502, 505, 513–14; Bretall, p. 222.

100. *Training*, pp. 84, 112; *Papers*, vol. 2, p. 6; *Fear*, p. 37.

101. *Journals*, p. 177.

102. *Papers*, vol. 2, p. 6; *Fear*, p. 37; *Postscript*, pp. 159, 173–74.

103. *Papers*, vol. 2, p. 24.

104. *Papers*, vol. 3, p. 363; *intelligere ut credam* means "to understand in order that I might believe," and *credere ut intelligam* means "to believe in order that I might understand." For more about Kierkegaard's radical disjunction of philosophy from religion, see "The Accession and Dismissal of an Upstart Handmaid," by Wayne P. Pomerleau, in *The Monist*, vol. 60, no. 2 (April, 1977), pp. 220–25.

105. *Fragments*, pp. 49, 55; Christian, pp. 299–300.

106. *Sickness*, pp. 147, 153, 163, 182, 201, 207, 205, as well as pp. 171, 173; see also *Fear*, p. 57; Bretall, pp. 126, 341, 344, 351, 366, 369, 371.

107. *Papers*, vol. 2, p. 113; *Present*, pp. 98–99; *Training*, p. 67; *Postscript*, pp. 369, 439, 296, 122, 218; *Papers*, vol. 2, p. 515; Bretall, pp. 409, 231, 246.

108. *Journals*, p. 250; *Love*, p. 20; *Attack*, p. 245; *Christian*, p. 299; *Papers*, vol. 2, p. 5; Bretall, p. 459.

109. *Stages*, p. 292; *Postscript*, pp. 19–20, 328, 333, 495, 546; *Attack*, pp. 142–43.

110. *Postscript*, p. 256; *Attack*, p. 271; *Journals*, pp. 225, 227; *Either/Or*, vol. 2, pp. 346, 350, 354; *Sickness*, pp. 179, 182; Bretall, pp. 464, 348, 351.

111. *Christian*, p. 247; *Fear*, pp. 47–48, 57, 33, 56, 59, 124; *Postscript*, p. 386; Bretall, pp. 125, 127–28.

112. *Fear*, pp. 65–67, 69, 77, 80; Bretall, pp. 130–32, 134.

113. *Journals*, p. 222.

114. *Fear*, p. 49; *Postscript*, pp. 367, 453; Bretall, p. 119.

9

James's Pragmatic Voluntarism

Life and Writings

William James's life began in New York City, where he was born on January 11, 1842, the eldest of the five children of Henry James, Sr., and Mary Walsh James. He was named after his paternal grandfather, William James, of Albany, who had emigrated from Ireland in 1789, participated in the opening of the Erie Canal, become a multimillionaire, and raised a large family with three wives. The last of these wives was Catherine Barber James, who was descended from officers of the American Revolution.[1] Their fourth child, Henry James, Sr., was born in Albany in 1811. Henry graduated from Union College in Schenectady, then studied at the Princeton Theological Seminary (1835–37) as preparation for the ministry; but he rebelled against his father's orthodox Presbyterian theology and dropped out of the seminary. In 1840 he married Mary Walsh, the sister of a friend who had also withdrawn from the seminary.[2]

Henry had broken with his father's strict Calvinism because of its teaching that the alienation between God and man is natural. Henry believed that man is naturally innocent, rather than naturally corrupt, becomes guilty as a result of selfish choices, and can save himself by viewing his own will as an instrument to the social welfare. These heterodox theological views so angered his father, William, that he unsuccessfully tried to disinherit Henry. After William died in 1842 (the same year the philosopher William James was born), Henry received a legacy from his grandfather's estate adequate to allow him to devote the rest of his life to studying and writing theology. He became a prominent American disciple of the Swedish mystic Emanuel Swedenborg, and the friend of Thomas Carlyle, Ralph Waldo Emerson, and other famous transcendentalists.

In 1843, the second child of Henry and Mary was born; this was Henry, Jr., who would become one of America's most important writers of fiction. Three more children followed—Garth Wilkinson ("Wilky") in 1845, Robertson ("Bob") in 1846, and Alice in 1848. It seems to have been a happy family life. They moved around a great deal between Europe and America, so that the five children were raised to be cosmopolitan. They had private tutors and attended progressive schools, including, for Wilky and Bob in 1859, the Sanborn School in Concord, which was run by a devoted abolitionist and friend of John Brown's. (This later led to the enlisting of Wilky and Bob in the Union Army during the Civil War and their subsequent running of a plantation in Florida where freed slaves were employed in decent working conditions.) The children acquired a command of European languages, in accordance with their father's ideal of cosmopolitan education.

Throughout childhood, William loved to draw. His brother Henry later wrote, "As I catch W.J.'s image, from far back, at its most characteristic, he sits drawing and drawing, always drawing."[3] Because William had decided to become a painter, the family settled at Newport, Rhode Island, in 1860. There William was able to study with the leading American portraitist, William Morris Hunt, and could work every day at Hunt's studio. Within a year, he gave up the idea of being a painter, having become convinced that he would never be better than mediocre at it. In 1861, he entered the Lawrence Scientific School at Harvard, his health already having become a serious problem (which kept him out of the Civil War). The focus of his studies shifted from chemistry to physiology, before he entered Harvard's Medical School at the end of 1863. But he took a year (1865–66) out of his time in medical school to join the Thayer expedition to Brazil, which was led by Louis Agassiz, the famous Swiss-born scientist; for James the trip was marred by poor health.[4]

Having returned from South America, James resumed work in medical school, and his family moved to Cambridge, Massachusetts. But again he was drawn away—this time to study physiology and medicine at the University of Berlin and recover his health (1867–68).[5] While in Europe he read Kant. As he writes his father, "I began the other day Kant's 'Kritik,' which is written crabbedly enough, but which strikes me so far as almost the sturdiest and *honestest* piece of work I ever saw." He also discovered the writings of a neo-Kantian, as he goes on to tell his father, "one Charles Renouvier, of whom I never heard before but who, for vigor of style and compression . . . is unequaled by anyone. He takes his stand on Kant."[6] Although unsuccessful at curing his unexplained back pains, he returned to Harvard, passed his medical exams, and received his M.D. in June of 1869. He did not wish to practice medicine, however,[7] and there seemed to be considerable uncertainty as to what he would do.

In late 1869, his neurotic symptoms became increasingly severe, leading to what we would call a nervous breakdown. His scientific training seemed to be pulling him away from belief in freedom of will (and hence in the significance of struggling for moral ideals) and hurling him into a position of hopeless materialistic determinism. This led to a brooding, depressing self-absorption. In a thinly veiled case history in his *Varieties of Religious Experience*, he movingly recalls the sight of an epileptic patient he had seen in an asylum he visited as a medical student, a young man, "entirely idiotic, who used to sit all day . . . with his knees drawn up against his chin." James could not shake off the awful realization that, if determinism is correct, there was nothing he could possibly do to prevent that vegetative state from befalling him: "*That shape am I*, I felt, potentially. Nothing that I possess can defend me against that fate, if the hour for it should strike for me as it struck for him." He says that he found himself reduced to "a mass of quivering fear" as a result of this horrible thought, after which "the universe was changed for me altogether. I awoke morning after morning with a horrible dread at the pit of my stomach, and with a sense of the insecurity of life that I never knew before."[8] He became a virtual invalid at his parents' home in Cambridge.

By the beginning of February 1870, he felt that a moral decision of great personal significance had to be made—either to commit himself intently to the life of moral activity or give it up as a groundless fantasy. He later admitted that there were times when "suicide seemed the most manly form to put my daring into."[9] In a now-famous diary entry of April 30, 1870, James explains how reading the voluntarism of Renouvier led him to the point of resolution:

> I think that yesterday was a crisis in my life. I finished the first part of Renouvier's second "Essais" and see no reason why his definition of Free Will— "the sustaining of a thought *because I choose* to when I might have other thoughts"—need be the definition of an illusion. At any rate, I will assume for the present—until next year—that it is no illusion. My first act of free will shall be to believe in free will.

From that point on, James started gradually recovering from his psychological disorders. He became increasingly able to affirm a life of "doing and suffering and creating."[10]

In August of 1872, when James's former chemistry professor, Charles William Eliot, now president of Harvard, offered him a position on the faculty as instructor of physiology, he was well enough to accept. This was the beginning of a career of more than a third of a century on Harvard's faculty. By 1873, he was instructor in anatomy and physiology. Ill health prompted him to travel to Italy for recuperation in 1873–74. In 1875, back at Harvard, he taught his first course on psychology, using the physiological approach he had learned from the Germans. In 1876, he established the first American psychological laboratory and was promoted to assistant professor of physiology. In 1877, his course on physiological psychology was offered by the philosophy department.

Around 1876, William's father was attending meetings of the Radical Club, of which a schoolteacher (the daughter of a medical doctor) named Alice Howe Gibbens was a member. Henry, Sr., returned home after one such meeting to announce that he had met William's future wife. Although William was less than eager to meet her, the thirty-four-year-old man and twenty-seven-year-old woman were, indeed, instantly attracted to each other. They married in Boston on July 10, 1878. The intelligent, witty, sensitive Alice understood and sympathized with his intellectual obsessions and emotional moodiness. They lived comfortably in Cambridge and later acquired a summer house in New Hampshire. William and Alice (like his parents) had five children, of whom the first two were named Henry (born in 1880) and William (1882); Herman (1884), Margaret Mary (1887), and Alexander Robertson (1890) were born after them.

In 1878, James agreed to write a textbook on psychology. (This was to take him twelve years, finally being published as *Principles of Psychology* in 1890.) But he was already becoming restless to move on to another discipline. Throughout much of this decade he had been an active member of a "Metaphysical Club," in which he discussed philosophical issues with such friends and fellow intellectuals as Chauncey Wright, John Fiske, Oliver Wendell Holmes, and Charles Sanders Peirce, the founder of American pragmatism.[11] In 1879, James began teaching philosophy at Harvard, becoming an assistant professor of philosophy the following year. By this time his writings were becoming increasingly focused on philosophy; his important essay on "The Sentiment of Rationality" was partly published in *Mind* in July 1879,[12] the latter part being an address he delivered to the Harvard Philosophical Club in 1880. He became pro-gressively disenchanted with psychology, referring to it as "a nasty, little subject" and becoming irritated when called a "psychologist."[13] He became a full professor of philosophy in 1885 and, in 1889, a full profes-sor of psychology.

In 1890, James's extremely important and influential *Principles of Psychology* was finally published. In June of 1878 (a month before he married), he had contracted with a publisher to write it. He was asked to produce a manuscript within a year; he made excuses and was given two years to complete it, little anticipating that it would take twelve. Having finished what he calls his "tedious book," he writes his publisher complaining about its excessive length (about 1400 pages):

> No one could be more disgusted than I at the sight of the book. No subject is worth being treated of in 1000 pages! Had I ten years more, I could rewrite it in 500; but as it stands it is this or nothing—a loathsome, distended, tumefied, bloated, dropsical mass.

About the same time, he writes his brother Henry,

> As "Psychologies" go, it is a good one, but psychology is in such an ante-scien-tific condition that the whole present generation of them is predestined to become unreadable old medieval lumber, as soon as the first genuine tracks of insight are made. The sooner, the better, for me![14]

Nevertheless, it was extremely successful, its most conspicuous disadvan-tage being its great bulk. So, the following summer James prepared an abridged version, which was published in 1892 as *Psychology: Briefer Course*. Between them, the two books were staples of psychological instruction, the larger, two-volume work being referred to as "James," while the shorter, single volume was nicknamed "Jimmy."[15] After 1892, James's attention to psychology diminished, being gradually confined to the relationship "between normal and pathological mental states" and the psychology of religious experience.[16]

In 1892–93, James took a sabbatical year in Europe with his family. As he writes about a month before they left, "Both Alice and I need a 'year off.' "[17] They spent time in Germany, Switzerland, Florence, and London. This break from his routine at the university allowed James to be relieved as director of Harvard's psychological laboratory.

After returning from Europe, James threw himself into philosophical teaching and lecture writing with vigor. In 1896, he offered his first course on the philosophy of Kant. An important collection of his lectures was published in 1897 under the title of *The Will to Believe and Other*

Essays in Popular Philosophy. He taught courses at Radcliffe College and in Harvard's summer school as well as his normally assigned ones for the university. In a pivotal lecture on "Philosophical Conceptions and Practical Results," delivered in 1898 at the University of California at Berkeley, he announced the development of pragmatism. In 1899, his *Talks to Teachers on Psychology and to Students on Some of Life's Ideals* was published; in the preface to that book he indicates that what he was energetically working to formulate philosophically at that time was "a definite view of the world and of our moral relations to the same."[18]

Unfortunately, part of what was driving James was a concern about money. His Harvard salary was relatively modest, and his books had yet to prove lucrative. As a regular faculty member, he found himself overwhelmed with ordinary responsibilities that cut into his time for research and writing. As he writes to Renouvier,

> Our University moreover inflicts a monstrous amount of routine business on one, faculty meetings and committees of every sort, so that during term-time one can do no continuous reading at all—reading of books, I mean. When vacation comes, my brain is so tired that I can read nothing serious for a month.[19]

In a letter to another friend, he writes, "Last year was a year of hard work, and before the end of the term came, I was in a state of bad neurasthenic fatigue, but I got through outwardly all right."[20]

Several years of this led to his physical breakdown of 1899. He traveled to Nauheim, Germany for recuperative treatment. He and Mrs. James also visited England, the south of France, Switzerland, and Rome, moving from place to place for the climate or to take the baths or to consult with medical specialists. Much of the reading he did was on religious experience, preparation for the future Gifford Lectures. He was homesick. In one of his letters from England, after expressing his appreciation of that country, he writes, "Still, one loves America above all things, for her youth, her greenness, her plasticity, innocence, good intentions, friends, everything."[21] He was invited to deliver the prestigious Gifford Lectures at the University of Edinburgh in 1901–2. After arriving there, he writes, "Edinburgh is surely the noblest city ever built by man." Yet a few days later he writes, "Beautiful as the spring is here, the words you so often let drop about American weather make me homesick."[22] But it was the delivering of these lectures at Edinburgh that marked a renewal of energy for James.

He writes that his twofold purpose in the Gifford Lectures is to defend "experience" against "philosophy" as "being the real backbone of the world's religious life" and to show that, however foolish particular "manifestations of religion may have been," the religious life "as a whole is mankind's most important function"; he describes his attempt to realize this twofold purpose as "*my* religious act."[23] In another letter he writes that the findings of religious experience do not require that we worship God "as the Theists do, in the shape of one all-inclusive and all-operative designing power," but can as well point to a "pluralistic" conception of God "in the shape of a collection of beings who have each contributed and are now contributing to the realization of ideals more or less like those for which we live ourselves."[24] The Gifford Lectures were published under the title of *Varieties of Religious Experience*, in June of 1902, after James had returned to America. They were a popular success and helped to alleviate his nagging financial worries. However, James himself was not entirely pleased with them. He had hoped that they would successfully combine the findings of religious psychology with the speculations of metaphysics; but, in fact, the former had quite dominated the latter. As he writes, with some annoyance, to F. C. S. Schiller, a fellow Pragmatist at Oxford, "The Gifford lectures are all facts and no philosophy."[25]

After returning to Harvard from Scotland, James tried to limit his teaching and to apply his energies to the development of his own philosophy. He was working on the essays and lectures that would later be published under the titles of *Pragmatism*, *A Pluralistic Universe*, *The Meaning of Truth*, and *Essays in Radical Empiricism*. His off-campus lectures were geared to honing ideas for these essays. He said that at this time he was busy trying to develop "my metaphysical system."[26] In the spring of 1905, James sailed away to visit Greece, having yearned for some time to see Athens for himself. On the way back he stopped at Rome where he delivered his address on "The Notion of Consciousness" (in French) at the Fifth International Congress of Psychology. In 1906, he took a leave of absence from Harvard to serve as visiting professor at Stanford University for the Spring term, but his lecture series there was interrupted by the great San Francisco earthquake.[27]

In November of 1906, James's lectures on *Pragmatism* were delivered at the Lowell Institute in Boston; he repeated them at Columbia University two months later and published them in the spring of 1907. In February 1907, he resigned all his official responsibilities at Harvard in order to devote his remaining energies to developing his philosophy. (In a touching final class meeting at Harvard, his undergraduates gave him a silver cup, while his graduate students presented him with an inkwell.) That month, anticipating a period of undisturbed productivity, he writes in a letter, "I expect to shed truths in dazzling profusion on the world for many years."[28] The following month, in another letter, he writes that a professor has two primary "functions: (1) to be learned and distribute bibliographical information; (2) to communicate truth." He admits to being far more dedicated to the latter than to the former purpose: "Hitherto I have always felt like a humbug as a professor, for I am weak in the first requirement. Now I can live for the second with a free conscience."[29] A couple of months after he resigned, he writes his son Bill, "I have got my 'Pragmatism' proofs all corrected. The most important thing I've written yet, and bound, I am sure, to stir up a lot of attention. But I'm dog-tired."[30]

Now sixty-five years old, James suffered from angina pectoris and chronic shortness of breath. He was invited to deliver the Hibbert Lectures at Manchester College, Oxford, and reluctantly consented; in these lectures of 1908 he deliberately attacked the absolute idealism so prevalent in England at that time. As he writes from the boat on the way over, "I have been sleeping like a top, and feel in good fighting trim again, eager for the scalp of the Absolute. My lectures will put his wretched clerical defenders fairly on the defensive."[31] But meanwhile, since the publication of *Pragmatism*, James found himself embattled. In a letter that he wrote immediately after attending what he called "a really delightful meeting" of the American Philosophical Association, at Cornell, James reports, "everyone cursed my doctrine and Schiller's about 'truth.'" He admits that his unfortunate, reckless, racy use of language makes it difficult for fellow intellectuals to give him a fair hearing: "I find that my free and easy and personal way of writing, especially in 'Pragmatism,' has made me an object of loathing to many respectable academic minds."[32] So in 1909, he worked on preparing for publication a collection of essays elaborating and defending his views, to be entitled *The Meaning of Truth.*

Early in 1910, James was having more trouble with his heart and decided to visit a specialist in Paris. He also wanted to take the medicinal baths at Nauheim, Germany, again. But he was unable to overcome his fatigue and returned home a few months later. It had become an ordeal for him to walk or talk or write. Upon arriving in America in mid-August, he went directly to his summer house in New Hampshire. Within two days it became obvious that he was dying, as he did on August 26th. His body was transported back to Cambridge, a funeral service was held in the college chapel, and, after cremation, his ashes were placed near his parents' graves in the Cambridge cemetery.

James's writings have mostly been mentioned already. His two great psychological works were *The Principles of Psychology*, published in two volumes in 1890,[33] and *Psychology: Briefer Course*, published in 1892.[34] Most of his important philosophical lectures and essays have been collected into books. Among these some will be most relevant for our purposes: (1) *The Will to Believe and Other Essays in Popular Philosophy*, first published in 1897;[35] (2) *The Varieties of Religious Experience* (the Gifford Lectures), first published in 1902;[36] (3) *Pragmatism: A New Name for Some Old Ways of Thinking* (the Lowell Institute Lectures), first published in 1907;[37] (4) *A Pluralistic Universe* (the Hibbert Lectures), first published in 1909;[38] (5) *The Meaning of Truth*, published in 1909;[39] (6) *Some Problems of Philosophy* (a textbook on which James was still working when he died), edited by his son Henry James, Jr., and published in 1911;[40] and (7) *Essays in Radical Empiricism*, edited after his death by Ralph Barton Perry and published in 1912.[41] Many of James's most important philosophical works have been anthologized in *The Writings of William James: A Comprehensive Edition*, edited by John J. McDermott,[42] to which cross-references will be made.

Theory of Knowledge

Psychology. James's psychology, which underlies his epistemology, portrays human consciousness as an ongoing "stream" rather than in terms of such metaphors as a container to be filled or Hume's **atomistic** "bundle of perceptions," for example: "Consciousness, then, does not appear to itself chopped up in bits. Such words as 'chain' or 'train' do not describe it fitly." In other words, he goes on to explain,

> It is nothing jointed; it flows. A "river" or a "stream" are the metaphors by which it is most naturally described. *In talking of it hereafter, let us call it the stream of thought, of consciousness, or of subjective life.*[43]

As an empiricist, James tries to observe and record the basic facts of our psychological experience:

> The first and foremost concrete fact which every one will affirm to belong to his inner experience is the fact that *consciousness of some sort goes on.* "States of mind" succeed each other in him.[44]

He expresses the same point differently in "The Will to Believe," when he writes,

> There is but one indefectibly certain truth, and that is the truth that pyrrhonistic scepticism itself leaves standing,—the truth that the present phenomenon

of consciousness exists. That, however, is the bare starting-point of knowledge, the mere admission of a stuff to be philosophized about.[45]

This fundamental fact of conscious activity is comparable to Descartes's starting point, the experience of thinking itself.

But, then, how are we to analyze this fundamental fact of conscious activity? James does so in terms of five general characteristics. "1) Every thought tends to be part of a personal consciousness." Thoughts are experienced as grouped together, each belonging with some others while being segregated from other collections of thoughts. But none are experienced as either radically isolated from all other thoughts or as free-floating. "The only states of consciousness that we naturally deal with are found in personal consciousnesses, minds, selves, concrete particular I's and you's." Furthermore, each mind has direct, immediate access only to its own thoughts and not to those of any other mind, "every thought being *owned.*" Thus, it is "*my thought,*" rather than thought in general, that is given as an object of experience. "2) Within each personal consciousness thought is always changing." Here James is referring to the constantly dynamic quality of our mental activity. Although mental states may have a certain duration, he says, "*no state once gone can recur and be identical with what it was before.*" No thought persists between one act of thinking it and another: "*A permanently existing 'idea' or 'Vorstellung' which makes its appearance before the footlights of consciousness at periodic intervals, is as mythological an entity as the Jack of Spades.*" Although we can think about or experience the same object more than once, each thought or experience has its own unique identity and integrity. "3) Within each personal consciousness thought is sensibly continuous." Balancing the constant change of consciousness is its experienced continuity. James analyzes this continuity in terms of two facts:

> 1. That even where there is a time-gap the consciousness after it feels as if it belonged together with the consciousness before it, as another part of the same self; 2. That the changes from one moment to another in the quality of the consciousness are never absolutely abrupt.

The continuity of consciousness, then, from one mental event to another, involves the fact that the events are "parts of a common whole," which is a personal self. James goes on to analyze the parts, within this continuous whole, as of two types. There are those thoughts on which consciousness tends to focus attention and those that move consciousness towards such objects of attention. "*Let us call the resting-places the 'substantive parts,' and the places of flight the 'transitive parts,' of the stream of thought*." James emphatically denies that mental transitions from one focal object to another should be viewed in terms of radical gaps:

> The transition between the thought of one object and the thought of another is no more a break in the *thought* than a joint in a bamboo is a break in the wood. It is a part of the *consciousness* as much as the joint is a part of the *bamboo*.

Within the continuity of consciousness, there is also a distinction between its focus and its fringe. "In all our voluntary thinking there is some topic or subject about which all the members of the thought revolve." But this focus of thought is experienced in the context of an enveloping sphere of awareness, its "*psychic overtone, suffusion,* or *fringe*," as James calls it. "4) It always appears to deal with objects independent of itself." Here James takes issue with the implications of Hegelian metaphysics: "For Absolute Idealism, the infinite Thought and its objects are one." He also rejects the "perfectly wanton assumption," which he says was "originated" by Kant, "that a thought, in order to know a thing at all, must expressly distinguish between the thing and its own self." Against the Hegelians, James insists on an ultimate distinction between subject and object of consciousness. Against the Kantians, he holds that "*thought may, but need not, in knowing, discriminate between its object and itself*." And, finally, "5) It is interested in some parts of these objects to the exclusion of others, and welcomes or rejects—*chooses* from among them, in a word—all the while." Thus, James characterizes consciousness in terms of "phenomena of selective attention and of deliberative will." Despite this emphasis on choice and will, however, he also notes that we humans generally tend to agree as to what interests us and commands our attention.[46] For James, whatever we say about any objects of experience, including religion and the idea of God, should be understood against the backdrop of this conception of the "stream" of consciousness, analyzable in terms of these five characteristics. This might seem to rule out philosophies of religion based, for example, on Humean atomism or Kantian transcendentalism or Hegelian idealism.

Among the phenomena of consciousness that we experience are acts of volition or will; they are experienced and not merely inferred. As he writes, "In a word, volition is a psychic or moral fact pure and simple." Nevertheless, it is parasitic on other conscious acts rather than being radically fundamental: "Reflex, instinctive, and emotional movements are all primary performances" of consciousness; by contrast, James maintains, "*voluntary movements must be secondary, not primary functions of our organism*," in the sense that they follow after primary acts of consciousness in a responsive manner. The exercising of will involves a "*fiat*, the element of consent, or resolve that the act shall ensue." For instance, we can conceive of the possibility of writing down an example of an act of will, choose to do so (with a sense of *fiat*, or "let it be done"), and then proceed to engage in the physical motions that will realize the imagined possibility. What can we here experience internally, prior to the deliberate motion of writing down the example?

> *An anticipatory image, then, of the sensorial consequences of a movement, plus (on certain occasions) the fiat that these consequences shall become actual, is the only psychic state which introspection lets us discern as the forerunner of our voluntary acts.*

When we consider whether to act in such a way as to try to realize a conceived possibility,

> we are said to *deliberate*; and when finally the original suggestion either prevails and makes the movement take place, or gets definitively quenched by its antagonists, we are said to *decide*, or to *utter our voluntary fiat* in favor of one or the other course.

Meanwhile, the ideas inclining us to and inhibiting us from action "are termed the *reasons or motives*" for the decision.[47]

James distinguishes among five types of decisions of which our wills are capable. "The first may be called *the reasonable type.* . . . in which the arguments for and against a given course" are consciously considered until the stronger arguments prevail and we will to act accordingly. Thus, you might decide to become a lawyer rather than a philosopher because you want a high-paying job and the evidence convinces you that there are more lucrative positions to be found in law than in philosophy. "In the *second type* of case our feeling is to a certain extent that of letting ourselves drift with a certain indifferent acquiescence in a direction accidentally determined *from without*." You might, for example, be torn between a career in law and one in philosophy, deciding on the former because you like this semester's prelaw teacher more than your current philosophy professor. "In the *third type* the determination seems equally accidental, but it comes from within, and not from without." Here, although you might be as torn as in the preceding example, because, once again, the evidence is inconclusive and the arguments indecisive, you might be moved to choose law because you woke up this morning feeling it would be fun to have the opportunity to defend or prosecute dramatic civil cases. "There is a *fourth form* of decision, which. . . . comes when, in consequence of some outer experience or some inexplicable inward change, *we suddenly pass from the easy and careless to the sober and strenuous mood*, or possibly the other way." Thus, you may have been aiming to be a philosopher because you consider it intellectually satisfying work that does not require long hours or much concerted effort and then decided to shift to law after hearing a lecture on the dire needs of the poor and disadvantaged in our society for legal assistance. "In the *fifth and final type* of decision, . . . we feel, in deciding, as if we ourselves by our own wilful act inclined the beam." You might be genuinely drawn to both law and philosophy and find the reasons for each equally compelling; without being moved decisively by either external circumstances or internal feeling or experiencing any sort of personality sea change, you might self-consciously commit yourself to law, rather than to philosophy, for no cogent reason you could articulate, merely as a matter of will. (This is the type of decision that is involved in what James calls "the will to believe," which we shall consider soon.) James points out that what distinguishes such a decision from the previous four types is "the *feeling of effort*," and he maintains that this conspicuous feeling of effort is experienced in "comparatively few" of the decisions that "most people" actually make.[48]

Thus far, for James, "attention with effort is all that any case of volition implies"; and the effort involved may be more or less consciously felt. *"The essential achievement of the will, in short, when it is most 'voluntary,' is to ATTEND to a difficult object and hold it fast before the mind. The so-doing is the fiat."* As we have seen, volition is a secondary act of consciousness, dependent on some more fundamental conscious act(s), so that the object of will *"is always an idea"* about which we can deliberate and on which we can act. It is in this sense that James concludes that "volition is primarily a relation, not between our self and extra-mental matter (as many philosophers still maintain), but between our self and our own states of mind." In this sense, one fundamentally chooses the idea of a potato as tasty and nutritious and only then proceeds to act in such a way as to order the vegetable that corresponds to that idea. Are these acts of volition ever free? James answers, "My own belief is that the question of free-will is insoluble on strictly psychologic grounds." Like Kant, he views the issue of freedom transcendentally, postulating it as a necessary condition underlying the possibility of moral action and responsibility: "It is a *moral* postulate about the Universe, the postulate that *what ought to be can be, and that bad acts cannot be fated, but that good ones must be possible in their place.*" James also points out that meaningful religious commitment presupposes free choice: "Thus not only our morality but our religion, so far as the latter is deliberate, depend on the effort which we can make. *'Will you or won't you have it so?'* is the most probing question." The classic text in which James discusses freedom at length (and one of the best of all his writings) is "The Dilemma of Determinism," where he speaks of freedom and determinism as two opposing "postulates of rationality"; in "The Sentiment of Rationality," he includes freedom in a list of four such postulates, along with God, moral duty, and immortality.[49]

In a section on "Voluntary Thought," James observes that the will, in the context of consciously considering ideas, can "*emphasize and linger over those which seem pertinent, and ignore the rest.*" Here we experience deliberate selective attention at work. "The solution of problems is the most characteristic and peculiar sort of voluntary thinking."[50] When one reflects on the difficulty of reconciling belief in the perfect, infinite God of the Judeo-Christian tradition with the fact that terrible evil sometimes seems to prevail in the world, one's thinking is quite deliberate and not merely reflex action. But this leads us to a final topic in the psychological background to James's epistemology, his theory of belief. It is only because people believe in the recalcitrant reality of evil and find it tempting to believe in the monotheistic God that they choose to agonize over the problem at all. So what is this psychic phenomenon of belief, and how is it associated with our conception of reality?

Belief. James begins his discussion of belief by observing that we are all aware of the common experience of distinguishing between imagining or conceiving of something, on the one hand, and believing in it, on the other, or between considering "a proposition and acquiescing in its truth. In the case of acquiescence or belief, the object is not only apprehended by the mind, but it is held to have reality. Belief is thus the mental state or function of cognizing reality." He proceeds to say that belief admits of a wide spectrum of commitment from that which is quite tentative and insecure, at one extreme, to "the highest possible certainty and conviction," at the other. Inquiry ends (at least temporarily) with the feeling of belief, and disbelief in something always involves believing in its opposite. Thus, James concludes, "*The true opposites of belief*, psychologically considered, *are doubt and inquiry, not disbelief.*" Beliefs are intellectually expressed by means of propositions which relate the subject of belief to the predicate(s) attributed to it.

> In every proposition, then, so far as it is believed, questioned, or disbelieved, four elements are to be distinguished, the subject, the predicate, and their relation (of whatever sort it be)—these form the object of belief—and finally the psychic attitude in which our mind stands towards the proposition taken as a whole—and this is the belief itself.[51]

If people believe that God is the supernatural Person who cares for the welfare of human beings, there is the feeling of conviction which is their belief and the proposition that they believe; the latter can be analyzed in terms of its subject (God), its predicate (the supernatural Person who cares for the welfare of human beings), and the relationship between its subject and predicate (in this case, that of identity).

To believe in something is to consider it real in some sense; and it is conflict with other objects of belief that bars us from conceiving of something as real.

> The sense that anything we think of is unreal can only come, then, when that thing is contradicted by some other thing of which we think. *Any object which remains uncontradicted is ipso facto believed and posited as absolute reality.*

The fact that you entertain a proposition at all indicates that there is some basis for considering it as real (in some sense of that word), though this fact can be outweighed by conflicting considerations. Why might you be tempted to doubt the reality of the perfect, infinite God you were taught to believe in as a child? The reality of evil in the world that you have come to believe in since childhood seems to conflict with that religious belief, so that you experience the indecisive tension of doubt. You find yourself confronted with options: you can simply repudiate your former religious belief; you can try to dismiss what you call evil as an illusion; you can find some way of resolving the apparent conflict between the two in such a way that you can believe in both.

> *The whole distinction of real and unreal, the whole psychology of belief, disbelief, and doubt, is thus grounded on two mental facts—first, that we are liable to think differently of the same; and second, that when we have done so, we can choose which way of thinking to adhere to and which to disregard.*[52]

James goes on to discuss various realms of reality to which we can consign objects of belief, "the many worlds" to which they might belong. "1. The world of sense, or of physical 'things' as we instinctively apprehend them" contains, for almost all of us, the realities "of shoes and ships and sealing-wax, of cabbages and kings," in the words of Lewis Carroll. "2. The world of science, or of physical things as the learned conceive them" contains electrons, forces, and the laws of motion. "3. The world of ideal relations, or abstract truths believed or believable by all" contains Aristotle's logical principle of noncontradiction, Pythagoras' geometrical theorem, and Kant's ethical categorical imperative. "4. The world of 'idols of the tribe,' illusions or prejudices of the race," includes the sense that the center of the Earth is absolutely down and the tendency to view the rest of the universe as moving around the Earth. "5. The various supernatural worlds" such as "the Christian heaven and hell" or the "various worlds of deliberate fable," such as the world of Graham Greene's fiction (which his fans and critics refer to as "Greeneland"). "6. The various worlds of individual opinion, as numerous as men are," including one's quite groundless belief in extraterrestrial intelligent creatures. "7. The worlds of sheer madness and vagary, also indefinitely numerous," comprising the Son of Sam's psychotic delusions. James writes, "*Every object we think of gets at last referred to one world or another of this or some similar list.*" When we ask about the reality of this piece of paper on which these words are printed, the reference is to the first world; when we question whether the principle of utility is, indeed, the ultimate criterion of moral decision making, we refer to the third world; when we wonder whether the title character sees a real dagger near the beginning of Act II of *Macbeth*, the reference is to the fifth world; etc. But, within each realm, ideas can genuinely present themselves to consciousness as candidates for belief.

> Each world *whilst it is attended to* is real after its own fashion.

For an object of thought to appear as real, it must be viewed as having some conceivable practical significance to the mind conceiving it; that is to say, "it must appear both *interesting* and *important*." We dismiss as unreal whatever has no conceivable connection to ourselves. Thus, "*reality means simply relation to our emotional and active life.*" This is a relational conception of reality. We consider real objects of belief

> *whatever things we select and emphasize and turn to* WITH A WILL. These are our *living* realities; and not only these, but all the other things which are intimately connected with these.

Thus, a person's conscious experience is the ground of all his belief, of all that (in any sense) he can consider real. "As Descartes made the indubitable reality of the *cogito* go bail for the reality of all that the *cogito* involved," James maintains that all beliefs as to what is real are "anchored in the Ego, considered as an active and emotional term. That is the hook from which the rest dangles, the absolute support." Finally, among the possible sets of ideas which we can believe in as real are entire theories. One might be committed to materialism or psychophysical dualism; one might believe in the worldview of Christianity or be an atheistic naturalist. And one can decide in which of two (or more) competing theories he shall commit himself to believe. But how are such decisions made? James's answer is in terms of a holistic (rather than a narrowly theoretical) view of human nature:

> *That theory will be most generally believed which, besides offering us objects able to account satisfactorily for our sensible experience, also offers those which are most interesting, those which appeal most urgently to our aesthetic, emotional, and active needs.*[53]

In determining our beliefs, we do not live by logic alone. In "The Sentiment of Rationality" James says,

> Pretend what we may, the whole man within us is at work when we form our philosophical opinions. Intellect, will, taste, and passion co-operate just as they do in practical affairs.[54]

These elements of James's psychology provide a foundation for his theory of knowledge, which, in turn, supports his views on God and religious faith.

Radical Empiricism. James's radical empiricism is of a piece with his psychological theory, in starting with the objects and operations of consciousness. "Radical empiricism consists first of a postulate, next of a statement of fact, and finally of a generalized conclusion," as he writes in the preface to *The Meaning of Truth*. He proceeds to identify each of these three elements. First, he says, "The postulate is that the only things that shall be debatable among philosophers shall be things definable in terms drawn from experience." By means of this postulate James launches a preemptive strike against rationalism, in general, and the absolute idealism of Hegel and his followers, in particular. "The statement of fact is that the relations between things, conjunctive as well as **disjunctive**, are just as much matters of direct particular experience, neither more so nor less so, than the things themselves." With this second element, James distances his own form of empiricism from the skeptical atomism of Hume and his followers. Third, he writes, "The generalized conclusion is that therefore the parts of experience hold together from next to next by relations that are themselves part of experience." Thus, without subscribing to Kant's transcendental philosophy, James thinks his own epistemology can account for the interconnections among the objects of consciousness without "throwing 'categories' over them like a net."[55] Viewed in this light, his form of empiricism stands as an alternative to the dominant theories of knowledge of his day.

In *Essays in Radical Empiricism*, James observes that all brands of rationalism attempt to "emphasize universals and to make wholes prior to parts in the order of logic as well as that of being." In his mind, Hegelian idealism is the prominent contemporary example of this. "Empiricism, on the contrary, lays the explanatory stress upon the part, the element, the individual, and treats the whole as a collection and the universal as an abstraction." James's own epistemology is empirical in this sense. "It is essentially a mosaic philosophy, a philosophy of plural facts, like that of Hume and his descendants." James is drawn to the empirical over the rationalistic option because he is convinced that the primary, immediate objects of consciousness are always particulars and their interconnections and that universals are secondary derivatives, inferred by the mind. He goes on to "add the epithet radical" to the description of his own brand of empiricism in order to distinguish it from the Humean kind. "To be radical, an empiricism must neither admit into its constructions any element that is not directly experienced, nor exclude from them any element that is directly experienced." The fault of the Humean is that he fails to acknowledge that we directly experience things, events, and ideas as already conjoined. James's empiricism is "radical" in its insistence that "*any kind of relation experienced must be accounted as 'real' as anything else in the system.*" Interconnections are part of the natural order, directly linking particulars.

> *Radical empiricism*, as I would understand it, *does full justice to conjunctive relations*, without, however, treating them as rationalism always tends to treat them, as being true in some supernal way, as if the unity of things and their variety belonged to different orders of truth and vitality altogether.

Thus, James defines his own epistemology as a middle-ground alternative between the Scylla of Humean atomism, on which the ship of epistemology would crash, and the Charybdis of Hegelian idealism, by which it would be swallowed. In *Essays in Radical Empiricism*, James refers to Kierkegaard's saying, "We live forward, but we understand backward."[56] From his point of view, the reconstruction necessary in our efforts to "understand backward" makes both rationalism and traditional empiricism static. What is needed is for understanding, like experience itself, to move forward, so that it might be as dynamic as life itself.

In his posthumously published *Some Problems of Philosophy*, James analyzes the relationship between our perceptions and our ideas in three successive chapters on "Percept and Concept." Through our senses, we experience things as phenomenal presentations, of which our thoughts are frequently representations. James holds that, since "concepts flow out of percepts and into them again, they are . . . interlaced." Rather than viewing percepts and concepts as radically different, the former leading to the latter as if on a one-way street, we should recognize that, as James writes, "Sensation and thought in man are mingled." At the level of unconceptualized perception, we experience reality as a welter of sensations, "a big blooming buzzing confusion." It is by means of concepts that we make ideal "cuts" of discrimination. "The great difference between percepts and concepts is that percepts are continuous and concepts are discrete" as to their particular meanings.[57]

Like Kant, James emphasizes the importance of both percepts and concepts as necessary conditions of human knowledge. He pointedly writes that "a man can no more limit himself to either than a pair of scissors can cut with a single one of its blades." Nevertheless, he observes with disapproval that "there has always been a tendency among philosophers to treat conception as the more essential thing in knowledge." He condemns this "Platonizing persuasion" that abstract ideas "ought to supersede the senses rather than interpret them," arguing against it "1. That concepts are secondary formations, inadequate, and only ministerial," presupposing and interpreting perception, "and 2. That they falsify as well as omit" by being static representations of a dynamic reality and by suggesting "that perceptual experience is not reality at all, but an appearance or illusion." James deplores this sort of "intellectualism," which he tends to identify with the Germans. He accuses Kant of denying the reality of the perceptual flux, of reducing it to "a mere apparitional birth-place for concepts."[58] He says elsewhere, "The true line of philosophic progress lies, in short, it seems to me, not so much *through* Kant as *round* him."[59] In writing of "that strange and powerful genius Hegel," James accuses him of "a vicious intellectualism," to the extent that he makes any sense at all. James later says, "Hegel wrote so abominably that I cannot understand him, and will say nothing more about him here."[60] Similarly, James takes to task the unconvincing abstractions of Leibniz's theodicy, wondering why his God should ever compromise the perfection of His "antecedent will" by translating it into the reality of imperfect creation.[61]

In contrast to the German philosophy professors in their ivory towers and out of touch with reality, James openly prefers the British empiricists, with their openness to new experience. He writes, in a letter of 1902 to Schiller, "Anyhow, *vive* the Anglo-Saxon amateur, disciple of Locke and Hume, and *pereat* the German professional."[62] Against the latter, in his 1898 lecture at Berkeley, he says, "I sincerely believe that the English spirit in philosophy is . . . on the saner, sounder, and truer path."[63]

Through a combination of perceptual experience and conceptual ideas, knowledge can be established as a relationship between consciousness and (some of) its objects. This assumes a "*dualism*," which "supposes two elements, mind knowing and thing known, and treats them as irreducible." James goes on to say, "*There are two kinds of knowledge* broadly and practically distinguishable: we may call them respectively *knowledge of acquaintance* and *knowledge-about*." Thus, I am acquainted with "the color blue when I see it, and the flavor of a pear when I taste it"; yet I could not describe them to anyone who is not already acquainted with them or something very like them. Nevertheless, I can claim a direct, first-hand experiential knowledge of them. By contrast, I might know a good deal about Hegel's Absolute Mind; but I certainly would not claim to be directly acquainted with any such ultimate Reality. Our knowledge is ordinarily articulated by means of a grammatical sentence which relates a "subject" with which we are somehow acquainted to a "predicate," which says something about it. We know the objects of acquaintance through intuitive feeling; what we know about them is grasped through conceptual thought: "Feelings are the germ and starting point of cognition, thoughts the developed tree."[64] Our percepts give us knowledge of acquaintance, while our concepts express knowledge-about.

It is experience which leads us to discriminate between greater and lesser degrees of conviction. "We are sure that fire will burn and water wet us, less sure that thunder will come after lightning, not at all sure whether a strange dog will bark at us or let us go by." We develop habits of expectation, thanks to which "we continually divine from the present what the future is to be." Experiences which have cognitive significance "influence the mind" by means of "habits and association." We formulate and communicate our knowledge in terms of propositions, which, for James, are of two types:

> I shall now in what follows call all propositions which express time- and space-relations empirical propositions, and I shall give the name of rational propositions to all propositions which express the results of a comparison.

As an example of the former, we can say that the chalkboard is green; to illustrate the latter, we may observe that the meaning of "good" differs from that of "evil." In addition to the data of consciousness (such as that about the chalkboard) derived from sensory experience, we have direct, immediate access to rational propositions like the latter, whether or not anything corresponding to them exists in the perceptual world.

> There is thus no denying the fact that *the mind is filled with necessary and eternal relations which it finds between certain of its ideal conceptions, and which form a determinate system, independent of the order of frequency in which experiences may have associated the conception's originals in time and space.*

(James is inclined to accept the characterization of these systems as *a priori* but hesitates because of the connotative baggage associated with such terminology; he says his views on this matter are basically those expressed in Book IV of the *Essay* by "the immortal Locke.") Three such systems of necessary relations are those of syllogistic logic, arithmetic, and geometry. Thus the first assures us that if Socrates is a man and all men are mortal, Socrates cannot be immortal; the second guarantees (to use Kant's example) that seven added to five always equals twelve; and the third rules out the possibility that any circle could be a rectangle.

> None of these eternal verities has anything to say about facts, about what is or is not in the world. Logic does not say whether Socrates, men, mortals or immortals *exist*, arithmetic does not tell us where her 7's, 5's, and 12's are to be *found*; geometry affirms not that circles and rectangles are *real*.

These abstract systems give us hypothetical knowledge, to the effect "that *if* these things are anywhere to be found, the eternal verities will obtain" in relation to them. Some rational propositions, such as that blue is different from yellow, have already been experientially verified, whereas others have not. Among the latter are metaphysical axioms, such as that of Leibniz, that "Nothing is or happens without a reason," or that of Hegel, that "The world is throughout rationally intelligible." James says that such principles should be considered "*postulates of rationality*, not propositions of fact," in that we demand that they be assumed for the purpose of making sense of experience and reality, although they have not been verified and may not be conclusively verifiable. He sounds rather like Kant when he says, "Where harmonies are asserted of the real world, they are obviously mere postulates of rationality, so far as they transcend experience." Leibniz's principle of sufficient reason is a basic postulate in metaphysical reasoning. "The widest postulate of rationality is that the world is rationally intelligible throughout, after the pattern of *some* ideal system."[65] This principle, as we have seen, is fundamental to the Hegelian metaphysical system. But even these abstract principles emerge from the world of conscious experience and have a functional value because they refer back to it somehow.

The epistemological insights of James discussed in this subsection are admirably worthwhile, made all the richer by being based on his expert study of human psychology. However, he is a great deal closer to Kant on these matters than he ever realized or was disposed to admit. His criticisms of Kant tend to be unfair and unfortunate. For example, Kant does not, as James claims, deny the reality of the perceptual flux, but only that we can know it as it is in itself. Second, James dismisses "the old debate as to whether the *a priori* truths are 'analytic' or 'synthetic' " in much too facile a manner, as "one of Kant's most unhappy legacies," which is "devoid of all significance," thus skirting the important epistemological issue of whether we can have knowledge which is informative, on the one hand, and universally and necessarily certain, on the other. And, third, James dogmatically rejects Kant's view "that the forms of our necessary thought are underived from experience."[66] He may or may not be correct against Kant on this matter, but he fails to argue his point convincingly. Their epistemological theories seem remarkably comparable, despite obvious methodological and terminological differences. It is too bad that James's animosity towards German philosophers prevented his entering into serious dialogue with Kant's theory of knowledge.

Pragmatism. James's pragmatism, probably the most well-known aspect of his philosophy, presents a method that is clearly empirical. As we have seen, for James, even metaphysical postulates must emerge from and refer back to conscious experience. The functional value of all percepts and concepts is experiential and essentially related to their possible use for persons. The eight lectures of *Pragmatism* begin with a rough analysis of two opposing types of philosophical approaches, which James labels the "tender-minded" and the "tough-minded." The former approach is typically (1) rationalistic (fundamentally based on "principles"), (2) intellectualistic, (3) idealistic, (4) optimistic, (5) religious, (6) committed to free will, (7) monistic, and (8) dogmatic; by contrast, the latter tends to be (1') empirical (fundamentally based on "facts"), (2') sensationalistic, (3') materialistic, (4') pessimistic, (5') irreligious, (6') fatalistic, (7') pluralistic, and (8') skeptical. Each type of thinker tends to view the other with suspicion, if not with disdain. "The tough think of the tender as sentimental and soft-heads. The tender feel the tough to be unrefined, callous, or brutal."[67] James realizes that it is difficult to find philosophers who are pure examples of either type. But he would generally classify Augustine, Anselm, Aquinas, Descartes, Leibniz, and Hegel in the "tender-minded" category, calling Locke and Hume "tough minded." He admits that there can be thinkers who are rather evenly balanced, saying, "Kant may fairly be called mixed."[68]

The problem is that few of us, given this set of alternative approaches, are disposed to be satisfied with either over the other. "Most of us have a hankering for the good things on both sides of the line. Facts are good, of course—give us lots of facts. Principles are good— give us plenty of principles." So, like Kant and James himself, we normally want the best of both approaches. But can they be coherently synthesized? This is what James describes as "the present dilemma in philosophy." Having exposed the problem, he is prepared to present his own synthesis:

> It is at this point that my own solution begins to appear. I offer the oddly-named thing pragmatism as a philosophy that can satisfy both kinds of demand. It can remain religious like the rationalisms, but at the same time, like the empiricisms, it can preserve the richest intimacy with facts.[69]

In its method, pragmatism will be fact-based and empirical, avoiding rationalism's intellectualistic idolatry of abstract principles; James will offer us a decidedly pluralistic, antimonistic worldview, which strives to be neither dogmatic nor skeptical, neither optimistic nor pessimistic (but rather "**melioristic**"), and is committed to both religious faith and free will. The remainder of James's lecture is a study of his attempt to develop and articulate this synthesis.

The most celebrated of these eight lectures, "What Pragmatism Means," explains and illustrates "*the pragmatic method*," which, James says, "is primarily a method of settling metaphysical disputes that otherwise might be interminable." As examples, he mentions the traditional debates between monists and pluralists, fatalists and indeterminists, materialists and idealists. In dealing with any such issue, we should raise the pragmatic question:

> What difference would it practically make to any one if this notion rather than that notion were true? If no practical difference whatever can be traced, then the alternatives mean practically the same thing, and all dispute is idle.

James is confident that disputes can be made to "collapse into insignificance" when subjected to this pragmatic test; yet he is curiously negligent about providing even a single example of a traditional metaphysical problem that can be so dissolved. Could this be because all such issues have been practically (and not merely theoretically) significant to people? For example, during the thirteenth century, Christian thinkers, including Bonaventure and Aquinas, debated about whether we can establish, by rational argumentation, that the world is not eternal. We might ask why the issue should be pursued with any seriousness. To do so is to raise the pragmatic challenge. A Jamesian might (although James himself does not) say that the issue did "collapse into insignificance" several centuries ago because it ceased to pass the pragmatic test,[70] whereas other metaphysical topics (such as those concerned with human freedom, immortality, and the existence of God) remain live issues for us human beings because they continue to pass the test.

James asserts that no significant difference in meaning fails to "*make a difference*" in experience; there is "no difference in abstract truth that doesn't express itself in a difference in concrete fact and in conduct consequent upon that fact, imposed on somebody, somehow, somewhere, and somewhen." Even if this difference is merely theoretical or potential, it is important in providing a stabilizing anchor for our conceptualization. "The whole function of philosophy ought to be to find out what definite difference it will make to you and me, at definite instants of our life, if this world-formula or that world-formula be the true one." The use of the personal pronouns here is significant, since meaning and meaningfulness are to be relative to persons. This relational view will make James's treatment of religious experience quite different from the logical, systematic demonstrations of medieval and early modern times. The pragmatic method, James admits, embraces the concrete facts, practical action, and open-mindedness of empiricism and turns away from the abstractions, absolute principles, and closed, dogmatic systems of rationalism. "At the same time it does not stand for any special results. It is a method only.... It has no dogmas, and no doctrines save its method."[71] It is open to the findings of experience in helping us to decide whether to commit ourselves to belief in God, freedom, objective moral values, immortality, etc.

This leads to James's relational view of truth, "*that ideas (which themselves are but parts of our experience) become true just in so far as they help us to get into satisfactory relation with other parts of our experience.*" This requires that those ideas relate new experiences to our "stock of old opinions" as smoothly as possible, sacrificing no more of the latter than is necessary. We should neither ignore nor deny the new experiences, on the one hand, nor play fast and loose with our worldview, on the other. "New truth is always a go-between, a smoother-over of transitions. It marries old opinion to new fact so as ever to show a minimum of jolt, a maximum of continuity." James is clearly developing a relational theory of truth here, which is quite different from the traditional conception of truth as absolute. "To a certain degree, therefore, everything here is plastic." This view stands in stark contrast to that of Augustine, Anselm, Aquinas, Descartes, Locke, Leibniz, and Hegel, for whom truth is fixed and given for our discovery and acquiescence. James staunchly opposes this view:

> Purely objective truth, truth in whose establishment the function of giving human satisfaction in marrying previous parts of experience with newer parts played no role whatever, is nowhere to be found.

He picturesquely adds, "The trail of the human serpent is thus over everything,"[72] especially in the areas of meaning and truth.

As an illustration, James critically considers the Hegelian notion of an Absolute Mind. Is it meaningful and true to affirm its reality? James sees both strengths and weaknesses in the notion, regarded pragmatically:

> Far be it from me to deny the majesty of this conception, or its capacity to yield religious comfort to a most respectable class of minds. But from the human point of view, no one can pretend that it doesn't suffer from the faults of remoteness and abstractness.

It is a noble abstraction, but one which fails to help us better understand and constructively deal with the particular facts of concrete experience. The comforting "cash-value" of the idea is that it assures us that "finite evil is 'overruled,' " affording us the luxury of a "don't-care mood" and assuring us that "moral holidays are in order." To this extent the notion has positive worth.

> *If theological ideas prove to have a value for concrete life, they will be true, for pragmatism, in the sense of being good for so much. For how much more they are true, will depend entirely on their relations to the other truths that also have to be acknowledged.*

The fact that belief in the Absolute confers "moral holidays" is an advantage; yet it still "must run the gauntlet of all my other beliefs." From this perspective it is seen as unacceptable because "it clashes with other truths of mine whose benefits I hate to give up on its account." It seems to conflict with James's beliefs in and commitment to human individuality and personal freedom and the importance of initiative and moral responsibility.

> But as I have enough trouble in life already without adding the trouble of carrying these intellectual inconsistencies, I personally just give up the Absolute. I just take my moral holidays, or else as a professional philosopher, I try to justify them by some other principle.[73]

James is ironically like Hegel in emphasizing a contextual view of truth but different in seeing it as relative to subjective needs and interests.

In his third lecture, James pragmatically considers several traditional metaphysical problems, including (1) what we can know of substance (material substance, spiritual substance, and personal identity), (2) "the debate between materialism and theism," (3) the issue of whether there is "*design in nature*," and (4) the question of free will. From a pragmatic perspective, personal identity, God, natural order, and freedom are all significant beliefs in that they point to "a world of promise"; by contrast, phenomenalism, materialism, cosmic chaos, and determinism support a worldview whose "sun sets in a sea of disappointment." The idea of God, in particular, is remarkably valuable in that

> it guarantees an ideal order that shall be permanently preserved. A world with a God in it to say the last word, may indeed burn up or freeze, but we then think of him as still mindful of the old ideals and sure to bring them elsewhere to fruition; so that, where he is, tragedy is only provisional and partial, and ship-wreck and dissolution not the absolutely final things.

It is easy to see how different is this approach from that of traditional philosophers. James says, "I myself believe that the evidence for God lies primarily in inner personal experiences" rather than in formal logical arguments. The "promise" or hope that values can be realized and main-tained is irrelevant to a purely objective view of meaning and truth but a crucial consideration for a pragmatic one.[74]

One of the oldest metaphysical issues and among those of the great-est interest to James is that of "The One and the Many," which is the subject of his fourth lecture. Is reality, taken as a whole, fundamentally characterized by unity or diversity? Hegel is an example of a rationalist who tends to submerge all particulars in cosmic unity (that of his Absolute Spirit), whereas Hume is a phenomenalist for whom the ("loose and separate") particulars of experience seem not to cohere in any under-lying unity. James sees both connections and "disconnexion among things," characterizing experience in terms of "definite networks" that are nevertheless not all-encompassing. He recommends that we

> equally abjure absolute monism and absolute pluralism. The world is One just so far as its parts hang together by any definite connexion. It is many just so far as any definite connexion fails to obtain. And finally it is growing more and more unified by those systems of connexion at least which human energy keeps framing as time goes on.

To the extent that he must come down on one side of the fence or the other, James, as an empiricist and a pragmatist, sides with the pluralistic view of reality. He admits that the monist's ideal of "total union" may become realized. "Meanwhile the opposite hypothesis, of a world imper-fectly unified still, and perhaps always to remain so, must be sincerely entertained."[75] This is all that moderate pluralism, as opposed to the absolute pluralism of Hume, would require.

In *Some Problems of Philosophy*, James reconsiders the problem, attack-ing (Hegelian) monism on four counts: "1. It does not account for our finite consciousnesses," with its view of the absolute as the only reality. "2. It creates a problem of evil" of a theoretical nature, given apparent imper-fection in a world whose source is absolute Perfection. "3. It contradicts the character of reality as perceptually experienced," in terms of the temporal changes, "novelties, struggles, losses, gains" evident in the world of sense. "4. It is fatalistic," in viewing mere possibility, "as distinguished from necessity on the one hand and from impossibility on the other," as "pure illusion." These are the crucial problems inherent in (Hegelian) monism. "Pluralism, on the other hand, taking perceptual experience at its face-value, is free from all these difficulties." Also, in its determinism, monism tends to either optimism (the view that things are determined to work out for the best, no matter what we do) or pessimism (that things are determined to work out for the worst, no matter what we do).

> Pluralism, on the other hand, is neither optimistic nor pessimistic, but melioristic, rather. The world, it thinks, may be saved, on condition that its parts shall do their best. But shipwreck in detail, or even on the whole, is among the open possibilities.

So, meliorism holds that things can improve if we strive to make them better; emphasis is placed on our initiative, effort, and responsibility. Finally, James notes a logical advantage that pluralism has over monism:

> It is not obliged to stand for any particular amount of plurality, for it triumphs over monism if the smallest morsel of disconnectedness is once found undeniably to exist. "Ever not quite" is all it says to monism; while monism is obliged to prove that what pluralism asserts can in no amount whatever possibly be true—an infinitely harder task.[76]

The fifth lecture of *Pragmatism* deals with its relation to common sense, which is depicted as "one great stage of equilibrium in the human mind's development," on which other stages, including the scientific and philosophical, have "grafted themselves" without "displacing it." Common sense has its own fundamental concepts, "of which the most important" are those of "Thing; The same or different; Kinds; Minds; Bodies; One Time; One Space; Subjects and attributes; Causal influences; The fancied; The real." We might notice here the similarity between James's concepts of common sense and Kant's forms of intuition and categories of the understanding. But whereas Kant views his as *a priori* structures of the mind, James argues for the evolutionary view "that *our fundamental ways of thinking about things are discoveries of exceedingly remote ancestors, which have been able to preserve themselves throughout the experience of all subsequent time.*" According to this view, such concepts were formed and evolved in human experience and were transmitted from one generation to the next, continuing to be used because they proved to be useful. "For all utilitarian practical purposes these conceptions amply suffice." But matters become more complex when we start wondering why things behave as they do and what are their natures in themselves. "Science and critical philosophy thus burst the bounds of common sense." These, then, are three distinct "well-characterized levels, stages or types of thought about the world we live in," each having its own pragmatic utility. "It is impossible, however, to say that any stage as yet in sight is absolutely more true than any other." We benefit from learning to operate at the scientific and philosophical levels yet cannot afford to disconnect ourselves from the more fundamental level from which they have emerged, which is the viewpoint of ordinary experience. "Common sense is the more *consolidated* stage, because it got its innings first, and made all language into its ally." Ordinary experience is conceptualized at the level of common sense, which generates the structures of natural language, in terms, for example, of subjects and predicates. Intellectual history is important because it hands down to us scientific laws and philosophical principles by which, like the concepts of common sense, our predecessors have "unified and straightened the discontinuity of their immediate experiences."[77] All of these are instruments we learn to use to render experience intelligible.

The most controversial of the eight lectures is the sixth one, "Pragmatism's Conception of Truth." It develops more thoroughly some of the ideas on truth indicated earlier (especially in the second lecture). Before the turn of the twentieth century, the two dominant philosophical theories of truth were the correspondence (for example, truth requires the conformity of mind and object) and coherence (for example, truth requires that ideas fit together consistently and comprehensively) theories. James does not repudiate these established theories so much as he absorbs them into his own pragmatic one. He accepts the old correspondence view that true ideas must "agree with reality," while pragmatically interpreting that notion in terms of "a *leading that is worth while.*" The same can be said of his appropriation of coherence theory: "The connexions and transitions come to us from point to point as being progressive, harmonious, satisfactory." Again, as he insists, an important part of the "reality" with which our ideas must agree is that insisted on by coherence theorists, namely "the whole body of other truths already in our possession."[78] Part of the genius of James is this ability to incorporate rival perspectives into his own unique synthesis.

Yet there are also problems with his theory, partially arising from "the unguarded language" which James himself later admitted plagued these lectures on *Pragmatism*,[79] four of which we shall consider here. He writes,

"*True ideas are those that we can assimilate, validate, corroborate and verify. False ideas are those that we can not.*" To whom does the pronoun "we" refer—each of us individually (a subjective interpretation) or all of us collectively (an intersubjective interpretation)? And does this mean that an idea that is not subject to actual corroboration now is *therefore* false? And, if it can be corroborated next year, does a false idea (for example, that the Sun revolves around the Earth) thereby become true? In a second passage, James says that the truth of an idea "*is*" the process "of its verifying itself, its veri-*fication*." The notion that truth is a dynamic process to which we can make a contribution, rather than a static fact independent of us, may be appealing. But ideas do not verify themselves; they are verified by persons like us. Yet to identify truth with our activity would seem to relativize it in a manner that is at least unorthodox and perhaps counterintuitive. Third, James identifies the truth of an idea with its utility: "You can say of it then either that 'it is useful because it is true' or that 'it is true because it is useful.' Both these phrases mean exactly the same thing." But to say that truth is a criterion of utility is not logically the same as saying that utility is a criterion of truth. Most philosophical traditionalists might agree that truth contributes to the utility of an idea, while staunchly denying that an idea's utility contributes anything to its truth. And, fourth, James maintains,

> "*The true,*" to put it very briefly, *is only the expedient in the way of our thinking, just as "the right" is only the expedient in the way of our behaving*. Expedient in almost any fashion; and expedient in the long run and on the whole of course.

A problem with this view results from the word "only," which gives the analysis the appearance of being reductionistic. Pragmatism's view that truth contributes to the success of our thought processes, and even that the latter is an indication of the former, is attractive. Yet this seems only one dimension of truth, which should be coordinate with the other dimension of adequately meeting the requirements of objectively given experience. As James himself says, "Woe to him whose beliefs play fast and loose with the order which realities follow in his experience; they will lead him nowhere or else make false connexions." The question is whether James is correct that ideas that thus "play fast and loose" cannot prove to be "expedient in the long run and on the whole."[80]

As an empiricist, James insists, "Truths emerge from facts; but they dip forward into facts again and add to them; which facts again create or reveal new truth (the word is indifferent) and so on indefinitely." This ongoing dynamic between facts and truths (both characterized as plural

rather than monolithic) is an exciting contribution to the history of epistemology. Yet James is anxious that we should not blur the distinction
between the two: "The 'facts' themselves meanwhile are not *true*. They
simply are. Truth is the function of the beliefs that start and terminate
among them." He accepts and employs Hume's view that "matters of
fact," to be verified or falsified by means of perceptual experience, are not
the only objects of our beliefs.

> *Relations among purely mental ideas* form another sphere where true and false
> beliefs obtain, and here the beliefs are absolute, or unconditional. When they are
> true they bear the name either of definition or of principles.

That all bachelors are unmarried is a matter of definition, and it is a basic
logical principle that any particular living thing is either subject to death
or not. These truths refer to our concepts. "Moreover, once true, always
true, of those same mental objects. Truth here has an 'eternal' character."
But when it comes to objects of perceptual experience, James warns, "The
'absolutely' true, meaning what no farther experience will ever alter, is that
ideal vanishing-point towards which we imagine that all our temporary
truths will some day converge." (This is a strong alternative to the
Cartesian demand for incorrigibility that has dominated so much of modern philosophy.) Even our conceptual systems, to the extent that they are
to apply (or be related) to the world of factual experience, should be
regarded as corrigible, however insecure this may make us feel.

> Meanwhile we have to live to-day by what truth we can get to-day, and be ready
> to-morrow to call it falsehood. Ptolemaic astronomy, euclidean space, aristotelian
> logic, scholastic metaphysics, were expedient for centuries, but human experience
> has boiled over those limits, and we now call these things only relatively true,
> or true within those borders of experience.

We have lived through the replacement of Ptolemaic astronomy by the
Copernican view of the solar system; Euclidean geometry is now seen as
only one of several legitimate ways of conceiving of spatial relationships;
Aristotelian logic, although still extremely important, has been challenged
by Hegel's dialectical reasoning; scholastic metaphysics is now widely
viewed as obsolete, supplanted, in some places, for example, by process
thought. This track record of intellectual history may well incline us to
give James's **fallibilism** a fair hearing. Despite the problems indicated,
James has given us the most dynamic theory of truth in the history of
philosophy up to his day. Its insistence that the "truth of an idea is not a
stagnant property inherent in it" but is rather an open-ended "process"
constitutes its primary importance and challenge.[81]

In his seventh lecture, "Pragmatism and **Humanism**," James moves from opposing "that typical idol of the tribe, the notion of *the* Truth," so cherished by rationalists, to the view of pragmatism as humanistic, "the doctrine that to an unascertainable extent our truths are man-made products." The word "unascertainable" is significant here; we cannot figure out to what extent our truths are given to us and to what extent we create them. Yet the human contribution, James avers, is undeniable. "Human motives sharpen all our questions, human satisfactions lurk in all our answers, all our formulas have a human twist." Against humanism, the absolutist insists that all truth concerns objective "Reality" and is not relative to human subjectivity. But James analyzes the "Reality" of which our truths must take account into three parts, all of which are to be viewed in relation to our human experience. The "*first* part of reality from this point of view is the flux of our sensations," given to us as factual data. "The *second* part of reality . . . is the *relations* that obtain between our sensations or between their copies in our minds"—that is, our ideas. "The *third* part of reality, additional to these perceptions (tho largely based upon them), is the *previous truths*" with which new experience must cohere. We enjoy "a certain freedom in our dealings with" all three of "these elements of reality," even with our basic sensations. "*That* they are is undoubtedly beyond our control; but *which* we attend to, note, and make emphatic in our conclusions depends on our own interests." Thus, we inevitably play a role in the determining of truth, even though it must relate to some given reality. "We receive in short the block of marble, but we carve the statue ourselves." We do employ identifiable concepts in the determination of truth.

> Superficially this sounds like Kant's view; but between categories fulminated before nature began, and categories gradually forming themselves in nature's presence, the whole chasm between rationalism and empiricism yawns.

From James's perspective, Kant's fixed, *a priori* categories represent a rationalistic given that transcends humanism, whereas his own mental concepts are "man-made," evolutionary, dynamic products of human development. Rationalism and pragmatism agree that, in some sense, truth must agree with "reality."

> The essential contrast is that *for rationalism reality is ready-made and complete for all eternity, while for pragmatism it is still in the making, and awaits part of its complexion from the future.*

These two views of reality make different appeals to different people. "On the one side the universe is absolutely secure, on the other it is still pursuing its adventures." At any rate, we have reached a point where differences in "*the theory of knowledge*" have generated different views of "*the structure of the universe itself.*" The difference is intrinsically related to that between pluralism and monism. "On the pragmatist side we have only one edition of the universe, unfinished, growing in all sorts of places, especially in the places where thinking beings are at work." This view allows for human innovation and creativity.

> On the rationalist side we have a universe in many editions, one real one, the infinite folio, or *édition de luxe*, eternally complete; and then the various finite editions, full of false readings, distorted and mutilated each in its own way.

The latter view tends to cosmic determinism, so that "the phrase *must be* is ever on its lips";[82] by contrast, pragmatism, with its commitment to human initiative, speaks of what *might* be.

The eighth lecture, "Pragmatism and Religion," translates this dichotomy into terms of salvation, distinguishing between religious thinkers "who insist that the world *must and shall be,* and those who are contented with believing that the world *may be,* saved." James holds that "the salvation of the world" is neither "impossible," as the pessimists believe, nor "inevitable," as optimists maintain. "Midway between the two there stands what may be called the doctrine of meliorism," which "treats salvation as neither necessary nor impossible. It treats it as a possibility, which becomes more and more of a probability the more numerous the actual conditions of salvation become." These conditions are (at least partially) supplied by human effort. James asks us to imagine "the world's author" making you an offer prior to creation, saying,

> I am going to make a world not certain to be saved, a world the perfection of which shall be conditional merely, the condition being that each several agent does its own "level best." I offer you the chance of taking part in such a world. Its safety, you see, is unwarranted.

This would be a world of real possibility with no guarantees.

> It is a social scheme of co-operative work genuinely to be done. Will you join in the procession? Will you trust yourself and trust the other agents enough to face the risk?

James thinks that most of us are "healthy-minded" enough that we would accept such an offer and that the resulting world of God's creation might be practically identical to the world in which we now actually live.

> Most of us, I say, would therefore welcome the proposition and add our *fiat* to the *fiat* of the creator. Yet perhaps some would not; for there are morbid minds

in every human collection, and to them the prospect of a universe with only a fighting chance of safety would probably make no appeal.

To such a person as Descartes or Hegel, who craves rational certainty, the "*must and shall be*" is absolutely necessary. "Pluralistic moralism simply makes their teeth chatter, it refrigerates the very heart within their breast." Against the thinkers of medieval and early modern times, James denies that logic can decide such an issue or should have veto power over an act of personal faith. He expresses his own faith commitment quite personally: "I find myself willing to take the universe to be really dangerous and adventurous, without therefore backing out and crying no play!" He goes on to say, "I am willing that there should be real losses and real losers, and no total preservation of all that is,"[83] provided that there is a chance of our realizing values through our own collaborative effort. This defense of personal faith commitment at the end of *Pragmatism* leads us to a final element of James's theory of knowledge.

Faith and the Will to Believe. James's view of faith and the "will to believe" argument effectively bring out his voluntarism, turning the focus of religious epistemology from abstract logic and theoretical reason to practical human interests and voluntary commitments. In addition to being one of his most famous (his critics might say infamous) essays, "The Will to Believe" is also among James's most important works because it presents (against so much of the history of modern philosophy) "a defence of our right to adopt a believing attitude in religious matters, in spite of the fact that our merely logical intellect may not have been coerced."[84] The very "intellectualism" that dominates most of modern philosophy would have us acknowledge that truth is always ready-made and (at least theoretically) available for apprehension, our job being to grasp it by means of certain knowledge.

It is important to recognize at the outset that the conceptual distinctions made near the beginning of the essay are not mere window dressing. James needs to establish clearly what "a *genuine* option" is because it is only to such possible faith commitments (and not even to all of them) that his argument is to apply. He writes that "an *option*" is a "decision between two hypotheses," calling a hypothesis "anything that may be proposed to our belief." Such a possible object of faith may be "either *live* or *dead*" for any given person at any given time. "A live hypothesis is one which appeals as a real possibility to him to whom it is proposed."[85] Although it is theoretically conceivable that we were not alive yesterday, it is practically impossible for us to believe that; so it is a dead hypothesis for us now.

James continues, "Options may be of several kinds. They may be— 1, *living* or *dead*; 2, *forced* or *avoidable*; 3, *momentous* or *trivial*." He speaks of one as "a *genuine* option when it is of the forced, living, and momentous kind." He then proceeds to explain each of these characterizations. "A living option is one in which both hypotheses are live ones" (in the sense explained in the preceding paragraph) for the person to whom (and at the time at which) they are proposed. As he says, for most Americans of his day, "Be an agnostic or be a Christian" was a living option; on the other hand, for most, "Subscribe to Shinto or to Islam" was a dead one. Second, he says, "Every dilemma based on a complete logical disjunction, with no possibility of not choosing, is an option" that is forced. This is a mutually exclusive "either-or," in which one must choose between the two hypotheses. Most of our options, such as "Either love me or hate me," are avoidable, in that we can avoid choosing between the two given hypotheses, by opting for a third (that has not been given) or by not choosing at all. His example of a forced option is, "Either accept this truth or go without it"; these are mutually exclusive and exhaustive alternatives. Third, an option is momentous if it is irreversible or so unlikely to recur that it approaches a once-in-a-lifetime opportunity. James uses the early-twentieth-century example of being invited to participate in a North Pole expedition. By contrast, he says, an "option is trivial when the opportunity is not unique, when the stake is insignificant, or when the decision is reversible if it later prove unwise."[86] Now James's argument, on behalf of the possible legitimacy of faith without evidence, is only meant to apply to options that are "genuine" in his sense of being living, forced, and momentous. If we fail to respect this fact, we are liable to indulge in the facile and unfair accusation that James is trying to give us a license to believe anything we please.

James presents the case against the "Will to Believe" position, which is classically represented, for example, by "Pascal's wager." In assessing the reasonableness of any gamble, we do well to consider the odds and the stakes. Pascal, suspicious of the arguments used to demonstrate "the God of philosophers and scholars," was doubtful that we can reckon anything of the odds for or against God's existence since there is no preponderance of evidence either way. This leaves us with only the stakes to consider. If we believe in God and act accordingly, we only "risk a finite loss" for the sake of the "infinite gain" of "eternal beatitude"; on the other hand, if we choose not to believe, we risk the infinite loss of eternal damnation for the sake of little or no gain. Regarded from such a calculating perspective, it might seem that commitment to faith is the reasonable choice. James acknowledges that such a cold-blooded, selfish approach to religious faith is unattractive:

> We feel that a faith in masses and holy water adopted willfully after such a mechanical calculation would lack the inner soul of faith's reality; and if we were ourselves in the place of the Deity, we should probably take particular pleasure in cutting off believers of this pattern from their infinite reward.

It is doubtful that we can force ourselves to believe something, unless we are already so inclined; and, even if we could, would not doing so be a contemptible hypocrisy (at least at the outset)? "The talk of believing by our volition seems, then, from one point of view, simply silly. From another point of view it is worse than silly, it is vile." We, like the audience to whom James initially delivered this lecture, want religious faith to be more genuine and more respectable. We seek objective grounds for believing and eschew wishful thinking. "Can we wonder if those bred in the rugged and manly school of science should feel like spewing such subjectivism out of their mouths?" James quotes the English mathematician/philosopher William K. Clifford (from "The Ethics of Belief," published in 1877), who had lost his faith after encountering the views of Darwin, as most vigorously expressing a critique of the "Will to Believe" position attributed to Pascal and to be advocated here: "It is wrong always, everywhere, and for every one, to believe anything upon insufficient evidence." This is expressive of the scientific intellectualism which was influential in James's day. But if Clifford represents the empiricist arm of modern intellectualism, an apt representative of its rationalistic arm is "Descartes, for instance, with his clear and distinct ideas guaranteed by the veracity of God."[87]

Against both arms of intellectualism James takes his stand. First of all, whether we are able to choose to believe in something depends on whether it is a live hypothesis for us. It is true, for example, that I cannot force myself earnestly to believe that I am the only living person in the universe, no matter how I might try to do so; but this is because the experiential evidence is such that I cannot even regard it as a living hypothesis to be taken seriously. "It is only our already dead hypotheses that our willing nature is unable to bring to life." To the extent that hypotheses are living for us, "our willing nature" has some leverage in dealing with them. James explains that by our "willing nature" he means not only "deliberate volitions" but "all such factors of belief as fear and hope, prejudice and passion, imitation and partisanship," and so forth. Second, James points out that, as normal human beings, we believe all sorts of things without having, or ever having had, first-hand evidence. As he says to his early-twentieth-century, ivy-league audience,

> Here in this room, we all of us believe in molecules and the conservation of
> energy, in democracy and necessary progress, in Protestant Christianity and the
> duty of fighting for "the doctrine of the immortal Monroe," all for no reasons
> worthy of the name.

Some of the items in this list may be out-of-date, but James's point still
applies today—that all of us base much of what we believe about this
world on the authority of others, that "not insight, but the *prestige* of the
opinions, is what makes the spark shoot from them and light up our
sleeping magazines of faith." Since our personal experience of the world
is so limited, this is as it must be: "Our faith is faith in some one else's
faith." James argues that this is so in connection with even the most fundamental and general matters:

> Our belief in truth itself, for instance, that there is a truth, and that our minds
> and it are made for each other,—what is it but a passionate affirmation of desire,
> in which our social system backs us up?

Our mental life comprises a constant dynamic between volitions and
belief. "There are passional tendencies and volitions which run before and
others which come after belief, and it is only the latter that are too late
for the fair." Those that are "too late" develop after beliefs have been
formed and run contrary to them. However, if (psychologically) we can
"will to believe" in live hypotheses and if (practically) everyday experience
indicates that we must do so, then the protests of critics like Clifford
seem like so much wailing in the wind. "Pascal's argument, instead of
being powerless, then seems a regular clincher,"[88] at least in dealing with
certain types of beliefs.

This leads to the position statement:

> The thesis I defend is, briefly stated, this: *Our passional nature not only lawfully
> may, but must, decide an option between propositions, whenever it is a genuine
> option that cannot by its nature be decided on intellectual grounds; for to say, under
> such circumstances, "Do not decide, but leave the question open," is itself a passional
> decision,—just like deciding yes or no,—and is attended with the same risk of losing
> the truth.*[89]

The two conditions given here should be carefully noted: (1) we must be
dealing with "a genuine option," and (2) it must be unresolvable by logical argumentation and scientific evidence, in order for James's "Will to
Believe" argument to apply. His claim is that religious beliefs can sometimes meet these conditions and thus qualify.

James explores the topic of "objective evidence"; having been trained
as a scientist, he values and desires it, to the extent that it is available. As
he says to his audience,

> You believe in objective evidence, and I do. Of some things we feel that we are certain: we know, and we know that we do know. There is something that gives a click inside of us, a bell that strikes twelve, when the hands of our mental clock have swept the dial and meet over the meridian hour.

Yet the extent to which such objective evidence can be achieved in factual matters is even more limited than Descartes's *cogito* would suggest: "There is but one indefectibly certain truth, and that is the truth that pyrrhonistic scepticism itself leaves standing,—the truth that the present phenomenon of consciousness exists." Beyond this and founded on this, philosophy offers various systems of rationally supported beliefs that necessarily fall short of meeting Clifford's exacting demands. "Objective evidence and certitude are doubtless very fine ideals to play with, but where on this moonlit and dream-visited planet are they found?" Thus, James takes his stand in opposition to all forms of dogmatism:

> I am, therefore, myself a complete empiricist so far as my theory of knowledge goes. I live, to be sure, by the practical faith that we must go on experiencing and thinking over our experience, for only thus can our opinions grow more true; but to hold any one of them—I absolutely do not care which—as if it never could be reinterpretable or corrigible, I believe to be a tremendously mistaken attitude.[90]

This fallibilist view of truth and knowledge runs counter to the apodeictic intellectualism that dominates modern philosophy from Descartes on.

James crystallizes the conflict between intellectualists, such as Descartes and Clifford, and voluntarists, such as Pascal and himself. He focuses on two of our "great commandments as would-be knowers" which seem fundamental: "*We must know the truth; and we must avoid error.*" Intellectualists and voluntarists alike, both absolutists and empiricists, wish to obey the positive *and* the negative injunctions. So far, so uncontroversial. The problem arises as to how to rank them in cases where they conflict.

> We may regard the chase for truth as paramount, and the avoidance of error as secondary; or we may, on the other hand, treat the avoidance of error as more imperative, and let truth take its chance.

Intellectualists such as Descartes and Clifford preach the latter alternative, while James is defending the former. The intellectualist "who says, 'Better go without belief forever than believe a lie!' merely shows his own preponderant private horror of becoming a dupe." To that extent his beliefs are guided by his personal preferences and passional nature. James admits that, to some extent, he can sympathize with this view: "For my own part, I have also a horror of being duped; but I can believe that worse things than being duped may happen to a man in this world." The issue concerns how much embarrassment we are willing to risk for the sake of believing in truths which might otherwise forever elude us. For James, the commandment, "Believe truth!" takes precedence over the one that says, "Shun error!" As he explains,

> Our errors are surely not such awfully solemn things. In a world where we are so certain to incur them in spite of all our caution, a certain lightness of heart seems healthier than this excessive nervousness on their behalf. At any rate, it seems the fittest thing for the empiricist philosopher,[91]

who is committed to using experience, in an open-minded way, to pursue truth.

As James admits, there are many cases where we can afford to play it safe and not risk error, but these are cases where the options are either trivial or avoidable.

> In scientific questions, this is almost always the case; and even in human affairs in general, the need of acting is seldom so urgent that a false belief to act on is better than no belief at all.

In considering whether to accept the wave theory or the particle theory of light and in deciding whether to believe that the Soviets used chemical warfare in Afghanistan, we can indefinitely postpone making a commitment. In such cases, as James argues, where the issue "is not momentous," because we can readily change our view, or "there is no forced option," we can afford to (and usually should) pursue the ideal of dispassionate caution. But this leaves open the question of whether there are forced options for which no "coercive evidence" is forthcoming. Of course, we would prefer that the issues about which we most care should be those for which the available evidence would be conclusive. Yet, as James wryly comments, "In the great boarding-house of nature, the cakes and the butter and the syrup seldom come out so even and leave the plates so clean."[92] Religious faith might turn out to be a prime example of an area in which things are not as neat as we would wish.

But are there, in fact, any such issues to which James's "Will to Believe" argument, properly qualified, applies? *Moral* questions immediately present themselves as questions whose solution cannot wait for sensible proof." Here he means to discuss issues of value, as opposed to those of fact. "Science can tell us what exists; but to compare the *worths* both of what exists and of what does not exist, we must consult not science, but what Pascal calls our heart." There are, of course, people who profess not to believe in any objective values, and James considers them impervious to falsification: "Moral scepticism can no more be refuted or proved by logic than intellectual scepticism can."[93] But the crucial question at stake here is whether, granting that point, we can legitimately commit ourselves to believing in such values.

In some areas of significant practical concern, James seems correct in maintaining that we legitimately can and sometimes should commit ourselves to believing in what scientific evidence and logical demonstration cannot substantiate. Should you commit yourself to this potential friendship or not? Should you marry that person, who may (despite appearances) be merely pretending to love you, or not? Ought you to accept this job offer, which would require you to move your family 2,000 miles across country, or not? In matters such as these, we shall find ourselves permanently paralyzed if scientific evidence and logical demonstration are to be regarded as necessary conditions for making a decision. But what, then, would follow? We would have to resign our lives to the avoidance of serious personal and professional commitment. What sort of lives would we be settling for in the absence of any freely chosen decisive feelings and actions? Our lives would be shallow, insignificant, and empty as a result.

As James holds, we do not and cannot live by knowledge alone. We strive for knowledge and cherish it where it is achieved. Yet we must accept the fact that it is not likely to permeate all the significant dimensions of our lives as human beings. Against the intellectualists, we should admit that, at times, it is precisely our decisive commitment which helps make the truth come into being where previously it was only a spectral possibility (for example, in friendship relationships).

> There are, then, cases where a fact cannot come at all unless a preliminary faith exists in its coming. *And where faith in a fact can help create the fact*, that would be an insane logic which should say that faith running ahead of scientific evidence is the "lowest kind of immorality" into which a thinking being can fall.[94]

Where enough is at stake, we do well to avoid succumbing to such a prejudice.

Are religious commitments, indeed, of the sort that would fall under James's "Will to Believe" argument? He argues that they can be. But in order to understand what distinctively religious beliefs are, we need to recognize the two basic claims that religion essentially makes: First, religion "says that the best things are the more eternal things, the overlapping things, the things in the universe that throw the last stone, so to speak, and say the final word." Religion generally holds that the values of the hereafter take precedence over those of the here and now. "The second affirmation of religion is that we are better off even now if we believe her first affirmation to be true." This signals that the option of commit-ting oneself to religion or refusing so to commit is *momentous*. "We are supposed to gain, even now, by our belief, and to lose by our non-belief, a certain vital good." The option is also *forced*

> so far as that good goes. We cannot escape the issue by remaining sceptical and waiting for more light, because although we do avoid error in that way *if religion be untrue*, we lose the good, *if it be true*, just as certainly as if we positively chose to disbelieve.

Either we commit ourselves to a particular set of religious beliefs at any given time or we do not. From this perspective, we cannot avoid the pos-sibility of error, if, as James maintains, no "sufficient evidence" is likely to be forthcoming in our natural lifetimes. The choice not to believe in such cases may be as mistaken as the choice to believe. James's verdict here seems accurate:

> Dupery for dupery, what proof is there that dupery through hope is so much worse than dupery through fear? I, for one, can see no proof; and I simply refuse obedience to the scientist's command to imitate his kind of option, in a case where my own stake is important enough to give me the right to choose my own form of risk.

In addition to being momentous and forced, the decision whether to adopt a religious view can be a *living* option for some of us, as it seems to have been for James himself. For such people, then, the commitment or lack of commitment to religious faith can take the form of a *genuine* option. And it could be that those who commit themselves to it help to realize its truth, contributing to the higher value of "the more eternal things" and helping to bring it about that believers "are better off even now."[95] What James is *not* suggesting, however, is that religious belief can make God exist; the most it can do is create conditions in which we can collaborate with an already existing God, whom we might come to know hereafter.

It is unfortunate that James called the essay "The Will to Belicve," suggesting wishful thinking and arbitrary whimsy to his critics. As he admits in *Pragmatism*,

> All the critics, neglecting the essay, pounced upon the title. Psychologically it was impossible, morally it was iniquitous. The "will to deceive," the "will to make believe," were wittily proposed as substitutes for it.[96]

In a letter of 1904, James expresses the conviction that it "should have been called by the less unlucky title the *Right* to Believe."[97] Near the end of the essay James anticipates the likelihood that members of his audience will reject out of hand a caricature of his view of faith as "defined by the schoolboy when he said, 'Faith is when you believe something that you know ain't true.'"[98] This is, of course, a ridiculous distortion of James's view since we can only know something if it is intellectually decidable, in which case one of his conditions does not apply; and if we know something to be untrue, it ceases to be a living option for us. But if that is an unfair parody of James's view of faith, what is an accurate characterization?

The answer can be found in "The Sentiment of Rationality," where James writes, "Faith means belief in something concerning which doubt is still theoretically possible; and as the test of belief is willingness to act, one may say that faith is the readiness to act in a cause the prosperous issue of which is not certified to us in advance." Two elements of this analysis (both of which Kierkegaard could appreciate) are worth highlighting. First, faith is not only compatible with doubt (as knowledge is not), but requires its possibility. And, second, far from being purely theoretical, faith is practically oriented toward action. James combines both points in two words, saying, "Faith is synonymous with working hypothesis."[99]

The appendix to *Some Problems of Philosophy* is entitled "Faith and the Right to Believe." There James analyzes and criticizes "Intellectualism," of both the rationalistic and the empiricistic varieties. Much of what he says at the beginning of the piece repeats the views of "The Will to Believe." But he also presents what he calls his "faith-ladder," consisting of seven steps, each lower step leading psychologically (but not necessarily logically) to the next one up:

> 1. There is nothing absurd in a certain view of the world being true, nothing self-contradictory; 2. It *might* have been true under certain conditions; 3. It *may* be true, even now; 4. It is *fit* to be true; 5. It *ought* to be true; 6. It *must* be true; 7. It *shall* be true, at any rate true for *me*.[100]

What we should note here is the gradual move from objective intellectualism to subjective voluntarism. The first step is a logical observation, which, if true, is true for everyone everywhere; the last step expresses a decision of personal will.

James delivered a lecture, "Reason and Faith," in San Francisco in 1906. The address was sent to the printer, but publication was halted by the great earthquake and San Francisco fire. The manuscript was not discovered and published until many years after James's death and consequently has remained rather unknown. There he considers the question of whether reason should be considered "all-sufficient" or is legitimately supplemented by faith. Reason, he says, is "a faculty of inference"; it can assert relationships on the basis of hypotheses, but should base its existential claims on experienced facts:

> *If* there be a God, Reason can be theistic and say that we exist alongside of him, or pantheistic and say that we are parts of him; but *that* there is a God, Reason can infer only from the facts of experience, from their character as needing a cause, or from the purpose they display.

Reason inferentially aims at knowledge. "Faith uses a logic altogether different from Reason's logic. Reason claims certainty and finality for her conclusions. Faith is satisfied if hers seem probable and practically wise." We see this distinction, in their approaches to God, represented, for example, by Aquinas and Descartes, on the one hand, and by Hume and Kierkegaard, on the other. Here James proceeds to present a modified view of his "faith-ladder" (this time without the numbered steps):

> Faith's form of argument is something like this: Considering a view of the world: "It is *fit* to be true," she feels; "it would be well if it *were* true; it *might* be true; it *may* be true; it *ought* to be true," she says; "it *must* be true," she continues; "it *shall* be true," she concludes, "*for me*; that is, I will treat it as if it were true so far as my advocacy and actions are concerned."

Here we see connections with Kant's view of faith as practically oriented toward action (we act as if we knew the object of our belief to be true) and with Kierkegaard's emphasis on the subjectivity of religious faith (as opposed to the objectivity of scientific reason). James immediately acknowledges that the "faith-ladder," although a sort of argument, is non-demonstrative: "Obviously this is no intellectual chain of inferences, like the Sorites of the logic-books." Now that analyses of the procedures of faith and reason have been advanced, let us return to the question: is reason "all-sufficient," as Hegel and his followers maintain, or not? James's answer is that it depends on how broadly one is willing to conceive of reason. "Now the advocates of Reason's all-sufficiency can follow either of two courses, but not both." First, they can adopt such a broad conception of reason that it can encompass the "reasonings" of faith. "They can approve of the faith-ladder and adopt it, but at the same time call it an exercise of Reason." It may well be that this would be the preferred option of a Hegelian. Or, second, they could, perhaps with Clifford, "forbid us the faith-ladder, as something liable only to mislead," urging us to wait for sufficient objective evidence. In conclusion, says James,

> If the word "Reason" be taken to cover the faith-process, then Reason is, indeed, all-sufficient. But if it is taken to exclude the faith-process, then its

insufficiency to found a man's religion solidly seems to me too obvious for any further discussion.[101]

It seems James would prefer to interpret reason broadly enough to include faith; but if a narrower view be insisted upon, disjoining it from faith, James would maintain (against intellectualists like Clifford) that reason, in that sense, is inadequate for human living.

James's conception of faith and the "Will to Believe" argument are appealing, as is the analogy of friendship. If I have been involved in hiring a junior colleague to work with me, may I legitimately believe, in the absence of objective evidence, that we shall become friends? Let us suppose that I not only lack "sufficient" evidence (however that vague word be defined), but that I have no objective evidence at all. Imagine that this junior colleague has no friendly feelings toward me at all at present, finds me personally unattractive, but wishes to be as obliging and polite as possible for purposes of job security (I have some input in determining his retention). It may be a living option for me whether I shall believe in this future friendship or remain professionally civil but personally aloof. It is a forced option in that I either shall or shall not believe that we will become friends (I am not interested here in a mere theoretical possibility, having moved further up the "faith-ladder" than that). And, because of my loneliness and lack of other prospects, it can be a momentous option. Now let us suppose that, under those circumstances, I commit myself, through an act of deliberate will, to believing that we will be friends and that I act accordingly toward him. Is this a legitimate commitment to faith on my part or am I being rash and morally irresponsible, as Clifford might object? It seems that James is importantly correct here, that I do have the right to believe in such a situation, that I am justified in acting in accordance with that faith, and that my doing so might very well help to establish the friendship relationship which, otherwise, would never develop. Finally, there is no reason why a commitment to religious faith is not essentially analogous to this rather commonplace example. But notice that there must be some experiential basis for choosing to believe. What, we might ask, could provide such a basis for faith in God? In order to answer this, we now turn to James's discussion of religious experience.

Religious Experience

Defining Religion. James's conception of religion is developed most thoroughly in *The Varieties of Religious Experience* (his Gifford Lectures).

As the title indicates, the entire book is concerned with religion. But emphasis should also be placed on the last word of the title, since the work is remarkably experiential in its perspective, in conformity with his theory of knowledge. The second word of the title is also significant; for James, true to his pluralistic vision of reality, refuses to adopt any dogmatic, reductionistic position that would rule out alternative conceptions. The book is subtitled "A Study in Human Nature," pointing to both James's humanism and its foundation in the natural world, and comprises twenty lectures and a postscript.

James professes to be "neither a theologian, nor a scholar in the history of religions, nor an anthropologist" but to be approaching the study as a professional psychologist. This will tilt the investigation away from any focus on "religious institutions" in the direction of "religious feelings and religious impulses." He distinguishes "between two orders of inquiry concerning anything," including religious experience: we may ask, first, what is its "nature" and try to answer by means of "an *existential judgment*" or, second, we may wonder about its "significance" and try to respond with "a *proposition of value*." James insists that "existential facts by themselves are insufficient for determining the value" of an experience. He is concerned to expose as shallow the reductionistic view of "medical materialism," which holds that religious experiences are insignificant or have no value because they are " 'nothing but' expressions of our organic disposition." Even granting the dubious premise on which this is based, the conclusion is a *non sequitur*. The value or lack of value of religious experience is not a function of its antecedent conditions but of its agreeableness in and/or usefulness for our lives: "It is either because we take an immediate delight in them; or else it is because we believe them to bring us good consequential fruits for life." So, our judgment concerning the value of any experience should be in terms of its "fruits" rather than its "roots." Anticipating the language of his developing pragmatism, James writes, "In other words, not its origin, but *the way in which it works on the whole*, is . . . our own empiricist criterion."[102] Thus he blocks all dogmatic attempts to dismiss out of hand an inquiry into religious experience.

James rejects all attempts to define religion narrowly. For example, many of us who have been raised in a monotheistic tradition might be tempted to define religion in terms of belief in a transcendent, personal, infinite God. But such a definition would exclude too much. James prefers to define religion more broadly in terms of "*the feelings, acts, and experiences of individual men in their solitude, so far as they apprehend themselves to stand in relation to whatever they may consider the divine.*" Several aspects of this definition are striking enough to be noteworthy. First, it focuses on feeling, action, and experience rather than on theoretical doctrines. Second, the emphasis is on religious individuals rather than on religious institutions, so that it is personal. Third, for James, it is important what religious persons do "in their solitude" rather than merely in community. Fourth, it is a matter of how they regard their relationship to "the divine" rather than of whether anything corresponding to "the divine" exists to which they can be actually related; in other words, it does not presuppose the reality outside the mind of what they believe in. And, fifth, the notion of "the divine" is deliberately left broad enough to encompass even "godless or quasi-godless" religions such as "Emersonian optimism" and certain forms of Buddhism. But the object of religious experience should be considered seriously and respectfully. Thus, says James, "The divine shall mean for us only such a primal reality as the individual feels impelled to respond to solemnly and gravely, and neither by a curse nor a jest."[103]

James analyzes religious belief further in terms of both an *existential judgment* and a *proposition of value*, which, of course, are interrelated. He says that religious faith "consists of the belief that there is an unseen order, and that our supreme good lies in harmoniously adjusting ourselves thereto." On this view, for example, Plato's philosophy, with its world of ideas and eternal souls, is religious, even without any reference to gods, goddesses, the demiurge, and so forth. For the religious person, the unseen realm of the divine is at least as real as the physical world of time and space.[104]

Types of Religious Consciousness. James's analysis of types of religious consciousness follows. He discusses two extreme types of religious consciousness, which he labels "healthy-mindedness" and "the sick soul." The former tends to religious optimism and joy. "Systematic healthy-mindedness, conceiving good as the essential and universal aspect of being, deliberately excludes evil from its field of vision." James sees the advance of Christian liberalism in his own day as "a victory of healthy-mindedness within the church over the morbidness with which the old hell-fire theology was more harmoniously related." James realizes that this ebullient form of religious thinking is easily dismissed by its critics— " 'scientists' or 'positivists,' they are fond of calling themselves"—as a naive "atavistic reversion to a type of consciousness which humanity in its more enlightened examples has long since left behind and outgrown." But James denies that science and religion are logical contraries, such that if either is true, the other must be false. He prefers to regard both of them as "genuine keys for unlocking the world's treasure-house to him who can use either of them practically," neither of which is "exhaustive or exclusive of the other's simultaneous use." (Some theological liberals today regard the creation-versus-evolution controversy as a phony fight on similar grounds.) The healthy-minded person might stress the saving efficacy of penitence for wrong-doing without brooding over it. "Repentance according to such healthy-minded Christians means *getting away from* the sin, not groaning and writhing over its commission." James praises Catholicism's "practice of confession and absolution" for helping to maintain a degree of healthy-mindedness.[105]

In contrast to this religious outlook, however, there is the "sick soul," which dwells "on the persuasion that the evil aspects of our life are of its very essence." This is a morbid pessimism which tends to cast a "joy-destroying chill" over our view of reality and is not easily or permanently dismissed by healthy-mindedness. Death, illness, disease, ignorance, want, etc., infect even nonreligious people everywhere with an understandable sense of sorrow and regret.

> This sadness lies at the heart of every merely positivistic, agnostic, or naturalistic scheme of philosophy. Let sanguine healthy-mindedness do its best with its strange power of living in the moment and ignoring and forgetting, still the evil background is really there to be thought of, and the skull will grin in at the banquet.

James uses an arresting simile to describe the attitude of the sick soul, for whom

> mankind is in a position similar to that of a set of people living on a frozen lake, surrounded by cliffs over which there is no escape, yet knowing that little by little the ice is melting, and the inevitable day drawing near when the last film of it will disappear, and to be drowned ignominiously will be the human creature's portion.

Of course, the sick soul recognizes that some people can divert their attention from their tragic fate. But, as James writes,

> The merrier the skating, the warmer and more sparkling the sun by day, and the ruddier the bonfires at night, the more poignant the sadness with which one must take in the meaning of the total situation.

Such a representation of the human condition graphically illustrates the morbid melancholy of the sick soul. As Walt Whitman was suggested as an example of healthy-mindedness, Leo Tolstoy is offered as an example of the sick soul. James emphasizes the natural antagonism between these two points of view. The "morbid-minded" regard the "healthy-minded" as "blind and shallow," whereas the attitude of the former strikes the latter as "unmanly and diseased." It is interesting that James's treatment of the problem of evil as a theoretical issue is mainly in connection with this contrast of extreme religious attitudes. Despite the bias of the descriptive labels James uses, he indicates his own sympathies for the perspective of the sick soul, saying that "there is no doubt that healthy-mindedness is inadequate as a philosophical doctrine, because the evil facts which it refuses positively to account for are a genuine portion of reality." To the extent that religions ignore or dismiss the evils of the world, they seem unreal. "The completest religions would therefore seem to be those in which the pessimistic elements are best developed. Buddhism, of course, and Christianity are the best known to us of these."[106]

Further, James acknowledges that, between the extremes of healthy-mindedness and the sick soul, "the concrete human beings whom we oftenest meet are intermediate varieties and mixtures." Another peculiar type is the religious schizophrenic whom James calls "the divided self." Such persons' lives are

> little more than a series of zigzags, as now one tendency and now another get the upper hand. Their spirit wars with their flesh, they wish for incompatibles, wayward impulses interrupt their most deliberate plans,

and they find themselves usually torn between healthy-mindedness and morbid-mindedness. The classic example of "the divided self," for James, is Augustine. Yet the divided self can also achieve integration, and again Augustine is an example of one who "emerged into the smooth waters of inner unity and peace." James says that religion is one important means, but still "only one out of many ways of reaching unity." The unification that can be achieved by the previously divided self is characterized as "a firmness, stability, and equilibrium succeeding a period of storm and stress and inconsistency."[107] Thus, in addition to the extreme forms of religious consciousness that James calls "healthy-minded," "morbid-minded," and "the divided self," there is also the more desirable and tranquil integrated sort.

Conversion. As a psychologist of religion, James takes seriously a wide variety of accounts of conversion experiences. There are, of course, numerous testimonies of radical changes of character; "if the change be a religious one, we call it a *conversion*, especially if it be by crisis, or sudden." One of the most famous and dramatic examples of this, of course, is that of Paul, who was converted to Christianity (from being a persecutor of Christians) while on the road to Damascus. James distinguishes between conversions of "the *volitional type*" (we might here recall the will to believe), in which "the regenerative change is usually gradual, and consists in the building up, piece by piece, of a new set of moral and spiritual habits," and "the *type by self-surrender*." Though not all of us are equally subject to conversion experiences, he identifies "two things in the mind of the candidate for conversion: first, the present incompleteness or wrongness, the 'sin' which he is eager to escape from; and, second, the positive ideal which he longs to compass." James delineates four characteristics of those who have had conversion experiences: "The central one is the loss of all the worry, the sense that all is ultimately well with one, the peace, the harmony" associated with achieving salvation. "The second feature is the sense of perceiving truths not known before," which once seemed bewildering mysteries. "A third peculiarity of the assurance state is the objective change which the world often appears to undergo" for the convert. Fourth, the "most characteristic of all the elements of the conversion crisis, and the last one of which I shall speak, is the ecstasy of happiness produced." James admits that some conversions are only temporary but avers that people everywhere are liable to lapse from all sorts of conditions; so cases of "backsliding" do not diminish the value of such experiences. But, he adds, "As a matter of fact, all the more striking instances of conversion . . . *have* been permanent."[108] We might observe that James neither suggests nor denies in these two lectures that any or all conversion experiences are tantamount to proof that any object of religious belief exists outside the mind of the convert.

Saintliness. Saintliness is perhaps more a sustained condition than a momentary experience; nevertheless, it is experienced by the saint, as are its effects by others. "The saintly character is the character for which spiritual emotions are the habitual center of the personal energy," as opposed, for example, to those of us who are driven by physical desires. James maintains that there is "a certain composite photograph of universal saintliness, the same in all religions," and proceeds to elaborate its features: "1. A feeling of being in a wider life than that of this world's selfish little interests; and a conviction, not merely intellectual, but as it were sensible, of the existence of an Ideal Power" beyond the physical realm. "2. A sense of the friendly continuity of the ideal power with our own life, and a willing self-surrender to its control. 3. An immense elation and freedom, as the outlines of the confining selfhood melt down" in the matrix of this continuity. "4. A shifting of the emotional centre towards loving and harmonious affections, towards 'yes, yes,' and away from 'no,' where the claims of the non-ego are concerned." These are all internal characteristics experienced by the saint, but they are typically accompanied by the external qualities (which others can experience) of asceticism, strength of soul, purity, and charity. One of James's favorite examples of a man in whom this profile seems realized is Ignatius Loyola, the sixteenth century founder of the Jesuits. The fruits of saintliness, according to James, are generally beneficial and attractive. He even holds that

> the saintly group of qualities is indispensable to the world's welfare. The great saints are immediate successes; the smaller ones are at least heralds and harbingers, and they may be leavens also, of a better mundane order.

But, again, we note (and James admits) that this is to comment on the utility rather than on the objective truth of the saint's religious beliefs.[109]

Mysticism. Next, James discusses mystical experiences. Where his discussions of conversion and saintliness were insightful and illuminating, that of mysticism is masterful. He points to its importance by expressing the opinion "that personal religious experience has its root and centre in mystical states of consciousness." Yet, even while attesting to the importance of mystical states, he admits that "my own constitution shuts me out from their enjoyment almost entirely, and I can speak of them only at second hand." Despite this handicap of not having personally experienced any mystical states, James promises, "I will be as objective and receptive as I can; and I think I shall at least succeed in convincing you of the reality of the states in question, and of the paramount importance of their function." Like his studies of conversion and saintliness, this one is founded on an immensely rich collection of case studies which we have not the time and space to consider here. James proposes four distinctive marks of mystical experience: "1. *Ineffability*," which means "that it defies expression, that no adequate report of its contents can be given in words" so that it "must be directly experienced" in order to be understood. "2. *Noetic quality*," which means that "mystical states seem to those who experience them to be also states of knowledge. They are states of insight into depths of truth unplumbed by the discursive intellect." James says that these first two characteristics, by themselves, can entitle a state of consciousness to be called mystical, but he proceeds to discuss two other marks which are typical. "3. *Transiency*," meaning that mystical states "cannot be sustained for long" but tend to pass rather quickly. "4. *Passivity*," meaning that "when the characteristic sort of consciousness once has set in, the mystic feels as if his own will were in abeyance, and indeed sometimes as if he were grasped and held by a superior power." James speaks of "the mystical group" of states of consciousness, as determined by the cluster of these four marks.[110] We should note that he does not define such states as *essentially* religious.

He considers four types of experiences which have these marks but do not necessarily have any religious significance. First, there is "that deepened sense of the significance" of something, which can suddenly sweep over us. " 'I've heard that said all my life,' we exclaim, 'but I never realized its full meaning until now.' " Second, there is the familiar psychological experience of *déjà vu*, "that sudden feeling, namely, which sometimes sweeps over us, of having 'been here before.' " Third, he says, "Somewhat deeper plunges into mystical consciousness are met with in yet other dreamy states," which can assume a sort of trancelike form. Fourth, there is "the consciousness produced by intoxicants and anaesthetics, especially by alcohol," which we would call drug-induced states. James testifies that he himself experimented with nitrous oxide (sometimes called "laughing gas"), as a result of which he became convinced "that our normal waking consciousness, rational consciousness as we call it, is but one special type of consciousness."[111]

He speaks of people of different cultures who have learned to place themselves in circumstances in which they are more susceptible to mystical experiences—for example, the yogis of India, the Sufis of Islam, the ancient Roman Plotinus, and Ignatius Loyola, John of the Cross, and Teresa of Avila in Christianity. Although religious mystics are varied in their interpretations of the objects of their experiences, James thinks that, in general, they tend toward optimism and monism, identifying the natural world with the supernatural and enjoying a confidence that events will ultimately transpire for the best. Despite the ineffable quality of their unique experiences, mystics do sometimes try to articulate their experiences, frequently resorting to such paradoxical "phrases as 'dazzling obscurity,' 'whispering silence,' 'teeming desert,' "[112] and so forth.

So far, James has confined himself to speaking of the experiences of mystical consciousness, not committing himself one way or the other on the issue of whether, and to what extent, it has objective validity. "My next task is to inquire whether we can invoke it as authoritative. Does it furnish any *warrant for the truth*" of any objects of religious belief? His balanced, nuanced answer comes in three parts.

> (1) Mystical states, when well developed, usually are, and have the right to be, absolutely authoritative over the individuals to whom they come.

In other words, the mystic himself is absolutely convinced of the legitimacy and verity of his experiences as religiously significant, and that conviction should be respected.

> (2) No authority emanates from them which should make it a duty for those who stand outside of them to accept their revelations uncritically.

That is to say, those of us who have not been blessed with such experiences need not feel obliged to accept the claim that they deliver superior truth.

> (3) They break down the authority of the non-mystical or rationalistic consciousness, based upon the understanding and the senses alone. They show it to be only one kind of consciousness. They open out the possibility of other orders of truth, in which, so far as anything in us vitally responds to them, we may freely continue to have faith.

Do they offer us higher truth? James is reluctant to answer definitely, not having enjoyed such experiences personally. He will only say that it is "an open question whether mystical states may not possibly be such superior points of view, windows through which the mind looks out upon a more extensive and inclusive world." All the mystical experiences from all of recorded history do not constitute proofs of any religious truths for those of us who, like James himself, have not had them. "They offer us *hypotheses*, hypotheses which we may voluntarily ignore" but which also could turn out to "be after all the truest of insights into the meaning of this life."[113]

Conclusions. James's conclusions from this study of religious experience may seem somewhat disappointing, given how impressive the study itself has been. After exploring the sadly minimal role philosophy can play in providing "a universal authority" for religious beliefs (we shall consider this in our next section), James turns, in his last two lectures, to these conclusions. As prelude to probing the truth of religious experience, he invokes the pragmatic principle: "the true is what works well, even though the qualification 'on the whole' may always have to be added." Included among the practical interests of any set of beliefs, James reminds us, is "their aesthetic value." He discusses the practical value of three elements of traditional organized religion, "Sacrifice, Confession, and Prayer." Sacrifice is "a religious exercise," calling for "offerings of the heart, renunciation of the inner self," which can generate spiritual improvements. Confession involves a "purgation and cleansing which one feels one's self in need of, in order to be in right relations to one's deity." And "in prayer, spiritual energy, which otherwise would slumber, does become active, and spiritual work of some kind is effected."[114] These are all subjective consequences of religious faith. So far, it seems that James's subjective view of truth (criticisms of which we considered earlier) leads to this inability or unwillingness to grapple with the issue of what object(s) there may be to which the evidence of religious experience points.

In his final lecture, James says, "In re-reading my manuscript, I am almost appalled at the amount of emotionality which I find in it." Indeed, in its focus on personal experience, it seems remarkably subjective. In keeping with this orientation, he summarizes "the religious life" in terms of three beliefs:

> 1. That the visible world is part of a more spiritual universe from which it draws its significance; 2. That union or harmonious relation with that higher universe is our true end; 3. That prayer or inner communion . . . is a process wherein work is really done.

He adds to these three beliefs two psychological characteristics of the religious believer:

> 4. A new zest which adds itself like a gift to life... 5. An assurance of safety and a temper of peace, and, in relation to others, a preponderance of loving affections.

The "critical Science of Religions" which James advocates can draw these generalizations from his empirical study, but this is only one of her tasks. "She has now to exert her critical activity, and to decide how far, in the light of other sciences and in that of general philosophy, such beliefs can be considered *true*." He is warning us not to expect too much when he adds, "Dogmatically to decide this is an impossible task."[115]

In analyzing religion into dimensions of thought and of feeling (both of which are "determinants of conduct"), James concludes,

> When we survey the whole field of religion, we find a great variety in the thoughts that have prevailed there; but the feelings on the one hand and the conduct on the other are almost always the same.

His conclusion is close at hand:

> The theories which Religion generates, being thus variable, are secondary; and if you wish to grasp her essence, you must look to the feelings and the conduct as being the more constant elements.

(We can note here that particular religious faiths might disagree; Christianity, for example, typically seems to regard the divinity of Jesus as essential.) But the "intellectual content" to which all religious experience clearly points can be expressed in terms of "a common nucleus" which comprises a sense of uneasiness about ourselves and the idea of a solution to this problem:

> 1. The uneasiness, reduced to simplest terms, is a sense that there is *something wrong about us* as we naturally stand. 2. The solution is a sense that *we are saved from the wrongness* by making proper connection with the higher powers.

James adds that in "more developed minds" the sense of wrongness typically assumes "a moral character, and the salvation takes a mystical tinge."[116] In Christianity, this "uneasiness" may be illustrated by the notion of sin, whereas the "solution" can be viewed in terms of moral reform as a prerequisite to salvation; in Buddhism, by contrast, the "uneasiness" has to do with a sense of universal suffering caused by the cravings of desire, and the "solution" is to overcome that desire.

So much for the general doctrines of religion. But we still must ask, "What is the objective 'truth' of their content?" James believes that the evidence of religious experience points to something "MORE" than can be found in the natural order, "with which our own higher self appears in the experience to come into harmonious working relation." It is difficult to determine the nature of this something "more," a controversy to be pursued by competing theologies. James's own attempt at definition may be somewhat less than satisfying:

> Let me then propose, as an hypothesis, that whatever it may be on its *farther* side, the "more" with which in religious experience we feel ourselves connected is on its *hither* side the subconscious continuation of our conscious life.

Although this is theologically thin, it is sufficient, James thinks, to refute the scientific (or quasi-scientific) dismissal of religion as "Pure anachronism," which he labels "the survival-theory," because it regards religion as "an atavistic relapse into a mode of thought which humanity in its more enlightened examples has outgrown," although it has unfortunately survived in the rest of us. James criticizes "the survival-theory" as "shallow," because it acknowledges only the objective part of reality, while denying that there is also "a subjective part" that is crucially important.[117] At any rate, this is about as far as his "critical Science of Religions" can take James. We have yet to examine his own view of God.

Theory of God

God's Existence. James's rejection of traditional arguments for God develops a thesis he had stated earlier in *Varieties*, "No religion has ever yet owed its prevalence to 'apodictic certainty.' " This statement expresses his rejection of attempts of traditional philosophical theology to demonstrate religious truths. He states his conviction "that feeling is the deeper source of religion, and that philosophic and theological formulas are secondary products," which should be classified as "**over-beliefs**, buildings-out performed by the intellect into directions of which feeling originally supplied the hint." James appreciates the service that the intellect thus strives to render: "To redeem religion from unwholesome privacy, and to give public status and universal right of way to its deliverances, has been reason's task." Yet there is a strain of "intellectualism" in traditional philosophical theology, which he openly sets out "to discredit" because he finds it pretentious and fraudulent: "It assumes to construct religious objects out of the resources of logical reason alone, or of logical reason drawing rigorous inference from non-subjective facts."[118] This is the project against which James's own philosophy of religious belief is directed.

His procedure is to take a critical look "first at the arguments by which dogmatic theology establishes God's existence, after that at those by which it establishes his nature." James views traditional arguments for God's existence as rationalizations supporting belief that has already been achieved rather than as the means effective to establish religious faith: "If you have a God already whom you believe in, these arguments confirm you. If you are atheistic, they fail to set you right." He briefly describes the cosmological argument, the argument from design, the moral argument, and the argument from general consensus or popular agreement, criticizing the first two. Against the first he observes, "Causation is indeed too obscure a principle to bear the weight of the whole structure of theology. As for the argument from design," he says, since the time of Darwin, "the benevolent adaptations which we find in Nature suggest a deity very different from the one who figured in the earlier versions of the argument." As he adds in a footnote, to be fair in our use of the argument from design, we would need to take into account the "*dis*order in the world" which we experience and attribute that to its designer as well as cosmic order. To acknowledge only the order of the universe in using the argument is one-sided and reflects our human bias.

> There are in reality infinitely more things "unadapted" to each other in this world than there are things "adapted". . . . But we look for the regular kind of thing exclusively, and ingeniously discover and preserve it in our memory.

Such considerations should make us reluctant to imagine that the argument from design can "constitute a knock-down proof" of the existence of the perfect, infinite God of monotheism. Still, like Hume and Kant, who also attacked their predecessors' traditional arguments for God's existence, James takes the argument from design more seriously than the others (not even mentioning the anti-empirical ontological argument). These criticisms of James are nothing new but follow in the footsteps of David Hume. Of all such arguments James concludes, "They prove nothing rigorously. They only corroborate our pre-existent partialities."[119] James is probably correct here; no argument for God's existence thus far developed has stood invulnerable to logical criticism.

"If philosophy can do so little to establish God's existence, how stands it with her efforts to define his attributes?" James reminds us that in the Christian tradition philosophical theology tries to argue that God is necessary and absolute, unlimited, infinitely perfect, one and unique, spiritual and simple, immutable, omnipresent and eternal, a self-sufficient, living, personal being with intelligence and will, the omniscient, omnipotent creator. These are all "metaphysical determinations" of God's essence. But there are also moral attributes: "God of course is holy, good, and just. He can do no evil," but in "creating free beings He *permits* it only."[120] Again this is the orthodox Christian conception of God, dating back, philosophically, to Augustine.

James finds the traditional arguments offered in support of the divine attributes even less convincing than those for God's existence and does not bother to refute them logically. Instead, he questions to what extent they are pragmatically meaningful to most of us human beings:

> If, namely, we apply the principle of pragmatism to God's metaphysical attributes, strictly so called, as distinguished from his moral attributes, I think that, even were we forced by a coercive logic to believe them, we still should have to confess them to be destitute of all intelligible significance.

Whether God is absolutely infinite, necessary, simple, and so forth, has no bearing on how we should lead our lives; "candidly speaking, how do such qualities as these make any definite connection with our life? And if they severally call for no distinctive adaptations of our conduct, what vital difference can it possibly make to a man's religion whether they be true or false?" From a pragmatic perspective, significance is relative to possible practical consequences, and James can see none for the metaphysical attributes of God.

> For my own part, although I dislike to say aught that may grate upon tender associations, I must frankly confess that even though these attributes were faultlessly deduced, I cannot conceive of its being of the smallest consequence to us religiously that any one of them should be true.[121]

James may be mistaken here. He includes aesthetic considerations as effective conditions of practical action. And for some thinkers, such as

Anselm and Kant, it is important to conceive of God in terms of certain metaphysical attributes, which do make a practical difference for those people.

Thus far, we have been discussing God's metaphysical attributes, as conceived by traditional philosophical theology.

> What shall we now say of the attributes called moral? Pragmatically, they stand on an entirely different footing. They positively determine fear and hope and expectation, and are foundations for the saintly life.

God's holiness orients the divine will toward the good, at which we too should aim; divine justice implies rewards for right conduct and punishment for wrongdoing; and God's love points to the possibility of forgiveness and mercy toward us who are weak. So here (unlike with the metaphysical attributes) there is pragmatic value to be detected. But what about the arguments that have been offered on behalf of God's moral attributes? "It stands with them as ill as with the arguments for his existence." James goes on to observe that "it is a plain historical fact that they never have converted any one who has found in the moral complexion of the world, as he experienced it, reasons for doubting that a good God can have framed it." And, of course, for many thoughtful people through the ages, the problem of evil has posed such a reason for doubt. Having criticized the arguments for divine existence, for God's metaphysical attributes, and for the divine moral attributes, as traditionally conceived, James concludes his findings against the religious philosophies of medieval and modern times:

> We must therefore, I think, bid good-by to dogmatic theology. In all sincerity our faith must do without that warrant.[122]

Religious experience and the will to believe must, on this view, stand without the support of any definitive logical argumentation.

Concept of God. James's conception of God is tentatively suggested in several scattered texts, without being systematically developed anywhere. Let us begin this subsection by focusing on some important passages at the end of *Varieties of Religious Experience*. James proposes to present his own "over-belief"—that is, his view of God over and above what he has analyzed as religion's "common and generic" doctrine of the divine—and admits that it may "appear a sorry under-belief" to many of us because it will still leave so many relevant issues undetermined. He believes in some supreme reality which is engaged with our visible world in an ongoing manner.

> God is the natural appellation, for us Christians at least, for the supreme real-
> ity, so I will call this higher part of the universe by the name of God. We and
> God have business with each other; and in opening ourselves to his influence
> our deepest destiny is fulfilled.

Pragmatically it matters to James that there be such a higher reality:

> God's existence is the guarantee of an ideal order that shall be permanently pre-
> served. This world may indeed, as science assures us, some day burn up or freeze;
> but if it is part of his order, the old ideals are sure to be brought elsewhere to
> fruition, so that where God is, tragedy is only provisional and partial, and ship-
> wreck and dissolution are not the absolutely final things.

This indicates a "cash-value" tied up with faith and prayer. So far, so
orthodox, it might appear. But, at the end of the lecture, James backs off
from any further analysis of God: "What the more characteristic divine
facts are, apart from the actual inflow of energy in the faith-state and the
prayer-state, I know not."[123]

In the postscript James classifies himself "among the supernaturalists
of the piecemeal or crasser type." He is not a naturalist because he believes
in an ideal realm that transcends the natural order. Nor does he subscribe
to the "refined" or "universalistic" supernaturalism made so fashionable by
the idealists of his time, whose view tends to hold that "the world of the
ideal has no efficient causality, and never bursts into the world of phenomena at particular points." As a pragmatist, James believes that the ideal
realm must significantly affect the facts of the natural order. As he writes,

> Notwithstanding my own inability to accept either popular Christianity or
> scholastic theism, I suppose that my belief that in communion with the Ideal
> new force comes into the world, and new departures are made here below,
> subjects me to being classed among the supernaturalists of the piecemeal or
> crasser type.[124]

James refuses to conclude that God must be unique and infinite, as
the Judeo-Christian tradition maintains. At the end of his lecture series,
he insists

> that religious experience, as we have studied it, cannot be cited as unequivocally
> supporting the infinitist belief. The only thing that it unequivocally testifies to
> is that we can experience union with *something* larger than ourselves and in that
> union find our greatest peace.

James's empirical study discloses an ideal power with which man can be
in communion and with which many of us might prefer to identify the
God of monotheism. But his point is that we need not feel compelled
to do so.

> All that the facts require is that the power should be both other and larger than our conscious selves. Anything larger will do, if only it be large enough to trust for the next step. It need not be infinite, it need not be solitary.

James suggests that it might even be an extension and collection of our spiritual selves "with no absolute unity realized in it at all. Thus would a sort of polytheism return upon us—a polytheism which I do not on this occasion defend."[125] It is not clear that James ever embraces this sort of "polytheism"; but the point to be made here is that his conception of God is nondogmatic and unorthodox. Let us now look elsewhere for its further definition.

Two of James's "essays in popular philosophy," "The Dilemma of Determinism" and "Reflex Action and Theism," have something to offer in this regard. Near the end of the former essay, having argued for an indeterministic universe of chance, James considers whether that view can be squared with belief in divine providence. His answer is that it can on a certain conception of God. In a memorable analogy, he compares God to a master chess player, who is engaged with us in the game of life, respecting our capacity to make our own choices. His knowledge is limited, encompassing past and present fact but the future only in terms of possibilities. If we amateurs played chess against a grand master, he would know all the possible moves we could make before we made our choices, which ones were statistically more probable and which less likely, and what the appropriate response would be to any move we might choose. Yet our moves would be genuinely our own and not determined for us. And the master chess player's victory would be practically assured, although it could not be certain beforehand how long the game would run or exactly which moves we would choose to make. James points out in a footnote that this model "leaves the creative mind subject to the law of time" and is incompatible with divine "timelessness," which James thinks stands in tension with a genuine belief in human freedom: "And is not the notion of eternity being given at a stroke to omniscience only just another way of whacking upon us the block-universe, and of denying that possibilities exist?" James is not only setting a distance between his own view of God and that of monistic idealism, but also identifying God as more of a person like us:

> So the creator himself would not need to know *all* the details of actuality until they came; and at any time his own view of the world would be a view partly of facts and partly of possibilities, exactly as ours is now. Of one thing, however, he might be certain; and that is that his world was safe, and that no matter how much it might zigzag he could bring it home at last.[126]

Thus, to the extent that he subscribes to his own analogy (and he probably does), James limits God's knowledge to past and present facts and future possibilities, placing God in time with ourselves.

James's essay "Reflex Action and Theism" was originally an address delivered at a Unitarian Ministers' Institute in 1881. There he argues

> that some outward reality of a nature defined as God's nature must be defined is the only ultimate object that is at the same time rational and possible for the human mind's contemplation. *Anything short of God is not rational, anything more than God is not possible.*

He proceeds to explain this thesis by observing that not just "any object of our loyalty" will prove worthy of being called "God," but that certain "intrinsic characteristics" must be attributed to the divine nature. "Now what are these essential features? First, it is essential that God be thought of as the deepest power in the universe; and, second, he must be conceived under the form of mental personality." We might observe that he does not say this "deepest power" need be omnipotent or the "mental personality" omniscient. Against Hegelian panentheism, James regards God as transcendent "and other than me," although in relation to man in that "both have purposes for which they care, and each can hear the other's call." James defines the divine personality in terms of "the reflex-action theory of mind," which he holds to be characteristic of our own mental nature:

> Any mind, constructed on the triadic-reflex pattern, must first get its impression from the object which it confronts; then define what that object is, and decide what active measures its presence demands; and finally react. The stage of reaction depends on the stage of definition, and these, of course, on the nature of the impressing object.[127]

Thus, unlike Kant, for example, who attributes to God an intellectual intuition which is radically different from our own sensible intuition, James, the empiricist, holds that the only sort of mental life of which we have any experience (and, therefore, any right to postulate in God) is our own, in terms of impressions, definition and decision, and reaction.

James explicitly embraces a theistic belief in a personal God with whom we can maintain ongoing relations. Theism, he says,

> by reason of its practical rationality, is certain to survive all lower creeds. Materialism and agnosticism, even were they true, could never gain universal and popular acceptance; for they both, alike, give a solution of things which is irrational to the practical third of our nature, and in which we can never volitionally feel at home.

Our "will to believe" is oriented toward ultimate meaning and significance, which only a personal God can provide for most people. Theism

makes a qualitatively different appeal from that of the ultimately impersonal and pointless universe of materialism. "At a single stroke, it
changes the dead blank *it* of the world into a living *thou*, with whom
the whole man may have dealings." Thus, James justifies the first half
of his thesis-statement italicized above: "Infra-theistic conceptions,
materialisms and agnosticisms, are irrational because they are inadequate
stimuli to man's practical nature." Now he must try "to justify the latter
half of the thesis." Pantheism and panentheism are "attempts to fly
beyond theism," by denying divine transcendence, to erase the duality
between natural man and the supernatural God, "and to transform it
into some sort or other of identity." In James's day, Hegel loomed as the
greatest proponent of this view. Its practical impossibility for James rests
on its implicit denial of our own individual identity and integrity (the
same issue against which Kierkegaard lodged his protest). My religious
relationship with God should be such that my personality, as well as
God's, is maintained. Yet this is not to deny any sort of union in that
relationship, as James explains:

> Now, it seems to me that the only sort of union of creature with creator with
> which theism, properly so called, comports, is of this emotional and practical
> kind; and it is based unchangeably on the empirical fact that the thinking sub-
> ject and the object thought are numerically two.

Emotionally, the religious relationship can take the form of love and
respect if we and God are committed to common values. Practically, we
will then find ourselves motivated to act in such a way as to help realize
these values.

> To co-operate with his creation by the best and rightest response seems all he
> wants of us. In such co-operation with his purposes, not in any chimerical spec-
> ulative conquest of him, not in any theoretic drinking of him up, must lie the
> real meaning of our destiny.[128]

This Jamesian analysis of the religious relationship as one of personal col-
laboration has not received sufficient scholarly attention.

Perhaps a reason this aspect of James's thought has been played down
is that it offends our traditional sense of God as omnipotent and infinite. In another of his "essays in popular philosophy," entitled "Is Life
Worth Living?," he makes the shocking suggestion that God's power and
reality might, to some extent, be a function of our support: "God himself, in short, may draw vital strength and increase of very being from
our fidelity."[129] We may well wonder how far James is willing to go with
this provocative suggestion. In *A Pluralistic Universe* (one of his last
books) he makes it clear that he rejects monism's "block-universe" and

all-encompassing Absolute, because of the problems they pose for human individuality and freedom:

> The line of least resistance, then, as it seems to me, both in theology and in philosophy, is to accept, along with the superhuman consciousness, the notion that it is not all-embracing, the notion, in other words, that there is a God, but that he is finite, either in power or in knowledge, or in both at once.

(Here, of course, lies a solution to the traditional problem of evil.) On this view we are not identical with God.

> Yet because God is not the absolute, but is himself a part when the system is conceived pluralistically, his functions can be taken as not wholly dissimilar to those of the other smaller parts,—as similar to our functions consequently.

Thus, for James, God becomes identified with man without becoming identical with him: "Having an environment, being in time, and working out a history just like ourselves, he escapes from the foreignness from all that is human, of the static timeless perfect absolute."[130] Although, from the perspective of orthodox Christianity, this may be an unorthodox conception of God, it is reasonable in light of James's radical empiricism and pragmatism.

In a letter of 1907, James repeats his denial of a Being who is infinite in both knowledge and power, saying, "The 'omniscient' and 'omnipotent' God of theology I regard as a disease of the philosophy shop." But there is one final item to add to this account. In 1904, James filled out a questionnaire sent out by a Professor James B. Pratt. In answer to the question, "What do you mean by God?," James responds, "*A combination of Ideality and (final) efficacity.*" He proceeds to say that God "*must be cognizant and responsive in some way*" as well as productive of effects. In response to the question, "How do you apprehend his relation to mankind and to you personally?," James answers, "*Uncertain.*" He says that his belief in God is based on neither argumentation nor personal experience of the divine presence, but on the "*whole line of testimony*" of others (such as are studied in his *Varieties*) which he considers "*so strong that I am unable to pooh-pooh it away.*"[131] James's God, then, is a supernatural person, who is limited and in time like us, to whom we can be related, with whom we can share spiritual values and cooperate for the sake of their realization. He views God as the object of experience rather than as the conclusion of a logical demonstration. Religious belief, for James, calls for personal commitment and pragmatic action rather than theoretical certainty; it is not a matter of objective intellect so much as one of subjective will.

Notes

1. *The Letters of William James*, ed. Henry James, in two volumes bound together (Boston: Little, Brown, & Company, 1926), vol. 1, pp. 2–5. This work will hereafter be called "*Letters.*"

2. Ibid., p. 8.   3. Ibid., pp. 22–23.

4. Ibid., pp. 31–32, 47, 53, 56, 60–61.

5. Ibid., pp. 84–85.   6. Ibid., p. 138.   7. Ibid., p. 140.

8. *The Varieties of Religious Experience*, by William James (New York: New American Library, 1958), pp. 135–36; see also *Letters*, vol. 1, pp. 145–46.

9. *Letters*, vol. 1, p. 148; see also p. 129.

10. Ibid., pp. 147–48.   11. Ibid., vol. 2, p. 233.

12. At the time James referred to "The Sentiment of Rationality" as "The only decent thing I have ever written"—*Letters*, vol. 1, p. 203.

13. Ibid., vol. 2, pp. 2–3.   14. Ibid., vol. 1, pp. 194, 294, 296.

15. Ibid., pp. 300–301.   16. Ibid., vol. 2, p. 3.   17. Ibid., vol. 1, p. 319.

18. *Talks to Teachers on Psychology and to Students on Some of Life's Ideals*, by William James (New York: W. W. Norton and Company, 1958), p. 19.

19. *Letters*, vol. 2, p. 45. James was never willing to serve as administrative chairman of his department.

20. Ibid., p. 47.   21. Ibid., p. 105.   22. Ibid., p. 146.

23. Ibid., p. 127; see also pp. 149–50.

24. Ibid., p. 155.   25. Ibid., p. 165.   26. Ibid., p. 172.

27. James went to San Francisco on the day of the quake to observe the situation and reports his observations in a paper "On Some Mental Effects of the Earthquake," included in *Memories and Studies*, by William James (Westport, CT: Greenwood Press, 1968), pp. 209–26.

28. *Letters*, vol. 2, p. 266.

29. Ibid., p. 268.

30. Ibid., p. 276. To his brother Henry, a few days later, he wrote, "I have just finished the proofs of a little book called "Pragmatism". . . . I should n't be surprised if ten years hence it should be treated as "epoch-making," for of the definitive triumph of that general way of thinking I can entertain no doubt whatever—I believe it to be something quite like the protestant reformation"—ibid., p. 279.

31. Ibid., p. 303.   32. Ibid., pp. 300–301.

33. *The Principles of Psychology*, in two volumes, by William James (New York: Dover Publications, 1950); this work will hereafter be called "*Principles.*"

34. *Psychology: Briefer Course*, by William James (New York: Henry Holt and Company, 1892); this work will hereafter be called "*Psychology.*"

35. *The Will to Believe and Other Essays in Popular Philosophy*, by William James (New York: Dover Publications, 1956); this work will hereafter be called "*Will.*"

36. *The Varieties of Religious Experience*; this work will hereafter be called "*Varieties.*"

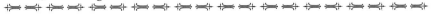

37. *Pragmatism* and *The Meaning of Truth*, by William James (Cambridge: Harvard Univ. Press, 1978).

38. *Essays in Radical Empiricism* and *A Pluralistic Universe*, by William James, ed. Ralph Barton Perry (New York: E. P. Dutton, 1971); the latter work will hereafter be called "*Universe*."

39. *Pragmatism* and *The Meaning of Truth*; the latter work will hereafter be called "*Truth*."

40. *Some Problems of Philosophy*, by William James (New York: Longmans, Green, and Company, 1911); this work will hereafter be called "*Problems*."

41. *Essays in Radical Empiricism* and *A Pluralistic Universe*; the former work will hereafter be called "*Empiricism*."

42. *The Writings of William James: A Comprehensive Edition*, ed. John J. McDermott (New York: The Modern Library, 1968); this book (which has recently been reprinted in paperback by the Univ. of Chicago Press) will hereafter be called "*Writings*."

43. *Principles*, vol. 1, p. 239; *Psychology*, p. 159; *Writings*, p. 33. For James's definition of "psychology," see the first paragraph of *Psychology*, p. 1.

44. Psychology, p. 152.

45. *Will*, pp. 14–15 (*Writings*, p. 725).

46. *Principles*, vol. 1, pp. 225–26, 230, 236–38, 243, 240, 258–59, 271, 274–75, 284, 289 (*Writings*, pp. 22–23, 26, 30–32, 36, 34, 48–49, 59, 61–62, 70, 74).

47. *Principles*, vol. 2, pp. 560, 487, 501, 528.

48. Ibid., pp. 531–34.

49. Ibid., pp. 567–68, 572–73, 579; *Will*, pp. 152, 95, 109 (*Writings*, pp. 592, 336, 344).

50. *Principles*, vol. 1, pp. 586, 584.

51. *Principles*, vol. 2, pp. 283–84, 287; "The Psychology of Belief," in *Mind*, vol. 14, no. 55 (July, 1889), pp. 321–22, 325.

52. *Principles*, vol. 2, pp. 288–90; "The Psychology of Belief," pp. 326–28.

53. *Principles*, vol. 2, pp. 292–93, 295, 297, 312; "The Psychology of Belief," pp. 329–31, 333, 346. Compare the last quote to *Will*, pp. 75–76, 146 (*Writings*, pp. 325, 588).

54. *Will*, p. 92 (*Writings*, p. 334).

55. *Truth*, pp. 172–73 (*Writings*, p. 314).

56. *Empiricism*, pp. 24–26, 70n. (*Writings*, pp. 195–96, 231n.); compare *Problems*, pp. 35–37.

57. *Problems*, pp. 47–50 (*Writings*, pp. 232–33); James writes of the infantile experience of the world as "one great blooming, buzzing confusion" in *Principles*, vol. 1, p. 488, and *Psychology*, p. 16.

58. *Problems*, pp. 74–75, 79, 81, 84 (*Writings*, pp. 243–47).

59. *Collected Essays and Reviews*, by William James (New York: Longmans, Green and Co., 1920), p. 437 (*Writings*, p. 361). Some begrudging admiration may be expressed when he says there, "Kant's mind is the rarest and most intricate of all possible bric-a-brac museums, and connoisseurs and dilettanti will always wish to visit it and see the wondrous and racy contents."

60. *Universe*, pp. 162, 174 (*Writings*, pp. 512, 521); *Problems*, p. 92 (*Writings*, p. 250); see also "On Some Hegelisms," in *Will*, pp. 263–98.

61. *Universe*, pp. 178–79 (*Writings*, p. 525); cf. *Pragmatism*, pp. 18–20 (*Writings*, pp. 370–71).
62. *Letters*, vol. 2, p. 165.
63. *Collected Essays and Reviews*, p. 436 (*Writings*, p. 361).
64. *Principles*, vol. 1, pp. 218, 221–22.
65. Ibid., vol. 2, pp. 619, 628, 644, 661–63, 669–70, 675, 677 (*Writings*, pp. 76, 84, 96–97, 110–12, 117, 122–23).
66. Ibid., pp. 661–62n., 664–65n. (*Writings*, pp. 110–11n., 113n.).
67. *Pragmatism*, pp. 13–14 (*Writings*, pp. 365–66).
68. *Problems*, pp. 36–37; see *Will*, pp. 66–67 (*Writings*, p. 319).
69. *Pragmatism*, pp. 14, 23 (*Writings*, pp. 366, 373).
70. Ibid., pp. 28, 30 (*Writings*, pp. 377, 379).
71. Ibid., pp. 30–32 (*Writings*, pp. 379–80).
72. Ibid., pp. 34–37 (*Writings*, pp. 382–84).
73. Ibid., pp. 40–43 (*Writings*, pp. 387–89).
74. Ibid., pp. 52, 55–56 (*Writings*, pp. 396, 398–99); see *Truth*, pp. 171–72 (*Writings*, p. 313).
75. *Pragmatism*, pp. 67, 76, 79 (*Writings*, pp. 408, 415, 417).
76. *Problems*, pp. 138–43 (*Writings*, pp. 267–70); see "A Pluralistic Mystic," in *Memories and Studies*, pp. 409–10.
77. *Pragmatism*, pp. 83–85, 89–92, 94 (*Writings*, pp. 420–21, 424–26, 428).
78. Ibid., pp. 96–98, 102 (*Writings*, pp. 429–32, 434).
79. *Truth*, p. 171 (*Writings*, p. 312).
80. *Pragmatism*, pp. 97–99, 106 (*Writings*, pp. 430–32, 438).
81. Ibid., pp. 108, 100–101, 106–7, 97 (*Writings*, pp. 439, 433, 438, 430). James published *The Meaning of Truth* as a "Sequel to Pragmatism" and a defence of his theory against his critics. See there, especially, "A Word More about Truth," "The Pragmatist Account of Truth and Its Misunderstanders," "The Meaning of the Word Truth," and "A Dialogue" for further detail.
82. *Pragmatism*, pp. 115, 117–20, 123–24 (*Writings*, pp. 449, 451–53, 456–57).
83. Ibid., pp. 135–42 (*Writings*, pp. 465–70).
84. *Will*, pp. 1–2 (*Writings*, p. 717).
85. Ibid., pp. 2–3 (*Writings*, pp. 717–18).
86. Ibid., pp. 3–4 (*Writings*, p. 718).
87. Ibid., pp. 5–8, 15 (*Writings*, pp. 719–21, 725). For the passage on the "wager," see *Pascal's Pensées*, trans. W. F. Trotter (New York: E. P. Dutton, 1958), #233, pp. 65–69.
88. Ibid., pp. 8–11 (*Writings*, pp. 721–22).
89. Ibid., p. 11 (*Writings*, p. 723).
90. Ibid., pp. 13–15 (*Writings*, pp. 724–25).
91. Ibid., pp. 17–19 (*Writings*, pp. 726–27).
92. Ibid., pp. 19–22 (*Writings*, pp. 728–29).
93. Ibid., pp. 22–23 (*Writings*, pp. 729–30).

94. Ibid., p. 25 (*Writings*, p. 731).

95. Ibid., pp. 25–27 (*Writings*, pp. 731–32); cf. *Will*, pp. 94–95n. (*Writings*, p. 336n.).

96. *Pragmatism*, p. 124 (*Writings*, p. 457).

97. *Letters*, vol. 2, p. 207.

98. *Will*, p. 29 (*Writings*, p. 734); cf. *Truth*, p. 172 (*Writings*, p. 313); see also *Varieties*, p. 173.

99. *Will*, pp. 90, 95 (*Writings*, pp. 333, 336).

100. *Problems*, pp. 221–24 (*Writings*, pp. 735–37); cf. *A Pluralistic Universe*, p. 277, where James speaks of the "faith-ladder" as an example of "life exceeding logic" (*Writings*, p. 809).

101. "Reason and Faith," by William James, *The Journal of Philosophy*, vol. 24, no. 8 (April 14, 1927), pp. 197–99. For more on James's epistemology and views on metaphysics, see *Twelve Great Philosophers*, by Wayne P. Pomerleau (New York: Ardsley House, 1997), pp. 378–400.

102. *Varieties*, pp. 22–23, 29–30, 33–34.

103. Ibid., pp. 42, 44, 47 (*Writings*, pp. 744, 746, 749).

104. Ibid., pp. 58, 72.   105. Ibid., pp. 83, 85, 104–5, 107, 113.

106. Ibid., pp. 114, 121–22, 137, 139.

107. Ibid., pp. 140, 142–47.

108. Ibid., pp. 162, 169, 171, 198–99, 203, 205.

109. Ibid., pp. 216–17, 290–91.

110. Ibid., pp. 292–94.   111. Ibid., pp. 294–98.

112. Ibid., pp. 307–8, 312–15, 319, 322.

113. Ibid., pp. 323–28; see "Does Reason Demand That God Be Infinite?," by Wayne P. Pomerleau, in *Sophia*, vol. 24, no. 2 (July, 1985), pp. 24–25.

114. *Varieties*, pp. 348, 350–52, 361.

115. Ibid., pp. 367, 370 (*Writings*, pp. 759, 761–62).

116. Ibid., pp. 380–81, 383 (*Writings*, pp. 771–72, 774).

117. Ibid., pp. 384–86, 371, 376–77 (*Writings*, pp. 775, 777, 762, 767–68).

118. Ibid., pp. 260, 329–31.

119. Ibid., pp. 333–35.   120. Ibid., pp. 335–37.   121. Ibid., pp. 339–40.

122. Ibid., p. 341.   123. Ibid., pp. 388–91 (*Writings*, pp. 779–81).

124. Ibid., pp. 392–93 (*Writings*, pp. 782–83).

125. Ibid., pp. 395–96 (*Writings*, pp. 785–86).

126. *Will*, pp. 180–82 (*Writings*, pp. 608–10).

127. *Will*, pp. 115–16, 121–23.

128. Ibid., pp. 126–27, 134–35, 141.

129. Ibid., p. 61.

130. *Universe*, pp. 269, 272 (*Writings*, pp. 802–3, 805).

131. *Letters*, vol. 2, pp. 269, 213–14.

10

Contemporary Perspectives

Debates

Classical vs. Contemporary Views. The conflict between the classical and contemporary views in the philosophy of religion centers around the problem of the meaningfulness of religious concepts. In previous chapters we have considered what some of the greatest philosophers in Western civilization, from Augustine to William James, have written about God and religion. We have studied their theories of knowledge, views on the relationship between faith and reason, positions on arguments for God's existence, ideas regarding the divine nature, and treatment of the problem of evil. Because of its philosophical character, this study has inevitably involved critical evaluation, rather than being purely expository. We have continuously probed for the rational grounds, evidence, and justification underlying these famous systems of thought; the disagreements surfacing among the great thinkers have provided us with a realization that even their knowledge-claims regarding God and religion were far from obviously true.

A radical question on which we have not yet had to spend much time must now be faced: what basis, if any, can we have to suppose that any of our attempts to speak (or even think) about God can be meaningful? If language requires an experiential foundation in order to make sense, if our normal human experience is of things of our natural world, and if religion is interpreted as referring us to that which transcends that natural world, then what sense can we possibly make of religious language? This issue cuts to the very core of the intelligibility of philosophical theology.

This is the sort of consideration which contemporary analytic philosophy raises in its most powerful form. This approach to philosophy, emphasizing conceptual elucidation, has dominated academic philosophy in most English-speaking countries (including our own) throughout this century. It seems appropriate that the significance of religious faith should be the focus of our concluding chapter.

The chapter will proceed in three main parts. This first section will consider two important debates, which were originally broadcast by the British Broadcasting Corporation in 1948–49. These provide an illuminating transition between the classical perspective presented in the previous nine chapters of this book, which is defended by English philosopher Frederick Charles Copleston, and the contemporary critique of that tradition, presented here by two of the most famous of English analytic philosophers, Bertrand Russell and Alfred Jules Ayer. The middle section of this chapter will deal with the challenges to the meaningfulness of religious language posed by Ayer and Antony Flew and with various responses to those challenges by Richard M. Hare, Basil Mitchell, Richard B. Braithwaite, and John Hick. Then the final section will be a broader study of Hick's still developing philosophy of religion, as an illustration of the fact that contemporary analytic philosophy can inspire new contributions to philosophical theology, even while challenging its very possibility.

Before plunging further, however, a few related disclaimers may be in order. First, this chapter, unlike all of its predecessors, makes no promise to deal with the ideas of the greatest philosophers in Western civilization. We shall be studying views developed after the First World War, which have therefore not yet had the same opportunity to stand the test of time, as have those of previous centuries. Our crystal balls are hopelessly cloudy. Some academics believe that Bertrand Russell, for example, has already achieved the stature of first-rate philosopher, while others do not. It is arguable, but not certain, that Hick's philosophy of religion will prove to be lastingly valuable. Second, the selection process that leads to our considering some thinkers here while ignoring others is even more subject to second-guessing than that of earlier chapters precisely because the sifting of intellectual history has not gone as far. Of course, there are those who will be outraged that thinkers they consider extremely important and/or provocative are omitted here. But we must pick and choose if we are to avoid a fruitless superficiality; the thinkers considered here will help crystallize the conflict between the great philosophers of past centuries who tended to presuppose the meaningfulness of theological concepts and contemporary analysts who challenge that meaningfulness or defend against that challenge. And, third, since this chapter does not deal with a single thinker as do its predecessors (or even with three famous thinkers, as our first chapter did), it is to be expected that the discussion will be more scattered and, thus, will achieve less depth. Yet its central emphasis will remain the defense of philosophical theology against the charge that it is doomed to meaninglessness.

Russell vs. Copleston. The debate between Russell and Copleston was first broadcast on the BBC in 1948. Born in 1872, the grandson of a British Prime Minister, Bertrand Russell was orphaned at the age of four. Though he alternately attended Episcopalian and Presbyterian churches as a small child, by eleven the boy had become a nonchurch-going follower of Darwin's. At eighteen he went to Cambridge University, from which he graduated. The debate with Copleston was published in 1957 in a collection of Lord Russell's writings on religion, under the revealing title, *Why I Am Not a Christian*; he died in 1970. By contrast, Father Copleston was a Jesuit priest, born in 1907 and educated at Oxford University. He entered the Roman Catholic Church in 1925, joined the Society of Jesus in 1930, and was ordained a priest in 1937. Copleston is best known for his monumental nine-volume *History of Philosophy* and was philosophically in the Thomistic tradition; he died in 1994. Given their backgrounds, it is predictable that Copleston and Russell advocate diametrically opposed positions.

The debate itself is comprised of five unequal sections: a one-page introduction, a rather long section on the cosmological argument from contingency, a brief treatment of religious experience, a slightly longer one of the moral argument, and a couple of pages of summary. The little introduction accomplishes two things quickly and clearly. First, agreement is reached as to what the two philosophers will mean by "God" for the duration of the debate, namely, "a supreme personal being—distinct from the world and creator of the world." In reflecting on the definition, we might observe that it does not capture everything that orthodox Jews, Christians, and Muslims believe about God (for example, no mention is made of infinite perfection), that it depicts God as a person rather than as merely an abstract metaphysical principle, and that it characterizes God as transcendent, ruling out pantheism. The second thing of importance in the introduction is the establishing of perspectives. Russell just says that "my position is agnostic," declining to argue for the atheistic view that there is no God. By contrast, Copleston adopts "the affirmative position that such a being actually exists, and that His existence can be proved philosophically" by "Leibniz's argument from 'Contingency.'"[1] This sets the stage for the longest section of the debate, dealing with metaphysical argumentation for God's existence.

Copleston states his version of the argument from contingency in a single paragraph. "First of all, I should say, we know that there are at least some beings in the world which do not contain in themselves the reason for their existence." These, by definition, are contingent beings, of which we ourselves are examples, in the sense that there is nothing about our nature which requires that we should have existed. "Now, secondly, the world is simply the real or imagined totality or aggregate of individual objects, none of which contain in themselves alone the reason for their existence." We might note that there is quite a leap from the first claim that we know some things are contingent to this second one that everything in the world is contingent. Third, given that each object of experience in the world is (allegedly) contingent, we are rationally driven to try to explain its existence by reference to some self-sufficient, noncontingent, necessary existing being; otherwise, we would be caught up in an infinite regress of causal explanations of contingent things in terms of other contingent things, in which case we would never achieve an ultimate and adequate account of anything at all. "So, I should say, in order to explain existence, we must come to a being which contains within itself the reason for its own existence, that is to say, which cannot not-exist."[2] This is an old, familiar metaphysical argument for God's existence, which we can trace back beyond Leibniz to medieval times; indeed, it is a variant of the third of Aquinas's "five ways."

We might analyze the subsequent debate regarding this argument in three parts:

1. Is it even meaningful to speak of God as a "necessary being," in contrast to the allegedly "contingent" beings of this world?
2. Can we make adequate sense of the idea of God as the ultimate "sufficient reason" of the entire "universe"?
3. How could we possibly justify applying "the concept of cause" to "the world as a whole"?

We shall consider each of these particular issues in turn; but notice how all three of them involve the importance of conceptual analysis and how collectively they raise a challenge against the assumed meaningfulness of theological language.

Russell reacts to Copleston's presentation of the argument from contingency by saying that "the best point at which to begin is the question of necessary being. The word 'necessary,' I should maintain, can only be applied significantly to propositions." Russell, one of the premier proponents of modern logic, holds that a necessary proposition is one the contradiction of which is logically impossible and that such a proposition "has got to be analytic." For example, "No bachelors are married" is such a proposition, and its contradictory, "Some bachelors are married," is linguistic nonsense. If we analyze the subject term, "bachelors," we see that it conceptually (i.e., by definition) contains the notion of being unmarried, so that the predicate term, "married," is logically incompatible with it. (Notice that Russell implicitly denies the Kantian view that there can be synthetic *a priori* propositions, which inform us about what is real because they are "synthetic" but which are also universally and necessarily true because "*a priori*.") Russell tries to attach some sense to Copleston's notion: "I could only admit a necessary being if there were a being whose existence it is self-contradictory to deny." Even if there were a God in the sense agreed upon at the beginning of this debate, it does not seem plausible to suppose that denying that there is would be tantamount to self-contradiction. Russell thus tries to take the high ground by defining "necessary being" in terms of logical propositions. With this reduction, the meaningfulness of "a contingent being" is also eliminated. He summarizes his view by saying, "I don't admit the idea of a necessary being and I don't admit that there is any particular meaning in calling other beings 'contingent.'" Copleston attempts to sever the connection between reality and logical propositions: "After all, a 'contingent' being is a being which has not in itself the complete reason for its existence. . . . A 'necessary' being, on the other hand, means a being that must and cannot not-exist." He accuses Russell of dogmatically dismissing metaphysical terms as meaningless, to which the latter replies, "I don't maintain the meaninglessness of metaphysics in general at all. I maintain the meaninglessness of certain particular terms." Unfortunately, Copleston fails to swing Russell over to accepting the meaningfulness of "necessary being" in his sense of the phrase, so it seems fruitless to proceed along this course. As Copleston concludes, "Well, we seem to have arrived at an impasse. To say that a necessary being is a being that must exist and cannot not-exist has for me a definite meaning. For you it has no meaning."[3]

Second, the discussion shifts to the consideration of regarding God as the "sufficient reason" of the "universe," and again Russell throws down the gauntlet. If God is to be so regarded, Russell demands a definition of "sufficient reason." Copleston replies that it is "an explanation adequate for the existence of some particular being," to which Russell retorts that then the notion of an adequate explanation requires conceptual elucidation. Copleston answers, "An adequate explanation must ultimately be a total explanation, to which nothing further can be added." Russell dismisses this as an unachievable goal not worth pursuing; Copleston replies, "To say that one has not found it is one thing; to say that one should not look for it seems to me rather dogmatic." Russell claims that, in addition to the problem of making any workable sense of the notion of "sufficient reason," there is also a problem with the concept of "universe"; though it is "a handy word in some connections," he does not "think it stands for anything that has a meaning." Copleston reiterates his sense of the universe as "the real or imagined totality" of phenomenal objects,[4] but Russell still regards that as a mere abstraction.

The third question to be disputed in connection with the argument from contingency is whether we can sensibly apply the concept of cause to the world as a whole. Russell argues, "The whole concept of cause is one we derive from our observation of particular things; I see no reason whatsoever to suppose that the total has any cause whatsoever." More dogmatically than Kant, he asserts that "the concept of cause is not applicable to the total" and that "the universe is just there, and that's all." But Copleston insists on asking (with Leibniz), "Why something rather than nothing, that is the question?" He agrees that the question would be "illegitimate," if the concept of "cause" itself "were meaningless or if it could be shown that Kant's view of the matter were correct." But Russell does not appear to hold the former and has failed to accomplish the latter. Copleston presents a logical argument to show that the world as a whole "must have a cause." But it is impotent here, since Russell repudiates the whole idea: "I do think the notion of the world having an explanation is a mistake. I don't see why one should expect it to have." They agree that it is "very difficult" to discuss an issue when one of the participants finds it meaningless and that they should "pass on to some other issue."[5]

That issue is religious experience. Copleston makes it clear immediately that he does not consider it to be "a strict proof of the existence of God"; yet he does maintain that "the best explanation of it is the existence of God." He explains that what he means by "religious experience" is a loving, but unclear, awareness of some object which irresistibly seems to the experiencer as something transcending the self, something transcending all the normal objects of experience, something which cannot be pictured or conceptualized, but of the reality of which doubt is impossible—at least during the experience.[6]

In response, Russell comments that it is "a very tricky affair" to try to argue "from our own mental states to something outside us" such as God and that religious experience tends to be extremely private. Nor does he accept Copleston's suggestion that God's existence is "the best explanation" of the fact that some people's lives have dramatically changed for the better following their religious experiences, which they believe to have been caused by God: "The fact that a belief has a good moral effect upon a man is no evidence whatsoever in favour of its truth."[7] So, it reduces to a difference of how causally to interpret religious experiences, which even Russell does not deny some people sincerely believe they have had. He and Copleston simply disagree as to whether an existing God is "the best explanation" available to us, neither of them offering much in the way of criteria for judgment.

The next portion of the debate deals with the moral argument, Copleston arguing that "all goodness reflects God in some way and proceeds from Him," whereas Russell holds that moral distinctions can be maintained without presupposing any participation in divine goodness. At this point, Copleston goes on the offensive, demanding what ultimate grounds Russell can have "for distinguishing between good and bad." Russell replies in terms of an analogy with color distinctions: as we discriminate "between blue and yellow" through visual experience, so we make moral distinctions on the basis of the intuition of feelings. Copleston objects that this reduces moral distinctions to the subjective, private criterion of personal feelings, pushing Russell to amend his position a bit: "You've got to take account of the effects of actions and your feelings towards those effects."[8] Thus, for Russell, moral distinctions become a function of both objective consequences and subjective feelings.

For Copleston, the only adequate explanation of the foundation of "absolute values" and an absolute moral law is "the hypothesis of a transcendent ground of value and of an author of the moral law." Russell repudiates the concept of the "absolute" in connection with values: "I don't think there is anything absolute whatever. The moral law, for example, is always changing"; and he holds that our sense of moral obligation is socially conditioned. Copleston admits that different cultures can disagree about the content of moral law. "But the form of it, what Kant calls the categorical imperative, the 'ought,' I really don't see how that can possibly be conveyed to anybody by nurse or parent." But Russell refuses to be driven to either moral skepticism or the belief that categorical obligation must be supernaturally derived: "Well, I think the sense of 'ought' is the effect of somebody's imagined disapproval, it may be God's imagined disapproval, but it's somebody's imagined disapproval."[9] So here again (as with the topics of proving God's existence and of religious experience) we see the two at loggerheads over what is the most meaningful or most adequate interpretation of experienced phenomena, neither of them able to convert the other.

In summary, Copleston observes that his position can be reduced to two theses:

> First, that the existence of God can be philosophically proved by a metaphysical argument; secondly, that it is only the existence of God that will make sense of man's moral experience and of religious experience.

He points out that Russell's view that "existing beings are simply there" and that they require no ultimate explanation "itself stands in need of proof," which Russell has not provided. He incisively concludes, "I think we have reached an impasse because our ideas of philosophy are radically different." His point seems to be well-taken in that he seems to regard metaphysics as philosophically fundamental, where Russell sees philosophy in terms of conceptual analysis. For his part, the latter says that, though he does not reject all metaphysics as "nonsense," he does so reject Copleston's usage of "contingent" as opposed to "necessary" being. Although he accepts the distinction between good and bad as legitimate, Russell says, "I cannot attribute a Divine origin to this sense of moral obligation, which I think is quite easily accounted for in quite other ways."[10] As with any debate, we have a tendency to ask, "Which side is right?" (or, worse, "Who won?"). But we shall postpone evaluation until we have analyzed the second debate, which raises some similar points, though in an even more radical fashion.

Ayer vs. Copleston. The debate between Ayer and Copleston was first broadcast on the BBC in 1949. Born in 1910 and educated at Oxford University, A. J. Ayer (who died in 1989) is most well-known for his book, *Language, Truth and Logic*, published in 1936, which popularized **logical positivism**, with its "principle of verification," calling into question the very possibility of metaphysics (including philosophical theology) as a meaningful inquiry. As might be expected, the debate between Ayer and Copleston is focused on this challenge.

Ayer begins the debate by saying that "logical positivism isn't a system of philosophy," but rather "a certain kind of attitude toward philosophical problems" which rejects "the possibility of philosophy as a speculative discipline." Thus, he rejects all metaphysics, as Russell had refused to do; and Ayer explicitly asserts (what Copleston had thought Russell implied) that "if philosophy was to be a branch of knowledge as distinct from the sciences it would have to consist in logic or in some form of analysis." Ayer analyzes propositions into two possible types:

> Formal propositions, like those of logic and mathematics, depend for their validity on the conventions of a symbol system. Empirical propositions, on the other hand, are statements of observation—actual or possible—or hypotheses from which such statements can be logically derived.

Metaphysical assertions are not designed merely to reveal interrelationships of abstract symbols; nor are they the sort of observation statements that are even potentially **verifiable** by natural means. "Consequently we reject metaphysics." If it is not legitimately speculative, then "if philosophy is to be a cognitive activity, it must be purely critical,"[11] its legitimate function that of conceptual elucidation.

While acknowledging that conceptual elucidation is "an extremely useful thing," Copleston objects to the view that "logical analysis is the only function of philosophy." Also, he points out, Ayer has stipulatively classified all "significant propositions" in such a way as either to reduce metaphysics to something other than what it is, such as analytic truths or scientific hypotheses, or to eliminate it altogether as meaningless. Yet metaphysical assertions, by their very nature, attempt to make informative, factual claims about "the transcendent." At this point Ayer presents his fundamental criterion of meaning:

> I hold the principle—known as the principle of verification—according to which a statement intended to be a statement of fact is meaningful only if it's either formally valid, or some kind of observation is relevant to its truth or falsehood.

He does not argue for this criterion of meaning but points out that the "transcendent statements" of metaphysics fail to meet its requirements.[12]

Copleston holds that Leibniz's metaphysical query as to "why there are phenomena at all, why there is 'something' rather than 'nothing,'" is meaningful to many thinkers, whether or not it can be definitively answered. Ayer responds that, far from being meaningful, it proves on analysis to be "self-contradictory," because any explanation, purporting to answer a "why" question, must be in terms of "a more general description," whereas metaphysics pretends to offer explanations that are nondescriptive. Copleston responds that this objection collapses the distinction "between a scientific question and a metaphysical question" and that the latter, unlike the former, does not seek the sort of explanation that is describable in terms of empirical observations; it rather explains "the existence of phenomena in general . . . in terms of a transcendent reality." Then, Ayer replies, that "transcendent reality" would have to function like a most "general scientific hypothesis." As a historian of philosophy, Copleston observes that great metaphysicians do not accept any such reduction:

> Neither . . . Hegel nor Thomas Aquinas supposed that one could investigate scientifically what they respectively believed to be metaphysical reality, but each of them thought that intellectual reflection can lead the mind to postulate that reality.

If the hypotheses of metaphysical explanations are not scientific, he protests, why should anyone presume they are empirically testable? Logical positivism is guilty of dogmatically rejecting as illegitimate all metaphysical inquiry, including Leibniz's question (which began this paragraph). Copleston continues:

> It isn't meaningful if the only meaningful questions are those which can be answered by the methods of empirical science, as you presuppose. In my opinion you are unduly limiting the "meaningfulness" to a certain restricted kind of meaningfulness,[13]

that of abstract systems and empirical science, so that, in effect, metaphysics is ruled out by definition.

Ayer demands, how can "a non-scientific explanation explain anything?" Because a metaphysical explanation allegedly transcends the realm of empirical observation, it cannot possibly be verified or falsified. "In fact it's not an explanation at all. It becomes empty of significance because it's consistent with everything." Second, any metaphysical explanation would have to be expressed in terms of

> a proposition that is both contingent and necessary—contingent—contingent insofar as it's got to describe the world, necessary insofar as it's not just something happening to be, but something that must be. But that's a contradiction in terms.

Although ducking the first problem, Copleston confronts the second directly, saying that though a metaphysical explanation must take contingent things into account, this does not require that it be "a contingent proposition" and that, after all, "the ontological explanation of the world" is not itself a proposition of any sort, but a "necessary being." He adds that reality is not reducible to statements:

> Well, the world doesn't consist of contingent propositions, though things may be expressed in contingent propositions. Nor should I say that a necessary being consists of necessary propositions.

When Ayer points out that it is common to distinguish between "necessary" and "contingent" propositions, Copleston agrees, but he immediately denies that "all necessary or certain propositions are tautologies" and asserts that some apply to actual things.[14] Thus, he is committed to the possibility of the Kantian "synthetic *a priori* propositions" which Ayer rejects.

This returns us to the latter's "principle of verification," which holds that "to be significant a statement must be either on the one hand a formal statement—one that I should call analytic—or on the other hand empirically testable." Ayer sounds like a pragmatist when he announces that understanding any statement means

> knowing what would be the case if it were true. Knowing what would be the case if it were true means being disposed to accept some situations as warranting the acceptance or rejection of the statement in question.

From this position he draws two radical conclusions:

> The statements to which no situations are relevant one way or the other are ruled out as non-factual. And, secondly, the contents of the statement, the cash-value, to use James's term, consists of a range of situations, experiences, that would substantiate or refute it.[15]

This serves as a provocative statement of the challenge of logical positivism. But we should notice that Ayer has not argued for his view, however clearly he may have articulated it.

Copleston acutely objects that Ayer's position is nonverifiable and involves circularity:

> If you say that any factual statement, in order to be meaningful, must be . . . verifiable by sense experience, then surely you are presupposing that all reality is given in sense experience.

This is tantamount to assuming that there can be no metaphysical reality, which is the very issue in question;

> and if you presuppose this you are presupposing a philosophical position which cannot be demonstrated by the principle of verification. It seems to me that logical positivism . . . presupposes the truth of positivism.

In reply, Ayer says he does not want to restrict experience to sense experience and would wish to include "introspectable experiences or feelings." Yet, he insists, the factual content of any statement can only be determined empirically. At this point Copleston makes a curious concession:

> I think I should probably be prepared to accept the principle if it were understood in a very wide sense—that is, if verifiable by experience is understood as including intellectual intuition, and also as meaning simply that some experience, actual or conceivable, is relevant to the truth or falsity of the proposition concerned.[16]

Of course, Ayer is unwilling to include Copleston's sort of "intellectual intuition" under the rubric of experience; therefore this option is not considered further.

Copleston maintains that Ayer's refusal to accept metaphysical statements as cognitively meaningful is merely another way of saying that they do not satisfy his principle of verifiability but that this is only significant if we have sufficient reason to accept that principle.

> All that is shown, it seems to me, is that metaphysical propositions do not satisfy a definite assumed criterion of meaning. But it does not follow that one has to accept that criterion of meaning.

Next, he provides an example of a meaningful statement which is, in principle, unverifiable (and, for that matter, unfalsifiable as well): "Atomic warfare will take place and it will blot out the entire human race." If at any time this prediction has not come true, it might still come to pass in the future (so that it is not **falsifiable**); on the other hand, if it ever did come true, Ayer would have to admit that it could not be empirically verified, since all humans would be dead. Still "most people would think that this statement has meaning." Ayer does not directly answer the first charge that he has merely stipulated a criterion of meaning without arguing for it. In response to the second, he admits that Copleston's apocalyptic example "describes a possible situation," so that it is presumably meaningful. Ayer tries to elude the problem by suggesting that we can imaginatively verify the statement through an extrapolation from past experience:

> Putting the observer outside the story, one knows quite well what it would be like to observe devastation and fail to observe any men. Now it wouldn't necessarily be the case that in order to do that, one had to observe oneself.[17]

This leads Copleston to propose an interesting alternative criterion of meaning:

> If I can at least imagine or conceive the facts, the existence of which would verify the proposition, the proposition has significance for me. Whether I can or cannot know that the facts correspond is another matter.

Ayer observes, however, that they must disagree about what it means to imagine or conceive of something:

> I want to say that having an idea of something is a matter of knowing how to recognize it. And you want to say that you can have ideas of things even though there's no possible situation in which you could recognize it because nothing would count as finding it.

But this is just another way of insisting that meaningful statements must be, at least in principle, verifiable at the level of knowledge. This is the point of contention rejected by Copleston:

> No. I should say that you can have an idea of something if there's some experience that's relevant to the formation of the idea, not so much to its verification.

For example, our idea of "a disembodied spirit," even if not verifiable in this life, is meaningful insofar as it is derived from "the idea of body and the idea of mind,"[18] both of which are rooted in experience.

Both Copleston and Ayer are empiricists of sorts, the former wishing to draw all our ideas, including that of God, from experience. However, says the latter, "My quarrel with you is not that you take a wider view of experience than I do, but that you fail to supply any rules for the use of your expressions." In other words, the claim that an idea is meaningful if it is drawn from some sort of experience relevant to its formation, without reference to any observation verifying it at the level of knowledge, is too fuzzy to be helpful. Ayer continues:

> It's not necessary that the observation should actually be made; there are cases, as you've pointed out, where for practical, or even for theoretical, reasons, the observation couldn't, in fact, be made, but one knows what it would be like to make it. The statements which refer to it would be said to be verifiable in principle, if not in fact.

Ayer acknowledges that his critic can accuse him of being "entirely arbitrary" in the formation of his position, as if the principle of verifiability were merely "a persuasive definition." But he insists that it can "yield valuable results in the way of analysis," whereas Copleston's metaphysical statements can serve no cognitive function at all. Although they are alleged to be

> ultimate explanations of fact, yet you admit that they're not explanations in any accepted sense of the term, and you can't say in what sense they are explanations. You can't show me how they're to be tested, and you seem to have no criterion for deciding whether they are true or false. This being so, I say they're unintelligible.[19]

In his concluding remarks, Copleston reiterates that experience must be relevant to the formation of metaphysical ideas and says, "A metaphysical proposition is testable by rational discussion, but not by purely empirical means." However, he does not explain what it means to test a statement "by rational discussion," and Ayer does not have the opportunity to challenge him on this point. Finally, Copleston aims an acute logical dilemma at the principle of verification, which must be "either a proposition or not a proposition." If not, then it is meaningless, on Ayer's grounds. "If it is a proposition it must be, on your premises, either a tautology or an empirical hypothesis." If the former, then it is factually uninformative and indicates nothing about metaphysical reality. And if the latter, "then the principle itself would require verification. But the principle of verification cannot itself be verified."[20]

A Critique of the Debates. A critical assessment of these two debates should not be reduced to the simplistic attempt to declare a winner in each case. Neither philosopher in either debate adequately justifies his position throughout. And both debates nicely bring out a collision between credible perspectives—the traditional view that philosophical theology is a meaningful intellectual enterprise and the contemporary position that linguistic analysis can expose its failure in this respect. But what may be most striking about the debates is how they illustrate—without any of the participants apparently intending to do so—William James's point about alternative postulates of rationality. Russell considers it reasonable to accept the world as "just there," with no ultimate explanatory cause; Copleston's sense of rationality requires that there be some such self-sufficient, adequate cause. Ayer regards it as fundamentally irrational to use metaphysical statements at all; for Copleston, philosophical reason inevitably pushes us to the sort of speculation about the nature of reality that can only be addressed through metaphysical statements. It does not appear that such postulates of rationality can ever be conclusively demonstrated or refuted. They rather function philosophically as axioms do in geometry—as unprovable foundations on the basis of which arguments can be developed for other elements of the system. This may well be why neither participant in either debate can convert the other to his point of view. Their very foundations for considering and discussing such matters are at loggerheads. But let us more specifically evaluate each of the two debates.

In the first it should be noted that Russell has the easier task, since he only denies the possibility of any theological knowledge, whereas Copleston presents and must defend an affirmative position. As we have seen, his version of the argument from contingency is subjected to three lines of attack. First, granted that there is established usage in logic for the distinction between "necessary" and "contingent" propositions, it does not follow, as Russell wants to suggest, that those adjectives cannot also be meaningfully applied to beings. On the other hand, Copleston would need to elaborate further upon his sense of a "necessary being" as one which "must" exist and "cannot not-exist." Copleston is correct that Russell is dogmatic in refusing to consider that such a use of language might be meaningful and that this is the primary reason further discussion of the point is aborted. Second, it seems that Copleston does a capable job of meeting Russell's demands that "sufficient reason," "adequate explanation," and "universe" be elucidated and that Russell again dogmatically refuses to entertain the ideas seriously. And, third, even if we accept (against Copleston) Kant's view that the application of concepts such as causality to that which transcends experience can never yield knowledge, Russell not only fails to argue for that view but carries it to the less defensible extreme of holding that the idea of causality cannot be meaningfully applied to the world at all and insisting that there neither is nor could be a causal explanation for the whole phenomenal world. Although the argument from contingency involves problems of the sort exposed by Kant, Copleston's views here seem more open-minded than those of the more dogmatic Russell.

On the topic of religious experience, however, Copleston fails to show in what sense God's existence is its "best explanation" or to justify the claim. Russell is correct in emphasizing (as James did) the difficulty of trying to provide any support for claims concerning reality outside the mind on the basis of such intensely private phenomena as religious experiences, as well as in denying that beneficial consequences for the believer provide any evidence on behalf of the belief itself.

On the issue of the moral argument, Copleston requires absolute values as a postulate of rationality, but Russell does not. There either are or are not absolute values, but it does not seem that we can know whether there are or not. Even those of us, like Copleston, who believe in them and distrust Russell's moral intuitions based on feelings can think Copleston is wrong in holding that God is the only adequate ground of absolute values. We might hold that absolute values are anchored in the nature of reason and that ethics is independent of theological commitments.

In the second debate Copleston has the easier task because it is Ayer's position of logical positivism that is presented and subjected to criticism. Copleston seems correct that Ayer's view of philosophy as reduced to logical analysis and precluding all speculative theorizing is excessively narrow; certainly, it flies in the face of two and a half millennia of the history of philosophy (though, of course, this fact does not prove it erroneous). Second, Copleston is correct that in this debate Ayer has merely stipulated a criterion of meaningfulness without presenting a shred of argumentation on its behalf. Third, Copleston successfully observes that metaphysical ideas and questions have been meaningfully considered by great thinkers for centuries without being treated as scientific hypotheses. And, fourth, he does well to criticize Ayer's confusion regarding necessary versus contingent propositions, on the one hand, and necessary versus contingent reality, on the other.

However, Copleston still fails to elucidate his concept of a necessary being cogently. Second, he does not show in what sense a nonscientific, metaphysical explanation can explain anything. Third, he dodges Ayer's challenge that a metaphysical assertion must be meaningless because it is consistent with any and all possible experience. In each of these respects he leaves something to be desired.

Copleston's attack on Ayer's position as itself nonverifiable and involving circularity is brilliant. His suggestion that the principle of verifiability might be acceptable if it allowed for intellectual (nonsensible) intuition is provocative. On the other hand, how could we conclusively resolve the issue of whether human experience in this life can include the sort of "intellectual intuition" required by Copleston and rejected by Ayer?

Next, Copleston's counterexample in terms of the atomic-warfare prediction is effective in pushing Ayer to expand his notion of verifiability to include imaginative verification based on an extrapolation from past experience. This move leaves logical positivism's criterion of meaning less rigorous but more acceptable, so that even Copleston can propose an acceptable version of it. Ayer raises a useful objection against this variant, however, in pointing out that Copleston is not prepared to provide any criterion for a recognition that does not involve sensible observation. Copleston's suggestion is fruitful, that the meaningfulness of an idea is a function of its being formed from an experiential basis rather than of its actual verification; but Ayer is correct that Copleston, with his talk of "intellectual intuition," fails to provide any clear standards of (even imaginative) identification such as are needed to ground any knowledge-claims. Finally, Copleston's logical dilemma aimed against Ayer's principle of verification is not merely a clever parting shot, but it effectively highlights the stipulative nature of this principle.

Each participant in the two debates does an impressive job of challenging the other's position and focusing on its points of vulnerability. Both debates provide valuable contexts in which the traditional perspective of philosophical theology can collide with that of contemporary analytic philosophy. The pivot point around which each debate revolves is the alleged meaningfulness or meaninglessness of religious language. Let us now see how this issue is played out, beginning with the challenges posed in Ayer's most celebrated book and in a provocative position paper by Antony Flew.

God-talk

Challenges to Theological Language. The challenges of Ayer and Flew to the meaningfulness of theological language hinge on demands for verification and falsification. In *Language, Truth and Logic*, his classic presentation of logical positivism, Ayer clearly aligns himself with the analytic tradition of Russell, which is derived from the empiricism of earlier British philosophers:

> Like Hume, I divide all genuine propositions into two classes: those which, in his terminology, concern "relations of ideas," and those which concern "matters of fact."

Like Hume, he holds that the former are "the *a priori* propositions of logic and pure mathematics," whose certainty and necessity are due to their being analytic. He considers the latter, by contrast, to be entirely "hypotheses, which can be probable but never certain," and he describes his view as "a thoroughgoing phenomenalism," saying that the philosophers of his own day with whom he identifies are those "commonly known as logical positivists."[21]

It is significant that the first chapter of Ayer's book is entitled "The Elimination of Metaphysics" and that it attacks the notion "that philosophy affords us knowledge of a reality transcending the world of science and common sense." Even a metaphysician must rest his arguments on premises derived from experience. If those premises are empirically anchored in sensation, then no allegedly "super-empirical" conclusions could be shown to follow from them. Yet Ayer realizes that a metaphysician (such as Copleston, for example) would wish to deny

> that his assertions were ultimately based on the evidence of his senses. He would say that he was endowed with a faculty of intellectual intuition which enabled him to know facts that could not be known through sense-experience.

But Ayer undercuts the entire dispute about his alleged capacity for "intellectual intuition" by holding that such a faculty, even if it did exist, could never yield any cognitively significant "statement which refers to a 'reality' transcending the limits of all possible sense-experience."[22]

He correctly points out that, "although Kant also condemned transcendent metaphysics" as an area of possible knowledge, Kant's critique was not "a matter of logic, but a matter of fact." Ayer is not merely saying that we happen to be so constituted that metaphysical knowledge is not available to us; he wants to deny its very possibility. He bases this denial, of course, on his verification criterion of meaning:

> We say that a sentence is factually significant to any given person, if, and only if, he knows how to verify the proposition which it purports to express—that is, if he knows what observations would lead him, under certain conditions, to accept the proposition as being true, or reject it as being false.

Yet he holds that any sentence whose "putative proposition is of such a character that the assumption of its truth, or falsehood, is consistent with any assumption whatsoever concerning . . . future experience" can be dismissed as either an empty tautology or "a mere pseudo-proposition." If the latter, it cannot be "literally significant," no matter how "emotionally significant" it may be to anyone.[23]

Ayer allows for "verifiability in principle" here. When he wrote the book in 1935, it was not technologically possible for anyone to verify "the proposition that there are mountains on the farther side of the moon." Yet we knew quite well what sort of observations could conclusively settle the issue, once we achieved the technological capacity to make them. Thus, even in 1935 Ayer was willing to say "that the proposition is verifiable in principle, if not in practice, and is accordingly significant," literally. He also allows for a "weak" sense of verification, whereby conceivable "relevant" observations can render a statement "probable" rather than "conclusively established" or "definitively confutable by experience." Indeed, he holds that all informative, significant statements are more or less probable hypotheses. Thus, he concludes that

> the question that must be asked about any putative statement of fact is not, Would any observations make its truth or falsehood logically certain? but simply, Would any observations be relevant to the determination of its truth or falsehood? And it is only if a negative answer is given to this second question that we conclude that the statement under consideration is nonsensical.[24]

It is precisely metaphysical assertions—including those of theology—which are so dismissed, since they are used neither for the purpose of expressing a mere tautology nor for that of advancing any empirical hypothesis.

Ayer applies all this to generate his critique of theology. When the philosophy of religion attempts to demonstrate God's existence, it requires premises that are known as certain, because otherwise the conclusion of the argument could never be presented as certain. But the only certain statements are *a priori* propositions, and these cannot establish anything about matters of fact and existence since they are mere tautologies. Only empirical propositions are relevant to matters of fact and existence. Yet Ayer insists that "no empirical proposition can ever be anything more than probable," since all empirical propositions are allegedly hypotheses. Thus, whether our premises are *a priori* or empirical, they are supposedly incapable of "demonstrating the existence of a god." Second, Ayer goes on to deny that we can ever prove that God's existence "is even probable." To say that "God probably exists" is to express "a metaphysical utterance which cannot be either true or false." The reason for this is that any true or false statement must be cognitively significant, as this one allegedly cannot be because it violates the verification criterion of meaning. Third, "by the same criterion, no sentence which purports to describe the nature of a transcendent god can possess any literal significance."[25] If Ayer is correct, philosophical theology is doomed to frustration and failure since nothing can be established regarding God.

Ayer is quick to distinguish his own position from both agnosticism and atheism.

> For it is characteristic of an agnostic to hold that the existence of a god is a pos-sibility in which there is no good reason either to believe or disbelieve; and it is characteristic of an atheist to hold that it is at least probable that no god exists.

Ayer's view is "actually incompatible" with all claims regarding even the possibility or impossibility of God's existence. He also tries to identify his position with one of orthodox theism:

> For we are often told that the nature of God is a mystery which transcends the human understanding. But to say that something transcends the human under-standing is to say that it is unintelligible.

This, Ayer holds, is equivalent to denying that it is cognitively signifi-cant. He also tries to connect his position with the orthodox view (for example, of Kierkegaard) that "God is not an object of reason but an object of faith."[26] However, against Ayer, we might observe that ortho-dox Christian theologians do not typically wish to dismiss God-talk as nonsensical, even when they insist that God transcends human experi-ence, is an object of faith rather than of rational knowledge, and cannot be adequately described by means of univocally significant religious lan-guage. This is because they see faith and reason as overlapping rather than as utterly divorced.

In 1946, Ayer wrote an introduction to the second edition of his book in which he admits that key aspects of his theory "call for some further explanation" but insists that "the point of view which it expresses is substantially correct." He has found a simpler way of formulating his "principle of verification"—namely, that a sentence has "literal meaning" if and only if the statement it is expressing is "either analytic or empirically verifiable." He admits that "the word 'meaning' is commonly used in a variety of senses," not all of which correspond to his sort of "literal meaning" or "factual meaning." Thus, it might seem dogmatic of him to insist that "a statement can properly be said to be either true or false" only if it satisfies his criterion of meaning. After all, he is stipulating what does and what does not count as cognitively meaningful. His response is that, "while I wish the principle of verification itself to be regarded, not as an empirical hypothesis, but as a definition, it is not supposed to be entirely arbitrary."[27] Unfortunately, despite this assertion, he fails to show that it should not be so regarded.

A few years after the publication of the second edition of Ayer's book, a little symposium paper by Antony Flew (an English philosopher born in 1923) appeared, called "Theology and Falsification." He begins with a parable, derived from John Wisdom's article, "Gods," about two explorers who discover a clearing in the jungle in which "many flowers and many weeds" were growing. One of them imagines that there must be a gardener who tends the plot, while the other denies it. They camp there and set up watch to decide the issue, yet never behold any gardener. The believer explains that it might be an invisible gardener; yet an electrified, barbed-wire fence and roving bloodhounds never indicate any evidence. The believer remains steadfast in his conviction, driving the skeptic to wonder aloud what conceivable difference there is between the believer's gardener and a figment of the imagination. Like a pragmatist (such as William James), the positivistic skeptic demands that beliefs make some pragmatic difference. The idea that there is some "gardener" who is identifiable by some normal means is interesting; but once it has been hedged and mitigated to the point where it can no longer make any practical difference, it becomes worthless from this point of view. As Flew strikingly puts it, "A fine brash hypothesis may thus be killed by inches, the death by a thousand qualifications."[28]

Flew contends that all uses of religious language which are compatible with any conceivable state of affairs—in other words, which are nonfalsifiable—are pseudoassertions. Even when theological utterances are used analogously (in the manner advocated by such different thinkers as

Aquinas and Kant), they must pass this test. The statement, "God loves us as a father loves his children," for example, looks like an assertion; and the person uttering it may, no doubt, intend it as an assertion. But, Flew maintains, "to assert that such and such is the case is necessarily equivalent to denying that such and such is not the case." On this view, a way to resolve doubt as to whether or not a speaker is uttering a genuine assertion "is to attempt to find what he would regard as counting against, or as being incompatible with, its truth."[29] If nothing could conceivably count against its truth—as is allegedly the case with the believer's utterance about a gardener—then it is a pseudoassertion.

Flew suspects this is the case with theological utterances. "We are reassured" to hear that "God loves us as a father loves his children." Yet how can we reconcile this notion with the reality of "a child dying of inoperable cancer of the throat"? We cannot help observing that the child's "earthly father is driven frantic in his efforts to help, but his Heavenly Father reveals no obvious sign of concern." Nor does Flew's sarcasm subside in the face of attempted qualifications that hold that God's love is different from "a merely human love" and is "an inscrutable love," because it doesn't seem to allow any sort of guarantees at all. He ends his little paper with a challenge:

> Just what would have to happen . . . to entitle us to say "God does not love us" or even "God does not exist"? I therefore put to the succeeding symposiasts the simple central questions, "What would have to occur or to have occurred to constitute for you a disproof of the love of, or of the existence of, God?"[30]

Although the manner of expression is different from Ayer's, Flew is issuing the same positivistic challenge against the very meaningfulness of theological language.

Radical Responses to Positivism. Radical responses to the challenges of positivism can be found in works by Hare and Braithwaite. These are "radical" responses in the sense that they agree that theological utterances are unfalsifiable and therefore not cognitive assertions at all. Richard M. Hare (an English philosopher from Oxford University, born in 1919) was among the symposiasts, to whom Flew was referring, who were to respond to his challenge. In defense of religion, Hare writes, "I must begin by confessing that, on the ground marked out by Flew, he seems to me to be completely victorious." Not wishing to hold that religious utterances are genuine assertions, Hare signals a shift of interpretation and offers an alternative parable of a lunatic who is convinced that all "dons" (tutors) want to murder him. Despite his meeting "the mildest and most respectable" dons, who never give the slightest indication of wishing to harm him in any way, the lunatic replies that they are so diabolically cunning that they never give themselves away. No amount or kind of evidence can sway the lunatic from his conviction, and we consider him "deluded." On Flew's grounds, his deluded theory about malevolent dons "asserts nothing" since no possible evidence will count against it.

> But it does not follow that there is no difference between what he thinks about dons and what most of us think about them—otherwise we should not call him a lunatic and ourselves sane, and dons would have no reason to feel uneasy about his presence.[31]

But then how should we interpret such a nonassertional theory which nevertheless makes an obvious difference in the context of human experience? Hare says, "Let us call that in which we differ from this lunatic, our respective *bliks*. He has an insane *blik* about dons; we have a sane one. It is important to realize that we have a sane one, not no *blik* at all." Although Flew is correct that such a "*blik*" is not an assertion, Hare adds, "nevertheless it is very important to have the right *blik*." And its importance is a function of its practical significance in our lives. Hare points out that our "*bliks*" can refer to everyday objects of use, such as automobiles. I can easily imagine what it would be like for the steering mechanism of an automobile to fail completely. It has never happened to me before, nor am I acquainted with anyone to whom it has happened. But how do I know it will not occur the next time I go for a drive?

> The truth is, I don't know; I just have a *blik* about steel and its properties, so that normally I trust the steering of my car; but I find it not at all difficult to imagine what it would be like to lose this *blik* and acquire the opposite one. People would say I was silly about steel.[32]

The notion of trust or the lack of it seems to be essential to Hare's concept of a "*blik*." This is why it has a practical significance, even if it fails the positivist criterion of falsifiability (or verifiability). He finds something like this concept in David Hume's view that our fundamental attitudes toward our world cannot be conclusively established or refuted by factual observation but rather underlie the way we interpret our observations. Although Hume does not specifically refer to what Hare calls a "*blik*," the concept does illuminate what Hume says, for example, of our beliefs in causality, order in the universe, and even God. "The mistake of the position which Flew selects for attack is to regard this kind of talk as some sort of *explanation*." Hume was more perceptive in viewing what Hare calls a "*blik*" as rather the foundation on which all explanations must be built.[33] Thus, on this interpretation, belief in God is not itself an explanation of anything, but rather a fundamental attitude toward reality and experience that provides a context within which explanations can be formulated.

Hare correctly points out "an important difference" between his examples and Flew's parable of the two explorers in the jungle.

> The explorers do not *mind* about their garden; they discuss it with interest, but not with concern. But my lunatic, poor fellow, minds about dons; and I mind about the steering of my car; it often has people in it that I care for.[34]

What Flew misses is the element of existential involvement in one's beliefs that gives Hare's "*bliks*" a practical significance. They need not meet Ayer's verification criterion of cognitive meaningfulness or Flew's falsification criterion of genuine assertions to be significant.

Richard B. Braithwaite (an English philosopher, born in 1900, from Cambridge University) offers another radical response to the challenge of positivism in *An Empiricist's View of the Nature of Religious Belief*, published in 1955. Like Hare, he defends the significance of religious utterances while conceding to Ayer and Flew that they do not communicate statements of fact or scientific explanations or logically necessary truths. Braithwaite admits that the verification principle of meaning "is in complete accord with contemporary philosophy of science, to which those following "the empiricist tradition in British philosophy," from Locke through Hume to Russell, must be respectful. He denies that religious utterances fall into any of the three categories of expressions to which that principle most clearly applies, namely, "statements about particular matters of empirical fact, scientific hypotheses . . . , and the logically necessary statements of logic and mathematics (and their contradictories)." First, they are not statements "about particular empirical facts," because they are not "testable by direct observation." Second, they are not "scientific hypotheses," since they are not "refutable by experience." Third, they do not "resemble the propositions of logic and mathematics in being logically necessary," because they purport to "assert existence" regarding God.[35] Thus, religious utterances cannot be shown to be meaningful in the ways appropriate to any of these three classes of statements.

But does it follow, as the logical positivists claim, that uses of theological language are meaningless pseudoassertions and that we should, in the spirit of Hume, "commit them to the flames"? Braithwaite points out (what Ayer admitted) that moral principles would be subject to the same verdict. This observation suggests that the positivist criterion of meaning is too narrow. "For moral statements have a use in guiding conduct; and if they have a use they surely have a meaning—in some sense of meaning." Thus, Braithwaite prefers Ludwig Wittgenstein's principle over that of the positivists, that "the meaning of any statement is given by the way in which it is used." He claims this "use principle" incorporates the "older verificational principle," in that the latter defines the way in which some—but not all—meaningful expressions are used. So what can be said about the use—and hence the meaning—of theological language? "The kernel for an empiricist of the problem of the nature of religious belief is to explain, in empirical terms, how a religious statement is used by a man who asserts it in order to express his religious conviction."[36]

Since Braithwaite wants to argue that a religious utterance fundamentally "is used as a moral assertion," he needs to explain "how moral assertions are used." Unlike Ayer and other logical positivists, he does not believe that moral assertions are essentially expressions of feeling. Instead they allegedly express the will to act in certain ways under certain circumstances, he says, adopting "a conative rather than an emotive theory" of ethics. This view of how moral assertions are used, he adds,

> is fully in accord with the spirit of empiricism, for whether or not a man has the intention of pursuing a particular behavior policy can be empirically tested, both by observing what he does and by hearing what he replies when he is questioned about his intentions.

When expressions of intentions to act are made as general policies of action or as instances of such general policies, Braithwaite calls them "moral assertions."[37]

He holds that the use of religious language essentially involves such "moral assertions," committing the user to adopt a particular sort of policy of action. As he says,

> The view which I put forward for your consideration is that the intention of a Christian to follow a Christian way of life is not only the criterion for the sincerity of his belief in the assertions of Christianity; it is the criterion for the meaningfulness of his assertions.

On this view, any given religious system, such as Judaism or Christianity, will comprise a "body of assertions . . . specifying a particular way of life." Thus, the assertions of Christianity are epitomized by the claim "that God is love (*agape*)"; and any Christian who maintains this can "be taken to declare his intention to follow an agapeistic way of life"—that is, to commit himself to a policy of loving conduct. The meaning of any given set of religious assertions, on this view, is a function of the "principles of conduct the asserter takes the assertions to involve," and these are revealed by physical and verbal behavior. So far Braithwaite is claiming "that the primary use of religious assertions is to announce allegiance to a set of moral principles." He adds that religious assertions typically concern internal as well as external behavior, that Christianity, for example, calls for a commitment to "an agapeistic frame of mind"[38] or an attitude of love toward others.

But there is still something missing in this account. For two or more different religious traditions may be committed to basically the same policy of action. For instance, Braithwaite admits that Judaism and certain forms of Buddhism may be as committed to "an agapeistic way of life" as is Christianity. And this possibility presents a problem:

> How then can religious assertions be distinguished into those which are Christian, those which are Jewish, those which are Buddhist, by the policies of life which they respectively recommend if, on examination, these policies turn out to be the same?

He offers a plausible, even ingenious, solution to this problem. Each religious tradition identifies its moral teachings with its own unique story or set of stories, the stories of Jesus providing a different paradigm from those of Buddha. Here is a crucial distinction between religion and (non-religious) morality: "A religious assertion will, therefore, have a propositional element which is lacking in a purely moral assertion, in that it will refer to a story as well as to an intention." It is not necessary, he adds, for the persons making religious assertions "to believe in the truth of the story involved" in them; all that is necessary "is that the story should be entertained in thought" by the person making them.[39]

On this view, people who subscribe to a Christian code of conduct (for example, the "agapeistic way of life") can regard Jesus as their model, thinking in terms of the examples of Christian stories, without literally believing that Jesus was divine as well as human, chose to suffer and die to redeem man's sins, rose from the dead three days later, and so forth. Braithwaite's point is well taken to the extent that we do not have to believe in a story literally to find it psychologically inspiring.

Even when a religious person does believe a story or set of stories, this belief is not reducible to statements of fact or empirically testable hypotheses or logically necessary propositions. As Braithwaite says, in summary of his view,

> A religious assertion, for me, is the assertion of an intention to carry out a certain behavior policy, subsumable under a sufficiently general principle to be a

> moral one, together with the implicit or explicit statement, but not the asser-
> tion, of certain stories. Neither the assertion of the intention nor the reference
> to the stories

involves belief of the sort that is amenable to the positivist's criterion of meaning, however.[40]

The views of both Hare and Braithwaite evade the challenges of positivism by admitting that theological language does not essentially involve statements that are empirically or logically verifiable or falsifiable. Both argue for a different kind of meaning that is a function of its practical implications. Thus, both defend the meaningfulness of religious discourse. Yet both are radical in that they disavow the need for any literally intended claims about matters of fact. Neither Hare's "*blik*" nor Braithwaite's "religious assertion" makes any empirical claims about whatever has been, is, or ever will be the case as a matter of fact. Both rather involve basic attitudes guiding action.

Orthodox Responses to Positivism. Orthodox responses to the challenges of positivism can be found in writings by Mitchell and Hick. Unlike Hare and Braithwaite, they try to defend religious assertions as making factual claims and therefore as cognitively significant in a traditional sense. Basil Mitchell (an English philosopher from Oxford University, born in 1917) was one of the original symposiasts responding to Flew's article, which he calls "searching and perceptive." Yet he criticizes it for ignoring the problem of evil, which recognizes that "the fact of pain counts against the assertion that God loves men." Unlike Flew's explorers, the religious believer is not a "detached observer" but cares about the suffering in the world's garden. The traditional problem of evil is a problem for the believer precisely because suffering obviously counts against his belief in the perfect, infinite God of monotheistic theology. "But it is true that he will not allow it—or anything—to count decisively against it; for he is committed by his faith to trust in God."[41]

Mitchell offers his own alternative parable to help illustrate this crucial distinction between "counting against" faith and having something "count decisively against" belief. He asks us to imagine a wartime situation in an occupied country, in which a partisan member of a resistance group meets a strikingly impressive stranger with whom he talks all night.

> The Stranger tells the partisan that he himself is on the side of the resistance—
> indeed that he is in command of it, and urges the partisan to have faith in him
> no matter what happens. The partisan is utterly convinced at that meeting of
> the Stranger's sincerity and constancy and undertakes to trust him.

They never again get together in such intimate circumstances. Subsequently, the Stranger is sometimes observed helping the resistance but at other times "is seen in the uniform of the police handing over patriots to the occupying power." Despite the latter observations, the partisan remains steadfast in his faith that it is all part of the Stranger's plan for the ultimate victory of the resistance. On several occasions, the partisan requests help of the Stranger; sometimes the requested assistance is given, but at other times it is not. On the latter occasions, the partisan assures himself, "The Stranger knows best." Meanwhile, the partisan's exasperated colleagues demand, "Well, what *would* he have to do for you to admit that you were wrong and that he is not on our side?" But there is no clear-cut answer possible. The partisan realizes that "the Stranger's ambiguous behaviour *does* count against" his being an ally. But he "does not allow anything to count decisively against the proposition 'The Stranger is on our side.' This is because he has committed himself to trust the Stranger."[42]

In Mitchell's parable the partisan represents the religious believer, the mysterious Stranger is God, the overnight meeting is religious experience, and the actions that count against the Stranger's being "on our side" stand for the evil, pain, and suffering in our world. It is impossible to say what it would take for the partisan to lose faith in the Stranger; but unless and until he does, he will not allow anything to count decisively against the Stranger's being "on our side." Likewise for as long as religious believers are committed to faith in God, they allow nothing to count decisively against God's love for humanity.

Mitchell points out a crucial difference between his view and Hare's: "The partisan admits that many things may and do count against his belief: whereas Hare's lunatic who has a *blik* about dons doesn't admit that anything counts against his *blik*. Nothing can count against *bliks*." Thus, for Mitchell, as against Hare, "theological utterances must be assertions. The partisan is making an assertion when he says, 'The Stranger is on our side.'" Likewise, the religious believer is making an assertion in saying that "God loves humanity." Mitchell considers such assertions, although not "conclusively falsifiable," to be explanations in some sense. The partisan's belief is used to explain the behavior of the mysterious Stranger. Similarly, the religious believer's faith is used to make sense of experience and reality. Such assertions, for the believer, function neither as "provisional hypotheses to be discarded if experience tells against them" nor as "vacuous formulae" to which experience is irrelevant and which are disconnected from life; they are rather "significant articles of faith" to which the believer is personally committed.[43]

John Hick (an English philosophical theologian born in 1922), like Braithwaite, prepared an influential response to logical positivism's challenge against the meaningfulness of religious language in the 1950s, without having been one of the original symposiasts immediately answering Flew. Hick's response appeared first in his 1957 book *Faith and Knowledge*, then, more succinctly, in a splendid paper, "Theology and Verification," first published in early 1960. Although he specifically addresses Flew rather than Ayer, as the title of his paper indicates, he ends up defending the possibility of verification rather than of falsification. He wants to face the problem squarely, acknowledging that theism appears to its critics to be "compatible with whatever may occur. But if this is so, we must ask: Does theism constitute a genuine assertion?" Further, he praises Flew for having "posed the question in a characteristically forthright and challenging way."[44]

Hick begins his article by pointing to the vagueness of the question of whether God's existence is verifiable. Not only is the very concept of verification imprecise, so that on some understandings of the term something might be verifiable, whereas on others it might not. But, further, "There are many different concepts of God, and it may be that statements employing some of them are open to verification or falsification while statements employing others are not." He proposes to argue that the existence of God, understood in accordance with the Christian concept of divinity, is verifiable in principle, holding that verification is essentially "the removal of ignorance or uncertainty concerning the truth of some proposition." When this is accomplished, an issue becomes "settled so that there is no longer room for rational doubt concerning it."[45] Thus, we see that Hick (like Mitchell and unlike Hare and Braithwaite) will treat God's existence as essentially a matter of fact and expressions concerning it as empirically meaningful assertions.

Hick notes that verification and falsification are usually "symmetrically related." The testing procedures that would verify a proposition, such as "There is a table in the next room," are the same as those that might falsify it—for example, going in there and looking around. Many of the thinkers considered in this section have focused on falsification as the more accessible of the operations in dealing with divine existence. As Hick writes,

> Antony Flew and others have raised instead of the question, "What possible experiences would verify 'God exists'?" the matching question "What possible experiences would falsify 'God exists'? what conceivable state of affairs would be incompatible with the existence of God?"

But Hick shrewdly points out that they are not always so symmetrical. "The hypothesis of continued conscious existence after bodily death," for example, involves a prediction which one could personally verify if it were true but which no one could falsify if it were not.

> That is to say, it can be false, but *that* it is false can never be a fact which anyone has experientially verified. But this circumstance does not undermine the meaningfulness of the hypothesis, since it is also such that if it be true, it will be known to be true.

Hick then points out that it should not be identified with a process of proving "logically necessary truths," since verification, by its very nature, deals with "only propositions concerning matters of fact." The best we can legitimately expect here is evidence sufficient "to exclude rational doubt."[46]

Having thus analyzed the concept of verification, Hick proceeds to make a case for the possibility of "**eschatological** verification" of the existence of the God of Christianity by telling a parable: "Two men are travelling together along a road. One of them believes that it leads nowhere; but since this is the only road there is, both must travel it." They are both completely unfamiliar with their surroundings and have no way of anticipating what lies ahead at any particular time in their journey. They encounter both pleasant and painful experiences along the way. The believer interprets the former as encouragements and the latter as tests of faith, whereas the skeptic "sees their journey as an unavoidable and aimless ramble," simply enjoying the pleasurable experiences and enduring the painful ones. They meaningfully disagree about what, if anything, awaits them at the end of the road (assuming there is one), being divided by "genuinely rival assertions" rather than by merely different feelings about their common experience. Likewise, the theist and the atheist meaningfully disagree regarding whether the road of human life will end with our natural death or whether that in turn will lead us to a supernatural experience of God. They can share the same experiences of and expectations about this life as they travel down the road.

> But the theist does and the atheist does not expect that when history is completed it will be seen to have led to a particular end-state and to have fulfilled a specific purpose, namely that of creating "children of God."

This is Hick's "idea of an eschatological verification of theism."[47]

It presupposes the meaningfulness of the notion of our having life-after-death experiences. To defend the intelligibility of this hypothesis, Hick offers us three scenarios for critical consideration. In the first, he asks us to imagine a person "at some learned gathering in this country" disappearing "suddenly and inexplicably" and "at the same moment an exact replica of him" appearing just as "suddenly and inexplicably" at a similar meeting in Australia. Puzzling though the phenomenon would be, he would think of himself as the same person; and we too would have to admit that "there is everything that would lead us to identify the one who appeared with the one who disappeared, except continuity of occupancy of space. In his second scenario, Hick asks us to imagine that, instead of disappearing, the person suddenly dies here in America. "Only, at the moment when the individual dies, a replica of him as he was at the moment before his death, complete with memory up to that instant, appears in Australia." This is more bizarre than the first scenario because of the presence of a dead body here in America. Yet, again, we would find ourselves driven to admit that "the same person who died has been miraculously recreated in Australia." In his third scenario, Hick asks us to imagine that after dying, "the replica, complete with memory, etc., appears not in Australia, but as a resurrection replica in a different world altogether, a resurrection world inhabited by resurrected persons." The person recalls the experience of what he took to be dying and supposes that at some point he became unconscious. "But how does he know that (to put it Irishly) his 'dying' proved fatal; and that he did not, after losing consciousness, begin to recover strength, and has now simply waked up?" Well, he encounters several friends, relatives, and people from prior history whom he knows to be dead and who report to him that he has just arrived in their world. Such inductive grounds, Hick adds, could accumulate "to the point at which they are quite as strong as the evidence which, in pictures one and two, convince the individual in question that he has been miraculously translated to Australia."[48]

Though these three scenarios admittedly strain the credulity of those of us who are empirically minded, there is nothing self-contradictory about any of them. We can imagine, at least to some extent, what it might be like for these thought experiments to be realized. Thus, unless we are already committed to the idea that verification (and falsification) must be achieved in this life and in accordance with previously established patterns of experience, there is no good reason to dismiss any of them as necessarily meaningless.

Yet mere survival after physical death is not yet sufficient to establish the meaningfulness of God's existence and the verifiability of theism, even if it is plausible. In connection with Hick's parable of the two men traveling together on a road, we can observe that two people who survived their own bodily deaths and were transported to another realm might still disagree about the existence of God. So Hick must go further to defend the verifiability of theism.

To do so, he suggests a combination of two possible experiences which

> would assure us beyond rational doubt of the reality of God, as conceived in the Christian faith. These are, *first*, an experience of the fulfillment of God's purpose for ourselves, as this has been disclosed in the Christian revelation; in conjunction, *second*, with an experience of communion with God as he has revealed himself in the person of Christ.

Nor need we know fully in advance the specific form that such fulfillment and communion are to take, any more than a small child must know before adulthood what it will be like in order to be able to recognize it when he has reached it. Indeed, Hick suggests, we may (like the child approaching adulthood) achieve a progressively better understanding of this supernatural destiny as we move in its direction.[49] At any rate, if he is correct, it is conceivable that we could survive our own physical deaths, know that we had done so, and experience both the fulfillment of what Christianity teaches is God's plan for us and communion with God as revealed through Christ. This would be tantamount to an eschatological verification of theistic belief. Thus, Hick believes that he has met the positivist's challenge of verification; and religious language has allegedly been shown, at least to this extent, to be meaningful.

A Critique of These Challenges and Responses. An evaluation of these challenges and responses must consider both the verification and falsification perspectives on theological language. This discussion will consist of two phases: first, a consideration of whether any compelling reason has been offered by Ayer or Flew for accepting the positivist criterion of meaning and what alternative might be preferable; and, then, a critique of the various responses to the positivist challenges that we have examined.

The main problem with the positivist criterion of meaning—whether in its verification or its falsification form—is that it dogmatically stipulates a standard of linguistic meaningfulness which is narrower than our ordinary usage. Granted that any utterance which is, in principle, verifiable or falsifiable can be cognitively significant. But why should we agree that *only* such utterances can be? The positivist's claim that such is the case is not itself verifiable or falsifiable but merely expresses a rule for what will be allowed to count as meaningful.

Why accept such a rule? Most of us would presumably agree with Copleston that his assertion concerning atomic warfare that will destroy all human life is meaningful, even though it rules out the possibility of any natural human verification or falsification. This is because, as Copleston indicates, we imaginatively identify a possible scenario with ideas derived from past experience.

But this seems to indicate that Braithwaite is correct in arguing that the criterion of linguistic significance we actually employ is broader than, though it includes, the criteria of positivism. It does seem to be something like Wittgenstein's principle that meaning is a function of usage. We use theological assertions to formulate and communicate ideas about God which are imaginatively related (by analogy, as Aquinas and Kant would say) to our past experience.

Thus, people who do not believe in current divine intervention in the natural order or mystical experience or life after death can still meaningfully think and speak of God by means of language drawn from previous experience. When they say that God designed the universal order in which humanity has evolved and cares about its welfare, their language leans on our experience of human design and caring for its significance. Even if we agree with them that no verification or falsification of the assertion will ever be forthcoming, we neither regard the assertion as gibberish nor reduce it to mere emotive connotations. Our sympathetic sense of how they are using language, which is grounded in our own comparable experience, provides us with some cognitive understanding of what they mean. This is because we share their use of the language without having to be committed to the possible verification or falsification of the assertion.

Let us now turn to an evaluation of the four responses to the challenges of Ayer and Flew. At the end of his symposium Flew had the opportunity to react to the perspectives of Hare and Mitchell. What he says against Hare not only seems correct but applies as well to Braithwaite's position. He points out that the analysis of "religious utterances as expressions or assertions" of attitudes (whether these be construed as Hare's "*bliks*" or as Braithwaite's commitments to a policy of action) "rather than as (at least would-be) assertions about the cosmos is fundamentally misguided." It is an "entirely unorthodox" conception of the way in which theological language is actually used by religious believers.[50]

The orthodox responses of Mitchell and Hick avoid this problem. Flew admits that Mitchell is correct in insisting that theism does traditionally allow "the problem of evil" to "count against" its assertions (or pseudoassertions) about God without acknowledging any incompatibility. The problem is that the God of Christianity, unlike Mitchell's mysterious Stranger, is omnipotent, omniscient, and perfectly good. Thus, the search for an explanation as to why God allows evil in the world inevitably slips into "the avoiding action of *qualification*."[51] It does not seem that Mitchell can ever offer a threshold beyond which what "counts against" belief in God will rationally "count decisively against" it. As long as religious believers maintain their faith commitment, they will not accept anything as falsifying their theological utterances. Flew is correct in arguing that they can always find some vague, speculative qualification that will save them.

Hick's response seems more satisfying. If we accept the sort of imaginative verification, related to past experience, that Copleston recommended, then Hick's "eschatological verification" seems adequate to confer meaning on (though not necessarily knowledge of) some religious doctrines. Although neither Ayer nor Flew allows for relevant experiences after death, as long as we can imagine what they might be like, there is no conclusive reason why our ideas of such experiences cannot be accepted as meaningful. This approach ties in well with the views of those religious traditions (such as Christianity) which link theological doctrines with thoughts of our supernatural destiny. Hick offers, however, not only a plausible response to the challenges of positivism, but a broader philosophy of religion of which it is a component part. Let us examine this next.

Hick

Faith and Knowledge. Hick's views on faith and knowledge are carefully presented in his first book, published in 1957, and are developed further in some of his later writings. The book, *Faith and Knowledge*, focuses on "a central problem in the epistemology of religion, namely the problem of the nature of religious faith." Hick holds that both the epistemological use of "faith" (*fides*), as indicating cognitive significance, and its nonepistemological use (*fiducia*), as indicating personal trust, are legitimate and that the latter logically presupposes the former; thus he is primarily concerned with "faith as cognition." The traditional cognitive view that we have inherited from medieval times (he calls it the "Scholastic view") is explicitly propositional: "Faith consists in assent to certain propositions which are believed to have been revealed by God." Hick cites Locke as a modern example of this conception of faith; but, in fact, it is the view that has dominated philosophical theology in the medieval and modern periods. The problem with it is that it rests on two presuppositions, both of which critically require justification: "(a) that there is a God and (b) that he has made the revelations alleged."[52]

Thus, we find Aquinas trying to demonstrate the "preambles" of faith as a foundation for "believing religious truths because they have been divinely revealed." Hick denies that "this scholastic conception of faith" captures the essence of the "vivid compelling sense" of divine presence and activity experienced by religious prophets, saints, and martyrs. "In fact Thomism was really describing the faith, not of the great religious geniuses, but of the simple medieval lay believer whose religion was essentially obedience to the church."[53] But at least this is a cognitive approach which seriously strives to establish objective truth.

By contrast, voluntarist theories of faith, as represented by Pascal's "Wager" passage and William James's "Will to Believe" argument, try to characterize it as a calculated kind of betting. On this view, we can have no compelling objective evidence for or against God and should opt for whatever belief(s) we think will offer us the most pragmatic payoff.

> But this again is remote from the state of mind of such men as the great prophets. They did not think of themselves as making a wager. They would never have granted the premiss that we cannot know whether God is real and therefore have to treat the question as a gamble.[54]

Hick's most general and most accessible philosophical book, *Philosophy of Religion*, contains a section on "Voluntarist Theories of Faith," in which he takes to task both Pascal and James. The former presupposes "an anthropomorphic (and to many people very unattractive) conception of God" and "assumes that God will be pleased by such a calculating and self-regarding attitude" as human belief deliberately adopted for the sake of a payoff. Hick finds James's view artificial and static, out of line, for example with "the kind of living religious faith that finds expression in the Bible." Second, despite James's attempts to limit his "Will to Believe" argument to genuine options that are not susceptible to any objective evidence, Hick worries that the view "constitutes an unrestricted license for wishful thinking." Finally, there is the problem of pragmatism's reduction of truth to utility: "The fruitfulness of a belief or of faith for the moral and religious life is one thing, and the reality or existence of what is ideated and assumed is another."[55] If anything, the voluntarist conception of faith seems even less acceptable than the traditional propositional view, and Hick must seek another alternative.

Hick argues against the traditional view of knowledge, which has dominated Western thought since "the time of Plato," as the "direct and infallible acquaintance with 'reality' (in ancient philosophy) or with 'truth' (in modern philosophy)." Since Descartes, this quest for certainty has focused on "propositions as the supposed objects of human knowledge" and has engendered the dogma that "to know anything is equivalent to being able to prove it." Not only is this view, which Hick labels "the infallibilist theory or definition of knowledge," dogmatic, but it is also counterproductive; for there is hardly any knowledge of this sort available to us. From this perspective, knowledge becomes an ideal out of "contact with common human experience"; almost everything (as Hume has argued) becomes relegated "to an inferior status of 'beliefs,'" so that skepticism is actually promoted rather than overcome. Furthermore, ordinary knowledge-claims at the level of common sense and science cannot be justified in the infallibilist sense. Even the intuitions of private sense data and our own mental states must be interpreted and fail to "yield knowledge of the structure and character of the world" apart from those interpretations. And our apprehension of analytic truths merely provides a cognition of "linguistic conventions," rather than conveying any factual information about reality. So in none of these areas can we seem to find knowledge that is "genuinely informative as well as certain."[56] This suggests that we should abandon the infallibilist model of knowing as an unreachable ideal.

Hick therefore seeks a "more modest" sense of knowledge. However, it must retain at least an element of psychological certainty. He approvingly quotes Locke's identification of knowledge and certainty, holding that the term "knowledge" must "not refer to a merely casual absence of doubt but to a stable and tested certainty which has withstood critical scrutiny." Hick admits that no precise amount of "critical scrutiny" can be specified as "necessary to constitute rational certainty." Although this might seem rather subjective, he argues that such "knowledge" is "objective in the sense that it is 'the same for everyone.' That which I know is in principle knowable by others." Even so, our very conviction that something "*is* objectively certain is itself a psychological certainty." Thus, although objectivity can sometimes accompany subjective certainty, the latter can never be replaced by the former. Hick points out an advantage implicit in his proposed view of knowledge as "rational certainty" when he writes,

> If we abandon the conception of knowledge as infallible and self-authenticating cognition, in favor of a more empirical description of it as rational certainty, we abandon also the idea that there is any one single and invariable way of coming to know.

He explains that, from this perspective, the ways of our gaining knowledge will be as varied as the possible grounds for "rational certainty; and there are as many types of ground for rational certainty as there are kinds of objects of knowledge."[57] Thus, the old isomorphic model of rationalistic proof no longer has the privileged status it assumed on the infallibilist theory.

In his analysis of "belief," Hick considers the contributions of the modern empiricists, Russell, Hume, and Locke. He quotes Russell as writing, "A belief, we may say, is a collection of states of an organism bound together by all having, in whole or part, the same external reference." But he rejects this analysis as too broad to be helpful since it would allow us to say that "the amoeba absorbing food *believes* that what it consumes is nourishing"; as Hick observes, this is too radical a "departure from normal usage." In our everyday lives we are ordinarily accustomed to believing, or "taking for granted," all sorts of things, which, as Hume noted, "are not arrived at by logical reasoning" and "cannot ultimately be vindicated thereby." Yet, following Locke, Hume tended to think of belief as largely "propositional."[58]

Hick identifies Locke as "the father" of the modern epistemological identification of beliefs with propositions. Locke's definition of belief as "the admitting or receiving any proposition for true" is acceptable to Hick as "a first approximation." But his own "fuller analysis" reveals four dimensions of belief:

> There is the entertainment of a proposition in thought; assent to this proposition, or the adoption or embracing of it as true; a resulting disposition to act, both in thought and in overt deed, upon the adopted proposition; and a disposition to feel an emotion of conviction toward the proposition whenever its truth is challenged.[59]

This is an obviously empirical analysis of the concept of belief.

After developing his theory of knowledge as rational certainty and his empirical analysis of belief, Hick argues for a view of religious faith as a noninferential (and unprovable) basic interpretation of one of the three main orders of situational significance in human experience (the natural, the moral, and the religious). The person of religious faith is not, as such, engaged in logical reasoning. "He professes, not to have inferred that there is a God, but that God as a living being has entered into his own experience." This awareness, far from being detached from ordinary experience, occurs in the context of the person's "material and social environment." It, like the context in which it occurs, is experienced as having a "familiar, intelligible character," which Hick labels "significance." For such is the nature of human consciousness. Here Hick is adopting "the Kantian thesis that we can be aware only of that which enters into a certain framework of basic relations which is correlated with the structure of our own consciousness." And, like a pragmatist (such as James), he holds that significance is practically oriented towards possible action: "Consciousness of a particular kind of environmental significance involves a judgment, implicit or explicit, as to the appropriateness of a particular kind, or range of kinds, of action in relation to that environment."[60] Yet another important fact is that any human experience, in order to become significant, must be interpreted.

Hick points out that there are two related but different meanings of "interpretation," both of which apply to the theistic interpretation of reality. First of all, "an interpretation is a (true or false) *explanation*, answering the question, Why?" For example, God's creative activity provides an interpretation, in this sense, of the fact that our planet is inhabited by persons who are capable of doing good and evil. Second, "an interpretation is a (correct or incorrect) *recognition*, or attribution of significance, answering the question, What?" For instance, God's ongoing relationship to human nature provides an interpretation, in this sense, of the object of religious experience. The experience to be interpreted (in both senses of the word) can never be so abstract as not to be situational or given in the context of "a state of affairs which, when selected for attention . . . , carries its own distinctive practical significance for us."[61] As humans, we typically live in a complex web of overlapping situations.

Yet Hick distinguishes "three main orders of situational significance, corresponding to the threefold division of the universe, long entertained by human thought, into nature, man, and God." The natural order is significant to us as our physical environment; the human world as an arena of moral relationships; and the supernatural realm as that in which we can relate to God. As the human world of moral relationships is "superimposed upon the natural world," so our relationship to the divine is never experienced—in this life, at least—as totally divorced from "the natural and ethical spheres." Further, all of "these three realms, the natural, the human, and the divine," require "a basic act of interpretation" in order to become personally significant. On this view, then, religious faith interprets reality in terms of "the divine presence within the believer's human experience." It involves, at least implicitly, the four dimensions of belief, being "not only a way of cognizing but also, and no less vitally, a way of living." And, although the person of faith may be unable to prove that or "explain *how* he knows the divine presence to be mediated through his human experience," religious interpretations can "qualify, as instances of rational certainty, for the title of knowledge" in as significant a manner as can natural and moral interpretations.[62]

In the early 1960s, Hick chaired a conference of papers, published under the title, *Faith and the Philosophers*. His own contribution, "Sceptics and Believers," probes the issue of how religious experience can be held to be "cognitively veridical" by analyzing the similarities and dissimilarities between it and perceptual experience. There are two main lines of similarity: first, both types of experience involve certain data which must be interpreted in the context of a situation; and, second, in the case of neither sort of experience "can we prove demonstratively, or even show it to be probable, that the object of our 'cognition' exists independently of those states of mind in which we suppose ourselves to be cognizing it." So far, it seems, we are dealing with analogous sorts of experience. But there are also at least three "important differences between sense perception and religious perception" which ought to be acknowledged: first, whereas sense perception is coercive, religious perception is not; second, whereas sense perception is universal among all humans, religious perception is not; and, third, whereas the former is "highly coherent, in that the perceived world exhibits continuity and order both in space and time," by contrast, "the religious awareness of different individuals varies greatly in degree of coherence."[63]

The question is whether these differences suffice to rule out the possibility that human cognition can be based on religious experience as it is on sense experience, and Hick means to defend that possibility. He does so by insisting that the root of all three of these differences is the fact that a person's "own free receptivity or responsiveness plays a part" in his religious consciousness. Nevertheless, "once he *has* become conscious of God that consciousness may possess a coercive and indubitable quality" for him comparable to that of sensory cognition. Second, given the fact that humans are free (rather than forced) to apprehend God's presence, it should not be "surprising that many are entirely or almost entirely without it." Third, "the lack of coherence among man's religious experiences" would likewise be a function of free human responses to God that would vary "both from person to person and from time to time in the same person."[64] But if we accept the view of *Faith and Knowledge* that cognition is "rational certainty," people who have freely responded to religious experience and for whom the consciousness of God has become coercive (i.e., "who cannot help believing") may be said to have religious knowledge.

Although it is nowhere near as philosophically celebrated as the material from *Faith and Knowledge*, the second chapter of Hick's *Christianity at the Centre*, entitled "How Do We Know?", is a valuable supplement (published more than a decade later). He expands the Wittgensteinian notion

of "seeing as" (the idea, for example, of your seeing an ambiguously executed line drawing "as your mind interprets it, *as* a duck or *as* a rabbit")
into the more general notion of "experiencing as" and comments, "We
experience situations in different ways as having different kinds of significance and so as rendering appropriate different practical responses." He
holds that this activity is "to an important extent" a matter of voluntary
choice on our part. His analysis of faith as interpretation is connected with
this notion of "experiencing as" in the following way:

> I am suggesting then that faith is to be equated with the interpretative element
> within our experience—in sense perception; in moral responses; and in religion,
> where it is the interpretative activity by which we experience life as divinely cre-
> ated and ourselves as living in the unseen presence of God.[65]

But such an interpretation of religious faith is as much a mode of knowledge (in Hick's noninfallibilist sense of the word) as are the interpretations of sense perception and moral awareness.

But is it rational to commit oneself to such religious faith? Hick
answers (as James might have) that "it is reasonable for some people, or
for some people at some times, and not for other people at other times."
A belief is "reasonable or rational" to the extent that it is held "on adequate grounds." But, unlike Kant, who clearly distinguishes between
rational faith and knowledge (no doubt because he holds an infallibilist
view of the latter), Hick identifies the two. He writes that

> the business of seeking knowledge is in practice simply the business of trying to
> come to reasonable or rational or adequately based beliefs. When we claim to
> know some matter of fact we are simply claiming to have adequate grounds for
> believing that same thing.

Yet different people (or even the same person at different times) will not
necessarily have comparably adequate grounds for believing anything,
since those grounds are always relative to empirical data. Thus,

> it is in principle quite possible for one person to have participated in experiences
> on the basis of which it is reasonable for him to believe in God and even unrea-
> sonable not to, while another person who has not participated in those experi-
> ences may equally reasonably not believe in God.[66]

Indeed, Hick considers this actually to be the case.

Can people reasonably believe, for example, in Jesus and follow the
Christian way of life? In doing so, they would be committing themselves
to the reasonableness of someone else's faith, since "Jesus' whole life was
coloured and dominated by his consciousness of God." But this pushes us
to the more fundamental question, "was it reasonable for Jesus to believe

in the reality of God?" It seems to Hick that his situational experience was such that "he could not help believing in God." Of course, this does not mean that his belief was true, since situationally "compelling delusions" can exist. But whether we think it was reasonable for Jesus to believe in God depends on whether we consider him to have been sane or insane. "If insane, we dismiss his distinctive beliefs along with himself. If sane, we acknowledge his right as a rational person to believe what his own religious experience compels him to believe." No objective, independent proof of his sanity or insanity is available to us. Contemporary believers' faith in Jesus' sanity must be relative to the experience they have which leads them to be responsive to Jesus. And so it is for all of us:

> If our own experience as a whole leads us to respond on his own terms to Jesus of Nazareth this response will then be as rational as we ourselves are. The moral is: if you trust in your own rationality then act upon what you cannot help believing.[67]

Practicing Christians experience reality as revealing the truth of Jesus' teachings. If their belief is compelling enough to constitute rational certainty on their part, then, on Hick's terms, they have religious knowledge.

Hick's Gifford Lectures, published in 1989 under the title, *An Interpretation of Religion*, contain a chapter on "The Rationality of Religious Belief." Again, he presses the analogy between religious experience and perceptual experience, arguing that "in the absence of adequate grounds for doubt it is rational to trust our putative experience." Some people do interpretively experience the world as manifesting God's presence. To the extent that such experience is compelling for them, it is reasonable for them to believe accordingly and might even be irrational not to trust it (since our experience is the only foundation for cognitive awareness available to us). "One who has a powerful and continuous sense of existing in the presence of God *ought* therefore to be convinced that God exists." Of course, we can be mistaken in what we reasonably believe. For example, "it was rational for people in the ancient world to believe that the earth is flat"; even though they were factually wrong, there was no way to determine the error in their time. We can accept the rationality of the ancients' belief while feeling obliged to reject believing in it ourselves, because it is incompatible with other beliefs to which our own experience leads us.[68] The notion that the Earth is flat was compelling in the context of ancient human experience but no longer is for us; whereas the ancients had no adequate grounds for doubting it, we do have grounds. Thus, it was reasonable for them to believe it but would be an unreasonable belief for us today.

What comparable parameters would apply to religious faith? Hick answers that "a rational person will only be open to accepting others' religious experience reports as veridical, and indeed will only trust his or her own religious experience, if the beliefs to which they point are such as one judges may be true." And it is precisely at this level of the "*important* possibility" of God's existence and presence that natural theology has a valuable role to play:

> Its office is not to prove the existence of God, or even to show it to be probable, but to establish both the possibility of divine existence and the importance (that is, the explanatory power) of this possibility.

(In the next subsection we shall consider Hick's critical analysis of the traditional arguments of natural theology.) If experience leads us to believe in any being, it is reasonable for us to do so, assuming that two conditions are met:

> One is that we have responsibly judged (or reasonably assumed) it to be possible for such an entity to exist. The other is that it seems to be given in our experience in a powerful, persistent and intrusive way which demands belief in its reality.[69]

Hick holds that natural theology can help us meet the first condition and that some people's religious experience is such as to allow them to meet the second.

We have already seen that Hick has serious reservations about Jamesian voluntarism. Yet he agrees with James that we live in "a religiously ambiguous universe" (which is susceptible to either a theistic or a naturalistic interpretation) and proposes a variant of the "Right to Believe" argument, which he thinks avoids the suggestion of "a licence for wishful thinking." He suggests that "we substitute compelling religious experience" for James's mere "will to believe" some "genuine option" that is neither provable nor falsifiable.

> Thus if in the existing situation of theoretic ambiguity a person experiences life religiously, or participates in a community whose life is based upon this mode of experience, he or she is rationally entitled to trust that experience and to proceed to believe and to live on the basis of it.

Of course, there remains "the ever-present theoretic possibility" that this belief is delusory. But, in Jamesian fashion, Hick avers that such a person can "rightly feel that it would be irrational to base life upon this theoretic possibility." As he rhetorically asks, "Why should one forego entry into a larger universe of meaning, which claims and seems to represent the actual structure of reality, simply because there is always the general possibility of delusion?"[70] On Hick's analysis, this person's rational certainty is both cognitively respectable and epistemologically responsible.

Five aspects of Hick's religious epistemology, as discussed here, seem particularly valuable. The first is his critique of the traditional "infallibilist" theory of knowledge; whether or not his analysis of knowledge as "rational certainty" is adequate, the history of modern philosophy has exposed the counterproductive tendencies of an excessively stringent model. Second, Hick's fourfold analysis of belief is useful as opening up its many dimensions. Third, his view of religious faith as a basic interpretation which must be situationally significant to the believer is important. Fourth, there is his treatment of the relationship between religious "experiencing as" and perceptual experience. And the fifth aspect is his defence of the rationality of religious faith for some people at some times.

God's Existence. Hick's analysis of arguments for God attempts to establish his claim that the role of natural theology must be other than that of proving (or even establishing as probable) anything. His *Arguments for the Existence of God* focuses on the four traditional approaches of the argument from design, cosmological reasoning, moral argumentation, and the ontological proof. All four of these approaches "are theistic in intent: the God whose existence they seek to prove, or to show to be probable, is the God of ethical monotheism (i.e. of Judaism, Christianity, and Islam)." In order for an argument to function as a "proof," it must meet three conditions, according to Hick: (1) its conclusion must validly follow from its premises; (2) all those premises must be true; and (3) the premises must be "acknowledged to be true by those to whom" the argument is addressed. Now we have already considered all four of these approaches; the purpose of this subsection is to examine Hick's assessment of them all. As we have seen, his general position is that, although none of the traditional arguments of natural theology succeeds as a proof, most of them do serve to "establish the *possibility* of God."[71]

The teleological (or "design") argument was discussed by such philosophers as Aquinas, Hume, and Kant. In Hick's view, the world of our experience is such as to exhibit an "immense number and variety" of data, some of which "point in one direction and some in the other"; that is to say, some of them (for example, religious experiences and moral intelligence) seem to support a theistic interpretation of reality, whereas others (for example, wickedness and suffering) might lead to a purely naturalistic one. But no combination of such data ever proves to be unequivocal. "There is no item offered as theistic or antitheistic evidence which cannot be absorbed by a mind operating with different presuppositions into the contrary view." Nor are we able to establish any objective basis for showing "one consistent and comprehensive world-view" (whether that of theism or that of naturalism) to be "inherently more probable than another." Thus, according to Hick, "the design argument neither proves the existence of a creative mind behind the physical universe nor in any objective sense shows this to be probable." Yet it is valuable. Insofar as it "focuses our attention upon aspects of the world that evoke a sense of wonder and an awareness of mystery" for which only theism provides an adequate solution, it points to God's possibility.[72]

Under the heading of "cosmological" reasoning Hick considers "the family of arguments," such as those used by Aquinas, Descartes, Locke, and Leibniz, "which proceed by means of the principle of sufficient reason from the non-self-explanatory character of the universe to a being whose existence is self-explanatory." Hick holds that "the nerve of this family of arguments," which he labels "the cosmological principle," is

> the claim that the space-time continuum, as a contingent, non-self-explanatory phenomenon, only becomes intelligible when seen in relation to an eternal self-existent being who has established it.

This claim arises in the context of something like Leibniz's principle of sufficient reason, which is not itself demonstrable but "is presupposed by so many of the processes of thought which we call rational as itself to count as a fundamental principle of rationality." But even if we accept it, we are not logically compelled to adopt the cosmological principle, since, "as *de facto* ultimates, God and the physical universe enjoy an equal status"; there does not even seem to be any greater probability in favor of either option over the other. On the other hand, it can be psychologically attractive to think that "*if* the existence of the universe, as an ordered cosmos, is ultimately explicable or intelligible it must be so in virtue of its dependence upon an eternal self-existent reality which is of the same order as conscious mind." Although the cosmological argument succeeds in highlighting the options of the "universe as brute fact or as divine creation, it does not provide any ground for preferring one to the other." In their famous debate, for example, Russell and Copleston adopt different options, neither being able to prove his point to the other. Yet, in highlighting the options, the cosmological argument "points very clearly to the possibility of God as the ground of the ultimate intelligibility of the universe in which we find ourselves, and of ourselves as part of it."[73]

The moral argument of Kant attempts to present God as a postulate of practical reason rather than as theoretically demonstrated by speculative reason. The argument presupposes two crucial claims—that morality is objective or absolute and that its ultimate source and/or warrant must be God—both of which are open to critical doubt. Hick's approach is to consider the practical implications of naturalistic humanism. Since it must view all value as "a correlate of either unfulfilled or fulfilled desire" and ultimate human motivations in terms of the pursuit of such value, it might have difficulty accounting for acts of "mortal self-sacrifice" which, by their very nature, preclude their agents' ever experiencing the desired values motivating them. Perhaps the naturalistic humanist would not be able (or even not wish) to justify such actions rationally. But many of us want to do so, and the theistic hypothesis makes it possible. Again, Hick only presents this as indicative of God's possibility and not as either a probability calculation or "a proof of divine existence. But to follow out the implications of our own moral insights and convictions is to raise a question to which the answer *may* be—God."[74]

Hick regards the "ontological argument," used by Anselm, Descartes, and Leibniz, to be philosophically "the most interesting of the traditional 'theistic proofs', involving as it does such fundamental concepts as perfection, deity, existence, and necessity—both logical necessity and the idea of necessary being." Yet, of all the traditional arguments for God, he also thinks this one "most definitively fails." Hick accepts the criticisms of Kant and Russell of the premise that existence is a predicate or perfection as destructive of the most famous traditional uses of the argument; as he writes, "existence is not a predicate in any sense that would validate the ontological argument." Another version of the argument, derived from Anselm's *Proslogium*, proceeds in terms of "necessary existence—meaning by necessary existence (a phrase which Anselm himself does not use) the existence of something which is such that it cannot be thought not to exist." Hick maintains that this version of the argument only shows that God "does not contingently not-exist. In being other than a non-existent-which-might-exist he *either* exists *or* is a non-existent which could not exist (i.e. whose existence is impossible). But what is not proved is that he exists." Unlike "the teleological, cosmological and moral arguments," in Hick's opinion, the ontological establishes nothing, not even "pointing to the *possibility* of God, by posing a question to which God might be the answer." Nor should this be surprising, he remarks, given its "purely *a priori*" approach.[75]

So, in Hick's judgment, none of the four traditional arguments for God proves logically cogent. "Neither those which undertake strictly to demonstrate the existence of an absolute Being, nor those which profess to show divine existence to be probable, are able to fulfil their promise." But the promise itself mistakenly identifies the rationality of belief with the soundness of logical inferences marshalled on its behalf. The problem is that this perspective seems to imagine

> people standing outside the realm of faith, for whom the apologist is trying to build a bridge of rational inference to carry them over the frontier into that realm. But of course this is not the way in which religious faith has originally or typically or normally come about.[76]

Hick has done an effective job of showing that most of the arguments we have been dealing with can serve to point to the *possibility* of divine reality. But, beyond this, as we saw in the preceding subsection, religious believers must consult their own experience as situationally significant in order to determine whether their faith provides them with an interpretation which will make life most meaningful. This part of the process is inevitably person-relative rather than objective.

The Problem of Evil. Hick's discussion of evil and the God of love may be the most intriguing contribution to theodicy developed in the twentieth century. If the existence of the God of ethical monotheism cannot be proved by logical argumentation, can it be disproved by reference to the fact of evil in the world? The purpose of theodicy is to show that that fact is compatible with such a God. Hick poses the issue on the very first page of his *Evil and the God of Love*: "Can the presence of evil in the world be reconciled with the existence of a God who is unlimited both in goodness and in power?" This problem of evil, as it is usually called, arises only in the context of belief in a God, such as that of the Judeo-Christian tradition, who is "at once perfectly good and unlimitedly powerful." Hick presents it in its classical dilemma form: "If God is perfectly good, He must want to abolish all evil; if He is unlimitedly powerful, He must be able to abolish all evil: but evil exists; therefore either God is not perfectly good or He is not unlimitedly powerful." The purpose of theodicy (a word constructed by Leibniz from Greek, meaning God's justice), then, is to develop a "defence of the justice and righteousness of God in face of the fact of evil."[77]

Since theodicy takes evil seriously, rather than denying or dismissing it (we shall consider this possible option again later), we need to be clear what sorts of phenomena are encompassed. Since at least the time of Augustine, whom Hick calls "the greatest theodicist of all," it has been standard practice to distinguish moral from natural or physical evil.

> Moral evil is evil that we human beings originate: cruel, unjust, vicious, and perverse thoughts and deeds. Natural evil is the evil that originates independently of human actions: in disease bacilli, earthquakes, storms, droughts, tornadoes, etc.

From Leibniz on, theodicists have also identified a third type, which he called "metaphysical evil," referring "to the basic fact of finitude and limitation within the created universe," and which is typically seen by Christian theodicists as the "ultimate cause" and/or the "ultimate occasion" of the other two kinds of evil.[78]

Hick devotes two chapters of his book (over fifty pages) to examining four aspects of Augustine's theodicy: (1) his negative conception of evil as a "privation of good"; (2) his "free-will defence" explanation of the source of evil; (3) his justification of imperfection in terms of the "principle of plenitude"; and (4) his "aesthetic" theme that evil is part of the harmonious good of God's creation. In subsequent chapters Hick discusses other traditional Christian theodicies, including those of Aquinas and Leibniz, both of whom fall generally within the Augustinian tradition.[79] Without tracking Hick's exposition of these various contributions to theodicy, let us observe that he does regard them as component elements of the same objectionable perspective.

His "most fundamental criticism" of all the representatives "of the Augustinian type of theodicy" focuses on its underlying "impersonal or subpersonal way in which God's relationship to His creation is prevailingly conceived." Rather than depicting man as "valued and loved for his own sake as finite personal life capable of personal relationship with the infinite divine Person," this perspective allegedly emphasizes the idea that "man is created to complete the range of a dependent realm which exists to give external expression to God's glory." But it is precisely "the category of the personal" that must be emphasized as intrinsically good.

> Instead of seeing the creation of man as determined by the exigencies of the universal chain of nature, we must see it as determined by God's free desire to create beings for fellowship with Himself. Instead of construing evil as metaphysical non-being, we must see it primarily as a failure in personal relationship.

From a Christian perspective, this special relationship between God and personal creatures is highlighted in the myth of divine Incarnation in Jesus, whose life expresses "the divine love for persons" through "activities of healing, teaching, challenging, forgiving—activities that are wholly personal in character."[80] Because Hick thinks that this emphasis on the personal relationship between God and man is given short shrift in the Augustinian tradition, he searches for an alternative within monotheistic thought.

He finds this alternative indicated in the work of a second-century Hellenistic Father of the Christian Church, Irenaeus (particularly in chapters 37–39 of the fourth book of his *Against Heresies*). "Irenaeus distinguishes between the image" of God in man, which "represents his nature as an intelligent creature capable of fellowship with his Maker," and "the likeness" of God, which "represents man's final perfecting by the Holy Spirit." Hick interprets this as meaning that man already "is made as person in the image of God" but "is only at the beginning of a process of growth and development in God's continuing providence, which is to culminate in the finite 'likeness' of God." On this view man was originally created by God as "an immature being" who must deliberately strive to become ready for "His highest gifts." Thus, on the one hand, there is a recognition of "man's finitude and weakness"; but, on the other hand, there is also a focus on his capacity to make more of himself through the proper use of "his cognitive freedom in relation to God, which is safeguarded by the ambiguities of God's self-revealing activity in history and by the corresponding need for an uncompelled response of faith on man's part."[81] Hick believes man can only develop into the "likeness" of God by facing and coping with the adversity of evil, so that it is a necessary condition of our self-development. (This notion will be elaborated upon later; our focus at the moment is on the suggestions of Irenaeus, rather than on the manner in which Hick develops them into an explicit theodicy.) There is a link, of course, between this Irenaean perspective on man, which Hick adopts, and his denial of our infallibly knowing God and of the logical cogency of arguments for God. Certainty regarding God would compromise our freedom to believe.

Hick specifies six points of contrast and then six similarities between the Augustinian and Irenaean theories, which we can briefly summarize, beginning with the former. First, whereas the Augustinian tradition is designed "to relieve the Creator of responsibility for the existence of evil," the Irenaean tradition "accepts God's ultimate omni-responsibility and seeks to show for what good and justifying reason He has created a universe in which evil was inevitable." Second, whereas the former tradition adopts the Neoplatonic view of evil as nonbeing, its principle of plenitude, and its aesthetic theme, the latter tradition makes no such commitment to philosophical Platonism. Third, whereas the former tradition tends to see "God's relation to His creation in predominantly non-personal terms," the latter insists that "man has been created for fellowship with his Maker and is valued by the personal divine love as an end in himself." Fourth, whereas the former looks to the past (for example, to some primal fall from grace) to account for evil, the latter "is eschatolog-ical" in looking to the future to justify evil in terms of a greater good to be achieved. Fifth, whereas "the doctrine of the fall plays a central role" in the former tradition, it "becomes much less important" in the latter. And, sixth, whereas the Augustinian tradition points to "a final division of mankind into the saved and the damned," the Irenaean one downplays the ideas of "permanently unexpiated sin and unending suffering."[82] It seems clear that, on all six of these points of contrast, Hick's sympathies lie with the Irenaean tradition against the Augustinian.

Yet he also delineates six significant similarities between the two per-spectives. First, there is a parallel between the aesthetic theme of the rel-ative perfection of the universe, in the Augustinian tradition, and the Irenaean idea of the eschatological perfection of personal creatures. Second, both traditions must "acknowledge explicitly or implicitly God's ultimate responsibility for the existence of evil," although the Augustinian is more reluctant to do so. Third, the idea of a fortunate evil is somehow common to "theologians in both traditions." Fourth, both "acknowledge logical limitations upon divine omnipotence, though neither regards these as constituting a real restriction upon God's power." Fifth, both traditions can encompass "the reality of a personal devil and of a community of evil powers," so long as this is not used as an ultimate solution to the prob-lem of evil. And, sixth, both can be open to God's having other purposes than those for human persons.[83] So these are six points on which there is no reason to prefer either tradition over the other.

The most important part of *Evil and the God of Love* is the chapter on "The Starting-point" of "A Theodicy for Today." Hick first points out that the Biblical Scriptures contain an implicit theodicy, in which genuine evil is recognized while God's good purposes in the world are affirmed. He sees his own concern as one of explicitly articulating that latent theodicy. It will not be part of his task to provide any knock-down, drag-out proof of anything.

> The aim of a Christian theodicy must thus be the relatively modest and defen-sive one of showing that the mystery of evil, largely incomprehensible though it remains, does not render irrational a faith that has arisen, not from the infer-ences of natural theology, but from participation in a stream of religious experi-ence which is continuous with that recorded in the Bible.[84]

This is, of course, a negative, rather than a constructive, task.

Hick wishes to distinguish among three different "facets of the Christian religion: Christian experience, Christian mythology, and Christian theol-ogy." The first is a Christian's experience of Jesus as Lord and Savior along with the effects of that experience on that person's life. The second encompasses "the great persisting imaginative pictures" associated with the Christian faith. And the third involves "attempts by Christian thinkers to speak systematically about God" in the context of their faith. Until recently, mythology and theology have been quite closely entwined in Christianity. Only lately has Christian theodicy been examined in such a way as "to identify as such its mythological basis, to apply a theological criticism to it, and then to go back to the data of Christian experience and build afresh," so that it can be made meaningful in the light of contemporary thinking.[85]

The most original and intriguing section of the book is that on "The 'Vale of Soul-making' Theodicy"; in that section Hick elaborates Irenaean ideas into a systematically developed view, which will constitute a valuable alternative to "the 'majority report' of the Augustinian tradition, which has dominated Western Christendom, both Catholic and Protestant, since the time of Augustine himself." He adopts Irenaeus' theory that "man, created as a personal being in the image of God, is only the raw material for a further and more difficult stage of God's creative work," whereby he will achieve "that quality of personal existence that is the finite likeness of God," as revealed in the person of Jesus. He sees this transition as one "from one level of existence, that of animal life (*Bios*), to another and higher level, that of eternal life (*Zoe*), which includes but transcends the first." This is compatible with a view of man as "a product of the long evolutionary process" of history.[86] But such an interpretation of human existence should spur us to reconsider our comfortable notion of its purpose.

Hick astutely points out that antitheistic critics (such as Hume, for example) for centuries have capitalized on the facile assumption that "the purpose of a loving God must be to create a **hedonistic** paradise; and therefore to the extent that the world is other than this, it proves to them that God is either not loving enough or not powerful enough to create such a world." Those (like Hume) who regard the problem of evil as reason not to believe in the God of ethical monotheism tend to "think of God's relation to the earth on the model of a human being building a cage for a pet animal to dwell in. If he is humane he will naturally make his pet's quarters as pleasant and healthful as he can." This critique tends to emerge out of the matrix of an Augustinian theory. But it is wholly inappropriate in the context of the Irenaean perspective, "confusing what heaven ought to be, as an environment for perfected finite beings, with what this world ought to be, as an environment for beings who are in process of becoming perfected." Hick prefers to conceive of humans as they presently are not

> on the analogy of animal pets, whose life is to be made as agreeable as possible, but rather on the analogy of human children, who are to grow to adulthood in an environment whose primary and overriding purpose is not immediate pleasure but the realization of the most valuable potentialities of human personality.

Although we wish our children to enjoy pleasurable lives, we also want them to develop such "values as moral integrity, unselfishness, compassion, courage, humour, reverence for the truth, and perhaps above all the capacity for love." Far from promoting these values, a life of unmitigated pleasure is likely to hinder their development.

> Rather, this world must be a place of soul-making. And its value is to be judged, not primarily by the quantity of pleasure and pain occurring in it at any particular moment, but by its fitness for its primary purpose, the purpose of soul-making.

But then the evil to be found in this "vale of Soul-making" (a phrase Hick found in a letter of April 1819, written by the poet John Keats to his siblings) can provide the very sort of adversity that will stimulate spiritual growth.[87]

In order for man to achieve this spiritual growth on his own initiative, rather than merely having it thrust upon him, he must be free to choose. This freedom, which involves the ever-present possibility of wrongful choice, requires that an "epistemic distance" be maintained "between God and man." Certain knowledge of God would compromise "human autonomy" and responsibility. Yet man's experience remains open to a theistic interpretation.

> Thus the world, as the environment of man's life, will be religiously ambiguous, both veiling God and revealing Him—veiling Him to ensure man's freedom and revealing Him to men as they rightly exercise that freedom.

Man's "natural origin and setting" provide this "religiously ambiguous" environment and "contribute to the 'epistemic distance' by which man is enabled to exist as a free and responsible creature in the presence of his infinite Creator."[88]

So, in general, metaphysical evil (or imperfection) is necessary to the extent that there are creatures at all; for, by definition, they must be limited at least with respect to genetic dependence. Natural evil, from an Irenaean perspective, is explicable as providing an environmental context in which the human person is pushed toward moral growth and spiritual development. Moral evil is a function of the "unpredictability" of human freedom, conceived in terms of "a limited creativity." Yet Hick does not pretend to have all the answers. He admits that there remains the problem of apparently "excessive or dysteleological suffering" and refuses to dissolve its mysterious quality:

> The mystery of dysteleological suffering is a real mystery, impenetrable to the rationalizing human mind. It challenges Christian faith with its utterly baffling, alien, destructive meaninglessness.

However, his Irenaean theodicy, "eschatological in character," leads him to "repudiate" the doctrine of "hell, in the traditional sense of eternal suffering inflicted by God upon those of His creatures who have sinfully rejected Him." Their suffering would be a pointless evil, permanently solidifying their sin.

> For the doctrine of hell has as its implied premise either that God does not desire to save all His human creatures, in which case He is only limitedly good, or that His purpose has finally failed in the case of some . . . of them, in which case He is only limitedly sovereign.

This does not necessarily compel allegiance to a theory of universal salvation since a third possibility of "divine annihilation" remains logically available. However, Hick is not inclined to adopt that alternative because it also seems to point to a partial failure in soul-making and an aspect in which "evil would have prevailed over good and would have permanently marred God's creation."[89] So, Hick's Irenaean theodicy tilts him toward universalism.

Let us now consider some of Hick's amplifications of his theodicy, developed since *Evil and the God of Love* first appeared. In 1968, two years after the publication of the original edition of the book, two of Hick's follow-up papers (both of which are now included in his *God and the Universe of Faiths: Essays in the Philosophy of Religion*) appeared in print, stimulated by the objections of critics. In "God, Evil and Mystery," he discusses the relationship between religious faith and the mysterious quality of evil.

> The starting point must be the acknowledgement that although Christianity (in its Irenaean version) claims that good is ultimately to be brought out of evil, so that all suffering is finally to become a stage in the sufferer's journey to the Kingdom of God, yet we cannot in the present life foresee in each particular case along what specific routes of future experience good is to be brought out of evil.

The mystery, then, is how evil which seems, from our present limited point of view, to occur "haphazardly, uselessly, and therefore unjustly" could possibly be justified. This certainly poses a serious challenge to the religious belief that even such evil as this contributes to a process of spiritual development. Yet this reinforces that "epistemic distance" from which our autonomous commitments must function. To speak of the reality of evil as mysterious is to indicate not only our present inability to understand it adequately, but also the "positive contribution" that lack of understanding makes to our motivation to struggle for moral improvement. "Thus, paradoxically, if this life is to be an ethical and spiritual preparation for participation in an infinite good, it must remain a matter of faith and not of sight that this is indeed the purpose that it serves." So the mystery of evil makes a "positive contribution" to our religious faith, rather than being merely a negative obstacle.[90]

In the second 1968 paper, "The Problem of Evil in the First and Last Things," Hick sets out to show how the Christian myths of the fall and eternal damnation have introduced conflicts into theodicy and how these conflicts can be profitably dealt with through demythologization. There are both an internal and an external problem with the doctrine of the fall. The former consists of a "radical incoherence" in the idea of creatures made good by God "deliberately and sinfully turning away from their maker"; and the latter involves an incompatibility between the idea of humans made "finitely perfect" by God and anthropological science's claim that we were continuous with and evolved from "lower forms of life." What is symbolically true in the myth of the fall is that there is a separation between us and God and that we can use our freedom in such a way as to reject God. That symbolic truth is preserved in the notion of man's "epistemic distance from God" without the conflicts posed by the myth. We have already seen that Hick rejects the myth of eternal damnation because it leaves part of God's plan for the ultimate well-being of personal creatures frustrated, part of the divine plan for salvation thwarted (and that this would apply even if we substitute the notion of extinction for damnation).

> The only real alternative, then, to a doctrine of lost souls, whether living in misery or having totally perished, is the contrary doctrine of universal salvation.

Thus, Hick expresses the "hope" (certainly not, he says, anything like "a scientific prediction") that, at some time to come, "all will be saved without their freedom being at any point overridden." This may require suffering comparable to that indicated by the "traditional Roman Catholic doctrine" of **purgatory**. For the symbolic truth of the myth of eternal damnation is that the deliberate rejection of good (and of God) is a real evil that must be purged and rectified. As autonomous persons, we remain morally responsible (and answerable) for our choices. But the goal could be achieved without the mythological notion that this suffering will ever take the form of "an everlasting suffering" such as compromises the infinite goodness of the God of ethical monotheism.[91]

In 1975, Hick chaired a symposium on "The Problem of Evil." In his chairman's "Remarks" at the end of the session, he defines theodicy as "a 'picture' of the universe or a hypothesis about the nature of the universe, a hypothesis or 'picture' in which evil can be seen as ultimately serving a good and justifying purpose" and reviews the elements of the one he advocated in *Evil and the God of Love*. But he emphasizes how "essential" he considers "human immortality" to be to the type of theodicy he defends. "For it is quite evident that the creating of human animals into children of God is not usually completed by the moment of bodily death and that if it is ever to be completed it must continue beyond this life." And again, he endorses the ideas of "universal salvation" and "an eternal heavenly life eventually supervening upon an intermediate or purgatorial postmortem existence."[92]

In "An Irenaean Theodicy," his contribution to *Encountering Evil: Live Options in Theodicy*, Hick holds that an acceptable "theodicy-hypothesis" must satisfy two conditions: it must be "internally coherent," and it must be "consistent with the data" of experience. "These two criteria demand, respectively, possibility and plausibility." And, as we have seen, he faults elements of the established Augustinian view on grounds of both coherence and consistency with experience and presents his alternative as preferable in both respects. He admits that the plausibility of this Irenaean theodicy depends on the eschatological presupposition of a "realistic possibility of an after-life" and that such a presupposition will make it suspect and dubious "in the minds of many today." Yet, as he points out, to the extent that this constitutes a serious problem, the Augustinian theodicy will be tarred by the same brush. Later, in a response to various critiques of his view, Hick points out that a theodicist who does not begin with independent grounds for affirming the goodness and infinity of God can be led by "the pressing fact of evil in its many forms" to believe in either "a good but finite" God or "an infinite but partly evil deity." But Hick counts himself among those who start "from a powerful sense of the reality and love of God, as known particularly through the life and teaching of Jesus and the religious tradition which has flowed from him."[93] Given this foundation, he embraces the Irenaean theodicy as one compatible with ethical monotheism's commitment to a perfectly good and infinite God.

In Hick's chapter on "The Problem of Evil" in his *Philosophy of Religion*, he nicely maps out the logic of the issue. After restating the problem in its traditional dilemma form, he points out that one possible solution, the dismissal of evil as "an illusion of the human mind," should be "ruled out immediately so far as the traditional Judaic-Christian faith is concerned," since this would belie "the stark realism of the Bible." Another possible solution, the denial of divine infinity (as, for example, in the view of God as less than omnipotent by "modern process theology"), is in tension with the orthodox Judeo-Christian conception of God. In between these extremes of denying evil and denying divine infinity are the Augustinian and Irenaean theodicies, the former of which Hick criticizes (as we have already seen) and the latter of which he advocates.[94]

His treatment of the issue in his recently published Gifford Lectures is quite brief (about four pages), due to his having discussed it so thoroughly elsewhere. "The reality and extent of evil," he acknowledges, "is indeed the most serious challenge that there is to theistic faith." Yet he defends the central claim of his theodicy: "Theism can by no means be inferred from the grim facts of suffering and wickedness, but it can, I think, be shown not to be necessarily incompatible with them."[95]

For two decades (between the publication of the original edition of *Philosophy of Religion* in the early 1960s and the publication of its third edition in the early 1980s), Hick developed an imaginative and impressive theodicy. He does an effective job of arguing its merits against the better established Augustinian view. Believers whose faith is warranted by their religious experience should find it an attractive alternative.

A Pluralistic Interpretation of Religion. Hick's pluralistic interpretation of religion has gotten him embroiled in theological controversies in recent years. The 1980s was a period of **ecumenical** initiatives in Christianity, and he did his part to contribute to them. Two of his books published in that decade (*God Has Many Names* and *Problems of Religious Pluralism*) contain opening chapters that chronicle some of these controversies encountered in his "Spiritual Journey" towards a more open theological perspective. As a young man he became a "conservative-**evangelical**" Christian and joined the Presbyterian Church of England; he served as a minister of a rural Presbyterian church in England before coming to America to teach philosophy. But his "questioning mind" and philosophical studies pushed him "to face challenges to the belief system within which his Christian faith was first made available to him" and gradually "to modify or discard many of its elements."[96]

This inevitably led to painful conflicts with his more conservative brethren. He admits to experiencing "an inner conflict between instinct and intellect," describing himself as temperamentally "conservative, cautious, timid and credulous" though led intellectually to liberal "conclusions that have got me into trouble." In America he tried to transfer his ministerial membership from a **presbytery** in England. He was interrogated by a **fundamentalist** who asked whether he "took exception" to "anything in the Westminster Confession of 1647." Hick honestly admitted to having reservations concerning several items, "such as the six-day creation of the world, the **predestination** of many to eternal hell, the verbal inspiration of the Bible, and the virgin birth of Jesus." The last item in particular (which Hick neither denied nor positively affirmed, being openly "agnostic about its historical truth" and holding that "it is not an essential item of Christian faith") aroused the opposition of the fundamentalists. Almost a year later, in 1962, the Judicial Commission of the New Jersey **Synod** sustained the presbytery's refusal to accept Hick, barring him from ministerial membership.[97] Since then, his writings seem to have become increasingly liberal.

A good place to begin a study of his contributions to religious pluralism is with the collection of his essays entitled *God and the Universe of Faiths*, published in 1973. The first chapter, on "Theology's Central Problem," was his inaugural lecture at the University of Birmingham. There he presents the problem of "the conflicting truth-claims of the different world religions" in personal terms: "If I had been born in India I would probably be a Hindu; if in Egypt, probably a Muslim; if in Ceylon, probably a Buddhist; but I was born in England and am, predictably, a Christian. However, these different religions each profess to be true" in a more (for example, Christianity) or less (for example, Hinduism) exclusive manner. Given conflicts among their essential doctrines, it is hard to see how they can all be true. But this leads to a curious dilemma for people who are committed to a particular faith. It would appear that they must either give up their allegiance to its truth-claims or relegate other religious faiths to the inferior status of falsehood or merely partial, qualified truth. "But to adopt the first option" is, in effect, "to commit religious suicide"; and "to take the alternative option . . . would be to imply that God has revealed himself to mankind in a remarkably limited and ineffective way."[98] But, so far, this is only to pose a problem and not to offer a solution.

Subsequent essays at least work toward such a solution. Hick observes that the Christian church as it now exists "is widely different from anything that can plausibly be said to have been intended by Jesus of Nazareth" and encompasses "an inherited set of ideas called christian theology," some of which Hick finds "either quite untenable or open to serious doubt" today. These include the doctrines of creation from nothing, the fall, the redemption, the virgin birth, the miracles, the resurrection, and eternal damnation. Hick proposes that we consider a particular religion (including that of Christianity) in which such doctrines arise as "a human phenomenon . . . whose history is part of the wider history of human culture." On this view, different religious traditions need not be regarded as "mutually exclusive entities" but can function as parallel phenomena within "a dynamic continuum." A practical implication of such a shift is that, on such a revised view, "it is not appropriate to speak of a religion as being true or false, any more than it is to speak of a civilization as being true or false."[99] The extent to which a religious perspective is personally meaningful and vitally important will be relative to particular experiences in particular cultures at particular times in history.

Hick tries to define "that which is most important in Christianity, the religious heart of the christian faith," in terms of both how its adherents live and the beliefs to which they subscribe. But both Christian beliefs and the activity of worship in which they are expressed undergo a process of change over the centuries. "The change has sometimes been rapid and obvious, and at other times so slow as to be barely perceptible; but it has been taking place all the time."[100] And this change has necessarily filtered through particular cultural experiences. Hick proposes a "Copernican revolution in theology," which will shift from viewing any particular religious tradition as central "to the realisation that it is *God* who is at the centre, and that all the religions of mankind, including our own, serve and revolve around him."[101]

Hick begins "The New Map of the Universe of Faiths" by defining religion as

> an understanding of the universe, together with an appropriate way of living within it, which involves reference beyond the natural world to God or gods or to the Absolute or to a transcendent order or process.

This conception of religion accommodates nontheistic, as well as theistic, faiths but not "purely naturalistic systems of belief, such as communism." Religions develop historically, as culture-situated responses to human experiences of the divine. "Seen in this historical context these movements of faith—the judaic-christian, the Buddhist, the Hindu, the Muslim—are not essentially rivals," despite their periodic conflicts. Each of them interprets religious experience through cultural filters.

> Thus Islam embodies the main response of the arabic peoples to the divine reality; Hinduism, the main (though not the only) response of the peoples of India;

> Buddhism, the main response of the peoples of South-East Asia and parts of northern Asia; Christianity, the main response of the European peoples, both within Europe itself and in their emigrations to the Americas and Australasia.

Although all the major religious traditions point to an "ultimate reality" that "transcends the grasp of the human mind," it can only be experienced, conceived of, and described by means of our limited categories, all of which might be "true" in the sense of referring to reality somehow experienced, yet none of which is "the whole truth." On this view, our religious ideas "are all images of the divine, each expressing some aspect or range of aspects and yet none by itself fully and exhaustively corresponding to the infinite nature of the ultimate reality." Yet, given contemporary developments in communication and transportation, we are becoming a kind of global community;

> now that the religious traditions are consciously interacting with each other in the "one world" of today, in mutual observation and dialogue, it is possible that their future developments may be on gradually converging courses.[102]

Yet this is not the end of the matter. Hick's own contribution to his anthology, *Truth and Dialogue in World Religions: Conflicting Truth-Claims*, acknowledges apparent conflicts among different religions' truth-claims. Christianity teaches that Jesus is the incarnate love of a personal God, whereas Islam professes belief in a personal God who does not become incarnate; Vedantic Hinduism's "ultimate reality, Brahman, is non-personal and only mythologically to be described as personal love," whereas Theravada Buddhism maintains that there is no God at all. "But how can it be true both that there is and that there is not a personal God; both that Christ is God incarnate, and that God does not become incarnate?" Hick suggests that God's infinity is such that it encompasses such apparently conflicting claims "as complementary rather than as rival truths."[103] It may be that any conception of God is a partially true perspective on ultimate reality, though none is wholly adequate, that the ultimate reality is personal in some respects but impersonal in others, that there is a sense in which the divine love has become incarnate, whereas in another this is impossible.

On this last issue, Hick became ensnared in another controversy over the publication (in 1977) of a book he edited, entitled *The Myth of God Incarnate*. As he reports in a later paper, that book developed three themes: first, "the historical thesis that Jesus did not teach that he was in any sense God incarnate and had no conception of himself as the Second Person of a divine Trinity"; second, that we can track the transition from the view of Jesus as God's prophet "to the properly incarnational doctrine which was finally established at the Councils of Nicaea and Chalcedon in the fourth and fifth centuries"; and, third, his own wish to interpret incarnational language mythically or metaphorically in order to facilitate "a genuine acceptance of religious pluralism." The book was a sensation, and reactions become nasty. Hick admits that "the title was more provocative than the book itself" and was the primary source of the heat generated. Yet he considers the episode successful in that the book did "make the body of church people and the general public aware of the historical and theological issues" that had been previously the province of scholars.[104]

Hick's own contribution to the book is entitled "Jesus and the World Religions." Jesus was a historical human being "who really lived in first-century Palestine"; but, says Hick, our "mental images of him" have evolved during centuries in response to our devotional ideals, "hopes and desires." Hick maintains that the doctrine of "God-the-Son-incarnate" is merely the Greco-Roman world's "way of conceptualizing" Jesus and that in our "new age of world ecumenism" we should accept "the mythological character of this traditional language," which can be divisive when a literal interpretation is demanded. (Likewise, in Buddhism the "human Gautama came to be thought of as the incarnation of a transcendent, pre-existent Buddha.") What does seem to have been exceptional about Jesus was his acute, intense consciousness of God, which informed his morally exemplary life. (Could the same not be asserted, perhaps in slightly modified language, of Gautama?) And it does seem clear that the historical Jesus saw himself as "called to be God's special servant and agent on earth." Decades after Jesus' death, the Gospels appeared describing him as divine (*Mark* 1:1; *John*, 1). This deification of Jesus became solidified in the Nicene Creed, which "asserts that Jesus was literally (not merely metaphorically) divine and also literally (and not merely metaphorically) human." But can we make sense of such an assertion on anything but a metaphorical interpretation? Despite centuries of theological discourse, "orthodoxy has never been able to give this idea any content. It remains a form of words without assignable meaning," traditionally consigned to the camouflage category of "mystery." This is a way of admitting that we can make no sense of something we are nonetheless committed to believing. But, given that such a literal interpretation divides (and alienates) the minority of humans who are orthodox Christians from all the rest of humanity that has ever lived on our planet, Hick prefers to adopt a "mythological" interpretation. A "myth," in his sense, is not a lie; rather it "is a story which is told but which is not literally true, or an idea or image which is applied to someone or something but which does not literally apply, but which invites a particular attitude in its hearers." Its "truth" must be of a "practical" sort, "consisting in the appropriateness of the attitude to its object." For Christians the practical truth of the myth of the Incarnation is that Jesus remains a unique model of love and goodness informed by a consciousness of the divine. Hick cites Mohandas Gandhi as an example of a non-Christian for whom a nonliteral interpretation allows a profound inspiration.[105]

Hick's *God Has Many Names* argues for "a world theology." While admitting that religions are relative to particular cultures, he maintains that theology need not be.

> Christian theology consists in a body of theories or hypotheses designed to interpret the data of Christian experience. Analogously, a global theology would consist of theories or hypotheses designed to interpret the religious experience of mankind.

Hick's pluralism is an alternative to explicit and implicit claims to religious exclusivity. He takes issue with the old Roman Catholic "dogma *Extra ecclesia nulla salus* (Outside the church, no salvation), with its nineteenth-century Protestant missionary equivalent (Outside Christianity, no salvation)." But he also rejects, as arrogant and arbitrary, more subtle contemporary versions, such as "Karl Rahner's picture of devout persons of other faiths as 'anonymous Christians.' " Hick writes that "The Christian View of Other Faiths" has undergone "three phases so far." The first was one of "total rejection . . . expressed in the dogma that non-Christians, as such, are consigned to hell." The second tried "to retain the words of the established dogma but to add a rider reversing its practical effect," by indicating that those formally outside the fold can "metaphysically" or spiritually be Christians "without knowing it." The third phase (represented by Rahner) involves stipulating that "all who are saved are to be called Christians" in some oblique sense, as when Hans Kung "distinguishes between the ordinary way of salvation within the world religions and the extraordinary way within the Catholic Church."[106] Although this development from phase to phase represents a growth in tolerance, even the third fails to represent authentic religious pluralism.

In the book's title essay, Hick adopts Kantian language to "distinguish between, on the one hand, the single divine noumenon, the Eternal One in itself, transcending the scope of human thought and language, and, on the other hand, the plurality of divine phenomena" appearing in both theistic and nontheistic religions. "Among the former are Yahweh (or Adonai), and Allah, and the God and Father of Jesus Christ, and Krishna, and Shiva"; while the nonpersonal conceptions of the Absolute include "the Brahman of advaitic Hinduism, the **Nirvana** of Theravada Buddhism, and the Sunyata of Mahayana Buddhism." All of these different human responses to religious experience are culturally conditioned. As Hick writes,

> When I say in a summarizing slogan that God has many names, I mean that the Eternal One is perceived within different human cultures under different forms, both personal and nonpersonal, and that from these different perceptions arise the religious ways of life which we call the great world faiths.[107]

The key word here, from the perspective of religious pluralism, is "different," as opposed to "better" or "superior" or "true."

In the preceding paragraph we saw that Hick appropriates Kantian language for explanatory purposes. Yet a qualification is in order, in that he holds that "the phenomenal world is the noumenal world as humanly experienced." Thus, he denies the Kantian dualism.

> The result is the distinctly non-Kantian thesis that the divine is experienced (rather than postulated, as Kant believed), but is experienced within the limitations of our human cognitive apparatus in ways analogous to that in which he argued that we experience our physical environment.

But human religious experience is characteristically diverse and points in the direction of pluralism. Hick claims that a compilation of all the gods whose names appear in religious literature "would probably form a list as long as the telephone directory of a large city." As Kant held that all knowledge of objects must be filtered through the categories of the understanding, Hick maintains that human religious experience can only occur "under some specific and relatively concrete divine image." Yet, though our religious experience is thus necessarily partial and relative, the absolute reality to which it refers is nonetheless real.[108]

Hick's *Problems of Religious Pluralism* defines it as "the view that the transformation of human existence from self-centredness to Reality-centredness is taking place in different ways within the contexts of all the great religious traditions." On this view, which he is advocating, "There is not merely one way but a plurality of ways of salvation or liberation." A more philosophical formulation of the same point consists of saying that "the great world faiths embody different perceptions and conceptions of, and correspondingly different responses to, the Real or the Ultimate from within the major variant cultural ways of being human." The religious responses of almost all human beings continue to occur within the cultural perspectives in which they were born through-out their entire lives. Yet

> it is an extraordinary, and to some a disturbing, thought that one's basic religious vision, which has come to seem so obviously right and true, has been largely selected by factors entirely beyond one's control—by the accidents of birth.[109]

The realization of this fact should enable us to try to move beyond the parochial presumption that ours is the only correct—or even necessarily most correct—religious perspective.

What should be the practical effect of this pluralistic approach? Hick discusses this near the end of *An Interpretation of Religion*:

> We ought then to consider the total belief-systems of the different traditions, composed as they are of elements of diverse logical types: experiential reports, mythologies, historical and trans-historical affirmations, interpretive schemes and concepts of the ultimate.

The apparent conflicts among such elements of diverse religious systems should be neither surprising nor threatening on "the pluralistic hypothesis that the great world traditions constitute different conceptions and perceptions of, and responses to, the Real from within the different cultural ways of being human." A tolerant quest for mutual understanding seems a healthier response to such differences than a hostile defensiveness or arrogant dismissal. Hick himself is advancing the cause of an "inter-faith dialogue," which may increasingly characterize our future.

> But if a world ecumenism does increasingly develop during the coming decades and generations this will not entail an eventual single world religion. The religious life of humanity will no doubt continue to be lived within the existing traditions, though with less and less emphasis upon their mutually exclusive claims.[110]

To those of us who identify religion with the practicing of love and respect, this should seem an attractive prognosis.

We have now considered Hick's (still developing) philosophy of religion in four dimensions: first, his critique of the infallibilist epistemology and proposal that religious faith can be knowledge in the sense of rational certainty; second, his analysis of the traditional arguments for God as generally establishing the possibility of divine reality though failing to prove logically cogent; third, his advocacy of the Irenaean theodicy as an orthodox Christian alternative to the more famous Augustinian solution to the problem of evil; and, fourth, his call for a more pluralistic interpretation of religion, which will view different faiths as complementary, rather than as conflicting, perspectives.

We have covered considerable conceptual (as well as historical) distance between the great medieval thinkers and John Hick. Yet, like Augustine, Anselm, and Aquinas, he is committed to the philosophical project of "faith seeking understanding." Like Descartes, he places philosophical theology in a foundation of epistemology. Like Locke, he adopts an empirical point of view and contributes to the growth of religious toleration. Like Leibniz, he uses logical reason to grapple with argumentation regarding God and theodicy. Like Hume, he is skeptical of philosophical theology's traditional claims to indubitable certainty. Like Kant, he uses a critical method to restrict the bounds of infallible knowledge and make room for reasonable faith. Like Hegel, he tries to construct a universal, comprehensive worldview. Like Kierkegaard, he emphasizes the personal experience of the individual religious believer. Like James, he stresses the practical relevance of our religious commitments and the need for respect for alternative perspectives. And, like other analytic philosophers of our own century, he appreciates the essential importance of language in our awareness and understanding.

Notes

1. "The Existence of God: A Debate between Bertrand Russell and Father F. C. Copleston, S.J.," in *Why I Am Not a Christian and Other Essays on Religion and Related Subjects*, by Bertrand Russell, ed. Paul Edwards (London: George Allen & Unwin, Ltd., 1957), pp. 144–45; this work will hereafter be called "Russell." It is also in *Classical and Contemporary Readings in the Philosophy of Religion*, 2nd ed., ed. John Hick (Englewood Cliffs: Prentice-Hall, 1970), pp. 282–83; this work will hereafter be called *"Readings."*

2. Russell, pp. 145–46; *Readings*, p. 283.

3. Russell, pp. 146–49; *Readings*, pp. 284–86.

4. Russell, pp. 150–51; *Readings*, p. 287.

5. Russell, pp. 151–55; *Readings*, pp. 288–91.

6. Russell, pp. 155–56; *Readings*, p. 291.

7. Russell, pp. 156–58; *Readings*, pp. 291–93.

8. Russell, pp. 160–62; *Readings*, pp. 294–96.

9. Russell, pp. 163–64; *Readings*, pp. 297–98.

10. Russell, pp. 166–68; *Readings*, pp. 299–301.

11. "Logical Positivism—a Debate," by Alfred J. Ayer and Frederick C. Copleston, in *The Logic of God: Theology and Verification*, ed. Malcolm L. Diamond and Thomas V. Litzenburg, Jr. (Indianapolis: Bobbs-Merrill, 1975), pp. 98–99; this work will hereafter

be called "*Logic*." A more complete version of this debate appears under the title "Logical Positivism: Discussion between Professor Ayer and Father Copleston," in *Readings in Religious Philosophy*, ed. Geddes MacGregor and J. Wesley Robb (Boston: Houghton Mifflin Company, 1962), pp. 328–29; this book will hereafter be called "MacGregor and Robb."

12. *Logic*, pp. 99–101; MacGregor and Robb, pp. 329–30.
13. MacGregor and Robb, pp. 332–34.
14. Ibid., pp. 337–39.
15. *Logic*, pp. 101–2; MacGregor and Robb, p. 345.
16. *Logic*, pp. 102–3; MacGregor and Robb, pp. 345–46.
17. *Logic*, pp. 103–6; MacGregor and Robb, pp. 346–48.
18. *Logic*, pp. 107–8; MacGregor and Robb, pp. 349–50.
19. *Logic*, pp. 116–17; MacGregor and Robb, pp. 354–55.
20. *Logic*, pp. 117–18; MacGregor and Robb, p. 355.
21. *Language, Truth and Logic*, by Alfred Jules Ayer (New York: Dover, 1952), pp. 31–32; this work will hereafter be called "Ayer."
22. Ayer, pp. 33–34; *Logic*, pp. 63–64.
23. Ayer, pp. 34–35; *Logic*, pp. 64–66.
24. Ayer, pp. 36–38; *Logic*, pp. 66–69.
25. Ayer, pp. 114–15; *Logic*, pp. 76–77.
26. Ayer, pp. 115, 118; *Logic*, pp. 77, 79.
27. Ayer, pp. 5, 15–16; *Logic*, pp. 81–82, 92.
28. *Readings*, pp. 464–65; *Logic*, pp. 257–58. Wisdom's version of the parable is in *Readings*, pp. 434–35, and *Logic*, pp. 164–65.
29. *Readings*, p. 465; *Logic*, pp. 258–59.
30. *Readings*, p. 466; *Logic*, p. 259.
31. *Readings*, p. 467; *Logic*, p. 260.
32. *Readings*, p. 467; *Logic*, pp. 260–61.
33. *Readings*, p. 468; *Logic*, pp. 261–62.
34. *Readings*, p. 469; *Logic*, p. 263.
35. *The Existence of God*, ed. John Hick (New York: The Macmillan Company, 1964), pp. 229, 231–34 (this book will hereafter be called "*Existence*"); *Logic*, pp. 127, 129–32.
36. *Existence*, pp. 235–36; *Logic*, pp. 132–33.
37. *Existence*, pp. 236–37; *Logic*, pp. 133–35.
38. *Existence*, pp. 239–43; *Logic*, pp. 136–39.
39. *Existence*, pp. 243–44, 246; *Logic*, pp. 140–42.
40. *Existence*, p. 250; *Logic*, p. 146.
41. *Readings*, p. 469; *Logic*, p. 263.
42. *Readings*, pp. 469–70; *Logic*, pp. 263–64.
43. *Readings*, pp. 470–71; *Logic*, pp. 264–65.

44. *Faith and Knowledge: A Modern Introduction to the Problem of Religious Knowledge*, by John Hick (Ithaca: Cornell Univ. Press, 1957), p. 148; this work will hereafter be called "*Faith*." The rest of this subsection will focus on Hick's article, but comparisons with pp. 150–62 of this book might be useful.

45. *Existence*, pp. 253–54; *Logic*, pp. 188–89.

46. *Existence*, pp. 257–59; *Logic*, pp. 192–94.

47. *Existence*, pp. 260–61; *Logic*, pp. 195–96.

48. *Existence*, pp. 263–66; *Logic*, pp. 198–201.

49. *Existence*, pp. 269–70; *Logic*, pp. 203–4.

50. *Readings*, p. 472; *Logic*, p. 267.

51. *Readings*, p. 472; *Logic*, pp. 266–67.

52. *Faith*, pp. v, xi–xii, xiv–xv.

53. *Christianity at the Centre*, by John Hick (New York: Herder and Herder, 1970), pp. 51–52; this book will hereafter be called "*Christianity*." See also *Philosophy of Religion*, by John Hick, 3rd ed. (Englewood Cliffs, NJ: Prentice-Hall, 1983), pp. 60–62, "The Propositional View of Revelation and Faith"; this work will hereafter be called "*Philosophy*."

54. *Christianity*, p. 52; see also "Voluntarist Theories of Faith," in *Faith*, especially pp. 46–57.

55. *Philosophy*, pp. 63–64, 66.

56. *Faith*, pp. 3–10.

57. Ibid., pp. 13–17, 21. 58. Ibid., pp. 26, 28–29. 59. Ibid., p. 30.

60. Ibid., pp. 109, 112–13; *Readings*, pp. 490, 492–93.

61. *Faith*, pp. 116, 120; *Readings*, pp. 495, 497–98.

62. *Faith*, pp. 121–22, 129, 132–33; *Readings*, pp. 498–99, 504, 506.

63. *Faith and the Philosophers*, ed. John Hick (New York: St. Martin's Press, 1966), pp. 242–45.

64. Ibid., p. 246. Cf. *Arguments for the Existence of God*, by John Hick (London: Macmillan, 1970), pp. 112–14; this book will hereafter be called "*Arguments*."

65. *Christianity*, pp. 53–55. Cf. *Philosophy*, pp. 70–72; *God and the Universe of Faiths: Essays in the Philosophy of Religion*, by John Hick (New York: St. Martin's Press, 1973), pp. 37–52, "Religious Faith as Experiencing-as" (this book will hereafter be called "*God*"); *Problems of Religious Pluralism*, by John Hick (New York: St. Martin's Press, 1985), pp. 16–27, "Seeing-as and Religious Experience" (this book will hereafter be called "*Pluralism*"); and *An Interpretation of Religion: Human Responses to the Transcendent*, by John Hick (New Haven: Yale Univ. Press, 1989), pp. 140–42 (this work, which is an expanded version of Hick's Gifford Lectures of 1986–87, will hereafter be called "*Interpretation*").

66. *Christianity*, pp. 57–58; cf. *Interpretation*, p. 211.

67. *Christianity*, pp. 60–62, 64.

68. *Interpretation*, pp. 215–19.

69. Ibid., pp. 219, 221. 70. Ibid., pp. 227–28.

71. *Arguments*, pp. vii, x, xiii; Hick also discusses these four types of arguments in Chapters 5 and 6 of *Interpretation*, as well as in Chapter 2 of *Philosophy*.

72. *Arguments*, pp. 30–31, 33–34; see also *Philosophy*, pp. 23–28, and *Interpretation*, pp. 81–94.

73. *Arguments*, pp. 37, 46–48, 50–51; see also *Philosophy*, pp. 20–23, and *Interpretation*, pp. 79–81.

74. *Arguments*, pp. 65, 67; see also *Philosophy*, pp. 28–29, and *Interpretation*, pp. 96–99.

75. *Arguments*, pp. 68–69, 83–84, 90, 99–100; see also *Philosophy*, pp. 15–20, *Interpretation*, pp. 75–79, and what Hick writes in *The Many-faced Argument: Recent Studies on the Ontological Argument for the Existence of God*, ed. John Hick and Arthur C. McGill (New York: Macmillan, 1967), pp. 209–18, 341–56.

76. *Arguments*, pp. 101, 107–8.

77. *Evil and the God of Love*, revised edition, by John Hick (San Francisco: Harper & Row, 1977), pp. 3–6; this book will hereafter be called "*Evil.*"

78. Ibid., pp. 12–13.   79. Ibid., pp. 37–38, 94–95, 154–68.

80. Ibid., pp. 193–94, 196, 198.

81. Ibid., pp. 211–13. In "An Irenaean Theodicy," Hick later writes that "Irenaeus' own terminology" regarding image and likeness "has no particular merit, based as it is on a misunderstanding of the Hebrew parallelism in Genesis 1:26; but his conception of a two-stage creation of the human, with perfection lying in the future rather than in the past, is of fundamental importance"—*Encountering Evil: Live Options in Theodicy*, ed. Stephen T. Davis (Atlanta: John Knox Press, 1981), p. 42.

82. Ibid., pp. 236–37.   83. Ibid., pp. 238–40.

84. Ibid., pp. 243–45; *Readings*, pp. 507–8.

85. *Evil*, pp. 245–46; *Readings*, pp. 508–9.

86. *Evil*, pp. 253–55; *Readings*, pp. 515–16.

87. *Evil*, pp. 256–59; *Readings*, pp. 517–19.

88. *Evil*, pp. 281–82, 316.

89. Ibid., pp. 276, 330–31, 335, 341–42.

90. *God*, pp. 58, 61.

91. Ibid., pp. 62, 64, 66–68, 70–73.

92. *Reason and Religion*, ed. Stuart C. Brown (Ithaca: Cornell Univ. Press, 1977), pp. 124–28. A book of Hick's which is not being analyzed here but which explores at length a theory of a possible human destiny is *Death and Eternal Life*, by John Hick (San Francisco: Harper & Row, 1976).

93. "An Irenaean Theodicy," pp. 39, 50–52, 63–64.

94. *Philosophy*, pp. 40–49, 54–56.

95. *Interpretation*, pp. 118, 121.

96. *God Has Many Names*, by John Hick (Philadelphia: The Westminster Press, 1980), pp. 15–16; this book will hereafter be called "*Names.*"

97. *Pluralism*, pp. 1–3.

98. *God*, pp. 16–17.

99. Ibid., pp. 92–93, 101–2.

100. Ibid., pp. 108, 110.   **101.** Ibid., p. 131.

102. Ibid., pp. 133, 137, 139–40, 146.

103. *Truth and Dialogue in World Religions: Conflicting Truth-Claims*, ed. John Hick (Philadelphia: Westminster Press, 1974), pp. 148, 152.

104. *Pluralism*, pp. 11–13.

105. *The Myth of God Incarnate*, ed. John Hick (Philadelphia: Westminster Press, 1977), pp. 168–69, 173, 177–78, 183.

106. *Names*, pp. 21, 27, 29, 31, 34; cf. *Pluralism*, pp. 31–34, and "Religious Pluralism and Salvation," by John Hick, *Faith and Philosophy*, vol. 5, no. 4 (October, 1988), pp. 375–76 (this last work will hereafter be called "Salvation").

107. *Names*, pp. 53, 59.

108. Ibid., pp. 83, 94, 103–6; cf. *Philosophy*, pp. 119–20, *Pluralism*, pp. 98, 104–5, "Salvation," p. 370, and *Interpretation*, pp. 233–34, 240–44.

109. *Pluralism*, pp. 34, 36, 73.

110. *Interpretation*, pp. 374, 376, 378–79.

Conclusion

$\mathcal{T}$he eminently quotable William James jokes that a philosopher, speculating about the nature of reality and theorizing about the ultimate causes of things, can be compared to a "blind man in a dark room looking for a black cat that is not there." To carry his analogy further, the philosopher of religion might be said to search for an invisible, inaudible, intangible cat that cannot be experienced, whether or not it is there. But the joke only works if we grant the positivists the controversial assumption that naturally verifiable sense experience is our only access to existential truth. If reason constitutes an alternative access and/or if there are other legitimate modes of experience than natural sense experience, the mischievous analogy collapses.

The general trend of our studies has been away from dogmatic claims to demonstrative knowledge and toward more flexibility and openness. We might track the main line of development of these studies as progressing through three stages, with one great thinker (Hegel) defying the generalization. Our three medieval philosophers, Augustine, Anselm, and Aquinas, and our first three early modern philosophers, Descartes, Locke, and Leibniz, represent the first of these stages, which exhibits a great confidence in the power of human reason to establish truths of religious faith through logical argumentation. The second stage, represented here by Hume and Kant, develops a radical critique of that first approach. Hegel responds to that critique by attempting to reconstruct rationalism on the basis of the new logic of the dialectic. But the more typical reaction is that of the third stage, which concedes the point of the Enlightenment critique and seeks alternative approaches: Kant himself turns to our moral experience as his source; Kierkegaard embraces faith beyond reason; James appeals to personal religious experiences; and contemporary analysts look to language as the key.

What has remained consistent throughout our studies is a focus on theories of knowledge as foundational for work in the philosophy of religion. As long as Western philosophers could comfortably commit themselves to traditional epistemologies (inherited from the ancient Greeks), they could trust reason to prove some of their religious doctrines. Once those epistemologies were fundamentally challenged, new approaches were in order. From Kant on (again Hegel is the exception to the rule), the trend has been away from theoretical, rational certainty toward more inclusive pluralism.

The historical development we have followed is indicative of a process of sixteen centuries in which theories have been tested and have given rise to countertheories. Thus, Western philosophies of religion build upon one another. Although countercurrents are always possible, we can detect a general flow of ideas in an identifiable direction. Meanwhile, the phenomena of religious faith and our desire to understand remain constant. If there is an ultimate causal Source of the world as we experience it, what reality could possibly be a more appropriate object of our attention? It would seem foolish to cut ourselves off from the highest Truth because we fear it may turn out to be an undetectable "black cat." To determine whether there is such an ultimate Reality, what its nature might be, and what we can know of its relation to ourselves has been the project of the great religious epistemologies from Augustine to John Hick.

Appendix
Two
Eastern Classics

In the last chapter, we saw John Hick advocating a religious pluralism that is open to the contributions of traditions other than our own. At the very end of *An Interpretation of Religion* he supportively anticipates the coming of a "world ecumenism" involving further cross-fertilization of ideas: "The religious life of humanity will no doubt continue to be lived within the existing traditions, though with less and less emphasis upon their mutually exclusive claims." The great world religions will maintain their own identities and integrity in the larger context of interreligious dialogue. "One will be a Christian or a Jew or a Muslim or a Buddhist or a Hindu or a **Taoist** or a Shintoist and so on who sees one's inherited tradition as one context of salvation/liberation among others."[1] In the spirit of this ideal, this Appendix will analyze two philosophical classics from Eastern cultures, the *Lao Tzu*, a text of Chinese Taoism, and the *Bhagavad-gita*, a seminal text of Indian Hinduism (both of which are available in several inexpensive English translations and are recommended reading). We shall not attempt to discuss the Taoist religion or Hinduism in general but shall confine our considerations to these two writings, trying to establish connections between their doctrines and key ideas of Christian philosophers of religion studied here.

The Lao Tzu

*I*f he is referring to the Taoist religion, John Hick can safely identify Taoism as "a quasi-theistic movement, though a highly philosophical one."[2] But the *Lao Tzu* or *Tao-te Ching* is too naturalistic to be identified with theism.[3] Though far less systematic than any of the works we have considered, this is a work of philosophy in the sense that it is a metaphysical theory, supported by some argumentation, developed to provide a foundation for both a worldview and practical conduct. The very title *Tao-te Ching*, literally "the classic of the Way and its virtue," reveals this fact. Although it later became a bible of the Taoist religion (*Tao-chiao*), it is a philosophical work of the Taoist school (*Tao-chia*), containing little distinctively religious doctrine. The author to whom it is traditionally attributed is called "Lao Tzu," although this is a title (meaning "Old Master") rather than a name. We know nothing for certain about this man, including even whether he was a single historical individual and, if so, in what century he lived (it could have been as long ago as the sixth century B.C. or as recently as the third century B.C.), facts which have been lost in the mists of time. Yet the *Lao Tzu*, as a book, is a rich repository of provocative ideas (now divided into eighty-one chapters) that live on and continue to invite our consideration.

From the outset Tao, the Way, is characterized, and yet we are warned that every attempt to characterize it is misleading: "The Tao that can be told of is not the eternal Tao; The name that can be named is not the eternal name." The eternal Way is "Nameless" because it is beyond the logical distinctions of language, which can only fracture the oneness of Tao. "The Nameless is the origin of Heaven and Earth; The Named is the mother of all things." Tao is the unified source as well as the path of all things. Our names introduce artificial distinctions among things. That which is "Nameless" (*wu-ming*) is nonbeing (*wu*), the subtle source of everything, from which originates the "Named" (*yu-ming*) or being (*yu*) to which that source leads: "Therefore let there always be non-being, so we may see their subtlety, And let there always be being, so we may see their outcome." We are told that there is a primordial identity of being and nonbeing, subsequent distinctions between them being reflected by a diversity of names. The profundity of both being and nonbeing generates the subtleties of reflective thought.[4] Likewise, in Western mystical literature (consider the treatment by William James), God defies logic and language and is "ineffable." For Kant, God is a noumenal idea that eludes the constitutive use of all concepts of understanding. Like the God of Christianity, Tao is the eternal source of all; yet, unlike the Christian God, Tao is not represented here as a transcendent or personal deity, and there is no hint of anthropomorphism.

"Being and non-being produce each other; Difficult and easy complete each other." Opposites, such as being and nonbeing, are not merely opposed to each other (as in Aristotelian logic) but complement each other and enhance the understanding of one another. The unity of Tao calls for a synthesis of all antitheses. Like Hegel's Absolute, Tao transcends and cannot be limited by ordinary logic, which fragments the unity of things. If Tao eludes logic and language, the wise man should teach silently and act "without action" (*wu-wei*), achieving naturally and without exertion: "Therefore the sage manages affairs without action And spreads doctrines without words."[5] These last admonitions are without parallel in the Western works we have studied and may strike us as rather paradoxical. But they advise a detachment from particular purposes based on selfish desires.

"Tao is empty (like a bowl). It may be used but its capacity is never exhausted. It is bottomless, perhaps the ancestor of all things." Here Tao is poetically compared to the void of a bottomless bowl, whose profundity can never be fathomed and whose inclusiveness is inexhaustible. The empty space of a bowl, its nonbeing, is even more useful than the stuff of which the bowl is made, its being. The nonbeing of Tao seems to be the primordial source of all things. "Deep and still, it appears to exist forever. I do not know whose son it is. It seems to have existed before the Lord."[6] Tao seems eternal in its profundity and tranquillity. It would be impossible to identify any origin for the Way. It is apparently older than even what some think of as the Lord of Heaven. Unlike the God of medieval Christians (e.g., Augustine, Anselm, and Aquinas), as well as of modern Christians (e.g., Descartes, Locke, Leibniz, and Kant), Tao is not a deity and allegedly has a priority over any deity in whom people may happen to believe.

"Heaven and Earth are not humane. They regard all things as straw dogs." Tao is always impartial rather than ever sentimentally playing favorites; it has no humane (*jen*), or inhumane, feelings but is impersonal. Everything is treated dispassionately, like cheap, economical "straw dogs" that are used as sacrificial offerings and then discarded. "Much talk will of course come to a dead end. It is better to keep to the center."[7] We might relate these passages to the Western problem of evil. Unlike

Augustine, Leibniz, and Hick, the *Lao Tzu* would suggest that we cannot penetrate it in such a way as to solve it. Our tedious explanations must ultimately end in silence, and we should exercise restraint in speaking about what we cannot comprehend.

Likewise, we should be restrained in our behavior, not overdoing things but prudently realizing when to quit: "To hold and fill a cup to overflowing Is not as good as to stop in time." The Way of Heaven indicates that we should do our work and, when it is done, modestly withdraw.[8] If we immoderately push things too far, our actions will generate opposite reactions (here we see an implicit use of dialectical thought emerging). Similarly, for such Christian thinkers as Augustine, Aquinas, and Kant, how we think about God should lead to practical implications for how we behave.

"Thirty spokes are united around the hub to make a wheel, But it is on its non-being that the utility of the carriage depends." The nonbeing of Tao is as real and as valuable as the hole in the hub of a wheel, without which an axle could not revolve at all. Likewise, the significance of Tao consists in its not being any particular thing. "Therefore turn being into advantage, and turn non-being into utility."[9] Things or beings (such as axles) have advantageous value, but nonbeing (like the hole in a wheel's hub) also has a useful function. By contrast, the God of Christian thought is traditionally conceived as ultimate Being, with nothingness or nonbeing viewed (e.g., by Augustine) as mere privation of being. In the West it is a minority view (e.g., of Hegel) that God incorporates both being and nonbeing.

> We look at it and do not see it; Its name is The Invisible. We listen to it and do not hear it; Its name is The Inaudible. We touch it and do not find it; Its name is The Subtle (formless).

Tao is subtle in that it is inaccessible to sense experience; it is not visible, audible, or tangible, as are things or beings. Because it is nonbeing, we cannot hope to grasp it conceptually. "Infinite and boundless, it cannot be given any name; It reverts to nothingness. This is called shape without shape, Form without objects. It is The Vague and Elusive."[10] As infinite, Tao eludes all the definitions of our logic and language; it is the formless form of nonbeing. Although Tao is infinite and immaterial, like the God of Christianity, it also incorporates the character of nothingness, which is foreign to the Christian God.

"The all-embracing quality of the great virtue follows alone from the Tao. . . . Eluding and vague, in it are things." Virtue (*te*) emanates from the all-encompassing, elusive Tao, the profound essence of all things. "Deep and obscure, in it is the essence. The essence is very real." Though Tao is imperceptible, this metaphysical "essence" (*ching*) is the ultimately true and "real" (*chen*). Through reflection "we may see the beginning of all things. How do I know that the beginnings of all things are so? Through this (Tao)."[11] We can only know the Way of things by means of the Way (Tao) itself. Likewise, in orthodox Christianity, virtue requires conformity to the will of God, the ultimate reality, with some combination of reason, conscience, and revelation being our access to the divine will. We might contrast the elusive obscurity of the Way with Descartes's paradigm of clarity and distinctness, so esteemed in modern Western thought.

"There was something undifferentiated and yet complete, Which existed before heaven and earth. Soundless and formless, it depends on nothing and does not change." Taoist **cosmology** holds that the reality of Tao pre-exists and is "the mother of the universe." It is all-encompassing and immutable; because it is intrinsically "undifferentiated," the distinctions of names inevitably prove inadequate to it. It is the Way, great, omnipresent, and one. "Man models himself after Earth. Earth models itself after Heaven. Heaven models itself after Tao. And Tao models itself after Nature."[12] There is a hierarchy of appropriate conformity: humans should conform to the Earth, Earth to Heaven, Heaven to Tao, and Tao to its own nature. In Christian cosmology, by contrast, a personal God pre-exists and creates our universe. Like Tao, this God is conceived of as eternal and immutable; but orthodox Christians view God as transcendent.

The simplicity of the eternal, essentially nameless Way may seem unobtrusive, yet ultimately all things must conform to it: "Tao is eternal and has no name. Though its simplicity seems insignificant, none in the world can master it." When things do conform to the Way, they are naturally "sweet." When we impose the artificial limits of names on the Way, we conceptually fragment its essential unity, which is poetically compared to the flow of all waters into the same great sea: "As soon as there are names, know that it is time to stop. . . . Analogically, Tao in the world may be compared to rivers and streams running into the sea."[13] Likewise, in Christian philosophy, it is thought (e.g., by Aquinas and Kant) that our concepts fail to capture God's essence and that the best we can do is use analogical language. But Taoist monism must be contrasted with the transcendent theism of orthodox Christianity (though it might be compared with Hegel's panentheism).

"Hold fast to the great form (Tao), And all the world will come." Those who conform to "the great form" of the Way are assured of ultimate safety, "comfort, peace, and health," in accordance with nature. It is natural that we try to see the Way, to hear it, and to make use of it; yet it perpetually and inevitably eludes our grasp: "We look at it; it is imperceptible. We listen to it; it is inaudible. We use it; it is inexhaustible."[14] These ideas, allowing for differences of terminology, are remarkably similar to the way Christians tend to think of God in relation to the supernatural destiny of humans.

"Tao invariably takes no action, and yet there is nothing left undone." The Way accomplishes everything yet "takes no action" (*wu-wei*). In its simplicity, the Way is "tranquil" because it is "free of desires." To the extent that we can conform to this ideal, our world will naturally be "at peace" as well.[15] By comparison, many Christian thinkers believe that we can gain everlasting peace by following the eternal, immutable will of God.

To get or obtain (*te*) the Way (Tao) is to achieve the highest virtue (*te*). It is so natural that one need not be consciously aware of it: "The man of superior virtue is not (conscious of) his virtue, And in this way he really possesses virtue." By contrast, lesser virtue is self-conscious and requires effort. Merely humane people strive without any ulterior motives, while the righteous strive, driven by ulterior motive, and the person of "propriety" (*li*) forces his efforts on others.

> Therefore when Tao is lost, only then does the doctrine of virtue arise. When virtue is lost, only then does the doctrine of humanity arise. When humanity is lost, only then does the doctrine of righteousness arise. When righteousness is lost, only then does the doctrine of propriety arise.

This implicitly criticizes those who try to talk of virtue without reference to the metaphysical doctrine of Tao that should underlie it. Without the Way, virtue is forced and unnatural; without virtue, one can only try to be humane; without humanity, we tend to settle for righteousness; and without righteousness, we must settle for the "superficial"[16] gestures of mere propriety. Likewise, for some Christians (like Augustine and Aquinas), true morality is lost when severed from God's will and then devolves into artificial conventions.

The unity of the Way is immanent in all things. "Of old those that obtained the One: Heaven obtained the One and became clear. Earth obtained the One and became tranquil. The spiritual beings obtained the One and became divine." The vitality of "myriad things"[17] stems from their sharing in the One. By contrast, except for Hegel, whose panentheistic God is immanent in all things, the Western thinkers we have studied tend to conceive of God as a transcendent Other.

"Reversion is the action of Tao." The process of the Way is cyclical and involves returning to the source of all reality. This dialectical process is such that, while the things of our world emerge from "being" (*yu*), being emerges from the "non-being" (*wu*) of the Way: "All things in the world come from being. And being comes from non-being."[18] Again, except for Hegel, the Christian thinkers we have studied tend to adopt a linear cosmology and to assign an ontological primacy to Being over nonbeing.

> When the highest type of men hear Tao, They diligently practice it. When the average type of men hear Tao, They half believe in it. When the lowest type of men hear Tao, They laugh heartily at it.

The Taoist Way is to be followed, not understood; merely believing in it, though better than derisively dismissing it, is not enough. "Tao is hidden and nameless. Yet it is Tao alone that skillfully provides for all and brings them to perfection."[19] Though obscure and indescribable, the Way naturally perfects everything. For many Christian thinkers, however, faith should lead to some understanding as well as to good practice.

"Tao produced the One. The One produced the two. The two produced the three. And the three produced the ten thousand things." In terms of causal efficacy, Tao is the source of the unity of all reality; that unity is the source of the opposites of active force (*yang*) and negative force (*yin*); these antitheses are synthesized in "the material force" of nature, which, in turn, is the source of the myriad things of our world, which are themselves harmoniously interrelated. "The ten thousand things carry the yin and embrace the yang, and through the blending of the material force they achieve harmony."[20] The dialectical monism of this passage again invites comparisons with Hegel. In general, Christian cosmology tends to conceive of the natural order as the product of God's creation and divine providence.

There is a dichotomy between inadequate appearances and the adequacy of reality: "What is most perfect seems to be incomplete; But its utility is unimpaired. What is most full seems to be empty; But its usefulness is inexhaustible. What is most straight seems to be crooked."[21] We typically fail to comprehend the richness and rightness of things as they naturally are. The distinction between appearance and reality is also among the oldest issues in the history of Western philosophy (consider, for example, Kant on phenomena versus noumenal reality). Many Christian theodicists (e.g., Augustine and Leibniz) view the problem of evil in the context of man's finite, limited, and even distorted perspective on reality.

"There was a beginning of the universe Which may be called the Mother of the universe." Tao is "the Mother of the universe," the nurturing source of its being and life. "He who has found the mother (Tao) And thereby understands her sons (things), And having understood the sons, Still keeps to its mother, Will be free from danger throughout his lifetime." We can only properly understand things (her children) by reference to Tao (their mother) but should maintain our focus on the Way rather than being distracted by things. "Close the mouth. Shut the doors (of cunning and desires). And to the end of life there will be (peace) without toil." The Way cannot be found in a life of mere sense experience and desire. "Open the mouth. Meddle with affairs. And to the end of life there will be no salvation."[22] Salvation can only come from within. Likewise, for most Christian philosophers, an adequate understanding of things must involve reference to God, as their creative Source, sensation and material desires tending merely to divert us from ultimate Truth.

"He who knows does not speak. He who speaks does not know." Mysticism teaches that the sage knows not to try to express the inexpressible Tao and that the person who presumes to speak of ultimate reality does not really comprehend it at all. "Close the mouth. Shut the doors." Empirical observations and physical activity directed toward external things do not help. "Become one with the dusty world. This is called profound identification."[23] We should achieve oneness with our world, base and dirty as it seems. True wisdom requires a "profound identification" (*hsüan-t'ung*, sometimes translated as "mystic unity") with all things. Christian mysticism (for example, as analyzed by James) emphasizes both the oneness of reality and the ineffability of mystical experience.

"Tao is the storehouse of all things. It is the good man's treasure and the bad man's refuge." Nothing escapes the power of the Way. It contains good people, who value it, and bad people, for whom it yet provides sanctuary, alike. "Even if a man is bad, when has (Tao) rejected him?"[24] The Way includes and accepts even those sinners who try to reject it. Likewise, in Christian thought, divine providence is comprehensive. Comparisons can be made with the idea of universal salvation adopted by Hick.

"Who knows why Heaven dislikes what it dislikes? Even the sage considers it a difficult question." The ways of Heaven are ultimately inscrutable. Yet the Way is properly responsive and provident:

> The Way of Heaven does not compete, and yet it skillfully achieves victory. It does not speak, and yet it skillfully responds to things. . . . It is not anxious about things and yet it plans well.

Tao encompasses everything: "Heaven's net is indeed vast. Though its meshes are wide, it misses nothing."[25] Again, this perspective compares neatly with Christian theists' views on divine providence.

"A good man does not argue; He who argues is not a good man." Genuine virtue is seen as incompatible with the habitual practice of argumentation. True wisdom is incompatible with complex, detailed, encyclopedic knowledge: "A wise man has no extensive knowledge; He who has extensive knowledge is not a wise man."[26] By Western standards, this Taoist opinion may seem rather anti-intellectual. The Christian philosophers we have studied have tended to believe in the power of reason to gain at least partial understanding of God based on the knowledge we can glean from our experience and critical reflection upon it. Yet they too would agree that mere knowledge and genuine wisdom are not identical.

This comparative analysis might be summarized by focusing on the grounds for belief, the object of belief, and the appropriate goal of belief. Whereas Christian philosophers tend to base religious belief on logical argumentation and/or on our rational reflection on experience, the *Lao Tzu* bases it on mystical insight. The God of orthodox Christianity is eternal, immutable, infinitely perfect, personal, supernatural, and transcendent, whereas the Tao is eternal, immutable, all-encompassing, impersonal, natural, and immanent. Unlike Christian philosophers who attempt to move from belief to knowledge motivating good action, the *Tao-te Ching* is suspicious of the pursuit of knowledge and more directly aims proper belief at living a good life. Because of his monism and dialectical method of thinking, Hegel compares more favorably with the *Lao Tzu* than does any other Western philosopher we have studied.

The Bhagavad-gita

The Hindu classic, the *Bhagavad-gita*, as John Hicks observes, "has long been in effect the bible of most Indians."[27] The *Bhagavad-gita* (Song of the Lord) is a poem that is a small part of the epic *Mahabharata*; we do not know how old it is, but it probably dates back to between the fifth and second centuries B.C. The scene is a battlefield on which the despondent warrior Arjuna has decided against doing his duty because he would be fighting against and trying to kill friends and kinsmen on the other side.[28] His friend and charioteer is Krishna, a human incarnation of the Lord God Vishnu, who explains why Arjuna must do his duty, by telling him of *Brahman*, the all-encompassing Absolute, its relation to God, to the human spirit, and to material nature, and the connection between religious faith and action. Like the *Lao Tzu*, the *Gita* (divided into eighteen chapters) is an ancient classic of mystical literature that does not primarily rest on logical argumentation, is philosophical in that it presents a metaphysical theory as a foundation for correct action, and is not systematic in the way that works of Western philosophy typically are, preferring the path of illuminating insight.

Krishna scolds Arjuna for his unmanly dejection and teaches that the soul or self is indestructible and eternal, though now embodied and subject to reincarnation. "Just as a person casts off worn-out garments and puts on others that are new, even so does the embodied soul cast off worn-out bodies and take on others that are new." Nevertheless, the self is "eternal" and "unchanging" throughout. We should care for it and its adherence to duty and "righteousness (*dharma*)" rather than for transient, perishable physical things. We must practice the *yoga*, or disciplined method of salvation, that will liberate the self from bondage to the modes of material nature. Through knowledge we can rise above dualistic oppositions to reach a higher unity. When we thus "attain to insight (*yoga*)," we shall be able to overcome sense attachment and selfish desire, to work without an anxious regard for external results, and to "attain to the bliss of God."[29] Likewise, Christian philosophy often calls for the overcoming of selfish desire and the performance of moral duty; for it too believes in an immortal (though not eternal) soul that is more precious than the body. The suggestion that we must rise above dualistic oppositions to higher unity invites comparisons to Hegel's dialectic.

In addition to "the path of knowledge for men of contemplation," there is a second way "of works for men of action." This is *karma-yoga*, the method of work. Like the *Lao Tzu*, Krishna does not advocate inactive quietism but preaches work without selfish attachment. The man of inaction "lives in vain"; we must work "to maintain the world-order." The evil of sin stems from craving desire and hostile anger. We should maintain a proper hierarchical balance, with the empirical mind controlling the senses, the higher intelligence controlling the mind, and the self or soul controlling intelligence.[30] This idea of a proper hierarchy can also be found in such Christian philosophers as Augustine and Descartes.

For those pursuing the *yoga* of knowledge, faith is a necessary condition. "He who has faith, . . . and who has subdued his senses, gains wisdom, and having gained wisdom he attains quickly to the supreme peace." So far this sounds like the medieval Christian ideal of faith seeking understanding. Yet already we get a glimpse into the theological direction this will take that is so different from that of orthodox Christianity, when the divine Krishna tells Arjuna that, through faith rising to wisdom, he will "see all existences without exception in the Self, then in Me."[31] Here we have an initial, fleeting suggestion of the qualified mystical monism that is to follow, which will dialectically combine a personal theism, comparable to that of most of the Christian thinkers we have studied, with a view (comparable to both the *Lao Tzu* and Hegel) that all is one.

The idea of the enlightened "self in union with the Divine" is gradually developed. The Deity is different from us, yet somehow one with us: "God is flawless and the same in all. Therefore are these persons established in God" when they have reached enlightenment. "Such a one who is in union with God enjoys undying bliss." Similarly, the person of unattached action (*yogin*) "becomes divine and attains to the beatitude of God." So the way of knowledge and the way of unselfish action can both lead us to a blissful oneness with God, "the supreme *nirvana*" that is the extinction of all desire and selfishness. A panentheism emerges when the divine Krishna speaks of the enlightened one "who sees Me everywhere and sees all in Me." As faith leads to wisdom, so wisdom leads to religious worship of and harmony with God—"he who full of faith worships Me, with his inner self abiding in me,—him I hold to be the most attuned to me."[32] We notice that no argumentation for any of this has been offered; it is, rather, a mystical insight into the nature of reality. The emphasis on knowledge as revealing an ontological unity between God and humans relates to Hegel's panentheism. Yet this is a qualified monism, in that God is depicted as personal, as involved with our world, even as incarnate in human form as Krishna.

More needs to be articulated concerning the divine Essence, with which we are allegedly to be unified. "Earth, water, fire, air, ether, mind, understanding, and self-sense" are said to constitute "the eightfold division" of God's "lower nature" or manifestation in the material world of transient phenomena. By contrast, God's "other and higher nature" is the soul or spirit, which is eternal. The divine Krishna proclaims, "I am the origin of all this world and its dissolution as well" and adds, "There is nothing whatever that is higher than I." This conception of God as the highest Reality and eternal source and teleological end of all creation, by itself, of course, is quite compatible with the divine essence as discussed by such orthodox Christian philosophers as Aquinas and Descartes. The idea that this God is personally identified with the incarnate person of Krishna can be compared to the incarnate God-man, Christ. But, of the various Western philosophers we have studied above, only Hegel teaches a panentheism like this one: "And whatever states of being there may be, ... I am not in them; they are in Me." God is characterized here as "changeless and supreme" in the higher divine nature, and also as omniscient yet unknowable: "I know the beings that are past, that are present, O Arjuna, and that are to come, but Me no one knows." It allegedly is only through the knowledge of God that we can "know the *Brahman* [or the Absolute] entire,"[33] of which God is a personal aspect.

Arjuna reasonably wonders about the nature of *Brahman*, or the Absolute Reality. Krishna responds, "*Brahman* [or the Absolute] is the indestructible, the Supreme" Reality that "brings all beings into existence" by means of "*karma*," the divine creative power. As was asserted of Tao, so *Brahman* is inconceivable and linguistically inexpressible in itself, the mystical mantra *Aum* being its most adequate formula. All beings are supposedly immanent in God, the personal aspect of *Brahman*; yet God transcends the phenomena of the world. In addition to this dialectical synthesis, we are also told that God is both "one" and "manifold," involving "being as well as non-being" (comparisons to both Tao and Hegel are obvious here). Arjuna acknowledges that Krishna is God and *Brahman* when he exclaims, "Thou art the Supreme *Brahman*, the Supreme Abode and the Supreme Purifier, the Eternal, Divine Person, the First of the gods, the Unborn, the All-pervading." Krishna responds, "I am the beginning, the middle and the very end of beings" (cf. the end of the Christian New Testament: "I am Alpha and Omega, the beginning and the end, the first and the last"— *Revelation* 22:13). Krishna announces, "I am the dialectic"—not merely expressing it but embodying it. He claims to be the source and necessary condition of all things, transcending them all: "I support this entire universe pervading it with a single fraction of Myself."[34] Likewise, the personal God of religion and the all-encompassing Absolute are ultimately one for Hegel, for whom philosophical reason is a more adequate access to Truth than religious faith.

What occurs next may seem particularly strange in the context of everything discussed in the ten chapters of this book. Arjuna mystically experiences an **epiphany** in which Krishna is transfigured into the universal divine form, which no natural human eye can behold. In this **theophany** Arjuna sees "the whole universe with its manifold divisions gathered together in one, in the body of the God of gods." This mystical experience of the infinite allegedly leads to the dialectical realization that "the Supreme" is both the Absolute *Brahman* and the personal God, by which the entire universe is pervaded, "boundless in power and immeasurable in might." Arjuna is naturally shaken by the tremendous experience, implores Krishna's forgiveness for any past impertinence, and begs for divine grace, which he is assured has been granted him. Krishna claims that it is people who are "possessed of supreme faith" who are best, though other devout people can also approach God. The way of devotion (*bhakti-yoga*) is said to be particularly dear to God.[35] This passage, so intensely mystical, stands in such stark contrast to the analytical and critical approaches of logical reason we have seen undertaken by most of the Christian philosophers studied that all we can do is emphasize the striking difference. What they have in common is the idea of faith leading to some sort of knowledge of God; but in one case the route is that of personal mystical experience, while in the other it is that of argumentation. James, we recall, had more confidence in the former than in the latter as a foundation for religion.

True knowledge, then, purportedly turns out to be nonlogical and suprarational. It alone can attain to "the Supreme *Brahman* who is beginningless and who is said to be neither existent nor non-existent," being dialectically beyond all the oppositions of ordinary thought. *Brahman* "is without and within all beings," both transcendent and immanent. It "is unmoving as also moving," that is, immutable yet also in process. It "is undivided [indivisible] and yet . . . seems to be divided among beings." Nature and spirit are both held to be eternal manifestations of *Brahman*, the former and not the latter being the true source of physical actions, including those of the warrior on the battlefield. All three of the modes or strands of material nature (lightness, energy, and heaviness) bind the spirit to the body and can generate evil. The first, lightness or "goodness (*sattva*)," binds the soul to happiness. "Passion (*rajas*)" or energy binds the soul to action. The third, heaviness or "dullness (*tamas*)," binds the soul to neglect. It is the soul that transcends these three modes and all selfish desire that "attains life eternal." Krishna, who claims to be the embodiment or "the abode of *Brahman*," maintains that only the person of such detachment "is fit for becoming *Brahman*."[36] Religion frequently calls for a transcendence of the merely natural. But whether we can or should try to overcome the oppositions of ordinary logical reason is controversial (Kant and Hegel, for example, disagreeing).

Krishna speaks of a "fragment [or fraction] of My own self, having become a living soul, eternal, in the world of life." Thus, like Hegel's Absolute, the God of the *Gita* is manifest in our world. Krishna describes himself as a knowing "Supreme Self," expressed in both "the perishable" realm of material nature "and the imperishable" realm of spirit, who enters into and sustains our world. Enlightened souls share in the divine nature.

In contrast, "the demoniac" souls, ignorant and selfish, choose to reject God. They are evil and are the source of evils; eventually they are cast into demons and "fall into a foul hell," the threefold gateway to which is comprised of "lust, anger, and greed."[37] Thus, the problem of evil is explained, as it is by orthodox Christian theodicy, in terms of a freely chosen rejection of the Good by the human soul. However, the Hindu "hell" involves a purging of evil preparatory to rebirth.

Corresponding to the three modes or strands of the natural world there are three types of faith ("good, passionate, and dull"). Likewise, there are three kinds of knowledge: good knowledge, "by which the one Imperishable Being is seen in all existences, undivided in the divided"; passionate knowledge, "which sees multiplicity of beings in the different creatures, by reason of their separateness"; and dull knowledge, which narrowly "clings to one single effect as if it were the whole, without concern for the cause, without grasping the real" at all. Through the highest faith and knowledge, a person allegedly "becomes worthy of becoming one with *Brahman*," the Absolute. What Arjuna cannot do is avoid taking action; he must freely choose whether to act well and wisely or ill and foolishly. He is assured that God loves him and that, if he chooses well and wisely, God will release him "from all evils," so that he "shall attain to the happy worlds of the righteous." Finally, Arjuna declares that all his doubts have been dispelled and that he is ready to act in accordance with duty.[38] Two observations are relevant here: first, the degrees of faith and knowledge do not adulate the way of logical reason so prized by many philosophers (an exception being Kierkegaard); and, second, faith and knowledge, as for Christian philosophers, though they are theoretical, are oriented toward practical conduct, which is susceptible to moral evaluation.

As was the case with the *Lao Tzu*, here we see some significant points of comparison with ideas of Christian philosophers of religion we have studied. But both of these classics of Eastern thought are fundamentally works of mystical literature that place little trust or emphasis on the sort of argumentation stressed by great Western philosophers (who inherited that orientation from ancient Greeks). Both of these Eastern writings highlight the unity of reality and a dialectical synthesis of opposites similar to what we find in Hegel but distinguishing them from more orthodox Christians from Augustine through Kant. At any rate, they are indicative of alternative perspectives that might be explored, if one were to pursue the sort of religious pluralism advocated by Hick. They might complement and enrich the theories of Western philosophers of religion on which the body of this book has focused.

* * * * *

Hick maintains that the great world religions "constitute different ways of experiencing, conceiving and living in relation to an ultimate . . . Reality which transcends all our varied visions of it." He takes Kant's famous distinction between noumenal Reality in itself and phenomenal appearances to our consciousness as his "starting point for a pluralistic epistemology of religion." We do not know noumenal Reality as it is in itself. Yet Hick considers particular religious traditions, such as Christianity, Taoism, and Hinduism, to be cognitive filters through which cultures can experience "divine *personae*" (such as the Christian God or Krishna) and "metaphysical *impersonae*" (such as Tao or *Brahman*) as phenomenal "manifestations of the Real."[39] One can only consider such matters from a particular human perspective, typically situated in some given culture. We who are part of Western civilization have our own intellectual history that provides us with a context for reflecting on our own religious traditions and a base from which we can explore others. That intellectual history has been nurtured by the ideas of renowned philosophers of religion, from Augustine to Hick, that we have studied.

Notes

1. *An Interpretation of Religion: Human Responses to the Transcendent*, by John Hick (New Haven: Yale Univ. Press, 1989), p. 379; this book will hereafter be called "*Interpretation.*"
2. Ibid., p. 257.
3. All references to this book will be to *The Way of Lao Tzu*, trans. Wing-tsit Chan (Indianapolis: Bobbs-Merrill, 1963). The interpretation adopted here follows Chan's extensive comments and notes. A compact but complete version of this translation can also be found in *A Source Book in Chinese Philosophy*, trans. and ed. Wing-tsit Chan (Princeton: Princeton Univ. Press, 1963).

4. Ibid., p. 97.	5. Ibid., p. 101.	6. Ibid., p. 105.
7. Ibid., p. 107.	8. Ibid., p. 115.	9. Ibid., p. 119.
10. Ibid., p. 124.	11. Ibid., p. 137.	12. Ibid., p. 144.
13. Ibid., p. 157.	14. Ibid., p. 162.	15. Ibid., p. 166.
16. Ibid., p. 167.	17. Ibid., p. 170.	18. Ibid., p. 173.

19. Ibid., p. 174.   20. Ibid., p. 176.   21. Ibid., p. 180.

22. Ibid., p. 192.   23. Ibid., p. 199.   24. Ibid., p. 210.

25. Ibid., p. 228.   26. Ibid., p. 240.

27. *Interpretation*, p. 254.

28. A complete copy of Sarvepalli Radhakrishnan's translation of this work is contained in *A Source Book in Indian Philosophy*, ed. Sarvepalli Radhakrishnan and Charles A. Moore (Princeton: Princeton Univ. Press, 1957); references to it are to this work. This one is to pp. 104–5.

29. Ibid., pp. 107–12.   30. Ibid., pp. 112–15.   31. Ibid., p. 119.

32. Ibid., pp. 121–26.   33. Ibid., pp. 127–29.   34. Ibid., pp. 129–38.

35. Ibid., pp. 138–44.   36. Ibid., pp. 146–50.   37. Ibid., pp. 151–54.

38. Ibid., pp. 155, 159, 161–63.

39. *Interpretation*, pp. 235–36, 240–42.

Bibliography

Anselm, *St. Anselm: Basic Writings*. Translated by S. N. Deane, 2nd ed. LaSalle, IL: Open Court Publishing Company, 1968.

Anselm of Canterbury, *Truth, Freedom, and Evil: Three Philosophical Dialogues*. Edited and translated by Jasper Hopkins and Herbert Richardson. New York: Harper & Row, 1967.

Aquinas, *Basic Writings of Saint Thomas Aquinas*. Edited by Anton C. Pegis. 2 vols. New York: Random House, 1945.

———, *On Being and Essence*. Translated by Armand Maurer. Toronto: Pontifical Institute of Mediaeval Studies, 1949.

———, *On the Truth of the Catholic Faith: Summa contra Gentiles: Book 1: God*. Translated by Anton C. Pegis. Garden City, NY: Doubleday, 1955.

———, *Truth*, Vol. 1. Translated by Robert W. Mulligan, S.J. (Chicago: Henry Regnery, 1952.

———, *Truth*, Vol. 2. Translated by James V. McGlynn, S. J. Chicago: Henry Regnery, 1953.

———, *Truth*, Vol. 3. Translated by Robert W. Schmidt, S. J. Chicago: Henry Regnery, 1954.

Augustine, *The Advantage of Believing*. Translated by Luanne Meagher, in *Writings of Saint Augustine*, Vol. 2. Edited by Ludwig Schopp. New York: CIMA, 1947.

———, *Against the Academicians*. Translated by Sister Mary Patricia Garvey. Milwaukee: Marquette University Press, 1957.

———, *The City of God*. Translated by Marcus Dods. New York: The Modern Library, 1950.

———, *The Confessions of St. Augustine*. Translated by John K. Ryan. Garden City: Image Books, 1960.

———, *Divine Providence and the Problem of Evil*. Translated by Robert P. Russell, in *Writings of Saint Augustine*, Vol. 1. Edited by Ludwig Schopp. New York: CIMA, 1948.

———, *The Enchiridion on Faith, Hope and Love*. Translated by J. F. Shaw, edited by Henry Paolucci. Chicago: Henry Regnery, 1961.

————, *Lectures or Tractates on the Gospel According to St. John*, Vol. 1. Translated by Rev. John Gibb, in *The Works of Aurelius Augustine*. Edited by Rev. Marcus Dods, Vol. 10. Edinburgh: T. & T. Clark, 1873.

————, *Letters*, Vol. 2. Translated by Sister Wilfrid Parsons, in *The Fathers of the Church*, Vol. 18. Edited by Roy Joseph Deferrari. New York: Fathers of the Church, Inc., 1953.

————, *Of True Religion*. Translated by J. H. S. Burleigh. Chicago: Henry Regnery, 1966.

————, *On Christian Doctrine*. Translated by D. W. Robertson, Jr. Indianapolis: Bobbs-Merrill, 1958.

————, *On Faith in Things Unseen*. Translated by Roy J. Deferrari and Mary Francis McDonald, in *Writings of Saint Augustine*, Vol. 2. Edited by Ludwig Schopp. New York: CIMA, 1947.

————, *On Free Choice of the Will*. Translated by Anna S. Benjamin and L. H. Hackstaff. Indianapolis: Bobbs-Merrill, 1964.

————, *Sermons on the Liturgical Seasons*. Translated by Sister Mary Sarah Muldowney, in *The Fathers of the Church*, Vol. 38. Edited by Roy Joseph Deferrari. New York: Fathers of the Church, Inc., 1959.

————, *The Soliloquies*. Translated by Thomas F. Gilligan, in *Writings of Saint Augustine*, Vol. 1, edited by Ludwig Schopp. New York: CIMA, 1948.

Ayer, Alfred Jules, *Language, Truth and Logic*. New York: Dover Publications, Inc., 1952.

Ayer, Alfred J., and Frederick C. Copleston, "Logical Positivism—a Debate," in *The Logic of God: Theology and Verification*. Edited by Malcolm L. Diamond and Thomas V. Litzenburg, Jr. Indianapolis: Bobbs-Merrill, 1975.

Bayle, Pierre, *Historical and Critical Dictionary: Selections*. Translated by Richard H. Popkin. Indianapolis: Bobbs-Merrill, 1965.

Brown, Stuart C., editor, *Reason and Religion*. Ithaca, NY: Cornell University Press, 1977.

Chan, Wing-tsit, translator, *The Way of Lao Tzu*. Indianapolis: Bobbs-Merrill, 1963.

————, editor and translator, *A Source Book in Chinese Philosophy*. Princeton, Princeton University Press, 1963.

Copleston, Frederick, S.J., *A History of Philosophy*, 9 vols. Garden City, NY: Image Books, 1962–77.

Davis, Stephen T., editor, *Encountering Evil: Live Options in Theodicy*. Atlanta: John Knox Press, 1981.

Descartes, René, *Descartes' Conversation with Burman*. Translated by John Cottingham. Oxford: Oxford University Press, 1976.

————, *The Philosophical Works of Descartes*. Translated by Elizabeth S. Haldane and G. R. T. Ross, 2 vols. New York: Cambridge University Press, 1968.

Diamond, Malcolm L., and Thomas V. Litzenburg, Jr., *The Logic of God: Theology and Verification*. Indianapolis: Bobbs-Merrill, 1975.

Dostoyevsky, Fyodor, *The Brothers Karamazov*. Translated by Constance Garnett. Edited by Manuel Komroff. New York: New American Library, 1957.

Hegel, G. W. F., *Early Theological Writings*. Translated by T. M. Knox. Philadelphia: University of Pennsylvania Press, 1971.

————, *Faith and Knowledge*. Translated by Walter Cerf and H. S. Harris. Albany: State University of New York Press, 1977.

————, *Hegel: The Letters*. Translated by Clark Butler and Christiane Seiler. Bloomington: Indiana University Press, 1984.

———, *Hegel's Lectures on the History of Philosophy*. Translated by E. S. Haldane. New York: The Humanities Press, 1955.

———, *Hegel's Logic*. Translated by William Wallace. Oxford: Oxford University Press, 1975.

———, *Hegel's Philosophy of Mind*. Translated by A. V. Miller. Oxford: Oxford University Press, 1971.

———, *Hegel's Philosophy of Nature*. Translated by A. V. Miller. Oxford: Oxford University Press, 1970.

———, *Hegel's Philosophy of Right*. Translated by T. M. Knox. New York: Oxford University Press, 1967.

———, *Hegel's Science of Logic*. Translated by A. V. Miller. London: George Allen & Unwin, 1969.

———, *Lectures on the Philosophy of Religion Together with a Work on the Proofs of the Existence of God*. Translated by E. B. Speirs and J. Burdon Sanderson. London: Routledge & Kegan Paul, 1968.

———, *Natural Law*. Translated by T. M. Knox. Philadelphia: University of Pennsylvania, 1975.

———, *On Art, Religion, Philosophy: Introductory Lectures to the Realm of Absolute Spirit*. Edited by J. Glenn Gray. New York: Harper & Row, 1970.

———, *Phenomenology of Spirit*. Translated by A. V. Miller. New York: Oxford University Press, 1979.

———, *The Philosophy of Fine Art*. Translated by F. P. B. Osmaston. London: G. Bell and Sons, Ltd., 1920.

———, *The Philosophy of Hegel*. Edited by Carl J. Friedrich. New York: Modern Library, 1953.

———, *Philosophy of History*. Translated by J. Sibree. New York: P. F. Collier and Son, 1900.

———, "Reason and Religious Truth." Translated by A. V. Miller, in *Beyond Epistemology: New Studies in the Philosophy of Hegel*. Edited by Frederick G. Weiss. The Hague: Martinus Nijhoff, 1974.

———, *Three Essays, 1793–1795*. Edited and translated by Peter Fuss and John Dobbins. Notre Dame, IN: University of Notre Dame Press, 1984.

Hick, John, *Arguments for the Existence of God*. London: Macmillan, 1970.

———, *Christianity at the Centre*. New York: Herder and Herder, 1970.

———, *Death and Eternal Life*, San Francisco: Harper & Row, 1976.

———, *Evil and the God of Love*, revised ed. San Francisco: Harper & Row, 1977.

———, *Faith and Knowledge: A Modern Introduction to the Problem of Religious Knowledge*. Ithaca, NY: Cornell University Press, 1957.

———, *God and the Universe of Faiths: Essays in the Philosophy of Religion*. New York: St. Martin's Press, 1973.

———, *God Has Many Names*. Philadelphia: Westminster Press, 1980.

———, *An Interpretation of Religion: Human Responses to the Transcendent*. New Haven: Yale University Press, 1989.

———, *Philosophy of Religion*, 3rd ed. Englewood Cliffs, NJ: Prentice-Hall, 1983.

———, *Problems of Religious Pluralism*. New York: St. Martin's Press, 1985.

———, "Religious Pluralism and Salvation," *Faith and Philosophy* 5, no. 4 (October, 1988).

———, editor, *Classical and Contemporary Readings in the Philosophy of Religion*, 2nd ed. Englewood Cliffs, NJ: Prentice-Hall, 1970.

———, editor, *The Existence of God*. New York: Macmillan, 1964.

————, editor, *Faith and the Philosophers*. New York: St. Martin's Press, 1966.

————, editor, *The Myth of God Incarnate*. Philadelphia: Westminster Press, 1977.

————, editor, *Truth and Dialogue in World Religions: Conflicting Truth-Claims*. Philadelphia: Westminster Press, 1974.

Hick, John, and Arthur C. McGill, editors, *The Many-faced Argument: Recent Studies on the Ontological Argument for the Existence of God*. New York: Macmillan, 1967.

Hume, David, *An Enquiry concerning the Principles of Morals*. Edited by J. B. Schneewind. Indianapolis: Hackett, 1983.

————, *Hume on Religion*. Edited by Richard Wollheim. Cleveland: World Publishing Co., 1969.

————, *An Inquiry concerning Human Understanding* and "An Abstract of *A Treatise of Human Nature*." Edited by Charles W. Hendel. Indianapolis: Bobbs-Merrill, 1955.

————, *The Letters of David Hume*. Edited by J. Y. T. Grieg. Oxford: Oxford University Press, 1932.

————, *Letters of David Hume to William Strahan*. Edited by G. Birnbeck Hill. Oxford: Oxford University Press, 1888.

————, *New Letters of David Hume*. Edited by Raymond Klibansky and Ernest C. Mossner. Oxford: Oxford University Press, 1954.

————, *Of the Standard of Taste and Other Essays*. Edited by John W. Lenz. Indianapolis: Bobbs-Merrill, 1965.

————, *A Treatise of Human Nature*. Edited by L. A. Selby-Bigge. Oxford: Oxford University Press, 1888.

James, William, *Collected Essays and Reviews*. New York: Longmans, Green and Co., 1920.

————, *Essays in Radical Empiricism* and *A Pluralistic Universe*. Edited by Ralph Barton Perry. New York: E. P. Dutton, 1971.

————, *The Letters of William James*. Edited by Henry James, in 2 vols. Boston: Little, Brown, & Co., 1926.

————, *Memories and Studies*. Westport, CT: Greenwood Press, 1968.

————, *Pragmatism* and *The Meaning of Truth*. Cambridge, MA: Harvard University Press, 1978.

————, *The Principles of Psychology*, in 2 vols. New York: Dover, 1950.

————, *Psychology: Briefer Course*. New York: Henry Holt and Co., 1892.

————, "The Psychology of Belief," *Mind* 14, no. 55 (July, 1889).

————, "Reason and Faith," *The Journal of Philosophy* 24, no. 8 (April 14, 1927).

————, *Some Problems of Philosophy*. New York: Longmans, Green, and Co., 1911.

————, *Talks to Teachers on Psychology and to Students on Some of Life's Ideals*. New York: W. W. Norton, 1958.

————, *The Varieties of Religious Experience*. New York: New American Library, 1958.

————, *The Will to Believe and Other Essays in Popular Philosophy*. New York: Dover, 1956.

————, *The Writings of William James: A Comprehensive Edition*. Edited by John J. McDermott. New York: The Modern Library, 1968.

Kant, Immanuel, *Anthropology from a Pragmatic Point of View*. Translated by Victor Lyle Dowdell. Carbondale, IL: Southern Illinois University, 1978.

————, *The Conflict of the Faculties*. Translated by Mary J. Gregor and Robert E. Anchor. New York: Abaris Books, 1979.

————, *Critique of Judgment*. Translated by J. H. Bernard. New York: Hafner Publishing Co., 1968.

——, *Critique of Practical Reason*. Translated by Lewis White Beck. Indianapolis: Bobbs-Merrill, 1956.

——, *Critique of Pure Reason*. Translated by Norman Kemp Smith. New York: St. Martin's Press, 1965.

——, *The Doctrine of Virtue: Part II of The Metaphysics of Morals*. Translated by Mary J. Gregor. New York: Harper & Row, 1964.

——, *Dreams of a Spirit Seer*. Translated by John Manolesco. New York: Vantage Press, 1969.

——, *Education*. Translated by Annette Churton. Ann Arbor: University of Michigan Press, 1960.

——, *Enquiry concerning the Clarity of the Principles of Natural Theology and Ethics*. Translated by D. E. Walford, in *Kant: Selected Pre-Critical Writings and Correspondence with Beck*. Translated by G. B. Kerford and D. E. Walford. Manchester: Manchester University Press, 1968.

——, *Grounding for the Metaphysics of Morals*. Translated by James W. Ellington. Indianapolis: Hackett, 1981.

——, *Kant—Philosophical Correspondence: 1759–99*. Edited and translated by Arnulf Zweig. Chicago: The University of Chicago Press, 1967.

——, *Kant: Selected Pre-Critical Writings and Correspondence with Beck*. Translated by G. B. Kerford and D. E. Walford. Manchester: Manchester University Press, 1968.

——, *Kant Selections*. Edited by Theodore M. Greene. New York: Charles Scribner's Sons, 1957.

——, *Lectures on Ethics*. Translated by Louis Infield. New York: Harper & Row, 1963.

——, *Lectures on Philosophical Theology*. Translated by Allen W. Wood and Gertrude M. Clark. Ithaca, NY: Cornell University Press, 1978.

——, *Logic*. Translated by Robert S. Hartman and Wolfgang Schwarz. Indianapolis: Bobbs-Merrill, 1974.

——, *The Metaphysical Elements of Justice: Part I of The Metaphysics of Morals*. Translated by John Ladd. Indianapolis: Bobbs-Merrill, 1965.

——, *Metaphysical Foundations of Natural Science*. Translated by James Ellington. Indianapolis: Bobbs-Merrill, 1970.

——, *A New Exposition of the First Principles of Metaphysical Knowledge*. Translated by F. E. England, in his *Kant's Conception of God*. New York: Humanities Press, 1968.

——, *Observations on the Feeling of the Beautiful and Sublime*. Translated by John T. Goldthwait. Berkeley: University of California Press, 1965.

——, *The One Possible Basis for a Demonstration of the Existence of God*. Translated by Gordon Treash. New York: Abaris Books, 1979.

——, *On History*. Edited by Lewis White Beck, translated by Lewis White Beck, Robert E. Anchor, and Emil L. Fackenheim. Indianapolis: Bobbs-Merrill, 1963.

——, "On the Failure of All Attempted Philosophical Theodicies." Translated by Michel Despland, in his *Kant on History and Religion*. Montreal: McGill-Queen's University Press, 1973.

——, *On the Form and Principles of the Sensible and Intelligible World*. Translated by G. B. Kerford, in *Kant: Selected Pre-Critical Writings and Correspondence with Beck*. Translated by G. B. Kerford and D. E. Walford. Manchester: Manchester University Press, 1968.

————, *The Philosophy of Kant*. Edited by Carl J. Friedrich. New York: Modern Library, 1949.

————, *Prolegomena to Any Future Metaphysics That Will Be Able to Come Forward As Science*. Translated by Paul Carus and revised by James W. Ellington. Indianapolis: Hackett, 1977.

————, *Religion within the Limits of Reason Alone*. Translated by Theodore M. Greene and Hoyt H. Hudson. New York: Harper & Row, 1960.

————, *What Real Progress Has Metaphysics Made in Germany Since the Time of Leibniz and Wolff?* Translated by Ted Humphrey. New York: Abaris Books, 1983.

Kierkegaard, Søren, *Christian Discourses*. Translated by Walter Lowrie. Princeton: Princeton University Press, 1971.

————, *Edifying Discourses: A Selection*. Edited by Paul L. Holmer, translated by David F. and Lillian Marvin Swenson. New York: Harper & Row, 1958.

————, *Either/Or*, in 2 vols. Vol. I translated by David F. Swenson and Lillian Marvin Swenson, Vol. II translated by Walter Lowrie, both revised by Howard A. Johnson. Garden City, NY: Doubleday & Co., 1959.

————, *Fear and Trembling* and *The Sickness unto Death*. Translated by Walter Lowrie. Garden City, NY: Doubleday, 1954.

————, *Johannes Climacus or, De Omnibus Dubitandum Est* and *A Sermon*. Translated by T. H. Croxall. Stanford: Stanford University Press, 1958.

————, *The Journals of Kierkegaard*. Translated and edited by Alexander Dru. New York: Harper & Row, 1959.

————, *A Kierkegaard Anthology*. Edited by Robert Bretall. Princeton: Princeton University Press, 1946.

————, *Kierkegaard's Attack upon "Christendom" 1854–1855*. Translated by Walter Lowrie. Princeton: Princeton University Press, 1968.

————, *Kierkegaard's Concluding Unscientific Postscript*. Translated by David F. Swenson and Walter Lowrie. Princeton: Princeton University Press, 1941.

————, *Kierkegaard's The Concept of Dread*. Translated by Walter Lowrie. Princeton: Princeton University Press, 1957.

————, *Letters and Documents*. Translated by Henrik Rosenmeier. Princeton: Princeton University Press, 1978.

————, *Philosophical Fragments or A Fragment of Philosophy*. Translated by David F. Swenson and revised by Howard V. Hong. Princeton: Princeton University Press, 1967.

————, *The Point of View for My Work As an Author*. Translated by Walter Lowrie. New York: Harper & Row, 1962.

————, *The Present Age* and *Of the Difference between a Genius and an Apostle*. Translated by Alexander Dru. New York: Harper & Row, 1962.

————, *Repetition*. Translated by Walter Lowrie. New York: Harper & Row, 1964.

————, *Søren Kierkegaard's Journals and Papers*. Edited and translated by Howard V. and Edna H. Hong, in 7 vols. Bloomington: Indiana University Press, 1967–78.

————, *Stages on Life's Way*. Translated by Walter Lowrie. New York: Schocken Books, 1967.

————, *Training in Christianity and the Edifying Discourse Which 'Accompanied' It*. Translated by Walter Lowrie. Princeton: Princeton University Press, 1944.

————, *Works of Love: Some Christian Reflections in the Form of Discourses*. Translated by Howard V. and Edna H. Hong. New York: Harper & Row, 1964.

Leibniz, Gottfried Wilhelm, *Leibniz: Discourse on Metaphysics, Correspondence with Arnauld, and Monadology*. Translated by George R. Montgomery. LaSalle, IL: Open Court, 1968.

———, *Leibniz Selections*. Edited by Philip P. Wiener. New York: Charles Scribner's Sons, 1951.

———, *Monadology and Other Philosophical Essays*. Translated by Paul and Anne Martin Schrecker. Indianapolis: Bobbs-Merrill, 1965.

———, *Philosophical Papers and Letters*, 2nd ed. Translated and edited by Leroy E. Loemker. Dordrecht: D. Reidel, 1970.

———, *Theodicy: Essays on the Goodness of God, the Freedom of Man and the Origin of Evil*. Translated by E. M. Huggard, edited by Austin Farrer. London: Routledge & Kegan Paul, 1951.

Lessing, Gotthold, "On the Proof of the Spirit and of Power," in *Lessing's Theological Writings*. Edited and translated by Henry Chadwick. Stanford: Stanford University Press, 1957.

Locke, John, *The Conduct of the Understanding*, in *The Works of John Locke*, Vol. 3. London: Thomas Davidson, Whitefriars, 1823.

———, *An Essay concerning Human Understanding*, in 2 vols. Collated by Alexander Campbell Fraser. New York: Dover, 1959.

———, *Essays on the Law of Nature*. Edited by W. von Leyden. Oxford: Oxford University Press, 1954.

———, *An Examination of P. Malebranche's Opinion of Seeing All Things in God*, in *The Works of John Locke*, Vol. 9. London: Thomas Davidson, Whitefriars, 1823.

———, *A Letter concerning Toleration*. Indianapolis: Bobbs-Merrill, 1955.

———, *The Reasonableness of Christianity* with *A Discourse of Miracles* and part of *A Third Letter concerning Toleration*. Edited by I. T. Ramsey. Stanford: Stanford University Press, 1958.

———, *Second Vindication of the Reasonableness of Christianity*, in *The Works of John Locke*, Vol. 7. London: Thomas Davidson, Whitefriars, 1823.

———, *Two Treatises of Government*. Edited by Peter Laslett. New York: New American Library, 1963.

MacGregor, Geddes, and Wesley Robb, editors, *Readings in Religious Philosophy*. Boston: Houghton Mifflin, 1962.

Montaigne, Michel de, *In Defense of Raymond Sebond*. Translated by Arthur H. Beattie. New York: Frederick Ungar, 1959.

Newton, Isaac, *Newton's Philosophy of Nature: Selections from His Writings*. Edited by H. S. Thayer. New York: Hafner, 1953.

Pascal, Blaise, *Pascal's Pensées*. Translated by W. F. Trotter. New York: E. P. Dutton, 1958.

Plato, *The Collected Dialogues of Plato*. Edited by Edith Hamilton and Huntington Cairns. New York: Pantheon Books, 1961.

Pomerleau, Wayne P., "The Accession and Dismissal of an Upstart Handmaid," *The Monist* 60, no. 2 (April, 1977).

———, "Does Reason Demand That God Be Infinite?", *Sophia* 24, no. 2 (July, 1985).

———, "Kierkegaard's Existential Critique of Modern Rationalists," *Explorations* 8, no. 2 (Winter, 1989).

———, *Twelve Great Philosophers*. New York: Ardsley House, 1997.

Radhakrishnan, Sarvepalli, and Charles A. Moore, editors, *A Source Book in Indian Philosophy*. Princeton: Princeton University Press, 1957.

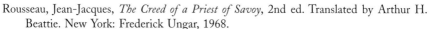

Rousseau, Jean-Jacques, *The Creed of a Priest of Savoy*, 2nd ed. Translated by Arthur H. Beattie. New York: Frederick Ungar, 1968.

Russell, Bertrand, *The Problems of Philosophy*. New York: Oxford University Press, 1959.

———, *Why I Am Not a Christian and Other Essays on Religion and Related Subjects*. Edited by Paul Edwards. London: George Allen & Unwin, 1957.

Russell, Bertrand, and Father F. C. Copleston, S.J., "The Existence of God: A Debate," in *Why I Am Not a Christian and Other Essays on Religion and Related Subjects*, by Bertrand Russell. Edited by Paul Edwards. London: George Allen & Unwin, 1957.

Smart, Ninian, editor, *Historical Selections in the Philosophy of Religion*. New York: Harper & Row, 1962.

Voltaire, *Candide*. Translated by Lowell Bair. New York: Bantam Books, 1959.

Wolff, Christian, *Preliminary Discourse on Philosophy in General*. Translated by Richard J. Blackwell. Indianapolis: Bobbs-Merrill, 1963.

Glossary

ABBACY (from the Latin *abbatia*, meaning abbey). The office, jurisdiction, or term of an abbot or abbess, the superior of an abbey of monks or nuns

ABBEY (from the Aramaic *abba*, meaning father). A monastery under the supervision of an abbot or a convent under the supervision of an abbess

ABSOLUTE SPIRIT/MIND/IDEA. The ultimate, unconditioned, uncaused, complete Reality, especially in Hegelian thought

ABSURD. Loosely, contrary to reason or the rules of logic; more precisely, for existentialists, lacking any ultimate rational explanation

ACCIDENT. An attribute or property of a thing that is not essential to its nature; more popularly, an unintended event

AD HOC (literally, in Latin, for this). For the particular purpose, situation, or problem at hand

AD HOMINEM (literally, in Latin, to the man). Focusing on an opponent rather than addressing his arguments, often in such a way as to appeal to prejudice, emotions, or special interests

ADVENTITIOUS. Coming from without, as from objects outside the mind (for Descartes); more commonly, accidental or casual

AESTHETIC (from the Greek *aisthetikos*, meaning pertaining to sense perception). Usually, dealing with beauty or emotional matters of taste; in Kant, the aesthetic examines the *a priori* conditions of sense experience

AESTHETICS (from the Greek *aisthetikos*, pertaining to sense perception). The branch of philosophy dealing with art and beauty

AETIOLOGY (from the Latin *aetiologia*, meaning a statement of causes). The study of causes, origins, or reasons

AGNOSTICISM. The view that something, especially the existence of God, cannot be known

ALIENATION (from the Latin *alius*, meaning other). The sense of estrangement from or foreignness to consciousness, especially as discussed by Hegel and existential thinkers

ALLEGORY (from the Greek *allegorein*, meaning to speak figuratively). The expression of truths or abstract points by means of fictional characters and actions used symbolically

ALTERNATIVE ARGUMENT (from the Latin *alter*, meaning other). An argument based on either-or alternatives

AMBIGUITY (from the Latin *ambigere*, meaning to wander about). Uncertainty of meaning, often due to words or phrases having two or more reasonable senses

ANALOGY. A resemblance or set of similarities between different things, sometimes used as a basis for an inductive inference; some theists, like Aquinas, regard analogy as the correct way to think and speak of God

ANALYTIC. Using or pertaining to the resolution of something complex into simpler elements (as in Descartes); an analytic judgment (since Kant) is one whose predicate term is already implicitly contained in its subject (e.g., "All bachelors are unmarried"), as opposed to a synthetic judgment

ANIMISM (from the Latin *anima*, meaning soul). The belief that natural objects and phenomena such as rocks have living souls

ANTHROPOMORPHISM (from the Greek *anthropos*, meaning human being, and *morphe*, meaning form). The attribution of human characteristics to something, such as God, which is nonhuman

ANTINOMY (from the Greek *antinomia*, meaning conflict in law). The mutual contradiction of two principles, each of which appears to be true and can be supported, especially in Kant

ANTIQUITY. Ancient times, before the Middle Ages—for our purposes, until the late fourth or early fifth century A.D.

ANTITHESIS (from the Greek *antitithenai*, to oppose). An idea or proposition set forth in opposition to another (as in Kant's discussion of the antinomies); in Hegelian thought, such opposition is the second phase of a dialectical process, leading to a synthesis of that antithesis and the thesis to which it is opposed

APODEICTIC (from the Greek *apodeiktikos*, meaning proving fully). Certainly true, clearly proven, or beyond dispute

APOLOGETICS (from the Greek *apologetikos*, meaning fit for defense). The branch of theology defending or trying to prove Christian beliefs

A POSTERIORI (literally, in Latin, from after). Following and dependent on some particular sense experience, empirical, as opposed to *a priori*

APPERCEPTION. Self-awareness, the mind's consciousness of its own inner states; in Kantian thought, it is the ego's awareness of a unity of self-consciousness

A PRIORI (literally, in Latin, from before). Knowable prior to, or independently of, particular sense experience, as opposed to *a posteriori*

ARCHBISHOP. The highest ranking bishop in a province, typically having ecclesiastical authority over it

ARGUMENT. A logical reasoning process designed to infer one proposition (the conclusion) from one or more other propositions (premises), which collectively are supposed to support it; more loosely, any dispute

ARGUMENT FROM DESIGN. An argument for the existence of God as the Designer responsible for the combination of order and complexity we experience in our world; also called teleological (from the Greek *telos*, meaning end or purpose) because it infers divine purpose from apparent cosmic order

ARGUMENT FROM GENERAL CONSENSUS. The argument that something (such as belief in the existence of God) must be true (or false) because most people consider it true (or false)

ATHEISM (from the Greek *atheos*, meaning godless). Disbelief in or denial of the existence of God or any gods

ATOMISM (from the Greek *atomos*, meaning indivisible). The view that reality is composed of tiny, indivisible physical particles; more generally, the tendency to analyze things in terms of basic, independent constituent elements

AUTONOMY (from the Greek *autonomos*, meaning self-legislating). Self-determination, the capacity and/or right to determine one's own views, values, and actions (in Kant, contrasted with heteronomy)

AVE MARIA (literally, in Latin, hail, Mary). A Roman Catholic prayer to Mary, the mother of Jesus of Nazareth

AXIOM (from the Greek *axioun*, meaning to think worthy). A foundational principle or allegedly self-evident truth

BAPTISM. A ceremonial application of water to a person, as a religious rite effecting or symbolizing spiritual cleansing—a Christian sacrament

BEATITUDE (from the Latin *beatus*, meaning blessed). Supreme happiness or felicity

BENEDICTINE. A member of, or pertaining to, the order of Roman Catholic monks (or nuns) founded by Benedict in the sixth century

BIBLICAL (from the Latin *biblia*, meaning books). Of, pertaining to, or contained in books of sacred Scriptures, such as the Old and New Testaments of the Christian Bible

BISHOP. A person with ecclesiastical supervision over churches in a district

BISHOPRIC. The diocese or jurisdiction of a bishop

BLASPHEMY (from the Greek *blasphemein*, meaning to speak profanely). An act or utterance of irreverence toward God

BUDDHISM (from the Sanskrit *Buddha*, meaning awakened or enlightened). A religion, based on the teachings of Gautama Siddhartha, called the Buddha, originating in India and later spreading through eastern and central Asia

CARTESIAN CIRCLE. A problem in Descartes's philosophy, arising from his claim that the reliability of all clear and distinct ideas depends on our knowledge of God, although that knowledge, in turn, is allegedly based on our grasp of clear and distinct ideas

CATEGORICAL. Unconditional or without exception; having to do with definite concepts or structures of understanding; in Kant, a categorical imperative is unconditionally obligatory, as opposed to a hypothetical imperative, which only applies conditionally

CAUSE. That which explains something, especially in terms of its origin or source of change, its sufficient condition(s); Kant identifies causality as one of the twelve categories or concepts of the understanding

CERTAINTY. The assurance that a belief is wholly reliable or that a proposition is indubitably known

CHRISTIANITY (from the Greek *Christos*, meaning anointed). A religion, based on the teachings of Jesus and accepting him as Christ, the Messiah prophesied in the Jewish Scriptures

CIRCULAR REASONING (or BEGGING THE QUESTION). The fallacy of assuming the conclusion of an argument in its premises

COGITO (from the Latin, *cogito, ergo sum*, meaning I think, therefore I am). Descartes's insight that I know I must mentally exist insofar as I experience any sort of thinking

COGNITION (from the Latin *cognitio*, meaning learning, acquiring knowledge). The act or faculty of knowing

COHERENCE. A relation between experiences, beliefs, or propositions that are logically compatible or consistent

CONCLUSION. In an argument, a proposition that is supported by one or more other propositions (the premises)

CONDITIONAL (or HYPOTHETICAL) ARGUMENT. A deductive argument involving one or more implications (conditionals)

CONJUNCTION (from the Latin *conjunctio*, meaning a joining together or combination). The act of joining together or the fact of things being combined; in logic, this refers to the uniting of propositions (the conjuncts), as by the word "and"; in order for a logical conjunction to be true, both of its conjuncts must be true

CONSISTENCY. The compatibility of things, actions, beliefs, or logical propositions that can coexist or be done or held without contradiction or be simultaneously true

CONSTITUTIVE. Forming a part of, helping to make up a whole; in Kant, ideas have a constitutive (as opposed to a regulative) function when they can lead to knowledge

CONTINGENCY. That which could be otherwise (as opposed to necessity)

CONTRADICTION (from the Latin *contradictio*, meaning a speaking against or refutation). Loosely, a denial or the act of opposing; in logic, the relationship between two propositions, such that it is impossible for both to be true or for both to be false

CONTRARY (from the Latin *contra*, meaning opposite or against). Loosely, what is opposed or the opposite; in logic, the relationship between two propositions, such that it is impossible for both to be true, although they could both be false

CONVERSE. Loosely, a reversal of ideas or an opposite assumption; in logic, a proposition obtained by reversing the subject and predicate terms of another proposition

COPERNICAN REVOLUTION. Kant's view that objects of experience need to meet the requirements of the mind, rather than the traditional view that the ideas of the mind must meet the requirements of objects of experience (analogous to Copernicus's adopting a new model of the solar system, as having all planets moving around the Sun, to replace the old model of the Earth as stationary in the middle of the universe, with all other heavenly bodies revolving around it)

CORRESPONDENCE THEORY. The traditional view that a belief or judgment is true if it conforms to reality, subscribed to by almost all Western philosophers before Kant; Kant's revolutionary proposal is that objects must conform to the requirements of the mind, rather than the other way around; after Kant, coherence and pragmatic usefulness become alternative criteria of truth

COSMOLOGICAL ARGUMENT. An argument purporting to prove the existence of God as the necessary, ultimate First Cause of the universe or cosmos, whose reality (by contrast) is regarded as contingent

COSMOLOGY. That area of inquiry that theorizes about the cosmos, or universe as an organized whole; for Kant, rational cosmology (along with rational psychology and rational theology) is one of the three branches of metaphysical speculation

COUNTEREXAMPLE. An instance that refutes a universal claim; for example, Europeans once believed that "all swans are white," until the counterexample of a black swan was discovered

DEDUCTION. Reasoning in which the truth of all the premises of an argument supposedly necessitates the truth of its conclusion as certain, as opposed to induction

DEISM (from the Latin *deus*, meaning god). The belief in a transcendent God who created or designed our world but does not intervene in it

DETERMINISM. The doctrine that every event in the universe, including every human action, is causally necessitated by antecedent conditions, to the exclusion of free will

DIALECTIC (from the Greek *dialektikos*, meaning discourse). A process of thought, whereby one thesis, or line of inquiry, leads to its opposite, or antithesis; Kant considers antithetical conflict an indication of metaphysical illusion, whereas Hegel sees it as an opportunity to advance rationally to a higher unity, or synthesis

DILEMMA (literally, in Greek, a dual or ambiguous proposition). Loosely, a choice between two undesirable alternatives; in logic, an argument based on a choice between alternatives, each of which seems unacceptable

DISJUNCTION (from the Latin *disjunctio*, meaning a separation). The act of separating or the fact of things being separated or disjoined; in logic, this refers to a relationship between (or among) propositions (as expressed with the word "or"), such that at least one of them is asserted to be true

DOGMA (literally, in Greek, opinion or belief). Loosely, any fixed belief that is not to be questioned; more specifically, a doctrine or set of teachings on faith or morals authoritatively proclaimed by a church or religious group

DOGMATISM (from the Greek *dogma*, meaning opinion or belief). In philosophy, unwarranted certainty in asserting any doctrine; since Kant, the word more specifically refers to metaphysical claims not grounded in a prior critique of the cognitive powers of reason

DOMINICAN. A member of, or pertaining to, the Roman Catholic Order of Preachers, founded by Dominic in the thirteenth century

DONATISM. A sect in North Africa that split from orthodox Christianity in the fourth century and taught that the sacraments are only valid when administered by holy men

DUALISM. The view that there are two irreducible sorts of reality, often physical and spiritual, or two irreducible components of human nature, such as body and soul (Descartes, for example, is a dualist)

ECUMENISM (from the Greek *oikoumenikos*, meaning of the whole world). Belief in or commitment to the worldwide unity of religious groups, transcending their doctrinal differences through mutual understanding and cooperation

EMPIRICISM (from the Greek *empeiria*, meaning experience). The theory that all synthetic or existential knowledge is derived ultimately from sense experience, as opposed to rationalism

ENCYCLICAL (from the Greek *enkyklios*, meaning circular or general). A letter, as by the Pope of the Roman Catholic Church, which is intended for general circulation

ENLIGHTENMENT. An intellectual movement, especially of eighteenth-century Europe and America, advocating the ideals of reason, science, liberty, and progress

ENS REALISSIMUM (literally, in Latin, the most real Being). A term Kant uses for God

ENTHUSIASM (from the Greek *enthousiazein*, meaning to be inspired or possessed by a god). Loosely, any acute eagerness or passionate feeling; rapturous zeal or religious fanaticism

ENTHYMEME (from the Greek *enthumeisthai*, meaning to have in mind or consider). A syllogism in which one premise, or even the conclusion, is merely implied rather than explicitly stated

EPIPHANY (from the Greek *epiphaneia*, meaning appearance or manifestation). A revelatory manifestation of a deity

EPISTEMOLOGY (from the Greek *episteme*, meaning knowledge, and *logos*, meaning an account). That area of philosophy dealing with the nature, conditions, and limits of human knowledge

EQUIVOCAL (from the Latin *aequivocus*, meaning equal in name). Having two or more equally appropriate meanings; ambiguous

ESCHATOLOGY (from the Greek *eschatos*, meaning last, and *logos*, meaning an account). The branch of theology that tries to give an account of the last things, death, judgment, Heaven, and hell

ESSENCE. The set of properties that characterizes something as the type of thing it uniquely is and that is necessary for it to be that sort of thing, as opposed to its accidents

ETHICS (from the Greek *ethos*, meaning custom). Moral philosophy, that area of philosophy that studies value judgments regarding "good" and "evil," "right" and "wrong," and obligation

EVANGELICAL (from the Greek *euangelos*, meaning bringing good news). Pertaining to, preaching, or following the Christian Gospels and their teachings

EVIL, PROBLEM OF. The puzzle as to how a perfect (e.g., omnipotent, omniscient, and infinitely good) God can be compatible with the reality of evil in the world

EXCLUDED MIDDLE, LAW OR PRINCIPLE OF. A basic law of Aristotelian logic asserting the disjunction of any (significant) proposition and its negation (e.g., there either is or is not a one-hundred-year-old philosopher now teaching in an American college)

EXCOMMUNICATION. Official ecclesiastical exclusion from communion or membership in a church

EXHAUSTIVE ALTERNATIVES. Two possibilities that are so related that no third alternative is possible (e.g., either eternal or not eternal)

EXISTENTIAL (from the Latin *existere*, meaning to stand out). Having to do with what exists; existentialists relate what exists to the dynamic reality of consciousness

EXISTENTIALISM. A philosophical movement that began in the middle of the nineteenth century and became popular in the twentieth, teaching that human consciousness is individual, is free rather than being determined by some alleged common essence, and is a source of values

FACULTY. An ability, capacity, or power, as of the mind, or of the soul, or of the body

FAITH. Loosely, belief or confidence; theologically, belief and trust in God and/or the teachings of religion, especially as based on the authority of revelation or a church

FALLACY. An error in reasoning, such that the conclusion of an argument does not logically follow from its premises

FALLIBILISM (from the Latin *fallibilis*, meaning capable of being deceived). The principle that some sorts of beliefs or propositions are inherently uncertain and possibly erroneous

FALSE DILEMMA. The fallacy of presuming that an either-or distinction is exhaustive (and/or mutually exclusive) when other alternatives exist (also called "bifurcation")

FALSIFIABILITY. The property of a statement or theory that it is capable of being refuted by experience

FIDEISM (from the Latin *fides*, meaning faith). The view that religious truth must be accepted purely on faith rather than justified by reason

FOREKNOWLEDGE. Knowledge, traditionally attributed to God, of that which is yet to be

FORM. The essential structure or nature of something; in Kant, the *a priori* element in experience whereby the data of sensible intuition are structurally organized by the mind

FUNDAMENTALISM (from the Latin *fundamentum*, meaning foundation). A religious movement calling for a strict adherence to traditional teachings and practices; in Protestantism, this typically involves belief in the inerrancy of the Scriptures, whose literal interpretation is seen as basic or fundamental

GENERALIZATION. An inductive inference that what is true (or false) of some observed individuals is probably also true (or false) of others that have not yet been observed

GNOSTICISM (from the Greek *gnosis*, meaning knowledge). A movement that became popular among early Christian heretical sects, associating the material world with evil, claiming that Christ was noncorporeal, and viewing salvation as attainable through esoteric knowledge of spiritual truth rather than through ordinary faith

GRACE (from the Latin *gratia*, meaning favor). Freely given, unmerited divine favor

GRATING (from the old French *grater*, meaning to scrape). Abrasive rubbing or scraping, as of the flesh for purposes of mortification

HAIR SHIRT. A garment of coarse haircloth, worn next to the skin by penitents and ascetics to mortify the flesh

HEDONISM (from the Greek *hedone*, meaning pleasure). The theory that pleasure is in fact (psychological hedonism) and/or should be in principle (ethical hedonism) our ultimate good

HENOTHEISM (from the Greek *heno-*, meaning one, and *theos*, meaning god). Belief in or worship of one god without denying the existence of other gods; it can be viewed as a transitional stage between polytheism and monotheism

HERESY (from the Greek *hairesis*, meaning choice). Religious opinion contrary to orthodox doctrine

HINDUISM (from the Persian *Hindu*, meaning an inhabitant of India). A system of religious beliefs and practices, originating in India and stemming from the ancient Vedic Scriptures

HOURS (from the Latin *hora*, meaning hour). In Christianity, the times or offices for daily prayer or liturgical devotion

HUMANISM. Any view (e.g., in James) emphasizing the value and dignity of human individuals

HYPOTHESIS (from the Greek *hupothesis*, meaning suggestion or supposition). An assertion that something may be the case; a proposition assumed as a basis for reasoning, argument, or action

HYPOTHETICAL ARGUMENT. An inference derived from at least one hypothetical, or conditional (e.g., if-then), premise

IDEALISM. The philosophical theory that reality is ultimately mental or spiritual in its nature and/or its origins (metaphysical idealism) or that we can only know minds and their ideas (epistemological idealism)

IDENTITY. The quality of remaining the same or the condition of two things being the same; in Aristotelian logic, the law of identity maintains that everything is what it is and cannot simultaneously be something other than what it is

IDOLATRY (from the Greek *eidolon*, meaning image or idol). The religious worship of idols or images of deities

IMMANENCE. Presence in something else, inherence, as opposed to transcendence; for example, the God of panentheism is immanent in the things of this world

IMMORTALITY. The unending existence of a soul or spirit, once it has begun to be

IMMUTABILITY (from the Latin *immutabilis*, meaning incapable of change). Unalterability, the property of not being susceptible to change

IMPLICATION (or CONDITIONAL). That which follows from something else; in logic, the relation of propositions, such that the truth of one of them can allegedly be inferred from the truth of the other or others

INCARNATION (from the Latin *incarnari*, meaning to be made flesh). The embodiment of a deity; in Christian theology, the embodiment of God in human form as Jesus

INCONSISTENCY. A logical conflict between two (or among more than two) statements, such that one (or more) of them must be false if the others are true

INDUCTION. Reasoning that takes the form of a probability argument, deriving a conclusion from the premise(s) as more or less likely, rather than as certain, as opposed to deduction

INEFFABLE (from the Latin *ineffabilis*, meaning inexpressible). Incapable of being expressed or described in words

INFERENCE. A process of deductive or inductive reasoning from one or more statements, called premises, to another, called the conclusion

INFINITE (from the Latin *infinitus*, meaning unlimited). Unbounded, without any limits (often said of God)

INNATE (from the Latin *innatus*, meaning inborn). Inborn, not derived from sense experience; Descartes and Leibniz believe we have some innate ideas, whereas empiricists deny such ideas

INTRINSIC. In itself, for its own sake, rather than as a means to something else, or instrumental; a different meaning is inherent or essential, as opposed to extrinsic or accidental

INVALID ARGUMENT. In deductive reasoning, an argument that is such that for some assignment of truth values, the premises are all true, yet the conclusion is false

JESUIT. A member of, or pertaining to, the Society of Jesus, a Roman Catholic religious order founded by Ignatius Loyola in the sixteenth century

KNOWLEDGE. Belief that is both true and justifiably held to be true (although some philosophers criticize and deny this traditional analysis)

LOGIC (from the Greek *logos*, meaning reasoning). The systematic study of reasoning and argumentation, often divided into deductive (or formal) logic vs. inductive (or informal) logic

LOGICAL POSITIVISM. A twentieth-century philosophical movement that began in the 1920s and flourished until the 1950s, which holds that any empirical statement must be, at least in principle, verifiable (or, sometimes, falsifiable), in order to be cognitively meaningful; this renders metaphysical (and theological) utterances literally nonsensical and reduces value (including ethical) statements to expressions of emotional preferences

LORD'S PRAYER. A Christian prayer taught by Jesus to his followers (*Matt.* 6:9–13; *Luke*, 11:2–4), also sometimes called the "Our Father"

MANICHEANISM. The teaching of the Babylonian Mani (a third-century religious leader who tried to synthesize Christianity and Zoroastrianism) of the dualistic Gnostic doctrine that there is a God of light and a powerful principle of darkness and evil

MATERIALISM. The theory that all reality is ultimately physical and that whatever we may regard as mental or spiritual is actually only an expression of some fundamentally material being

MEDIEVAL (from the Latin *medium aevum*, meaning the middle age). Of or pertaining to the Middle Ages

MELIORISM (from the Latin *melior*, meaning better). In James, the view that the world, however good or evil it may be, can become better if we freely act to help improve it

METAPHYSICS (from the Greek *meta*, meaning after, and *phusika*, meaning physics). That area of philosophy that studies the nature of ultimate reality and the fundamental structures of being

MIDDLE AGES. That period of Western history between antiquity and modernity—i.e., from the late fourth or early fifth century to the end of the fourteenth century

MIND. Individual (or cosmic) consciousness; a psychological self or soul (or an intellectual aspect of the self or soul)

MIRACLE (from the Latin *miraculum,* meaning object of wonder). An extraordinary event, surpassing all known human powers or natural forces, ascribed to divine intervention or supernatural causality

MODERNITY (or **MODERNISM**). That period of Western history extending from the beginning of the seventeenth century; when contrasted with contemporary times, modernity ends early in the twentieth century

MODUS PONENS (from the Latin *modus,* meaning manner, and *ponens,* meaning asserting). A valid deductive argument form that asserts an implication, then affirms its antecedent as true, and concludes that the consequent must also be true

MODUS TOLLENS (from the Latin *modus,* meaning manner, and *tollens,* meaning denying). A valid deductive argument form that asserts an implication, then denies that its consequent is true, and concludes that its antecedent must also be false

MONAD (from the Greek *monos,* meaning alone). An elementary, indivisible, spiritual substance, especially in the philosophy of Leibniz

MONASTERY (from the Greek *monazein,* meaning to live alone). A residence for people, especially monks, living under vows, in seclusion, as a religious community

MONASTICISM. A movement in which people withdrew from the secular world to live in religious communities under vows, such as those of obedience, chastity, and poverty

MONISM (from the Greek *monos,* meaning alone or single). The view that ultimately only one type of substance or only one numerical being is real

MONOTHEISM (from the Greek *monos,* meaning single, and *theos,* meaning god). The belief or doctrine that one God exists, as opposed to polytheism

MORAL ARGUMENT. In Kant, the postulation of God as practically necessitated by our moral consciousness

MYSTERY. A doctrine, usually associated with religion, that defies complete rational understanding

MYSTICISM (from the Greek *mystikos,* meaning initiated into mysteries). The belief that union with and/or direct knowledge of God, spiritual truth, or ultimate reality can be attained

NATURALISM. The view that everything can, at least in theory, be explained in terms of natural realities, their actions, and their interrelationships, as opposed to supernaturalism

NATURAL SELECTION. The Darwinian principle that organisms with heritable variations that are better adapted to their environment are more likely to survive and successfully propagate

NECESSARY CONDITION. That without which something else could not be or occur; for example, knowing a language is a necessary condition of your understanding another person's biography

NECESSITY. That which could not be otherwise than it is, as opposed to contingency

NEGATION (from the Latin *negare*, meaning to deny). Generally, a denial; in logic, the claim or assertion that a proposition is false

NEOPLATONISM. A philosophical movement, in which Plotinus was prominent, based on Platonic ideas, beginning in Alexandria in the second century A.D. and extending to at least the fifth century

NIRVANA (literally, in Sanskrit, extinction). In Buddhism, the blessedness characterized by a liberation from the cycle of death and reincarnation through the extinction of the self; in Hinduism, a similar state attained through the union of the self with Brahman and the suppression of individuality

NOETIC (from the Greek *noetikos*, meaning intellectual). Cognitive, having to do with the rational activity of intellect

NOMINALISM (from the Latin *nominalis*, meaning belonging to a name). The theory that only particulars exist and that the only universals are names, the products of human language

NONCONTRADICTION, LAW OR PRINCIPLE OF. The Aristotelian law of thought that no proposition (or statement) and its negation (or denial) can both be true of the same thing(s) at the same time in the same respect

NON SEQUITUR (literally, in Latin, it does not follow). An inference whose conclusion does not logically follow from the premises

NOUMENON (plural, **noumena**). In Kant, a rational idea, transcending all possible experience, of a thing-in-itself, as the unknowable ground of phenomenal appearances

OMNICOMPETENCE. Ability and/or authority to deal with everything

OMNIPOTENCE (from the Latin *omnipotens*, meaning almighty). The quality or state, as in God, of having unlimited power

OMNISCIENCE (from the Latin *omnis*, meaning all, and *scientia*, meaning knowledge). The quality or state, as in God, of knowing everything

ONTOLOGICAL ARGUMENT. An *a priori* argument purporting to deduce the necessary existence of God from the very idea of God as an infinitely perfect Being; though Kant gave it this name, the argument originated with Anselm and was used by Descartes

ONTOLOGY (from the Greek *onta*, meaning really existing things, and *logos*, meaning an account). The study of being; that branch of metaphysics which speculates about the essential characteristics of Being as such, as opposed to the study of particular beings

ORDINATION (from the Latin *ordinare*, meaning to appoint). The act or ceremony of holy orders, whereby a person is made a priest or appointed to the ministry of a church

ORIGINAL SIN. In Christian theology, the tendency to commit evil supposedly innate in all humans, as inherited from Adam, the first man, who deliberately disobeyed the manifest will of God

OVER-BELIEFS. In James, those religious beliefs a person holds over and above the core beliefs common to religions generally; for example, a Christian might subscribe to the over-belief that Jesus Christ was literally and uniquely God, whereas a Jew or Muslim would not

PAGAN (from the Latin *paganus*, meaning a villager or rustic). A person who is not Jewish, Christian, or Muslim, especially one who subscribes to a polytheistic religion

PANENTHEISM (from the Greek *pan*, meaning all, *en*, meaning in, and *theos*, meaning god). The view that God is immanent in the world without being simply identical with the world (as in pantheism)

PANPSYCHISM (from the Greek *pan*, meaning all, and *psyche*, meaning soul). The doctrine, associated with Leibniz's theory of monads, that all of nature essentially consists of psychic centers

PANTHEISM (from the Greek *pan*, meaning all, and *theos*, meaning god). The view that God and the world are simply identical, with individual things being mere modifications, moments, or phenomenal appearances of God and with God being absolutely immanent without transcending the world in any respect

PANTHEON (from the Greek *pan*, meaning all, and *theos*, meaning god). A temple dedicated to all the gods or the collection of all the deities of a particular people

PAPACY (from the Greek *papas*, meaning bishop). The office or jurisdiction of a pope, the Bishop of Rome in the Catholic Church

PARADOX (from the Greek *paradoxos*, meaning contrary to opinion). A seemingly absurd or self-contradictory view, often based on apparently sound reasoning from plausible assumptions (an ancient example was the saying of Epimenides the Cretan that all Cretans always lie)

PARALOGISM (from the Greek *paralogos*, meaning contrary to reason). In Kant, any of four fallacious arguments meant to prove something about the nature of the soul or pure ego; loosely, a piece of false reasoning, an illogical argument

PELAGIANISM. The theological doctrine propounded by Pelagius (and opposed by Augustine) that denies original sin and affirms that the human will can do good without the assistance of divine grace; early in the fifth century, the Roman Catholic Church condemned it as heresy

PHENOMENALISM. The view (as in Hume) that we can only be aware of appearances or sense data and never of things-in-themselves; this leads some phenomenalists to conceive of physical objects, such as sticks and stones, as mere sets of appearances or enduring possibilities of sensation

PHENOMENOLOGY. Broadly, the study of appearances providing the content for all empirical knowledge; in Hegel, it is the study of the mind by way of the hierarchy of phenomena it considers; in the twentieth century, it is a philosophical movement (from Husserl) which uses introspective analysis to describe in depth the various forms of intentional consciousness

PHENOMENON. Generally, an object of experience; more specifically, an appearance or object of perception; in Kant, opposed to noumenon

PHILOSOPHES (literally, in French, philosophers). The eighteenth-century philosophical thinkers of the French Enlightenment, including Voltaire, Condorcet, and the editors of the great *Encyclopedia* (Diderot and d'Alembert)

PHILOSOPHY (from the Greek *philosophos*, meaning loving wisdom). The most general systematic rational inquiry; philosophers disagree about its proper definition, but the one used here is critical reflection on basic concepts, assumptions, and principles related to any areas of experience and/or reality

PHYSICOTHEOLOGY. Kant's name for that branch of philosophical theology that argues from design to prove God's existence

PIETISM (from the Latin *pietas*, meaning dutifulness or piety). An evangelical reform movement in the German Lutheran Church, during the seventeenth and eighteenth centuries, emphasizing personal piety over against religious formalism

PLATONISM. The idealistic and dualistic philosophy associated with Plato, especially as it affirms the transcendent reality of eternal, ideal forms, accessible to reason alone, and regards the phenomena of the spatio-temporal, sensible world as derivative and transitory

PLURALISM. The view (as in James) that reality comprises many distinct substances or kinds of substance (vs. dualism and monism)

POLYTHEISM (from the Greek *poly*, meaning many, and *theos*, meaning god). The worship of or belief in many gods, as opposed to monotheism

POSITIVISM. A philosophical system (associated with Auguste Comte in the nineteenth century) recognizing only positive facts and observable phenomena as adequate sources of knowledge and rejecting metaphysics and theology as idle speculation

POSTULATE (from the Latin *postulare*, meaning to demand). An indemonstrable rational hypothesis used as a fundamental assumption of a system of thought; in Kant, freedom, God, and immortality are the three postulates of practical reason demanded by morality

POTENTIALITY. The capacity of a thing to undergo change or become different, sometimes opposed to actuality

PRAGMATISM (from the Greek *pragma*, meaning deed or action). A philosophical movement of the late nineteenth and twentieth centuries (beginning with Peirce and popularized by James), emphasizing the practical usefulness of ideas and beliefs as the criterion of their meaning and truth

PREDESTINATION (from the Latin *praedestinatus*, meaning foreordained). The act whereby the divine will supposedly foreordained all things; the doctrine that God has predetermined everything, especially the salvation of particular souls

PREDETERMINISM. The theory that every event is necessitated according to fixed causal laws; fatalism adds to this the idea that nothing we can do will affect the outcome that is determined; the theological view of predestination identifies God's will as the original source of all predeterminism

PREMISE. In an argument, a proposition or statement that is used to provide support for the conclusion

PREORDINATION. *See* Predestination

PRESBYTERY (from the Greek *presbyteros*, meaning elder or priest). An ecclesiastical assembly of ministers and elders in a jurisdiction of the Presbyterian Church

PRESUPPOSITION. An assumption, especially of an argument

PRIOR (literally, in Latin, superior). A superior in a monastic order or religious house, sometimes next in rank below an abbot

PRIVATION (from the Latin *privatus*, meaning deprived). An act, state, or result of deprivation or loss; the lack or absence of a good, desirable, or natural quality

PROCESS-OF-ELIMINATION ARGUMENT. An argument built on alternatives, all but one of which are ruled out, leaving the remaining one as the necessary conclusion

PROCESS THOUGHT/PHILOSOPHY/THEOLOGY. A contemporary theory analyzing reality in terms of dynamically changing events rather than static substances; Hegel seems to anticipate this movement

PROOF. Evidence establishing a fact or an argument establishing a conclusion; often identified with a demonstration, as leading to certainty (though Hume distinguishes a proof as an argument from experience)

PROPHECY (from the Greek *prophetes*, meaning interpreter or spokesman, especially for a god). The foretelling or prediction of future events; divinely inspired utterance, exhortation, or writing, particularly in religious Scriptures

PROPOSITION (from the Latin *propositio*, meaning what is put forward or proposed). A statement or what is expressed by a declarative sentence relating a subject term to a predicate term in such a way that the statement as a whole can be regarded as true or false; an example of a proposition is provided by the sentence, "The book is on the table."

PROVIDENCE (from the Latin *providere*, meaning to foresee or watch out for). The foreseeing care and guidance of God over the world of creatures

PURGATORY (from the Latin *purgare*, meaning to purify). A state of spiritual cleansing, according to the Roman Catholic Church, in which the souls of the dead are purged of venial (or lesser) sins or atone for mortal (or graver) sins of which they have been absolved, in order to render them worthy of the eternal happiness of heaven

RATIONALISM. The philosophical theory that some synthetic or existential knowledge is derived from reason rather than from sense experience, as opposed to empiricism

REALISM. Generally, the view that some condition or sort of entity exists independently of the human mind; common-sense realism (condemned by its critics as "naive realism") holds that perception normally grasps external objects directly or reveals them to us as they really are

REASON. Generally, the intellect, the capacity for abstract thought, logical inference, and comprehension; in Kant, reason is the intellectual faculty that engages in metaphysical speculation, as opposed to understanding, which is the intellectual faculty capable of knowledge; some philosophers (such as Kant) distinguish between theoretical reason, which pursues knowledge, and practical reason, whose deliberations are oriented toward action

REDUCTIO AD ABSURDUM (literally, in Latin, reduction to absurdity). The refutation of a proposition by demonstrating the absurdity to which it leads when followed to its logical conclusion

REDUCTIONISM. The view that all reality and/or value can (and should) be resolved into one sort of thing; a materialist, for example, reduces all mental activity to physical processes

REFUTATION. The disproof of an argument or the demonstration that a position is false or erroneous

REGULATIVE (from the Latin *regula*, meaning a rule). Serving the heuristic function of guiding further thought and action, as opposed (in Kant) to the constitutive function of ideas that can lead to knowledge

RELATIVISM. The view that truths and values vary among different individuals and/or cultures rather than being absolutely binding

RELIGION (from the Latin *religare*, meaning to bind back). A set of beliefs and practices related to human reverence for some ultimate power(s) recognized as creating and/or governing the universe; the service and worship of God or supernatural forces

RESURRECTION (from the Latin *resurrectus*, meaning risen again). Returning to life after being dead

REVELATION (from the Latin *revelare*, meaning to uncover or reveal). Something disclosed or revealed, especially as divine truth

SACRAMENT (from the Latin *sacer*, meaning holy or sacred). A formal religious ceremony or act deemed to have sacred significance, especially one considered to have been instituted or recognized by Christ

SALVATION (from the Latin *salvare*, meaning to save). The saving of a soul from sin and/or its admission to eternal happiness

SCHOLASTICISM (from the Greek *skholastikos*, meaning learned). The educational tradition (both philosophical and theological) of medieval universities, often as influenced by Aristotle, its masters being scholastics or "schoolmen"

SCRIPTURES (from the Latin *scriptura*, meaning writing). Sacred religious writings, such as the books of the Old and New Testaments of the Christian Bible

SECT (from the Latin *secta*, meaning a pathway or following). A religious group that has broken away from an established church or is regarded as heretically deviating from orthodox tradition

SEE (from the Latin *sedes*, meaning seat). A bishop's official seat, center of authority, office, or jurisdiction

SELF-EVIDENT. So obviously true (or false) as to require no justification (or refutation)

SIMONY. The buying and selling of ecclesiastical privileges, pardons, or offices

SIN. A transgression of a religious law; a condition of estrangement from God as a result of violating divine law; some Christians distinguish between "venial," or lesser, sins and "mortal" sins, which are grave enough to merit damnation

SKEPTICISM (or SCEPTICISM) (from the Greek *skeptesthai*, meaning to consider or examine). The doctrine that knowledge is unobtainable, in some or even all areas of inquiry; many of the greatest philosophers (e.g., Augustine, Descartes, and Kant) try to refute skepticism

SOLIPSISM (from the Latin *solus ipse*, meaning oneself alone). The theory that all that is real is one's own mind and its states of consciousness (metaphysical solipsism) or that the only things one can know to exist are one's own mind and its states of consciousness (epistemological solipsism)

SOPHISM (from the Greek *sophisma*, meaning a trick or clever device). A specious argument used for displaying cleverness or for deceiving people

SORITES (from the Greek *soros*, meaning heap or pile). A form of argument in which a series of incomplete syllogisms is so arranged that each premise's predicate is also the subject of the next proposition, forming a chain connecting the subject of the first premise to the predicate of the last in the conclusion

SOUL. Broadly, the principle of life in a living thing; more commonly, a spiritual substance that is or can be the subject of conscious thought

SOUNDNESS. The quality of a valid deductive argument, all of whose premises are true

STOICISM (from the Greek *stoa*, meaning a portico or covered porch). An ancient (Greek and Roman) philosophical movement, emphasizing rational will, mastery of one's passions, doing one's duty, and detachment from external things, over which one has no ultimate control

SUBJECTIVISM. The theory that all knowledge and/or value is relative to an individual subject's mental states or experiences, as opposed to objectivism

SUBLATION. In dialectical (e.g., Hegelian) philosophy, the resolution of opposites, or antitheses, into a higher unity, or synthesis; Hegel's word for it, *Aufhebung*, simultaneously means cancellation, preservation, and elevation

SUBSTANCE (from the Latin *substare*, meaning to stand under). An independently existing entity, supporting, or providing the foundation for, its phenomenal appearances and properties

SUFFICIENT CONDITION. That which is adequate to bring about something else, so that whenever the first occurs, the second will as well; for example, a pet's being a dog is a sufficient condition for its also being a mammal

SUMMUM BONUM. Literally, in Latin, the greatest good

SUPERSENSIBLE. In Kant, beyond the physical realm of possible sense experiences

SYLLOGISM (from the Greek *syllogismos*, meaning a reckoning together). A deductive argument with two premises and a conclusion

SYNOD (from the Greek *synodos*, meaning meeting or assembly). A council or assembly of ecclesiastical officials; in the Presbyterian Church, an ecclesiastical court representing several presbyteries

SYNTHETIC. Combining elements together to form a greater whole; a synthetic judgment (since Kant) is one whose predicate term adds new information not even implicitly contained in its subject (e.g., "All bachelors are frivolous"), as opposed to an analytic one; in dialectical reasoning (as in Hegel), synthesis is the higher unity of opposed antitheses

TABULA RASA (literally, in Latin, scraped or shaved tablet or, more loosely, a blank slate). A metaphor for the human mind as devoid of ideas prior to sense experience, as opposed to the doctrine of innate ideas

TAOISM (from the Chinese *tao*, meaning the way). A philosophy, attributed to Lao Tzu in China, advocating simplicity and harmony with nature; also the religion, originating in China, developed from a mixture of Taoist philosophy, folk religion, and Buddhism

TAUTOLOGY (from the Greek *tautologos*, meaning repeating what has been said). Loosely, a repetition of the same ideas, though, perhaps, in different words (e.g., "visible to the eye"); in logic, a proposition that is necessarily true by definition because its predicate is already contained (at least implicitly) in its subject term (e.g., "All bachelors are unmarried")

TELEOLOGICAL ARGUMENT. *See* Argument from design

TELEOLOGY (from the Greek *telos*, meaning end, and *logos*, meaning an account). The study of reality as oriented toward natural ends or, in rational beings, as having purposes; Aquinas is a teleological thinker

THEISM (from the Greek *theos*, meaning god). Belief in the existence of God or gods

THEODICY (from the Greek *theos*, meaning god, and *dike*, meaning justice or right). The attempt to justify the goodness and justice of God in light of the reality of evil in order to solve the problem of evil rationally

THEOLOGY (from the Greek *theos*, meaning god, and *logos*, meaning an account). The study of God; we can distinguish between rational theology, which is part of philosophy, and revealed theology, which is not, because it is based on revelation

THEOPHANY (from the Greek *theophaneia*, meaning a manifestation of a god). A revelatory manifestation of a deity

THESIS (from the Greek *tithenai*, meaning to put or place). An idea formulated or a proposition put forward; in Hegelian thought, this represents the first phase of a dialectical process in which that thesis is placed in opposition to another (its antithesis), leading to a higher unity of the two (their synthesis)

THINGS-IN-THEMSELVES. Independent realities transcending the realm of phenomenal appearances; for Kant, they are humanly unknowable, though we have (noumenal) ideas of them

TRANSCENDENCE. That which is higher than or beyond the realm of natural experience, as opposed to immanence—e.g., the God of deism is transcendent; for Kantians, that which is transcendent is necessarily unknowable

TRANSCENDENTAL. In Kant, having to do with the *a priori* necessary conditions of organized experience (e.g., time and space), of knowledge (e.g., the concepts of the understanding), of metaphysical speculation (the ideas of pure reason), and so forth

TRIADIC. Threefold or pertaining to a triad, or group of three (things, properties, ideas, etc.)

TRINITY (from the Latin *trinitas*, meaning triad). In Christian theology, the unity of three divine Persons—the Father, the Son, and the Holy Spirit—in one Godhead

TRUTH. Traditionally, the conformity of what is said or thought with fact or reality, though this interpretation has been challenged by some modern philosophers; Christians sometimes refer to God as the ultimate Truth

TRUTH TABLE. A schematic device for analyzing logically related truth values in (propositional) logic

TRUTH VALUES. Truth or falsehood, as they apply to propositions

UNIVERSAL. As an adjective, pertaining to an entire class or all-encompassing, rather than partial or particular; as a noun, a general concept (such as "tree") common to a number of particulars (such as pines, maples, walnuts, oaks, etc.) or an abstract idea (such as justice, truth, beauty, goodness, and equality)

UNIVERSALISM (from the Latin *universus*, meaning entire or whole). The doctrine of universal salvation, that all souls will eventually be saved; loosely, the view that something applies to a whole

UNIVERSALIZABLE. Able to be reasonably applied to all actions of a particular sort in morally similar circumstances; Kant uses universalizability as a criterion for testing whether the maxim of an action is morally justifiable

UNIVOCAL (from the Latin *univocus*, meaning having one meaning). Having only one proper meaning; unambiguous

UNSOUND. Loosely, not well-founded; in logic, an unsound argument is invalid and/or contains at least one false premise

VALID ARGUMENT. In deductive reasoning, an argument that is such that whenever the premises are all true, the conclusion must also be true

VALIDITY. In logic, the quality of a deductive argument, such that its conclusion necessarily follows from the conjunction of its premises; loosely, cogency

VERIFIABILITY. The property of a statement or theory that it is capable of being proved to be true

VIRTUE (from the Latin *virtus*, meaning excellence or manliness). A morally excellent or good habit or quality of character

VOLUNTARISM (from the Latin *voluntas*, meaning will). The doctrine that will is the fundamental principle in human experience and/or in all of reality

VOLUNTARY. Resulting from free choice rather than constrained or extrinsically determined, as opposed to both involuntary and nonvoluntary

ZOROASTRIANISM. The dualistic religious system, taught by the Persian Zoroaster, emphasizing a struggle between a good force of light and an evil force of darkness

Index

K

Kant, Immanuel, 268–329, 501–3, 507,
 511, 514, 517, 528, 563–64, A2–A5,
 A7, A13–A15
 and Anselm, 30, 296, 301–2, 305
 and Aquinas, 43, 45, 52, 296, 301, 318
 and Augustine, 8, 296, 316
 and Descartes, 72, 88, 92, 270, 280, 296,
 301, 303, 306
 and Hegel, 296, 318, 335–37, 340–56,
 359–60, 362–63, 366–75, 386
 and Hick, 532, 535, 538, 540, 555–56,
 558
 and Hume, 224–25, 251, 263, 271, 281,
 283–87, 296, 301, 308, 316, 318–20,
 329
 and James, 296, 301, 317, 433–34, 436,
 442, 444, 446, 448, 450, 452–53,
 458, 462, 473, 485, 487, 490,
 494n.59
 and Kierkegaard, 296, 316, 318, 401,
 408, 411, 415–16, 423–26
 and Leibniz, 158, 166, 177, 179,
 269–70, 272–73, 283–84, 286, 296,
 301, 303, 305–6, 326
 and Locke, 134, 139, 269, 273, 296,
 301, 316
Kierkegaard, Søren, 391–427, 515, 564,
 A14
 and Augustine, 419
 and Descartes, 407–8
 and Hegel, 367–69, 371, 375, 386,
 402–3, 405–6, 408–11, 414–16,
 419–20, 423–25
 and Hick, 558
 and Hume, 263, 408
 and James, 403, 418, 449, 472–73,
 491
 and Kant, 296, 316, 318, 401, 408, 411,
 415–16, 423–26
 and Leibniz, 408
 and Locke, 131, 408, 422
Königsberg, 268–72, 274, 276–77, 279,
 285, 330n.5, 335
Krishna, A9–A13, A15

L

La Flèche College, 67, 69, 73, 81, 101,
 206, 214
Lao Tzu, A1–A11, A14
Leap (of faith), 371, 406, 416–17, 419–20,
 423, 430n.80, 431n.93
Leibniz, Gottfried Wilhelm, 149–98, 500,
 502, 505–6, 563, A3–A4, A7
 and Anselm, 160
 and Aquinas, 160, 178, 180, 194,
 199n.27
 and Augustine, 191, 193–94
 and Descartes, 70–71, 79, 87–88, 93, 96,
 99, 104n.108, 149–50, 152, 154–55,
 158–61, 163–64, 166–68, 171–72,
 175, 179–80, 182–83, 186, 188, 192,
 197, 201n.81
 and Hegel, 339, 356, 375
 and Hick, 539–42, 558
 and Hume, 162, 164, 166, 177, 179,
 198, 199n.18, 203, 213–16, 220, 224,
 239, 249, 255–57, 263
 and James, 167, 450, 452–53, 455
 and Kant, 158, 166, 177, 179, 269–70,
 272–73, 283–84, 286, 296, 301, 303,
 305–6, 326
 and Kierkegaard, 408
 and Locke, 111, 149–50, 152, 158–59,
 161–67, 171, 175, 180, 182–83, 185,
 199n.29
Leipzig, 149–50, 152, 154
Locke, John, 105–44, 519, 563, A3
 and Aquinas, 39
 and Descartes, 70–73, 82, 88, 95, 101,
 109–13, 116, 118–19, 121–22, 125,
 132, 143, 144n.8–9
 and Hegel, 350–52, 362, 369, 375
 and Hick, 529, 531–32, 539, 558
 and Hume, 114, 116, 122, 127, 137,
 204–5, 214–16, 218–19, 221, 223–24,
 230, 239, 254, 263
 and James, 140, 450, 452–53, 455
 and Kant, 134, 139, 269, 273, 296, 301,
 316
 and Kierkegaard, 131, 408, 422